Final. Chp. 1-15

70 ques. ch. 1-11

30 ques. ch. 12-15

RESEARCH METHODS FOR CRIMINAL JUSTICE AND CRIMINOLOGY

Dean J. Champion

California State University, Long Beach

PRENTICE HALL, Upper Saddle River, New Jersey 07458

Library of Congress Cataloging-in-Publication Data
Champion, Dean J.
  Research methods for criminal justice and criminology /Dean J.
Champion.
  p. cm.
  ISBN 0-13-572876-2
  1. Criminology—Methodology. 2. Criminal justice, Administration
of–Methodology. I. Title.
HV6018.C43   1993
364'.072–dc20   92-24748
                                                       CIP

Editorial/production supervision and interior design: Eileen M. O'Sullivan
Cover design: Bruce Kenselaar
Manufacturing buyer: Ed O'Dougherty
Acquisitions Editor: Robin Baliszewski
Editorial Assistant: Rose Mary Florio
Prepress buyer: Ilene Levy

 © 1993 Prentice-Hall, Inc.
Simon & Schuster / A Viacom Company
Upper Saddle River, New Jersey 07458

Printed in the United States of America
10 9 8 7 6 5 4 3

ISBN 0-13-572876-2

Prentice-Hall International (UK) Limited, *London*
Prentice-Hall of Australia Pty. Limited, *Sydney*
Prentice-Hall Canada Inc., *Toronto*
Prentice-Hall Hispanoamericana, S.A., *Mexico*
Prentice-Hall of India Private Limited, *New Delhi*
Prentice-Hall of Japan, Inc., *Tokyo*
Prentice-Hall of Southeast Asia Pte. Ltd., *Singapore*
Editora Prentice-Hall do Brasil, Ltda., *Rio de Janeiro*

For my "Uncle Bill,"
William A. Hackett

Contents

Contents   ix

Preface

RESEARCH METHODS FOR CRIMINAL JUSTICE AND CRIMINOLOGY is about how to conduct research and statistically analyze it. Within the social sciences, a broad range of research techniques, data collection strategies, and analytical tools exists that serves the needs of most scholars who conduct independent research investigations. Although certain research procedures and statistical techniques may be relevant only for certain specialized types of investigations, there are numerous techniques and procedures that may be generalizable and applicable to most fields, including criminology and criminal justice.

LEVEL OF BOOK

This text book has been written with the beginning student in mind. Therefore, much of the technical language and symbolic notation used to describe methodological and statistical strategies has been simplified. At the same time, consideration has been given to those who may wish to use this book as a reference or guide in their future research work. Thus, several topics have been included that are often given extended coverage in more advanced texts. Again, a major objective has been to describe and explain some of the more complex methodological and statistical procedures in an understandable manner. A useful feature that enhances student comprehension of more difficult material is the extensive use of examples drawn from the criminological and criminal justice literature. Students should relate well to this material and find particular applications of concepts and strategies reasonably easy to understand.

ORGANIZATION

The book has been organized as follows. First, "doing research" is explained in Part I. This explanation includes a discussion of some of the kinds of research topics undertaken by investigators in criminology and criminal justice. An integral part of any research activity is the creation of a theoretical scheme or explanatory framework that accounts for relationships between things. The role of theory in the research process will be described. Since the research enterprise is a process, this process consists of several important parts. Each part will be given appropriate attention. Like a chain that is no stronger than its weakest link, the research enterprise is no better than the weakest part or stage of that enterprise.

When investigators do research, they ordinarily begin with an idea of what they wish to study and how they intend to study it. Those who choose to study juvenile delinquency, for instance, will approach this topic from one explanatory perspective or another—perhaps the idea that delinquency is largely the result of family instability, or that it is largely the result of the significant influence of one's peers who may be delinquent, or that it is largely the result of cultural deprivation. These are frames of reference or ways of looking at and accounting for the phenomenon to be studied. Researchers also formulate a research plan to implement their study, whatever it may be. The plan may be a research proposal, including specific objectives or goals and ways by which they can be achieved. Throughout the entire process, these researchers are mindful of a code of ethics that operates to objectify their investigations and causes them to refrain from engaging in conduct that would call their integrity or methods into question.

Each research plan includes provisions for collecting data or information about the problem studied. Several different data collection methods will be described, including observation, questionnaire administration, interviewing, and the analysis of reports and other published information available in libraries. These comprise the subject matter of Part II. Because much criminological research involves contacting others and soliciting information concerning their ideas and attitudes about things, attention is also given to the measures we use to quantify the information collected. Do our measures of things have validity; that is, do these measures actually measure what we say they measure? Are these measures reliable? Can we depend upon them to give us consistent results over time? Accordingly, Part III examines ways of measuring things and evaluating their reliability and validity.

A general objective of the research enterprise is to verify or refute the explanations we have chosen to account for criminological phenomena. We subject our theorizing to different types of testing. There is much diversity in the ways theories are tested, ranging from highly qualitative tests (i.e., use of observation, interviewing, and other non-mathematical data-gathering), to highly quantitative ones (i.e., the use of correlations, sophisticated statistical models, computer simulations, and other mathematical analyses). For those tests of theory that are heavily quantitative, an array of statistical techniques and tools exists. These procedures aid in describing the data we have collected and making inferences about the general adequacy of our theories or explanatory schemes. Parts IV and

V describe a wide variety of statistical tests that are used by criminologists and criminal justice scholars in making decisions about their data. These decisions invariably influence their impressions about the utility of their theories.

Often, the application of statistical procedures is more of an art form rather than a mechanical, perfunctory process. Each research investigation poses particular problems for researchers that differ from other projects. Thus, it is important to retain a high degree of flexibility so that easier adaptations to unusual situations may be made whenever they are encountered. <u>Almost every research project has a degree of serendipity, where investigators discover unexpected events that were not anticipated.</u> Finally, every research project should be regarded as a tentative reflection of social reality. No single project, regardless of its magnitude, is the final word on any research topic. Replication of research, time and time again, is crucial as we move forward to establish greater certainty about the events we study. Therefore, researchers are at the same time both pioneers and verifiers. They pave new paths in less explored subject areas, and they add to the growing body of literature about these same subject areas through their inquiry.

- learning things for the study

USING THIS BOOK MOST EFFECTIVELY

Perhaps the best way to approach the material in this book is as a collection of strategies for problem-solving. Each strategy that might be employed in the investigation of particular criminal justice-related or criminological problems has weaknesses and strengths, limitations and benefits. These features must be weighed carefully as they are considered for application in problem-solutions. The problems are research questions, questions about criminological and criminal justice-related factors about which we seek information and answers.

Because the research process is multidimensional and involves numerous phases or stages, each exhibiting technical and sometimes complicated procedures, it might be helpful to regard this "collection of strategies" from the standpoint of building blocks. Thinking of a pyramid, base blocks form the foundation, and blocks on higher levels can only be supported by the foundation we have provided. Thus, our knowledge of research methods proceeds accordingly, as we master knowledge of basics and proceed to more technical strategies in later chapters. And, like the pyramid which, once in place, is a beautiful, complete assemblage of blocks, the research process unfolds similarly to yield a distinctive "whole" that can best be appreciated when viewed as an interconnected constellation of numerous components.

Our general intention is to improve our understanding of the events that occur around us. Perhaps our investigations will lead to certain practical policy decisions. However, our investigations may be unrelated to public policy or to anything of practical value other than a simple understanding and appreciation for why certain events occur. My position is that we should seek a healthy balance between our practical, substantive concerns and our theoretical ones. While some research may have direct relevance for a particular intervention program to be used for parolees in halfway houses to assist in their community reintegration, other research may not be adapted easily to any helping program. This state of affairs is perhaps as it should be, especially in view of the great diversity of interests among criminologists and criminal justice scholars, the problems they select for study, and the ways they choose to investigate these problems.

SPECIAL FEATURES AND ANCILLARIES

The book has several special features. These are as follows:

- Complex statistical formulae have been minimized, with careful, step-by-step instructions about how to complete one's calculations.
- All statistical and methodological procedures are fully explained and their interpretation is simplified with examples from the criminological literature.
- Current illustrations have been extracted from the literature of criminology and criminal justice. Approximately ten leading journals were selected and abstracts of articles were extracted for the period, 1985–1990. Topics for illustrations were deliberately chosen because of their variety and because of their topical importance in view of their frequency of treatment in the professional literature. All statistical procedures covered in this book were found among these articles, and the ideas from these articles were the basis for each example provided.
- Questions are provided at chapter ends for review. Key terms are in the beginning of each chapter.
- Chapters containing statistical tests also have problems to solve at the conclusion of each chapter. Answers to all computational problems are provided in an appendix so that students may check the accuracy of their computations and learn from mistakes they may have made.
- Interpretive tables are included in an appendix, including a table of squares and square roots and a table of random numbers. All interpretive tables for statistical procedures include headnotes or footnotes describing fully how they are to be used; thus, it is unnecessary to go back in the book to where these procedures were originally discussed in order to see how observed statistical values should be interpreted.
- Instructional aids include an instructor's manual and a computerized test bank of 2,000 questions and problems and are available for examination preparation. Versions of the computerized test bank are available in either IBM, Macintosh, or Appleworks formats. Additionally, transparencies are available for key tables and charts throughout the text.

ACKNOWLEDGMENTS

Ronald E. Vogel, Ed.D., California St. Univ., Long Beach
James S. E. Opolot, Ph.D., Texas Southern University
Jeanne B. Stinchcomb, Ph.D., Florida International University
David Neubauer, Ph.D., University of New Orleans

Dean J. Champion

PART 1
Theory and Research in Criminal Justice: Getting Started

Part I is an introduction to the process of criminological research. Chapter 1 provides an overview of this process, including some answers to the general question, "Why should we do research?" The research process is an orderly sequence of events comparable to a chain with numerous links. The analogy that a chain is no stronger than its weakest link is applicable here. The quality of research depends on the strength, and quality, of individual parts of the research chain. Investigators make the critical assumption that patterns exist for most observed social behaviors. The research process attempts to unravel and discover these patterns. Several other assumptions made by criminologists and criminal justice scholars are discussed, as well as various functions that research methods perform.

In Chapter 2 we discuss the relationship between theory and methodology. Different theories are used by criminologists to explain and predict relationships between different variables that they examine. An array of research methods and statistical procedures are utilized to test these theories. Different types of theory are described, including inductive and deductive theory. Integral parts of theories, variables, are also described, as well as several of their important functions in the research process. Investigators seek to discover causal relations between variables, although the subject of causality is approached cautiously. Causality is established whenever one variable is consistently related to another variable, such that the occurrence of one variable means the particular occurrence of the other variable. Thus each criminological event is believed to be precipitated, preceded, or "caused" by one or more other variables. We devise theories as explanations of relationships between different variables, and certain associations among variables are anticipated. Over time, the accumulation of scientific evidence leads us to favor certain theories over others, and to discard those that have little predictive value.

Theories are formulated in the context of frames of reference or views toward particular problems that are adopted by criminologists. In Chapter 3 we examine the role of frames of reference in the research enterprise and how we choose topics for subsequent investigation. Several considerations made by criminologists and criminal justice scholars are described. Ideal criteria are often established when selecting methodological strategies for use in our research. However, most studies are conducted within the context of various constraints that frustrate these ideal criteria we have established. Thus an ideal–real gap emerges that must be acknowledged and addressed.

In Chapter 4 we describe several popular research designs and objectives. Exploratory, descriptive, and experimental research designs are described, and their limitations and strengths are discussed. Investigators may conduct large-scale surveys, or they may limit their efforts to one-shot case studies. Each of these designs has strengths as well as weaknesses. Several criteria guide a researcher's selection of study designs. Experimental designs are described, including the classical experimental design. Such designs enable us to differentiate between independent samples and related ones, and to describe the ways in which such samples can be created for experimental purposes.

1

The Research Enterprise in Criminal Justice and Criminology

KEY TERMS

Applied research

Causality

Descriptive research

Experimental research

Explanation

Exploratory research

Longitudinal research

Prediction

Pure research

Qualitative research

Quantitative research

Research

Research process

Statistics

Here are some potential research questions for criminologists:

> Are blacks who murder whites more likely to receive the death penalty than whites who murder blacks (Keil and Vito, 1989)?
>
> Can private industry provide greater flexibility and cost-effectiveness in the managership of jails and prisons than that provided by government administration and regulation of these facilities (Bowditch and Everett, 1987)?

What causes perceptions of powerlessness among correctional officers in prisons, and how can these perceptions of powerlessness be changed or improved (Walters, 1988)?

Despite a U.S. Supreme Court ruling (*Tennessee v. Garner*, 1985) restricting the use of deadly force by police when apprehending fleeing felons, what administrative and legal controls should be implemented among police departments to regulate conditions under which police officers use their firearms to subdue violent felons (Fyfe, 1988)?

Do those who plead guilty to criminal charges through plea bargaining receive greater judicial leniency in sentencing than do those who are convicted of crimes through jury trials (Champion, 1988)?

Does an increase in the nation's arrest rate mean a rise in crime (*Uniform Crime Reports*, 1989)? In the criminal justice system, are female felons treated more leniently than male offenders (Wilbanks, 1986)?

Each of these questions and thousands of others are asked often in criminological and criminal justice research. Annually, thousands of articles are published, papers presented, and reports prepared to provide tentative answers to such questions. These are research questions, or questions that must be investigated more thoroughly before final and conclusive answers can be provided. This chapter is about the research enterprise or process. Various essential components of this process are presented and defined.

What do investigators do when they "conduct research"? This book answers that question, and this chapter presents an overview of the research process. Additionally, several important functions performed by the research enterprise are described. An integral feature of the research enterprise is statistical analysis and description. Although a more extended treatment of statistical techniques and tests is presented much later, in Part IV, here we examine briefly how statistics and research are closely intertwined. Finally, to do research and pursue the research enterprise fully, several assumptions must be made about the targets of our investigations. These will be identified and discussed.

OVERVIEW OF THE RESEARCH PROCESS AND STATISTICAL ANALYSIS

The Research Enterprise

The research process or research enterprise consists of all activities that pertain to problem formulation and definition. It includes developing a theoretical explanation for why problems exist; collecting information that will verify or refute the explanation of problems; analyzing, presenting, and interpreting this information; and drawing tentative conclusions that will either support or refute the theoretical explanation provided. More simply, you become interested in certain events and why those events occur. You conjecture about what causes these events. A reasonable explanation for the event occurs to you, but you are uncertain about it. You seek out and collect evidence that will enable you to test your explanation of the event and determine if it is useful. You examine your evidence and evaluate whether the explanation of the event is acceptable or feasible. The strength of the evidence you have gathered may require that you collect additional evidence and retest the explanation elsewhere, in new social settings. You repeat this process until you achieve an acceptable level of certainty about why the event has occurred.

A study by John Whitehead (1986) provides a useful illustration. Whitehead was interested in the phenomena of job burnout and dissatisfaction among male and female probation and parole officers. *Burnout* is a phenomenon characterized by emotional exhaustion, feelings of overextension and fatigue, depersonalization, and cynicism. *Job dissatisfaction* relates to discontent with one's work, job pressures, and feelings of unfulfillment. Whitehead became interested in these phenomena in part because of his general interest in probation and parole work and because larger numbers of women were entering this work during the 1980s.

At the time that Whitehead's research was conducted, there was much concern among criminal justice scholars about the high degree of labor turnover among correctional officers, including those officers involved in probation and parole work. Furthermore, among many of those officers who remained in their jobs, seemingly large numbers of officers were expressing disenchantment with their work, with their growing client caseloads, and with greater pressures from administrators. Also, some evidence about burnout among professionals in other occupational areas suggested that women are more susceptible than men to burnout. Because Whitehead was interested in factors that influence the quality of work performance of probation and parole officers, and because larger numbers of women were entering these work roles, he wondered whether women would experience greater burnout than men, as had been reported previously by other investigators. Would gender differences explain burnout and job dissatisfaction differences among probation and parole officers in a current investigation?

The "problem" (not a "problem" in the sense that I have a health problem or there is a problem with this appliance) or "question" of interest to Whitehead was whether female probation and parole officers are different from their male counterparts in job burnout. A second question related to the first was whether women would reflect greater job dissatisfaction than would men. Whitehead examined the professional literature about burnout and dissatisfaction, thus providing a skeletal rationale for the relation between gender and job burnout/dissatisfaction.

He mailed questionnaires to 1500 probation and parole officers in New York, Indiana, Connecticut, and Pennsylvania. (See Chapter 6 for an in-depth discussion of questionnaire construction and administration.) Whitehead himself had formerly worked in a New York probation department, and in his judgment, each locale selected appeared to be typical of other geographical areas. Also, these states employed large numbers of female probation and parole officers, and there was a good chance that Whitehead could obtain sufficiently large numbers of both male and female officers to make comparisons of their job burnout/dissatisfaction levels. (See Chapter 5 for an extended treatment of sampling procedures.) Two-thirds of the questionnaires were returned, with 41 percent consisting of responses from female officers.

Whitehead asked the officers questions that touched on social and psychological factors (attitudes including burnout and job dissatisfaction measures), demographic information (rural–urban background), personal characteristics (gender, age), and work characteristics (time on the job, years of probation and parole work). These data enabled him to determine whether male and female officers differed in their degree of burnout and job dissatisfaction.

Initial impressions of Whitehead's results seem disappointing since he found no significant differences between male and female officers in their job burnout and dissatisfaction levels. However, several male and female officers reported some burnout and some dissatisfaction with their work. Whitehead was not disappointed with these results. He attempted to explain his findings. First, one-third of his original sample did not respond. This nonresponse impaired the representativeness of his study and may have affected the findings adversely. Second, the men and women involved in his study had also reported similar pay, similar caseloads, similar promotional opportunities, and similar degrees of role conflicts in dealings with clients. Third, Whitehead speculated that some degree of self-selection may have occurred, and that those females entering probation and parole work may have been more masculine than other females who make different career choices. Thus their responses might be expected to be more similar to those of their male counterparts. Whitehead concluded his investigation by recommending further examination of these phenomena in other localities by other researchers. The groundwork for further study had been provided.

What if Whitehead had found that female officers had extraordinarily high levels of burnout and dissatisfaction compared with male officers? Would he have concluded that "females are more inclined toward burnout and dissatisfaction than males"? Probably not. Whitehead realized that his study would not provide final or conclusive answers to his research questions. However, he knew that his study would provide tentative support for his beliefs about probation officer burnout, or that these beliefs would be refuted by what he found. Thus, regardless of whether Whitehead had found significant differences or no differences among males and females in their burnout and dissatisfaction levels, he knew that the study would have to be repeated several times before his gender explanation of burnout and dissatisfaction would have credibility among other researchers.

Depending on the subject matter of one's study and its extensiveness, the research enterprise is a more or less elaborate plan that we use for answering questions of interest to us. This plan will vary in complexity and sophistication. Others may or may not be involved directly as research participants. In Whitehead's study of burnout and dissatisfaction among probation and parole officers, he mailed questionnaires to people and relied on the information derived from the returned questionnaires. Whitehead may have chosen not to mail questionnaires to these persons. Instead, he may have decided to visit them personally or have arranged to have others visit them. Using these different methods of gathering data, he could have asked these officers questions directly about their work and work-related attitudes.

Some problems studied by researchers may not easily be investigated by mailing questionnaires or conducting interviews. If we want to know whether the crime rate is increasing faster than the rate of normal population growth in the United States, an analysis of public documents compiled by the FBI, U.S. Department of Justice, and U.S. Bureau of the Census may be necessary. In such investigations, it is unlikely that others will have to be contacted directly for information about these research questions.

Some investigators spend several decades compiling information about problems they have selected for study in *longitudinal research*. For instance, Wolfgang (Wolfgang, Figlio, and Sellin, 1972) studied a large Philadelphia birth cohort, nearly 10,000 boys born in Philadelphia in 1945, and tracked them through official records until 1963. A *birth cohort* is comprised of all children born in a particular geographical area during a specified time interval, such as a month or year, in this case, 1945. Among other things, Wolfgang wanted to describe the characteristics and behavioral patterns of chronic recidivists, or persistent juvenile offenders. In 1975, he conducted a further analysis of a sample of these persons at age 30 to see how many committed crimes as adults and became career criminals (Wolfgang, 1983). For comparative purposes, Wolfgang selected a much larger birth cohort of over 28,000 boys and girls born in 1958 and tracked them through official records for a similar 18-year period.

Wolfgang's research, regarded as classics by many criminologists, revealed that (1) a small core of offenders, approximately 6 or 7 percent, accounted for over 60 percent of all crimes committed by the 1945 cohort, and (2) the 1958 cohort had a violent offense rate almost three times as large as the 1945 cohort. Wolfgang speculated that successive generations of juveniles were committing increasingly violent offenses compared with earlier generations. Despite the magnitude of Wolfgang's analysis and the large samples studied, these investigators never regarded their findings as conclusive about chronic offender behavior patterns and characteristics. Nevertheless, it is noteworthy that Wolfgang spent over 30 years patiently investigating this phenomenon. This type of study, longitudinal research, is very laborious, because it spans a fairly lengthy time period and involves tracking the same sample at different time intervals.

Beginning students should recognize that generally, the pace of research is slow. Some topics, such as job burnout among probation and parole officers, are not investigated frequently, whereas other topics, such as the causes of delinquency, are investigated often. Therefore, research information in different topic areas accumulates at an uneven rate.

Research may also be pure or applied. *Pure research* is often more difficult for students to understand and appreciate because it may have intuitive relevance only for those investigators who do such research. It does not excite everyone to know that reported crime in the United States increased at a higher rate during the 1980s compared with general population growth. But for conflict theorists, crime rate fluctuations may enable them to draw parallels between crime and changing political, economic, and social conditions. It does not always matter that the terms used to describe crime in relation to politics, social, and economic conditions are diffuse or intangible.

Consider the following statement formulated in the context of conflict theory: "Capitalist interests have perpetrated an exploitative system wherein the rich dominate the poor. Laws are the manipulative tools of the capitalist class, and state repression of working class interests is evident in the differential punishments society imposes for street crimes compared with anti-trust or white-collar crime." Such statements would be difficult, but not impossible, to test scientifically. Who makes up the "capitalist class" or the "working class"? What are "capitalist interests"? Pure research is often undertaken simply for the purpose of knowing. "Knowledge for the sake of knowledge" underscores what motivates many pure researchers. When you ask such persons what of a practical nature can be done with the research they have conducted, they may or may not be able to tell you. Questions about the practical aspects of their work are often considered irrelevant and not at issue.

Applied research is research undertaken mostly for practical reasons. Whitehead's study of burnout among male and female probation and parole officers has an applied dimension. One practical outcome of knowing more about burnout and its causes is learning about how it can be prevented. Preventing or reducing burnout and job dissatisfaction may help to head off large amounts of labor turnover in the correctional field. How can the job performance of correctional officers and relations between offender-clients and their probation or parole officers be improved? What types of interventions in prisons help to rehabilitate inmates or enhance a parolee's reintegration into the community? What can the courts and prosecutors do to streamline case processing and make this part of the criminal justice process more efficient and fair? Which jurors should be selected who will be likely to be favorable toward particular types of defendants? What kinds of training should police officers receive to improve their relations with community residents? How can crime in neighborhoods be reduced? These are applied research questions.

Pure (or basic) and applied research can also be distinguished by the influence of such research on various community programs and public policies. Investigations of job burnout and dissatisfaction may change how administrators in probation agencies supervise their officers and assign them duties. Studies of peer-group influence on juvenile delinquency may help to establish intervention programs where delinquent peers are used to "undo" delinquent behaviors through self-study and individual counseling (Empey and Erickson, 1972).

Research is not always exclusively pure or applied. It may be both simultaneously. Studies of judicial discretion in sentencing offenders may show sentencing disparities that are explained by race, ethnicity, gender, or socioeconomic status. Radical or critical criminologists may investigate sentencing patterns in different jurisdictions and find these disparities. Their work may show support for the influence of social class on the ciminal justice system (a pure research objective), but it may also lead to sentencing reforms to remedy sentencing disparities because of race, gender, or social class, such as a shift from indeterminate to presumptive sentencing (an applied research objective).

Statistical Analysis

One of the last courses taken by many students in criminal justice and criminology is statistics. For many students, statistics is like a red flag, a frightening and seemingly difficult hurdle to overcome. Doesn't it involve lots of numbers and complex formulas, and don't you have to be a mathematical whiz kid to complete such a course satisfactorily? Isn't it painful? Don't most students who take such courses fail or do poorly? The subject of statistics should not be threatening or painful. Although it may not be the most exciting topic studied in a criminal justice program, it is no more painful, threatening, or difficult than other courses in methods of research.

Statistics has several meanings. First, it is a field of study. Second, it often refers to numerical evidence that has been compiled, such as the "vital statistics" compiled by the U.S. Bureau of the Census. Those who respond to questions asked by census takers or who complete and return U.S. Bureau of the Census questionnaires become a part of the vital statistics of the U.S. population for particular years. The birth rate, death rate, murder rate, the Philadelphia Phillies' batting average, the average height of Mrs. Jones' third-grade class in Rapid City, South Dakota, the average number of dropouts at the University of Kentucky, and the average yards gained per game by the Miami Dolphins are all statistics. Thus statistics may refer to hundreds of descriptive indicators of things.

A third meaning of statistics is a collection of tests and techniques used to describe and make decisions and inferences about collected research data. Statistics may enable researchers to determine the degree of association between things, such as the relation between the length of time that parolees have spent in prison and the length of time on parole before some of them commit new crimes. Other statistical techniques help to determine many factors simultaneously or the causal influence of multiple factors on a single event. How do age, gender, socioeconomic status, race, history of drug use, employment status, and family stability relate to one another, and what is their collective impact on recidivism? Some of these statistical procedures help to determine whether differences exist between groups on some measured characteristic. For instance, Whitehead used statistical tests to determine whether males differed significantly from females in their job burnout and dissatisfaction scores.

Four chapters of this book (Part IV) are devoted to statistical techniques that are useful for those in criminology and criminal justice programs. Statistical analysis is an integral feature of many research projects, although some types of research do not use statistics. In these projects, investigators obtain information about things by observing others. Their observations may be presented in lengthy written accounts and inferences about social patterns may be drawn from these observations.

Using or not using statistical procedures distinguishes between *quantitative research* and *qualitative research*. Those involved in quantitative research are considered "data crunchers" or "number crunchers." They are sometimes criticized by others for their strong, quantitative orientation. However, quantitative criminologists may believe that there is too much subjectivity in qualitative research, and that numerical quantities and sophisticated applications of statistics can improve the quality and objectivity of data analysis and interpretation. Both perspectives have much to offer. In a sense, each makes important contributions that are offsetting positive qualities. Thus claims that quantitative analyses of data are better or more important than qualitative analyses of data are unjustified.

One important theme throughout all statistics-oriented chapters in Part IV is learning to determine when, where, and why statistical procedures should be applied in research. Statistics enters the research process largely in the data analysis and interpretation phase. Various statistical tests and descriptive procedures are helpful to researchers as they present their work to others and evaluate the significance of their findings. No statistical procedures presented in this book involve calculations beyond simple addition, subtraction, multiplication, division, and square-root skills. Since pocket calculators are inexpensive and available in all colleges and universities, even computing square roots has been reduced to mere button pushing. Even so, a table of squares and square roots for numbers 1 to 1000 is provided in Appendix A for easy reference.

WHY DO RESEARCH?

Some of the major reasons for conducting criminological research include (1) acquiring knowledge for the sake of knowledge, (2) determining answers to practical questions, (3) adding to the growing body of knowledge in the profession, and (4) acquiring useful knowledge and skills to transmit this information to others and direct their investigations.

1. Some people are interested in simply knowing about things. The "knowledge for the sake of knowledge" position has been related to pure research. The practical implications of pure research are often not apparent. In fact, the practical ends served by such theorizing are simply ignored. Thus the objective is to study the complexities of explanations, not to solve current social problems.

2. Some practitioners seek answers to practical questions. Regardless of their "rightness" or "wrongness," decisions are made about public policy or program components. For example, research investigations of judicial sentencing patterns in certain jurisdictions have disclosed evidence of sentencing disparities. Although these disparities may not be overt, it is strongly implied by researchers that subtle, yet significant disparities exist. Thus state legislatures may seek to correct these disparities by modifying their state sentencing systems. This is not intended to mean that all judges are biased or deliberately sentence offenders of different genders or races to different incarcerative terms despite their offense similarities. Rather, legislatures may wish to take preventive action to eliminate possible allegations or the appearance of judicial favoritism or wrongdoing.

3. Most investigators wish to add to the growing body of knowledge in each criminological or criminal justice topic area. Whether we are interested in the relation between age and crime or offense escalation among juveniles arrested for status offenses, our knowledge of these and other topics is enhanced through objective research that is conducted. Any profession is noted for a body of grounded literature pertaining to specific subject areas. Systematically undertaken research can do much to enhance the sophistication of this body of literature so that others may benefit from it.

4. A fourth reason relates to understanding the work reported by other investigators and how such work relates to our professional interests. Students entering criminology or criminal justice will carve out an interest area or area of specialization. They will read research reported in various professional journals and trade publications, and it is in their best interests to acquire extensive knowledge of the work of others. If they should eventually teach subjects reflecting their areas of specialization, their previously acquired information will be an invaluable resource from which to draw examples and illustrations. They will be more capable of directing the research of students to seek to conduct their own investigations of topics of interest to them.

FUNCTIONS OF RESEARCH AND STATISTICS

Research methods and statistics as applied to criminal justice and criminology fulfill several important functions. These functions are (1) exploratory, (2) descriptive, (3) experimental, and (4) decision making.

Exploratory Functions

In some areas of criminology and criminal justice, little is known about observed events. Why do serial murderers kill? Why do spouses abuse each other and their children? What types of policing are best for particular neighborhoods or communities? What influence does the gender of criminal defendants have on juries comprised of the opposite gender? Are older judges more lenient than younger judges in sentencing older offenders? While some research exists to provide partial answers to these and other questions, few answers are presently available that adequately account for them.

For instance, a correctional innovation introduced on a limited scale in recent years is electronic monitoring (Ball and Lilly, 1985). Many legal, moral, and ethical questions have arisen about the use of electronic monitoring and its subsequent application for managing larger offender populations. While preliminary reports have been completed about the cost of using these systems in various jurisdictions, there are still unanswered questions about the technological implications of electronic monitoring and the logistical problems to be solved if such equipment is to be used on a large scale. Therefore, exploratory studies are being undertaken to answer some of these questions. (A more detailed explanation of exploratory studies is presented in Chapter 4.)

Exploratory studies also identify factors that seem to have more relevance than others for explaining things. Exploratory studies narrow our investigations to explanations of events that are more promising than others. For instance, electronic monitoring has raised constitutional questions such as the right to privacy. The U.S. Supreme Court has not ruled on the constitutionality of electronic monitoring in supervised release programs, and few, if any, jurisdictions have statutes that prohibit its use. An exploratory study might disclose little about the constitutionality of electronic monitoring, and therefore we might be better off studying the cost and logistical implementation of such monitoring in communities.

Descriptive Functions

Although descriptive research objectives are discussed in greater detail in Chapter 4, it is timely here to mention that descriptive research has a more focused quality than its exploratory counterpart. A study by Marquart and Roebuck (1986) of prison guards in a maximum-security institution described extensively the interactions among several correctional officers and inmates. (Although the American Correctional Association, the American Jail Association, and other interested correctional agencies have agreed to use "correctional officer" or "jail officer" as more professionally descriptive than the term, "guard," in references to those who manage inmates in prisons and jails, "guard" is used here because Marquart's participant observation in a prison was in the context of his role as a guard and was a part of his article title.)

These researchers were looking at specific types of interaction relating to rule enforcement and inmate norms that had been described previously by other researchers. How far will guards go to overlook inmate infractions in exchange for information about inmate contraband? What sanctions exist for prison correctional officers who use excessive force in subduing unruly inmates? These and several other questions were raised and examined. Therefore, they undertook their descriptive study with a fairly concise set of research objectives and behaviors to study and describe. Their investigation was rich with descriptive detail, as they outlined various incidents and correctional officer–inmate dialogue. Descriptive research sets the stage for more controlled experimentation later, where certain factors may be manipulated and controlled observations may be made.

Experimental Functions

The experimental function of research pertains to the amount of control researchers exercise over the variables (factors) or subjects (persons) they study. Experimental research is designed to see which factors make a difference in modifying a particular outcome. A standard type of experimental research is called the "before–after" method or design. Ordinarily, the experimental subjects (persons who are being studied by the researcher) are examined in one time period, administered a stimulus (an experimental factor or variable), and then examined again in a second time period. Comparing their time 1 and time 2 scores supposedly discloses the impact of the experimental factor on their behavior.

An example of an experimental study is reported by Sechrest (1989). Sechrest studied the influence on recidivism rates of "boot camps" or basic training camps designed for younger offenders in Florida. These are camps equated with "shock incarceration," where short-term exposures to highly regimented, military-like programs are offered to youthful offenders who have originally been sentenced to 10 years or less for certain crimes. These programs stress discipline, counseling, and different kinds of training that prepare participants for acceptance of personal responsibilities and decision making when freed. In Florida, for instance, the average boot camp experience is about 245 days (8 months), and this figure is about 20 percent of the average sentence lengths originally imposed.

Actually, Sechrest did not use a single group of offenders in a before–after test. Rather, he compared one group of offenders with another according to certain personal, social, and criminal characteristics. Thus the two groups differed primarily on the basis that one group participated in boot camp while the other was subject to standard incarceration in prison and later paroled. Follow-up investigations of these subjects showed that boot camp participants had a return-to-prison rate of about 6 percent compared with an 8 percent return-to-prison rate for the other group. Lopsided numbers of persons in the two samples (143 boot camp participants and 400 other inmates of prisons) were cited by Sechrest as a study limitation, although the ages and general backgrounds of all of those studied were similar. Although these findings are not clear-cut and cannot permit us to conclude that boot camps reduce recidivism drastically, the study itself is illustrative of a comparison of samples over time.

One convenient way of distinguishing between these different studies and the functions they serve is to envision a continuum of uncertainty and certainty such as the one shown below.

Uncertainty———————————————Certainty

Exploratory————→Descriptive————→Experimental

As we move from the extreme left (uncertainty), our studies change in quality from exploratory, to descriptive, to experimental. Thus experimental studies are those characterized by a high degree of certainty. What this means is that our knowledge of which factors are important has increased to the point that we can conduct specific tests and exert some degree of control over various factors. However, it is unlikely that any study ever reaches absolutely the right extreme of total certainty. Some studies are closer to the certainty end of the continuum than others. Those closer to the uncertainty end of the continuum are more likely to be exploratory or descriptive studies than experimental ones.

Decision-Making Functions

The major functions of statistics in research are to help us describe the phenomena we study, make decisions about our observations, and identify relationships between two or more variables. For instance, suppose that we are interested in the frequency of inmate lawsuits filed against prison officials and correctional personnel. We study two prisons, noting that prison A has an inmate-grievance counsel, where a board comprised of inmates hears complaints and allegations against prison officials lodged by other inmates. In prison B there is no inmate board. Assuming that the two prisons are of equal size, suppose the rate of lawsuits filed in prison A is 3 per 100 inmates, whereas in prison B the rate is 7 per 100 inmates.

Statistics can give us an objective appraisal of the significance of difference between these rates, although by inspection we can see that the two rates are numerically different. That they differ is important, but for statistical purposes, we want to determine if these differences are "significant," where statistical significance is evaluated according to certain "chance" expectations about whatever we observe. In Chapters 16 and 17 we discuss statistical significance in depth.

SOME BASIC ASSUMPTIONS ABOUT CRIMINAL JUSTICE AND CRIMINOLOGY

All scientific inquiry is based on several important assumptions. These assumptions relate to the predictability and regularity of any relation between two or more variables. A high degree of predictability and regularity among variables exists in the field of chemistry, for instance. Particular combinations of certain chemicals have regular, recurring, and predictable outcomes or reactions that can be forecast accurately in advance of their combination. Such predictability and regularity are more apparent among variables associated with the hard sciences (chemistry, biology, physics, engineering), where the controlled variables are tangible. Their interrelations with other variables, as well as environment factors, are heavily controlled. Interactions of measured amounts of different chemicals under certain temperatures for designated time periods reflect the high degree of variable control achieved by chemistry, for example. But people are not chemicals and cannot be studied under such controlled conditions.

In criminology and criminal justice, many of the variables we study, such as attitudes, ideas, and opinions, are less tangible than chemicals. Therefore, the presence or absence of these social and psychological variables must be inferred largely from other, indirect, indicators. Attitudinal phenomena are not immediately apparent through observation, although the influence of attitudes or an assessment of their existence can be made by constructing various attitudinal scaling devices.

Greater measurement difficulties associated with certain variables do not automatically exclude them from scientific investigation, however. It means that social scientists must make extraordinary efforts to establish these more elusive phenomena as behavioral predictors. Whereas chemists can measure quantities of chemicals and observe their effects on other chemicals, criminologists must devise indirect indicators of attitudinal variables in order to assess their effects on behaviors. Attitudes cannot be seen, but their presence may be inferred from how persons behave or respond to questions about their feelings and thoughts. Thus attitudinal measures require a high degree of empirical proof of their accuracy and consistency. This is a major reason why we spend so much time studying the validity (accuracy) and reliability (consistency) of our attitudinal measures. (See Chapters 9 and 10 for a more extended discussion of validity and reliability of measuring instruments.)

Research in criminal justice and criminology attempts to explain and predict relations between variables. What is the influence of diet on criminality? Do convicted black offenders receive harsher sentences than those of convicted white offenders? What barriers slow the influx of women into correctional officer and probation/parole officer work roles? How do our perceptions of powerlessness influence our adaptability to our jobs? What factors reduce stress and burnout? Is there a rise in female delinquency, and if so, why? Are successive generations of delinquents more violent than previous generations of delinquents? Can criminals be rehabilitated? If so, what intervention strategies seem to work best for purposes of rehabilitation? These questions require considerable research before conclusive answers can be provided. Before undertaking any investigation of relations between these and other variables, several assumptions are made by criminologists and criminal justice scholars. These assumptions are not unique to criminology or criminal justice. Rather, they extend to all types of scientific inquiry. In the present instance, these assumptions have been adapted to fit criminology and criminal justice applications.

1. *A pattern exists among certain variables of interest to criminologists.* This assumption is generally accepted by those conducting criminological research. If we do not believe that there is a pattern associated with certain variable interrelationships, prediction, forecasting, and regularity cannot be assumed. This means that relations between sentencing and race, between perceptions of powerlessness and job adaptation, between delinquency and family influence or socioeconomic status, between diet and criminality, and between attitudes of male administrators and correctional officers and female entry into corrections work are random. Few of us believe that these and similar variable interrelations are purely random.

2. *Patterns of variable interrelationships can be described and used as the bases for hypothesis tests.* This assumption stems from the first. It coincides with the empirical nature of criminological phenomena. It means that we can use the identifiable patterns of interrelationships between variables for the purpose of testing our theories about these variables. (See Chapters 2 and 3 for a more extensive discussion of theory and hypothesis formulation.)

3. *A causal relation exists between certain criminological variables.* While we are interested in establishing cause–effect relations among the variables we study, it is also true that causal relations between phenomena are difficult to establish. Nevertheless, a major aim of criminologists is to determine which variables cause other variables to occur and to describe these causal relationships. For example, if we believe that judges are racially prejudiced to a degree in the sentences they dispense and that such prejudice leads to sentencing disparities attributable to racial factors, these sentencing disparities may be minimized or eliminated entirely by restricting judicial sentencing discretion. Restricting judicial sentencing discretion may be accomplished by modifying existing sentencing structures to a guidelines-based scheme, where judges must impose sentences within certain ranges for different crimes if offenders are convicted of these crimes. Although other variables may be manipulated to invoke the desired responses or outcome, such as greater fairness in sentencing, the fact is that we can sometimes effect changes in one variable by manipulating other variables that are causally related to it.

Some Basic Assumptions about Criminal Justice and Criminology   **15**

4. *Relevant variables for criminologists and criminal justice scholars are empirical and amenable to measurement.* This means simply that we can identify variables and their interrelations with other variables, and can measure their existence. If we study the influence of peer groups on delinquency, for example, this means that we must devise a measure of peer-group influence. Definitions of delinquency are reasonably standardized, although there are some jurisdictional variations regarding whether certain behaviors should be classified as delinquency. Despite this variability, delinquency is easily conceptualized, although peer-group influence is less concrete.

5. *Inconsistencies exist among studies of the same phenomena, and these inconsistencies are not necessarily indicative of nonrelations between various phenomena.* Smith and Jones might find, for instance, that criminal behavior tends to decline with increasing age. However, Anderson and Freedman may find that the incidence of crime among the elderly is increasing annually. What should we conclude about the relation between age and criminal behavior? Apparent contradictory findings should not discourage us from pursuing our research interests enthusiastically. After all, there are different jurisdictions involved, different samples of criminals investigated, different types of crime examined, and a myriad of other factors that can explain away these inconsistencies. Thus research is cumulative, and through replication and repetition, our knowledge about variable interrelations is greatly enhanced. Eventually, we discover general patterns of relations between variables, although these patterns may exhibit occasional inconsistencies. Again, we must not be too hasty and conclude that because inconsistencies in findings exist, there must not be any continuity in the interrelationships of variables investigated.

These are only a few of many assumptions made about our fields of inquiry. Criminology and criminal justice offer a wealth of interesting information for research. Investigators are limited only by their imaginations of what can be studied and how. In subsequent chapters, we examine more closely the notions of theory, frames of reference, variables, and hypotheses, and how each of these relates to the research process.

SUMMARY

The research enterprise consists of all activities related to problem formulation and investigation, and the theorizing and data collection that result in the verification or refutation of explanations for different phenomena. A distinction is made between pure and applied research, where pure research seemingly has nonutilitarian objectives, whereas applied research is closely connected with social action to effect change. Research involves collecting and analyzing data. Statistical procedures are applied in most research investigations to corroborate our beliefs about the interrelations between variables. Statistical procedures are an assemblage of tests and techniques that enable us to describe and make decisions about the data we have collected. Research projects where statistics are not used are qualitative, whereas those projects using statistical analyses are quantitative. Much research exhibits both qualitative and quantitative dimensions.

Research is conducted for many reasons. People are interested in knowing about things, why they occur, and how they can be controlled. Research fulfills exploratory, descriptive, and experimental functions. Each of these functions is dependent on how much we actually know about the phenomena we investigate and how tightly we can control the environment where these phenomena are studied. Assumptions made by criminologists and criminal justice scholars about the data they study include the idea that there are distinguishable patterns of interrelation between variables that can be identified. Furthermore, these patterns can function as the foundations for subsequent hypothesis tests and an eventual verification or refutation of theory.

QUESTIONS FOR REVIEW

p. 7-9 1. What is the distinction between pure and applied research? Must any research be either pure or applied? Why or why not?

2. What is a research question? Formulate five research questions apart from those presented in the text and list them. You may turn to the research literature in professional journals for your answers.

4+6 3. What is the research process? What are some functions of the research process?

7 4. What is longitudinal research? What is an example of it?

9-10 5. What are several meanings associated with statistics? How are statistics and research methods interrelated?

10-11 6. What are some of the more important reasons that criminologists and others do research?

11-13 7. What are three general functions performed by research and statistics? Describe each of these functions. How does our degree of certainty about subject matter relate to these functions?

14-15 8. Criminologists and criminal justice scholars make various assumptions about their fields and the data they collect. What are some of these assumptions, and why are they important?

2

Theory and Research in Criminal Justice and Criminology

KEY TERMS

Assumptions

Causality

Concepts

Contingent conditions

Continuous variable

Contributory conditions

Convention

Deductive theory

Definitions

Dependent variable

Discrete variable

Empirical generalizations

Explanation

Independent variable

Inductive theory

Method of agreement

Method of concomitant variation

Method of difference

Necessary conditions

Prediction

Propositions

Spuriousness

Sufficient conditions

Theory

Variables

INTRODUCTION

This chapter is about theory and how it relates to the research process. Theory is defined, and several important functions of theory are described. There are different types of theory that criminologists and criminal justice scholars can use when conducting their investigations. Some of the more important types of theory will be illustrated.

All theories are comprised of several variables. These represent the phenomena to be explained as well as various phenomena used to explain them. Variables are conceptualized in alternative ways. Because the particular methods of data collection and statistical procedures that we will eventually choose to use are largely dependent on the nature of the variables we are investigating, it will be important to illustrate different ways in which variables can be conceived. Variables are an integral part of theories and perform several important functions. These functions will be identified and described.

Social scientists, criminologists, and criminal justice scholars seek to establish causal relations between variables, although it has been noted that causality is difficult to establish when the variables investigated are somewhat elusive empirically. Theories tie variables together in logical ways, and research permits investigators to explore the validity of these relationships. Thus there is a complementarity between research and theory, where each assists the other. Like the horse and carriage, theory and research, for all practical purposes, are quite compatible. Each may be defined and described independently, but both depend on each other for their maximum utility. Investigators almost always use theory to guide their research activity, and their research activity leads to either refutation or confirmation of their theories. The value of both theory and research will also be explored.

THEORY DEFINED

Some writers regard theory as a collection of concepts. Others say that theory is an interconnected set of hypotheses. Other writers say that theory is a set of concepts plus the interrelationships that are assumed to exist among those concepts (Selltiz, Wrightsman, and Cook, 1976:16). Another way of viewing theory is as a *system of explanation*. Some scholars regard theory as a conceptual scheme, a frame of reference, or a set of propositions and conclusions. If we consult a dictionary, theory is a mental viewing, a contemplation, conjecture, a systematic statement of principles, or a formulation of apparent relationships or underlying principles of certain observed phenomena that has been verified to some degree (Guralnik, 1972:1475).

All of these definitions of theory are true. Yet no single definition pulls together all of theory's essential elements. Theory *is* a conceptual scheme, a set of propositions and/or concepts, a contemplation, conjecture, a statement of principles, and a formulation of relationships of observed phenomena. Perhaps one of the clearer and more comprehensive definitions of theory may be gleaned from a synthesis of two definitions provided by Robert Merton (1957:96–99) and the late theorist, Arnold Rose (1965:9–12). According to these social scientists, *theory* is an integrated body of assumptions, propositions, and definitions that are related in such a way so as to explain and predict relationships between two or more variables.

Assumptions, Propositions, and Definitions

First, let's distinguish between assumptions and propositions. Assumptions are similar to empirical generalizations or observable regularities in human behavior (Merton, 1957:95–96). For our purposes, *assumptions* are statements that have a high degree of certainty. These are statements that require little, if any, confirmation in the real world. Examples of assumptions might be, "All societies have laws," or "The greater the deviant conduct, the greater the group pressure on the deviant to conform to group norms." Other assumption statements might be, "Prison inmates devise hierarchies of authority highly dependent on one's physical strength and abilities," or "Most types of deliquency are group-shared phenomena," or "Most delinquents commit delinquent acts in the company of other delinquents." While some of us may take issue with these statements, there is little need to verify each of them. Social scientists and criminologists have found extensive support for each. We take these statements for granted.

In contrast, *propositions* are also statements about the real world, but they lack the high degree of certainty associated with assumptions. Examples of propositions might be, "Burnout among probation officers may be mitigated or lessened through job enlargement and giving officers greater input in organizational decision making," or "Two-officer patrol units are less susceptible to misconduct and corruption than one-officer patrol units." Other propositions might be, "Reducing prison overcrowding will result in a proportionate decrease in inmate discontent and prison condition-related court litigation." Each researcher has more or less strongly held beliefs about the truth or certainty of these statements. Sometimes, the same statement may be labeled as a "proposition" by one researcher and an "assumption" by another researcher. Depending on one's experience with the subject matter being investigated, varying degrees of certainty are associated with different statements made about the real world.

Theories consist of *both* assumptions and propositions. At any given point, researchers will construct theories that contain assumptions and propositions, although over time, these various statements change in the degree of certainty that we associate with them. Accruing research in a given subject area will eventually transform propositional statements into assumptions. Many of our assumptions have evolved from the propositional statements of earlier times. As more research is conducted and information is compiled, we gradually improve our understanding of why certain events occur. We become more certain about things.

Other components of theories are *definitions*. Definitions of terms we use or definitions of the factors we consider significant in influencing various events assist us in constructing a logical explanatory framework or theory. A common problem is that often, the same terms are assigned different definitions by different investigators. If we use the term *peer influence* in a statement about delinquents and their delinquent conduct, how should peer influence be defined? How should stress be defined if we are investigating the relation between stress and probation officer power within a probation agency? How should power be defined? As we will see later, there is a conceptual "Tower of Babel" phenomenon in most sciences, as different investigators assign different meanings to the same terms. Differences in the definitions assigned common terms sometimes explain inconsistencies in research findings.

When different definitions are given to a common term, it is likely that researchers will arrive at different conclusions about variable interrelationships in independent investigations. For instance, researcher Smith might study probation agency A. If Smith defines "stress" as physical fatigue and exhaustion, this may characterize how probation officers in probation agency A feel while performing their jobs. However, if researcher Jones studies probation agency B and defines stress as an increasing inability to perform a variety of tasks involving conflicting expectations and the psychological frustration resulting from such role performances, it is likely that Jones will find that the probation officers studied in agency B may not exhibit "stress" in the same way as officers exhibit it in agency A. This is one of the many explanations we give for contrary or inconsistent findings when the "same" variables are researched by different investigators. Researchers Smith and Jones are using the same terms, but their different definitions of those terms yield different kinds of associations with other important variables.

In criminology and criminal justice, theory is utilized frequently to account for most phenomena. In most criminology and criminal justice books, for example, theories of deviant conduct and crime are presented that link these phenomena with glandular malfunctions, early childhood socialization, unusual chromosomatic patterns such as the "XYY syndrome," body types, peer-group associations and influences, criminal and delinquent subcultures, feeblemindedness and/or mental impairment, differential association, broken homes, cultural deprivation, anomie, social bonding, opportunity, hedonism, class conflict, unequal access to success goals, labeling, learning, cognitive developmentalism, behaviorism, gender, race, age, ethnicity, and social power differentials. For each of these linkages, such as the link between crime and labeling, for instance, an explanatory scheme is advanced that accounts for how labeling is related to criminal behavior.

Labeling theory, for example, explains deviant and criminal conduct by focusing on social definitions of acts of crime and deviance rather than on the acts themselves. Some of the assumptions underlying labeling theory are (1) that no act is inherently criminal; (2) that persons become criminals through social definition of their conduct; (3) that all persons at one time or another conform to or deviate from the law; (4) that "getting caught" begins the labeling process; (5) that persons defined as criminal will, in turn, cultivate criminal self-definitions; and (6) that they will eventually seek out and associate with others who are similarly defined and develop a criminal subculture (VanderZanden, 1984:206; Bernstein, Kelly, and Doyle, 1977; Lemert, 1951).

The impact of social influence is strong in labeling theory. Accepting the definitions of others and acquiring self-definitions of criminality seems to lead to further criminal behavior. While the empirical evidence to support labeling theory as a "good" explanation for criminal conduct is inconsistent and sketchy, it is nevertheless an explanation accepted by more than a few criminologists. Some scholars might regard labeling theory as grounded conjecture, where occasional instances of support for the labeling perspective have been observed.

Another theory of criminality is the *XYY syndrome*. Sociobiologists and geneticists have studied the chromosomatic patterns of many criminals in an attempt to link these patterns with different types of criminal conduct. X and Y are sex chromosomes that persons inherit from their parents. Male infants are typified with an XY chromosomatic pattern, while females are typified by an XX pattern. Y chromosomes are considered "aggressive"; X chromosomes are considered "passive."

Spectacular new events such as mass or serial murders stimulate interest in criminological theories. When Richard Speck murdered eight student nurses in Chicago during the 1960s, he was eventually studied by sociobiologists. They found that Speck had an unusual XYY chromosomatic pattern, with an extra Y chromosome. This "aggressive" chromosome provided at least one instance of support for the idea that crime and chromosomatic patterns are related. In Speck's case, his mass murders of nurses were thought attributable, in part, to his highly "aggressive" genetic structure. However, subsequent tests of chromosomatic patterns among incarcerated criminals, even violent offenders, have failed to disclose a systematic relation between chromosomes and particular criminial behaviors (Shah and Roth, 1974; Mednick and Volavka, 1980). In fact, Shah and Roth (1974) found that only 5 percent of a large sample of criminals had the XYY pattern. Although this percentage is slightly higher than that estimated for the general U.S. population, it is not significant as a consistent predictor of criminal behavior.

In both the labeling and XYY syndrome theories, various phenomena, social definitions, and self-definitions of certain behaviors and chromosomatic patterns are highlighted and featured as primary causes of other criminal behaviors. Those who use these explanations for criminal conduct write elaborate arguments to provide logical and plausible support for their beliefs. Eventually, research is conducted that provides some degree of support for these assertions and explanations. If researchers look hard enough, they can find support for their theorizing *somewhere*. Richard Speck's case was considered "proof" of the plausibility of the XYY syndrome, although this proof was insufficient to justify incarcerating all persons with an XYY chromosomatic pattern because of some suspected propensity to commit mass murder. These examples illustrate two important functions of theory: *explanation* and *prediction*.

Explanation and Prediction

Explanations of events are often given higher priority than are predictions of events. There is not much difference between explanation and speculation. Brainstorming and thinking up ideas about which factors seem to create probation officer burnout, delinquency, or rising crime rates usually involves much speculation, often mislabeled as "theorizing." When criminologists say, "My theory about why this or that occurs is . . .", what they usually mean is that their belief is that a particular factor seems responsible for causing some event. They speculate about what causes an event to occur. Seldom do they sit down and patiently and painstakingly develop a systematic explanatory scheme linking certain events with their believed "causes" of those events. True theorists among criminologists and criminal justice scholars are comparatively few in number.

Theories can be rank-ordered according to their ability to predict things. Theories with the greatest predictive utility are used more often, while those lacking predictive utility or promise are discarded and forgotten. Anyone can explain anything, but that does not mean that the explanations advanced are good ones. Often, the "acid test" is whether theories can predict events adequately or accurately.

Judges and parole boards, for example, are in the business of predicting behavior. Judges must make decisions about whether to place convicted offenders on probation or to incarcerate them for specific time periods. Parole boards must decide whether certain prisoners should be released from prison short of serving their full sentences. Different sentencing and early-release criteria are applied by judges and parole boards in their decision-making activity. In most instances, their decisions are influenced, in part, by references to rational, nonrational, and/or irrational criteria, such as race, ethnicity, age, gender, socioeconomic status, prior record, drug or alcohol dependency, presence or absence of a family support system, nature of the conviction offense, compliance or noncompliance with prison rules and regulations, acceptance of responsibility for their criminal actions, and the prestige of their defense attorneys. These decisions may also be guided by abstract references to vague theories, partial theories, or syntheses of several contrasting theories of crime and criminal conduct.

Decisions made by judges and parole boards are flawed in various ways. Many offenders placed on probation or granted parole eventually recidivate and commit new crimes. The criminal justice system considers these cases "failures." Such "failures" are empirical evidence of poor judicial and parole board judgment to forecast the future behaviors of probationers and parolees.

Consistent with the idea that theories may be evaluated as either good or bad on the basis of their degree of predictive utility, sometimes theories may be considered more less important according to the types of policy decisions that are influenced by them. Early in the twentieth century, for example, when the scientific community of criminologists believed heredity to be an important factor in causing criminality, prisoners in various states (e.g., Oklahoma and Virginia) were sterilized so that they would be incapable of fathering children. At the time, sterilization seemed to be a sound and logical step that society could take to prevent the birth of future criminals.

During the rehabilitation era of 1940–1970, for example, many prisons offered educational and vocational–technical training, as well as counseling programs for inmates. These programs were believed to be remedies for various inmate deficiencies, since many prisoners lacked formal education, vocational skills, and a basic understanding of the etiology of their criminal conduct. However, sterilization [subsequently declared unconstitutional in *Skinner v. Oklahoma* (1942)] and many rehabilitative programs for inmates have failed to decrease or reduce criminality. In recent years, while most prisons have continued to offer a broad range of inmate programs, the emphasis in corrections has shifted from rehabilitation to crime control. This is evidenced by the great increase in probation and parole programs in recent years that stress close or intensive offender monitoring or greater probation/parole officer–offender/client contact.

TYPES OF THEORY

Although there are many kinds of theorizing, in this discussion we focus on two of the more popular types: deductive theory and inductive theory.

Deductive Theory

Deductive theory is more common than inductive theory in social science today. It is based on deductive reasoning from the work of the early Greek philosopher, Aristotle (384–322 B.C.). Logical statements are *deduced* or derived from other statements. Typically, assumptions are made and conclusions are drawn that appear to be logically connected with these assumptions. A common example is, "All men are mortal. Aristotle is a man. Therefore, Aristotle is mortal." Symbolically, "All *A*'s are *B*'s; *C* is a *B*, therefore, *C* is also an *A*."

In research, any event that needs to be explained provides a foundation for deductive theory building. Some examples of "problems" or "unanswered questions" or "occurrences" may be:

1. Sentencing disparities among judges
2. Juvenile deliquency
3. Child sexual abuse or spousal abuse
4. Crime among the elderly
5. The prisonization process
6. Probation/parole officer burnout and stress
7. Prosecutorial discretion
8. Social class variations in crime rates

Researchers will choose problems of interest to them, and then they will devise an explanation for their problems. They will include in their explanation certain assumptions, propositions, and definitions of terms. The interrelatedness of these linakges among assumptions and propositions is a logical formulation. From this logical formulation, deductions may be made. These deductions are always considered to be tentative deductions. They must be tested by gathering data.

Through data gathering and analysis, researchers learn whether their deductions are valid. If the data suggest that these deductions should be questioned, further testing is done in other settings. Even if findings support certain deductions, further tests are ordinarily conducted, since these investigators want to be certain of their conclusions.

One example of deductive theorizing is Johnson's (1986) study of family structure and delinquency. Johnson reexamined the "broken home–delinquency" relation by using self-reports from 700 high school sophomores. Because of space limitations in professional journals, researchers are not always able to elaborate their theories for readers. Rather, they provide a sketchy view of their assumptions and propositions and how they are interconnected. Johnson's reported research is no exception. Johnson acknowledges initially that "broken" homes have, for many years, been thought to be a major factor in the cause of juvenile delinquency (p. 65). Also, he acknowledges that there is general, although inconsistent, support for this view in the professional literature.

A careful reading of his introduction and the discussion of what he found when the responses of 700 youths were examined permits us to identify several of his theoretical premises. For instance, Johnson observes that the process whereby delinquency and "broken homes" become related begins by a family breakup. The family breakup reduces the quality of parent–child relationships, possibly through the physical and/or psychological separation inherent in the breakup. The breakup, like ripples in a pond, influences different dimensions of a youth's life. Problems of familial breakups may lead to school difficulties, where the child has difficulty concentrating on schoolwork. Furthermore, Johnson notes that often, official agencies respond to children from broken homes in different ways compared with their responses to children where the children's homes are intact. Johnson's crucial question is, "Is there in fact an association between family structure and delinquency?" (p. 66). His data disclosed support, although moderate, for the claim that family structure is related to delinquency. Considerable statistical evidence is presented to support his tentative conclusions.

Although Johnson prepared a more elaborate version of these events and the interrelatedness of his basic assumptions and propositions, the skeletal aspects of his theorizing are there. Several traumatic events in a child's life trigger assorted problems of adjustment to other life events. We glean from his analysis that there are psychological rewards that youths obtain from intact familial experiences, and that physical separation minimizes or frustrates the youth's fulfillment of these rewarding experiences. School difficulties, one possible product of such frustration at home, generate further adjustment problems for affected youths. One product of such frustration is the commission of delinquent acts. Johnson does not claim that all youths from broken homes will become delinquent. Rather, he indicates that disruptive homes contribute with other factors in youths' lives to elicit delinquent behaviors. His discussion of these other factors (e.g., gender, age, and race of juveniles, mothers–stepfather/father–stepmother situations, and official reports from police versus self-reports from delinquents themselves) are excellent suggestions for follow-up research projects to be pursued by other interested investigators.

Johnson's study is largely deductive, where various assumptions and propositional statments have been made about the association between familial stability and propensity of juveniles toward delinquent conduct. A more comprehensive or sophisticated analysis of the problem would encompass an explanation or delineation of the nature of psychological rewards stemming from intact families, the reasons for mother–stepfather/father–stepmother differences in the incidence of delinquent behaviors among their respective children, and a detailed outline of why various "agents of society" would be inclined to respond differently toward children from intact homes compared with children from family breakups. Specific agencies of society could be identified, and a rationale could be given in each instance for why these agencies would respond in peculiar or unique ways to youths from broken homes. All of this would be encompassed within a more comprehensive and sophisticated theoretical framework. Space limitations for journal articles do not permit more extensive discussions of theory, however.

Johnson started by making a theoretical sketch of the relation between broken homes and delinquent behavior, and he found a setting where his theorizing could be tested. His data analysis led him to some of the conclusions noted above. He logically deduced an explanation for delinquent behavior and sought empirical confirmation or refutation of his explanation. All of this was accomplished through deduction.

Inductive Theory

Induction is a process whereby a specific event is examined and described, and where generalizations are made to a larger class of similar events. Suppose that we wanted to devise an explanation for why offenders become recidivists and commit new crimes. Through induction, we could examine a sample of known recidivists from Connecticut prisons, inmates who have a history of prior convictions. As the result of our observations and analyses of the Connecticut inmate sample, we might conclude that our recidivists are younger black males who have alcohol/drug dependencies, are in the lower socioeconomic strata, were unemployed or underemployed when originally arrested and convicted, and have less than a high school education. From these observations, we might make several generalizations about the broader class of recidivists nationally.

Or perhaps we are interested in learning about those persons most likely to "fail" while on parole or in probation programs. Again, judges and parole boards wish to know which criteria seem most relevant in forecasting the successfulness of prospective probationers and/or parolees. Observing samples of New York probationers and parolees who have been incarcerated or reincarcerated for violating one or more program conditions will enable us to delineate some of their social, demographic, and psychological characteristics and backgrounds. From our descriptions of New York probationers and parolees who have "failed" while on probation or parole, we might generalize to the broader class of probationers and parolees on a nationwide basis.

Now, let's back up for a moment and see what has been done in each of the instances mentioned above. In both cases, samples have been obtained and described. Then these descriptions have been generalized to the broader class of persons represented by the samples. Are these generalizations we have made in each instance "good generalizations"? Should we therefore deny parole or probation to *all* young black male offenders with drug or alcohol dependencies who were unemployed or underemployed when they were initially arrested and convicted and who lack a high school education? This general policy would prompt much controversy, to say the least.

In both instances, we have examined the "events" (i.e., the samples of Connecticut inmates and New York probationers and parolees who have failed) and described various characteristics of these events. Then we have attempted to generalize to the broader class of similar events. Clearly, our research goals include both explanation and prediction. We will tentatively explain recidivism and probation/parole program failures by using the characteristics of samples of inmates and program failures as predictors. But we must now turn our energies in the same direction as deductive theorizing. We must see whether these predictors or characteristics will permit us to forecast recidivism and program failures in advance of their potential recidivism and program failure.

Using deduction, we *abstract by generalizing*. Using induction, we *generalize by abstracting*. Although both deduction and induction help us achieve common research objectives, including data gathering and theory verification, they lead us to these objectives through different paths. In a deductive context, we state what we believe is a rational theory to explain some event, such as delinquency. Then we will obtain samples of delinquent and nondelinquent youths to test the adequacy of our theory. However, using induction, we may examine a few delinquents and nondelinquents, describe their similarities and differences, and attempt to generalize the characteristics uniquely possessed by these delinquents to a larger class of delinquents nationally. But again, we must follow up on our induction with an empirical test situation and determine whether the characteristics we have identified on a smaller scale help us to predict delinquent behavior on a larger scale.

The distinction between deduction and induction can also be made according to whether we construct a logical explanatory and predictive scheme and observe facts consistent with that scheme, or whether we observe certain facts and generalize from the facts observed. It has been noted that "there are those who feel that the entire research process is initiated with theories. Deduction occurs when we . . . gather facts to confirm or disprove hypothesized relationships between variables [derived from theory]. Whether there were facts that precipitated the [theory] does not really matter. What matters is that research is essentially a hypothesis-testing venture in which the hypotheses rest on logically [if not factually) deduced relational statements" (Black and Champion, 1976:65). Thus deduction and induction are simply alternative ways of constructing theory.

VARIABLES AND THEORY

Variables refer to any phenomena that can assume more than one value. Again, there are varying definitions of variables. Two alternative definitions are that variables are "categories that may be divided into two or more subcategories" (Fitzgerald and Cox, 1987:311) and "concepts that have been operationalized or 'concepts that can vary' or take on different values of a quantitative nature" (Hagan, 1989:15). Both of these alternative definitions of variables are true. However, the first definition above is preferred because it avoids the use of such terms as "operationalization" and "concepts." In the context of this book, these terms have particular meanings, discussed at length in Chapter 9.

What are "phenomena that can assume more than one value"? First, *any* attitudinal phenomena we can name (e.g., prejudice, achievement motivation, burnout, work satisfaction, alienation, positive feelings toward police officers) are variables. We can have much burnout, low work satisfaction, strong positive feelings toward police officers, a high degree of alienation, and low achievement motivation. Precisely what are meant by "high," "low," "strong," and "high degree" depend on how we measure these phenomena. Again, in Chapter 9 we describe variable measurement in detail.

Other phenomena that can assume more than one value are:

1. Gender
2. Social class
3. Race
4. Ethnicity
5. Political affiliation
6. Religious affiliation
7. Urban–rural background
8. Age
9. Income
10. Types of crime
11. Crime rates, delinquency
12. City size and population
13. Judicial, prosecutorial, and parole board discretion
14. Police–community relations
15. Employment discrimination

Sometimes, use of the term *value* is misleading. For example, *gender* assumes more than one "value." The values are *subclasses* on the gender variable, including "male" and "female." Different values on the "type of crime" variable might be "violent offenses" and "property offenses." Different values on the political or religious affiliation variables might be "Democrat," "Republican," "American Independent," "Catholic," "Protestant," and "Jewish." These are more like *designations* than values in a numerical sense. It is helpful to think of these variables simply as consisting of different subclasses. Also, we decide which subclasses will be used in our research for any variable.

Any research "problem" we choose to investigate is also a variable. *We use other variables to explain the variable we are investigating.* We illustrate the interconnectedness of these variables (the variable to be explained and the explanatory variables) in our theory. Thus our definition of theory makes more sense now as "an integrated body of assumptions, propositions, and definitions that explain and predict the relationship between two or more variables." One of these variables is the "problem" we wish to explain, and one or more "other" variables are used to explain or account for the existence of the problem (i.e., the variable to be explained).

Variables, essential to all theories, perform different functions. To best portray these functions, some distinctions between variables can be made. These include considerations of variables as (1) independent, (2) dependent, (3) discrete, and (4) continuous.

Independent Variables

Independence and *dependence* mean that some variables cause changes in other variables, while some variables are influenced by other variables. *Independent variables* are those that elicit changes in other variables. *Dependent variables* are those whose values are affected by independent variables. Two illustrations assist us in understanding these differences between independent and dependent variables and their interrelation.

Gunderson (1987) investigated the relation between the types of uniforms worn by police and their degree of credibility in the eyes of the public they serve. Three types of police uniforms (e.g., blazers and slacks, Eisenhower jackets and slacks, and standard paramilitary uniforms) were chosen for investigation by Gunderson. These different types of uniforms were subclasses of the variable "type of uniform." Gunderson wanted to know whether wearing one type of uniform or another had any significant influence on officer self-perceptions of professionalism and whether the public would perceive officers wearing certain kinds of uniforms as more or less professional.

It is quite clear here that "self-perceptions of professionalism" and "public perceptions of police professionalism" were the designated variables thought by Gunderson to be influenced by the independent variable "type of uniform." His findings supported the idea that officers who wore blazer uniforms not only had higher self-perceptions of professionalism, but they were also regarded by the public as more professional than officers wearing other uniform styles. Although this research was not conclusive, it illustrates what an independent variable is and how it functions in relation to other variables.

The Gunderson study was fairly matter of fact, and it was reasonably easy to measure "type of uniform" and "self-perceptions of professionalism." Often, however, certain variables may be more elusive, and their relationships with other variables must be inferred largely from independent, abstract criteria. For instance, Anson (1983) investigated the relation between inmate ethnicity and suicide rates among prisoners in state and federal prisons. Anson noticed that different state and federal prisons exhibited different rates of inmate suicide. Attempting to explain this problem, "prison suicide rates," Anson conjectured that the proportionate ethnicity of particular inmate populations might have something to do with the prison suicide rates. He devised a theoretical scheme wherein "ethnicity of prison population" was designated as the independent variable. Subclasses on this variable were varying proportions of ethnic inmates in the prisons he examined. His ethnic/racial categories included blacks, whites, Orientals, Hispanics, and Indians.

Anson observed that prisons with higher inmate suicide rates also had larger proportions of white inmates. In fact, he eventually concluded from his research that the following ethnic groups may be ordered from the highest to the lowest on self-inflicted injuries: Indians, blacks, Orientals, Hispanics, and whites. Therefore, "proportion of inmate ethnicity/race" was considered to be the independent variable and a prime factor in prompting self-inflicted injuries among inmates, including suicides. Again, while Anson's findings are not conclusive and do not necessarily typify inmate suicides in all U.S. prisons or jails, the example serves to illustrate the "function" of an independent variable in relation to one or more other variables, in this case, inmate suicides.

Dependent Variables

Dependent variables are those phenomena that derive their values largely from the influences or actions of other variables. In the Gunderson and Anson studies mentioned above, "self-perceptions of professionalism," "perceptions by the public of police officer professionalism," and "inmate suicides" were dependent variables. Virtually any problem we choose to investigate becomes a dependent variable.

In criminology and criminal justice, dependent variables are easy to identify. Often, they are "standardized" as dependent variables. That is, their use as either independent or dependent variables is fairly consistent from study to study. A silly but informative illustration is the gender–delinquency relation. Which variable, gender or delinquency, would be the more likely choice as the independent variable in relation to the other? Obviously, differences in gender are far more likely to produce changes in delinquent behavior rather than delinquent behavior producing changes in gender. Dependent variables from various components of the criminal justice system might be:

1. Probation officer burnout and stress
2. Crime rates
3. Prisonization
4. Prosecutorial, judicial, and parole board discretion
5. Police officer discretion to use deadly force in apprehending fleeing offenders
6. Police professionalism
7. Police misconduct
8. Inmate suicides
9. Inmate rioting frequency
10. Inmate rehabilitation
11. Parolee and probationer success in conditional intermediate punishment programs
12. Turnover among correctional personnel

This list is endless. These are common dependent variables, since we so often wish to explain their occurrence or development. However, we should not always assume that these and other variables are "fixed" as permanent dependent variables. Sometimes, we formulate complex combinations of variables in our research plans. In the examples presented thus far, we have looked at "two-variable" relations, where one variable was related or interconnected with one other variable. What if we wanted to relate more than two variables? Adding other variables to our analysis of some research problem might be illustrated as follows.

Suppose that we wish to study the relation between type of correctional officer supervision, correctional officer stress, and correctional officer turnover. We may read research reports indicating that if correctional officer supervisors were to involve their correctional officer subordinates in decision-making power more often, they might reduce the amount of burnout or stress experienced by correctional officers. Also, burnout reductions may incline correctional officers to consider remaining for longer employment periods with their prisons or jails. We have just linked three variables together. We will need to explain how each relates to the other, but this will be done in our theoretical scheme. The three-variable linkage we have formulated might look as shown in Figure 2.1.

Notice in the diagram that correctional officer self-perceptions of involvement in decision making and subsequent perceived burnout and stress are considered influenced by behaviors of correctional officer supervisors: namely, their consideration of subordinates in decision-making matters. Notice also that these correctional officer feelings of burnout and stress are linked in an implied causal fashion with labor turnover. Therefore, if you are the boss and do not give your workers power in decisions affecting their work, they will stress out, burn out, and quit.

In the case in Figure 2.1, correctional officer burnout/stress is functioning in a dual capacity: It is a dependent variable in relation to correctional officer supervisor consideration, and it is an independent variable in relation to officer labor turnover. Labor turnover, is, of course, the major dependent variable in this example. Usually, when researchers formulate theories to explain things, they specify which variables will be considered relevant and how they will be used—as independent, as dependent, or as both independent and dependent under certain circumstances. It is important to maintain a high degree of flexibility when considering how variables function in theoretical schemes. Under most circumstances, many variable treatment and definitional options are available to the investigator.

Discrete Variables

Discrete variables are phenomena that have a limited number of exclusive subclasses. *Gender* is a discrete variable, for all practical purposes. You are either "male" or "female." You cannot be in the two subclasses simultaneously. *Type of crime* is also a discrete variable. Divisions or subclasses on this variable include violent and property crime, misdemeanor and felony, or some other discrete designation. There are exceptions, of course. In biology, varying the amount of

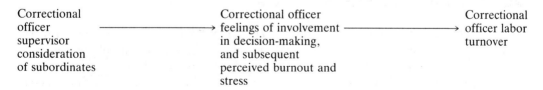

Figure 2.1 Hypothesized Relation Between Correctional Officer Supervisor Consideration of Subordinates, Correctional Officer Self-Perceptions of Involvement in Decision-making, and Correctional Officer Labor Turnover.

Variables and Theory

estrogen, androgen, or testosterone in the bodies of males and females may make them more or less male or female. In fact, biologists may be able to make a convincing case for "degrees of maleness or femaleness." Also, criminals may commit several types of crime during a crime spree. They may steal a car, burglarize a dwelling, rob a bank, kill a teller, and kidnap the bank president. Later, they may assault a police officer, resist arrest, and commit perjury on the witness stand at their trial. For convenience, however, criminologists will probably place them in one criminal category or another, depending on the type of research conducted. They will be classed as "violent offenders" (most likely) or possibly as "property offenders" (least likely).

Continuous Variables

Continuous variables are phenomena that can be infinitely divided into a variety of subclasses. All attitudinal variables are continuous variables. Income is a continuous variable. The crime rate is a continuous variable. Each of these phenomena may assume an infinite or nearly infinite number of values. As a practical matter, however, and largely for the convenience of the researcher and reader, virtually every continuous variable is reduced more or less arbitrarily to a limited number of discrete categories. For instance, we could report incomes of 50,000 city residents to the penny. Will Smith earns $30,267.83 per year, and Phil Jones earns $16,271.26 per year. But more often than not, income is reported in a series of discrete categories, such as "high income," "moderately high income," "moderately low income," and "low income." Dollar amounts can be assigned each of these categories so that we will know where to place Will Smith and Phil Jones. Zero dollars to $5000 will define the "low income" category, while $5000 to $10,000 will define the "moderately low income" category. The "high income" category may be $30,000 or over, depending on the community we study and how we have chosen to define our categories.

Again, the subjective element is present here. We usually decide how many categories or subclasses will comprise given variables, and we usually make up our own definitions or criteria for those categories or variable subclasses. These decisions we make are often arbitrary, although in later chapters we will see that certain guidelines, conventions, or standards may be invoked for the construction of variable subclasses.

CAUSAL RELATIONS BETWEEN VARIABLES

One long-range aim of theoretical schemes is to identify *causal relationships* between two or more variables. Logically, if we know what variable or variables cause another variable to occur or change in value, we might be able to exert some control and produced expected and desirable outcomes. When elementary school teachers hear about some of their former third- or fourth-graders who are now teenagers and who have committed serious offenses, they might say, "I just knew so-and-so was going to turn out that way—you just 'know' about certain children like that! Something could have been done earlier to prevent that!," what they are alluding to may be an intervention program of some sort that may have "caused" the child to grow up differently and not become delinquent. Although it is often difficult for teachers to define the specific nature and properties of an effective intervention program that might deter children from becoming delinquents, it is significant that they believe that "something" could and should have been done (as an intervention) for certain "problem children," whomever they are, and that "something" could have "caused" a different outcome.

Some of the research described in this chapter has causal overtones. Johnson's (1986) study of delinquency and intactness of families stressed family stability as a contributing factor. Why? Gunderson's (1987) study of police officer uniforms and self-perceptions of professionalism also implied causality between self-perceptions and type of uniform worn. Does wearing a particular type of uniform "cause" police officers to adopt more favorable self-perceptions of professionalism? Can we directly improve the perceptions of community residents of the professionalism of their police officers by changing officer attire? How does the type of uniform worn by police officers influence community perceptions of officer professionalism? And why? Can we decrease suicide rates in prisons by adjusting the racial and ethnic compositions of inmate populations in various ways? What proportion of whites and blacks is considered ideal for preventing or at least minimizing suicides? And why is this proportionate distribution relevant?

Most of the research in the professional literature avoids using "cause–effect" phraseology. Rather, more conservative tones are ordinarily adopted. Statements such as "There is an apparent association between X and Y," or "There may be a connection between X and Y," or "Evidence suggests that X may contribute to Y" are typical of the conclusions drawn by most researchers. And this is precisely how it ought to be. We may be in the business of attempting to establish cause–effect relationships between variables, but we also understand that it is a very difficult business.

John Stuart Mill (1806–1873), an English philosopher and political economist, was an early scientist who recognized certain problems of establishing cause–effect relationships between variables. He formulated three different methods whereby cause–effect relationships could be implied. These included the method of agreement, the method of difference, and the method of concomitant variation. Mill said that the *method of agreement* states that if the circumstances leading up to a given event have in all cases one factor in common, this factor may be the cause sought. The *method of difference* states that if two sets of circumstances differ in only one factor, and the one containing the factor leads to the event and the other does not, we may consider the factor to be the cause of the event. The *method of concomitant variation* states that if variation in the intensity of a given factor is followed by a parallel variation in the effect, this factor is the cause (Mill, 1930: 32–33).

Mill illustrated these principles, in part, by using a "rat" analogy. Suppose that we have two batches of rats, under identical circumstances, that are fed identical diets, except that one batch of rats also receives a certain drug. The fact that all rats in the batch with the included drug die immediately might be grounds to conclude that the drug killed the rats. Mill contended that although this might be so, it did not prove absolutely that the drug killed the rats. He reasoned that the result may be due to chance, or that the rats probably would have died anyway from natural causes. The difficulty, noted by Mill, is connected with the expression "identical circumstances." No two circumstances are ever exactly identical. At the very best, they must differ either in time or in place and will in fact differ in a practically infinite number of other respects as well (Mill, 1930:32–33).

Gunderson's (1987) study of the type of police uniform and self- and public perceptions of officer professionalism highlights some of the cause–effect difficulties noted by Mill. Were public perceptions of the types of uniforms worn by police officers influenced by contemporary fashion trends? Did residents of different races or ethnicities regard different uniform styles differently? Perhaps some of the officers wearing particular types of uniforms were disliked by specific community residents interviewed. Perhaps those officers who had low self-perceptions of professionalism had deep-seated personality problems or underconfidence, and that these problems would not be mitigated significantly by changing uniforms. Maybe height, weight, or gender of officers wearing particular uniforms functioned in various ways to alter resident perceptions of their professionalism. Perhaps a self-selection process had occurred, where certain officers chose to wear particular types of uniforms and "felt better" and "more professional" as a result. Again, the list of possible explanations for differential reactions to uniform type is endless.

Establishing cause–effect relations between variables also causes us to regard certain antecedent variables (i.e., variables or conditions that precede any observed associations between other variable interrelationships) as either necessary, sufficient, contributory, or contingent. *Necessary conditions* are those that must occur if the phenomena of which they are a "cause" are to occur. For example, permanent blindness involves destruction of the optic nerve, a necessary condition. *Sufficient conditions* are those that are always followed by the phenomena of which they are "causes." Corneal damage or a trauma to one's retina may be sufficient to cause blindness, although corneas may be replaced or repaired, traumas to retinas may heal or be relieved, and blindness may be cured (Selltiz et al., 1959).

Contributory conditions influence the occurrence and degree of change in other phenomena. Contributory conditions are not necessarily followed by the caused event. Rather, contributory conditions or variables, acting with other conditions or variables, operate to change dependent variables. For example, using drugs or alcohol does not automatically lead to criminal behavior, although drugs and alcohol are often identified as contributing factors that may make it easier for some persons to commit crimes by lowering their inhibitions. Probation and parole programs almost always require that clients refrain from using drugs and alcohol because of their close association with program failures. *Contingent conditions* are those acting as "intervening links" in the presence of an observed relation between two other variables (Selltiz et al., 1959:81).

Much of the research conducted today in criminology and criminal justice identifies contributory conditions, or those variables that precede other variables. Few researchers make cause–effect statements. In fact, several contemporary statistical procedures show predictable "contributions" of certain independent and intervening variables on dependent variables. These procedures include inter-correlations among variables, although they are also designed to disclose cause–effect path relationships. Ultimately, we attempt to identify the direct and indirect influences of certain variables on others. If cause–effect relations between variables are established later, this is a fringe benefit of our work.

It is possible to generate various combinations of variable functions by using necessary, sufficient, contributory, and contingent variable criteria. For instance, a variable might be a necessary (and obviously a "contributory") condition, but it may be insufficient to bring about a given phenomenon. Or a variable may be a contributory condition but not necessary for a given phenomenon to occur. Variables can function as sufficient, but not necessary, and so on. The point is that almost every variable can be treated in several different ways simultaneously in relation to other variables in the analysis and determination of a causal relation. The theoretical scheme we devise to account for given phenomena in criminology and criminal justice provides the necessary structure for showing the precise relation or contribution of each variable in relation to other variables used in our hypotheses.

Hyman (1955), Hirschi and Selvin (1967), and others recommend the inclusion of intervening variables in any causal analysis of variable interrelationships. They say that holding a match to a pile of leaves is a cause of their bursting into flames, although we cannot describe fully the intervening chemical reactions. It makes a difference whether the leaves are wet or dry (Hirschi and Selvin, 1967:123–130; Black and Champion, 1976:41–42). On the subject of explaining and predicting the incidence of delinquency, for instance, Hirschi and Selvin note that they have detected at least six "false criteria of causality" in their investigations of delinquency literature. These are to:

1. *Falsely assume that to be causal, relations between variables must be perfect.* Relations between social and psychological variables are seldom perfect. For example, possessing greater verbal skills and higher education may enable many police officers to relate more effectively with community residents. However, not every police officer possessing greater verbal skills and higher education always relates well with the public. Some less-educated officers do well in their community relations. Nevertheless, better verbal skills and higher education seem helpful in fostering better police–community relations. Therefore, police officer recruits may be selected, in part, because of their better verbal skills and higher degrees of education. The relation between police–community relations and verbal skills and educational attainment is not perfect, but there does appear to be a general relationship.

2. *Falsely assume that causal relations are equivalent to characteristics.* Variations that occur infrequently in variables are not necessarily characteristic variations. Many psychological variables are beyond our immediate grasp. If we hire correctional officers who seem to be confident and secure and capable of handling stress, the instruments we use as indicators of these traits are imperfect. Thus, when some officers "crack" under the pressure of a prison riot, for example, these exceptions do not typify all correctional officer reactions to stress-producing situations. Rather, they indicate the presence of individual factors that were previously unknown or beyond the scope of our existing measures of one's confidence and ability to handle stress.

3. *Falsely assume that variables whose relations are restricted to a specific social context can be used to comprehend relations between similar variables in other contexts.* We may find, for example, that probation officers who take a course on report writing may do quite well in writing presentence investigation reports for convicted offenders and have higher self-esteem. However, it cannot be assumed that police officers who take the same report-writing course will necessarily do a better job of writing accident or arrest reports in their own work or have higher self-esteem.

4. *Falsely assume that intervening variables eliminate the original causal relation observed between two variables.* Variables that add to our overall comprehension of an original relation between variables do not necessarily diminish the importance of the original relation we observed between those variables. An original relationship may be observed between delinquency and working mothers. However, it may be that continuous adult supervision may be more important in influencing one's delinquency than whether or not the mother works. However, the fact that many mothers who work also have delinquent children suggests that the absence of mothers in the home during the workday may be a contributing factor to delinquency. The importance of whether or not mothers work in helping to explain delinquency should not be discounted, simply because other variables seem to intervene in this original association.

5. *Falsely assume that measurable variables are not causes.* Some researchers believe that the "real" causes of criminological events lie beyond our immediate grasp and outside the realm of our methodological sophistication. Most variables can be measured. Not all measures we devise for these variables are necessarily good measures, but this does not prohibit us from exploring cause–effect relationships between variables. If the true causes of criminological phenomena were indeed beyond our methodological grasp, applications of science in criminology and criminal justice would be worthless. Current evidence suggests that these fields are expanding and growing in theoretical and methodological sophistication and not throwing in the scientific towel.

6. *Falsely assume that relationships between variables are dependent on other variables and that the independent variable is not a cause of the dependent one.* Some researchers mistakenly believe that single independent variables are incapable of inducing specific outcomes or changes in dependent variables, and that relationships between all variables are necessarily complex ones. No doubt this line of thought has contributed to the greater use of complex methodologies and statistical procedures, where less complex strategies might be equally adequate for explaining and predicting things (Hirschi and Selvin, 1967:123–130; Black and Champion, 1976:41–42). Obviously, criminological events are complex. Single-factor explanations of events may be incomplete, but a certain amount of predictive power can be attributed to each independent variable.

One additional topic deserves addressing in our discussion of causal relations between variables. This is *spuriousness*. Often, we cite agreement or concomitant variation among variables as evidence of a causal relation between them. One example suggested by Riley (1963) and mentioned briefly above is the relation between working/nonworking mothers and delinquent/nondeliquent status of children. Obtaining records of 100 delinquent boys and 100 nondelinquent boys, for instance, may yield a table such as that shown in Table 2.1.

We may tentatively conclude from these data that 75 percent of the mothers who work have delinquent children, whereas 75 percent of the mothers who do not work have nondelinquent children. One implication is that if the mother works, this contributes to delinquency. It makes a case for encourging mothers to stay at home and be with their children. An appropriate rationale for this case can be created easily, including home stability, the importance of mother in child-rearing, and so on. However, what if we were to take into account another variable, such as "continuous supervision by an adult" and see whether this modifies our original data pattern? Table 2.2 shows our data recast, where continuous/noncontinuous adult supervision has been taken into account, and where the working/nonworking status of mothers is observed in relation to delinquent/nondelinquent status of children.

In Table 2.2, all of the delinquent children are found in the category where children do not receive continuous adult supervision, regardless of whether the mother works or does not work. Furthermore, all of the nondelinquent children are found in the category where children are continuously supervised by an adult. This "washes away" or overrides the original relation we presumed existed between working mothers/nonworking mothers and delinquency of children. This brief exercise illustrates the potential impact of an additional variable on an original two-variable relation. This is spuriousness. *Spuriousness* is an apparent relation

TABLE 2.1 RELATION BETWEEN WORKING/NONWORKING STATUS OF MOTHERS AND DELINQUENT/NONDELINQUENT STATUS OF 200 BOYS

		Mothers:		
		Work	Do not work	Total
Children are:	Delinquent	75	25	100
	Nondelinquent	25	75	100
	Total	100	100	200

TABLE 2.2 RELATION BETWEEN WORKING/NONWORKING STATUS OF MOTHERS AND DELINQUENT/NONDELINQUENT STATUS OF CHILDREN, CONTROLLING FOR CONTINUOUS/NONCONTINUOUS SUPERVISION OF CHILDREN

		Adult supervision of children				
		Continuous		Noncontinuous		
		Mother works	Mother does not work	Mother works	Mother does not work	Total
Children	Delinquent	0	0	75	25	100
	Nondelinquent	25	75	0	0	100
	Total	25	75	75	25	200

Causal Relations between Variables

between two variables that is subsequently explained by the presence of an additional, unknown, variable. The potential for spuriousness in any variable interrelationship is an additional important reason for us to exercise caution when interpreting our research findings and drawing conclusions about observed relationships.

Testing for spuriousness is not difficult. Much depends on our actual knowledge of the research problem and whether possible alternative explanations for variable interrelationships exist. Additional time and patience are required, as the researcher puts each of these alternative explanations of the originally observed outcome to rest through empirical tests and tabular arrangements such as those illustrated in Tables 2.1 and 2.2. If an originally observed relation between variables is later determined to be spurious, much has been accomplished. Researchers can then focus more of their attention on those variables that were largely responsible for the spuriousness.

THE COMPLEMENTARITY OF THEORY AND RESEARCH

There is an inevitable interplay between theory and research. More often than not, theory is a guide for subsequent research activity. Theory focuses our research in particular directions, and it directs us to examine certain variables and disregard the influence of other variables. Thus theory is like "blinders" on horses: Horses see directly ahead and are less disturbed or distracted by events not directly in their field of vision. Theory is also value-laden, because it is formulated in the context of our beliefs about what causes certain events. If we believe that criminal behavior is a function of glandular malfunction, we will be unlikely to focus our attention on delinquent subcultures or the socialization process of differential association. Instead, we will look at potential relations between different types of crime and glandular irregularities or problems among criminals. However, if we adopt labeling theory as our favored explanation for criminal behavior, we will be concerned with public reactions to and definitions of crime and the criminal's response to such reactions. We will not conduct biochemical analyses of criminals to determine the possible presence of glandular irregularities.

Research enables us to test our theories empirically. We can evaluate whether our theories are adequate at accounting for events we attempt to explain. Our predictions of events can be supported or refuted, depending on what we observe from the collected data. We may discover things about our data and the events we attempt to explain that were formerly unknown, or if they were unknown, were considered unimportant or inconsequential at the time. Upon further analysis, however, it seems that certain variables have taken on greater importance to us. This is sometimes called *serendipity*, where we find out important things about the people we study that we were not looking for initially. On these occasions, we might reformulate our theoretical schemes and include these formerly unknown or "unimportant" variables. Thus research that we conduct may suggest theories, the application of different strategies to collect and analyze data, or the modification of existing theories according to newly discovered criteria.

THE VALUE OF THEORY

Often, distinctions among social scientific fields have been made according to their theoretical sophistication. Some evidence exists that criminal justice has not advanced theoretically to the same degree as criminology (Willis, 1983; Conley, 1979; Morn, 1980). Despite this evidence or its validity, there is a strong trend within criminal justice departments in the United States to improve the current state of theory throughout the discipline (Henderson and Boostrom, 1989).

Theoretical sophistication has also been equated with the degree of professionalization in any academic discipline (Dingwall and Lewis, 1983). One reason for the perceived absence of theory in criminal justice has been its historical emphasis on process and application within the criminal justice system. In contrast, criminology has historically emphasized crime causation (Henderson and Boostrom, 1989:37) Whatever the merits of these arguments, the fact is that theory is receiving greater attention from both criminologists and criminal justice scholars alike. Theory is increasingly perceived as the integrating medium through which the administration of justice, the criminal justice system, and explanations of crime can be productively blended.

Intermediate punishment programs such as intensive supervised probation, furloughs, work/study release, and home incarceration/electronic monitoring must increasingly respond to questions about those inmates and criminal candidates most likely to benefit from these supervisory services. In turn, these services may be treated by criminologists as intervening factors in theoretical schemes, where these factors may change criminal behaviors and reduce recidivism in different ways. Theory not only functions to explain and predict events, but it acts as a general policy guide for how offenders are or should be processed throughout the criminal justice system. The observed factual information—crime rates, recidivism rates, crime escalation, effects of decriminalization, plea bargaining, shock probation, short- or long-term incarceration—all conspire to tell us something about the validity of theories we have formulated.

THE VALUE OF RESEARCH

By the same token, research provides support for or refutes our theorizing. Generally, research activity advances our knowledge about things, raising our level of certainty about why events that are of interest to us occur in ways that they do. Much of the research used in examples above throughout this chapter will benefit greatly from additional research. We may eventually be able to describe fully the process whereby police officers acquire professional attitudes about themselves and how the types of uniforms they wear influence this process. We might eventually learn the true relation between delinquency and homes that are not intact. Furthermore, some day we may be able to predict with amazing accuracy those settings where inmate suicides will be highest, and we may be able to structure things or juggle inmate environments in ways that curb inmate suicidal propensities.

Research is not limited exclusively to testing theories, however. Some research is evaluative, where we seek to discover the efficacy of a particular intervention strategy or the influence of certain factors on others. Of course, we can carry our research findings into the classroom to enhance our lectures on specific subjects. Student interest in course content is frequently stimulated by presenting some of the findings from new research on selected subjects. Research uncovers topic areas that need further study. Research suggests ideas that might be useful in modifying older theories or developing new ones.

SUMMARY

Theory and research are closely interconnected. Theory is an integrated body of assumptions, propositions, and definitions that are related in such a way as to explain and predict relationships between two or more variables. Key components of theory include assumptions or empirical generalizations, observable regularities about social behavior, and propositions or statements about the real world that have less certainty associated with them. The basic functions of theory are to explain and predict. Two major types of theory include deductive theory and inductive theory. Deductive theory results when we assemble a set of interrelated more-or-less factual statements and derive statements from them which can be empirically tested. Inductive theory occurs when we observe specific incidents or events and attempt to generalize from them to larger populations or more general and similar events.

Variables are components of theory. Variables are phenomena that may assume two or more values. Variables may be dependent, where their values depend on other variables, or they may be independent, where they influence other variables. Variables may also be continuous or discrete. Causality may be inferred from observed relationships between variables. Sometimes, spuriousness among variables causes us to draw misleading conclusions about their supposed interrelation. Spuriousness occus when another, possibly unknown variable influences others so that they appear related when, in fact, they are not related causally.

Theory focuses our research activities. In turn, research enables us to test the predictive utility of the theories we formulate. Theory also pulls together the research efforts of many investigators who work on similar subjects, but who also work on those subjects independently. Research also suggests new ideas and highlights variables that may have been overlooked previously as important causes of events we wish to explain. Theoretical sophistication is also often equated with the professionalization of a scientific field. The greater the theoretical sophistication, the greater the professionalization. In recent years, substantial improvements have been made in criminological and criminal justice theories.

QUESTIONS FOR REVIEW

1. What is meant by *theory*? What are two important functions of theory? Give an example from the criminology or criminal justice literature to highlight each of these important functions.

2. What are several key elements of theory? Define each.

3. What are variables? How are variables utilized in research? Show at least four functions performed by variables. Give an example of each from your own experience.

4. What conditions must prevail for causality among variables to be established? Do these conditions mean that a cause–effect relation between variables exists if we adhere to them? Why or why not?

5. What are three methods proposed by John Stuart Hill whereby we can demonstrate causality?

6. Differentiate between assumptions, propositions, and definitions.

7. Which is more important for theories: explanation or prediction? Give a brief rationale for your choice.

8. What is the importance of convention relative to variables and how they are used or conceptualized in the research literature? Give an example.

9. Distinguish between independent and dependent variables. Select an article of your choice from the criminal justice or criminological literature, and isolate those variables designated as independent and dependent. How can variables perform both independent and dependent functions simultaneously? Explain and give an example.

10. What are five false assumptions about causality highlighted by Hirschi and Selvin?

11. What is spuriousness? Why is it an important consideration when attempting to establish a causal relation between two or more variables? Give an example of spuriousness apart from the example provided in the text.

12. Discuss the interplay between research and theory and how each complements the other.

3

Frames of Reference and Problem Formulation

KEY TERMS

Analysis of secondary sources
Frame of reference
Nonresponse
Reactivity
Reliability

Social desirability
Theory
Validity
Values

INTRODUCTION

This chapter is about frames of reference or ways of looking at problems that are of interest to criminologists and those who study the criminal justice system. In the first part of the chapter we examine different kinds of frames of reference that guide researchers in their various projects and investigations. Several topics for investigation by criminal justice experts and criminologists are listed and described.

Since many persons entering these areas as scholars may be overwhelmed by the wide array of interest areas to pursue, some attention will be devoted to examining the decision-making process of determining what should be studied. Whenever investigators are deciding what to study, they must consider their limitations as well as their strengths as researchers. How accessible are the elements or persons they plan to study? What must be assumed ideally about their research objectives and how to attain them? What realistic considerations must they take into account that will alter whatever it is they are attempting to do?

Since virtually every research project begins with an idea of something to study, certain topics are more easily accessible than others. Those researchers interested in studying inmates of jails or prisons must not only plan on obtaining permission from jail or prison authorities to study inmates, but they must also obtain permission from inmates themselves. In these heavily controlled settings, obtaining permission from correctional authorities and/or inmates to study them may be difficult or impossible under certain circumstances. Thus we examine some of the ideal and real considerations researchers must make whenever they decide to study specific groups or organizations.

WHAT ARE FRAMES OF REFERENCE?

A *frame of reference* is the way researchers or investigators view the problem selected for study. It is the approach chosen for problem-solving situations. Several examples from criminology literature will be helpful here. Suppose that we were interested in studying the influence of various deterrents to criminal behavior? How might we approach this subject and investigate it?

In their study of police behavior and its influence on crime deterrence, Kohfeld and Sprague (1990) were interested in examining the relevance of intervening variables such as social structure and demography on the police action–criminal reaction relation. These researchers outlined their frame of reference explicitly. "Several general theoretical ideas guide this analysis, but probably the most fundamental is the notion that the interaction between criminals and police is demographically embedded" (Kohfeld and Sprague, 1990:112). Thus the demographic approach was chosen by these researchers as their frame of reference or way of approaching the problem. They argued that demography enhances police response to criminal acts (e.g., burglaries, robberies), police make arrests or at least conduct investigations of crimes, criminals become aware of the time and spatial factors associated with such police responses to criminal activity, and that these "general communication phenomena" change as demography varies (p. 131). Their demographic argument is based, in part, on the logic and work of the Chicago School, led by Ernest W. Burgess and Clifford R. Shaw, where demography was viewed as "causing, and geographically configuring the occurrence of, crime" (p. 113).

Alternative frames of reference toward crime deterrence include the risk of imprisonment, as perceived by criminals, police aggressiveness, and family disruption. Sampson (1986) has reviewed the literature and examined the influence of police aggressiveness in response to crimes committed in their communities, family disruption, and the likelihood of incarceration associated with specific criminal acts. Sampson considered crime deterrence in the context of macrolevel social control. Through an investigation of crime rates in different cities, he found, for instance, that lower robbery rates occurred in those jurisdications having a high risk of jail incarceration.

Interestingly, he also found that certain communities having a high proportion of family disruption (through divorce or desertion, as examples) also had higher crime rates than did communities with less family disruption. He reasoned here that the greater the family disruption, the less likely family members were to become involved in anticrime community organizations, neighborhood watches, and the like. Also, where police response to criminal acts was rapid and "aggressive," lower robbery rates were found. Although the results of the research he reported were inconclusive, they suggested various "avenues" or frames of reference for approaching crime deterrence.

A leading explanation for crime deterrence is based on the utilitarian rational choice model of Becker (1968) and Ehrlich (1975) (Sampson, 1986:274). These researchers have asserted that much crime is committed because the utility of the criminal behavior or the expected benefits accruing as the result of that activity outweigh the benefits that might otherwise accrue to criminals from other, possibly legal, activities (Sampson, 1986:274). Thus, if the expected benefits derived from crime are frustrated or hindered by police or community residents, the likelihood of criminal behavior as utilitarian activity decreases.

Each of these frames of reference functions like blinders on a horse. For instance, carriage horses wearing blinders are prevented from seeing directly to either the left or right, and thus they are inclined to move in the direction intended by the carriage driver. Frames of reference function similarly. While the researcher knows or is aware of other possible explanations for or approaches to the problem under investigation, selecting one frame of reference over others diverts the researcher's attention in one direction only, and other possible explanatory factors are given lower priority.

Let's look at another example of a frame of reference. Suppose that we wished to examine the phenomenon of spousal abuse. Why do spouses physically assault one another, often causing serious bodily harm and psychological trauma? This phenomenon has become an increasingly important research topic in recent years, in part because more spouses are reporting such abuse and initiating prosecutions against their mates in formal court proceedings (Gelles and Mederer, 1985).

There is an equally broad range of explanations for and approaches to spousal abuse as exists for crime deterrence. Summarizing much research conducted by others, Burgess and Draper (1989) report that spousal abuse is attributed to ecological instability, underemployment, financial pressures (which no doubt stem, in large part, from underemployment), anxiety, and alcohol abuse. If we were to adopt ecological instability as our frame of reference to account for a high incidence of spousal abuse, this might refer to relocating frequently to new geographical areas (perhaps in search of employment or better promotional opportunities). Such moves might involve a loss of immediate kin support or signify changes in the marital balance of power. Financial pressures, underemployment, and alcoholism might suggest a high degree of marital tension over how money is spent or allocated, disputes over who should make such decisions on the basis of each spouse's relative contribution to family income, and loss of inhibitions resulting from alcohol intake.

In fact, DeMaris (1989) investigated 295 males in Baltimore, Maryland, who were referred by the court to a domestic violence treatment facility between July 1985 and June 1986. Of these original 295 subjects, 198 completed the program. Those who failed to complete the program tended to be younger, have lower incomes, and have assorted alcohol-related problems. Thus such findings would support certain frames of reference as more useful (e.g., immaturity, loss of inhibitions) compared with others (e.g., demographic factors, sociobiology, mental illness, loss of kin support). Other explanations for spousal abuse suggest that abusers were abused as children by their own parents (Johnston, 1988; Seltzer and Kalmuss, 1988). Further, there is a "universal risk" theory that has prompted a frame of reference that considers all women at risk and subject to wife battering largely as the result of liberal and radical feminist movements within a predominantly patriarchal society (Schwartz, 1988).

Choosing a Frame of Reference

One's choice of frame of reference is based on several factors. First, when a review of recent literature is undertaken, investigators learn which frames of reference seem most popular. Although the popularity of a certain frame of reference compared with others may be indicative of its "success" as a frame of reference in explaining some phenomenon, it may not necessarily be the best frame of reference to use. However, new investigators may select more popular frames of reference as a conservative move, particularly if they are new to the discipline and are hesitant to risk selecting less popular frames of reference for their investigations. Another reason why a certain frame of reference is chosen over others is that perhaps the researcher is simply more familiar with it and believes it is the best one to use unless a better alternative appears. Yet other researchers may select particular frames of reference that reflect their earlier coursework and experience. Thus their choices of frames of reference might be rooted more firmly to a degree of rationality rather than to more elusive, vague beliefs that certain frames of reference "seem" better than others.

Values and Frames of Reference

Values and frames of reference are closely connected. *Values* are standards of acceptability that we acquire from our peers or from society in general. Values cause us to prioritize, or to allocate greater importance to some things and less importance to others. Thus each of us learns to value things differently, and these differences explain, in part, the diversity of approaches to various subjects or the different frames of reference chosen to accout for or explain events.

There is a strong element of subjectivity reflected in our values. It follows, therefore, that the research we conduct is to some extent subjective. Most often we choose the topics we will investigate. Certain topics are chosen over others frequently because we may regard them as more interesting. We may choose one frame of reference over another, simply because we find it more interesting or regard it as more important. Our choice of *methodology*, how we will collect data and analyze it, may also be viewed as reflecting our priorities and interests, although we may be limited in other respects by the fact that we are unaware of certain research strategies as alternatives. All of these choices are value-laden choices.

Apart from the requirements of degree programs and the personal preferences of the professors who guide us in our undergraduate and graduate research, the decisions we make often reflect our own value system. The fact that our decisions are closely linked with our values is not necessarily bad. But we need to recognize the influence of values in our research choices at the outset, lest we label someone else's research choices and approaches as poor or irrelevant. The "state of the art" today in criminology and criminal justice is such that no single frame of reference in any particular area is considered the "best" one. There is currently ample room for differences of opinion about how events ought to be explained. And you will always have a chance to link your frame of reference to the event you wish to explain through the medium of *theory*.

FRAMES OF REFERENCE AND THEORY

A frame of reference points us in a given direction as we attempt to unravel the complexities of criminological problems. The frame of reference is crucial at the outset, since it is the foundation of our explanation for why certain problems exist or events occur. The way we decide to view the problem under investigation is also the way we have chosen to explain it. The next step in the research process is to enunciate, articulate, or spell out in plain language how your explanation of the event or problem relates to the problem in some logical fashion.

Thus frames of reference and theory are, for better or worse, inevitably related. Our theory consists of numerous statements reflecting linkages between variables. If we are studying crime deterrence, for example, and we decide to use a demographic approach, our theory becomes the explanatory and predictive tool we will use to show how it came to be that crime deterrence and demographics are related. If we choose to view crime deterrence largely as a function of police aggressiveness or family instability, we must demonstrate the possible causal relation between crime deterrence and police aggressiveness or between crime deterrence and family instability in your theory or theoretical scheme. If we study spousal abuse and wish to explain it or account for it by using underemployment or alcoholism as predictor variables, our theoretical scheme should lay out our reasoning for why spousal abuse and underemployment or why spousal abuse and alcoholism are related.

Some researchers specialize in theory construction, and they heavily stress the importance of different theoretical components, such as axioms, propositions, assumptions, and postulates. In a logical fashion, they weave an explanatory and predictive web that yields certain "tentative" conclusions (hypotheses) that may be tested empirically. It is insufficient, for instance, to say simply that because someone is unemployed or underemployed, he will feel bad and beat his wife. It is insufficient also to say simply that if one consumes considerable alcohol, he will become drunk and physically abuse his spouse. Everyone wants to know why these events are related or interconnected. Why should underemployment or unemployment contribute to or cause spousal abuse? Why should family instability raise crime rates? Why should large alcohol consumption precipitate family violence?

As we attempt to explain the "whys" involved, you continue asking why, until we have exhausted this explanation or have given a reasonably full account of how the events are related. What is "reasonable"? Again, value judgments enter the picture, and we must rely on our own standards and assessments about how much completeness in our explanations of things is an adequate amount of completeness. No one agrees on how "complete" our theoretical explanations ought to be. In fact, theory is perhaps the weakest link in the chain of events we regard as the research process. This is because it is difficult to develop theory or construct theory or create theory.

At least the frame of reference we adopt in relation to any given problem or event focuses our attention on a limited number of explanatory options. But remember, that whenever we choose one frame of reference over others, we are "blinding" ourselves to those other options. Our choices may not be the best ones, and our results may be inconclusive as good explanations for and predictors of the problems we investigate. This is one reason for why so much replication and reinvestigation occurs in any kind of social research, criminological or otherwise. Perhaps this is as it should be, considering how science operates and affects what we do. We acquire knowledge and certainty about things slowly, and we continually subject our views and explanations for things to experimentation and empirical testing. Gradually, some explanations of things emerge as better predictors than other explanations. Over time, we develop a stronger sense of what fits and what does not fit, of what seems to work and what does not seem to work.

DECIDING WHAT TO STUDY: TOPICS OF INVESTIGATION FOR CRIMINAL JUSTICE AND CRIMINOLOGY

A strong interest in doing research in criminal justice and criminology means that certain topics will be chosen for investigation. If you happen to be in a criminology or criminal justice department and are working toward an undergraduate or graduate degree, and/or are working for a professor as a research assistant as a part of a larger grant project, deciding what topics to study may not be one of your options. In short, you may already be locked into a particular topic and expected to investigate a particular aspect of it. However, in most departments and in most other academic scenarios, there is a great latitude extended to researchers regarding what they decide to study and how they decide to study it.

It is unnecessary to list every interest area in criminology and criminal justice where research may be conducted. At professional meetings, for instance, criminologists and those with criminal justice interests convene annually to present papers or give reports about research they have conducted. These papers are quite diverse and reflect the many differences among these investigators. Inspecting the program for the annual meeting of the Academy of Criminal Justice Sciences held in Nashville, Tennessee in March 1991, for example, disclosed that over 200 panels, workshops, and roundtables were presented, with an average of three or four papers per session. These panels included topics such as the impact of AIDS in law enforcement, psychosocial aspects of criminal behavior, police officer safety, a historical perspective of women in criminology, crime control trends, the sexual integration of prison and jail guard forces, community corrections models, victimization, crime prevention strategies, police education, electronic monitoring and house arrest, sentencing policies, elderly abuse, prisoner rights, juvenile gang patterns and trends, and corrections institutional management. The program for the American Society of Criminology annual meeting, held in San Francisco, California in November 1991 disclosed similar diversity of subject matter and paper topics. The subject matter of criminology and criminal justice is boundless. While there are some standard topic areas related to different components of the criminal justice system, there is an infinite number of subtopics they may be investigated. In the area of prosecution and the courts, for example, plea bargaining has been a popular topic for investigation. What factors influence prosecutorial discretion? How do race, ethnicity, gender, and socioeconomic status influence the plea bargaining decision and the contents of a plea bargain agreement? What are the implications of different types of sentencing schemes for various types of offenders? Are defendants more likely to receive greater leniency from judges at the time of sentencing if they pleaded guilty through plea bargaining or if the guilty verdict was rendered against them by a jury through a jury trial?

Regarding jury trials, many researchers have investigated the jury deliberation process. What are the dynamics of jury deliberations? Does racial and/or gender composition of juries make a difference and influence these deliberations, depending on the race or gender of defendants? Can jury verdicts be predicted with any degree of accuracy? Are smaller juries more likely to reach consensus compared with larger juries? Is there an optimum jury size? What can prosecutors and defense attorneys do to influence juries one way or another, unfavorably or favorably, toward defendants? These are just a few of the many questions researchers raise when investigating juries, jury deliberations, and other jury-related factors.

When police officers are investigated, some researchers focus on factors that influence the exercise of police discretion in effecting arrests of suspects. Does a more educated police officer relate to the community better than a less educated officer? What types of training should police officers receive to prepare them for the realities of police work? Is there a distinctive police personality? How much stress do police officers experience while on the job? What coping mechanisms are put into play as a means of handling such job stress? How do stress and burnout affect job performance? Are one- or two-officer patrol units more effective in combating crime? Again, there is a virtually limitless range of topics within the component of law enforcement that may be selected for scientific study.

Before we make a final decision about what to study, however, we should assess our abilities, our personal strengths and weaknesses, and our interests. Sometimes, inexperienced researchers will identify grandiose research problems that are well beyond their means, both personally and financially. The topics selected are noteworthy, but often, the study objectives are unobtainable, simply because they are beyond the investigator's financial means. We might wish to conduct a study of a large sample of all officers of the Los Angeles Police Department. But we quickly find that the cost of such a study would be prohibitive. This is one reason why professors, researchers, and others apply for grants from different funding agencies, both public and private, in order to secure appropriate funding for their investigations. Perhaps we want to study a sample of district attorneys in various cities in several states. Maybe we do not at first consider the travel time involved, the appointments we would have to make, and other logistical factors that would make it possible for our study to materialize.

If we plan to study others in public organizations or agencies, one of the first things we do is assess our connections. Do we know anyone who can help us get our "foot in the door"? Are we personally employed at an agency that would allow us to study it? In short, we identify who we know relative to the problem we intend to study, or we assess the connections of friendly others who may be in a position to help us in your research endeavors. If our choice is to do library research and rely exclusively on the contents of documents and other library materials for our information, it is unnecessary to obtain permission from anyone or go through the often difficult and tedious process of gaining access to organizations and agencies. But even if "quiet" research is done on our own in library settings, there are still practical concerns that must be addressed beyond our immediate research interests. We must pay attention to some of the dilemmas that often arise between what ideally should be done and what, in reality, can be done. This is the ideal–real scenario that is common to all researchers in all subject areas.

IDEAL AND REAL CONSIDERATIONS IN FORMULATING RESEARCH PROBLEMS

It is difficult to refrain from structuring ideal research scenarios for yourself as you prepare to examine one topic or another. One major reason is that most of your academic work in preparation for research, your statistics and methods courses, has presented you with the ideal way of proceeding under maximally ideal conditions. Many of the articles you have read describing the research of others may have given you the impression that everything proceeded smoothly, without complications of any kind. Few research reports contain detailed descriptions of data gathering, of the actual interviews conducted, of the reactions of others to being observed by the researcher and the researchers' assistants. We seldom hear about having doors slammed in the researchers' faces, of investigators being told off by various irate respondents who have been sent questionnaires by anonymous persons and agencies for the past 10 years or longer.

This does not mean that making ideal plans for investigating certain research problems is necessarily bad or should be discouraged. What it does mean, however, is that often, our ideal conceptions of how to proceed may be fraught with problems, hurdles, and all manner of obstacles from the outset. And that even if everything seemingly were to go smoothly and perfectly as we planned initially, other obstacles of a theoretical or philosophical nature might intervene and affect adversely the interpretations we have made of our findings. It is good to devise our research plans in ways that adhere to the ideal formulations and conceptions we have learned. But at the same time, we must recognize that in all likelihood, those ideal scenarios that we have structured will not be realized fully, and that we will fall to some extent short of them. This is the "gap" between the ideal and real worlds. The standards to guide us are in place at all stages of the research enterprise.

The reality is that some departure from these standards is inevitable, and it is the price paid for engaging in research of any kind. Therefore, we must prepare ourselves for these "less than perfect" experiences and what we will say about our work when it is completed. The researcher decides almost everything about the implementation of a research project and oversees it through its completion. But dealing with people poses various risks and certain problems that widen the ideal–real gap. Even in those research situations where secondary sources are exclusively relied upon for research information in libraries, certain problems exist such that we must readjust our original objectives and procedures at various research stages.

At the outset it is imperative that some consideration be given to both ideal and real situations that may be confronted as the investigation progresses. Below are several pitfalls that may or may not occur in the research we conduct. We cannot forecast their occurrence, but we should be made aware that certain of these pitfalls may be encountered along the way, and that it might be wise to store up various strategies or "plan B's" in such cases. When things do not go the way we want, when we rely on someone to provide us with certain important information and they let us down and fail to provide it, when the findings, for some reason, turn out precisely opposite the ways we originally predicted, when we are promised access to an organization and that access is later denied—these are some of the real experiences that frustrate our investigative efforts and contribute to the ideal–real gap. The list below is by no means exhaustive, but it does provide you with an indication of the sorts of things to be aware of, to possibly anticipate, as the research investigation proceeds.

1. *A common pitfall is not containing one's research objectives within manageable limits.* When a topic is selected, there is a frequent tendency to be too ambitious and extend the problem boundaries beyond your personal means. Researchers must carve out investigations that can be completed within reasonable time frames. It would be foolish, most likely impossible, for graduate students to design a longitudinal study over a 10-year period (e.g., observing a cohort of youths from age 11 until they reach age 21 for purposes of determining factors that may influence some of them to adopt delinquent behaviors), for example, since the graduate schools of their universities limit the time students have to complete their

degree work. In many cases, students must finish their research work (e.g., their dissertations and theses) within a six-year or nine-year period, after they have completed their coursework. These are maximums, and few students ever stay that long in any given graduate department. Thus much of the research conducted by graduate students is of short duration. Also, it is common to define a topic in such a diffuse way that there are many loose ends. The researcher will never be able to "connect" these loose ends within a reasonable time frame.

2. *If permission is required to study certain elements, it may not be granted.* Some investigators may wish to study a sample of juveniles at a secure detention facility or inmates in a prison or jail. They may do all of their preliminary work, prepare their research design, write their study objectives, define their population to be studied, and construct measuring instruments and questionnaires. Then, when they approach the target institution with their study proposal, permission to interview, observe, or in other ways examine the detained delinquent youths is denied by institution authorities. Even when permission to study a particular setting is granted in advance, that permission may be withdrawn later with little or no notice.

3. *When samples of persons are designated for study, some of those persons selected may refuse to participate.* If you mail questionnaires to certain respondents, they may trash your questionnaires. If you visit certain people with the idea of interviewing them, they may refuse to be interviewed. No matter how well you plan ahead and identify certain persons for investigation, little, if anything, can be done to force them to comply with your requests. Even when your research does not involve people directly and your research efforts are exclusively library related, it is not always the case that the materials you examine will be directly relevant for your specific research interests. Any time that data have been collected by others, their personal objectives may not coincide directly with yours. Therefore, if you design a research project involving collecting certain secondary source material in the library, that material may not exist, or it may not exist in the form that would best fit your own objectives. Thus researchers often adjust their original investigative sights to fit the data available.

4. *The instruments designated for studying various samples may be deemed unsuitable, because they may "trigger" actions on the part of participants that may be detrimental to the goals of the organization.* If the proposed research is "threatening" in any way to the participants or those in charge of specific settings, they may refuse cooperation. Asking prisoners whether their grievance procedures are adequate, for instance, may evoke negative, and unwarranted, responses. It may even provoke lawsuits filed by inmates against corrections officials if the inmates believe they should be entitled to a grievance procedure they do not already have. Questionnaires are not only a source of information for the investigator, but they can also educate respondents about things that are not always favorable for the organization. For instance, considering the example above, asking penitentiary inmates whether they have inmate grievance committees or various privileges may precipitate minor rioting if they have no such committees or lack certain privileges. Thus seemingly innocent-appearing questionnaires can be a key source of future respondent discontent.

can't be done again   *, valid*

5. *The measures selected for use in the research project may lack validity and reliability.* (See Chapters 9 and 10 for a more in-depth discussion of these phenomena.) This means that despite everything else going well for the researcher, there is always a problem relating to the adequacy of measures measuring what they are supposed to measure, and also the extent to which these measures are measuring phenomena consistently. As we will see in subsequent chapters, measuring social phenomena accurately is a complex task. While these measurement problems will be addressed in later chapters, it is important at the outset to recognize that our measures of social and psychological variables are flawed in various respects. We explore some of these flaws later, especially in Chapters 9 and 10.

6. *The problem selected for investigation has been researched heavily in the past.* Regardless of how recent one is to a field of study, there is the matter of selecting a researchable problem and a solution that have already been implemented and found to be unproductive. This means that recent familiarity with the topic area may not disclose previous approaches that are considered unnoteworthy. The researcher needs to experiment with different research methods, and also with different frames of references, before actually implementing a research project. It is confusing, and especially frustrating, for a researcher to investigate a problem in a certain way that may have been researched earlier using the same approach, the same explanation, and the same investigatory techniques.

7. *The data collection methods selected for use may not be the best for the problem under investigation.* Sometimes, researchers will select problems for investigation that lend themselves to specific kinds of data collection techniques. Some techniques may be more appropriate for certain kinds of research compared with others. Again considering the example of inmates above, it would be unreasonable, for instance, to expect researchers to investigate inmate grievance procedures in prisons through the use of surveys (e.g., questionnaire administration). The superficial nature of responses to questionnaires would not provide researchers with a complete picture of the grievance process used by inmates. There might be some hesitancy on the part of correctional officials to disclose their own procedures for processing grievances, and inmates may not be entirely truthful about the administrative and internal grievance mechanisms that are currently in place for the resolution of interpersonal or legal problems, especially when they are required to do so in writing. If the wrong people see their written responses, certain inmates may be subject to reprisals later or have certain privileges withdrawn. Personal interviews and observations of the grievance process in action would be better depictions of what is going on and why.

8. *Depending on the data collection method used, respondents may say things that they believe the researchers want to hear but which are not necessarily true.* Investigators have termed these types of responses *social desirability*. Social desirability is the propensity of respondents to place themselves in a favorable light when being interviewed or questioned. Black interviewers, for instance, may not obtain truthful answers from white respondents if the subject area has racial overtones. Topics such as race prejudice or the death penalty issue are touchy subjects for many persons, and often there is an element of cat-and-mouse interplay between an interviewer and an interviewee. Once interviewees sense that the interviewer has a particular attitudinal disposition or mind-set, they may say and do things that they believe the interviewer wants to hear or see. Regardless of whether they are wrong in their beliefs, their statements of opinion and belief are nevertheless distorted to conform to an acceptable social image. Social desirability is an important contaminating factor discussed in greater detail in Chapters 8 to 10.

9. *The samples selected may not be representative of the population from which they have been drawn.* While sampling will be discussed at length in Chapter 5, for the present it is important to understand that those persons who are subsequently studied may not necessarily be typical of the population at large. If investigators study police officers in Omaha, Nebraska, for example, how do we know that Omaha police officers are typical of police officers in other jurisdictions, such as Los Angeles, Chicago, or New York? We do not know how typical they are. Thus some caution should be exercised in generalizing our findings to settings beyond those under immediate study. There is little that researchers can do to influence the representativeness of the samples they obtain for research investigation. There are absolutely no guarantees that certain samples are better than others.

10. *If subject participation is coerced, responses may not be an accurate portrayal of their "real world."* Studies of detained juveniles, jail or prison inmates, or probationers and parolees are basically studies involving a degree of coercion. If permission is granted to study persons with any of these or similar characteristics, such research may be tainted by respondent retaliation because of the coercive nature of their involvement. These are captive audiences. Inmates of prisons and jails may deliberately lie to researchers. Detained juveniles may overdramatize their involvement in delinquent activities and "confess" to juvenile acts they never committed or contemplated committing. Probationers and parolees studied by investigators may feel "compelled" to participate in research projects because of their belief that failure to comply might dispose their probation/parole officers to file negative reports about them. Again, the coercive nature of their involvement raises the serious question of the meaningfulness of their responses. It is not so much that they will say what they think we want to hear, but rather, they may say what they *want us to hear.* We have no direct ways of controlling for the influence of coercion on participant responses. We can recognize some of the elements of coercion in the research we conduct and act accordingly and cautiously when interpreting our data.

As noted above, this is not a comprehensive listing of all of the ideal–real problems that can influence the research enterprise. However, the listing does bring to our attention the idea that many factors can operate in a variety of ways to complicate or frustrate our research efforts and shake the investigation's ideal foundations. Throughout the book, you will detect a strong element of conservatism. This is not political conservatism, but rather a conservatism that urges us to be cautious when collecting data, analyzing it, and drawing conclusions about it. There are simply too many weak points in the research process where things can go wrong. Murphy's Law may apply here. If something can go wrong, it probably will go wrong. Although investigators should be prepared to accept some failure in their work, they should bear in mind simultaneously that research itself has many rewarding features as well.

SUMMARY

Frames of reference are ways of viewing research questions or problems. Every investigator approaches a topic for study from a particular point of view, and this frame of reference functions to limit one's scope of investigation to select dimensions. Our value systems are instrumental in the decisions we make to study things in certain ways. The fields of criminal justice and criminology are broad enough that a virtually unlimited number of topics are available for scientific investigation. We are limited only by our own imaginations.

Certain pitfalls confront us as we embark on the research enterprise. Some of these pitfalls include being overly broad when formulating our research objectives and not anticipating difficulties of collecting the actual data we will need to subject our explanations of problems to empirical test. Because of the coercive nature of some of our research, participants may not be truthful in their responses; they may deliberately lie and say things they think we want to hear or things they want us to hear. In those investigations where samples of persons are to be obtained, some of those selected for study may choose not to participate. We may not necessarily choose the best procedures for collecting the data, or our analyses may be flawed by nonresponse and misinterpretations of collected information. Our instrumentation may lack validity and/or reliability, meaning that our measures may not measure what we think we are measuring or they may not be measuring certain attitudinal phenomena consistently.

These problems are only a few of the many potential obstacles confronting researchers as they prepare to conduct their investigations of specific topics. Whether data are to be collected directly from others or from library sources such as historical records, archival information, or public and private documents, we may not be able to get the precise information we seek. Thus it is necessary to retain a degree of flexibility so that adjustments in our research efforts may be made when appropriate. There is an ideal way to proceed in most research, although real-world events such as some of the problems noted in this chapter may interfere with or frustrate our investigative efforts. Therefore, there is an ideal–real discrepancy that must be considered in any research undertaken.

QUESTIONS FOR REVIEW

1. What is social desirability? How can it distort responses to survey instruments or questionnaires? Is reactivity the same as social desirability? Why or why not? Explain.

2. What is a frame of reference? Do all criminologists and criminal justice scholars use the same frames of reference in approaching a common research problem such as juvenile delinquency? Why or why not?

3. How do values influence our decision making at different stages of the research process? Can you think of any stages of the research process where our values have little or no impact? If so, what are these stages, and why would our values be of little consequence?

4. How do you believe nonresponse might cause our samples to be unrepresentative of the populations from which they are drawn?

5. What are some elements of coercion in data collection? How might coercing respondents into responding cause distortions to occur in our collected data? Think of two situations (apart from those mentioned in the text) where coercion might be found in the research process.

6. Why is our instrumentation important in testing our theoretical schemes?

7. How do frames of reference influence theoretical schemes? What is the relation between explanations for research questions or problems and theoretical schemes?

8. Why is it important for researchers to consider both ideal and real aspects of the research process?

9. Who chooses our research problems? What factors can you think of that influence our choice of research topic? In each case, explain how the factor mentioned influences our research choices.

10. Do certain research questions lend themselves to one specific data collection technique and not to any others? If so, what are they?

11. Suppose that you decide to study a group of juveniles in detention in a small community. Before you conduct your study, what are some considerations you should make?

12. Who selects frames of reference for our research investigations? What criteria do we often use for selecting certain topics for study and specific frames of reference?

4

Research Designs

KEY TERMS

After-only design
Before–after design
Case study design
Classical experimental design
Control
Control group
Cross-tabulation
Descriptive design
Experimental design
Experimental group
Experimental variable
Exploratory design

Frequency distribution control
  matching
Group distribution matching
Individual matching
Matching
National Youth Survey
Panel
Persons used as their own controls
Random assignment
Research design
Survey design
Treatment variable

INTRODUCTION

The research interests of criminologists and criminal justice scholars are limited only by their imagination. Any social setting is a potential target for scientific examination, whether it is a prison or probation agency. Despite the diversity of subject matter that criminologists and criminal justice scholars might study, all types of social scientific research are characterized by a limited number of types of *research plans* or *research designs*. Research designs are detailed plans that specify how data should be collected and analyzed.

In this chapter we describe various types of research designs, including explorative, descriptive, and experimental plans. The goals and functions of these research designs are discussed. Given the space limitations, it is not the intention of this chapter to cover all possible designs that may be applied in criminological research. Rather, several plans have been selected for discussion that appear to have the greatest amount of utility in terms of their frequency of usage throughout the research literature.

RESEARCH OBJECTIVES AND DESIGNS

As we have seen in previous chapters, the goals of researchers may be conventionally grouped according to (1) exploration, (2) description, and (3) experimentation. No single research design is universally applicable for all investigators at any particular time. Each type of research design functions to allow researchers to conduct their social inquiries in different ways and at different levels of sophistication. Selecting the appropriate research design, therefore, is dependent, in part, on the types of questions researchers wish to answer. Often, several research design objectives may be combined in the same research project to shed light on specific social questions. However, most research projects will probably emphasize one design over the others. Decisions about selecting the best designs must be made by considering the weaknesses and strengths of each design relative to the others. There is no prohibition that would prevent researchers from customizing their investigations with elements of several different types of research designs.

Exploration and Exploratory Objectives

Research designs may have predominantly exploratory objectives. Exploratory research is characterized by several features. First, it is assumed that investigators have little or no knowledge about the research problem under study. A general unfamiliarity with a particular group of people does not provide investigators with much opportunity to focus on specific aspects of the social situation. Exploratory research has as one of its chief merits the fact that potentially significant factors may be discovered and may subsequently be assessed and described in greater detail with a more sophisticated type of research design.

For instance, if researchers wanted to study social interaction patterns among inmates in prison systems but knew little or nothing about the structure and functioning of penal institutions, an exploratory research project would be in order. Such was the case in the early 1930s when Joseph Fishman described inmate subculture and sexual aggression. Little was known about prisoners and prison life, and even less was known about their sexual aggressiveness and patterns of sexual assault. Fishman was a federal prison inspector who became interested in depicting various dimensions of prisoners' lives. In 1934 his work *Sex in Prison* was published. Although this classic work described the prevalence and nature of inmate homosexuality behind prison walls, it also acquainted the outside world with several new concepts and inmate jargon that suggested to other researchers a new and rich source in need of greater social description. Fishman used the term "subculture" to describe unique social arrangements among the separate, smaller social system of prisoners behind prison walls but within the greater societal culture.

Fishman's work stimulated other investigators to describe similar prison environments and inmate culture. Donald Clemmer wrote *The Prison Community* in 1940, which described inmate subculture in the Menard, Illinois Penitentiary. Clemmer was a correctional officer who spent nearly three years observing inmate life and interviewing various prisoners. Especially noteworthy was his description of how new inmates were introduced to prison life. He described new inmates using inmate jargon. Thus new inmates or "fish" would undergo a certain amount of "prisonization" (a term equivalent with the sociological concept of socialization, or learning through contact with others), where older inmates would take them aside and tell them about the do's and don't's of prison life at Menard. *Prisonization* was the descriptive term that portrayed inmate customs and who controlled the flow of scarce prisoner goods and contraband as well as certain inmate privileges.

The works of Fishman and Clemmer stimulated other social scientists to provide more detailed descriptions of prison life in later years. For example, one of the most precedent-setting classic studies of prison life is *The Society of Captives* (1958), written by Gresham Sykes. Sykes acknowledged the influence of both Fishman and Clemmer on his own research and writing when depicting inmate culture at the New Jersey State Maximum Security Prison at Trenton. His analysis of prisoner culture introduced us to terms such as "rat" (an inmate who informs or squeals on other inmates), "merchant" (an inmate who barters scarce goods in exchange for favors), and "real man" (an inmate who is loyal and generous but tough in his relations with other inmates). Sykes extended his analysis of prisoners to include a description of the inmate code and pecking order. Subsequently, descriptive works appeared by Schrag (1961), Cressey and Irwin (1962), and Irwin (1970, 1980, 1985).

The distinguishing feature of exploratory studies is that relatively little is known about the target of one's research. Thus investigators who wanted to study delinquent gangs in the 1940s and 1950s had to become acquainted with gang norms and patterns of formation and persistence before they could conduct more sophisticated descriptive investigations. Today, many metropolitan police departments have special gang divisions and specialty teams of officers whose exclusive function it is to monitor gang movements and activities in their jurisdictions. For uninitiated observers several decades ago, the significance of different types and colors of wearing apparel among juvenile gang members would be largely unknown. Currently, much descriptive information is available about gang members, their colors and signs, and the meaning of certain types of graffiti in their "turfs" or neighborhood territories. Thus in many schools throughout the United States today, both teachers and students who are not gang members refrain from wearing certain-colored clothing for fear of being victimized by juvenile gangs. It has been found, for instance, that random driveby shootings of innocent bystanders are perpetrated by juvenile gang members in part based on the "wrong" colors worn by pedestrians.

Exploratory studies therefore serve primarily to acquaint researchers with the characteristics of research targets that should be described or examined more extensively. Another example of early exploratory research would be the initial investigations conducted by researchers into our drug culture of the 1920s and 1930s. At one time in our history, marijuana was believed to cause irreversible insanity and cause persons to murder others. Gradually, we have learned much about marijuana and other drugs, and under certain medical conditions, different types of drugs have potential therapeutic value for such disorders as glaucoma. Thus over a 60-year period we have gradually moved our level of inquiry about the social, biological, and psychological influence of different drugs from exploration to description, and from description to experimentation.

Today, there is considerable room for more exploratory research in criminal justice and criminology. Contemporary exploratory investigations are being conducted about the influence and impact of using female correctional officers to supervise male inmates in prisons and jails. Fairly new programs are in the early stages of implementation pertaining to allowing female inmates to have overnight or weekend visits with their infant children on prison grounds. Another area to be explored in greater detail is the phenomenon of co-correctional institutions, where both male and female inmates are permitted common access to certain recreational facilities during daytime hours. These "revolutionary" developments in the 1990s will no doubt be commonplace and deserving of "ho-hums" from social scientists in the year 2050. Presently, however, they are very innovative and very controversial.

Description and Descriptive Objectives

Much of the criminological literature is replete with descriptive studies of all types. Description is the most common design objective in criminology and criminal justice. Before we can discover *patterns* for various phenomena, such as sentencing disparities, prison violence and rioting, civil disorder, probation and parole officer burnout and stress, law enforcement officer misconduct or use of excessive force, or any other event we wish to explain, we must first acquire large amounts of descriptive information about these phenomena.

Description means pretty much as it sounds. We select settings for investigation, we target particular features of those settings for special attention, and we describe in various ways whatever we find. Different data collection strategies can be used for this purpose. In Chapters 6 to 8 we examine questionnaires, interviewing, observation, and the analysis of secondary sources as some of the many ways information may be obtained about social settings and the people within them. All of the information derived from such data collection strategies provides rich descriptions that often have explanatory value for researchers. It should be noted, however, that description, true scientific description, is considerably more structured than casual descriptions of social settings. Researchers know in advance what they wish to describe, and their accumulated data reflect a focus on specific social and psychological dimensions of persons and their environments. The work of Long, Shouksmith, Voges, and Roache (1986) is an example of a descriptive study.

These researchers were interested in describing stress levels among a group of New Zealand prison staff and assessing the impact of such stress on their levels of health. Long, Shouksmith, Voges, and Roache noted that "research in prisons has tended to concentrate almost exclusively on the culture, social structure, and rehabilitation of inmates, and it is only relatively recently that more attention has been given to prison staff" (1986:331). The research subjects consisted of 575 volunteer staff from 17 different penal institutions in New Zealand. These were prison officers, ranking officers, and instructors. Questionnaires were used to collect the data, and the length of questionnaire administration varied between one and two hours. Using previously devised instruments, these researchers obtained information about sources of work-related stress, a life events measure, a general health questionnaire, a personality measure, and questions of social and demographic interest, such as age, length of service, satisfaction in remaining in the prison service, the likelihood of taking another job if offered, and the respondent's possible intention to resign within the next six months. Forty-eight variables were described for these employees.

Some of their findings were as follows. Ranking officers made more frequent visits to medical practitioners compared with the other officers. The various health measures were correlated with several job stressors, and significant associations were found between these stressors and staff relationships, task pressures, relationships with inmates, promotion, and physical environment. Based on their analysis of data, these investigators concluded that the most effective approach for attacking the problems of work-related stress would be to improve staff relations and promotion policies and create more stable relationships between staff and inmates. Further, these researchers recommended that significant changes should be made by reorganizing shift work and working hours to alleviate task pressures inherent in the job and by offering various forms of support to families who have to live with and on the job. These researchers faulted the New Zealand prison system in terms of the nineteenth-century environment and the depressing "behavior settings" it manifested. They recommended that staff training should be geared, in part, to help officers cope more effectively with the behavioral settings in which they find themselves (1986:341–343).

Contrasted with exploratory studies, descriptive designs are more specific in that they direct our attention to particular aspects or dimensions of the research target. The heuristic value of descriptive studies must be considered a major contribution as well. Descriptive studies may reveal potential relationships between variables, thus setting the stage for more elaborate investigations later. In the research by Long, Shouksmith, Voges, and Roache, several important relationships among different variables were disclosed. Subsequently, revised training programs for prison officers can be examined to see experimentally whether debilitating job stress is decreased substantially. Reorganized shift work and job hours for employees can be studied to see if stress emanating from family conflicts is reduced to a significant degree. The point of a descriptive design is that it enables us to move forward to the most valuable type of investigation—experimentation. This is the type of investigation where it is possible to establish cause—effect relationships between variables.

Experimentation and Experimental Objectives

Designs with the objective of experimentation implicitly include the control of variables. Researchers experiment by observing the effects of one or more variables on others, under controlled conditions.

The use of the term control in criminological investigations has several connotations. First, control means to hold constant one or more factors while others are free to vary. For instance, if the variable *gender* were believed to be a crucial factor in an experimental situation, gender is controlled by observing the differential reactions of males and females in relation to some specific stimulus or an experimental variable. An experimental variable might be a sound, an electric shock administered to the skin, a dosage of some drug, a changed social situation, such as replacing a lenient supervisor with one who is strict, or any other external condition to which the sample of males and females is exposed. If we control for the variable *age*, this variable is said to be held constant. In other words, how do all individuals between the ages 16 and 19 behave compared with individuals in the age category 20 to 23 when exposed to a common stimulus?

An illustration of how variables are controlled is shown below and is based on a research idea by Kowalski, Shields, and Wilson (1985). These researchers conducted a descriptive study of female murderers in Alabama during the years 1929–1971. Among other things, they wanted to know about the contributory effects of alcohol and other possibly precipitating events, as well as whether there has been increased use of firearms among female offenders. Among the descriptive information they compiled were questions about race, age, the nature of the victim—offender relationship, and the type of weapon used. Table 4.1 shows an hypothetical distribution of race and the method whereby victims were murdered.

TABLE 4.1 HYPOTHETICAL RELATION BETWEEN RACE AND METHOD USED BY FEMALE OFFENDERS TO COMMIT HOMICIDE

Method of murder	Race of offender	
	Black $(N_1 = 125)$	White $(N_2 = 140)$
Shooting	36%	64%
Stabbing	55%	10%
Beating	3%	18%
Other	6%	8%
Total	100%	100%

In Table 4.1, the variable *race* has been controlled and divided into two categories, "black" and "white." An inspection of this *cross-tabulation* (i.e., the method of murder has been cross-tabulated with the race of offenders) shows that the majority of black murderesses stabbed their victims, while a majority of white murderesses used a firearm. A substantial number of white offenders murdered their victims by beatings, whereas beatings accounted for very few murders by black offenders. Had we wished to "experiment" with the variable *race* and determine its relation with the method whereby these murders had been committed, Table 4.1 would have given us the relevant information we would need.

More elaborate tables can be constructed, and several variables may be controlled simultaneously. Suppose that we wished to determine whether one's race has any bearing on the original charges filed and the final charges associated with the murder conviction. Some hypothetical information are shown in Table 4.2.

In Table 4.2 it would appear that 60 percent of the black offenders were charged with first-degree murder initially and that that charge was the subsequent conviction offense. This figure is contrasted with only 20 percent of the white offenders who were originally charged with first-degree murder and eventually convicted of it. It would also appear that a substantial portion of white offenders had the charges against them reduced to less serious charges compared with black offenders. For instance, about 7 percent of the black offenders had their second-degree murder charges reduced to manslaughter, whereas 60 percent of the white offenders had their second-degree murder charges reduced to manslaughter. Although these findings are hypothetical, they demonstrate certain possibilities that tentative conclusions about variable interrelationships may be drawn from cross-tabulations such as these.

Another meaning of the word *control* is a reference to groups or individuals who are not exposed to experimental variables, whatever they might be. For instance, if we were to administer a particular drug to persons in one group and withhold the drug from persons in another group, the group receiving the drug would be called the *experimental group*; the group not receiving the drug would be called the *control group*. Ordinarily, the reactions of the experimental group

TABLE 4.2 HYPOTHETICAL CROSS-TABULATION OF ORIGINAL CHARGES FILED AND EVENTUAL CONVICTION OFFENSE, BY RACE

| | Original Charge | | | | | |
| | First-degree murder | | Second-degree murder | | Manslaughter | |
Final charge	Black ($N = 50$)	White ($N = 55$)	Black ($N = 20$)	White ($N = 60$)	Black ($N = 55$)	White ($N = 25$)
First-degree murder	60%	20%	23%	10%	5%	0%
Second-degree murder	30%	50%	70%	30%	35%	15%
Manslaughter	10%	30%	7%	60%	60%	85%
Total	100%	100%	100%	100%	100%	100%

and the control group are observed and compared. Differences between the two groups are attributed largely to the effects of the experimental stimulus, or in this case, the drug.

In such experimental situations, it is assumed that the two (or more) groups are equated in some way. Persons or groups are *matched* in some respect, or persons are used as their own "controls" in a before–after experiment. That is, persons are measured according to some characteristic in one time period, and then the same persons are measured again according to that same characteristic in a later time period. In the interim, researchers introduce some experimental variable that is predictably designed to change behaviors. In the general case, it would be predicted that the dependent variable measured in the first time period would change between the first and second time periods. The experimental variable, an independent variable, would be regarded as responsible for any score changes observed between the two time periods, since its introduction was the only new event to influence dependent variable values. In Chapter 5 we examine different types of strategies that researchers might use to equate groups for experimental purposes. Experimental studies may be more or less elaborate or sophisticated in terms of the number of variables used and controlled.

SOME CONVENTIONAL RESEARCH DESIGNS

In this section we examine several conventional research designs used by criminologists and criminal justice scholars to answer various types of questions. Perhaps the two most popular research designs chosen by investigators are surveys and case studies. A third, more complex design is the classic experimental design.

Surveys

Survey research is defined simply as gathering information about a large number of people by interviewing a few of them (Backstrom and Hursh, 1963:3). Hyman (1955) differentiates between exploratory and descriptive surveys, and although no formal definition of survey design is apparent in his classic work, the meaning of survey research implicit in his writing is very similar to that described by Backstrom and Hursh. Generally, survey designs are specifications of procedures for gathering information about a large number of people by collecting information from a smaller proportion of them.

Survey researchers apply at least three standards in their research work that center around the *quality* of data collected. First, the quality of surveys depends, in part, on (1) the number of people obtained for the study, (2) the typicalness of persons sampled in relation to the populations from which they are drawn, and (3) the reliability of data collected from them. (Sampling and sample representativeness are discussed at length in Chapter 5, and the reliability and validity of measures are discussed in Chapter 10.)

An example of survey research is a study by Johnson (1986), who examined the association between family structure and delinquency. Johnson selected three high schools "in a large American city" and distributed questionnaires to 734 high school sophomores. Data were collected pertaining to age, race, gender, status of parental arrangement (i.e., whether the real fathers and mothers were in the respondents' homes or whether stepmothers or stepfathers were present), the quality of school experiences, social class, and the frequency of self-reported delinquent behavior. On the basis of these survey results, Johnson found low correlations between family stability and delinquent conduct. He did find, however, that daughters of single mothers and sons of mother/stepfather combinations tended to report more contacts with police and the courts than sons and daughters whose real mothers and fathers were together in their homes. Johnson addressed the representativeness of his sample by noting that the schools contained approximately equal numbers of males and females and served a variety of socioeconomic and racial groups, and thus it "approximates the situation of the vast majority of non-rural American youth" (1986:67).

Another example of a survey design is the well-known *National Youth Survey* (NYS), an ongoing longitudinal (over time) study of delinquent behavior and alcohol and drug use among the American youth population. The NYS uses a fairly typical sample of youth ranging in age from 11 to 17. Self-report questionnaires are administered, where youths disclose whether they have committed any status or criminal offenses and whether they have been apprehended for any of these offenses. The NYS utilizes this sample of youth over successive time periods as a panel. A *panel* is a designated sample that is studied repeatedly over time, and comparisons are made between "panels" or the responses given by these youths within each time frame. Krisberg et al. (1987) used the NYS to investigate the differential rates of incarceration of minority youth. Key research findings were that minority youth were being incarcerated at a rate three to four times that of white youths, and that over time, minority youth incarcerations are increasing proportionately. Self-reports of delinquent conduct among both whites and minorities disclosed similar patterns, and thus one's minority status is seen as a primary predictor of subsequent incarceration or involvement with police compared with being white.

Both of these studies involve somewhat superficial examinations of data. This is not an unfavorable observation. Survey designs are superficial by their very nature. In each case, limited numbers of social and personal characteristics are solicited from respondents. These characteristics are tabulated and analyzed statistically. They yield broad conclusions about large aggregates of persons. No attempt is made to conduct in-depth investigations of family systems, personality systems, or any other intimate details of participants' lives. Details such as these are disclosed by means of an alternative design known as the case study. Case studies are examined in the next section.

Advantages and disadvantages of surveys. The major advantages of survey designs are the following:

1. Surveys can provide information about a large number of persons at relatively low cost.

2. Generalizability to larger populations of elements is enhanced because of the larger numbers of persons who are included in survey designs.

3. Surveys are flexible enough to permit the use of a variety of data collection techniques.

4. Surveys sensitize researchers to potential problems that were originally unanticipated or unknown.

5. Surveys are useful tools that enable investigators to verify theories.

Some of the disadvantages of survey designs are:

1. Surveys are superficial reflections of population sentiments.

2. Surveys, particularly political surveys, are unstable reflections of population characteristics.

3. Researchers have little or no control over individual responses in surveys.

4. Statements about populations from which samples are drawn are tentative.

Case Studies

Although some investigators might claim that case studies are not "designs" in a technical sense, case studies are one of the most popular types of research designs used by criminologists and other social scientists today. *Case studies* are relatively thorough examinations of specific social settings or particular aspects of social settings, including detailed psychological and behavioral descriptions of persons in those settings. Words such as "intense" and "in-depth" characterize the type of information yielded by case studies, whereas survey designs yield data of a superficial nature, as we have seen. An example of a case study is the work of Charles (1989).

Charles investigated the social and psychological impact and effects of electronic monitoring on six juvenile delinquents. Charles conducted in-depth interviews with probation officers, parents/guardians of the juveniles, the juveniles themselves, and probation department administrators. His close contact with juveniles themselves disclosed details about wearing electronic wristlets associated with electronic monitoring programs that he would not have known had he not conducted the case study. For example, one activity, "hanging out," frequently led to delinquent acts, since youths who hung out were bored, with little or nothing to do. Charles found that youths could avoid trouble in their schools by using their wristlets as a "crutch" to withstand peer pressure and refuse invitations to "mess around," "hang out," and commit delinquent acts (Charles, 1989:168). The wristlet worn by these participating youths also reminded others of their probationary status. Thus Charles was able to penetrate the social worlds and minds of these boys to a limited degree and to understand their motives and rationales for different behaviors.

One interesting characteristic of case studies is that much rich information about social settings is disclosed. Another example of such research is an ambitious case study undertaken by Frazier and Bishop (1990). In 1987, these researchers sent observers and interviewers to Florida's 67 county jails to investigate booking and inmate processing. They were particularly interested in the extent to which Florida jails were in compliance with a general mandate to remove juvenile offenders from adult jails and lockups. Jail personnel were interviewed, and the ways and places in which juveniles were processed and detained were observed. Approximately 13 percent of all juvenile jail admissions were considered out of compliance with the Juvenile Justice and Delinquency Prevention mandate.

Through conversations with jail officials and other personnel, Frazier and Bishop found that both law enforcement officers and jail officials held basic misconceptions about detaining status offenders. Although holding status offenders in adult jails is a violation of Florida law, 237 cases in 1985 and 219 cases in 1986 were reported where status offenders were held for various periods in these county jails. Some officials believed that status offenders could be held in adult jails, as long as sight and sound separation was provided, or as long as they were placed in general holding areas and not in individual cells. Interviews and casual conversations also disclosed that many jail officials were resistant to unwanted reform and had complacent attitudes about jailing juvenile offenders of any kind.

A good point to be made here is that this quality of information could not have been obtained through more superficial survey instruments. It took an intense investigation and description of these settings, together with detailed interviews with jail officials and examinations of jail records, before such information emerged. After all, not many jail officials are going to admit to violating any Florida statute on an anonymous questionnaire mailed or distributed to them. Further, they are probably not going to say that they have complacent attitudes about whether juveniles are jailed in their facilities, or that they are stubborn or resistant to juvenile jailing reforms. Case studies therefore provide us with an in-depth grasp of social environments. However, because they consume so much time and energy of researchers, they are not conducted on the same broad magnitudes as surveys. This is one reason why both types of designs have offsetting weaknesses and strengths.

Advantages and disadvantages of case studies. Some of the more important advantages of case studies for criminologists are:

1. Case studies are flexible in that they enable researchers to use multiple data-gathering techniques, such as interviewing, observation, questionnaires, and examinations of records and statistical data.

2. Case studies may be conducted in almost any type of social environment.

3. Case studies offer specific instances of tests of theories. If researchers have adequately prepared a theoretical framework within which to cast the research activity, case studies provide them with an opportunity to test theories. Thus case studies may be viewed as a test of a more general theory to the same degree that survey designs are able to achieve this objective. Surveys make possible certain generalizations to the extent that the elements surveyed are representative of the population from which they are drawn. Similarly, a case study design has as its major concern typicalness for purposes of generalizability. An intensive case study may be as generalizable as more superficial surveys to larger social situations or aggregates.

4. The flexibility of case studies may be extended to virtually any dimension of the topic(s) studied.

5. Case studies may be inexpensive, depending on the extent of inquiry involved and the type of data collection techniques used. A researcher's costs may be kept to a minimum if data can be collected firsthand. It is not unusual to find researchers conducting case studies of social settings of which they are a part. This stems from the fact that their affiliation with the organization or group studied supports or helps to legitimize their research efforts. They are not outsiders and do not encounter refusals as often as outsiders. For instance, James Marquart became a prison correctional officer ("prison guard") when he conducted his participant–observation research into officer–inmate interactions within a maximum-security Texas prison anonymously referred to as the Eastham Unit (Marquart, 1986). His participation in the prison as a correctional officer enabled him to assess critical interpersonal situations between officers and inmates that otherwise would not be accessible to other casual observers. Some of his work is highlighted under observational techniques discussed in Chapter 8.

The most prominent disadvantage of case studies is that they have limited generalizability. Although they are geared to provide detailed information about social units, they are often criticized for being quite limited in scope and insufficient for meaningful generalizations to be made to larger social aggregates. Representativeness, however, is a primary question in the assessment of the quality of survey information as well. On a theoretical level, it may be argued that findings from case studies lend support to or provide refutation of theories. Researchers do not regard case study findings as conclusive proof of anything. Neither do survey researchers. Only through the accumulation of information from many case studies and many surveys investigating similar phenomena can we begin to generate statements about the social world that have little or no exception.

Comparison of Surveys and Case Studies

Figures 4.1 and 4.2 illustrate more clearly how each type of research design treats the social aggregates studied and their generalizability to larger populations. Figure 4.1 shows that a survey derives elements from the total population, which is generally known. Characteristics of a sample of elements are generalized tentatively to the entire population of elements. Figure 4.2 depicts case studies in relation to an "unknown" population. The typicality or representativeness of the case under investigation is unknown and is all but impossible to assess. However, because social situations are usually involved, certain theoretical propositions and hypotheses can be put to the test, again on a tentative basis.

It is clear that both types of research designs discussed above may be used for hypothesis testing. In fact, in some instances, both types of study designs may be used to test the same hypotheses. Case studies appear to have greater utility for hypothesis tests about certain structural and procedural characteristics (e.g., mobility patterns, status relations, interpersonal characteristics) of specific social units (e.g., organizations, small groups, cliques, communities). In addition to their descriptive value, surveys are of great utility for testing hypotheses about

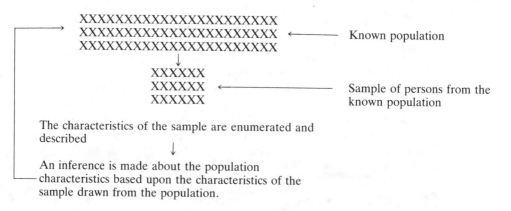

XXXXXXXXXXXXXXXXXXXXXXXX
XXXXXXXXXXXXXXXXXXXXXXXX ←————— Known population
XXXXXXXXXXXXXXXXXXXXXXXX
              ↓
          XXXXXX
          XXXXXX ←————————————— Sample of persons from the
          XXXXXX   known population

The characteristics of the sample are enumerated and
described
              ↓
An inference is made about the population
characteristics based upon the characteristics of the
sample drawn from the population.

Figure 4.1 An illustration of the Generalizability of Samples Studied with
Survey Designs.

large social aggregates (e.g., female criminals between the ages of 20 and 25,
background differences of convicted felons, sentencing disparities among judges
that pertain to racial or ethnic factors, or describing the social and demographic
characteristics of juvenile delinquents).

Classical Experimental Design

Experimental research designs generally are those that seek to control conditions
within which persons are observed and analyzed. The nature and types of experimental designs ranges from simple to complex and is quite varied. In any
discussion of experimental designs, two types of groups must be distinguished: (1)
experimental groups and (2) control groups. Conventionally, *experimental groups*
are those exposed to experimental variables or treatment variables. Also conventionally, *control groups* are those not exposed to experimental variables but
are compared with experimental groups to determine an experimental variables'
effects. Seahrest

Control groups are used in experimental designs in order for comparisons to
be made between them and experimental groups. The major problem related to
using control groups with experimental groups is the degree of their similarity.
For instance, an experiment with a particular type of drug used with a control
group consisting entirely of women will demonstrate questionable results compared
with an experimental group consisting entirely of men. We cannot say that the
two groups are equated in any meaningful way because the two groups differ quite
dramatically in their gender composition. Therefore, researchers attempt to equate
control and experimental groups on as many salient dimensions as possible (e.g.,
gender, age, rural or urban background, socioeconomic status, years of education,
and certain personality dimensions). Then when theorized changes occur within
the experimental group but not within the control group, investigators may tentatively infer a cause–effect relation between the experimental variable and the

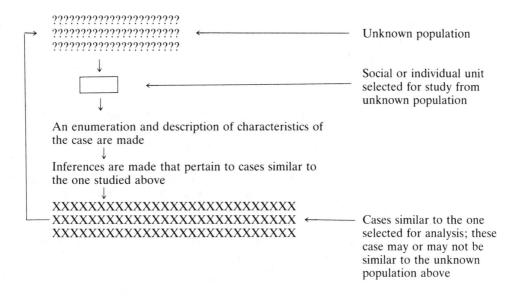

```
???????????????????????
???????????????????????          ←─────────────────  Unknown population
???????????????????????
          ↓
       ┌──────┐
       │      │               ←─────────────────  Social or individual unit
       └──────┘                                   selected for study from
          ↓                                       unknown population

An enumeration and description of characteristics of
the case are made
          ↓
Inferences are made that pertain to cases similar to
the one studied above
          ↓
XXXXXXXXXXXXXXXXXXXXXXXXXXXX
XXXXXXXXXXXXXXXXXXXXXXXXXXXX  ←───────  Cases similar to the one
XXXXXXXXXXXXXXXXXXXXXXXXXXXX            selected for analysis; these
                                       case may or may not be
                                       similar to the unknown
                                       population above
```

Figure 4.2 An Illustration of the Generalizability of Samples Studied with Case Study Designs.

changed behavior, whatever it might be. Behavioral changes are more likely attributable to the experimental variable than to pronounced differences between the experimental and control groups.

To achieve equivalence between two or more groups designated for experimentation, social scientists can use (1) individual matching, (2) persons as their own experimental controls, (3) group or frequency distribution control matching, or (4) random assignment.

Individual matching. Individual matching is the most difficult method of equating two or more groups. If researchers wanted to match 25 persons in an experimental group with 25 other persons according to several important characteristics, it is often necessary that a large population base must exist to find sufficient numbers of persons who will match up with those in the experimental group. Usually, experimenters will want to match persons according to their gender, age, years of education, socioeconomic status, occupation, race or ethnicity, and perhaps, some additional personality factors. The addition of each new matching characteristic greatly limits the available pool of persons from which matching individuals may be drawn. And assuming that "matches" can be made, there are no guarantees that those who are found to match others will participate in one's research as a part of the control group. Even if persons participate later who have been matched with others on certain characteristics, there is a definite likelihood that the two groups will remain unmatched on numerous other important characteristics. Thus if differences are later observed between the two groups on some dependent variable, it will be unknown whether the experimental variable caused changes in variable values or if unknown differences between the two groups were responsible for these discrepancies. Figure 4.3 illustrates individual matching.

Use of persons as their own experimental controls. One way of overcoming the "matching" problem and equating persons more directly is to use persons as their own controls in an experimental situation. Therefore, a target sample of persons is identified, measures on some dependent variable are taken, the group is exposed to some experimental variable, and then measures are again taken on the dependent variable. Score changes observed under this circumstance cannot be attributed to differences between individuals, since the same persons who were tested in the first time period were also tested in the second time period. An example of persons used as their own controls is illustrated in Figure 4.4.

In Figure 4.4, the same persons are measured on some dependent variable in two or more time periods. Perhaps a new program is being implemented in a parole agency to bolster morale and work attitudes, or to improve interpersonal relations. The new program is the experimental variable. Perhaps the researcher has a "quality of life" scale that measures contentment with the working environment and one's work associates. Scale scores in time 2 and are compared with these same scale scores in time 1, and differences observed are attributed more to the new program rather than to "individual differences" between the two groups in the two time periods, since it is the same group in both time periods.

Group or frequency distribution control matching. Sometimes investigators will equate groups according to group properties rather than on the basis of individual attributes. Group matching or frequency distribution control matching might be used here. For instance, if the experimental group has an average age of 34.1, an average years of education of 14.9 years, a male/female proportionate distribution of 35/65, and is 85 percent white and 15 percent black, a control group is sought with similar group properties. Group properties are emphasized

EXPERIMENTAL GROUP   CONTROL GROUP

Individual: MATCHED WITH: Individual:

1(---)7
2(---)8
3(---)9
4(---)10
5(---)11
6(---)12

Figure 4.3 A Hypothetical Illustration of Individual Matching.

Individual: Individual:
```
1⟨ ------------------------------------------     --------------------------------------------------- ⟩1
2⟨ ------------------------------------------     --------------------------------------------------- ⟩2
3⟨ ------------------------------------------     --------------------------------------------------- ⟩3
4⟨ ------------------------------------------     --------------------------------------------------- ⟩4
```

Figure 4.4 A Hypothetical Illustration of Persons Used as Their Own Controls in a Before-After Experiment.

here, since it is easier to match on group properties than on individual ones. Figure 4.5 shows an example of group or frequency distribution control matching.

Random assignment. The fourth and poorest method for equating groups is to select them from an overall sample by means of random assignment. Thus we might draw a sample from some population, such as a sample of students from a large introductory criminal justice course. Suppose that we drew a sample of 20 students from a large class. Using random assignment, we would place 10 students in the experimental group and 10 students in the control group. Figure 4.6 shows how random assignment would divide these persons.

In Figure 4.6, 20 students have been numbered from 1 to 20. Using a random procedure, each of the 20 students is placed in either the experimental group or the control group. It is believed by some researchers that random assignment results in making the two groups equivalent for experimental purposes in the same sense that matching equates groups on selected characteristics. Unfortunately, it does not. There is no reason to believe that *any* sample, regardless of its original heterogeneity, can be subdivided to yield two equivalent samples such as are illustrated in Figure 4.6. There are too many individual differences between persons to make any experimentation meaningful here. The researcher's best and simplest option is to use a sample of persons as their own controls over several different time periods.

EXPERIMENTAL GROUP N = 100	CHARACTERISTICS USED FOR MATCHING PURPOSES	CONTROL GROUP N = 100
34.1 ⟨--------------------------------------- 1.	Average age --⟩	34.2
14. 9 ⟨--------------------------------------- 2.	Average years of education----------------------------⟩	15.3
35/65 ⟨--------------------------------------- 3.	Male-female composition------------------------------⟩	33/67
83.9%⟨--------------------------------------- 4.	Percentage favorable --------------------------------⟩ toward issue X	81.8%
etc. ⟨-- etc.	--⟩	etc.

Figure 4.5 A Hypothetical Example of Group Matching or Frequency Distribution Control Matching.

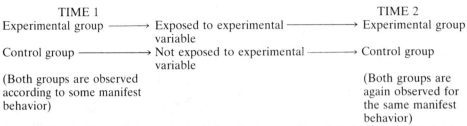

```
Random                                                          Random
Assignment                      ORIGINAL GROUP              Assignment
EXPERIMENTAL GROUP                  N = 20                 CONTROL GROUP
```

Individual #:   Individual #:
  20   1
  2   15
  19   16
  3   4
  11   13
  12   5
  7   9
  10   8
  6   14

Figure 4.6 A Hypothetical Illustration of Random Assignment.

With these concepts in mind, we can now look at a typical experimental scenario where an experimental and a control group are used. Figure 4.7 shows an hypothetical experimental situation involving one experimental group and one control group.

The classical experimental design is easily illustrated by an example provided by Goode and Hatt (1952:76–78): "In its simple statement, it can be formulated in this fashion: If there are two or more cases, and in one of them observation Z can be made, while in the other it cannot; and if factor C occurs when observation Z is made, and does not occur when observation Z is not made; then it can be asserted that there is a causal relationship between C and Z." Figure 4.8 illustrates the classical experimental design defined by Goode and Hatt.

Suppose that we were to observe two random samples of parolees over a two-year period. Both samples of parolees have similar prior records, and all parolees were earlier convicted of robbery. Further suppose that previous information

```
        TIME 1                                                 TIME 2
Experimental group ———→ Exposed to experimental ———————→ Experimental group
                        variable
Control group ——————→ Not exposed to experimental ————→ Control group
                        variable
(Both groups are observed                              (Both groups are
according to some manifest                             again observed for
behavior)                                             the same manifest
                                                      behavior)
```

Potential result: The experimental group should change, either in behavior or attitude, in response to the experimental variable, whereas the control group should remain the same from one time period to the next.

Figure 4.7 A Hypothetical Illustration of an Experiment with An Experimental Group and a Control Group.

about these parolees indicates that one sample has a history of drug/alcohol abuse, while the other sample of parolees does not show any drug or alcohol use or dependencies. From the literature we know that if it is going to occur at all, recidivism usually occurs with a two-year interval from the time inmates are paroled from prison. If we observe these two samples of parolees over the next two years, we might find that *no* parolees within the group with no drug or alcohol abuse history have recidivated, while *all* parolees in the group with a history of drug/ alcohol abuse have recidivated and have been returned to prison. This hypothetical example would suggest that a history of drug or alcohol dependency or abuse would be a strong predictor of subsequent recidivism among parolees. Unfortunately, our findings about parolees and other groups throughout the criminal justice system are not that clear-cut. We usually find perhaps higher rates of recidivism within one group compared with another, or we might find higher levels of work satisfaction among one group of parole officers compared with another. Seldom, if ever, do we find "all" or "none" differences that might be suggested under a pure or perfect classic experimental design format.

The *idea* of "all" or "none" is important, however. Thus if the presence of certain factors triggers certain events or behaviors, even a greater frequency of those events, and the absence of those same factors does not elicit the same events or behaviors, or if the same events or behaviors are not elicited as frequently, we might view these factors and events/behaviors as causally related. Goode and Hatt (1952:78–81) caution, however, that when it comes to "proof" of the effectiveness or impact of an experiment, the classical experimental design has certain weaknesses. Some of these weaknesses are that (1) researchers are unable to control all relevant variables in the research project; (2) there is a lack of clarity in the causal relation between the two variables; (3) there are unpredictable effects produced by the factor of time; and (4) there may be an oversimplification of cause– effect relations between the different variables.

Modifications of the Classical Experimental Design

The classical experimental design has manifested itself in different forms in the criminological literature. Variations of it include (1) the after-only design and (2) the before–after design.

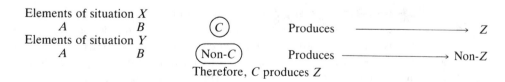

Elements of situation X
$\quad A \qquad B \qquad \;\; \textcircled{C} \qquad\qquad$ Produces $\qquad\qquad\longrightarrow Z$
Elements of situation Y
$\quad A \qquad B \qquad \boxed{\text{Non-}C} \qquad$ Produces $\qquad\longrightarrow$ Non-Z
$\qquad\qquad\qquad$ Therefore, C produces Z

Figure 4.8 The Classical Experimental Design.

After-only design.   The after-only design seeks to compare an experimental group with a control group *after* an experimental variable has been introduced to one group but not the other.   Sometimes, the terms "experimental group" and "control group" are loosely defined.   In some instances, these terms may refer to similar neighborhoods or similar cities.   For instance, police departments throughout the United States have experimented with various police patrol methods either to prevent crime or decrease it.   An example is the Tampa, Florida, Police Department.

Believing that a "back-to-the-people" program might be helpful in reducing Tampa crime, the Tampa Police Department inaugurated *sector patrolling*, where police officers would be assigned particular city sectors.   Offices were established in each sector and manned 18 hours a day.   Police officers were assigned to patrol specific neighborhoods and became familiar with residents and merchants.   Supposedly, reported crime in those areas of the city receiving sector patrolling, compared with other city areas, decreased "significantly" during the first six months of the program and greater police–citizen cooperation occurred (Smith and Taylor, 1985).   In this case, the "experimental group" was comprised of those city sectors receiving sector patrolling, while the "control group" consisted of those city areas not receiving sector patrolling.

On a more conventional and smaller scale, suppose that a state were to change the type of administrative leadership in several of its probation departments in various cities.   State officials might believe that different, more authoritative leadership might improve officer accountability and responsibility.   Assuming that we had measures of officer accountability and responsibility, those offices undergoing this administrative change (the experimental group, in this case) could be contrasted with those offices with no administrative changes (the control group, in this case).   Subsequently, the two sets of offices would be compared in an after-only contrast, and any differences in officer accountability and responsibility would be noted.   Theoretically, those offices that underwent adminsitrative changes would subsequently have greater officer accountability, as indicated by the appropriate instruments.

Unfortunately, the after-only design fails to identify the respective conditions of the experimental and control groups before changes have occurred.   Thus it is difficult to make conclusive statements about any observed differences between the experimental and control groups that might be more attributable to general differences within the groups themselves rather than to the experimental variable.   One weakness of the after-only design is that unless some method has been used to establish the equivalency of the experimental and control groups, it is impossible to assess the impact of the experimental variable with certainty.

Before–after design.   An improvement over the after-only design, the before-after design consists of obtaining measures on some dependent variable for two groups that are presumed equivalent for experimental purposes, introducing an experimental variable to one group and withholding it from the other, and comparing the two groups after the experiment has been completed.   An example of the before–after experiment, again using police patrol styles as the theme, is the work of Kelling et al. (1974), who conducted what became known as the classic Kansas City Preventive Patrol Experiments between June 1972 and September 1973. Funded by a grant from the Police Foundation, the Kansas City Police Department varied the numbers of routine preventive patrols within 15 of Kansas City's beats. The beats were divided into three groups of five each. In the "control" beat grouping, patrols were continued according to previously "normal" patterns. In the two "experimental" beat groupings, routine patrols were both increased and eliminated. In one experimental beat grouping, known as the "proactive" beats, the "normal" one-car patrols were increased to three-car patrols. In the other experimental beat grouping, the "reactive" beats, all one-car patrols were removed, and police officers serviced those areas strictly on the basis of calls from residents who reported crimes as they occurred.

It was expected, and predicted, that crime would increase in the reactive beats, decrease in the proactive beats, and remain about the same in the "control" beats. The experiment failed to produce these results. Crime remained about the same or occurred with about the same frequency in all beats, regardless of the patrol style used. These results generated much controversy, since police agency funding is based, in part, on the argument that more police presence tends to deter crime. Clearly, this was not the case, at least in those experimental and control beats studied. In fact, since crime did not increase in those areas where police patrols were withdrawn, some citizens questioned the value of police patrols in *any* city sector. In all fairness to the Kansas City Police Department, some experts surmised that criminals "thought" that police patrols were continuing as usual. After all, how were criminals supposed to know that the city was experimenting with varying police patrol styles? Thus a "phantom effect" was described to account for the lack of increased crime in those areas not patrolled by police.

The principal advantage of the before–after experimental design is the ability of the researcher to evaluate experimental and control group subjects both before and after experimentation, and to isolate and eliminate (or take into account or into consideration) extraneous factors that might otherwise obscure the true effect(s) of the experimental variable. In the Kansas City study, for instance, crime rates in various beats were known before the experiment was conducted. Thus comparisons were easily made among beats after the experiment ended to determine the experimental effects on crime rates of varying the intensity of police patrols. Again, reference may be made to Figure 4.7, where the before–after experimental design is illustrated.

There are other, more advanced types of experimental designs, although their use in criminological research is somewhat limited. An analysis of 15 major journals in criminology and criminal justice for the period 1980–1990 disclosed few instances of articles containing complex experimental methodology. In fact, the bulk of articles containing research findings include more simple tabular presentations and descriptive materials (independent analysis conducted by author, 1991). (Some of the journals surveyed included *Criminology, Justice Quarterly, Law and Society Review, Criminal Justice Review, Journal of Criminal Law and Criminology, Journal of Criminal Justice, Crime and Delinquency, American Journal of Criminal Justice, Journal of Crime and Justice, Social Problems*, and *Journal of Police Science and Administration.*) More specialized experimental procedures are described in more advanced texts (see Judd, Smith, and Kidder, 1991).

SUMMARY

Research designs are detailed plans that specify how data are to be collected and analyzed. Major designs and design objectives include exploration, description, and experimentation. Exploratory studies assume that investigators know little or nothing about the research problem or sample studied. Thus the primary aim of exploratory research is to yield fruitful avenues that can be explored and described in greater detail with more sophisticated descriptive designs. Descriptive designs are intended to disclose patterns of behavioral or attitudinal characteristics among samples of respondents. Experimentation involves controlling key variables that are believed to affect dependent variables. *Control* means to hold constant certain factors while other factors are free to vary.

Experimentation involves the identification of experimental and control groups. Experimental groups are those that receive the experimental variable or treatment variable, while control groups are those not exposed to the experimental variable. Experimental and control groups are presumed equated, although this presumption varies according to the method whereby researchers attempt to achieve group equivalencies. Four methods are used for achieving equivalence between two or more groups. These include individual matching, using persons as their own controls in before–after experiments, group distribution matching or frequency distribution control matching, and random assignment. Using persons as their own controls is perhaps the best method for establishing equivalency, while random assignment is the poorest method.

Conventional types of designs include survey designs and case studies. Survey designs gather information about a large number of persons by studying a smaller sample of them. Questionnaires are often used in survey research. Case studies involve relatively intense investigations of smaller numbers of cases. Survey designs are considered superficial indicators, while case studies provide in-depth information about the subjects studied. Both types of designs have offsetting weaknesses and strengths. Experimental designs include the classical experimental design, and two related designs, the after-only design and the before–after design. In these experimental design cases, attempts are made by researchers to determine the effects of independent variables by comparing experimental and control groups under different circumstances.

QUESTIONS FOR REVIEW

1. What is a research design? Identify two major types of research designs and discuss briefly their major objectives and limitations.
2. What are three major research objectives? Give some examples of each different from those in the chapter and that are drawn from your own perusal of criminal justice literature.

3. How does the amount of information we have about a given sample to be studied influence our study design choices? Explain.

4. Define *control*. Illustrate how different variables might be manipulated or controlled by the investigator.

5. What is cross-tabulation? Give an hypothetical example of variable control in a cross-tabulation using at least three variables of your choice.

6. Differentiate between experimental groups and control groups. In what sense might the term "group" be used when the research target might be more broadly conceived? *Hint:* Review the Kansas City Preventive Patrol Experiment.

7. What are four methods whereby groups are equated for experimental purposes? Describe each and discuss their respective limitations.

8. What is a survey? In what sense is a survey considered superficial? Discuss.

9. What is a case study? What are some drawbacks of case studies? In what respects can case studies be more informative than surveys?

10. Describe the classic experimental design by using hypothetical variables of your choice from the research literature.

11. What factors influence the quality of survey information?

12. What are panels, and how are they used in criminological research? How are self-reports relevant for studies that use panels?

13. What are after-only experimental designs? How are these designs variations of the classical experimental design?

14. How does a before–after experimental design improve on after-only designs? Discuss briefly.

Joseph Mengala
- Angel of Death
- infected people w/ disease
- used people as guinnea pig
- observe how they died.

Tuskegee Study
- withheld penecilin.

- Stanley Milgram
   - Obedience to Authority
   - Wanted to discover the cause of the
     Hallocaust.
   - Volunteers were recruited to act as
     teachers.
   - Shocking the students w/ high voltage.

PART 2
Data Collection Alternatives

In Part II we describe several popular data-gathering tools, including questionnaires, interviews, and observation. Before these data-gathering strategies are used, however, investigators must identify populations of elements in advance and draw samples from them for subsequent study. In Chapter 5 we define sampling and present an array of sampling procedures that investigators will find useful for their own analyses of social events. Key concerns among researchers are the extent to which their samples of elements are generalizable to larger populations of them, and whether their samples are typical of the populations from which they are drawn. One class of sampling plans is probability sampling, where probability theory enhances the generalizability of one's results. Another class of sampling plans is nonprobability, where generalizability to larger populations is limited. Several types of probability and nonprobability sampling plans are described, together with their respective weaknesses, strengths, and suggested applications. The chapter concludes by identifying several important sampling problems and describing how these problems might be minimized or resolved.

In Chapter 6 we describe questionnaires and their general purposes. Questionnaire administration is the most popular data-gathering technique in criminology. Data from questionnaires are coded and transferred to data-retrieval systems, such as personal computers, for statistical analyses. Questionnaire construction will be described, with illustrations provided from existing criminological literature. Different types of response patterns are discussed. The advantages and disadvantages of using questionnaires in social research will be presented. Several types of questionnaire administration are depicted, such as mailed questionnaires and face-to-face administration. Questionnaire construction is not without its problems, and several of the more important problems and issues associated with questionnaires, their construction, and use are discussed.

Another popular data-gathering tool is the interview. In Chapter 7 we describe the interviewing process. Interviews enhance the information provided through questionnaire administration. Often, researchers supplement their questionnaire administration with interviewing. Interviews may be either structured or unstructured, depending on the social circumstances. Interview schedules or interview guides may be devised to assist researchers in their data collection, whenever interviewing is used. The functions of interviews will be described, together with a general discussion of their weaknesses and strengths as data-gathering strategies. Several problems will be identified that influence the quality of information yielded through interviewing.

In Chapter 8 we examine both observation and secondary source analysis. Investigators often find that observing others depicts a different social dimension from those provided through questionnaire administration and interviewing. Two kinds of observation, participant and nonparticipant, are described, utilizing examples from the criminological literature. The analysis of secondary sources, such as public or private documents commonly found in library collections, are frequently tapped by researchers as rich sources of information about crime and crime trends. However, since such information has often been compiled for purposes other than those presently intended by investigators, there are limitations associated with this type of information. These limitations are described, together with some of the positive features contained by such data. Again, examples from the current criminal justice and criminological literature are used to illustrate how such techniques are applied in social research.

-Zimbardo, Phillip.-
   -Simulated Prison at Stanford.
   -12 guards 12 inmates· Volunteer
   - no physical Abuse.
   -See how the react.
   - discontinued 6 days after Started.
         Should have lasted 2 weeks
   -Classic Research.

Tea Room Trad. Laud Humphrey
   - nobody volunteered
   - homosexuals in male restroom.
   - copied license #'s + interviewed them
      at home.

*Project Camelot - US. Research.
Student + Peasant. - in Chili.*

5 — *Test Oct. 27*

Data Collection Strategies I: Sampling Techniques, Purposes, and Problems

KEY TERMS

Accidental samples
Area samples
Cluster samples
Convenience samples
Dense sample
Disproportionate stratified random
   samples
Elements
Equality of draw
Fishbowl draw
Independence of draw
Independent sample
Judgmental samples
Multistage samples
Nonprobability sample
Population
Potentates
Probability sample
Proportionate stratified random
   samples

Purposive samples
Quota samples
Randomness
Random sample
Related sample
Sample
Sample size
Sampling
Sampling fraction
Saturation samples
Simple random sample
Single samples
Snowball sampling
Stratified samples
Subpopulation
Subsample
Systematic samples
Table of random numbers
Two- or *k*-samples

INTRODUCTION

A major component of most research projects is *sampling*. Essentially, sampling involves targeting populations and selecting some persons from them for subsequent investigation. For instance, researchers may wish to study correctional officers from jails and prisons in order to compare their degrees of professionalism. Or researchers may want to know opinions of experts in community-based probation agencies about agency volunteers and how the effectiveness of these volunteers is determined. Other investigators may want to see whether shock probationers make better adjustments in their communities than offenders who do not participate in shock probation. Some researchers may want to profile the characteristics of convicted female murderers currently serving time in penitentiaries.

Each topic raises several common questions. These are (1) "*Where* will their data be obtained?" and (2) "*How* will they get it?" Many researchers know in advance where their data can be found. Also, they have a general idea about how they will get the data needed to answer their research questions. Perhaps they have important contacts within various institutions and agencies. Some researchers may be employees of organizations they wish to study. Using your organizational contacts or the contacts of others is a good means of initially getting one's "foot in the door" to conduct research.

A third question suggested by each of these topics is: "What *sampling process* will be used to obtain persons from the larger category of those we wish to study?" Because there are so many different topics, so many target audiences available for study, and so many different conditions that might exist whenever studies are conducted, no single sampling method has universal application. Over the years, many sampling techniques have evolved for use in different types of social research. Each technique has different strengths and weaknesses, depending on the unique circumstances of its application.

The organization of this chapter is as follows. First, several conventional types of sampling methods are identified and described. Sampling fulfills several important functions. These functions are outlined. Questions about why we sample are answered. All of the major sampling plans discussed here have been grouped into *probability sampling plans* and *nonprobability sampling plans*. Respectively, these plans either permit or do not permit generalizations to populations we have selected for study. Several types of probability and nonprobability sampling plans have been devised to meet investigator needs under different types of research conditions. Each of these types of sampling plans is illustrated, and the weakness and strengths of each are discussed. Suggested applications are made for each type of plan in relation to problems that may be investigated in criminal justice or criminology.

Finally, several important sampling issues are examined. Investigators may want to know whether their samples are representative or typical of the general class of persons they are studying. What factors intervene to affect the representativeness of samples adversely or favorably? What should researchers do if some persons they want to study refuse to participate or fail to return their mailed questionnaires? What should be the appropriate sample size? Some samples are difficult to access, since permission may be required to study them. Prisoners and juveniles are examples of persons requiring the consent of others before they may be studied. Some persons may not require the permission of others before they can be studied. But they may be nearly inaccessible as well. Judges and prosecutors are often insulated from researchers by a protective group of assistants and a loyal secretarial pool. Thus the broad class of *potentates* is examined as a sampling problem and consideration. These and other issues are presented and discussed below.

WHAT IS SAMPLING?

Statisticians refer to the units they study as *elements.* Elements refer either to things or people. Thus we may study light bulbs, shoes, telephones, or people, and in the general case, our references to them will be "elements." In the social sciences, "a study of 100 elements" means that researchers are studying 100 persons. Usually, these persons have characteristics of interest to the researchers. These characteristics may be male juvenile delinquents, female murderers, probation officers, defense attorneys, juvenile court judges, intake officers, jail or prison inmates, correctional officers, wardens or superintendents, or volunteers in a community-based correctional agency. Because of our research interests, we seek information about these persons. *Sampling* means to take a proportion of persons from the whole class of persons about which we seek information.

Populations and Parameters

Populations comprise the entire class or aggregate of elements about which one seeks information. For example, we may seek information about the inmates in the Kentucky State Penitentiary. We may want to study Illinois probation officers. Or we may seek information about juvenile delinquents in Las Vegas, Nevada. Therefore, the three populations about which we seek information are *all* inmates at the Kentucky State Penitentiary, *all* probation officers in the state of Illinois, and *all* juvenile delinquents in Las Vegas, Nevada. In each of these cases, the characteristics of these populations of elements are designated as *parameters*. Thus the average caseload of all Illinois probation officers is a parameter. The average height of juvenile delinquents in Las Vegas, Nevada is also a parameter or population characteristic. We want to know about these and other characteristics or parameters of these populations.

But because of the sheer magnitude of these populations, it is frequently difficult for researchers to study all of the population elements. We can appreciate this difficulty more easily by imagining what our task would involve if we wanted to study *all* probation officers or juvenile delinquents or inmates in the entire United States! Imagine the time, money, and personpower it would require to complete this task. However, our task of studying these populations is greatly simplified if we are less ambitious and choose to study only samples of elements taken from these populations.

Samples and Statistics

Samples are proportions or smaller collections of elements taken from the larger population of them. Using the population examples above, samples of them would be (1) a sample of all Kentucky State Penitentiary inmates, (2) a sample of all Illinois probation officers, and (3) a sample of all Las Vegas, Nevada juvenile delinquents. If the Kentucky State Penitentiary inmate population consists of 1200 inmates, we might study 200 of these inmates as our sample of elements. The characteristics of our inmate sample would be designated as statistics. Statistics are characteristics of samples of elements taken from a population of them. Some sample statistics might be the average age of a sample of Las Vegas, Nevada juvenile delinquents or the average caseload of a sample of Illinois probation officers. Table 5.1 illustrates the population–sample relation.

Generalizability and Representativeness

A persistent worry researchers have about studying samples of elements rather than entire populations of them is whether their samples are *representative* of those populations. Can investigators make generalizations about populations of elements by only studying samples of them? How do we know if our samples are representative of the populations from which they were taken? *As long as we*

TABLE 5.1   DISTINCTION BETWEEN A POPULATION AND A SAMPLE

Population (100%)	Sample (20%)
1. All Kentucky State Penitentiary inmates	1. Some Kentucky State Penitentiary inmates
2. All Illinois probation officers	2. Some Illinois probation officers
3. All Las Vegas, Nevada juvenile delinquents	3. Some Las Vegas, Nevada juvenile delinquents
Some characteristics of elements:	
1. The average age of all inmates in the Kentucky State Penitentiary	1. The average age of the sample of inmates in the Kentucky State Penitentiary
2. The average caseload of all Illinois probation officers	2. The average caseload of the sample of Illinois probation officers
3. The male/female proportion of all Las Vegas, Nevada juvenile delinquents	3. The male/female proportion of the sample of Las Vegas, Nevada juvenile delinquents

study samples of elements rather than entire populations, we will never know if our samples are representative of those populations.

Generally, sample representativeness is assumed or implied, depending on how the sample is selected and its size in relation to the population. If we must choose between two samples of different sizes that have both been selected using the same sampling procedure, the larger sample would be assumed to be more representative of the population than would the smaller sample. If different sampling procedures were used, however, we could not make this statement about the two samples, regardless of their respective sizes. Thus the size of the sample alone does not make the sample representative of its population. For instance, if we wanted to generalize about all incarcerated adult offenders in the United States, but if we select a sample of 20,000 offenders from half of all U.S. maximum-security penitentiaries only, we would have no inmate representation from jails (facilities that house short-term or less serious offenders) or other, less secure, incarcerative facilities. Although quite large, our sample of prison inmates would be unrepresentative or atypical of all inmates, since only the most serious and long-term offenders would be included in our sample, and all short-termers in jails or less serious offenders housed in medium- or minimum-security facilities would be excluded.

In another research situation, investigators may have responses from 350 out of 375 inmates of a particular prison. If the investigators want to generalize only to the inmates of that prison, the sample size of 350 is considered quite large for generalization purposes. Over 90 percent of all inmates have been obtained. However, what if the researcher wants to use the sample of 350 inmates and generalize to all inmates of all U.S. prisons? Because of the dramatic shift from the population of a single prison to the population of all U.S. prisons, the sample of 350 inmates diminishes in significance when we attempt to generalize from it to all U.S. prison inmates. Therefore, answers to questions about the representativeness and generalizability of one's sample on the basis of its size are *relative*. Much depends on what the researcher wants to do with the results and how large the sample is in relation to the population from which it was drawn.

The examples above have been used in connection with generalizability and representativeness of samples that involved studies of persons directly—prison inmates, probation officers, and juvenile delinquents. What about studies of element characteristics that involve persons only indirectly? What if we want to investigate files, records, documents, or other informative sources that provide in-depth data about individuals?

For example, a young police officer with the Long Beach, California Police Department (LBPD) was interested in studying the changing pattern of juvenile delinquency and demographic changes in the city of Long Beach over a 30-year period. He was working on a master's degree and wished to study this topic for his master's thesis project. One dimension of his study was the changing ethnicity of the Long Beach population during the period 1960–1990. During that period of time, a great influx of persons of Oriental and Spanish descent occurred throughout the city and contiguous areas near Long Beach. Because of his employment with the LBPD and friendship with record keepers in the department, he had access to the files of all juvenile arrests during that entire period. Among other things, he wanted to see whether there had been any change in patterns of delinquency during the period 1960–1990 that might correspond with (or be related to) changes in the ethnic distribution of Long Beach residents during that same period.

His solution to this problem required access to demographic information about Long Beach, together with access to the LBPD juvenile arrest files. While *any* files of juveniles are difficult to obtain in any jurisdiction under ordinary circumstances because of statutory provisions that preserve the confidentiality of this information, his position as a police officer, together with interest of the current police chief in promising research projects by his officers, meant that there were optimum circumstances for completing the project, or at least this particular phase of it. However, when he first examined the juvenile arrest files, he quickly found that there were 3000 or more juveniles arrested each year by Long Beach police. If he were to examine all years and examine all records, this would mean having to read 100,000 or more arrest records for the 30-year period. Working on his own after working hours, he would never be able to perform this herculean task.

Eventually, he decided to select approximately 200 juvenile arrest cases for study each year, using five-year intervals. Thus, commencing with 1960, he would obtain 200 juvenile arrest records. Continuing his work, he would also obtain 200 juvenile arrest records from the files for the years 1965, 1970, 1975, 1980, 1985, and 1990. This would give him a total of 1400 juvenile arrest records, a much more manageable number to analyze. Still remaining would be the problem of how such records would be obtained for each of those years from the existing files. He decided to use a procedure that will be described later in the present chapter. In this instance, samples of *records*, rather than people, are drawn. The basic principles for obtaining samples of records or people are the same.

THE DECISION TO SAMPLE

When the research design has been formulated, specifications have usually been made whether to include elements. An analysis of much of the current literature in criminal justice and criminology shows that the bulk of it describes data collected from samples. The decision to sample is made on the basis of at least three criteria: (1) the size of the target population, (2) the cost of obtaining the elements, and (3) the convenience and accessibility of the elements.

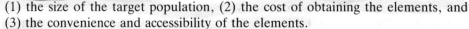

Size of the Target Population

How large is the target population? If researchers want to study the effectiveness of defense counsels in criminal cases, for instance, their target population might be all licensed criminal lawyers in the United States or all criminal defense counsel who are members of the American Bar Association. Perhaps the investigator wishes to study how AIDS inmates are segregated and treated in prisons and jails. Maybe the project is focused on the amount of knowledge correctional officers have about their legal liabilities in their interactions with inmates. These are fairly large populations, and it would be a demanding task to study all of these elements, even if they could be identified and contacted. Bureaus of social research, survey research centers, and most other large-scale public or private research organizations have the resources to conduct research projects on a grandiose scale. Nevertheless, even these large bureaus with extensive resources limit the scope of their inquiry to samples of elements rather than entire populations. However, most independent researchers must engage in small-scale studies with limited funds, unless one's project is funded by the Department of Justice, Bureau of Justice Statistics, or some other public or private funding agency.

Cost of Obtaining the Elements

How much money is available for the study? The cheapest ways of collecting data include observing others or going to libraries and analyzing information from surveys and reports. The *Uniform Crime Reports*, *National Crime Survey*, or the *Sourcebook of Criminal Justice Statistics* contain much information about crime and criminals. Another excellent source of data relevant to crime and the criminal justice system is the *National Archive of Criminal Justice Data*, which is sponsored by the Bureau of Justice Statistics, U.S. Department of Justice and operated by the Inter-university Consortium for Political and Social Research headquartered in Ann Arbor, Michigan (National Archive of Criminal Justice Data, 1990). Working through universities and colleges, professors, students, and others may access all types of information, including data sets, surveys, and statistical compilations about runaways, truants, prison and jail inmates, judicial decision guidelines, career offender characteristics, national crime figures, and correctional facility censuses. Nominal fees are charged for such services, which have been converted into computer-readable formats.

Convenience and Accessibility of the Elements

In the case of the young Long Beach police officer who wanted to study delinquency and ethnicity in the example presented earlier, having access to a "difficult-to-access" population was a definite advantage. The data needed, "confidential" juvenile records, were convenient and accessible. However, if someone wishes to interview AIDS inmates in prisons and how they are treated, permission must be obtained first from the wardens or superintendents of those facilities. Then the consent of those inmates with AIDS is required. The best research plans may be devised, *but they may never be implemented*, simply because of the *inaccessibility* of the target population.

Briefly summarizing, decisions to sample are based, in part, on the size of the population, the anticipated cost of the study in relation to the budget of the researcher, and the convenience and accessibility associated with obtaining the elements. Other factors are involved in this decision as well. Some of these factors are discussed later in the chapter.

SOME FUNCTIONS OF SAMPLING

The functions of sampling include (1) economizing resources, (2) manageability, (3) meeting assumptions of statistical tests, and (4) meeting the requirements of experiments.

Economizing Resources

Sampling saves researchers time, money, and personpower. Fewer elements are selected, less expense is incurred as the result of sending fewer questionnaires to respondents or interviewing fewer of them, and fewer assistants are necessary to help perform these necessary chores.

Manageability

Sampling helps to make data tabulation and analysis more manageable. It is easier to tabulate information from smaller numbers of elements. Also, many statistics programs for personal computers have data limitations, where the number of variables is restricted and smaller sample sizes are recommended. But "small" numbers of variables and sample sizes are not necessarily small. One computer program may prescribe, "This program may only be used for data sets with 40 or fewer variables and sample sizes of 1200 or less." This statement covers 99 percent of all research projects conducted by criminologists and criminal justice scholars. Much of the time, samples analyzed in the current literature (e.g., articles, reports) contain fewer than 500 elements.

Meeting Assumptions of Statistical Tests

Certain assumptions associated with statistical test applications are satisfied. Probability sampling is a requirement of all statistical procedures involved in statistical inference and decision making. Other assumptions must be satisfied as well, besides the probability sampling requirement. *The importance of meeting the assumptions is that meaningful and valid interpretations of test results can be made only if these assumptions are fulfilled.*

Also, each statistical test and measure of association has a "recommended sample size range" where optimum sample sizes are specified. Some procedures are designed for small samples, where "small" means 12 persons or less. Other procedures prescribe a range from 25 to 250 persons for optimum application. Applying these tests outside these sample ranges can be done, but the reliability and dependability of these tests are adversely affected. We cannot be sure of what the numerical test results mean under these less-than-optimum conditions. It will be helpful to review this chapter again as Chapters 14 to 17 are studied. Many of the terms subsequently introduced here are applied in actual test situations in later chapters.

Meeting the Requirements of Experiments

Certain types of research experimentation require that samples be of specified sizes. In some experimental situations, *several* samples of elements must be obtained. A requirement of an experiment might be that the samples should be of equal size and that they share other characteristics or similarities. For instance, these sample similarities may be equivalent proportions of males and females, equivalent proportions of different offense categories, or equivalent proportions of years on the job, depending on the target population being investigated. Specialized statistical procedures have been devised to analyze these unusual experimental situations as well. Some of these specialized statistical tests are presented in Chapter 17.

PROBABILITY SAMPLING PLANS

Probability sampling plans are those that specify the probability or likelihood of inclusion of each element drawn from a designated population. Technically, the following facts need to be known by the researcher in advance of selecting the sample:

1. The size of the target population or universe from which the sample will be obtained must be known. (The term *universe* is used interchangeably with *population*, since it refers to all persons about which one seeks information.)

2. The desired sample size must be specified. 1 in 10 of 250

3. Each element in the population or universe of elements must have an equal and an independent chance of being drawn and included in the sample.

Symbolically, when comparisons of population and sample sizes are made, N is the actual population size and n is the desired sample size. Under many conditions, these ideal criteria can be invoked. If we are seeking information about all inmates in a particular state penitentiary, a complete listing of inmates is available for our use in identifying all population elements. Another example is provided in a study by Larzelere and Patterson (1990). These researchers investigated the influence of parental management as a primary antecedent of delinquency. They believed that parental management skills would override factors such as socioeconomic status (SES), divorce, and exposure to criminal elements as contributors to juvenile delinquency.

To test certain hypotheses, these researchers identified a target population of youths in advance from the Oregon Youth Study (OYS). Among other things, the OYS identified those schools in the Eugene–Springfield area that had the highest per capita juvenile arrest rates. They drew their sample of youths from "all fourth-grade boys in these schools" (1990:308). Since there were existing records of these youths in the Eugene–Springfield area, it was relatively easy for them to draw the desired number of elements from these records. Similarly, membership lists of various organizations, such as the American Correctional Association, the American Probation and Parole Association, the American Jail Association, or the American Bar Association, will help us to identify various aggregates or potential target populations and enumerate them.

Some populations of elements are more elusive and cannot be enumerated easily, if at all. Studies of the parental characteristics of abused children are difficult to conduct, since child abuse is infrequently reported. Even if it is reported, many cases are not handled by courts but rather, by referrals to social welfare agencies. Prostitution and illegal gambling are other phenomena that are difficult to study, since the incidence or extent of these activities is largely hidden or unknown. Even if we know about the target population and where it can be located, there may be serious logistical problems encountered when attempting to sample from it. Knowing about the population of all jail inmates in the United States is theoretically possible, but our attempt to enumerate them would be frustrated by the fact that this population changes daily through admissions and releases.

A practical approach is best for dealing with large populations of elements. We will scale down our target population to a more manageable level. If we wish to study inmates, correctional officers, or juvenile delinquents, we can limit the scope of our investigation to a particular jurisdiction, such as a state, county, city, or suburb. Even if these smaller populations of elements do not include everyone, we can nevertheless conduct meaningful research and suggest to others that our findings are *potentially generalizable to other settings*. Researchers will often make qualifying remarks or statements in their work that highlight deficiencies in the target population or problems that occurred in the selection of sample elements.

Natural conditions may exist that limit the population's magnitude. For example, Meadows and Trostle (1988) studied police misconduct in the Los Angeles, California Police Department for the years 1974–1986. They wanted to describe the nature of the misconduct alleged as well as the legal outcome. The city attorney's office permitted them to examine 79 "closed" cases during that time interval. From their research report, it is unknown whether these 79 cases represented a small or a large proportion of the total number of police misconduct cases handled by the city attorney's office between 1974 and 1986. Under these circumstances, the researchers had no alternative but to label their sample "nonprobability," since it was not possible to enumerate all cases from which their sample was obtained.

In another study, Walters (1988) wanted to examine correctional officers' perceptions of powerlessness in their work. *Powerlessness* was defined as the probability that individuals could not determine the occurrences or outcomes they seek. Walters wanted to know if powerlessness was perceived by correctional officers, and whether powerlessness was the result of specific environmental factors and self-concepts. Walters identified a large prison in the "Intermountain West." The facility housed 750 inmates and employed 193 correctional officers. Walters sent questionnaires to all 193 officers, but only 126 completed questionnaires were returned, for a 65 percent response rate. In this study, no attempt was made to enumerate all of the officers. Rather, the entire population of 193 was targeted, although only two-thirds responded. However, two-thirds of the population of officers is a rather large proportion under the circumstances. Despite this large proportion of responses, the sample cannot be considered a probability sample. The reasons for officer nonresponse are unknown, but Walters' results may have been quite different had some or all of these nonrespondents actually responded and returned their completed questionnaires.

Randomness

The crucial features of probability sampling plans have to do with the equality and independence of drawing or selecting elements for inclusion in our samples. Actually, equality and independence are essential defining characteristics of *randomness*, which is the process of selecting elements such that each element has an equal and independent chance of being included. Randomness is the primary control governing all probability sampling plans. Equality of draw refers to giving all elements in the population an equal chance of being included in the resulting sample. Independence means that the draw or selection of one element will not affect the chances of the remaining elements of being drawn later.

Equality of draw is simply illustrated by the following hypothetical example. Suppose that we were studying defense attorneys in Detroit, Michigan. Our records might show that there are 2000 defense attorneys in Detroit. We will use a sampling method that will give each of these 2000 attorneys 1/2000 of a chance of being included in our sample. If our sample were of size 50,000, everyone should have 1/50,000 of a chance of being included. If our sample were 100, everyone would have 1/100 of a chance of being included. This is what is meant by giving everyone in the population an equal chance of being included.

Independence of draw means that the draw of any particular element will not influence the chances of other population elements of being included in the sample. An example known as the *fishbowl draw* will be used to illustrate what is meant by independence. First, all elements in the population are enumerated from 1 to N. Second, their numbers are placed on identical slips of paper. Next, these slips are placed in a fishbowl. Next, someone who is blindfolded reaches into the bowl and selects slips of paper, one at a time. Then the numbers are recorded, and those persons matching the numbers become a part of our sample.

Suppose that our target population consists of 100 elements. We number each person from 1 to 100, write these numbers on slips of paper, and place them all in a fishbowl. After mixing the slips of paper in the bowl, we reach in, blindfolded, and select the first slip of paper. Our first selection is a random one, since all element numbers were in the bowl and each had 1/100 of a chance of being included on the first draw. However, we have withdrawn one slip of paper. That leaves 99 pieces of paper in the bowl. The next time we dip into the bowl to retrieve a slip of paper, the remaining elements will have 1/99 of a chance of being included in our sample. Thus continuous draws of slips of paper from the bowl will slightly increase the chances of the remaining elements of being included (e.g., 1/98, 1/97, 1/96, etc.). These are not independent draws, since the chances of the remaining elements of being included in our samples are increased each time a slip of paper is removed from the bowl. Therefore, we will not have a random sample using this method.

What if we replace the slips of paper once we have drawn them? This way, there would always be 100 slips of paper in the bowl, and each person would have 1/100 of a chance of being drawn each time. Actually, this is an appropriate strategy for ensuring both independence and equality of draw, and it has been given a name by statisticians: *sampling with replacement*. The earlier method of withholding slips of paper from the bowl, once we have selected and recorded them, also has a name: *sampling without replacement*. In the social sciences, *all* probability sampling plans as well as *all* of the statistical tests used that require probability samples as one of their requisite assumptions assume that sampling with replacement has been used.

However, when sampling with replacement is used, some of us are going to worry about drawing slips of paper from the bowl that have been drawn before. Under these circumstances, the best procedure is to continue drawing slips of paper from the bowl, with replacement, until *n* desired elements are obtained. Simply skip or ignore those numbers that have already been drawn, replace them in the fishbowl, and continue to draw slips until you have selected *n* different numbers. Better procedures are available for selecting random samples of elements other than the fishbowl draw. We can obtain randomness by using either (1) a table of random numbers or (2) a computer-determined draw.

Simple Random Sampling and Random Numbers Tables

A *table of random numbers* is almost exactly the way it sounds. It is a table of digits randomly derived, where no digit occurs in any particular sequence and no digit occurs any more frequently than any other digit. Table A.2 in Appendix A is a table of random numbers. Examine Table A.2 and observe that digits have been "bunched up" into groups of five rows and five columns, with spaces above and below as well as on either side of these bunches. *There is no significance attached to these particular groupings.* The blank spaces between the bunches of digits are simply for reading ease. Imagine what this table would look like if all of these bunches of digits were pushed together toward the centers of the pages. Below is reproduced a segment of the first page of Table A.2, specifically the two bunches of digit groupings in the upper left-hand corner.

10097	32533
37542	04805
08422	68953
99019	02529
12807	99970

We use this table as follows. First, we identify our target population. Suppose that it is an inmate population at the Colorado State Penitentiary and that the population of inmates is $N = 850$. Suppose that we wish to draw a sample n of 50 from this population of 850. We first assign these inmates numbers from 001 to 850 and then we select 50 *different* random numbers from Table A.2. We begin this task by counting the number of digits in our population N, or three digits: 8, 5, and 0. We will move through this table in a systematic fashion, examining groupings of three digits each. Let's decide to start our election of sample elements with the first three digits shown in the upper left-hand corner of page 468. These are the digit groupings reproduced above for your convenience. Let's record the first three digits, 1, 0, and 0. For our purposes, this is inmate 100. Moving directly downward in the table, we pick up the next three digits immediately below 100, or 375. This is inmate 375. Continuing to move downward toward the bottom of the table, we select 084 or inmate 84, then 990, the 990th inmate, and 128, the 128th inmate. Did you just sense something wrong? Yes. The "990th inmate" does not exist, since our population size extends only to 850 inmates. Therefore, we skip or ignore all inmate numbers that do not fit the limits of our population.

When we reach the bottom of page 468, our last three-digit grouping is 690, or inmate 690. Where do we go from here? We go back to the top of the page, almost where we started initially. But now we move over to the right precisely one digit, and then pick up the next three-digit sequence. In this case, it will be 009, or the ninth inmate. The next, moving downward directly is 754, or inmate 754, 842 or the 842nd inmate, 901 (skip it), 280 or the 280th inmate, and so on, until we again reach the bottom of the page. We repeat this process by moving to the top of the page, moving over precisely one digit, selecting the next three-digit sequence, which is 097 (inmate 97), and move downward again, making our selections. The next time we go back to the top of the page, we will move over to the right again one digit and pick up the next three digits. In this case, we will pick up 973. The next three-digit groupings below this one in the example above are 420, 226, 190, and 079, respectively. Again, *ignore* the spacing between these bunches of digits. The spaces mean nothing. They are there to make it easier on our eyes to obtain samples from this table. We continue our selection process until we have identified 50 *different* random numbers for our desired sample size. By definition, this is a random sample of 50 elements from our population of 850.

Researchers often have access to computer systems with programs capable of generating n random numbers from a population of N elements. This is a computer-determined random sample. In fact, this is precisely how Table A.2 was generated by the Rand Corporation—by computer. Thus the computer-determined draw and a draw of elements from a table of random numbers are synonymous.

Simple random samples are samples of size n taken from a population size of N. An example of simple random sampling is provided in a study by Crouch and Marquart (1990). These researchers were interested in the effects of prison reforms introduced by the Texas Department of Corrections (TDC) during a period of massive court-ordered reforms, 1978–1981. They wanted to know whether significant changes occurred in prison conditions, violence levels, and perceptions of safety among prisoners before, during, and after court-decreed reform implementation. Using TDC-assigned six-digit numbers that identified each inmate, Crouch and Marquart obtained simple random samples of inmates from different prison units, eventually drawing 614 numbers or about 5 percent of the inmate population. However, 123 inmates were not available when these researchers collected their data. Some were ill, others were on furloughs, and others were in solitary confinement. Thirty of the available inmates refused to participate. Therefore, what started out as an ideally selected random sample of TDC prison inmates eventually atrophied at 461 inmates.

What should we call this sample of a simple random sample? First, the sample is no longer a random sample. Of the 614 inmates originally selected (the actual simple random sample), 153 inmates were either unavailable or refused to participate (1990:107). This nonresponse represents nearly 25 percent of the original sample. Who knows what effect this significant number of inmates would have made had it been included in the final data analysis? What happened in Crouch's and Marquart's study is what happens in almost every study researchers conduct. They failed to get all of the elements they originally selected. This is where our ideal—real gap in being procedurally correct and following rules of sample selection to the letter is most evident. However, Crouch and Marquart made the statement "These refusals showed no pattern that would bias the sample" (1990:107). Unless we know what their responses would have been to the questions we wanted to ask, we have no way of knowing what impact their inclusion would have had on the final outcome. They refused to participate for various reasons. This certainly makes them different from those who did participate. For all we know, they may have been the hardcore leadership of the Mexican Mafia or Aryan Brotherhood, and their responses to questions about prison violence and inmate safety would have been most enlightening. When confronted with sizable non-response, it is best simply to acknowledge it and not comment about its significance, nonsignificance, or biasing effects. Let the reader judge accordingly.

Advantages and disadvantages of simple random sampling plans. Simple random sampling plans have the following advantages:

1. All elements in the population are selected randomly, each having an equal and an independent chance of being included. Theoretically, at least, the sample obtained will have a good chance of being representative of the population.

2. This plan is used in conjunction with all other probability sampling plans. It serves as the foundation upon which all types of random samples are based.

3. Of all the probability sampling plans, it is the easiest to apply.

4. The true composition of the population does not need to be known in advance. Simple random samples theoretically reflect all important segments of the target population to one degree or another.

5. The amount of *sampling error* can be computed easily. A more extensive discussion of sampling error is presented later in this chapter, but briefly, sampling error is the degree of departure of various sample statistics from their respective population parameters. Ordinarily, larger samples have less sampling error than smaller samples.

The disadvantages of simple random sampling plans are:

1. These plans may not exploit fully the knowledge researchers may have of the target population studied. Sometimes, researchers may know more about certain characteristics of the population that would enable them to draw more representative samples using an alternative probability sampling plan, such as a stratified random sample. Simple random sampling ignores these valuable characteristics. For instance, in sampling from a prison inmate population using simple random sampling, suppose that there are 20 inmates out of 800 who have AIDS. Unless something is done to provide for the inclusion of AIDS inmates, it is likely that because of their few numbers, they will not be included in the subsequent sample. Again, a stratified random sample would overcome this limitation.

2. Compared with stratified random samples of the same size, there is usually more sampling error in simple random samples. This is because stratified random samples use more information about the population to enhance representativeness, whereas such information is not ordinarily considered under the simple random sampling format.

Stratified Random Sampling

Stratified random sampling plans take into account one or more population characteristics. "Stratifying" means to *control* for one or more variables and ensure their subsequent inclusion in a sample. If we study probation officers and determine from the population of them that 30 percent are nonwhite and 70 percent are white, we can "stratify" on race/ethnicity and ensure that both whites and nonwhites will be included. Further, suppose that 10 percent of the population consists of females. We can stratify on gender as well, and we can ensure that some of the female probation officers will be included in our sample. Thus stratifying means to take one or more variables into account in our sample selections and ensure their inclusion. Two types of stratified random sampling plans are presented here: (1) disproportionate stratified random sampling and (2) proportionate stratified random sampling.

Disproportionate stratified random sampling. When investigators possesses some knowledge concerning the target population, such as its offense characteristics, race, gender, or some other variable, they may select their samples such that one or more of these characteristics are represented. These types of sampling plans are improvements over simple random sampling, since it is entirely possible when selecting a simple random sample that some of these relevant characteristics will not be included. To use disproportionate stratified random sampling, researchers divide their population into categories on those variables considered important. Then they select their sample from each of these subcategories.

For example, McShane (1987) studied prison inmates in the Texas Department of Corrections (TDC). She wanted to know whether inmates who are illegal aliens, alien inmates, receive differential punishment and more severe punishments than do nonalien inmates. At the time of her study, McShane found that the TDC had 27 prison units housing 36,653 inmates. About 1500 of these were alien inmates. Because she wanted a substantial number of alien inmates to compare with nonalien inmates, it would be unlikely using a simple random sampling plan that she would randomly include many alien inmates. She decided to divide the entire inmate population into *subpopulations* of alien and nonalien. Next, she drew two separate simple random samples, *subsamples*, one from the alien inmate population and one from the nonalien inmate population.

Her alien inmate subsample consisted of 590 prisoners, while her nonalien subsample consisted of 603 prisoners. These different subsamples, roughly equivalent in size, were subsequently examined. If McShane had combined these subsamples into one large sample, her overall sample, randomly selected, would be disproportionate in relation to the general inmate population on the alien/nonalien variable. About 1.6 percent of the TDC inmate population consisted of alien inmates. However, her sample was made up of about 50 percent alien inmates. Therefore, these inmates were disproportionately represented or overrepresented in her sample. Accordingly, nonalien inmates were underrepresented in the sample, since they made up nearly 99 percent of the TDC inmate population.

While McShane made direct comparisons of the two subsamples of inmates according to various factors such as sentence lengths, good time credit, and status level, she had other investigative options. She could have combined the two subsamples into one large sample of 1193 (590 + 603 = 1193) and made other analyses of her data. She would have referred to the combined subsamples as a "disproportionate stratified random sample, stratified according to alien/nonalien inmate status." Using some general figures that roughly parallel those reported by McShane, Table 5.2 illustrates disproportionate stratified random sampling for the TDC inmate population.

Advantages, disadvantages, and uses of disproportionate stratified random sampling. The major advantage of disproportionate stratified random sampling is that it enables researchers to guarantee that specific characteristics or important variables that exist in the population will also be represented in their samples. The disadvantages are:

1. This sampling method does not give each of the subpopulations (total alien and total nonalien inmates in the TED population in this case) weight in the sample in accordance with their proportionate weight in the population. In this respect, the resulting sample is less representative of the population. However, an overriding consideration is the guaranteed inclusion of small numbers of elements that possess desired traits or characteristics, so that meaningful comparisons may be made between subsamples.

2. This method requires some in-depth knowledge about the target population in advance. This information is not always available, depending on the target population investigated. In McShane's case, TDC files helped her to determine those belonging in one subpopulation or another so that she could draw simple random samples from them.

TABLE 5.2 DISPROPORTIONATE STRATIFIED RANDOM SAMPLING ILLUSTRATED FOR 36,000 TEXAS DEPARTMENT OF CORRECTIONS INMATES, CONTROLLING FOR ALIEN/NONALIEN STATUS

Population (Stratified by Alien/Nonalien Status)			Sampling Method	Sample	
Alien inmates	2,000	(1.6%)	Simple random	600	(50%)
Nonalien inmates	34,000	(98.4%)	Simple random	600	(50%)
Total	36,000	(100.0%)		1,200	(100%)

↳ Not Proportionate ↑

3. Whenever samples are stratified on any variable, there is the possibility that classification errors may arise. In studies of the influence socioeconomic status (SES) on delinquency, for instance, one's SES and the type of delinquency may be defined according to several broad categorizations. Subpopulations of persons on the SES variable will be identified, as well as subpopulations of juveniles on the delinquency variable. Some of these elements may be improperly assigned to certain categories. A nonviolent property juvenile offender might be misclassified as a violent offender, or persons classified as upper-class may really be middle-class. Using simple random sampling, however, will minimize errors that may result from misclassifications of elements.

Serious
"mis-classification"

Same proportion in population & Sample.

3. Proportionate stratified random sampling. The major difference between disproportionate and proportionate stratified random sampling plans is that in proportionate plans, stratified characteristics exist in samples in the same proportionate distribution as they exist in the population. In McShane's study of TDC inmates, for example, it would have been easy to sample these inmates proportionately instead of disproportionately. She would have proceeded to identify the two subpopulations the same as before, but in the present instance, her interest would be in carrying over the proportionate distribution of alien/nonalien status into her resulting sample. For example, if she knew that 1.6 percent of the 36,000 TDC inmate population were aliens and 98.4 percent were nonaliens, her sample would be made up of 1.6 percent aliens and 98.4 percent nonaliens. For comparative purposes, let's assume that she wanted a large sample of 1200.

Wishing to preserve the proportionate distribution of alien/nonalien status, she would ensure that 1.6 percent of 1200 ($0.016 \times 1200 = 19$) or 19 aliens would be included, and 1181 nonaliens would be included. This would make her resulting sample a "proportionate stratified random sample, controlling for alien/nonalien status." Table 5.3 illustrates this procedure. In each case, McShane would simply calculate how much of her sample should consist of persons exhibiting certain characteristics. Since alien inmates made up 1.6 percent of the population, her sample of 1200 should have this proportion included, or $(0.016)(1200) = 19$. Nineteen of these 1200 sample elements should be alien inmates, provided that she wanted to have a proportionate stratified random sample, stratified according to alien/nonalien inmate status.

TABLE 5.3 PROPORTIONATE STRATIFIED RANDOM SAMPLING ILLUSTRATED FOR 36,000 TEXAS DEPARTMENT OF CORRECTIONS INMATES, CONTROLLING FOR ALIEN/NONALIEN STATUS

Population (Stratified) by Alien/Nonalien Status)		Sampling Method	Sample	
Alien inmates	2,000	Simple random	19	(1.6%)
Nonalien inmates	34,000	Simple random	1,181	(98.4%)
Total	36,000 (100%)		1,200	(100%)

Advantages and disadvantages of proportionate stratified random sampling. The advantages of this sampling method are:

(1.) Proportionately stratifying a sample on one more important characteristics enhances the representativeness of the sample in relation to the population.

(2.) The resulting sample is superior to a simple random sample of the same size as the basis for estimates about population parameters or characteristics.

(3.) The amount of sampling error in proportionate stratified random samples is generally less than that found in simple random samples of the same size. This is because there are more similarities between the sample and the population that have been controlled.

The disadvantages of this sampling method are:

(1.) The researcher needs to know something in advance about the composition of the population to ensure proportionality on one or more characteristics. Like disproportionate stratified random sampling, this information is not always readily available.

(2.) Compared with simple random sampling, this method is more time consuming, since subpopulations of elements with certain characteristics must be identified first before random samples can be taken from them.

(3.) Similar to the disproportionate stratified random sampling, stratifying always creates the possibility that misclassifications may occur regarding population element placements in one sample or another. Simple random sampling overcomes misclassification problems.

Area, Cluster, or Multistage Sampling

If we consider that disproportionate and proportionate stratified random sampling are two different types of probability sampling plans, *area sampling*, also known as *cluster* or *multistage sampling*, is a fourth type. Area (sometimes *areal*) sampling is used primarily for the purpose of surveying public opinion about issues within a vast geographical territory, such as a country, state, or city. Area sampling has its origin in agriculture. Farming experiments were often conducted to determine the effects of various types of fertilizers and soil nutrients as well as various planting methods on crop yield. A map of some specified acreage would be identified, and vertical and horizontal grids would be drawn for the entire area, creating numerous smaller squares or land plots. These squares would be enumerated, and a simple random sample of squares would be obtained by using the table of random numbers. Once the sample of land squares was obtained, the researcher would combine them into one large sample of land squares, calculate crop yield for the aggregate of squares, and compare the yield with the yield of some other aggregate of squares taken from land treated by different nutrients or fertilizers.

Social science applications of this method have been closely connected with public opinion polling and survey designs in field research. Thus geographical divisions and horizontal and vertical gridlines are designated on a map of some previously identified territory, community, or neighborhood. Squares of smaller portions of territory are formed by the intersecting gridlines. These squares are numbered, and a simple random sample of squares is obtained. These individually selected squares are again crisscrossed with horizontal and vertical gridlines, the resulting squares are numbered, and a simple random sample of territorial squares is again taken from each of the previously drawn squares. This process involves different sampling stages: hence the term _multistage sampling_. This probability sampling method is illustrated in Figure 5.1

Suppose that the geographical territory was a part of the United States as pictured in Figure 5.1. Note that vertical and horizontal grids have been drawn and squares numbered. A simple random sample of these squares is obtained using the table of random numbers that we have already discussed. These squares comprising our initial sample are known as first-stage units. We subdivide each of these first-stage units or territorial squares as shown, using similar horizontal and vertical gridlines. We number these resulting squares and take simple random samples of them. We continue this procedure, possibly through a second stage to third-stage units as shown. We then combine all of the third-stage units into one large sample. This becomes our probability sample for a large geographical territory. From here, we identify persons who dwell within the territories of the squares we selected. Perhaps one of our third-stage units is a 6-square-mile area in Kansas.

Five farms are located within this area, as shown in Figure 5.1. We might send an interviewer to the area to interview the heads of all families living in this "cluster" of farms: hence the name "cluster sampling." This saves a lot of interviewer travel time, since interviewers only have to go to a few localities and interview all or most of those who live there.

Numerically, we might begin area sampling by selecting 10 squares from the original grid. Once these 10 squares (first-stage units) have been identified, each is vertically and horizontally crisscrossed again to yield numerous squares that are numbered. Suppose that we take 10 squares at random from each of the first 10. This will give us 100 squares (second-stage units). We can grid these squares with vertical and horizontal lines, thus creating numerous other squares. Of course, these squares are becoming smaller and smaller geographical areas. Taking 10 squares from each of these 100 squares will give us 1000 squares (third-stage units as shown in Figure 5.1). Then, clusters of elements living in those third-stage units are interviewed or surveyed.

If it occurs that one of these squares is a city block of large apartment buildings in Los Angeles, it might be cost-prohibitive to canvass all persons living in that block of apartments. Perhaps we will interview every tenth family throughout all of these apartment buildings in the block. Actually, this is using *systematic sampling* (discussed below as a nonprobability sampling plan) with a probability sampling plan, but it does save us some time, particularly if we are conducting interviews.

Although area or cluster or multistage sampling is conducted primarily by demographers and pollsters, criminologists and criminal justice scholars might be interested in soliciting opinions about different controversial issues, such as abortion or the constitutionality of the death penalty. On the basis of survey data, researchers may eventually influence public policy relating to these issues.

Advantages and Disadvantages of Area Sampling

Area sampling includes the following advantages:

1. It is much easier to apply compared with simple random sampling, whenever large populations are studied or when large geographical areas must be canvassed. It is easier in the sense that researchers do not have to have predetermined lists of elements who inhabit the areas selected. Random geographical areas are included, and these are believed representative of the general population.

2. Compared with other sampling methods, especially where large geographical territory is involved, area sampling is less expensive. Interviewers may concentrate their efforts in specific regions, and consequently they save time and money by not having to travel great distances to interview different people living at random points in a geographical area.

3. Not everyone may respond when contacted by the researcher. Since clusters of elements are sampled, however, individual refusals are less harmful to the sample's representativeness than in a simple random sample of elements from the entire territory.

4. If field research crews or work units are dispersed throughout a state or territory, cluster sampling saves them time and money by focusing their efforts in selected areas. This advantage is even more relevant for large research corporations than for individual investigators.

5. This sampling method offers flexibility, since a combination of sampling strategies might be employed to sample elements from densely populated areas.

The disadvantages of area sampling are:

1. There is no way to ensure that each sampling unit included (second-or third-stage units) will be of equal size as the researcher exercises little control over the size of each cluster sampled. This may introduce some bias in the final sample obtained.

2. Area samples have a greater amount of sampling error than do simple random samples of the same size.

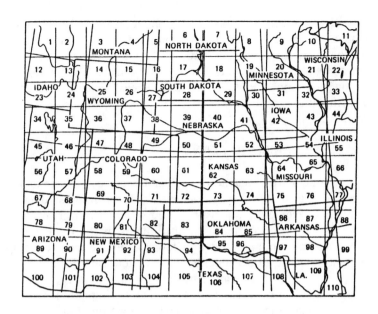

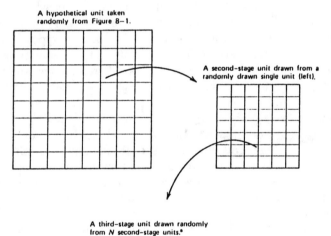

A hypothetical unit taken randomly from Figure 8–1.

A second-stage unit drawn from a randomly drawn single unit (left).

A third-stage unit drawn randomly from N second-stage units.[a]

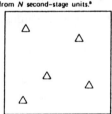

[a] $\triangle$ = a farm home or other dwelling unit within a third-stage unit.

Figure 5.1 illustration of area sampling

Probability Sampling Plans

3. It is difficult to ensure that all elements surveyed in all clusters are independent of one another. For instance, someone interviewed in one cluster area may be visiting relatives. That person may travel to another area and be interviewed by other researchers involved in the same research project. Thus the same person's opinion would be counted at least twice. The chances of this event occurring are remote, however.

NONPROBABILITY SAMPLING PLANS

Many types of research designs do not require that random samples should be obtained. Rather, investigators may only be interested in obtaining sufficient numbers of elements to satisfy limited research objectives. Perhaps the investigator is testing certain research instruments or the readability of questionnaires. Only a sufficient number of warm bodies would be required to assist the researcher in pretesting these instruments. It is often unimportant if these persons have characteristics that are similar to those in the intended target population.

Some types of research are such that it is <u>impossible</u> to enumerate population elements in advance to draw random samples from them. For instance, if we were interested in describing the behaviors of looters who steal from others in the aftermath of natural disasters, such as earthquakes or floods, these types of events cannot be forecast with any accuracy. Also, some types of behaviors that we might want to examine pertain to satanic cults and nefarious rituals carried out in secret away from the prying eyes of others. If researchers should gain access to such groups, the formality of obtaining random samples of elements would have to be abandoned.

The main distinction between probability and nonprobability sampling plans is that probability samples use randomness as the primary control feature and nonprobability sampling plans do not. Randomness permits inferences to be made about population characteristics based on observed sample characteristics. Random samples of elements are commonly considered generalizable to larger populations from which they are drawn, within a probabilistic context. In the case of nonprobability samples, we cannot make inferential statements of any value about population parameters. We do not know what populations our nonprobability samples represent or typify. But this limitation does not mean that such samples are without merit. On the contrary, much of what we do in criminal justice and criminology is based on descriptions of nonprobability samples.

Another compelling argument suggesting that nonprobability samples have heuristic value is that often, researchers begin their investigations ideally seeking random samples to study. As so often happens, however, these researchers frequently fail to obtain all persons they originally included in their sampling plan. Relatively few research projects report that all of those originally selected for inclusion in the sample are subsequently included and studied.

MacKenzie and Shaw (1990) were fortunate in this respect in their investigation of inmate adjustment to shock incarceration. Shock incarceration involved placing convicted offenders in jail for a period of up to six months. These persons were then brought back into court, and provided that they behaved well while in jail, were paroled under intensive supervision. The shock of confinement does much to induce conformity to societal rules and parole program conditions. MacKenzie and Shaw studied inmates who participated in a Louisiana Department of Public Safety program known as IMPACT, the Intensive Motivational Program of Alternative Correctional Treatment. They wanted to know whether the shock incarceration program was more effective than plain "flat time" or incarceration at changing offender attitudes and behaviors. They asked all 90 offenders who were entering the IMPACT program during a specified time interval if they would like to participate in their research. All offenders agreed to participate. This 100 percent response is rare in any social scientific project.

Nonprobability samples are categorically easier to obtain than are probability samples. In this section, seven nonprobability sampling plans are presented: (1) accidental sampling, (2) systematic sampling, (3) purposive or judgmental sampling, (4) quota sampling, (5) snowball sampling, (6) dense sampling, and (7) saturation sampling.

Accidental Sampling

Accidental sampling, sometimes known as *convenience sampling*, is exactly what it sounds like. Researchers make virtually no effort to identify target populations in advance and ensure all elements an equal and an independent chance of being included. Rather, they attempt to obtain as many persons as they believe will make it possible for them to test their theories and the hypotheses derived from them. The "roving reporter" interviewing passersby on the street is obtaining an accidental sample of respondents. Persons who call others at random by telephone and solicit their opinions about different controversial issues are obtaining accidental samples. The professor who distributes questionnaires to large sections of criminal justice or criminology courses and surveys students has acquired an accidental sample.

An example of obtaining an accidental sample is a study of social attitudes about offense seriousness and punitive severity by Durham (1988). Durham obtained 276 responses to a survey instrument he administered to several classes of undergraduate criminology students. The classes were large, "convenient," and accessible. Durham acknowledged at the outset that there were various limitations associated with using undergraduates in his sample. Nevertheless, his findings were of interest and will be useful to others studying similar phenomena. Durham never said that his sample was typical of the general population. Rather, he interpreted his findings in the context of the accompanying limitations he had previously acknowledged.

The primary advantages of accidental sampling are convenience and economy. The disadvantages include limited generalizability, considerable bias, and no evidence of a probability sample. Regarding bias, researchers often select elements because of their particular location in relation to the researcher. In Durham's study, for example, the elements were students in large classrooms. Durham distributed questionnaires to several classrooms of criminology students. He did not go to classes consisting of engineering students, education students, or history students. If researchers study their own organizations, they do not know whether their organizations are typical or atypical of other organizations like theirs. The major drawback of accidental sampling is that researchers have little or no idea about what population the sample is supposed to represent. This fact explains the limited generalizability, the bias, and the nonprobabilistic nature of such samples.

Systematic Sampling

Systematic sampling is a popular technique for selecting elements from alphabetized listings or other compilations of elements. Basically, it involves selecting every *n*th person from a list, whether the list is a telephone directory, inmate listing, or the membership list of a national or local professional association. In some instances, lists may not be involved. If investigators wish to canvass a particular geographical territory, such as a city block or small community, they can anticipate in advance how many persons or households exist. Then, they can select every *n*th household in the neighborhood or community for inclusion in their systematic sample.

This technique has a probability sampling aspect, although it is not a probability sampling plan. When investigators determine the size of the target population, they calculate how many persons they want to include in their sample. Then they divide the population by their desired sample size and derive their value of *n*. For instance, if a listing of persons contained 5000 names, and if researchers desired a sampling size of 200 elements, they would need to select every *n*th person, where $n = N/n$ or $5000/200 = 25$. Thus every 25th person on the list or every 25th household in the neighborhood or community would be contacted.

An illustration of the application of systematic sampling is found in the work of Kenney (1986). Kenney wanted to investigate the influence and effectiveness of various citizen groups that are created to combat street crime. In this particular study, Kenney focused on the group known as Guardian Angels. The Guardian Angels formed in 1979 and originally patrolled subways in New York City in an effort to minimize muggings and other subway crimes. One aspect of his investigation involved direct interviews with subway passengers about their perceptions of the effectiveness of the Guardian Angels. Therefore, a systematic sampling of subway passengers was obtained, consisting of passengers who were contacted while exiting subways as well as those waiting on subway platforms. Kenney notes that "individual passengers were then chosen in a systematic manner until the assigned number of interviews was completed" (Kenney, 1986:484). About 79 percent of all passengers contacted by Kenney and his assistants responded to face-to-face interviews. We are not informed by Kenney's report as to the magnitude of *n* in "every *n*th person being selected," although Kenney's resulting sample was substantial, consisting of 2693 passengers.

Advantages and disadvantages of systematic sampling. The primary advantages of systematic sampling are:

1. This method is easy to use, especially contrasted with having to use a table of random numbers in the identification of elements.

2. Because it is a nonprobability sampling form, mistakes in drawing certain elements are relatively unimportant. Mistakes might occur if one miscounts on the listing of elements and draws the 51st person instead of the 50th person, for example. This mistake is trivial.

3. If checks are employed to verify the accuracy of sample selection, systematic sampling makes it easier to spot mistakes that might have been made in counting. However, questions about the accuracy of systematic sampling are relatively unimportant, again because of the nonprobabilistic nature of the method.

4. Systematic sampling is a fast method for obtaining a sample. If researchers are in a hurry to make their sample selections, systematic sampling would be much faster than any of the probability sampling methods discussed earlier.

The major disadvantages of systematic sampling are:

1. Systematic sampling systematically excludes persons from being included in the selected sample. Thus it is not a probability sampling method. Representativeness and generalizability are affected adversely as a result.

2. If the listing of elements is alphabetically arranged, some degree of ethnic bias will enter the picture. Sampling error will be increased accordingly, as some groups with minority/ethnic surnames, Oriental or otherwise, are selected less frequently compared with selections of names beginning with "Mc," "Smith," "Jones," "Anderson," or "Johnson." This bias will affect the generalizability of findings accordingly.

3. If the listing of elements is arranged according to some other characteristic, such as "severity of offense," "educational level attained," "age," or some other similar ordered characteristic, some bias will be introduced. Those characteristics most frequently listed will be overrepresented; less frequently listed characteristics will be underrepresented.

Purposive or Judgmental Sampling — *those that know & have been there long & know the study.*

Purposive or *judgmental sampling* involves handpicking elements from some target population. The researcher's intent is to ensure that certain elements will be included in the resulting sample. Because some or most elements will be included in the sample deliberately and others will be excluded deliberately, purposive sampling is a nonprobability sampling form. Why would researchers want to sample in this fashion? One explanation is that the investigators might have extensive familiarity with the population to the extent that they know those elements who would be most representative of it. Because of their knowledge about the population, the researchers may, in fact, be able to obtain a sample that would be better (i.e., more representative) than any probability sampling plan would yield.

Purposive or judgmental sampling has been used in the social sciences, particularly where studies of small communities are involved. Someone who is well known in the community and is familiar with most residents is asked to handpick representative numbers of elements who typify the range of community sentiment

ask those who really know & been there awhile

on some issue. Thus if a researcher wanted to know community sentiment about abortion, or civil rights issues, or capital punishment, the handpicked sample, the "judgmental" sample, would be a good indication about what the community at large thought about the issue.

Because the application of judgmental sampling has been sparse in the criminal justice literature, an hypothetical illustration will be used, based on an actual study conducted by Charles (1989). Charles studied the effectiveness of electronic monitoring used to monitor the whereabouts of selected juveniles. Because of the initial costs of establishing electronic monitoring programs, not all jurisdictions have them. Those jurisdictions that use this equipment usually operate it with relatively few offenders. Charles studied juveniles who were adjudicated delinquent and sentenced to the Indiana Boys School in Fort Wayne (Allen County), Indiana.

In Charles' study, youths who wanted to participate in the electronic monitoring program and not enter the Indiana Boys School could volunteer. Probation officers would select those youths deemed to be the most acceptable electronic monitoring candidates. Hypothetically, suppose that Charles wanted to evaluate the effectiveness as it might influence recidivism of boys who represented several offending categories. He might select some boys who were violent offenders, some who were property offenders, and perhaps some who were status offenders but had violated court orders. Working with probation officers who knew all the boys and were familiar with their backgrounds, Charles could handpick those youths believed to be "typical" of different offender categories. This would enable him to obtain a reasonably representative sample for study, although it would not be a random one.

The major advantage of judgmental samples is that certain elements will definitely be included in the resulting sample. If researchers know a great deal about the populations of elements they are studying in advance, this handpicked sample could be a better representation of the population than would be possible using any probability sampling method. Additional advantages are that this method is less cumbersome than probability sampling plans. The elements selected are probably more accessible to the researcher and relate most directly to one's study objectives. On the negative side, no amount of judging can forecast accurately that the sample will be a truly representative one. Unknown biases may enter into the selection process and make the sample quite atypical. There are generalization problems, as well, since these samples do not conform to the requirements of probability sampling. Tests of statistical significance and inference would be inappropriate here and their use undermined by the nonprobabilistic nature of sample selection.

Finally, an extensive amount of information about the population is required in advance of such element selections. This is seldom the case when researchers approach the target population for the first time. Thus judgmental sampling plans are applied only infrequently in criminology or criminal justice research projects, although some investigators regard their representativeness as superior to all probability sampling plans.

Other Nonprobability Sampling Strategies

Four additional sampling plans merit discussion here: quota sampling, snowball sampling, dense sampling, and saturation sampling. Of these four lesser-known sampling strategies, quota sampling is, on the basis of its use in criminology and criminal justice research, the most popular of these other sampling methods.

same distribution

Quota sampling plans. *Quota sampling* is obtaining a desired number of elements from the population by selecting those that are most accessible and have certain characteristics of interest to the researcher. The selection of elements is comparable to proportionate stratified random sampling, without randomness as the primary control. These characteristics might be age, gender, race, ethnicity, type of offense, profession, or any other factor that might be measured. Investigators want to obtain persons that possess certain characteristics that typify some population, and they want to obtain similar proportions of these characteristics in their samples. Thus if a population is known to consist of 80 percent whites and 20 percent blacks, efforts will be made to secure a sample consisting of 80 percent white and 20 percent black participants. Quota sampling has been called the "poor man's proportionate stratified sample." *because not a*

A hypothetical illustration is provided by reference to a study of staff perceptions of volunteers in a correctional program conducted by Lucas (1987). In Lucas's original study, he wanted to sample probation and parole officers in Missouri and obtain perceptions from them about the quality of performance of volunteers in a state-sponsored Volunteers in Corrections (VIC) program. Lucas determined that there were 300 officers working in 28 districts in five state regions. In the actual study, Lucas limited his investigation to seven of the 28 districts. But suppose that Lucas had wanted to obtain a quota sample of probation and parole officers statewide? Further suppose that he determined that of the 300 probation and parole officers, 60 percent (180) were male, and 40 percent (120) were female. Also, suppose he learned that 10 percent (30) of these officers were black (15 males and 15 females) and 90 percent (270) were white (165 males and 105 females).

Let's assume that Lucas wants to obtain one-third of these officers (100) from the state for study. But he wants to use a quota sample, controlling for gender and race. Therefore, he would need to obtain 60 males and 40 females. Ten percent of his sample of 100, or 10 elements, would need to be black. Since half of the blacks are female, he would want to include five black female and five black male probation and parole officers. Of the 270 whites, 165 (61 percent) are males and 105 (39 percent) are females. Therefore, of the remaining 90 elements he wants in his sample, 61 percent need to be males and 39 percent need to be females. This breaks down to a 54–36 split. Thus he would select 54 white male officers and 36 white female officers for his remaining 90 elements. Combining these subsamples of male and female blacks and whites will give him a quota sample, controlling for race and gender. Concerning his choice of elements, they do not have to be randomly selected. He would begin his search in any of the 28 districts and obtain sufficient numbers of respondents that fit these desired characteristics. Remember that Lucas has not done any of these things. We are merely using his research topic to illustrate *hypothetically* how quota sampling might be applied in that *real* situation.

Advantages and Disadvantages of Quota Sampling

The advantages of quota sampling are best appreciated when contrasting this sampling method with probability sampling plans. Quota sampling is considerably less costly than probability sampling method. Furthermore, if quick, crude results are desired that will satisfy certain short-range research objectives, quota sampling is useful. Finally, use of quota sampling ensures the inclusion of certain types of elements, whereas simple random sampling might not. The major disadvantages of quota sampling are that while the most accessible elements are included that fit the desired characteristics of the researcher, these elements may not be typical of the rest of the population. There is limited generalizability, since this sampling method is a nonprobability one. Some bias may enter his selection procedure as the result of misclassifying elements. Of course, this may happen in any stratified sampling plan when we control for the inclusion of specific variables. Finally, although certain variables can be controlled for and their inclusion assured by quota sampling, other relevant variables perhaps unknown to the investigator might be better to use and have greater theoretical significance compared with the control variables he has chosen.

Snowball sampling. For special sampling situations, Coleman, Katz, and Menzel (1957) have suggested *snowball sampling* as a type of relational analysis. These researchers were interested in studying the diffusion of medical information among physicians. Snowball sampling, so-called because of the "snowball effect" achieved by the method itself, relies on the use of initial element contacts to furnish researchers with additional element contacts, and so on, until some constellation or social network is outlined. These researchers asked several physicians to name other physicians with whom they shared information about new pharmaceuticals or drugs. Those physicians named were contacted by researchers and asked the same question: "With whom do you share information about new drugs or pharmaceuticals?" These physician-respondents would supply additional names of other physicians; these would be contacted and asked the same question, until eventually, Coleman and his associates observed various group patterns.

Applications and Limitations of Snowball Sampling

Some possible applications of snowball sampling in criminology and criminal justice might be discovering inmate communication and goods distribution networks in prisons and jails. Snowball sampling could be used to discover drug-distribution patterns in cities or the recreational patterns of and interpersonal relationships among undercover law enforcement officers who work irregular hours and shifts. The major advantage of this technique is that it permits researchers to chart social relationships that are difficult to detect using conventional sampling strategies.

But statistical procedures might have limited application in these situations, since randomness is not assured. Further, if the population is large, the number of social networks detected might become unwieldy.

Dense and saturation sampling plans. Both dense sampling and saturation sampling are intended to overcome the deficiencies of a lack of randomness and small sample size that may hinder generalizability. Coleman (1959) suggested these sampling methods as they might be applied to the study of large-scale organizations. However, his work has been extended by others to applications in a variety of fields.

The theory behind dense and saturation sampling is fairly simple. If your sample size is substantial enough in relation to the population from which it was drawn, it will not make much difference whether randomness was used in the draw of sample elements. Coleman said that "*dense sampling* is sampling densely." Coleman elaborated further. He indicated that dense samples would involve the use of at least 50 percent of all population elements. Thus if the population consisted of 500 juvenile delinquents, the dense sample would be any 250 delinquents or about 50 percent of them. The overwhelming numbers of such a sample, even obtained accidentally, would be sufficient to warrant some amount of generalizing to and inferences about populations.

Saturation sampling, according to Coleman (1959), is almost like not sampling at all, since almost everyone in the population is subsequently included in the sample. When criminologists and criminal justice scholars send out questionnaires to all target population elements or seek to interview most if not all of them, saturation sampling is probably the method employed. Crank et al. (1986) used saturation sampling in their study of police chief cynicism among all Illinois police chiefs. They sent questionnaires to all 771 police chiefs in all jurisdictions, although the return rate was about 67 percent (519 chiefs responded). This large return was boosted, in part, by several follow-up letters to those chiefs who did not initially respond. According to Coleman's guidelines, their sample would be somewhere between a dense sample and a saturation sample. Nevertheless, the sheer numbers of police chiefs involved in their research seem convincingly representative of most police chiefs in Illinois. Of course, about a third of these chiefs did not respond, and again, we have no way of evaluating the influence of their impact on the final results had their responses been included and reported.

Virtually any occasion when researchers seek to include *all* respondents suggests that a saturation sample has been obtained. An example of saturation sampling applied to records and files is illustrated. A study of spousal abuse conducted by Bersani, Chen, and Denton (1988) is an example. Among other things, these researchers wanted to know about the effectiveness of certain treatment programs offered to those convicted of spousal abuse. Through previous agreements with judges in six municipal courts "in a city with well over 200,000 population," these researchers obtained a handpicked sample of convicted spousal abusers between October 1983 and May 1985. A therapeutic program called "Time Out" was being offered to spousal abusers in an effort to help them change their behaviors and choose nonviolent solutions to resolve marital conflict. Judges agreed to refer only those convicted offenders who had not been charged with domestic violence in the four years prior to their present convictions until the desired sample size had been obtained. Eventually, a sample of 120 males was obtained through this purposive sampling method. This sample represented almost all offenders processed during the targeted 1983–1985 dates.

If the target population is fairly small, and if the instrumentation selected is not time consuming, dense and saturation sampling plans might be useful since they do not require time-consuming randomness procedures. The results of any research are almost certainly applicable to the general population, since so much of it is included in the samples obtained. The size of the target population is relative. Generally, any population of 1000 or more would be considered a large population. If interviewing were proposed for such an investigation, the costs of interviewing using a dense or saturation sampling format would be prohibitive. Distributions of questionnaires to these elements for data collection purposes would be another matter altogether. In cases where survey instruments are used, such as questionnaires, dense or saturation samples would be extremely valuable in terms of their generalizability. Nevertheless, the technical requirements of probability sampling plans would not be fulfilled, and therefore, statistical applications would have to be viewed with caution.

TYPES OF SAMPLING SITUATIONS

The types of sample situations presented here include studies of single samples of elements (sometimes called "one-shot studies"), studies of two samples, and studies of k samples.* A further distinction is whether the two- or k-sample situations involve independent or related samples. These terms are defined below.

Single-Sample Situations

The most common research scenarios are studies of single samples at one point in time. A professor may administer a questionnaire to several classes of criminology students and combine these questionnaires to form a large sample. An investigator may study decision making of the Utah Parole Board. Another may describe jail inmate characteristics in a particular county jail. Another researcher may study a sample of New York City delinquents. All of these studies have in common the fact that a particular population has been targeted and a sample has been drawn from it. It makes no difference whether these elements have been selected randomly or chosen as the result of saturation or dense sampling. A single sample is described, interviewed, questioned, and/or observed. Statistical tests applied

---

*k technically means "two or more." Applied to samples, k would mean "two or more samples." However, several statistical tests of significance of difference, presented in Chapter 17, are conventionally categorized as "two-sample" and "k-sample" tests, where k is understood to apply to situations involving more than two samples.

to such sample situations are referred to simply as "single-sample tests of significance."

It is a common misconception that single samples of elements must be taken from a specific location. For instance, a study of Ohio forensics experts taken from numerous Ohio counties is simply a single sample of Ohio forensic experts. It is not a study of numerous samples of forensic experts taken from assorted Ohio counties. An investigation of Tennessee circuit court judges will probably involve responses from judges in many county jurisdictions throughout the state. The resulting sample will be referred to simply as a "single sample of Tennessee circuit court judges."

Two- and *k*-Sample Situations

Researchers may wish to investigate two or more samples for comparative purposes. For example, Fagan, Forst, and Vivona (1987) studied two samples of chronically violent juvenile delinquents to determine whether racial factors were important in affecting their likelihood of being adjudicated in juvenile court or being transferred to criminal court jurisdiction for adult processing. Are more minority youths transferred to criminal courts compared with white youths charged with similar offenses? Since transfer implies that these youths are either too dangerous for juvenile court sanctions or beyond rehabilitation, a comparison of two samples of chronically violent juvenile offenders was made. These investigators drew two samples of delinquents from juvenile court records and court petitions. Controlling for previous offense behaviors and juvenile records, these researchers examined two large samples of youths. One sample of youths had been adjudicated and sanctioned by juvenile courts. The other sample consisted of those youths who were designated for transfer to criminal courts. The study disclosed minimal differences in treatment between the two samples of juveniles examined.

Statistical tests have been formulated to fit two-sample situations. Two-sample tests of significance of difference determine whether two samples of elements differ significantly on some characteristic or exhibit only nonsignificant differences. "Significance" has a special meaning in statistics and is discussed in detail in Chapter 14.

All *k*-sample situations are simply extensions of the two-sample case. For example, Fagan, Forst, and Vivona (1987) could have studied the influence of race among three samples of juvenile probationers, juvenile parolees, and juvenile detainees. Additional samples of juveniles could be obtained by considering whether the detention facilities were operated publicly or privately. Another example might involve an investigation of three samples of inmates under minimum-, medium-, or maximum-security confinement conditions. Additionally, an investigator might describe five different types of administrative styles in five different police departments. Samples of police officers from each of these departments could be collected and studied according to whether they differ on self-perceptions of professionalism. Thus this would be a *k*-sample situation or a five-sample study of police officers.

Independent Samples

For the two- and k-sample cases or situations, specific statistical tests have been devised for application according to whether the samples are independent or related. *Independent* samples are those that contain elements that are mutually exclusive of one another. The study by Fagan, Forst, and Vivona (1987) described above involved two independent samples of juvenile delinquents. The hypothetical five-sample study of police officers would be a five-independent-sample situation or a K-independent sample case. Elements in one sample are *mutually exclusive* of those in the other sample or samples. In these situations, the samples were drawn separately, each from a particular population of elements. Independent samples may be established by other means, however.

Suppose that a researcher has obtained a large sample of 400 prison inmates. If the researcher desired, the entire sample of 400 inmates could be described, and hypotheses relevant to that sample could be tested. Single-sample statistical tests would be applied for more extensive data analyses. But the original sample of 400 could also be broken down or *stratified* according to type of conviction offense. This would be equivalent to treating various subsamples of elements as separate samples under either proportionate or disproportionate stratified random sampling discussed earler in this chapter. Perhaps the researcher wanted to divide inmates according to whether they were violent or property offenders. A division of inmates according to this dichotomy, violent or property offenders, might yield 200 violent offenders and 200 property offenders. This would be a two-independent-sample scenario. This scenario has been created artificially by dividing the original sample according to criteria deemed important by the investigator.

It is apparent that similar breakdowns could be completed according to age, race, ethnicity, security level, years of confinement, inmate gang membership, or any other relevant variable. If these 400 inmates belonged to five different gangs and the researcher separated them according to their particular gang affiliation, the result would be a five-independent-sample case. Membership in one gang would rule out membership in the other gangs. The different gang subdivisions would be mutually exclusive of one another. Therefore, it is not necessary to visit five different prison sites to obtain five different samples of offenders. All of this can be accomplished by drawing one large sample of inmates initially and subdividing them later on selected variables.

Related Samples

Two or more related samples involve two- or k-sample cases, where the samples are *not* mutually exclusive of one another. Related samples are useful whenever researchers conduct experiments and wish to know whether the experimental variable induces changes on some behavioral or attitudinal dimension. If the samples are related, they are treated as though they are equivalent. Thus any differences observed between the related samples on some measured characteristic are believed attributable to the experimental variable rather than to other extraneous factors, such as individual differences among sample elements. There are three ways of obtaining related samples. These include (1) using individual elements as their own controls in before–after experiments, (2) matching elements among samples, and (3) group or frequency distribution control matching. These types of related samples were discussed in Chapter 4 in connection with experimental groups.

4). *random assignment*

SOME SELECTED SAMPLING PROBLEMS

In this concluding section, we examine several important sampling issues that often arise in the course of one's research. No hard-and-fact rules exist to function as standards against which our own research efforts can be assessed. The fact that gaps frequently exist between what ideally ought to be done to obtain samples and what actually occurs generates several questions that have no universal answers. We might rely to some extent on conventions followed by one discipline or another. In criminology and criminal justice, there are conventional guidelines that we may use for decision making, but individual research circumstances and limitations frequently require departures from these guidelines. Issues selected for discussion include (1) determining the sample size, (2) the problem of nonresponse, (3) evaluating the representativeness of samples, (4) the relation of sampling techniques and statistical analyses, (5) the ideal–real gap in sampling procedures, and (6) the inaccessibility of potentates and special populations.

Determining Sample Size

How large should our samples be in relation to the populations from which they are drawn? For purposes of generalization and statistical inference, a conventional rule of thumb is that the sample size, n, should be 1/10 of the population size, N, or $n/N = 1/10$. This is called the *sampling fraction*. Applying this rule of thumb, if the population size is 500, the sample size should be 50. If the population size is 20 million, the sample size should be 2 million. However, this particular rule of thumb leads to unwieldy sample sizes whenever larger populations of elements are involved. Few researchers have the resources to obtain samples of 2 million elements. Do we necessarily need 2 million elements to make inferences about 20 million elements? No. Fortunately, the 1/10 rule of thumb becomes less important and may even be ignored whenever one's target population reaches or exceeds 2500 elements. Although this "2500" figure is somewhat arbitrary, note that the 1/10 rule would yield a sample size of 250 in this instance. Larger populations would yield sample sizes larger than 250.

There are several logical reasons for limiting our sample sizes and violating the 1/10 rule of thumb by drawing samples that account for less than 10 percent of their respective population sizes. The first reason is that we can manage smaller samples more easily than larger ones. Sample sizes of 150 to 250 are more manageable than sample sizes of 1000 or more. Second, samples that are extremely large are not proportionately more informative than smaller samples. A "diminishing returns" effect occurs as we increase our sample sizes substantially. In

Some Selected Sampling Problems   **113** short, we do not "double" the accuracy of our sample statistics as estimates of population parameters if, for example, we were to double our sample sizes from 250 to 500. As more persons are added to our samples, particularly where our samples are already fairly large, many of these additional elements have characteristics similar to those elements we have already obtained. Thus our larger samples are more costly than smaller samples, but they are not *substantially* more accurate for making inferences about population values. Provided that a probability sampling plan is used for one's sample selection, larger samples are generally more accurate than smaller samples for estimating population parameters. But the point is that this improvement in accuracy is only minimal in relation to the greater cost of obtaining additional elements.

A third reason relates to the statistical procedures we may use for data analyses. Most statistical procedures are designed to be applied to sample sizes of 250 or less. As we will see in Chapter 17, most tests of statistical significance are maximally efficient when they are applied to sample sizes within designated ranges, sometimes called *reasonable operating ranges*. For instance, some statistical tests discussed elsewhere require that one's sample size consist of fewer than 25 elements (e.g., Fisher's exact test) (Siegel, 1956; Champion, 1981).

Some statistical procedures have even smaller sample-size requirements for their legitimate application (e.g., the randomization test for two independent samples and the randomization test for matched pairs) (Siegel, 1956; Champion, 1981). Other procedures require sample-size ranges of from 25 to 250 (e.g., the chi-square test) (Champion, 1981). When statistical tests are applied to samples beyond these reasonable operating ranges, the statistical results are distorted. The nature of this statistical distortion is the *inflation* of our numerical results. Thus researchers may erroneously interpret certain statistical findings as significant when, in fact, the magnitude of one's sample size has *caused* unusually large and distorted statistical results. In Chapter 14 we address the issue of statistical significance in relation to samples of different sizes.

Certain statistical procedures have been proposed as objective means for determining one's sample sizes, given the size of the target population and other factors. However, *all* of these procedures are artificial contrivances and have inherent weaknesses. None of these procedures is qualitatively better than the 1/10 rule of thumb discussed above. For discussions of these exotic procedures, the reader is referred elsewhere (Blalock, 1972). Even if ideal sample sizes for research purposes could be forecast with great accuracy, almost all investigators have seen their ideal sampling plans dashed because of nonresponse.

Nonresponse and What to Do About It

Nonresponse is the proportion of the originally selected sample not included in the final sample studied by the investigator. If researchers have used a table of random numbers to identify 100 sample elements from their target population of 1000 elements, nonresponse occurs when one or more of these sample elements is not included in the final sample studied. For example, if questionnaires are mailed to 5000 persons and 2000 of them do not return their completed questionnaires,

30% resp.
avg.

this is a nonresponse of 2000/5000 or 40 percent. Nonresponse is not limited to questionnaire administration. Interviewers may attempt to interview certain subjects, only to be refused. Often, those selected for interviews may not be at home or keep their appointments with interviewers. Some persons, by virtue of their status, are simply inaccessible. (See the discussion of potentates below.)

Almost all studies that describe and analyze samples drawn from larger populations have some degree of nonresponse. The amount of nonresponse varies among studies and no standards exist that define normal nonresponse rates. Different textbooks report "average" nonresponse rates from 20 to 70 percent, although these estimates are largely impressionistic. An analysis of social science literature suggests that "average response" rates to mailed questionnaires are about 30 percent. On the average, the response to direct interviews is much higher, since this data collection method involves face-to-face contact between the interviewer and interviewee.

Professors and other researchers who administer questionnaires to students in large classrooms frequently report response rates of 100 percent. High response rates in these "captive audience" situations are commonplace, since classrooms are implicitly coercive settings. Sometimes teachers will require student compliance in completing administered questionnaries as one of several course requirements, or additional points will be awarded to those students who respond. Thus many students participate to avoid being penalized. (See Chapter 6 for a discussion of questionnaire administration and accompanying issues and problems.)

The major problem with nonresponse is that it affects adversely the typicality or representativeness of one's sample in relation to the population from which it was drawn. If ideal criteria are applied in one's initial sample selection, nonresponse detracts from these ideal sampling objectives. There is little we can do about it. We can encourage those who did not respond originally to reconsider. This is often done through follow-up letters to nonrespondents, if mailed questionnaires are used. These follow-ups require that we somehow keep track of and identify those who do and do not respond. But anonymity cannot be assured under this circumstance. And we often offer anonymity to potential respondents as a means of encouraging them to return completed questionnaires that contain personal and/or confidential data. But even follow-up letters usually result in small increases in the final response rate. Among other strategies that have been used to prompt larger response rates are (1) using hand-stamped postage (compared with metered postage) on return envelopes to "personalize" them, (2) cover letters that appeal to one's altruistic spirit, (3) offers of goods and money for responding, (4) prizes awarded based on lottery selections from among those who respond, (5) special delivery follow-up letters to nonrespondents, (6) direct telephone calls to all nonrespondents, and (7) home visits to nonrespondents.

Sometimes for experimental purposes, researchers will deliberately *oversample* in order to obtain a desirable sample size. For example, if investigators want to obtain 200 elements in their final sample, and if they are using mailed questionnaires, they may send questionnaires to 600 elements, anticipating that their nonresponse will be about 65 percent. Unfortunately, the original 600 elements selected may have comprised an ideal random sample drawn from a table of random numbers. Excluding 400 of these elements (through nonresponse) from the resulting data analysis means that the sample is not a random one, despite the fact that the final sample consists of 200 elements, a desirable sample size. Therefore, oversampling is recommended only when investigators require minimum sample sizes for anticipated experimental research and the research designs they have formulated or for the application of particular statistical procedures.

Is the Sample Representative?

How do we know if a sample is representative of the population from which it was drawn? Never. Assessing sample representativeness accurately requires considerable knowledge about the population and its characteristics. If such knowledge about the population were possessed, it is unlikely that we would need to draw samples from it. Of course, we may select sample elements according to their known distribution in the population. We may know the different types of offenders in a state prison or local jail. Or we may know the gender and educational distribution of law enforcement officers in a large city. Or we may know some of the superficial characteristics of state correctional officers from personnel files or state records. These information sources may enable us to judge whether our samples exhibit certain population characteristics. Thus we may say that our samples *appear* typical according to gender distribution, age distribution, educational level, type of offense, length of confinement, prior record, and any other recorded population information. But thousands of other variables, attitudinal and otherwise, characterize the populations we study. Controlling our sample selections according to those criteria we know about will make those samples representative of their parent populations only for those criteria. Remaining uncontrolled are thousands of other individual, social, and psychological attributes and characteristics that may render our samples atypical or unrepresentative. We cannot possibly know when our samples are truly representative or unrepresentative of their parent populations in all respects, however.

Sampling and Statistical Analysis

Noted earlier was the fact that particular statistical applications may require samples of certain sizes. Ordinarily, investigators know in advance of conducting their data analyses which statistical techniques they intend to apply. Their familiarity with these statistical techniques will often indicate the sample sizes required for those intended statistical applications. Furthermore, *any* inferential tasks to be performed require the use of a probability sampling plan when a sample is acquired. Randomness is an assumption underlying all statistical inference and decision making. Therefore, if we wish to generalize about population parameters on the basis of certain sample statistics or characteristics, our sample must be a random one. However, whenever the samples we obtain are less than random, as is the case when there is substantial nonresponse, the typicality and representativeness of our samples are ruined, and any generalizations and inferences about population parameters made from observed sample characteristics are similarly affected.

The purist view is that to apply statistical tests meaningfully, all assumptions and requirements underlying those tests must be met fully. Failing to meet one or more assumptions underlying certain statistical tests will automatically void the test results. However, if the purist view were adopted by all criminologists and criminal justice scholars, most research work that involves the application of statistical procedures would come to a grinding halt. This is because most research conducted in these fields and all other social sciences fails to satisfy completely all statistical test assumptions. But violating one or more statistical test assumptions is more the norm rather than the exception. The purist view is not particularly popular among social scientists. Ultimately, researchers apply various statistical tests, despite certain assumption violations, and report their findings with conventional cautions. Every piece of research examined should be given the appropriate degree of credibility commensurate with the studys' shortcomings.

Ideal and Real Sampling Considerations

The quest to obtain samples that meet ideal criteria is a noble one. But it is unrealistic to expect that all of our sampling plans will fall into place as anticipated. Whether we use the 1/10 rule of thumb or some exotic procedure for determining the desired sample size, Murphy's law is likely operative to taint our work. *Murphy's law* states that "whatever can go wrong will go wrong." Nonresponse is one of these "taints." Additionally, we will see that many other events and factors may occur and operate to contaminate our research efforts. Our choice of sampling plan is only one of the many links in the chain of events we know as the research enterprise. We must be prepared to deal with whatever elements we eventually obtain, regardless of our original ideal considerations. Eventually, we do the best we can with what we have, and we encourage others who read our work to assess its importance in view of existing research limitations.

Potentates: Juveniles, Prisoners, and Permission to Sample Special Populations of Subjects

Potentates are those who require special permission to study them. Criminologists and criminal justice scholars who study the criminal justice system often find that "gaining access" to specific populations targeted for study is difficult. It is not particularly easy for researchers to obtain samples of prison or jail inmates or to gather large samples of delinquent offenders in various detention facilities. Studying probation officers, criminal court judges, law enforcement officers, federal judges, correctional officers, and district attorneys are not easy tasks. These persons are usually insulated from the general public by secretarial hierarchies, locked gates, and a general aversion to being studied by anyone.

Studies of juvenile delinquents are sometimes difficult to conduct because of the confidential nature of record keeping relating to them. Not all juvenile courtrooms are open to the public, and court dispositions and adjudications relating to juvenile offenders are considered restricted material. Even if investigators wish to examine juveniles in school settings and obtain self-report information about delinquent conduct, permission must first be obtained from principals and teachers. There is often resistance to such investigations for a variety of reasons. School board and parental opposition to having their children involved in any type of research asking them to disclose personal details of their lives are barriers to certain kinds of research. Questionnaires are sometimes perceived as threatening or informative. Checklists of infractions and law violations may be interpreted by some juveniles as expected behaviors. In a sense, questions dealing with prohibited behaviors may prompt some youths to engage in those behaviors or at least be more susceptible to involvement in delinquent conduct.

Studying lawyers and district attorneys may be difficult, since their time is often limited by large numbers of clients and high caseloads. The sponsorship of research by a major college or university might help researchers gain access to some of these persons. Snowball sampling might be used as a means of obtaining an introduction to different attorneys, especially if some of their attorney-friends have referred interviewers to them.

Sometimes there are organizational constraints that restrict access to particular populations. If an investigator wished to study FBI agents, for example, local FBI offices do not disclose information to the public about their present roster of agents, where they live, or how they may be contacted. FBI agents usually have unlisted telephone numbers, live quietly and anonymously in neighborhoods for many years, and are advised by their superiors to refrain from divulging any information about their jobs. If you happen upon FBI agents at social gatherings, chances are that these agents will reply "government service" when you ask them about their occupation or profession. This high level of secrecy about one's affairs is primarily a function of the organization itself, in much the same way that the Central Intelligence Agency would control the behaviors of its operatives.

In sum, any research plan must realistically evaluate the accessibility of target populations. It is one thing to write a research plan; it is another thing to implement it. When researchers apply for research funds from public agencies or private foundations, it is conventional for them to include supporting documentation and letters from those they intend to contact. This information lets the funding agency know that the researchers have anticipated certain data collection problems and have engaged in preliminary efforts to ensure that this data can be obtained if the study is funded.

SUMMARY

Sampling is the process of obtaining a proportion of persons from the larger class of persons about which we seek information. Target populations are described according to their characteristics. These characteristics are known as parameters. Sample characteristics are known as statistics. Two major types of sampling plans are probability and nonprobability. Probability sampling plans include simple random samples, proportionate and disproportionate stratified random sampling, and cluster or area sampling. Nonprobability sampling plans are accidental sampling, systematic sampling, judgmental or purposive sampling, quota sampling, snowball sampling, dense sampling, and saturation sampling.

Different types of sampling situations include analyses of single samples of elements at a given point in time and analyses of two or more samples of elements. For the two- and k-sample cases, the samples may be either independent or related. Independent samples are mutually exclusive of one another. Related samples mean that the samples exhibit some equivalency, either through matching on an individual or group basis or by using persons as their own controls in before–after experiments. In any type of sampling situation, several issues arise concerning determinations of sample size, assessing sample representativeness, and gauging the accessibility of elements.

Sample representativeness can be ascertained only to the extent that we are familiar with various population characteristics. Most research projects are affected by nonresponse, where a portion of those surveyed do not respond to questionnaires or simply refuse to be interviewed. Thus originally selected samples seldom resemble the final samples that are studied by researchers. Potentates and inaccessible elements further detract from a sample's representativeness, since permission from others is often required before these elements can be contacted and questioned. Relatively inaccessible elements include populations of prison or jail inmates, judges, and juvenile delinquents. These populations of elements are insulated in various ways by organizational or statutory constraints. Researchers acknowledge these problems and limitations and proceed with their investigations accordingly. The significance of any study must be assessed in the context of any prevailing limitations associated with one's research plans.

QUESTIONS FOR REVIEW

1. Differentiate between probability and nonprobability sampling plans. Review briefly their general functions and limitations.
2. What are some major considerations in deciding to sample? Discuss these considerations briefly.
3. Discuss some of the problems researchers might have when studying potentates.
4. Sometimes, systematic sampling is considered a probability sampling plan. What is the basis for this thinking? What can be said of systematic samples that might disqualify them as probability sampling plans?
5. What are some general rules that apply to determining one's sample size? Are extremely large samples necessarily better than smaller sample sizes? What factors should be considered when determining one's sample size?
6. What are some of the primary advantages of judgmental or purposive sampling plans? In what sense might some researchers consider them to be superior to probability sampling plans?
7. What is the primary control factor in probability sampling plans? Why is it important? How can this factor be achieved when samples are selected from target populations?
8. Distinguish between independence and equality of drawing sample elements.

9. Differentiate between independent and related samples. What are at least three ways that related samples may be obtained?

10. What is sample representativeness? Can we ever guarantee that a sample of elements will be representative of the population from which it is drawn? Why or why not?

11. What is an accidental sample? Under what circumstances might accidental samples be the only samples available for study?

12. Define and differentiate between population parameters and sample statistics.

13. What is nonresponse in sampling, and how can it be affected?

14. Why is there often a gap between ideal sampling plans and real samples of elements obtained by the researcher?

15. What is the influence of statistical tests and techniques on sampling decisions?

16. When would area or cluster sampling be appropriate to apply? Identify at least three different situations where such a technique would be useful.

6

Data Collection Strategies II: Questionnaires

KEY TERMS

Altruistic appeals
Egoistic appeals
Face-to-face questionnaire
  administration
Fixed-response items
Mailed questionnaires
Nonresponse

Open-ended items
Pilot studies
Pretest
Questionnaire
Self-administered questionnaires
Triangulation

INTRODUCTION

The most popular data-gathering tool used in criminological research today is the questionnaire. *Questionnaires* are self-administered inventories that seek descriptive information about people and their opinions about things. From our earliest years in school, we are accustomed to completing questionnaires. Schools solicit information from us about our personal backgrounds; our previous educational experience, including high schools and elementary schools attended; where we live;

121

the occupations or professions of our parents; and our immediate and long-range interests, including our declared academic majors and professional ambitions. Perhaps you have been in a class where your instructor has distributed questionnaires in connection with a research project being conducted, or maybe the instructor has distributed questionnaires to you and your classmates on behalf of someone else conducting research.

In this chapter we describe questionnaires and their functions generally and distinguish between different kinds of questionnaires used for data-gathering purposes. Questionnaires are relatively easy to construct, although there are several important guidelines to follow when developing questions as well as alternative responses for them. Thus attention is given to questionnaire construction and format as well as to some of the guidelines associated with the proper administration of questionnaires to others. Some of the problems associated with the construction and administration of questionnaires are discussed. The weaknesses and strengths of questionnaires as data-gathering tools are also examined.

QUESTIONNAIRES IN CRIMINAL JUSTICE RESEARCH

Each of the data-gathering tools discussed in this and subsequent chapters should not be viewed in isolation. That is, we must consider questionnaires as one of *several* data-gathering strategies we might employ to gather information about people and their characteristics. It is not unusual for researchers to use several types of data-gathering tools in the same research project. For example, if we were to study law enforcement officers in a particular city, we might obtain information from them through questionnaires. Further, we might observe several officers as they conduct their patrol activities. Also, we might interview them at different times to determine why particular actions were undertaken. We might even supplement all of this information with reports about the police department generally, its organization and operation, and its change over time. Whenever two or more data-gathering tools or strategies are used by researchers for investigating the same social aggregate (e.g., a police department, community corrections agency, probation office, jail inmates, or juvenile delinquents), this practice is known as *triangulation*. Therefore, we would practice triangulation if we used both questionnaires and interviews, and possibly observation, in our investigations of law enforcement officers and their patrol activities.

The majority of criminologists and criminal justice scholars probably use two or more data-gathering techniques in their investigations of social phenomena. Triangulation is discussed in greater detail in Chapter 8, but for the present we can appreciate the fact that different types of information are yielded about the people we study, depending on the data-gathering procedures we use.

To describe fully the research contributions and limitations of these different data-gathering tools, in specific chapters we highlight each technique and illustrate its applications. It will become more apparent that certain deficiencies inherent in one type of data-gathering tool will probably be compensated for or overcome by simultaneous use of alternative data-gathering tools.

Throughout the criminal justice system, there are numerous aggregates about which we seek information. We have mentioned law enforcement officers as one important aggregate. Others include prosecutors, judges, court officials, defense attorneys, correctional officers, community corrections workers and ancillary personnel, and of course, clients. Clients may be defendants, convicted misdemeanants or felons, probationers, jail or prison inmates, or parolees. Clients may be further distinguished according to whether they are divertees, halfway house members, work or study releases, furloughees, shock probationers, or those participating in home confinement or electronic monitoring programs.

The literature in criminal justice and criminology is abundant with studies where questionnaires have been used as the principal data-gathering tool. For instance, one of the more ambitious (because of the large number of persons sampled) research projects was a national study undertaken by the Research Triangle Institute for the National Institute on Alcohol Abuse and Alcoholism (Rachal et al., 1975). A two-stage stratified cluster sample of 15,000 students in grades 7 to 12 was obtained from the 48 contiguous U.S. states. Each student was asked to complete an anonymous, self-administered questionnaire, which included items on drinking behavior, contexts and consequences of drinking, deviant behavior, and selected demographic, attitudinal, and personality characteristics. A response rate of 72.2 percent was obtained. This information was subsequently coded and became an interesting data set available for analysis by interested researchers.

In 1989, a study utilizing these data was completed and published by Thompson (1989). Thompson was interested in learning whether gender- or ethnicity-related drinking patterns among teenagers could be identified. He was also interested in whether socioeconomic status differences exerted any noticeable impact on drinking behaviors and if different types of socialization experiences seem to modify drinking habits between various age groupings. In this case, a ready-made data set was available to Thompson, based on the numerous questionnaires completed by randomly selected samples of students in 1974.

Although using existing information from previously administered questionnaires is a definite advantage for many researchers, other investigators find it necessary to devise their own instruments and tailor them to fit particular target audiences. For example, Colley, Culbertson, and Latessa (1986) analyzed the roles of probation officers, including the diverse and often contradictory demands that probation agencies make of those performing such roles. These researchers wanted to compare current probation officer educational and training programs with the actual tasks performed by such officers while performing their duties. One commonly used method to evaluate personnel needs in organizations is job analysis, which includes task analyses, job inventories, and descriptions of job elements and critical incidents.

Colley, Culbertson, and Latessa found little, if any, evidence of the use of job analysis for assessing probation officer work roles in the criminal justice literature. Thus these investigators sought to devise instrumentation that would be capable of identifying tasks comprising the probation function and that would determine those skills most necessary to perform the real tasks associated with probation work (1986:68). More simply, they wanted to identify the most essential elements that would fit into a competency-based probation officer training program. Presumably, such a competency-based program could be implemented in various jurisdictions to improve overall probation officer work performance and maximize the services and benefits they might render to their probationer-clients.

Starting from scratch, these investigators compiled an extensive list of tasks derived from the literature about probation officer training needs, training methods, and preexisting probation officer job descriptions. They also conducted face-to-face interviews with a sample of probation officers from both rural and urban counties to determine directly their individual responsibilities and job assignments. This permitted them to make comparisons between verbal responses given by these officers and the list of tasks they had compiled earlier.

Eventually, these researchers devised a three-part questionnaire. These parts assessed the frequency with which different listed tasks were performed, the relative importance of each task to the probation officer role and function, and a general information section, including questions about age, gender, race, job experience, education, and size of caseload. These investigators subsequently administered the final version of their questionnaire to 240 Illinois adult probation officers, or about one-half of the Illinois probation officer force.

Two extremes are portrayed here. In the first instance above, Thompson (1989) utilized information from questionnaires originally administered in 1974. No new questionnaire construction was necessary, since existing questions and scales yielded a data set containing much valuable information. In the second instance, Colley, Culbertson, and Latessa (1986) constructed their questionnaire instrumentation completely from scratch. They, too, analyzed some of this data they eventually collected, although both studies involved quite different statistical analyses and methodological objectives.

Frequently, investigators may build questionnaires that consist, in part, of original question items and, in part, of preexisting scales that purportedly measure certain phenomena. This practice is perhaps most common, since there are many existing scales that measure important social and attitudinal variables that are theoretically intertwined with criminal justice and criminological questions. Using existing scales exposes these instruments to further empirical testing, experimentation, and verification, while those using such scales benefit by not having to create their own measures. However, regardless of the popularity of certain existing scales, not everyone finds them suitable for particular research applications. One or more questionnaire items may not "fit" the intended audience. Therefore, some customizing is necessary to produce questionnaires that are directly relevant for certain samples of elements.

FUNCTIONS OF QUESTIONNAIRES

Two basic functions of questionnaires are (1) description and (2) measurement.

Description

The information acquired through questionnaire administration may provide descriptions of individual and/or group characteristics, such as gender, age, years of education, occupation, income, political and religious affiliation, civic group or fraternal order membership, urban or rural background, and job status.

Describing elements serves several useful purposes. For instance, knowledge of the age distribution of a sample of law enforcement officers may provide researchers with plausible explanations for certain group phenomena that occur on the job, including clique formations, liberal or conservative positions on social issues, intraofficer esprit de corps, and the type and amount of possible officer misconduct. Are younger officers more inclined to use excessive force when taking suspects into custody? The educational characteristics of particular employees may help to account for different assessments of job content, supervision, job satisfaction, and work quality. Are more educated police officers more effective at resolving domestic disputes or quelling civil disorders? What factors seem most important for improving police–community relations?

Accurate descriptions of elements in any social setting can benefit researchers in many ways. Insight, explanation, and prediction are but a few of the many contributions questionnaires make to social inquiry.

Measurement

A primary function of almost every questionnaire is the measurement of individual and/or group variables, particularly attitudinal phenomena. Questionnaires may contain single or multiple items (i.e., questions about issues or simple statements) used in combination that are designed to measure various attitudinal phenomena, such as group cohesiveness, peer-group influence, burnout and stress, alienation, professionalism, job security, role clarity, anxiety, or sexual permissiveness. The list of attitudinal dimensions that may potentially be tapped by questionnaires is endless. Annually, improvements are made on existing questionnaire measures, and new questionnaire instruments are continually being constructed as well.

TYPES OF QUESTIONNAIRES

Questionnaires are often classified according to whether they include fixed-response or open-ended items. Sometimes, questionnaires contain *both* fixed-response and open-ended items.

Fixed-Response Questionnaires

Fixed-response questionnaires consist of items (questions or statements) that have a finite list of alternative responses. Respondents are asked to select from among a number of fixed choices and check the responses that best fit them. Informational items with fixed choices include the following:

---

1. My age is: (*Check one*)

    _____   Below 18

    _____   18–21

_____ 22–25
_____ 26–29
_____ 30 or over

2. My political affiliation is: (*Check one*)
_____ Republican
_____ Democrat
_____ Independent

Fixed **3.** The amount of formal education I have completed is: (*Check one*)
_____ Less than eighth grade
_____ Completed elementary school, some high school
_____ High school graduate, no college
_____ High school graduate, some college, did not graduate
_____ College graduate, no advanced graduate work
_____ College graduate, some graduate work completed
_____ Completed a graduate degree (master's, doctorate, etc.)

Besides informational items, which may also include questions about race, ethnicity, income, occupation/profession, or rural–urban background, several items may be combined to form a scale. Below are three partial sets of items that form scales that purportedly measure group cohesiveness, desire for changing work tasks, and work alienation.

PARTIAL SET OF ITEMS 1

Group Cohesiveness Scale (Partial List of Items)

Below are various statements about your work group. Check the response that fits you best. (Responses include "strongly agree," "agree," "undecided, probably agree," "undecided, probably disagree," "disagree," and "strongly disagree.")

1. "Do you feel that other members of your work group give you ample consideration whenever issues concerning job matters are discussed?" (*Check one*)
_____ My opinion is considered very important by other group members.
_____ Group members are fairly interested in my opinion.
_____ Group members are somewhat disinterested in my opinion.
_____ Group members ignore my opinion when job matters are discussed.

2. "To what extent do you and/or other members of your work group refer to your group as 'we' or 'us'?"
_____ To a great extent (very frequently)

_____ To some extent (fairly frequently)

_____ To a small extent (fairly infrequently)

_____ To no extent at all (seldom, if ever)

3. "How would you characterize the way the members of your work group get along?"

_____ We get along better than most groups.

_____ We get along about the same as other groups.

_____ We get along less than other groups.

_____ We seldom, if ever, get along well.

4. "To what extent do you feel other members of your work group would come to your aid if you were in trouble involving your work tasks?"

_____ My work group members would come to my aid without question.

_____ My work group members would be fairly indifferent about my problems.

_____ I feel that I am on my own and cannot depend on other work group members for assistance if I get into trouble on my job.

PARTIAL SET OF ITEMS 2

Desire for Changing Work Tasks (Partial List of Items)

Each statement below (not reprinted here) is followed by the responses "strongly agree," "agree," "undecided, probably agree," "undecided, probably disagree," "disagree," and "strongly disagree." Please check the response for each item that best fits you.

1. On my job it is important to me that I do new things frequently.
2. Changing my job to meet changing technology in the workplace would be very disturbing to me.
3. I like a job where I can perform the same tasks routinely every day.
4. Work of an assembly-line type appeals to me.
5. I dislike frequent disruptions of my work routine.
6. I like my present job and would feel bad about having to perform different tasks.
7. Doing a variety of things on the job each day helps make me feel that time goes by more quickly.
8. I would tend to feel comfortable performing almost any job at my place of work, should higher-ups decide to switch me around frequently from one job to another.

PARTIAL SET OF ITEMS 3

Work Alienation (Partial List of Items)

Each of the statements below (not reprinted here) is followed by the responses "strongly agree," "agree," "undecided, probably agree," "undecided, probably disagree," "disagree," and "strongly disagree." Select the response for each item that fits you best.

1. On my job it is possible to make errors without too much disruption.
2. The way I do my work is important to my fellow employees.
3. My co-workers often think that getting the job done is more important than the people who do the job.
4. If I ever stay home from work, this department would be in a real bind.
5. A person who likes to do work that requires thinking would like to perform my job.
6. Things are really regimented around here.
7. When I come to work each day, I look forward to a new and challenging experience.
8. Sometimes I wonder just how important I really am around here.
9. I think my job is too mechanical and repetitive.

These various types of fixed-response items contain certain implicit assumption about the target audience. First, an assumption is made that the target sample has meaningful knowledge about the subject matter of the questionnaire. Second, it is assumed that the researcher knows enough about the sample under investigation to be able to anticipate the types of responses that would likely be expected and given. A third assumption is that most, if not all, questions asked were relevant to the basic research questions as shaped by the manifest goals of the researcher. A fourth assumption is that the responses people give are truthful reflections about them and how they feel. The latter assumption focuses on the accuracy of questionnaires and whether they provide reliable information about the target sample. These issues will be examined at length in Chapter 10. The matter of measuring accurately or "scaling" certain social and psychological phenomena, such as attitudes, is investigated at length in Chapter 9.

Fixed-response items may be constructed to fit an infinite number of response patterns. In the examples above, a format was used employing "strongly agree" and "strongly disagree" options. Other possible formats may include arrays of options according to "favorable–unfavorable," "most intense–least intense," "strong–weak," "all–none," "everybody–nobody," and "positive–negative." Your choices of response options are limited only by your imagination. There are no "standard" or "conventional" response options universally used or accepted by all researchers.

Open-Ended Questionnaires

Open-ended questionnaires consist of questions that require short or lengthy written replies by respondents. Below are some examples of open-ended items.

1. What is the title of your present position with this probation agency?
   _____

2. What are your primary responsibilities or duties? Please specify.
   _____
   _____
   _____

3. What are the chances for your advancement to a higher position in this agency in the future? Please explain. _____
   _____
   _____
   _____

4. What are your recommendations for an "ideal" work setting? _____
   _____
   _____
   _____

5. Do you feel that the present method of evaluating work quality is fair?
   Yes _____ No _____ Uncertain _____ (*Check one*)

6. Why do you feel this is so? Please explain: _____
   _____
   _____
   _____

In these instances, rather than anticipate particular responses from the target sample through fixed-choice items, investigators simply provide several pages of open-ended items that request respondents to indicate their opinions and elaborate about them in some detail. Exploratory and descriptive research designs might be more likely to include open-ended items if questionnaires are used for survey and investigative purposes.

Combinations of Fixed-Reponse and Open-Ended Items

Many questionnaires consist of items that are of both the fixed-response and open-ended varieties. If there is the likelihood that not all alternative categories for particular questions can be anticipated in advance, an "other" category is often included along with the other fixed choices. For instance, if we were to distribute questionnaires to a sample of residents in ethnically heterogeneous communities, such as Los Angeles, New York, Miami, or Chicago, and if we were to include an item about one's religious affiliation, it would be awkward to attempt a complete listing of all possible religious affiliations for these respondents. In Los Angeles, for example, there are large numbers of Cambodians, Laotians, Vietnamese, Chinese, Japanese, Indians, and numerous persons from the Middle East. Therefore, an item might be constructed as follows:

My religious affiliation is (*Check one or designate your faith in the space provided below*)

_____ Catholic
_____ Protestant
_____ Jewish
_____ Other. If "none," write "none." Please specify. _____

There may or may not be sufficient numbers of "other" responses to justify creating additional categories when we begin our data analysis. Perhaps 85 percent of our sample of city residents are primarily Catholic, Protestant, and Jewish, but 10 percent are Buddhist (a major religion of India and China) and 4 percent are Shintoist (the major religion of Japan). One percent might consist of 30 other religious faiths, with two or three respondents associated with each. Assuming that religious affiliation is an important variable in our theory, we would probably want to use the five religious categories where sizable numbers of respondents are found. For this particular part of our data analysis, we might omit those in the "other" category, since statistical manipulations of such small numbers of respondents would be meaningless.

Preliminary Comparison of Fixed-Response and Open-Ended Items

It is apparent that certain variables are taken into account more easily and directly by using fixed-response items. For example, gender, years of education, race, and political affiliation are almost always confined to a limited number of fixed-answer alternatives. For some variables, such as religious affiliation, "other" categories may be created and used together with a fixed-response format.

Most attitudinal measures in questionnaires are in fixed-response formats. These fixed-response formats enable researchers to score responses easily, sum individual item values, and determine overall raw scores for particular variables. Comparisons may be made directly between people or groups who possess certain raw scores or who fall within certain score ranges.

Survey research and the use of questionnaires are virtually inseparable, since it is almost always the researcher's intention to canvass large numbers of respondents who may be dispersed over large geographical areas. Questionnaires, particularly mailed questionnaires, enable researchers to acquire large amounts of data from large numbers of persons at minimal cost. Depending on what is known about the intended targets of questionnaires, these instruments will vary in their sophistication and format. Before we examine the task of constructing questionnaires, it is helpful to highlight some of the major weaknesses and strengths of fixed-response and open-ended questionnaire formats for particular research purposes.

Advantages and disadvantages of fixed-response questionaires.   Among the major advantages of fixed-response questionnaires are the following:

1. Fixed-response items are easy to score and code.   [Coding is a procedure whereby researchers assign numbers to particular types of responses (e.g., Democrat = 1, Republican = 2, Independent = 3, etc.)   in order to distinguish responses from one another in subsequent data analyses.   Coding is discussed in Chapter 9].   Researchers can more easily transfer the data from questionnaires containing fixed-response items to computers where data may be stored for subsequent statistical treatment and analysis.

2. No writing is required of respondents.   Respondents merely check the responses that best typify them.   In cases where respondents cannot adequately express themselves verbally, the fixed-response item is definitely an advantage.

3. Fixed-response items facilitate completion of questionnaires.   Lengthy questionnaires with fixed-response items are completed more rapidly compared with those containing large numbers of open-ended items.

4. If questionnaires are mailed to designated respondents, there is greater likelihood that respondents will complete and return questionnaires more frequently if little or no writing is involved in their completion.

Some of the disadvantages of fixed-response questionnaire items include the following:

1. Researchers may not be able to anticipate or think of all relevant response alternatives.   As noted previously, fixed-response items require some familiarity with the population under investigation.   If respondents are forced to make choices among several alternatives that do not fit them, researchers may obtain erroneous or misleading information.

2. Fixed-response items, especially those in attitudinal scales (i.e., with "strongly agree" and "strongly disagree" response patterns), may lead respondents to lapse into a *response set*.   A response set is a particular response pattern that has nothing to do with question or statement content, but rather, is designed almost exclusively to complete the questionnaire rapidly or "get it over with quickly."   Some respondents have been known to check the first responses for all statements or question items, regardless of whether such responses are true of them.   For example, someone might check the "strongly agree" response to the statement "I like my job."   Later, in the same set of items, they will also check "strongly agree" in response to the statement "I hate my job."   It is apparent that they do not read the statements or questions asked.   They are either bored with the questionnaire or consider the researcher's intrusion into their time as offensive.   Thus sometimes researchers build in "lie factors" that seek to detect set responses whenever it is suspected that they are being given.   Lie factors are nothing more than including several statements that are directly contradictory.   Either agreements with both statements or disagreements with them means inconsistency, a contradiction in response, and a possible set response.

Advantages and disadvantages of open-ended questionnaires.   Some of the major advantages of open-ended questionnaires are as follows:

1. Open-ended items are particularly useful when researchers have little or no information available about the samples studied.   Respondents are least restricted in terms of their possible answer choices that they can provide in response to specific questions.

2. In certain instances, open-ended items are helpful to researchers because they provide insights into one's thoughts and behaviors.   There is always the possibility that researchers can anticipate many responses that respondents might give, but often, the flexibility of open-ended items will elicit unanticipated and insightful replies from respondents.   These responses will enhance the investigator's understanding of what is going on and why.

Some of the disadvantages of open-ended questionnaires are the following:

1. For open-ended items, written answers from respondents may be so diverse that researchers may find them difficult to code or classify into convenient categories.   Also, different respondents may appear to provide similar responses to the same item on a questionnaire, when it fact, the meaning and importance that each respondent attaches to the particular reply may be considerably different.   Thus, although several respondents might be placed in common categories for purposes of classifying them on some measured characteristic, the results of such classifications may be erroneous or misleading.

2. A bias exists in open-ended questionnaires that stems from several sources. At the outset, persons who cannot express themselves adequately on paper (and also orally) will be combined unfairly with more fluent persons.   Therefore, an educational bias exists initially, particularly if the target population from which the sample is drawn is quite heterogeneous in this respect.   By the same token, questionnaires in the general case (i.e., those containing both open-ended and fixed-response items) are subject to a similar type of educational bias.   Not every respondent is equally adept in the art of self-expression.   The socioeconomic factor may yield misleading results and incorrect interpretations of findings as well.   Persons of different socioeconomic backgrounds or professions and occupations may not view issues the same way, nor will they necessarily use the same vocabulary to describe their feelings or attitudes.   The wording of questionnaires at the outset has certain built-in biases that must be considered in assessing the quality and meaning of information obtained.

3. A third disadvantage of open-ended items is that they are time consuming to complete.   If researchers mail questionnaires to respondents, response rates will be lower where open-ended items are used than in situations where fixed-response items are used exclusively.   Many persons feel that they do not have the time or interest to sit down and write out lengthy replies to questions. Face-to-face interviews appear to be more successful, with better response,

than self-administered open-ended questionnaires. (Interviewing is discussed in Chapter 7.)

4. Applicable to both open-ended questionnaires and fixed-response questionnaires is the possibility that significant portions of heterogeneous urban populations may not understand English. Large numbers of immigrants from Asian, Middle Eastern, and European countries in the last several decades have created ethnic enclaves in many cities throughout the United States. Thus, when heads of households are surveyed using mailed questionnaires, it is very possible that a language other than English may be native to these heads of households. If English cannot be read or understood, certain respondents may simply discard the questionnaires they receive. Further, a significant minority of citizens are illiterate despite the fact that their native language is English.

QUESTIONNAIRE ADMINISTRATION

Basically, there are two methods for administering questionnaires to target samples of elements. These are (1) the mailed questionnaire and (2) face-to-face questionnaire administration.

Mailed Questionnaire

Survey researchers utilize the mailed questionnaire extensively in canvassing large numbers of subjects located over broad geographical territories. This method consists simply of mailing questionnaires of variable lengths to previously designated subjects. Instructions for completing the questionnaire and returning it are usually enclosed, and a stamped return envelope is provided. Researchers want to maximize the rate of return whenever questionnaires are mailed. They may enclose cover letters designed to familiarize respondents with their study and the reasons it is being conducted.

After questionnaires have been mailed initially, a waiting period of about two weeks passes while researchers collect questionnaires from early respondents. If some attempt has been made to identify respondents within the questionnaires themselves, researchers can determine from master lists of respondents which ones have returned their questionnaires and which ones have not returned them. Those who have not yet returned their questionnaires may be sent *follow-up letters* with additional questionnaires included. A statement might be included, such as, "We recently sent you a questionnaire concerning [some topic] and we have not yet heard from you. Your responses are important to us. Because of the possibility that you may not have received the questionnaire we recently sent you, we are sending you another for your convenience, together with a stamped preaddressed envelope so that you may complete and return the questionnaire easily. We hope to hear from you soon. Thank you in advance for your important participation in our research project."

Response to mailed questionnaires varies among survey research projects. No one knows what a normal response rate is for any target response audience. Estimates of what is "normal" range from 30 to 75 percent. In the social sciences, return rates to mailed questionnaires are usually expected to be about one-third. Thus if we were to mail 1000 questionnaires to a random sample of city residents, we might expect about 330 to be returned. Naturally, if we receive larger numbers of completed questionnaires, this will enhance the representativeness of our respondents relative to the overall questionnaire mailing, which is usually based on some type of random sampling plan. Later in this chapter we examine the issue of nonresponse, or those instances where persons receive questionnaires but for various reasons elect not to return them. The rate of return for any mailed questionnaire depends on many factors, some of which are also discussed.

Face-to-Face Questionnaire Administration

Another common method of distributing questionnaires is face-to-face. Researchers may distribute questionnaires directly to target audiences. Many students have been a part of a target audience in the classroom, where investigators might pass out questionnaires to them during class time. Students are frequent target audiences of researchers because they are easily accessible and investigators can obtain direct responses to their questionnaires from large numbers of students in a matter of minutes.

Unfortunately, selecting students in the classroom for questionnaire administration has led some scholars to allege that over the years, we have learned a great deal about students and their attitudes about things. But students are atypical of the population at large in several respects. Their general educational level is somewhat higher than the average community resident. Further, many students in colleges and universities may be from elsewhere geographically. Thus if students at some university are used for a professor's attitudinal research, and if that research is connected with one or more community issues, student responses may be interesting but irrelevant in relation to those issues.

Besides administering questionnaires to students in classrooms, investigators can visit work settings and distribute questionnaires directly to employees. Prisons may permit researchers to canvass prisoners about various matters through self-administered questionnaires distributed to various inmates by correctional officers. A primary advantage of such direct distributions of these questionnaires is that students or prisoners or employees may ask researchers for clarification about any statement or question that may be ambiguous or confusing to readers. But the primary advantage is that a large proportion of those who receive questionnaires will probably complete and return them. Thus a high return rate is virtually guaranteed. Such guarantees cannot be made regarding mailed questionnaires.

Comparison of Mailed Questionnaires with Face-to-Face Questionnaire Administration

It should be apparent that the major benefit of mailed questionnaires is economy. Mailed questionnaires, therefore, are an inexpensive means of obtaining information about particular target samples. Some of the drawbacks to mailed questionnaires include the fact that you never are sure who completes and returns the questionnaires you have distributed. If researchers send questionnaires to organizational leaders in community corrections agencies, a secretary or volunteer worker in the agency may actually complete the questionnaire and return it. However, it is assumed by the researcher that directors or agency heads were the ones who responded to the questions. Another drawback is that researchers have no way of assuring that people will return the questionnaires they have been sent. Thus in most research projects involving mailed questionnaires, nonresponse is significant and limits the generalizability of subsequent research findings.

Another drawback of mailed questionnaires is that respondents may misinterpret certain statements or misread questions and provide answers that are unrelated to the intended statement meanings. Without the presence of the researcher as a resource, respondents must determine for themselves what the statements mean or how questions should be interpreted. Some inaccurate information is therefore expected among the returned questionnaires.

On the positive side, mailed questionnaires allow respondents the option of completing the instrument in the privacy of their own homes or work settings, with a high degree of privacy and anonymity. If sensitive issues are being probed, or if personal behaviors or attitudes are being solicited, such as indicating one's participation in illicit drug use or sexual experiences, heightening respondent anonymity will improve the odds of greater return rates. Respondents might be more inclined to return questionnaires that contain sensitive materials if they believe their responses will be treated confidentially and anonymously. In such situations, however, follow-up letters that contain extra questionnaires might serve notice to potential respondents that the researchers know who they are and that they did not respond initially. Relatively little research has been conducted about the distinction between those topics considered sensitive and those labeled as innocuous. What is considered sensitive by one person may not be considered sensitive by another.

The major advantages of face-to-face questionnaire administration are that (1) researchers know who are completing the questionnaire, (2) a high rate of questionnaire completion and return is expected, and (3) investigators are present to clarify any statements or questions that might otherwise be misinterpreted by respondents. A disadvantage is the fact that researchers must actually be present during the questionnaire administration, and that this presence might involve extensive travel to diverse locations.

QUESTIONNAIRE CONSTRUCTION

For the average person, a questionnaire is likely to be viewed as a simple device that anyone can create or throw together, given the time and interest. For serious scientists who do social research, however, the construction of questionnaires is serious business and considered a complex task. In many instances, before the final form of a questionnaire is determined for general distribution to a target sample, researchers will probably revise it several times. These revisions include modifications of question or statement wording and actual questionnaire content and length. Most researchers would probably agree that constructing a "good" questionnaire for any target audience is a tedious and arduous task. However, despite their best efforts, researchers have never devised the perfect questionnaire. Every questionnaire suffers from at least a few imperfections that neither the researchers nor their assistants detected during its preparation.

In this section we examine some of the major factors that researchers must take into account when constructing questionnaires for selected target samples. Let's begin by considering some of the questions that arise in the initial stages of questionnaire preparation:

1. What is the definition of the population about which we seek information?
2. What is the socioeconomic and/or educational level of people who will receive and complete our questionnaires?
3. What kinds of facts do we want to know about them?
4. How accessible are these people for research purposes?
5. How will we administer the questionnaire?
6. What kinds of response patterns will we use in our questionnaire construction?
7. How long should we make the questionnaire? *as short as can.*
8. How much control will we be able to exert over ensuring their responses to our questionnaire?

Ideally, every element in the population to be studied should be identified and given an opportunity to be included in the research project as recommended in Chapter 5. The socioeconomic level or educational background (if known) of the intended target population will enable the researcher to design questions or formulate statements at a particular level of readability commensurate with that of the respondents. If there is a strong likelihood that the population contains a substantial number of persons who might have difficulty with the English language for one reason or another, interviewing might be a better strategy, although it will be considerably more expensive in time and money.

The kinds of things we want to learn about the sample will directly determine the content of our questionnaires. Some of the standard social and demographic items are age, gender, occupation/profession, years of education, and race/ethnicity. Other items are included as needed. For example, if we are studying probation officer burnout, we would want to include a scale that measures burnout. If we wish to assess job performance and cross-tabulate it with other variables, including burnout, we would need to include various measures that would enable us to evaluate one's job performance or effectiveness. We can use existing measures devised by other researchers or we can create our own measures.

The length of questionnaires is a controversial matter and has never been resolved. Some investigators have argued that in the case of mailed questionnaires, shorter questionnaires are preferable to longer ones. The idea is that people will be more inclined to spend their time completing and returning shorter questionnaires than longer ones. Unfortunately, no one knows what the guidelines are for determining whether any given questionnaire is long or short. For instance, postcard questionnaires have been used in the past for soliciting public opinion about a few issues. Two or three statements can be printed on a self-addressed, stamped postcard which can easily be mailed back to researchers. These are considered "short" questionnaires. In another instance, all faculty at a small college were required to complete a 110-page questionnaire, printed on both sides of each page, that solicited information about their teaching duties, college functions, and numerous other items. This questionnaire was administered as part of a general accreditation program the school was pursuing. One hundred percent compliance was obtained from all faculty at the college, since turning in completed questionnaires to the payroll office was the only way faculty could receive their paychecks during the month the questionnaire was distributed. This type of questionnaire would be considered "long." But most questionnaires we are familiar with are somewhere in between postcard length and 110 pages.

Questionnaire length is a matter of personal preference and standards. One consideration that provides a good standard for limiting questionnaire length is how long it will take to complete. Extremely lengthy questionnaires can cause some respondents to become test-weary. Tired respondents may become somewhat careless in the responses they give, and they may drift into response sets.

Questionnaire length is also influenced by organizational time constraints. If you approach a police department and attempt to get departmental approval to administer questionnaires to all officers beginning various shifts, you will not be particularly persuasive if you tell the watch commander that the questionnaire will take about an hour to complete. You would be better off limiting questionnaire administration to 15 minutes or less. And even this short time interval may be considered "too long" by the target agency or department. Questionnaires sent to persons in their own homes and on their own time may be lengthier and take longer to complete. But again, you must balance questionnaire length against factors that would enhance the likelihood of increasing the rate of returns.

The length of the questionnaire is generally a function of the amount and type of information sought. If we assume that investigators are operating within a theoretical context and that the variables being studied are limited, the length of the questionnaire will be determined by the inclusion of those scales necessary to measure the limited number of variables examined. Researchers should not "throw in" extraneous scales or include variables that are detached from or irrelevant for their theoretical schemes. But sometimes, novice researchers will add other variables simply because they are interesting. A good rule of thumb is to include only those relevant variables that enable you to carry out your research objectives fully. Leave out other variables that might be more suitable for a subsequent investigation.

Selecting the Questions

Because the primary functions of questionnaires are description and measurement, researchers have a variety of options for selecting items for inclusion. Several classic sources exist that either tell researchers where to find existing measuring instruments in questionnaire form or provide them with compilations of measures themselves (see Miller, 1977; Bonjean, Hill, and McLemore, 1967). Investigators will often want to combine several relevant existing measures with items of their own or even newly devised scales (see Chapters 9 and 10). However, many existing scales, such as those that might be included in Bonjean, Hill, and McLemore (1967) or Miller (1977), are probably dated culturally or contain questions using phraseologies that might have different meanings in the 1990s than they had in the 1960s or 1970s. The researcher may sometimes be able to adapt older existing scales to fit present problems by changing the wording of various statements. Basically, the originally devised scales are used, but they have been given an upbeat treatment by investigators who have modified certain statements to fit the present research problem.

Whenever *any* scale is used in research, whether it is a previously constructed scale or a newly devised one, researchers should perform various tests to determine whether the items are clearly worded or are fairly internally consistent with one another. Such tests, known as *pretests*, involve administering early versions of questionnaires to audiences similar to those targeted for one's research. For example, if researchers wanted to administer questionnaires to a sample of Indiana prison correctional officers, they might want to pretest their questionnaires by giving them to samples of jail correctional officers or to others who perform similar work. Jail correctional officers in the researcher's local community might be more accessible for study than prison correctional officers, where access to the prison environment is extremely limited. Sometimes, these pretests are designated as *pilot studies*, because they involve "trial runs" of questionnaires before audiences similar to those where the final form of the questionnaire is to be administered. Thus pilot studies are small-scale implementations of the actual studies researchers are prepared to conduct. They enable investigators to detect faults associated with their research instruments and obtain ideas about how best to carry out the final project.

For example, these pretests are helpful in that they help researchers to detect spelling errors, awkward wordings of questions or statements, or possibly irrelevant items that do not apply to correctional officer duties or functions. Also, investigators may subject their scales to preliminary tests to determine whether they seem to provide accurate indications of the degree to which certain characteristics are possessed by respondents. These are *validity* and *reliability* checks, and several such checks or tests are discussed at length in Chapter 10. The procedures discussed in Chapter 10 assist investigators in determining the accuracy and consistency of the scales they intend to use.

Including items whose primary function is description is a fairly easy task for seasoned researchers. But precautions need to be taken, particularly with reference to the question wording. For instance, if investigators wanted to estimate the amount of marijuana consumption among an aggregate of college students, they might draw a probability sample and ask them the following question:

"How often do you smoke marijuana per month?"
or
"How many 'joints' do you smoke per week?"

These questions are equally presumptuous in that it is assumed that students who answer such questions actually smoke marijuana, when in fact, none of them may do so. Such questions, labeled "husband-beating-wife" questions, are similar to the question, "When was the last time you beat your wife?" The ridiculousness of this question is apparent. First, it assumes that respondents are married (which may not be true). Second, it assumes that all respondents are male (which may not be true). Third, it assumes that all respondents beat their wives (which may not be true). It is imperative that researchers refrain from assuming too much about the target population.

Provided that investigators have established or legitimized their research purpose with the target audience (particularly where information is requested concerning possible law violations by respondents), a safer and more reasonable approach to the marijuana question would be:

"Have you ever smoked marijuana?"

If the respondent's reply is "yes," the researcher can use the *follow-up question:*

"Do you smoke marijuana currently?"

Again, if the respondent's answer is "yes," the "frequency" question may be asked safely:

"How often per week (or month) do you smoke marijuana?"

Such types of questions are often asked in annual surveys of high school and college students by investigators who want to describe unreported crime. Thus *self-reports* are used to tap amounts of crime or infractions of the law that perhaps are undetected by police. Juveniles often disclose greater amounts of delinquency through self-reports than are reported by the *Uniform Crime Reports* or other official sources of illegal acts.

Caution should also be exercised when interpreting answers persons give to questions or statements. For instance, several interpretations may be made about the extent of one's professionalism as a police officer, depending on the answer given to the following question:

"How many journals, periodicals, or other police officer-oriented materials do you subscribe to on an annual basis?"
_____ None
_____ One or two
_____ Three or four
_____ Five or six
_____ Seven or more

If certain police officers subscribe to *no* journals or police-oriented periodicals, does this mean that they lack professionalism? Are officers who subscribe to "seven or more" periodicals more professional than those who subscribe to only "three or four" periodicals? We have no way of controlling for the types of periodicals referred to in the item above. Are these equipment magazines that advertise police officer weapons and accessories? Are these journals from a peace officer's association, such as *Police Chief*, that contain research articles about police work? Are these magazines about hand-to-hand combat or developing better public relations skills? We have no way of equating one's numbers of magazine subscriptions with one's degree of police officer professionalism.

We can ask police officers how professional they believe they are relative to their work. Or we can ask certain officers to evaluate the professionalism of other officers. All of these questions are contingent upon what we mean by the term "professionalism." But questionnaires are designed to function as indicators of the extent to which these various phenomena are possessed by our respondents. By probing and seeking answers to questions that relate logically to professionalism, such as membership in professional organizations, taking courses that improve one's performance on the job, or enrolling in workshops that are geared to enhance one's professional skills, we can acquire a fairly good understanding or impression of one's degree of professionalism. However, we do not know whether these officers will necessarily do better jobs at enforcing the law or refraining from using excessive force. Indicators of one's attitudes suggest only a possible propensity to behave in given ways. Often, there are discrepancies between what our indicators reveal on questionnaires and the ways people actually behave in the real world.

RESPONSE AND NONRESPONSE: SOME CONSIDERATIONS

Survey researchers who utilize questionnaires in their investigations are concerned about maximizing the number of respondents who are contacted initially. Also, they are concerned about the potential effects of nonresponse, if any, particularly in mailed-questionnaire situations. Below are listed some of the more important factors that affect the rate of response to questionnaires generally. Many of the factors identified are particularly relevant for mailed questionnaires, although most pertain to all types of questionnaire administration.

Questionnaire Length

Much attention has been given to questionnaire length. As we have seen, there are no consistent standards that distinguish short questionnaires from long ones. The common belief held by many researchers is that shorter questionnaires tend to be returned more often than longer ones. However, at least one study has investigated the influence on response rate of "apparent" questionnaire length. Researchers sent 3000 questionnaires to random samples of residents in three cities: Knoxville, Chattanooga, and Memphis, Tennessee (Champion and Sear, 1969).

The questionnaires pertained to NASA spending and were directed to household heads. All 3000 questionnaires had the same content; that is, all questionnaires were exactly the same in wording. However, the researchers spaced the question items differently so that three different questionnaire lengths were produced. The questionnaire lengths were three, six, and nine pages, respectively. Basically, the same questions were cramped into three pages, spread out over six pages, and even more spread out over nine pages. Thus respondents received questionnaires where some only appeared to be longer or shorter than others. Interestingly, nine-page questionnaires were returned more often than either six- or three-page questionnaires. This finding suggests that at least for questionnaires within these page ranges, "apparently" longer questionnaires do not necessarily lead to lower return rates among respondents.

Other investigators might consider any questionnaire under 10 pages to be short, whereas other researchers would invoke different standards of questionnaire length. We might assume, however, that generally, keeping a questionnaire as short as possible while including only the relevant scales and question items designed to accomplish one's research objectives will elicit the highest return rates under most conditions.

Questionnaire Content

Questionnaires that contain controversial material or that request respondents to reveal intimate details of their personal lives may elicit both high and low response rates, depending on the topics investigated and the target audience. It is entirely likely that some individuals will find material on some questionnaires to be offensive and "immoral," whereas others will find the same material interesting, "titilating," or "arousing." It would be logical to expect differential response rates from such diverse groups.

Some people may regard questionnaires as an invasion of their privacy and simply refuse to answer on such grounds. Others may see questionnaires as an opportunity to express their feelings about important issues, and therefore the questionnaire functions as a means of tension release or frustration reduction as well as a data-gathering tool.

Anonymity

Another common assumption is that people are more likely to respond to questionnaires to the extent that their anonymity is preserved or maintained. Sensitive items related to racial or religious attitudes or to sexual behavior may appear to be less threatening to the extent that respondent anonymity is preserved. On the other hand, because of certain psychological and/or social factors presently unidentified, persons may derive some gratification (to ego, sexual prowess, etc.) from disclosing sensitive information about themselves to others. No consistent pattern is evident in the literature concerning the influence of anonymity on response rates.

Other Factors

If questionnaires are mailed to respondents, factors such as the *type of postage used* (i.e., metered, hand-stamped, special delivery), type of cover letter attached (appeals to respondent egoism or altruism), rewards for responding (money, turkeys, opportunities to express opinions), and the socioeconomic status of the target sample are considered to be influential to different degrees for eliciting greater rates of response. If questionnaires are administered on a face-to-face basis, such factors as the appearance or ethnic/racial origin of the investigator or questionnaire administrator, the readability of the questionnaire, and the types of responses required must be considered important in determining response rates. When questionnaires are administered on a face-to-face basis, many problems are encountered similar to those encountered by interviewers. (See Chapter 7 for an extensive discussion of interviewing and interviewing problems.)

What about Nonresponse?

Two of the most frustrating questions investigators must deal with are "Who are the *nonrespondents*?" and "What would be the outcome of my results if the nonrespondents were somehow added or included as a part of all data analyzed?" There are various ways of identifying nonrespondents, particularly in a mailed questionnaire situation. Lists of individuals are compiled to whom questionnaires are sent. Those who respond and return the questionnaire are simply checked off these lists. Those who do not return their questionnaires may be sent *follow-up* letters to remind them to return the questionnaires they received. Under such conditions, it is ethical to advise respondents that their identities are known in advance and that the researcher will know if they have not responded to the mailed questionnaire.

Another method is simply to code each questionnaire or the return envelope with a number that refers to specific respondents. However, respondents will notice the number. This absence of anonymity may inhibit their response, but it will also explain why they receive a follow-up letter from researchers later if they do not respond to the original questionnaire mailed. A questionable practice is using some sort of invisible ink or coding procedure on the questionnaires or return envelopes to identify all respondents. Respondents may be unaware that their questionnaires have been coded so that if they are returned, researchers will know who they are. Researchers may or may not advise respondents about this lack of anonymity. Various professional associations, such as the Academy of Criminal Justice Sciences, the American Society of Criminology, and the American Sociological Association presently scrutinize various research practices such as these and seek to implement safeguards that will protect human subjects that are contacted by social investigators.

If researchers have made no provisions for identifying nonrespondents, they have little or no hope of being able to describe the characteristics (social, psychological, socioeconomic) of nonrespondents and contrast them with the characteristics of those who have responded. Obviously, the respondents and nonrespondents differ in at least one important respect—some of them returned the questionnaires and some did not return them. Would the inclusion of information from the nonrespondents be significant enough to change or alter one's research findings to any degree? We do not know. It would be wrong to think that the inclusion of the information from nonrespondents would make *no* difference to one's results, but we cannot calculate the impact unknown information might have to our final results. Considering response rates as varying from 30 to 60 percent, these rates would be associated with nonresponse rates of from 70 to 40 percent. These are sizable numbers of respondents, and it may be safely speculated that had they been included in one's data analysis, their information yielded would have made some difference. However, from a philosophical viewpoint, the effect of nonrespondents on the original research outcome is almost always purely speculative.

SUMMARY

Questionnaires are self-administered inventories that describe and measure information about people, their social characteristics, and their opinions about things. Questionnaires are perhaps the most popular data collection strategy researchers use to gather information about groups. Each data collection strategy (e.g., questionnaires, observation, interviewing) possesses weaknesses and strengths relative to other strategies, although researchers frequently employ multiple data collection techniques when conducting investigations and triangulate their findings by comparing the results obtained from these different strategies.

The major functions of questionnaires are description and measurement. Questionnaires may consist of exclusively fixed-response items, where all statements have previously designated answer options, and open-ended items, where respondents must provide written replies to questions asked. Fixed-response items are more easily completed by respondents, and many investigators feel that such questionnaires have a higher rate of return compared with open-ended questionnaires that take more time and depend on written answers from respondents. Educational and socioeconomic factors may inhibit responses to open-ended items as well.

Questionnaires may be mailed to respondents or distributed to them in face-to-face situations with investigators. Constructing questionnaires is time consuming and complex. Investigators should be sensitive to questionnaire length, inclusion of sensitive items that solicit intimate details of respondents' lives, and possible illiteracy among certain respondents, where English may not be understood by a portion of the target population or where many elements in the population have a poor grasp of it. Some amount of nonresponse is expected in most projects where questionnaires are used, although mailed-questionnaire situations are those having the greatest amount of nonresponse. Anonymity, type of postage used, and types of cover letters that have egoistic or altruistic appeal may be used to increase response rates. Follow-up letters may be used to solicit questionnaires from those who were unresponsive to the initial mailings of questionnaires. No one knows about those who do not respond, although their inclusion in the final results might have profound effects on the findings. Various methods for assessing characteristics of nonrespondents were discussed.

QUESTIONS FOR REVIEW

1. What are questionnaires? Identify and discuss briefly their major functions.
2. Describe triangulation. What are some primary purposes of triangulation?
3. Identify two types of questionnaire administration. Discuss briefly the weaknesses and strengths of each administration method.
4. Differentiate between fixed-response and open-ended items. What are the positive and negative features of each type of item? Discuss each.
5. What is a response set? Can researchers do anything to control for response sets and their occurrence when constructing their questionnaires? What can be done? Discuss briefly.
6. What are some primary drawbacks to using open-ended items on culturally diverse populations?
7. What are some limitations and advantages of using existing scales devised by other researchers?
8. What are mailed questionnaires? How much nonresponse is usually anticipated in mailed-questionnaire situations? What can be done to decrease nonresponse?
9. What are some important questions that we must consider before constructing our questionnaires?
10. What are follow-up letters? What are their purposes? Are there any ethical considerations to be made when sending out follow-up letters? Discuss briefly any ethical considerations that you might list.

7

Data Collection Strategies III: Interviews

KEY TERMS

Focused interview
Interview
Interview guide
Interview schedule

Social desirability
Structured interview
Unstructured interview

Michael McShane, a 15-year-old boy, was attacked by 30 members of a delinquent gang in a New York City park one hot summer evening in 1958. He was brutally killed. Subsequently, Edward R. Murrow interviewed several of the juvenile gang members for NBC Radio. Murrow interview with juvenile gang member:

Question: "Can you tell me what happened then?"

Answer [from 14-year-old]: "The other guys were all over him, you know, they was kickin', punchin', stompin', stabbin'. I couldn't get near him. I had a baseball bat. And then someone stabbed him with a bread knife."

Question: "Did you ever get near enough to hit him?"

Answer: Yeah, he was all messed up. The guys backed off, I got up close, but he was all messed up. I hit him a few times, you know, around the legs, with my bat. That's the least I could do, was to hit him a little. He was real messed up."

Question: "What about you? [gesturing to 11-year-old]. Are you the one who had the bread knife?"

Answer: "Yeah, I had a bread knife."

Question: "Did you stab the boy with the bread knife?"

Answer: "Yeah, I stabbed him good. I knew, you know, that that would sort of be good for my 'rep (reputation). You know, like, I wanted other guys to say, 'There goes a cold killer.' That would've given me a bigger 'rep, a bigger buildup, you know."

Question: "What about you? [gesturing to 13-year-old]. What weapon did you have?"

Answer: "I had a chain and a knife. I had it [the chain] wrapped around my fist."

Question: "Did you hit him, too?"

Answer: "Yeah, I hit him. I hit him good in the mouth, once in the back, I think."

Question: "What about the knife? Did you stab him with the knife also?"

Answer: "Yeah, I kinda stabbed him once, you know, in the stomach or chest . . . I don't know . . . maybe the back . . . anyway, I stabbed him with my knife."

Question: "Why did you do that?"

Answer: "I always wanted to know what it would feel like to stick a knife through human bone. You know, and, too, I wanted people to respect me for what I had done there."

(Excerpts from Edward R. Murrow interview with members of New York City gang known as the Egyptian Kings and Dragons in 1958, after boy, Michael McShane, was attacked by about 30 gang members and killed.)

INTRODUCTION

One of the most direct data-gathering tools is the interview. An *interview* is verbal communication for the purpose of acquiring information. Investigators target a sample of respondents and ask them questions directly. In this chapter we examine the interviewing process and how criminologists and criminal justice scholars can make use of interviews to acquire data in their research. First, several types of interviews are described as well as their general functions. Like questionnaire construction, some planning is necessary to construct appropriate interviewing tools. Thus we look at how interviews are arranged and conducted.

Since interviews involve direct contact between researchers and respondents, any anonymity respondents might otherwise enjoy, such as that accruing from self-administered mailed questionnaires, is eliminated. A different kind of information is obtained through interviews, and therefore, we will assess interviews in terms of their weaknesses and strengths relative to other data collection procedures. Further, the relatively close interpersonal nature of interviewing is inherently flawed by various factors. An interviewer's appearance, race or ethnicity, manner of speech, and several other factors combine to influence the types of responses interviewees provide. Thus several key problems associated with the interview are identified and discussed.

INTERVIEWS IN CRIMINAL JUSTICE RESEARCH

The interview is a very time-consuming, yet valuable data-gathering tool that can disclose much about various types of social settings and the people within them. Interviewers are at liberty to go well beyond the limited boundaries of questionnaires, even open-ended ones, and to probe respondents for additional, insightful information about themselves, their work, and those with whom they work. There are no restrictions relating to the conditions under which interviews may be conducted. If we consider each component of the criminal justice system, no single component is immune from an interviewer's questions.

For instance, we can interview police officers and their administrators to inquire about their work roles and how they are performed, how police officers react to job stress and life-threatening situations, their reactions to different patrol styles, and a host of other considerations. Prosecutors and judges may be interviewed to determine their prosecutorial and sentencing priorities, which types of cases are most and least preferred, and their reactions to different types of sentencing reforms. Defendants, inmates, probationers, and parolees may also be interviewed to determine their reactions to different types of prison or jail conditions, the quality of various community-based correctional programs and their interpersonal relations with those who supervise them. Juvenile gang members may be questioned about their behavioral patterns, reasons for fighting other gangs, and their gang formative processes. The portion of the late Edward R. Murrow's interview (at the beginning of this chapter) with gang members from the New York City gang the Egyptian Kings and Dragons proved quite insightful about the motives the boys had for killing another teenager suspected of being a rival gang member. The types of respondents and the ranges of questions they might be asked are virtually unlimited.

Most students are familiar with the results of several common interview applications, such as the *National Crime Survey* (where random households are targeted and occupants questioned about crimes they have experienced during the past year or some other time interval), the *National Youth Survey* (where samples of high school students disclose through interviews the incidence and types of crimes they have committed but have not been apprehended for committing), and the U.S. Census, where random samples of households throughout the United States are contacted and interviewed concerning specific demographic, social, and socioeconomic characteristics.

The characteristic features of interviews include the following:

1. *Questions are asked and responses are given verbally.* The verbal nature of the questions emphasizes three points about interviews that are not sufficiently stressed in our original definition. First, interviews are not simply conversational exchanges between interviewers and interviewees. They are conversations wherein the major thrust is obtaining verbal answers to questions put verbally. Second, these verbal exchanges need not be on a face-to-face basis, even though they usually are. Sometimes, interviews with others are conducted over the telephone. Finally, interviewing may be conducted with more than one interviewee, such as interviews of partners, such as husband/wife, two patrol officers, or small groups of prisoners who cell together.

2. *Information is recorded by investigators rather than respondents.* The fact that interviewers record information provided by respondents underscores the greater accuracy of interviewing regarding information obtained. Interviewers may take notes, mark interview schedules or guides, or tape-record these verbal exchanges with audio or videotaping devices.

3. *The relationship between interviewers and interviewees is structured.* First, this relationship is transitory. It has a fixed beginning and a fixed point of termination. Second, the relation is one where the participants are usually strangers. Even if these persons are not strangers to one another, the nature of the interviewer–interviewee relation is one of scientific objectivity, where most, if not all, threats are removed that might otherwise hinder or frustrate honest responses to one's questions.

4. *There is considerable flexibility in the interviewing format.* Few other data-collection tools offer such a large range of question-asking formats to investigators. It seems at times that the only limitation is the ingenuity of interviewers. Such an amount of structural variability allows for greater mutual understanding of both the questions by interviewers and the answers given by interviewees.

Some researchers deliberately choose interviewing, in part, because it permits them the opportunity of moving into unexpected or uncharted areas. Even the most standardized interviews do not prohibit such spontaneity of exploration both before and after the data have been compiled through the interview.

TYPES OF INTERVIEWS

Interviews are either (1) unstructured or (2) structured.

Unstructured Interviews

Unstructured interviews are much as their name implies. Investigators might be charged with finding out about parent–child relations relative to a sample of juvenile delinquents. They might conduct informal, unstructured interviews with several delinquents to determine what they can about how these juveniles define their relations with their parents. The interviews may vary greatly in the time taken to complete them, from one juvenile to the next. Further, not all questions asked of one juvenile may necessarily be asked of another. Also, the order of questions is irrelevant, as long as interviewers "cover their bases" and get all relevant material they can from the youths they interview.

Another feature of unstructured interviews is that interviewers do not need special interviewing training. They may record any observations they make and their own interpretations or impressions of any answers given. The interviews are also characterized as free-flowing, with the direction and depth of interviews determined by situational factors. If certain juveniles are obviously reluctant to talk about certain background factors, interviewers can shift gears to discuss other areas of interest. Thus unstructured interviews are the closest thing to the spontaneity inherent in natural conversation.

There are several advantages of unstructured interviews. First, the interview itself approaches natural conversation. Subjects interviewed might feel more at ease in responding to an interviewer's questions. Second, interviewers are guided in their questions by the types of responses given. Thus there is less likelihood that interviewers will infuse their own values and biases into the interview itself. Third, unstructured interviews offer the greatest degree of flexibility and serendipity. Researchers can spend as much time as they wish probing certain aspects of answers persons give in order to develop certain emerging themes.

One problem with unstructured interviewing, however, is that there may be *incomparability* of information derived from one interview that might be contrasted with information from other interviews. Since there is no systematic control over the question-asking procedures, the reliability of data is thrown into serious question. Also, much wasted time may be spent with respondents who have little or nothing to add to the knowledge interviewers have already obtained from others. Sometimes, interviewers may engage in repetitive or unproductive conversations with respondents.

Another problem is that some respondents may choose this opportunity to use interviewers as "therapists." For instance, one interviewer who studied employees in a large probation department reported that one older probation officer, a 63-year-old, was being singled out for early retirement. The probation officer did not want to retire early, but probation office administrators were dissatisfied with his performance, which was diminishing rapidly. The officer continually forgot to keep appointments with various probationer/clients, failed to submit presentence investigation reports with the court, and failed to comply with other rules and regulations associated with probation officer work. In short, administration wanted to get rid of him. Since civil service regulations were in effect at the time and mandatory retirement could not be enforced until one reached 70 years of age, one's early retirement was not mandatory. Therefore, the administration sought to make his life as uncomfortable as possible, hoping that eventually, he would take the "hint" and resign of his own accord.

The interviewer who interviewed this elderly probation officer found himself in the role of "therapist," since the probation officer poured out his life experiences and disclosed what had been happening to him on the job. At one point, the probation officer broke down and cried. The interviewer was in an awkward situation, since it would not be appropriate simply to get up and leave. The interviewer decided to hear him out, and this "interview," a tape-recorded one, lasted nearly seven hours. The interviewer finally was able to "get away" by noting that the sun was setting, his wife had dinner waiting, and his tape recorder had run out of tape.

Another drawback of unstructured interviewing is that there are no guarantees that the interview will be fruitful or insightful. However, this limitation may be a function of the original research enterprise implemented. If researchers have such poorly conceived research problems that unstructured interviewing is chosen as a data-gathering option, the investigators' own lack of problem conceptualization may enhance any shortcomings of unstructured interviewing. This is not meant to suggest that such unstructured interviewing is chosen only when researchers have poorly conceived research plans. Rather, it is simply *more likely* that unstructured interviews will be used whenever researchers are uncertain of the information desired from target audiences or if they believe that something new or insightful will be disclosed.

Closely related to this possible drawback is the fact that considerable time must be allocated to devising categories into which one's responses from an unstructured interview can be classified. If several interviewers are involved in the data collection effort, problems may arise relating to interinterviewer reliability. Different interviewers may ask different questions, or they may code similar responses to the same questions differently. For these and other reasons, most researchers prefer more structured interviews to less structured ones, since greater ease in coding and systemization of information derived are achieved. Some unstructured interviews are given *some* structure by using interview guides. *Interview guides* consist of lists of predetermined questions and/or topics about which researchers seek information. Since these questions and/or topic areas are anticipated in advance, some thought may be given to the codes devised for probable replies from respondents.

Structured Interviews and the Focused Interview

Contrasted with interview guides and unstructured interviews, *structured interviews* consist of a predetermined list of fixed-response questions or items. For the most part, interviewers adhere rather closely to the predetermined question list.

Structured interviews reflect a high degree of interviewer control. Such interviewer control may be exercised over the time taken to complete the interview, interviewer clarification of any confusing questions or answers received from respondents, and limiting the questions to those factors relevant for the problem being investigated. In contrast, unstructured interviewing lacks such controls. Often, it is important for those interviewed to know how much time the interview will take to complete. Interviewing is sometimes conducted on one's job. Sometimes, employers will allocate times when interviewing may be conducted. These "infringements" on a company's time must be controlled carefully, since researchers do not want to jeopardize their chances of studying the same setting at a later date.

Telling interviewees that the interview will take only 15 minutes, and subsequently conducting an interview that takes two hours, will do nothing but antagonize respondents and make them resistant to being interviewed again. Research projects where the same samples are studied over several different time periods rely on access to the same samples, and therefore good public relations skills are essential to permit study completion.

Actually, a structured interview utilizes an interview schedule. An *interview schedule* is a questionnaire consisting of a list of predetermined questions and fixed-response replies that interviewers can fill in themselves when they conduct interviews. Often, a copy of the interview schedule is given to respondents so that they may read it along with the interviewer. If respondents think of answers that are not among those provided by fixed responses, the interviewer can write in their verbal replies or tape record them.

One type of structured interview is the focused interview (Merton, Fiske, and Kendall, 1956). *Focused interviews* are interviews with respondents who have shared some common experienced that has, in turn, been carefully scrutinized by investigators to generate hypotheses about the effects of the experience on participants. The interview context focuses on the actual effects of the experience as viewed by the participants. Thus applications of focused interviews may be directed toward samples of shock probationers or those who participate in electronic monitoring or home confinement in community-based correctional programs. Focused interviews may be conducted with police officers who have received special types of training relating to resolutions of marital disputes. It is apparent that focused interviews may be used in close conjunction with experimental types of research designs, where it is important to assess the effects of experiments on subject behaviors and attitudes.

Bahn and Davis (1991) were interested in describing the social psychological effects of the status of probationers. They wanted to learn from probationers themselves whether the probation experience was helpful and if it stigmatized them in their communities. Bahn and Davis used self-administered questionnaires and focused interviews with samples of probationers to learn about their feelings and attitudes toward their probation program. They obtained a sample of 43 probationers and exposed them to three data-gathering instruments: (1) a questionnaire, consisting of 16 open-ended questions, administered in an interview format; (2) a scalogram, consisting of 15 items, with five choices for each item, which had been devised especially for the study by these authors; and (3) the Self-Attitude Inventory (SAI), a self-concept scale. The open-ended questions that comprised their focused interview are shown in Table 7.1.

Bahn and Davis were able to learn much about probationers and their feelings through the use of these questions. They found, for instance, that probationers generally received considerable assistance from their families and friends, and even from some employers. Interestingly, these researchers found that the stigma of being on probation was not as stigmatizing as many people think. For example, these probationers reported that most of their friends did not avoid them. However, they were hesitant to disclose their probationary status to employers for fear

TABLE 7.1 OPEN-ENDED QUESTIONS ADMINISTERED TO 43 PROBATIONERS BY BAHN AND DAVIS

1. Have you told your family, relatives, and friends that you are on probation? Why or why not?
2. Have any of your family, relatives, or friends been in trouble with the law?
3. Have the actions or what was said to you by your family or friends changed in any way after they found out that you were on probation?
4. Have any of your family, relatives, or friends helped you since you were on probation? In what way? Before probation?
5. Have you told your boss that you were on probation? Why or why not?
6. Do you think about the fact that you are on probation very often? Is it something that's on your mind?
7. Is there anything you especially like about your probation?
8. Is there anything you especially dislike about your probation?
9. What would you like to go on between me and you? What would you like to talk about?
10. What do you think the purpose of probation is?
11. Has your life changed since you have been placed on probation? How?
12. Are you afraid or anxious about probation? Why?
13. Have you felt depressed since you have been on probation? Why?
14. Do you think of yourself as a criminal since you have been on probation? Why or why not?
15. Do you think your arrest was justified? Why or why not?
16. Do you think the judge should have placed you on probation for the offense? Why or why not?

Source: Questions reproduced from Bahn and Davis (1991:24).

of being fired. They told the investigators that their behaviors had changed to the extent that they no longer associated with other criminals and that they tended to avoid using drugs and alcohol.

As an indication of how a scenario might develop between probationers and their probation officers, we might envision the following hypothetical interview, using one of Bahn's and Davis's questions (P = probationer, PO = probation officer).

PO: "Are you afraid or anxious about probation?"

P: "Yes."

PO: "Why?"

P: "Well, for one thing, you know . . . you always think they're looking over your shoulder. Like, they might be looking for a reason to bust you, or to run you in for something. I don't know . . . it just makes me feel uncomfortable."

PO: "But you haven't broken the law. You've told me that probation helps you go straight. Do you feel like law enforcement officers might pick on you more than someone else if a crime occurs and you happen to be near there?"

P: "Yeah, well, not exactly. It's just that . . . well, what if you happen to run into somebody accidentally . . . you know . . . on the street . . . you are walking along one day, and this guy comes up to you, and he says, 'Hey, Joe, long time no see.' And suppose it's a guy you knew had committed crimes. You begin thinking, are they watching me, are they testing me?

You don't really know for sure whether it's a test or whether it's just an accident . . . you know, you don't really have a whole lot of privacy . . . you want to feel like you're free, being on the outside and all . . . but they still have you . . . you are still controlled by the system . . . they can still put you away if they want . . . for any reason. . . . "

PO: "But you have to do something pretty serious to get your probation revoked."

P: "Well, yeah, I know . . . but I suppose . . . I guess, it's like they might think the wrong thing, seeing you with someone else who's maybe a criminal or former criminal, like maybe, you are still doing your old thing and all . . . I don't know . . . there are just those times when I feel, like, I feel the system is looking at me and thinking I'm going to screw up. . . . "

PO: "Are you afraid about your own willpower or will to avoid things that might get you into trouble?"

P: "Well, yeah. You know, like I might want a drink, or maybe I want to get high, or do some coke. But, you know, they got these checks, where they might come around and test me . . . I never know when to expect them . . . what if you only screw up once, have one little drink, and the next minute they're there wanting to test your pee. You don't know when they are coming around, or if they're watching . . . you get to where you don't trust anybody anymore, because there's so much at stake."

PO: "And so, being free on probation maybe doesn't mean that you are as free as everyone else?"

P: "Exactly. Anybody else, you know, they can get in a car and drive to Mexico, Canada, out of state, wherever, and who cares? But me, I drive out of the county and my PO might make a federal case out of it. I'm even afraid of the mail I get. . . . "

PO: "What do you mean, 'Afraid of your mail?'"

P: "Well, you know, you're always getting things in the mail even if you didn't order them . . . well, once I got this sporting goods catalog from some company back East . . . there were guns advertised in there . . . I was looking at the catalog one day when my PO paid me a visit . . . saw that magazine, about had a fit . . . wanted to know if I was going to order a gun by mail . . . I said, 'Hey, not me, I don't want no trouble . . . I just got this thing in the mail . . . I didn't even ask for it . . . you know, it's the little things that really screw you up . . . you don't have to do anything, just be there in the wrong place at the wrong time . . . I guess what really bothers me the most, why I worry, is that I never know when I am going to be in the wrong place at the wrong time. I don't even sometimes want to go out at night because of that."

Although this exchange between a probation officer and probationer is hypothetical, it is apparent that much enriching detail may be furnished the interviewer when the respondent is able to answer freely. The interviewer may probe at various points to seek clarification of particular points. We can learn from the interview above. For instance, probationers may feel certain pressures about being on probation that would be considered commonplace occurrences for most other people. Also, there is a psychological strain that persists among many probationers, no doubt owing to the possibility that they might be in the wrong place at the wrong time. Thus there is a persistent threat to their freedom that is inherent in their probationer status. Although probation revocation today is much more involved than it once was, it nevertheless exists as an option available to probation officers and judges if probationers violate one or more of their program conditions.

Telephone Interviews

Interviews may be conducted by telephone. To some extent, at least, a degree of anonymity between interviewers and interviewees is created. But because of this physical separation, interviewers may not see puzzled expressions on interviewee's faces, or they may not know the exact identity of those interviewed. Nevertheless, the telephone interview may be used as a relatively inexpensive way of obtaining information directly from respondents.

In one profitable use of telephone interviewing, this writer was hired by an attorney to conduct telephone interviews with various persons in an east Tennessee community. A local citizen had been arrested and charged with murder and conspiracy to commit murder. He had been linked with several others and was allegedly involved directly in the murder of a North Carolina man. His trial was scheduled soon in that community, but his attorney believed that the press had prejudiced prospective jurors. Thus the attorney sought a change of venue for his client, so that the trial might be held in another community where publicity was not as significant.

This writer called approximately 300 persons in the community and asked them various questions about their knowledge of the case. Among the questions asked were whether those contacted were voting citizens, whether they could be called for jury duty, and whether they had formed an opinion about the guilt or innocence of the defendant; if so, what was that opinion? Did they know any family members of the person charged with the murder? The results showed that most citizens had followed the case closely in their local newspapers. Furthermore, most citizens contacted had formed opinions. Most believed the defendant guilty of the murder and that he should be sentenced to death. On the basis of these telephone interview results, the attorney was able to convince the presiding judge to move the case to another county where it was believed that a fair trial could be conducted.

There is little disputing the fact that greater precision is achieved as the investigator's knowledge of the target population increases. The more closely investigators can approach the narrow objectives of the focused interview, the greater the likelihood that they will acquire more precise data. There is also a better chance that they might make full use of the advantages inherent in interviews generally.

There are three clear advantages of structured interviews. First, data from each interview may be compared and equated with data from other interviews.

Second, there are fewer problems of recording and coding data. Thus greater precision in measurement is achieved. Third, the more highly structured the interview, the less likely it is that attention will be diverted to extraneous, irrelevant, and time-consuming conversation.

On the other hand, as interviews become increasingly structured, they tend to lose the spontaneity of natural conservation. In addition, there is the danger that investigators have structured the interview in such as way that the respondent's views are minimized and the investigator's own biases about the problem are highlighted. Finally, the possibility of exploration and probing further, although not absolutely eliminated, is less likely to occur in structured interviewing than in unstructured interviewing.

FUNCTIONS OF INTERVIEWING

The major functions of interviews are (1) description and (2) exploration.

Description

Information obtained from interviews is particularly useful for describing various dimensions of social reality. With certain exceptions, such as certain forms of observation, no other type of research data-gathering tool performs this descriptive function as well. Most people spend much of their time with others in some sort of verbal exchange or dialogue. Being able to capture the question-and-answer process as an unfolding dimension of this dialogue permits us to catch a glimpse of social life as it is lived. Compared with the relatively stale and abstract nature of statistical results, interviewing can yield a "gut-level" understanding of how people think and behave that is more reflective of social reality than summarizing certain survey questionnaire results. Edward R. Murrow's interview with delinquent gang members at the beginning of this chapter evidenced the kind of enriching detail and insight that we frequently obtain from interviews which would be missed through self-administered surveys.

Can you imagine, for instance, giving these same delinquent gang members a self-administered questionnaire designed to investigate the same murder incident? "Please place a check in the space that best fits you." "What type of weapon did you use in the attack on the youth?" "On the average, how many times did you strike the boy with your weapon?" (*Check one*) "What reasons can you cite for why you attacked the boy?" (*Check as many reasons as apply—list of reasons attached*) Needless to say, much will be lost in this highly superficial survey that was originally captured in Murrow's probing interviews with gang members.

Exploration

Another purpose of interviewing is to provide insights into unexplored dimensions of a topic. Surveys of work done usually scratch only the surface and yield only superficial details about the phenomena we wish to explain. However, interviews invite more in-depth probing and detailed descriptions of people's feelings and attitudes. For instance, evidence in the criminal justice literature suggests that private counsel tend to have greater plea bargaining successes with prosecutors than do public defenders. Thus if defendants charged with various crimes attempt to plea bargain or negotiate favorable sentences in exchange for guilty pleas, they will probably receive more lenient treatment if they are represented by private counsel than by public defenders. Some of the logical reasons for this are that in many jurisidictions, public defenders are often new attorneys with little trial experience. Furthermore, private counsel probably have developed reputations and associations with various prosecutors, so that their bargaining powers are favorably enhanced. Do prosecutors view public defenders different from private counsel, and if so, how will these different views influence prosecutorial decision making and the plea bargains eventually worked out between counsel?

Among the various studies examining prosecutorial decision making relative to plea bargaining, Champion (1988) examined prosecutorial discretion and the relative influence of private counsel and public defenders on their plea bargain decisions. In the jurisdictions examined, it was found that private counsel generally were able to negotiate more favorable plea bargains for their clients than were public defenders. Further, of those cases that eventually went to trial, private counsel had a greater success rate through client acquittals. Prosecutors in these jurisdictions were interviewed to see whether they view public defenders and private counsel differently. One interview proved illuminating in that it explained some of the informality associated with plea bargaining that is often hidden from public view. Behind-the-scenes plea bargaining is inherently secretive, since no one knows the final contents of a plea bargain until it is accepted by the presiding judge. Regarding his interactions with private counsel compared with public defenders, one prosecutor said:

> One problem with public defenders is that they get stuck with a lot of cases they don't want. They don't get paid much for these cases. It's in their best interest to get their clients to cop pleas [plead guilty] and get it over with. Usually, they come to me and ask me what I recommend. If I say, 'I think a year in jail and two years probation sounds good,' they often agree with that without making a counteroffer. But if defendants can get themselves some high-powered counsel, well . . . let's put it this way. I know most of the big criminal attorneys in this town on a first-name basis and associate with several of them regularly. They know what and how I think and I know how and what they think. They make me an offer, and you know, more often than not, they know I'll probably go for it. They're not pushovers. I don't bluff as much with them as I do with PDs [public defenders].

In this interview, the intent of the interviewer was to find out whether prosecutors view public defenders differently than privately appointed counsel. It was apparent from these few statements what this particular prosecutor thought about public defenders. However, he said something else of interest that aroused the interviewer's curiosity. He said, "I don't *bluff* as much with them [privately appointed counsel] as I do with PDs." The fact that he brought up "bluffing" led the interviewer to try and find out more about prosecutorial bluffing. The interviewer said:

Interviewer: "What do you mean by 'bluffing?' "

Prosecutor: "Oh, you know. Whenever we have a weak case, perhaps a witness is unreliable, evidence is scarce, but, you know, we think we have the guy who did the crime, because of other things . . . we might push them hard, the PDs . . . to get them thinking we have more against their clients than we actually do. You'd be surprised how much of the time it works. Not all of our cases are airtight. So we do a little bluffing."

Interviewer: "You said that you don't do that as much, bluffing, with private counsels. Why not?"

Prosecutor: "Well, most of them know me and how I operate. Some of them have even been PDs. I've been at this job for nine years. Plus, they do their own research on a case, do their homework. They have a pretty good idea whether or not I've got a solid case. If they even smell a bluff, you can bet they'll call me on it. I've had 'em do it to me. But then, sometimes it backfires."

Interviewer: "What do you mean?"

Prosecutor: "Sometimes they think I'm bluffing and I'm not. They have pushed it in some cases, in really important cases, and they've gone to trial. I've got a perfect track record with them on that . . . when I really know down deep that I've got a solid case, and they're stupid enough to push it to trial, probably because they think I've got a weak case . . . I beat 'em."

Interviewer: "Why is it easier to bluff PDs?"

Prosecutor: "For one thing, none of them want to go to trial. They don't want to drag things out. Most of their clients are sleaze-bags, anyway, and they're probably guilty, know their guilty. We just let them think we're going to play hard ball with 'em, and most of the time, it works. We make an offer, they accept it. Bam! That's it!"

Interviewer: "Do you have many PDs call your bluff?"

Prosecutor: "Sometimes. We sit on the case for a few weeks, let them steam a little . . . then we drop it. So what? We didn't lose anything by trying. It works both ways, you know."

Interviewer: "What do you mean, 'It works both ways' "?

Prosecutor: "Defense attorneys do it to us, bluff."

Interviewer: "Do you know when they're doing it?"

Prosecutor: "Some of the time. There are some attorneys in town that do a good job at it. If I've got a weak case, I'm not going to take the chance, I mean, I'm not going to lose something for nothing. We usually work something out."

Interviewer: "Plea bargain?"

Prosecutor: "Yeah. Some attorneys I know let me know up front what they have and what they think I have. They make *me* an offer. You know, it kind of shakes you up, they come to you and try to dictate *their* terms."

At this point, the interviewer learns something else about the prosecutor/defense attorney relation. This is, "who" initiates the plea bargain offer and terms. A follow-up to this might be:

Interviewer: "Is there any pattern to this? I mean, do you get many defense attorneys coming to you with offers?"

Prosecutor: "Not too often. I'd say about 20 to 30 percent of the time."

Interviewer: "Is there any, do you think that those situations, where offers are made by these attorneys . . . are these situations the kind where they might have strong cases . . . as opposed to you going to them with an offer?"

Prosecutor: "Definitely. If they come to me with an offer . . . now I'm not going to say this as a policy thing . . . but if they come to me with an offer, I'll seriously consider it. I want to know what . . . I mean, I don't know what they have in their favor, but they must have something, you know, for them to come to me with the offer. If it is a "no time" deal . . . they don't want their client to do time . . . maybe probation, something like that . . . I'll probably think they've got a strong defense. It makes me think twice about pushing them."

Interviewer: "Now, let me see if I understand this. Would you say that, well, if you initiate a plea bargain, you've got a weak case, but if they initiate a plea bargain, they've got a weak case?"

Prosecutor: "No. It depends on *when* they bring me an offer. If they hit me with a plea bargain offer early on, like within a week or so after their client's been booked . . . they might have a weak case. But then again, we don't get approached that often. Most of the time, we approach them. I'll say this, and that is, if *we* approach *them* early with a plea bargain, we probably have a weak case. Not always, you know. But the sooner we send out an offer, well, we're hoping for a quick decision."

Interviewer: "So you think it makes a difference, who makes the offer to begin with, the attorney or the prosecutor?"

Prosecutor: "Definitely. You have to know these guys to figure out whether . . . you have to figure they've either got a weak case, and they might be bluffing, but they also might have a strong case . . . I'll bet they have a strong case if they come out with an offer of probation for a cop [guilty plea] to a lesser charge."

Interviewer: "So, it's more likely that if you make a plea bargain proposal to some attorney, especially early in the case, you might not have a particularly strong case?"

Prosecutor: "Something like that. That doesn't mean that we have a weak case. It might mean that we don't have the kind of evidence we want to be sure about nailing 'em. We've got evidence, but a lot of it might be circumstantial. First, we believe their guy's guilty. We're not going to purposely set up some shmuck and bluff him into a cop. But we're not going to lay down, either, especially when we've got incriminating stuff against the guy . . . also, you've got to understand . . . the longer you wait, well, the evidence might get cold. Witnesses might forget, move away, die. Attorneys are smart, too . . . they might try to delay things . . . you know, delays almost never hurt their cases. We had one guy, a vehicular homicide case . . . a waiter at a local restaurant . . . he was crocked, driving home from work one night. Ran over two drunks fighting in the middle of the road near his apartment. Killed 'em both. They dragged that [case] out for a year and a half . . . never did come to trial . . . the girlfriend of the two guys he killed [who was watching the guys fighting when they were killed] moved out of state. We lost track of her, couldn't get her here if we wanted. Anyway, it turns out these two guys were always in and out of jail . . . long records. Trash. Whose going to get up tight about running over trash like that? We settled the damn thing by putting the guy on probation for three years . . . he plead guilty to reckless driving. Can you beat that? Anyway, there would have been a problem or two with vehicular homicide . . . for one thing, you know, he didn't leave work that night thinking, 'I'm going to go out and run over two drunks fighting in some road.' We had a real problem with intent. Also, there was contributory negligence. The street wasn't lit up, either . . . some problem with the street lights. The trial, if there had been one, would've been a mess. Turned out the kid's dad was a physician, plenty of money. Also got himself the best criminal attorney in town. We knew it'd be tough initially, but when he got that attorney . . . well, I wasn't going to push it."

This interview was one of the more interesting conducted. It is apparent that the prosecutor's answers often open up areas previously unexplored by the interviewer. The prosecutor's comment about "hiring the best criminal attorney in town" could have led to questions about defense attorney quality and whether those who can afford the best attorneys receive more lenient treatment than do indigent clients. Suffice it to say that the interview functions as an exploratory tool every bit as much as it functions as a descriptive instrument.

INTERVIEW CONSTRUCTION

Constructing interview items is comparable to constructing questionnaires (see Chapter 6). Investigators who plan to use interview schedules, more highly structured interviewing formats, include standardized items. Thus interviewers *must* ask fixed numbers of questions, usually with fixed responses. If items are open-ended, interviewers must either record a respondent's replies by hand or tape-record them in some fashion. More structured interviewing instruments may be coded more easily. Also, data from several different interviews may be compared directly.

Focused interviews, those that solicit information from subjects exposed to common stimuli or events, are structured to disclose specific details about one's experiences. The more investigators know about the target audience, the greater the precision that interviews may achieve. An excellent illustration of a structured, focused interview, with open-ended options and space for interviewer notes, is the survey instrument for the *National Crime Survey* (NCS), a portion of which is shown in Figure 7.1.

Figure 7.1 shows a portion of the survey instrument used by the U.S. Department of Justice in its *National Crime Survey*. This instrument contains several parts, including a basic screen questionnaire that collects information about respondent characteristics. On the basis of respondent replies, a Crime Incident Report is completed, which is a lengthy, 28-page questionnaire. Some sample items have been included in Figure 7.1, beginning with page 11 of the actual Crime Incident Report and continuing through page 15, which includes item 18b. Observe that space is provided for interviewer notes and for open-ended replies by respondents. Subsequently, these data are easily coded and transmitted to computer programs for various types of analyses. These analyses yield numerous tabular data, cross-tabulating social and individual characteristics (age, race, age, victim–offender relationship) with different types of crime (robbery, assault, burglary, rape).

CONDUCTING INTERVIEWS

Gaining Access to Organizations

Conducting interviews varies in formality depending on the nature of the research, the sophistication of the interviewers, and the scope of the research plan. If employees are to be interviewed at their work settings, permission must be obtained from superiors to interview these subjects. If researchers are connected with a well-known sponsoring agency, such as the Bureau of Justice Statistics, National Institutes for Mental Health, or National Opinion Research Center, they stand a much better chance of gaining access to prospective interviewees than do investigators who are conducting research independently.

Sometimes, it is desirable to preface requests to interview employees with a letter, on official letterhead, indicating the purposes of the interviews and research objectives. It is advantageous to point out how the research might benefit those interviewed or the organizations who employ them. A subsequent face-to-face meeting with higher-ups can clarify any misconceptions that management might have about permitting interviewers access to their employees. Even then, access to employees may be denied. Perhaps the organization can be persuaded to permit investigators to interview employees at their homes, on their own time. This tactic has the advantage of leading subjects to believe their organizations are sponsoring or condoning the interviews, and their cooperation with interviewers is enhanced.

If interviews are to be conducted on a door-to-door basis, there is no need to obtain permission beforehand. However, interviewers must spend considerable time visiting each home and explaining their research purposes. Again, such interviewing is enhanced to the extent that researchers have the sponsorship of

OMB No. 1121-0111: Approval Expires December 31, 1987

NOTICE — Your report to the Census Bureau is **confidential** by law (U.S. Code 42, Sections 3789g and 3735). All identifiable information will be used only by persons engaged in and for the purposes of the survey, and may not be disclosed or released to others for any purpose.

FORM **NCS-1 and NCS-2**
(4-10-86)

U.S. DEPARTMENT OF COMMERCE
BUREAU OF THE CENSUS

ACTING AS COLLECTING AGENT FOR THE
BUREAU OF JUSTICE STATISTICS
U.S. DEPARTMENT OF JUSTICE

NATIONAL CRIME SURVEY

NCS-1 BASIC SCREEN QUESTIONNAIRE

NCS-2 CRIME INCIDENT REPORT

NCS 1 and 2

PGM 2

Sample	Control number				HH No.
	PSU	Segment	CK.	Serial	
J ___					

ITEMS FILLED AT START OF INTERVIEW

1. Interviewer identification
Code Name
[201]

2. Unit Status
[202]
1 ☐ Unit in sample the previous enumeration period — *Fill 3*
2 ☐ Unit in sample first time this period — *SKIP to 4*

3. Household Status — *Mark first box that applies*
[203]
1 ☐ Same household <u>interviewed</u> the previous enumeration
2 ☐ Replacement household since the previous enumeration
3 ☐ Noninterview the previous enumeration
4 ☐ Other — *Specify* ⌐

4. Line number of household respondent
[204] _____ *Go to page 2*

TRANSCRIPTION ITEMS FROM CONTROL CARD

5. Special Place type code
[205]

6. Tenure
[206] 1 ☐ Owned or being bought   2 ☐ Rented for cash   3 ☐ No cash rent

7. Land Use
[207] 1 ☐ Urban   2 ☐ Rural

8. Farm Sales
[208] x ☐ Item blank   1 ☐ $1,000 or more   2 ☐ Less than $1,000

9. Type of living quarters
Housing unit
[209]
1 ☐ House, apartment, flat
2 ☐ HU in nontransient hotel, motel, etc.
3 ☐ HU permanent in transient hotel, motel, etc.
4 ☐ HU in rooming house
5 ☐ Mobile home or trailer with no permanent room added
6 ☐ Mobile home or trailer with one or more permanent rooms added
7 ☐ HU not specified above -- *Describe* ⌐

OTHER unit
8 ☐ Quarters not HU in rooming or boarding house
9 ☐ Unit not permanent in transient hotel, motel, etc.
10 ☐ Unoccupied site for mobile home, trailer, or tent
11 ☐ Student quarters in college dormitory
12 ☐ OTHER unit not specified above – *Describe* ⌐

Use of telephone
10a. Location of phone — *Mark first box that applies.*
[210]
1 ☐ Phone in unit . . . .
2 ☐ Phone in common area (hallway, etc.) . . . .
3 ☐ Phone in another unit (neighbor, friend, etc.) . .
4 ☐ Work/office phone . . . .
5 ☐ No phone — *SKIP to 11a*
} *Fill 10b*

10b. Is phone interview acceptable?
[211] 1 ☐ Yes   2 ☐ No   3 ☐ Refused to give number

TRANS. ITEMS FROM CONTROL CARD — Cont.

11a. Number of housing units in structure
[212]
1 ☐ 1-*SKIP to 12*   4 ☐ 4   7 ☐ Mobile home or trailer – *SKIP to 12*
2 ☐ 2   5 ☐ 5-9
3 ☐ 3   6 ☐ 10 +   8 ☐ Only OTHER units

11b. Direct outside access
[213]
1 ☐ Yes   3 ☐ Don't know
2 ☐ No   x ☐ Item blank

12. Family income
[214]
1 ☐ (a) Less than $5,000   8 ☐ (h) 20,000-24,999
2 ☐ (b) $5,000- 7,499   9 ☐ (i) 25,000-29,999
3 ☐ (c) 7,500- 9,999   10 ☐ (j) 30,000-34,999
4 ☐ (d) 10,000-12,499   11 ☐ (k) 35,000-39,999
5 ☐ (e) 12,500-14,999   12 ☐ (l) 40,000-49,999
6 ☐ (f) 15,000-17,499   13 ☐ (m) 50,000-74,999
7 ☐ (g) 17,500-19,999   14 ☐ (n) 75,000 and over

PGM 3   ITEMS FILLED AFTER INTERVIEW

13. Proxy information — *Fill for all proxy interviews*

a. Proxy interview obtained for Line No.	**b.** Proxy respondent		**c.** Reason *(Enter code)*
	Name	Line No.	
[301]	[302]		[303]
[304]	[305]		[306]
[307]	[308]		[309]
[310]	[311]		[312]

Codes for item 13c
1 – 12 – 13 years old and parent refused permission for self interview
2 – Physically/mentally unable to answer } *FILL INTER-COMM*
3 – TA and won't return before closeout }

14. Type Z noninterview

a. Interview not obtained for Line No.	**b.** Reason *(Enter code)*	**Codes for Item 14b**
[313]	[314]	1 – Never available . . .
[315]	[316]	2 – Refused . . . .
[317]	[318]	3 – Physically/mentally unable to answer — no proxy available } *FILL INTER-COMM*
[319]	[320]	4 – TA and no proxy available . . . .
		5 – Other. . . . .
		6 – Office use only

▶ *Complete 17 — 28 for each Line No. in 14a.*

15a. Household members 12 years of age and OVER
[321] _____ Total number

15b. Household members UNDER 12 years of age
[322] _____ Total number
0 ☐ None

16. Crime Incident Reports filled
[323] _____ Total number — *Fill BOUNDING INFORMATION*
0 ☐ None

Notes

Figure 7.1

PERSONAL CHARACTERISTICS

17. NAME (of household respondent)	18. Type of interview	19.₁ Line No.
Last	PGM 4	
	401	402
First	1 ☐ Per. — Self-respondent	
	2 ☐ Tel. — Self-respondent	
	3 ☐ Per. — Proxy } Fill 13 on cover page	
	4 ☐ Tel. — Proxy	
/////////	5 ☐ Noninterview – Fill 19–28 and 14 on cover page	Line No.

20. Relationship to reference person	21. Age last birthday	22a. Marital status THIS survey period	22b. Marital status LAST survey period	23. Sex	24. Armed Forces member	25. Education – highest grade	26. Education –complete that year?	27. Race	28. Hispanic origin
403	404	405	406	407	408	409	410	411	412
1 ☐ Reference person		1 ☐ Married	1 ☐ Married	1 ☐ M	1 ☐ Yes		1 ☐ Yes	1 ☐ White	1 ☐ Yes
2 ☐ Husband	Age	2 ☐ Widowed	2 ☐ Widowed	2 ☐ F	2 ☐ No	Grade	2 ☐ No	2 ☐ Black	2 ☐ No
3 ☐ Wife		3 ☐ Divorced	3 ☐ Divorced					3 ☐ Amer. Indian, Aleut, Eskimo	
4 ☐ Own child		4 ☐ Separated	4 ☐ Separated						
5 ☐ Parent		5 ☐ Never married	5 ☐ Never married					4 ☐ Asian, Pacific Islander	
6 ☐ Brother/Sister			6 ☐ Not inter- viewed last survey period					5 ☐ Other	
7 ☐ Other relative									
8 ☐ Non-relative									

PGM 5

29. Date of interview

501			
	Month	Day	Year

30. Before we get to the crime questions, I have some questions that are helpful in studying where and why crimes occur.

How long have you lived at this address?

Enter number of months OR number of years. If more than 11 months, enter number of years and leave months blank.

502 _____ Months (1–11) — **SKIP** to 31

OR

503 _____ Years (Round to nearest whole year) — *Fill Check Item A*

CHECK ITEM A How many years are entered in 30?

☐ 5 years or more — **SKIP** to Check Item B
☐ 1–5 years — **SKIP** to 32

31. How many people 12 years of age or older were living in your previous household, including you?

504 _____ Number of people 12 +

32. Altogether, how many times have you moved in the last 5 years, that is, since_____ , 19_____?
(Mo. of Int.) (5 yrs. ago)

505 _____ Number of times

CHECK ITEM B Is the respondent 16 years or older?

☐ Yes — Ask 33
☐ No — **SKIP** to 35a

33. Did you work at a job or business LAST WEEK? (Do not include volunteer work or work around the house)

INTERVIEWER — If farm or business operator in the household, ask about unpaid work.

506 1 ☐ Yes — **SKIP** to 35a
2 ☐ No

34a. Did you work at a job or business DURING THE LAST 6 MONTHS?

507 1 ☐ Yes — Ask 34b
2 ☐ No — **SKIP** to 35a

34b. Did that job/work last 2 consecutive weeks or more?

508 1 ☐ Yes
2 ☐ No

35a. Does anyone in this household operate a business from this address?

509 1 ☐ Yes — Ask 35b
2 ☐ No — **SKIP** to 36

35b. PERSONAL — Fill by observation.
TELEPHONE — Ask.

Is there a sign on the premises or some other indication to the general public that a business is operated from this address?

510 1 ☐ Yes
2 ☐ No

Notes

Figure 7.1 (*Continued*)

FORM NCS-1 (4-10-86)

36. Now I'd like to ask some questions about crime. They refer only to the last 6 months—

between _____ 1, 19___ and _____, 19___. During the last 6 months, did anyone break into or somehow illegally get into your (apartment/home), garage, or another building on your property?

☐ Yes — How many times?⤸ _____
☐ No

37. (Other than the incident(s) just mentioned) Did you find a door jimmied, a lock forced, or any other signs of an ATTEMPTED break in?

☐ Yes — How many times?⤸ _____
☐ No

38. Was anything at all stolen that is kept outside your home, or happened to be left out, such as a bicycle, a garden hose, or lawn furniture? (other than any incidents already mentioned)

☐ Yes — How many times?⤸ _____
☐ No

39. Did anyone take something belonging to you or to any member of this household, from a place where you or they were temporarily staying, such as a friend's or relative's home, a hotel or motel, or a vacation home?

☐ Yes — How many times?⤸ _____
☐ No

40. What was the TOTAL number of motor vehicles (cars, trucks, motorcycles, etc.) owned by you or any other member of this household during the last 6 months? Include those you no longer own.

[511]
0 ☐ None — SKIP to 43
1 ☐ 1
2 ☐ 2
3 ☐ 3
4 ☐ 4 or more

41. Did anyone steal, TRY to steal, or use (it/any of them) without permission?

☐ Yes — How many times?⤸ _____
☐ No

42. Did anyone steal, or TRY to steal parts attached to (it/any of them), such as a battery, hubcaps, tape-deck, etc.?

☐ Yes — How many times?⤸ _____
☐ No

43. The following questions refer only to things that happened to YOU during the last 6 months —

between _____ 1, 19___ and _____, 19___. Did you have your (pocket picked/ purse snatched)?

☐ Yes — How many times?⤸ _____
☐ No

44. Did anyone take something (else) directly from you by using force, such as by a stickup, mugging or threat?

☐ Yes — How many times?⤸ _____
☐ No

45. Did anyone TRY to rob you by using force or threatening to harm you? (other than any incidents already mentioned)

☐ Yes — How many times?⤸ _____
☐ No

46. Did anyone beat you up, attack you or hit you with something, such as a rock or bottle? (other than any incidents already mentioned)

☐ Yes — How many times?⤸ _____
☐ No

47. Were you knifed, shot at, or attacked with some other weapon by anyone at all? (other than any incidents already mentioned)

☐ Yes — How many times?⤸ _____
☐ No

48. Did anyone THREATEN to beat you up or THREATEN you with a knife, gun, or some other weapon, NOT including telephone threats? (other than any incidents already mentioned)

☐ Yes — How many times?⤸ _____
☐ No

49. Did anyone TRY to attack you in some other way? (other than any incidents already mentioned)

☐ Yes — How many times?⤸ _____
☐ No

50. During the last 6 months, did anyone steal things that belonged to you from inside ANY car or truck, such as packages or clothing?

☐ Yes — How many times?⤸ _____
☐ No

51. Was anything stolen from you while you were away from home, for instance at work, in a theater or restaurant, or while traveling?

☐ Yes — How many times?⤸ _____
☐ No

52. (Other than any incidents you've already mentioned) was anything (else) at all stolen from you during the last 6 months?

☐ Yes — How many times?⤸ _____
☐ No

53. Did you find any evidence that someone ATTEMPTED to steal something that belonged to you? (other than any incidents already mentioned)

☐ Yes — How many times?⤸ _____
☐ No

54. Did you call the police during the last 6 months to report something that happened to YOU which you thought was a crime? (Do not count any calls made to the police concerning the incidents you have just told me about.)

[512] ☐☐ ☐☐ ☐☐

☐ No — SKIP to 55
☐ Yes — What happened?⤸ _____

CHECK ITEM C Look at 54. Was HHLD member 12 + attacked or threatened, or was something stolen or an attempt made to steal something that belonged to him/her?

☐ Yes — How many times?⤸ _____
☐ No

55. Did anything happen to YOU during the last 6 months which you thought was a crime, but did NOT report to the police? (other than any incidents already mentioned)

[513] ☐☐ ☐☐

☐ No — SKIP to Check Item E
☐ Yes — What happened?⤸ _____

CHECK ITEM D Look at 55. Was HHLD member 12 + attacked or threatened, or was something stolen or an attempt made to steal something that belonged to him/her?

☐ Yes — How many times?⤸ _____
☐ No

CHECK ITEM E Who besides the respondent was present when screen questions were asked? (If telephone interview, mark box 1 only.)

[514]
1 ☐ Telephone interview — Go to Check Item F

Personal interview— Mark all that apply.
2 ☐ No one besides respondent present
3 ☐ Respondent's spouse
4 ☐ HHLD member(s) 12 +, not spouse
5 ☐ HHLD member(s) under 12
6 ☐ Nonhousehold member(s)
7 ☐ Someone was present — Can't say who
8 ☐ Don't know if someone else present

CHECK ITEM F If self-response interview, SKIP to Check Item G
Did the person for whom this interview was taken help the proxy respondent answer any screen questions?

[515]
1 ☐ Yes
2 ☐ No
3 ☐ Person for whom interview taken not present

CHECK ITEM G Do any of the screen questions contain any entries for "How many times?"

☐ Yes — Fill Crime Incident Reports.
☐ No — Interview next HHLD member. End interview if last respondent.

FORM NCS-1 (4-10-86)

Figure 7.1 (*Continued*)

Page 3

Conducting Interviews

NOTICE – Your report to the Census Bureau is **confidential** by law (U.S. Code 42, Sections 3789g and 3735). All identifiable information will be used only by persons engaged in and for the purposes of the survey, and may not be disclosed or released to others for any purpose.

Notes

FORM **NCS-2**
(4-10-86)

U.S. DEPARTMENT OF COMMERCE
BUREAU OF THE CENSUS

ACTING AS COLLECTING AGENT FOR THE
BUREAU OF JUSTICE STATISTICS
U.S. DEPARTMENT OF JUSTICE

CRIME INCIDENT REPORT

NATIONAL CRIME SURVEY

N C S

2

I N C I D E N T   R E P O R T

PGM 6

1a. LINE NUMBER ⟶ | 601 | _____ Line number

1b. SCREEN QUESTION NUMBER ⟶ | 602 | _____ Screen question number

1c. INCIDENT NUMBER ⟶ | 603 | _____ Incident number

CHECK ITEM A Has this person lived at this address for more than 6 months? (If not sure, refer to item 30, NCS-1.)
☐ Yes (Item 30 – more than 6 months) – **SKIP** to 2c
☐ No (Item 30 – 6 months or less) – Ask 2a

2a. You said that during the last 6 months –
(Refer to appropriate screen question for description of crime.)
Did (this/the first) incident happen while you were living here or before you moved to this address?
| 604 | 1 ☐ While living at this address
2 ☐ Before moving to this address

2b. In what month did (this/the first) incident happen?
(Show calendar if necessary. Encourage respondent to give exact month.)
| 605 | ☐☐ ☐☐ – **SKIP** to Check Item B
Month   Year

2c. You said that during the last 6 months –
(Refer to appropriate screen question for description of crime.)
In what month did (this/the first) incident happen?
(Show calendar if necessary. Encourage respondent to give exact month.)
| 605 | ☐☐ ☐☐
Month   Year

CHECK ITEM B Is this incident report for a series of crimes? (Note – Series must have 3 or more similar incidents which respondent can't recall separately.)
| 606 | 1 ☐ Yes – Ask 3a (Note – Reduce entry in screen question if necessary.)
2 ☐ No – **SKIP** to 4b

3a. Altogether, how many times did this happen during the last 6 months?
| 607 | _____ Number of incidents

3b. In what month or months did these incidents take place?
If more than one quarter involved, ASK ↗
How many in (name months)?
INTERVIEWER – Enter number for each quarter as appropriate. If all are out of scope, end incident report.

Number of incidents per quarter			
Jan., Feb., or March (Qtr. 1)	April, May, or June (Qtr. 2)	July, Aug., or Sept. (Qtr. 3)	Oct., Nov., or Dec. (Qtr. 4)
608 ____	609 ____	610 ____	611 ____

4a. The following questions refer only to the most recent incident.
Was it daylight or dark outside when the most recent incident happened?
| 612 | 1 ☐ Light – **SKIP** to 5
2 ☐ Dark – **SKIP** to 5
3 ☐ Dawn, almost light, dusk, twilight – **SKIP** to 5
4 ☐ Don't know – **SKIP** to 6a

4b. Was it daylight or dark outside when this incident happened?
| 612 | 1 ☐ Light – Ask 5
2 ☐ Dark – Ask 5
3 ☐ Dawn, almost light, dusk, twilight – Ask 5
4 ☐ Don't know – **SKIP** to 6a

5. About what time did (this/the most recent) incident happen?

During day
| 613 | 1 ☐ After 6 a.m. – 12 noon
2 ☐ After 12 noon – 6 p.m.
3 ☐ Don't know what time of day

At night
4 ☐ After 6 p.m. – 12 midnight
5 ☐ After 12 midnight – 6 a.m.
6 ☐ Don't know what time of night

Or
7 ☐ Don't know whether day or night

Figure 7.1 (*Continued*)

6a. *ASK OR VERIFY —*
Did this incident happen inside the limits of a city, town, village, etc.?

614   1 ☐ Outside U.S. — *SKIP* to 7
     2 ☐ Yes (inside limits) — Ask 6b
     3 ☐ No (outside limits) — *SKIP* to 6c

6b. **What is the name of that city/town/village?**

615   1 ☐ Same city/town/village as present residence — *SKIP* to 7
     2 ☐ Different city/town/village from present residence —
       Specify ⤵

       _____

6c. *ASK OR VERIFY —*
In what State and county did it occur?

616   ☐☐☐☐☐

     State _____ County _____

6d. *ASK OR VERIFY —*
Is this the same State and county as your PRESENT RESIDENCE?

617   1 ☐ Yes
     2 ☐ No

7. **Where did this incident take place?**
Mark (X) only one box.

AT OR IN RESPONDENT'S HOME OR LODGING

618   1 ☐ At or in own dwelling, or own attached garage
       (Always mark for break-in or attempted break-in of
       same) . . . .
     2 ☐ At or in detached buildings on own property, such
       as detached garage, storage shed, etc. *(Always*
       mark for break-in or attempted break-in of same) . .
     3 ☐ At or in vacation home/second home . . . .
     4 ☐ At or in hotel or motel room respondent was
       staying in . . . .
         } *SKIP to 9a*

NEAR OWN HOME

     5 ☐ Own yard, sidewalk, driveway, carport *(does not*
       include apartment yards) . . . .
     6 ☐ Apartment hall, storage area, laundry room *(does*
       not include apartment parking lot/garage) . . . .
     7 ☐ On street immediately adjacent to own home . . . .
         } *SKIP to 8b*

AT, IN, OR NEAR A FRIEND/RELATIVE/NEIGHBOR'S HOME

     8 ☐ At or in home or other building on their property . .
     9 ☐ Yard, sidewalk, driveway, carport . . . .
    10 ☐ Apartment hall, storage area, laundry room *(does*
       not include apartment parking lot/garage) . . . .
    11 ☐ On street immediately adjacent to their home . . . .
         } *SKIP to 8b*

COMMERCIAL PLACES

    12 ☐ Inside restaurant, bar, nightclub . . . .
    13 ☐ Inside other commercial building such as store,
       bank, gas station . . . .
    14 ☐ Inside office, factory, or warehouse . . . .
         } *Ask 8a*

PARKING LOTS/GARAGES

    15 ☐ Commercial parking lot/garage . . . .
    16 ☐ Noncommerical parking lot/garage . . . .
    17 ☐ Apartment/townhouse parking lot/garage . . . . . .
         } *Ask 8a*

SCHOOL

    18 ☐ Inside school building . . . .
    19 ☐ On school property (school parking area, play area,
       school bus, etc.) . . . .
         } *Ask 8a*

OPEN AREAS, ON STREET OR PUBLIC TRANSPORTATION

    20 ☐ In apartment yard, park, field, playground *(other*
       than school) . . . .
    21 ☐ On the street *(other than immediately adjacent to*
       own/friend/relative/neighbor's home) . . . .
    22 ☐ On public transportation or in station (bus, train,
       plane, airport, depot, etc.) . . . .
         } *SKIP to 8b*

OTHER

    23 ☐ Other — *Specify* ⤵

       _____
         } *Ask 8a*

Figure 7.1 *(Continued)*

FORM NCS-2 (4-10-86)

8a.	*ASK OR VERIFY —* **Did the incident happen in an area restricted to certain people or was it open to the public at the time?**	`619` 1 ☐ Open to the public 2 ☐ Restricted to certain people (or nobody had a right to be there) 3 ☐ Don't know 4 ☐ Other — *Specify*_____
8b.	*ASK OR VERIFY —* **Did it happen outdoors, indoors, or both?**	`620` 1 ☐ Indoors (inside a building or enclosed space) 2 ☐ Outdoors 3 ☐ Both
8c.	*ASK OR VERIFY —* **How far away from home did this happen?** *PROBE —* **Was it within a mile, 5 miles, 50 miles or more?** *Mark (X) first box that respondent is sure of.* *Then **SKIP** to Check Item C.*	`621` 1 ☐ At, in, or near the building containing the respondent's home/next door . . . 2 ☐ A mile or less . . . . 3 ☐ Five miles or less . . . . 4 ☐ Fifty miles or less . . . . 5 ☐ More than 50 miles . . . . 6 ☐ Don't know how far . . . . *}* **SKIP** to Check item C
9a.	**Did the offender(s) live (here/there) or have a right to be (here/there), for instance, as a guest or a repairperson?**	`622` 1 ☐ Yes — **SKIP** to Check Item C 2 ☐ No 3 ☐ Don't know
9b.	**Did the offender(s) actually get in or just TRY to get in the (house/apartment/building)?**	`623` 1 ☐ Actually got in . . . 2 ☐ Just tried to get in . 3 ☐ Don't know . . . . . 4 ☐ Didn't try to get in — **SKIP** to Check Item C *}* Ask 9c
9c.	**Was there any evidence, such as a broken lock or broken window, that the offender(s) (got in by force/TRIED to get in by force)?**	`624` 1 ☐ Yes — Ask 9d 2 ☐ No — **SKIP** to 9e
9d.	**What was the evidence? Anything else?** *Mark (X) all that apply. Then **SKIP** to Check Item C.*	**Window** `625` 1 ☐ Damage to window (include frame, glass broken/removed/cracked) . . . 2 ☐ Screen damaged/removed 3 ☐ Lock on window damaged/tampered with in some way . . . . 4 ☐ Other — *Specify* _____ **Door** 5 ☐ Damage to door (include frame, glass panes or door removed) . . . . . 6 ☐ Screen damaged/removed . . . . . . `626` 7 ☐ Lock or door handle damaged/tampered with in some way . . . . . . 8 ☐ Other — *Specify* _____ **Other** 9 ☐ Other than window or door – *Specify* _____ *}* **SKIP** to Check Item C
9e.	**How did the offender(s) (get in/TRY to get in)?** *Mark (X) only one box.*	`627` 1 ☐ Let in 2 ☐ Offender pushed his/her way in after door opened 3 ☐ Through OPEN DOOR or other opening 4 ☐ Through UNLOCKED door or window 5 ☐ Through LOCKED door or window — Had key 6 ☐ Through LOCKED door or window — Picked lock, used credit card, etc., other than key 7 ☐ Through LOCKED door or window — Don't know how 8 ☐ Don't know 9 ☐ Other — *Specify* _____
CHECK ITEM C	Was respondent or any other member of this household present when this incident occurred? If not sure, ASK — **Were you or any other member of this household present when this incident occurred?**	`628` 1 ☐ Yes — Fill Check Item D 2 ☐ No — **SKIP** to 27a, page 18
CHECK ITEM D	Which household members were present? If not sure, ask.	`629` 1 ☐ Respondent only — Ask 10 2 ☐ Respondent and other household member(s) — Ask 10 3 ☐ Only other HH member(s), not respondent — **SKIP** to 28, page 18

FORM NCS-2 (4-10-86)

Figure 7.1 *(Continued)*

10.	ASK OR VERIFY — **Did you personally see an offender?**	630	1 ☐ Yes 2 ☐ No
11a.	**Did the offender(s) have a weapon such as a gun or knife, or something to use as a weapon, such as a bottle or wrench?**	631	1 ☐ Yes — *Ask 11b* 2 ☐ No — *SKIP to 12a* 3 ☐ Don't know — *SKIP to 12a*
11b.	**What was the weapon? Anything else?** *Mark (X) all that apply.*	632 *	1 ☐ Hand gun (pistol, revolver, etc.) 2 ☐ Other gun (rifle, shotgun, etc.) 3 ☐ Knife 4 ☐ Other sharp object (scissors, ice pick, axe, etc.) 5 ☐ Blunt object (rock, club, blackjack, etc.) 6 ☐ Other — *Specify* ⤸
12a.	**Did the offender(s) hit you, knock you down or actually attack you in any way?**	633	1 ☐ Yes — *SKIP to 15a* 2 ☐ No
12b.	**Did the offender(s) threaten you with harm in any way?**	634	1 ☐ Yes — *SKIP to 14* 2 ☐ No
13.	**What actually happened? Anything else?** *Mark (X) all that apply. Then **SKIP** to 19a, page 16.*	635 *	1 ☐ Something taken without permission . . . . . . 2 ☐ Attempted or threatened to take something . . 3 ☐ Harassed, argument, abusive language . . . . . 4 ☐ Forcible entry or attempted forcible entry of house/apt. . . . . 5 ☐ Forcible entry or attempted forcible entry of car . . . . 6 ☐ Damaged or destroyed property . . . . 7 ☐ Attempted or threatened to damage or destroy property . . . . 8 ☐ Other — *Specify* ⤸ *SKIP to 19a, page 16*
14.	**How were you threatened? Any other way?** *Mark (X) all that apply. Then **SKIP** to 19a, page 16.*	636 * 637 *	1 ☐ Verbal threat of rape . . . . 2 ☐ Verbal threat to kill . . . . 3 ☐ Verbal threat of attack other than to kill or rape . . . . 4 ☐ Weapon present or threatened with weapon . 5 ☐ Shot at (but missed) . . . . 6 ☐ Attempted attack with knife/sharp weapon . . 7 ☐ Attempted attack with weapon other than gun/knife/sharp weapon . . . . 8 ☐ Object thrown at person . . . . 9 ☐ Followed or surrounded . . . . 0 ☐ Other — *Specify* ⤸ *SKIP to 19a, page 16*
15a.	**How did the offender(s) attack you? Any other way?** *Mark (X) all that apply.*	638 * 639 * 640 *	1 ☐ Raped 2 ☐ Tried to rape 3 ☐ Shot 4 ☐ Shot at (but missed) 5 ☐ Hit with gun held in hand 6 ☐ Stabbed/cut with knife/sharp weapon 7 ☐ Attempted attack with knife/sharp weapon 8 ☐ Hit by object (other than gun) held in hand 9 ☐ Hit by thrown object 10 ☐ Attempted attack with weapon other than gun/knife/sharp weapon 11 ☐ Hit, slapped, knocked down 12 ☐ Grabbed, held, tripped, jumped, pushed, etc. 13 ☐ Other — *Specify* ⤸
15b.	**Did the offender(s) THREATEN to hurt you before you were actually attacked?**	641	1 ☐ Yes 2 ☐ No 3 ☐ Other — *Specify* ⤸

Figure 7.1 (*Continued*)

FORM NCS-2 (4-10-86)

Conducting Interviews

16a. What were the injuries you suffered, if any? Anything else?

Mark (X) all that apply.

642
* 0 ☐ None — **SKIP** to 19a
  1 ☐ Raped
  2 ☐ Attempted rape
  3 ☐ Knife or stab wounds
  4 ☐ Gun shot, bullet wounds
  5 ☐ Broken bones or teeth knocked out
  6 ☐ Internal injuries
  7 ☐ Knocked unconscious
  8 ☐ Bruises, black eye, cuts, scratches, swelling, chipped teeth
  9 ☐ Other — *Specify* ⤵

_____

CHECK ITEM E Refer to 11b.
Did the offender have a weapon other than a gun or knife? (Is box 4—6 marked?)

☐ Yes — Ask 16b
☐ No — **SKIP** to 17a

16b. Were any of the injuries caused by a weapon (other than a gun or knife)?

643
1 ☐ Yes — Ask 16c
2 ☐ No — **SKIP** to 17a

16c. Which injuries?

Enter code(s) from 16a.

644
* ☐ Code   ☐ Code   ☐ Code

17a. Were you injured to the extent that you received any medical care, including self treatment?

645
1 ☐ Yes — Ask 17b
2 ☐ No — **SKIP** to 19a

17b. Where did you receive this care? Anywhere else?

Mark (X) all that apply.

646
* 1 ☐ At the scene
  2 ☐ At home/neighbor's/friend's
  3 ☐ Health unit at work, school, first aid station at a stadium, park, etc.
  4 ☐ Doctor's office/health clinic
  5 ☐ Emergency room at hospital/emergency clinic
  6 ☐ Hospital (other than emergency room)
  7 ☐ Other — *Specify* ⤵

_____

CHECK ITEM F Refer to 17b.
Is "Hospital" (box 6) marked?

☐ Yes — Ask 17c
☐ No — **SKIP** to 18a

17c. Did you stay overnight in the hospital?

647
1 ☐ Yes — Ask 17d
2 ☐ No — **SKIP** to 18a

17d. How many days did you stay (in the hospital)?

648
_____ Number of days

18a. At the time of the incident, were you covered by any medical insurance, or were you eligible for benefits from any other type of health benefits program, such as Medicaid, Veterans Administration, or Public Welfare?

649
1 ☐ Yes
2 ☐ No
3 ☐ Don't know

18b. What was the total amount of your medical expenses resulting from this incident (INCLUDING anything paid by insurance)? Include hospital and doctor bills, medicine, therapy, braces, and any other injury-related expenses.

INTERVIEWER — *Obtain an estimate, if necessary.*

650
$ _____ . 00 Total amount
0 ☐ No cost
x ☐ Don't know

Notes

Figure 7.1 *(Continued)*

well-known research agencies. Although it may be ideal to contact subjects in advance by telephone, many subjects to be interviewed do not have telephones or may have unlisted numbers. Thus investigators may have to take what they can get through door-to-door contacts. The best advice to interviewers is to expect the worst, but hope for the best, interviewing conditions. Poor weather, vicious dogs, and other distractions quickly transform one's ideal plans into reality, which often is far from optimum interviewing conditions.

Dressing Appropriately

It is important for interviewers to adapt to the settings they are investigating. If executives of a large organization are being interviewed, it would be advantageous for interviewers to dress rather formally, in attire similar to those being interviewed. However, if interviewers are conducting interviews in run-down neighborhoods, formal attire is inappropriate. Casual attire is less likely to arouse the suspicions of those interviewed. Detectives often wear coats and ties, and interviewees may suspect interviewers of being law enforcement personnel. This may cause prospective respondents to become uncooperative and refuse to answer an interviewer's questions.

Since much research is conducted by investigators working independently, it is unlikely that they will have an adequately trained interviewer pool. Only major research organizations have this degree of sophistication and training capability. Assuming, then, that most interviewers will enter the field relatively untrained, their "training" will often consist of learning some general guidelines, or do's and don'ts, associated with conducting interviews.

An interviewer's primary objective is to obtain the most accurate data from respondents. It is important, therefore, to put respondents at ease during the interview. Even the most unskilled interviewers become more at ease themselves when conducting interviews after they have participated in 10 or 20 of them. The more experienced the interviewer, the easier it becomes to create good interviewer–interviewee rapport and obtain desired information. Interviewers, therefore, should not over- or underdress in relation to those interviewed. Further, interviewers should remain interested in one's answers yet relatively neutral, depending on an interviewee's responses. For instance, if the interviewee discloses some sexual indiscretion, admits to a crime, or says his salary is $500,000 per year, the interviewer should refrain from smiling, laughing, frowning, or deeply inhaling suddenly. These are some of the "don'ts" of conducting interviews. It is also possible to get too close to those interviewed. The objectivity of the interview may be impaired when either the interviewer or interviewee becomes overly friendly. Offers of alcoholic beverages or soft drinks during the interview should be avoided.

Interviewing May Be Dangerous

There is no such thing as the "perfect interview." Even the most seasoned interviewers encounter unusual situations for which there are no ready-made solutions. For instance, this writer interviewed 33 women who worked in a large

Indiana bank. The interviews were conducted at the women's homes, on Saturdays and Sundays, when they would be available to answer questions. One woman in her late 40s was interviewed on a Sunday afternoon. The interviewer placed a tape recorder in the middle of the floor, started it, and then sat on a sofa in the woman's living room opposite the woman, who sat in a chair. A large German shepherd dog rested nearby.

The purpose of the interview was to solicit opinions about certain job changes occurring at the bank. The women's work roles were changing because of the introduction of new computer equipment. The researcher wanted to know how their individual work roles would be affected. As the interviewer asked the woman various questions about her job and her interpersonal relations with co-workers, a man burst through the front-porch screen door into her living room. He cursed at the woman, calling her a whore and other unflattering names. He turned to the interviewer, called him things that would make a sailor's ears burn, and began ranting and raving about the house, breaking lamps and ceramic objects. The interviewer discreetly packed up his notes and tape recorder and quickly left. The man burst from the house and jumped into his car. He followed the interviewer for miles, at high speed, throughout the city, until the interviewer finally lost him in a back alley. Later, the woman called the interviewer, apologized, and explained that the man was her ex-husband, who had been in the war. It seems that he was suffering from shellshock and had other mental problems. She had divorced him a few years back, but he continued to visit her occasionally. The interviewer had indeed picked the wrong day to conduct his interview.

Hazards are also encountered by those who conduct research in high-crime areas. More than one interviewer has been mugged or assaulted in the course of conducting research. Perhaps one reason that mailed questionnaires are so popular is that they avoid certain problems that may arise in face-to-face interview situations, especially in areas of high crime or under circumstances that may jeopardize their safety. For example, some interviewers who have interviewed delinquent gang members have reported receiving threats or obscene telephone calls from various gang members subsequent to those interviews. Physical damage to an interviewer's property, such as an automobile, might occur if interviewees suspect that the information they provide might be used against them in some way.

ADVANTAGES AND DISADVANTAGES OF INTERVIEWS IN CRIMINAL JUSTICE RESEARCH

The major advantages of interviews are:

1. They enable investigators to obtain desired information more quickly than with data-gathering methods such as mailed questionnaires.
2. They permit investigators to be sure that respondents understand questions and interpret them properly.

3. They allow greater flexibility in the questioning process.

4. They permit much more control over the context within which questions are asked and answers given.

5. Information is more readily checked for its validity on the basis of nonverbal cues from respondents.

It is clear that other forms of data collection, such as observation and questionnaire administration, share certain of these advantages. However, none of these offers such a unique combination of advantages as interviews. But interviewing is not without flaws. Several disadvantages of interviewing are as follows:

1. Whenever persons are asked questions in a face-to-face situation, any anonymity of response is lost. It is generally believed that anonymity heightens one's objectivity in responses given, such as is the case with self-administered questionnaires mailed to strangers. But interviews are direct. If some of the questions pertain to intimate details of persons' lives, there is the possibility that they will not disclose some of this information to interviewers. Or if any information is disclosed, it may not be true. One of the more frequent contaminators that interferes with accurate information about people is social desirability. Social desirability is giving false but favorable information about yourself either to the interviewer or on paper in a self-administered questionnaire situation. Thus a respondent may be prejudiced toward a minority, but if the respondent is asked whether he is prejudiced, he might say "no" simply because it is undesirable to say "yes." Therefore, respondents may say what they think the interviewer wants to hear.

2. Interviewers may become tired as they conduct several interviews during the day. Their minds may wander or they might be distracted by environmental factors. Therefore, their own reliability in recording responses accurately may not be consistent from one interview to the next.

3. If unstructured interviews are used, there is the real possibility that inter-interviewer reliability may be poor. This is because each interviewer will give different priorities to or show greater interest in certain topics compared with others. This makes it difficult to compare interview results from different interviewers.

4. Interviews may take different amounts of time to complete. Each respondent may prolong the interview by becoming enmeshed in certain questions or by unnecessary elaboration on particular topics. It takes considerable tact on the part of interviewers to terminate one's responses without appearing rude or disinterested.

5. If interviewers tape-record their interviews, transcribing these recordings takes time. If they make notes about one's responses, they may distract respondents with their note pads and pens.

SUMMARY

Interviewing is perhaps the most direct way of gathering information about people and their opinions. Interviews are either unstructured or structured. Unstructured interviews, closely connected with exploratory research, delve into subject matter about which the investigator knows very little. Responses are largely open-ended, and interviewers may probe at length, depending on the types of details respondents disclose about themselves and what they are thinking. Unstructured interviews utilize interview guides or loosely constructed sets of questions. It is not a requirement that all of these questions be asked of all respondents in any consistent manner. Situational factors strongly influence question selections. Structured interviews, on the other hand, utilize interview schedules. These devices are fixed-response questionnaires, although some open-ended items may be included.

The major functions of interviewing are description and exploration. Interviews are characterized by eliciting verbal replies to questions by interviewers. Information is recorded by interviewers themselves to enhance the accuracy of data gathering. Interviews are flexible. Structured interviewing permits comparability between interviews. Focused interviews are directed at obtaining specific types of information from respondents who have had shared unique experiences, such as disaster survivors, prison inmates, judges, or prosecutors. Constructing focused and structured interviews is comparable to questionnaire construction. Interviewers should dress appropriately, according to the target audiences interviewed. Gaining access to these audiences may be difficult, especially if those interviewed are employees of an organization. Interviews permit investigators to clarify questions for respondents, to control the environmental conditions within which the interview is conducted, and to probe or follow-up certain answers with more questions if spontaneous responses seem insightful. Anonymity is lost in interviewing, however, and social desirability emerges as a significant contaminating factor.

QUESTIONS FOR REVIEW

1. What is the focused interview? Give some examples of how focused interviews might be applied.
2. Differentiate between unstructured and structured interviews. Under what circumstances would investigators want to use each type of interview? What general kinds of research plans might be associated with these two types of interviews?
3. What is social desirability, and how might it emerge to influence respondent truthfulness during an interview?
4. What are some major functions of interviews?
5. What are some major disadvantages of interviewing?
6. What types of things can interviewers do to make the interviewing process go more smoothly for targeted respondents?

7. What are some characteristic features of interviews?

8. Differentiate between interview schedules and interview guides. Under what types of circumstances might each of these instruments be used?

9. What is a telephone interview? What are some purposes and advantages of telephone interviews? Can you anticipate any problems with telephone interviews? List several potential problems and discuss them briefly.

10. What are some potential hazards faced by interviewers, especially those who conduct research in high-crime neighborhoods?

8

Data Collection Strategies IV: Observational Techniques and the Use of Secondary Sources

KEY TERMS

Archival analysis
Content analysis
Experimental social research
External validity
Historical method
Internal validity

Key informant
Nonparticipant observation
Observational research
Participant observation
Secondary source analysis

INTRODUCTION

This chapter has a dual focus: the examination of two remaining data-collection techniques used by criminologists for research purposes. These are the techniques of observation and secondary source analysis. Rivaling interviewing as the most direct access to information that people possess is observation. In the broadest sense, researchers are constantly observing human conduct. Whether investigators are distributing questionnaires in the classroom or listening to remarks made by interviewees, they watch others and their expressions. They carefully scrutinize the circumstances under which their investigations are conducted. Sometimes,

174

these researchers learn more by watching people than by recording whatever they say.

In this chapter we examine observation as a data collection tool. For criminologists and other social scientists, observation is much more than merely sitting in some social setting watching others behave. Criminologists who use observation for data collection purposes usually are trained to look for certain kinds of things, to structure their observations of others with specific goals in mind. Therefore, scientific observation differs from casual observation in that it is focused and linked closely with one's research objectives. Like marks made by respondents on questionnaires, observers code and classify their observations to make sense out of whatever they have seen. Observers may be actual participants in the activities they are observing or they may be on the periphery of interaction as outsiders "looking in." Thus a distinction is made between participant and nonparticipant observation. We define each and examine their respective weaknesses and strengths as research tools.

Besides observing others, researchers may inspect various resource materials in libraries or elsewhere. Government publications, especially those produced by the National Institute of Justice Bureau of Justice Statistics, are quite useful to investigators as information sources. Any information compiled by others, including public or government-sponsored research publications or reports or analyses, as well as those made by private organizations, is lumped under the broad designation *secondary source analysis*. Usually, available public or private data have been collected for other purposes, not necessarily those of immediate interest to the investigator. These sources may include statistical information, archival data, case histories, letters, reports, diaries, life histories, newspaper and magazine articles, and any other available published material. Various types of secondary source materials are described, and certain weaknesses and strengths of secondary source analysis are discussed.

WHAT IS OBSERVATION?

To appreciate the distinctiveness of observation as a data-gathering tool, we must distinguish between observations of a casual nature or those that might be by-products of one's investigations and observations that are used exclusively and fundamentally for data-gathering purposes. It has often been said that those using observation are probably "seasoned," which means that they know pretty much what to expect in advance of their observations. This comes from having been there before, regardless of the types of studies being conducted. Most serious observers have some firsthand on-the-scenes contact with studies they are conducting.

If properly conducted, observation is characterized by the following:

1. Observation captures the natural social context where persons' behaviors occur.

2. Observation grasps significant events or occurrences that might influence the social interactions of participants.

3. Observation determines what makes up reality from the world views, the outlooks, and philosophies of those observed.

4. Observation identifies regularities and recurrences in social life by comparing and contrasting data obtained in one study with those obtained in studies of other natural settings.

These characteristics of observation set it apart from casual, sporadic, and spontaneous observations made by researchers as they conduct their investigations with other types of data-gathering tools. These characteristics also highlight the distinction between observational research and experimental social research. In experimental research, observations are made, but events have been manipulated deliberately to effect certain results. Observational research, in contrast, seeks to preserve the natural context within which observed behaviors occur.

MAJOR PURPOSES OF OBSERVATION

The major purposes of observation in criminological research are:

1. *To capture human conduct as it actually happens, to permit us to view the processual features of behavior.* Whenever persons are interviewed or respond to questionnaires, these are more-or-less static glimpses of how people think and feel about things. Most observers claim that the difference between what people say and do is great. Observation reflects a dimension of reality that is untapped by other data-gathering methods.

2. *To provide more graphic descriptions of social life than can be acquired in other ways.* Thus observation supplements the factual information disclosed from other data-gathering methods. For example, we may describe delinquent behavior in terms of its incidence or frequency. However, observational methods may reveal what delinquents actually do to get into trouble. How do juveniles go about vandalizing businesses and homes, taking drugs, or stealing automobiles? Observation enriches our descriptions of social life and enables us to illustrate behaviors more graphically. Toward the end of this chapter, triangulation is discussed. As we have seen in previous chapters, triangulation involves the application of two or more data-gathering tools (e.g., combining interview data with questionnaire and observational information) when investigating a particular subject area. Observation may be combined with other data-gathering strategies to provide us with a more complete picture of the behaviors of others.

3. *To learn, in an exploratory sense, those things that should receive more attention by researchers.* Often, observational findings suggest topics for future research that were unanticipated by investigators when their studies were commenced.

TYPES OF OBSERVATION

Two major types of observation are described here: (1) participant observation and (2) nonparticipant observation.

Participant Observation

viewed as an insider ←

Participant observation is the structured observation of social settings of which the observer is a part. This is a popular form of observation, since researchers may find it convenient to describe settings wherein they work or the groups in which they have membership. One of the best illustrations of participant observation is some research by James Marquart (1986a,b).

Marquart participated in a project designed to evaluate correctional officer training, supervision, and turnover in the Texas prison system (1986a:16). While working on his doctorate in sociology in 1979, Marquart met with officials connected with the Texas Department of Corrections (TDOC) and explained his interests. The TDOC had recently been involved in highly publicized litigation involving allegations of brutality against inmates. One of Marquart's study objectives was to observe actual officer–inmate interactions to determine whether these allegations were true. Also, he wished to describe the "building tender system" or the pattern in many prisons of using more dominant/aggressive inmates to control other inmates.

Webb's Monara Penit. Observ.

Marquart became a "prison guard" in Eastham Unit (a pseudonym), a maximum-security facility housing 3200 prisoners over age 25 who had been incarcerated three or more times (1986b:16). (The choice of the term "guard" is Marquart's, and it was used by different officers in the prison to describe themselves. However, in the late 1980s, the American Correctional Association and American Jail Association independently endorsed proposals to reject "guard" terminology in favor of "correctional officer." It is believed by these and other related organizations that "correctional officer" conveys a degree of professionalism that "guard" lacks. Furthermore, "correctional officer" seems to imply some degree of training and greater responsibility over inmates than "guard," which some critics regard as "passive monitoring of inmate behavior." At the time Marquart's research was conducted, however, "guard" was a commonly used term for the activities and duties Marquart and his other work associates performed.)

Although Marquart acknowledged some difficulty being accepted by the prisoners and other prison guards, he was eventually able to build rapport and acquire both guard and inmate trust (1986b:22). An example of one of his guard experiences describes the enriching detail that can only come from participant observation. In this case, the use of force by other guards was obviously excessive, but both prisoners and guards alike seemed to accept its occurrence. One of Marquart's guard associates recalled the following:

> I was sitting at the Searcher's desk and Rick (convict) and I were talking and here comes Joe (convict) from 8-block. Joe thinks he knows kung-fu, hell he got his ass beat about four months ago. He comes down the hall and he had on a tank top, his pants were tied up with a shoelace, gym shoes on, and he had all his property in a

sack. As he neared us, Rick said, "Well, Joe's fixing to go crazy again today." He came up to us and Rick asked him what was going on and Joe said they (staff) were fucking with him by not letting him have a recreation card. I told him, "Well, take your stuff and go over there to the Major's office," and there he went. Officer A went over and stood in front of Joe, so did Officer B who was beside Joe, Officer C was in back of A, and two convicts stood next to Officer A.

Inmate James, an inmate who we "tuned up" in the hospital several days before, stood about ten feet away. All of a sudden Joe took a swing at Officer A. A and B tackled Joe. I ran over there and grabbed Joe's left leg while a convict had his right leg and we began kicking his legs and genitals. Hell, I tried to break his leg. At the same time B was using his security keys, four large bronze keys, like a knife. The security keys have these points on them where they fit into the locks. Well, B was jamming these keys into Joe's head. Joe was bleeding all over the place. Then all of a sudden another brawl broke out right next to us. Inmate James threw a punch at Officer D as he came out of the Major's office to see what was going on. James saw Joe getting beat and he decided to help Joe out. I left Joe to help Officer D. By the time I got there (about two seconds), Officer D and about six convicts (building tenders) were beating the shit out of James. Officer D was beating James with a blackjack. Man, you could hear the crunch noise every time he hit him. At the same time, a convict was hitting him in the stomach and chest and face. These other inmates were kicking him and stomping him at the same time. It was a wild melee, just like being in war.

I got in there and grabbed James by the hair and Officer D began hitting him, no love taps. He was trying to beat his brains out and yelling, "you motherfucker, you think you're bad, you ain't bad, you motherfucker, son of a bitch, you hit me and I'll bust your fuckin' skull." I think we beat on him alone for ten minutes. I punched him in the face and head. Then Officer D yelled "Take him (James) to the hospital." Plus we punched and stomped him at the same time. At the hospital, Officer D began punching James in the face. I held his head so D could hit him. Then D worked James over again with a blackjack. We then stripped James and threw him on a bed. D yelled at James, "I'm going to kill you by the time you get off this unit." Then D began hitting him in the shins and genitals with a night stick. Finally, we stopped and let the medics take over. James had to leave via the ambulance. Joe required some stitches and was subsequently put in solitary.

This was clearly a dimension of prison life Marquart saw that most researchers with conventional research instruments might never see. Can you imagine a formal interview in the home of one of these officers: "Do you hit inmates with your blackjack?" "Do you use excessive force on any inmate to obtain his compliance with prison rules?" How many officers are going to admit to that? Few, if any.

Marquart's participation as a prison guard made him very much aware of some of the shortcomings of participant observation. As a guard, his relationships and rapport with inmates was changed accordingly. Because of his status, he would not become privy to certain types of inmate information. Interestingly, he might have acquired some "guilty knowledge" about drug use or other rule violations, but he did not report such infractions to authorities. He believed that this "guilty knowledge" created an ethical dilemma, although he attempted to walk the fine line of civility and legality. Additionally, much of the brutality he witnessed was difficult for him to accept emotionally. Also, since others knew that he was not "really" a guard, his views of what occurred may have been manipulated by other guards to a degree. However, Marquart believed that he had acquired sufficient credibility and was honest enough to solicit true reactions from those with whom he worked.

Nonparticipant and Unobtrusive Observation

The other type of observation investigators might conduct is nonparticipant observation. *Nonparticipant observation* is structured observation of others with or without their knowledge and without actually participating in the behaviors and activities being observed. In this situation, researchers conduct observations of various social settings from the sidelines. Their observations of others may or may not be known to those being observed.

For example, Humphreys (1970) and his associates observed homosexual exchanges that occurred in the rest rooms of public parks. They secreted themselves in the rest rooms, where they had a vantage point to see possible homosexual interactions. They observed numerous occurrences of homosexual behavior, followed certain persons and obtained their automobile license numbers, and determined their identities and residence information. Later, some of those who had been seen committing homosexual acts were visited by researchers on some other pretext. Humphreys claimed that although this type of observation raised certain ethical questions, it nevertheless provided him with valuable data about attitudes concerning homosexuality from those he observed.

Many nonparticipant observers believe that the naturalness of the settings they observe yields more accurate information about social reality than what we might expect from contrived experiments in laboratory settings. Observing persons in their natural habitats is certainly not demanding on any investigation, and *field notes* may be taken to record one's observations. Field notes are simply written entries in a field diary to refresh one's memory about what has been observed. *Field research*, or any research conducted in the natural habitat of those observed, builds on whatever is observed and the interpretations we make of these observations.

As we have advanced technologically, it is now possible to record what is observed through video cameras. Such observations may be done secretly, so that those observed will be unaffected by the intrusion of cameras into their social interactions. Several different law enforcement agencies, such as the FBI, have used videotaping to record illegal activities. The effectiveness of sting operations has been enhanced through videotaping, as criminals are filmed in the act of committing various crimes. Criminologists have used videotaping for diverse purposes. For example, some criminologists have videotaped citizen reactions to vandalism. In one instance, an unattended automobile parked on the street was broken into by paid stooges of the researchers, and reactions of passersby to this breaking and entering were photographed. Several interesting observations were made about citizen apathy or noninvolvement in events that affect others. Certain theories about victimization and public response to being victimized can be recorded and tested.

ADVANTAGES AND DISADVANTAGES OF OBSERVATION
IN CRIMINOLOGICAL RESEARCH

Neither participant nor nonparticipant observation are physically demanding on investigators. Some amount of skill is required, however, in order to record whatever is observed accurately. Nonparticipant observers may choose their settings at will, as well as the times when their observations will be conducted. Thus there is great flexibility associated with this data collection method. Observed behaviors may be either anticipated or unanticipated. Unanticipated observations may form the basis for new research into previously unexplored areas. Observing what is anticipated may enhance theory verification. Observation is also a cheap method of acquiring data. It costs little or nothing to look at others.

An investigator's choice of participant or nonparticipant observation often depends on the nature of the research being conducted. If private clubs, gangs, prisons, or other "closed" organizations are to be studied, it is necessary to penetrate these settings either obtrusively or unobtrusively. James Marquart became a prison correctional officer temporarily in order to gather information about officer–inmate interactions. Frequently, researchers will go "underground" to infiltrate groups or organizations they plan to study. This may be the only way that such phenomena may be studied scientifically. On other occasions, researchers may have to solicit the help of others to become informants for them as group or organization members. Juvenile gangs may be studied, for instance, by enlisting the cooperation of one or more gang members to report on gang activities and member behaviors. The use of *key informants* is one method whereby researchers may obtain access to restricted organizations and acquire greater knowledge about them.

The researcher's gender may influence what is studied and how it is studied. For example, Jackie Wiseman (1970) was interested in studying skid row alcoholics. Wiseman had several choices. She could walk up and down skid row, make random observations, conduct random interviews with alcoholics and street people, and generally conduct conventional interviewing and nonparticipant observation. She could pretend to be an alcoholic and attempt to "blend in" with other skid row inhabitants as one of them. Or she could enlist the aid of one or more skid row people and use them as key informants. Wiseman's observations are insightful here, as she explains how she resolved this data-gathering problem:

> On Skid Row, observations were made both by myself in the company of a paid "guide," and by paid male observers. My observations were confined to those activities in which a woman can take part on the Row without causing undue comment—walking around during the day, sitting in bars, eating in cafeterias, cafes, and shopping in grocery stores.
>
> Four male observers walked the streets of Skid Row with the men at night, stood talking to them on the street, drank in taverns with them, and met them at the bars returning from jail. These observations were spread in time through one year.

Findings were further supplemented by published observations of the Skid Row area by other researchers.

On Skid Row, I passed as a woman friend of a presumed resident there, as a woman looking for a lost boyfriend, and as a woman who had returned to the area after some absence and was looking for a bartender friend. In Christian Missionary prayer meeting and in free soup lines, I merely joined the men and a few women recipients. At the various screening sessions held at stations on the loop, [police officers] were kind enough to allow me to sit in and pass as a secretary who was taking medical notes.

In the Jail and the State Mental Hospital, no attempt to pass was made for two different reasons: in an all-male world like the Jail, it would be virtually impossible; in a calmly coeducational and research-oriented environment like the State Hospital, it seemed unnecessary. The first night at the Hospital, when I was introduced to the men in one of the alcoholic wards, they gallantly included me in a late night party based on food raided from the kitchen. From then on they treated me as one of the family.

However, while there were a greater many scenes I could observe, it became apparent that as a woman, or as a researcher, access was denied to some areas of the loop. Especially acute problems were presented by the County Jail and the Christian Missionaries (in addition to Skid Row at night where a woman attracts attention no matter how innocuously she is dressed).

For these three areas, as well as a fourth (the courts) where time was at a premium, observers were hired. In jail, at the Christian Missionaries, and on Skid Row they were participant observers, unknown to their subjects as researchers. Recruiting observers for the Jail posed several problems. Obviously, I could not ask someone to commit a crime so as to be sentenced to the County Jail. On the other hand, there was a need for someone who could participate unnoticed in prisoner activities. The decision was to recruit within the Jail. Young men who were not in jail for alcoholism were selected. There were four observers in all. These men were not used simultaneously, but two were observing and recording for three weeks and then two others working for the same period of time approximately six months later— some time after the first two had been released. In this way, it was hoped that collusion between observers would be prevented (Wiseman, 1970:276–277).

Therefore, Wiseman effectively blended several different strategies—use of key informants, participant observation, the use of volunteers, and simple non-participant observation—to obtain her data. She was able to collect considerable data from her own observations and experiences as well as from those she paid to observe others.

Some of the limitations of observation as a data-gathering tool are that (1) the desired events to be observed may not occur; (2) certain actions of those observed may be wrongly interpreted by observers, since they are not directly involved with what is going on; (3) the observed behaviors may be atypical of the normal behaviors of those observed, given the time when the observations are conducted; and (4) it is impossible to ask those observed for explanations of their conduct, without disclosing one's identity as an observer. Two additional limitations are (5) the impact of the observer on the observed and (6) the impact of the observed on the observer.

IMPACT OF THE OBSERVER ON THE OBSERVED

A classic illustration of the impact of the observer on those being observed is the small-group experiment conducted in two rooms. One room, the experimental setting, contains a small group seated around a table. A one-way mirror is on one wall in the room, and it is known by those observed that one or more observers are viewing them from an observation booth or room on the other side of the mirror. Theoretically, those being observed eventually "forget" that others are watching them, and thus they behave more "normally." Critics of such experimentation indicate that those observed cannot possibly forget about the fact that they are being observed. Thus their actions are restrained or inhibited. They cannot act normally, since they are not in a normal setting, unhindered by observations made of them by others. A major criticism of such small-group research is that it is contrived and not indicative of real-world conditions. Experimenters counter by arguing that such settings are mostly ideal, since they are not cluttered with extraneous factors that might otherwise jeopardize the normal actions or behaviors of those observed. Both views have some validity.

An early study where observation was used, and where the influence of the observer on the observed was significant and eventually apparent, was the classic "Hawthorne studies." These were a series of studies conducted at the Hawthorne, Illinois plant of the Western Electric Company. This company manufactured telephone components. One experiment involved observations of workers who were wiring telephone equipment. Experimenters manipulated the number of rest pauses of these workers, the times when they took their lunch breaks, and even room temperature.

One experiment, known as the "illumination experiment", involved the use of a dimmer switch in the work area. Experimenters believed that worker productivity would increase if the lighting intensity in the room was raised. An observer sat in the room and watched workers perform their jobs. As the room was made brighter by raising the lighting intensity, worker productivity climbed. Experimenters argued accordingly that if the room lighting were decreased, productivity would drop also. Thus they dimmed the lights, although productivity continued to increase. Eventually, the room was lighted with the equivalent of moonlight, and worker productivity hit an all-time high. Later, workers disclosed in interviews that although they did not know the purpose of these experiments, they believed the company wanted them to produce as much as possible, even under conditions of moonlight. They believed that the entire company was watching them as an example. Thus they deliberately worked hardest when conditions of work were most adverse to them. This phenomenon became known as the "Hawthorne effect," and currently, such an effect is used to explain certain behaviors of those observed when they know they are being observed by researchers.

Another dimension of the impact of observers on the observed occurs whenever observers are actual participants in the social events observed. If observers are a part of the social situation they are observing, they may be "too close to" the situation to retain their objectivity about it. Further, their own input into what is going on may actually influence the behaviors of others in ways that detract from the naturalness of these settings. Therefore, participant observers may (1) develop friendships with certain group members they are observing, and these friendships, in turn, may bar them from access to information about others; or (2) observers may profess to believe various things about group ideas and goals, and these beliefs may alter the belief systems of those being observed.

IMPACT OF THE OBSERVED ON THE OBSERVER

Another belief is that if persons know they are being observed, they may behave according to whatever they think the observers expect. For example, if school teachers are being evaluated by their principals or department chairs, they may dress especially nice for these occasions. Further, they may prepare "canned lectures" or lessons that highlight their particular teaching skills. Thus observers develop impressions of these teachers that may or may not be accurate portrayals of their "average" teaching conduct. There is every reason to believe that if observers make their presence known to others, the validity of whatever is observed may be seriously questioned. This is a phenomenon similar to social desirability, where those observed behave in ways they believe are anticipated or expected by observers.

Investigators who use observation of any kind as a data-gathering tool should be sensitive to their own influence on those who are observed. Attempts should be made to inform readers about any influence their presence as observers may have had on reported findings. As we have seen, observation can be an excellent source of enriching detail to supplement otherwise drab statistical presentations and summaries of tabulated information from questionnaires. One general vulnerability of observation is that it often lacks well-established, coherent, methodological protocol for its implementation. The benefits of its use in criminological research are realized only to the extent that its users are skilled and aware of its potential as well as its limitations.

ANALYSIS OF SECONDARY SOURCES

It is possible to engage in research projects throughout one's career without having any direct contact with human subjects. Some investigators spend their entire professional careers studying secondary sources. *Secondary sources* are any information originally collected for purposes other than their present scientific one. For criminologists and criminal justice scholars, much use is made of publications generated by the U.S. Department of Justice Bureau of Justice Statistics. The

Uniform Crime Reports, published annually by the Federal Bureau of Investigation, is also tapped as a primary crime information source.

Since 1977, the National Archive of Criminal Justice Data has been operating at the Interuniversity Consortium for Political and Social Research in Ann Arbor, Michigan. This archival network makes available substantial information to analysts, policymakers, and researchers in all criminal justice fields. Data from the archive are made available to over 350 colleges and universities throughout the United States without charge. Private researchers are assessed modest fees to access this information for their own investigative purposes (National Archive of Criminal Justice Data, 1990:iii).

Major Features of Secondary Sources

Secondary source materials are characterized by the following:

1. *Secondary source materials are ready-made.* Any student may visit a local school or public library to discover a vast amount of ready-made data available for analysis of any kind.

2. *Secondary source materials have been collected independent of an investigator's research purposes.* Researchers seek out secondary sources that contain some or all of the information they might need to answer their research questions. Often, research projects are designed around available information from secondary sources. Thus one's research is tailored to fit existing data sets. This is different from formulating a research project in advance, not knowing whether data are available that can answer one's research questions.

3. *Secondary sources are not limited in time and space.* This means that investigators who use such sources did not have to be present when and where these data were gathered.

Types of Secondary Sources

There is practically no limit to the sorts of materials that can serve the purposes of scientific exploration. From the most private items, such as personal letters, diaries, logs, and appointment books, to the most systematically accumulated and distributed documents such as the publications of the U.S. Census Bureau, a bewildering array of information awaits investigators.

Secondary sources may be either public or private. Public data sources are most frequently national agencies and departments that publish and distribute information relative to their functions and goals. All types of data are compiled. Any public information source is directly accessible by researchers, and ordinarily, research costs associated with obtaining their data are low. Private sources include voluntary agencies or associations, bureaus, and societies. These organizations also publish and distribute data about their functions and goals, usually as technical reports or bulletins. Such information may or may not be distributed to all libraries. Often, researchers must do some detective work to determine whether certain types of information are available and where such data may be obtained.

CONTENT ANALYSIS

When investigators have targeted their research objectives, and if these objectives may be achieved in full or partially through the analysis of secondary sources, these researchers may engage in content analysis. *Content analysis* is the systematic qualitative and quantitative description of some form of communication. Thus the contents of communications of different kinds are examined for the purpose of discovering patterns and meanings. Three examples of content analysis drawn from the criminological literature are illustrated below.

Holmes and Taggart (1990) wished to compare the fields of criminology and criminal justice. They were interested in determining whether the two fields have experienced similar professional growth patterns as evidenced by the quality and sophistication of the major journals within each field. One indicator of the degree of professionalism of any academic discipline is the methodological sophistication of its publications.

These researchers focused on three major journals: *Criminology*, *Journal of Criminal Justice*, and *Justice Quarterly*. The journal *Criminology* is published by the American Society of Criminology, while the *Justice Quarterly* is published by the Academy of Criminal Justice Sciences. The *Journal of Criminal Justice* is an independent publication, publishing high-quality articles of broad criminological and criminal justice interest and distributed by the University of Michigan. These three journals enjoy considerable prestige in both the criminological and criminal justice academic communities.

Holmes and Taggart conducted a content analysis of all research articles in these journals for the period 1976–1988 with the exception of the *Justice Quarterly*, which originated in 1984. The articles in this journal were analyzed for the years 1984–1988. A total of 966 articles were examined. These investigators created 10 topical categories according to which all articles could be classified. Some of these categories included law enforcement and crime prevention, crime causation/social control, courts, corrections, statistics/methods, and discipline/profession. Also, seven variables were examined, including the article topic, methodological orientation, research design, data source, time orientation, and statistical techniques used.

They rank-ordered the three journals according to each of these criteria and drew various conclusions about comparative journal sophistication. Regarding topics addressed, for example, Holmes and Taggart found that *Criminology* focused primarily on crime causation/social control, juvenile delinquency, and the courts, while the *Justice Quarterly* contained articles that emphasized the courts, corrections, law enforcement, and crime causation/social control. Thus there were subtle differences in those articles receiving publication priority. *Criminology* contained articles that emphasized hypothesis testing to a greater degree than *Justice Quarterly*, and the *Justice Quarterly* seemed to promote more articles that were concerned with problem delineation. More descriptive research articles were found in the *Justice Quarterly* than in *Criminology*. An illustration of what these investigators found is shown in Table 8.1.

TABLE 8.1. DISTRIBUTION OF TOPICS APPEARING IN *CRIMINOLOGY, JOURNAL OF CRIMINAL JUSTICE,* AND *JUSTICE QUARTERLY* ARTICLES

Topic	Crim. Rank	Crim. %	JCJ Rank	JCJ %	JQ Rank	JQ %
Crime causation/social control	1	26.1	5.5	9.0	3	13.6
Juvenile delinquency	2	17.2	10	2.4	10	2.5
Courts	3	12.1	3	12.2	1	21.2
Other	4	9.4	8	8.3	5	10.2
Corrections	5	8.5	2	16.1	2	19.5
Law enforcement	6	8.0	1	19.0	4	11.9
Statistics/methods	7	6.2	7	8.5	8.5	4.2
Discipline/profession	8	5.3	4	9.2	7	5.1
Public opinion/relations	9	5.0	9	6.3	8.5	4.2
Policy/planning	10	2.3	5.5	9.0	6	7.6
	$N = 437$		$N = 411$		$N = 118$	

Source: Malcolm D. Holmes and William A. Taggart, "A Comparative Analysis of Research Methods in Criminology and Criminal Justice Journals," *Justice Quarterly*, 7:421–437 (1990).

An inspection of Table 8.1 enables us to determine the types of articles that are featured most among these journals. The predominance of certain subject matter suggests editorial priorities, which, in turn, are presumably influenced by the academic disciplines themselves.

Thus considerable research about the courts, corrections, and law enforcement is featured in *Justice Quarterly* articles, whereas predominant topics in *Criminology* pertain to crime causation, social control, and juvenile delinquency. Articles about juvenile delinquency are ranked tenth in the *Justice Quarterly* relative to their frequency. This is only one analysis of several that might be made from this and similar tables.

For instance, Holmes and Taggart were able to detect certain convergences over time, where articles in all these journals tended to exhibit similar statistical, theoretical, and methodological characteristics. Articles from these journals in earlier issues tended to be differentiated from one another more clearly, although recent journal issues were less distinct. These researchers concluded that although certain differences in journal content continue to exist, more recent journal articles exhibited growing use of correlational research designs, cross-sectional data, and multivariate research designs. Therefore, the contents of these journals, when analyzed over time, seem to reflect the relative age and development of these respective fields.

The second example, a study by Walker (1986), illustrates the potential of content analysis for discovering certain "hidden" messages or meanings contained in verbatim transcripts of legal proceedings. Walker conducted a sociolinguistic examination of the contextual features of court transcripts. She obtained responses from 27 judges, consisting of both trial court and appellate judges. Among other things, she asked judges to report their reading habits relative to trial transcripts. She wanted to know whether these judges believed it important to include actual witness speech characteristics in these written transcripts, such as pauses during testimony, "uh's," hesitations, poor grammar, false starts, stammers, laughing, crying, whispering, sighing, or shouting.

Apart from these judges' opinions about what should or should not be included in trial transcripts, many of the judges believed that the transcripts should be as accurate as possible. One judge said that "laughter and shouting are direct indications of [the deponent's] state of mind and may assist in proper meaning [being] given to statements—others may or may not go to state of mind or meaning— usually more to physical state" (Walker, 1986:421).

Walker discovered several curious inconsistencies among judges about their views concerning transcript completeness and accuracy. She says, "I found it curious, for example, that a total of 84 percent of the respondents considered the parenthetical [shouting] to be acceptable (i.e., objective), despite its close semantic connection to anger. Yet I cannot imagine any judge ever tolerating, nor any court reporter ever inserting the parenthetical [angrily] in a transcript. Equally curious was the finding reported . . . that allows the inference to be made that for some judges, at least, silent pauses are considered objective facts, while 'spoken' hesitations are not. Such an evaluation really stretches the definition of objectivity and leads inevitably to problems with interpretation, raising the question of who is competent to make the distinction between a fact and an interpretation" (Walker, 1986:423).

The third example is a study by Klofas and Weisheit (1987) of the historical evolution of the insanity plea in Illinois. To some extent, it involves *archival analysis*, since these investigators delved into historical records and court documents to discover patterns. It is also an example of how evidence disclosed by content analysis may be used as the basis for policy decision making by legislative bodies. Klofas and Weisheit were interested in tracing the transformation of "not guilty by reason of insanity" (NGRI) to the more current "guilty but mentally ill" (GBMI) statute, which was established in 1981 by the Illinois legislature.

These investigators examined the contents of court data from Cook County (Chicago) to determine and document the extent to which GBMI has gradually replaced NGRI. Besides charting the frequency of use of these statutes, these researchers also noted the type of disposition (e.g., plea bargaining, bench or jury trial). Their content analysis of case dispositions and the frequency of use of NGRI and GBMI led them to conclude that "GBMI cases are typically resolved differently from NGRI cases" (Klofas and Weisheit, 1987:43). Interestingly, they found that although the number of GBMI cases has increased over the years, a commensurate decrease in the number of NGRI cases has not been observed.

These investigators were able to show that by leaving the insanity defense virtually intact in Illinois and *adding* the GBMI statute, the legislature actually compounded rather than resolved the fundamental issues surrounding the insanity defense. Their research is important, in part, because it suggests misuse of the GBMI statute apart from its original application, and that GBMI "may be used to provide excuses for behavior rather than to hold offenders accountable" (Klofas and Weisheit, 1987:49). One implication is that the Illinois legislature, as well as the legislatures of states where similar statutes have been enacted, must face an important policy decision in future years as it attempts to further clarify the insanity issue. Thus a very important policy issue has been highlighted by using a fairly simple, inexpensive content analysis tool in analyzing insanity defense cases over a period of years.

When investigators such as Klofas and Weisheit examine documents over an extended period of time, there are natural occurrences or events that may intervene to frustrate their research efforts. For instance, a police officer in Long Beach, California, wanted to study gang formation patterns and membership over an extended period, from 1960 to 1990. He had access to all juvenile files, consisting of arrest reports and considerable personal and demographic information about juvenile arrestees. He wanted to compare these files over a sample of years. A secondary objective was that he wanted to see whether juvenile crime changed during this 30-year period. He designated specific years to study, using five-year intervals. However, when he inspected available files and records, he found that the forms for logging juvenile arrests had changed several times. Information provided on certain forms in 1960, for instance, was not provided in 1970, and so on. This irregularity made it difficult for him to code the information he wanted. Also, not all arresting officers were equally proficient in completing these arrest reports. He soon found that many juvenile arrest documents were poorly completed and unusable. This is one of the major hazards of using secondary source materials.

ADVANTAGES AND DISADVANTAGES OF SECONDARY SOURCES

The major advantages of analyzing secondary sources are:

1. There is considerable savings of time and money, since ready-made data are analyzed and are accessible to the public.

2. Information compiled often pertains to large aggregates of people and their characteristics. Thus generalizations to larger populations have greater legitimacy than those based on relatively small samples of elements.

3. Information from secondary sources may be triangulated with information obtained through interviews, observation, and questionnaires to yield more reliable data.

4. Researchers avoid potential ethical problems and harm to human subjects by studying documents rather than people directly.

The major disadvantages of secondary source analysis are:

1. Data have been collected for other purposes and may incidentally be related to the researcher's goals and interests. Specific questions that researchers would prefer to ask may not be included in available data.

2. There is no way that researchers can reconstruct missing data in available secondary sources. Nonresponse in secondary source materials is a "given," and the incompleteness of information may be an important limitation that can affect data reliability.

3. Researchers must often speculate about the meaning of phraseology in various documents, and they lack the opportunity of obtaining further clarification from respondents.

4. Researchers must devise codes to classify the contents of documents analyzed. If their analyses are conducted over time, it is possible that missing information may exist to frustrate their coding efforts.

In sum, the use of secondary sources in criminological research is widespread. The strengths of using secondary sources far outweigh any limitations or disadvantages. Secondary source materials are often used to supplement one's research efforts where alternative data collection procedures are used. Therefore, an additional, inexpensive mechanism exists for bolstering a study's internal and external validity. External validation is important because it pertains to a study's generalizability to other settings and elements. A close correspondence between what is generally known about a given topic as revealed by data in secondary source materials and the information disclosed by a given study attests to the study's generalizability. Internal validity reflects the study's quality and internal consistency. Thus information derived from questionnaires may be compared with various secondary source materials as a means of verifying its accuracy and dependability.

SUMMARY

Observation and the analysis of secondary sources are two relatively inexpensive data collection techniques employed by researchers to provide enriching detail to their investigations. Scientific observation is systematic and controlled. Criminologists who observe others engage in controlled or structured observation, where they seek to discover patterns of behavior and interaction. They may use participant observation, where they might actually be a part of the groups they observe. Also, they may use nonparticipant observation, where they are not directly involved in the social exchanges they observe. Their observations may or may not be known to those being observed.

Researchers who use observation must be sensitive to the fact that their presence, either as participants or as nonparticipants, may influence the actions or behaviors of those being observed. Also, those who are being observed may behave in ways which they believe are expected by their observers. Thus investigators must gauge the impact of the observer on the observed as well as the impact of the observed on observers.

The analysis of secondary sources is widespread throughout criminology and criminal justice. Available documents from the Bureau of Justice Statistics and other government agencies is exploited extensively by researchers. The accessibility of large amounts of data, together with the low cost of information retrieval, make the analysis of secondary sources an attractive investigative option for those investigators with limited research funds. But secondary sources have been collected for other purposes, and investigators must often adapt their own studies to conform to the limitations of secondary sources they analyze. Despite these flaws, secondary source materials provide much enriching information to supplement data derived from questionnaires, interviews, and other data collection strategies.

QUESTIONS FOR REVIEW

1. What is secondary source analysis? What are some examples of public secondary sources?
2. What is nonparticipant observation? What are some limitations of nonparticipant observation regarding the reliability of whatever is observed and its meaning? Explain.
3. What is participant observation? How can researchers who engage in participant observation "get too close to" the subjects being observed? What can be done to avoid this problem?
4. Who is a key informant? What are some purposes of key informants? What are some problems that can be anticipated from using key informants in research?
5. What is content analysis? How can content analysis be used to affect policy decision making? Give two examples.
6. What are some major problems associated with content analysis?
7. If you plan to use content analysis over a lengthy period such as five or ten years, what types of problems might occur to interfere with your coding of data? Explain.
8. In what sense is observation a source of enriching detail to supplement questionnaire information?
9. How does observation conducted by criminologists differ from everyday random observations by others?
10. In what ways are participant and nonparticipant observation structured? Explain.
11. What are some hazards of doing participant observation with criminals and street people?
12. What are the major limitations and strengths of secondary source analysis?

PART 3
Measurement and Data Presentation

We are now ready to consider several ways in which our variables can be defined and conceptualized so that we may use them for purposes of hypothesis testing. One of the most important phases of the research enterprise is measuring variables. We provide textbook definitions for variables whenever we use them in our theories. These are nominal definitions, and we give them meanings that embellish their importance in relation to other variables. However, these definitions are not particularly suited for use in hypothesis testing and various statistical applications. We must change or transform these variables into measurable quantities.

In Chapter 9 we define measurement and illustrate how variables are transformed into quantities that can be manipulated arithmetically. This process is known as operationalization, and it details how our nominal definitions can be "raised" to numerical quantities. An important feature of the measurement process is distinguishing between different levels of measurement, where the numbers assigned to the variables we use have different meanings depending on what the numbers represent. Several conventional scaling procedures are described, including Likert, Thurstone, and Guttman scaling, together with the semantic differential. Criminologists are interested in crime rates and trends, and various strategies for conceptualizing these phenomena are presented. Whenever variables are measured, several key measurement issues must be addressed. Several of these issues are identified and discussed.

In Chapter 10 we discuss two important features of measuring instruments: validity and reliability. Respectively, these terms refer to properties of measures that reflect their accuracy and dependability in social research. Several types of validation are identified and their operations described. Four different ways of measuring an instrument's reliability are also presented. In each case, illustrations from the criminological literature assist us in understanding how these procedures can enhance our measures in criminal justice research. Also, several important factors are discussed that influence a measure's validity and reliability. Several solutions are provided for minimizing any measurement problems that we may encounter in our investigative efforts.

In Chapter 11 we discuss various ways that collected data can be portrayed graphically so that investigators can illustrate what they have found. Such descriptive techniques include bar graphs, pie charts, frequency distributions, frequency polygons, histograms, and tabular presentation. We also discuss the criteria we use to decide how best to portray the data we have collected so that its meaning will be enhanced for others.

In Chapter 12 we explain how personal computers can be used in criminological research. Considerable technological changes have been made in both the hardware and software programs available to investigators in recent years. Currently, an abundant number of statistical analysis programs are available from which researchers may choose. Depending on the software chosen for statistical analyses, the operations investigators must learn are more or less simple. One of the most popular statistical packages currently marketed is the Statistical Package for the Social Sciences (SPSS). This tool enables investigators to do virtually anything they want with the data they have collected, including graphic displays and complex tabular presentations. Several illustrations are provided to show how such programs may be used.

In Chapter 13 we show the general relation between hypotheses and theories. Good theories generate numerous testable hypotheses. In turn, these hypotheses must be converted into forms that enable us to test them empirically. Several types of conventional hypothesis formats are described, including research, null, and statistical hypotheses. Various functions of hypotheses are listed and discussed. Hypotheses also differ in their complexity. Thus one additional feature of this chapter is the elaboration of different types of hypotheses to be used in conjunction with single-variable analyses, two-variable analyses, and k-variable analyses. Finally, interpretive guidelines are presented that assist us in evaluating the results of our hypothesis testing.

9

Measurement of Variables in Criminal Justice and Criminology

Not an Exam

KEY TERMS

Coefficient of reproducibility
Concepts
Constructs
Cornell technique
Epistemic correlate
Guttman scales
Intensity continuum
Item weights
Likert scaling
Method of equal-appearing intervals
Method of summated ratings
Multidimensional scales

Nominal definition
Nominal level of measurement
Operational definition
Operationalization
Reliability
Reproducible scales
Scalogram analysis
Semantic differential
Set response
Thurstone scaling
Unidimensionality
Validity

INTRODUCTION

One of the most important links in the research chain involves the measurement of variables. How do we know when probation officer stress levels and burnout are high or low? How do we know if prospective parolees will be dangerous to the community? How do we know how much peer-group pressure is exerted on juveniles to prompt them to commit delinquent acts? How do we know if sentencing disparities exist among judges and whether sentences imposed are harsh or lenient? How do we know whether crime is increasing or decreasing? These are measurement questions. Quite often, tests of our theories about behaviors and events depend on our ability to measure crucial variables.

In this chapter we define measurement and highlight its importance in the research process. Chapter objectives include (1) illustrating the relation of measurement to theory and the research process generally; (2) describing different levels of measurement and their relation to the data collection process; (3) highlighting some of the more important scaling procedures used for measuring criminological phenomena, including attitudes; and (4) illustrating several theoretical and substantive measurement issues in criminal justice research.

MEASUREMENT OF VARIABLES IN CRIMINOLOGY AND CRIMINAL JUSTICE

In Chapter 2 we examined variables in criminological research and different variable attributes. Variables are quantities that assume more than one value, and they may be discrete, continuous, dependent, or independent. All attitudinal phenomena are variables. Race, ethnicity, gender, political affiliation, religious affiliation, income, age, education, occupation/profession, and nationality are variables in the sense that they may assume different values. The persons we study have these and many other characteristics. Our attempts to describe persons and differentiate between them according to these and other characteristics involve measurement.

Some of the earlier definitions indicated that it is "the correlation with numbers of entities that are not numbers" (Cohen and Nagel, 1934) or "the assignment of numerals to objects, events, or persons, according to rules" (Stevens, 1951). A subsequent definition referred to measurement as "the procedures by which empirical observations are made in order to represent symbolically the phenomena and the conceptualizations that are to be explained" (DiRenzo, 1966).

Bailey (1987:60) has added to the previous definitions by stating that measurement is "the process of determining the value or level, either qualitative or quantitative, of a particular attribute for a particular unit of analysis." Bailey distinguishes between qualitative and quantitative measures by whether labels or names are applied to variables or whether numbers are applied to them. If labels or names are applied, such as eye or hair color, religion, political affiliation, or gender, he would describe these variables as qualitative. Descriptions of prison inmates, including "real man" or "punk," would also be qualitative. Age, income, years of education, and all attitudinal phenomena could be expressed in quantitative terms, and numerical values would be applied to them.

For our purposes, *measurement* is the assignment of numbers to social and psychological properties of individuals and groups according to rules, and correlating these numbers with these properties symbolically. Another way of viewing measurement is the process of using numerical expressions to differentiate between people and groups according to various properties they possess. These properties are largely behavioral and attitudinal characteristics that are amenable to measurement.

The primary functions of measurement are to:

1. Describe social and psychological phenomena empirically
2. Render data amenable to some kind of statistical manipulation or treatment
3. Assist in hypothesis testing and theory verification
4. Enable researchers to differentiate between people according to various properties they possess

Descriptions of Social and Psychological Phenomena

Exploratory and descriptive studies of criminological events depict both social settings and characteristics of persons in those settings. For example, jail overcrowding is sometimes used to explain the incidence of inmate suicides or unrest. Overcrowding is conceptualized in different ways, such as the amount of cell square footage available to inmates, the number of beds per cell, the number of inmates confined per cell, and the actual capacity of the jail facility in relation to its rated capacity. Different quantitative expressions of this phenomenon can be correlated with suicide rates, inmate anxiety, and the incidence of rioting. Describing the characteristics of burnout can help us acquire a better understanding of the effectiveness or ineffectiveness of police officers or others exposed to hazardous or life-threatening situations.

Rendering Data Amenable to Statistical Treatment

Another function of measurement is to bring various phenomena into a form that enables researchers to manipulate it statistically. To make sense out of data collected from different sources and respondents, it is often helpful to transform the data into numerical quantities. Once data have been cast into some kind of numerical form, we can apply various statistical tools and analyze the data more effectively.

Suppose that researchers inspect recidivism rates of probationers (i.e., their arrests or convictions for new crimes while on probation) in a given state. They note that in some cities, the recidivism rate among probationers is higher than in other cities. Believing that these different rates of recidivism among probationers might be attributable, in part, to differences in the ways these probationers are managed or supervised, these researchers place themselves in several probation offices for two weeks and observe what is going on around them. They observe interactions of probation officers and their clients, supervisory practices, and the general office setting. They probably take notes about what they observe. Further, they might ask questions of officers about different ways their jobs are performed or how they feel about their work. At the end of their observation, interviewing, and questionnaire administration, they will have compiled a good bit of information about the persons in the probation office. What can they do with these data they have collected? To make sense out of their observations of probation officer behaviors, they may find it helpful to classify their observations into different categories.

Perhaps one result of their investigation is the finding that in those cities with higher probationer recidivism rates, the caseloads of probation officers generally seem much higher than the caseloads of officers in cities with lower probationer recidivism rates. Probation officer caseloads are easily quantified. We can count the numbers of probationers that each officer is assigned. What about less obvious dimensions of the probation officer–probationer relation? What if there are certain probation offices with lower client caseloads but higher probationer recidivism?

Observations made by these researchers may lead them to conclude that in these particular offices, probation officers do not seem especially interested in probationer problems. Probation officers in these departments may relate to probationers in an impersonal fashion, whereas in other comparable departments, probation officers may seem to take more of a personal interest in their clients. If we are going to make sense out of these observations, we are going to have to translate "appears more impersonal or distant" or "seems to take more personal interest in probationers" into numerical quantities. We are going to have to measure these probation officer–client interactions in some way. Once we have measured these types of interactions, we can compare them with different office policies about how offenders ought to be supervised, or caseloads of officers, or size of office, or any other relevant variable. After these variables have been quantified in some way, it will then be possible to apply various statistical procedures to these data to enhance our understanding of what is going on and why.

Assisting in Hypothesis Testing and Theory Verification

An important function of measurement is to permit us to verify theories and test hypotheses derived from them. Perhaps investigators learn from their investigations of various probation offices that each is somewhat autonomous from the others, and that chief probation officers administer office procedures and policies according to their personal discretion. Researchers may suspect that the probation officer–client relation is influenced greatly by office policy. Perhaps certain offices are more rule-oriented and bureaucratic than other offices. Perhaps caseload assignments are quite different from one office to the next. These investigators may conjecture about the degree of formality in probation office operations and the relation of formality–informality to probation officer–client interactions. Certain organizational theories may be used to explain probation office behaviors and conduct. Measurement of the degree of formality–informality as well as the nature of probation officer–client interactions will permit researchers to test hypotheses about these variable interrelationships. Tests of hypotheses derived from theory are also tests of the theories from which those hypotheses were derived.

The nature of caseload assignments may have some explanatory value and account, in part, for probation officer–probationer interactions. In some offices, caseloads are determined by dividing the total number of probationers by the number of officers. This method gives each probation officer a caseload equivalent to other officers. But in another probation office, caseloads may be more specialized. Some probation officers may be assigned principally those probationers who have serious drug or alcohol dependencies. Other probation officers may be assigned violent offenders to supervise, including convicted rapists and robbers. Specialized caseload assignments such as these are often determined on the basis of a probation officer's skills and interests. Thus it may be that where caseloads are specialized and tailored to fit particular officer interests, the probation officer–client relationship may be more personalized. The officer takes greater interest in those clients supervised and relates better to their individual problems and needs. In more generalized caseload assignment situations, probation officers may have such diverse clientele that they cannot conceivably relate to all probationer problems and needs. These officers may feel frustrated and overworked. To insulate themselves from the complexities of these diverse relations, they may bureaucratize their behaviors and relate to their clients impersonally, on a "strictly business" basis.

Measurement permits us to evaluate these settings and the personnel within them. We can characterize office settings and caseload assignment policies according to various criteria and correlate these factors with other variables. In the general case, if a hypothesis concerns the relation between two variables, X and Y, and is of the form

"As X increases, Y increases,"

we must be able to conceptualize variables X and Y in such a way that this hypothesis can be tested. If variable X is *office formality* and variable Y is *probationer recidivism rates*, a hypothesis might be as follows:

"As the formality of probation office policy increases, recidivism rates among probationers will increase."

Both *formality or probation office policy* and *recidivism rates of probationers* will have to be measured. By the same token, if variable X is *nature of caseload assignments* and variable Y is *probationer recidivism rates*, we might develop the following hypothesis:

"Recidivism rates among probationers will be lower where specialized caseload assignments are made for probation officers compared with offices using generalized caseload assignments."

For both of these hypotheses, we can measure probationer recidivism by the proportion of probationers who are arrested for new crimes. If there are 100 probationers and 20 are arrested for new crimes, the recidivism rate (using this measure) is $20/100 = 0.20$. If there are 300 probationers and 90 of them are arrested for new crimes, the recidivism rate would be $90/300 = 0.30$, a higher rate of recidivism.

We have created categories for office formality/informality and for the nature of caseload assignments. In each, we have supplied hypothetical recidivism rates for aggregates of probationers. From the ways the data are arranged, it would seem that probation office formality is associated with higher recidivism rates of probationers, while informality is associated with lower probationer recidivism rates. Also, those offices making specialized caseload assignments seem to have less probationer recidivism associated with them compared with those offices making generalized caseload assignments. The tables we develop are relatively simple, but they illustrate how we might translate office characteristics into categorical expressions and contrast them with offender recidivism rates. Measurement would help us test our hypotheses about the influence of office environments on client recidivism.

	Office Procedures	
	Formal	Informal
Recidivism rate of probationers	.40	.30

or

	Nature of Caseload Assignment	
	Specialized	Generalized
Recidivism rate of probationers	.15	.30

Differentiating between People According to Properties They Possess

One of the primary functions of measurement is to allow us to make distinctions between people according to certain properties they possess. Suppose that we are looking at five large tables in a room. Each table is slightly different from the rest and of a different color. We might wish to know which table is longest, which is heaviest, which is widest, and which is tallest. One solution to our problem is to grasp a ruler as our measure of length, width, and height and compare the five tables. We can bring in scales and weigh each table as well. These two measuring instruments, the ruler and the scales, help us answer our questions about the different properties of length, width, height, and weight shared by these five tables.

However, what if we are looking at several people and wish to know whether they differ regarding their age, educational attainment, job satisfaction levels, morale, stress and burnout, job proficiency, and attitudes toward supervision. The ages and levels of educational attainment for these persons are not difficult to determine. We may have access to employee information that tells us their ages and amounts of formal education. Or, when asked, these persons may tell us their ages and amounts of education. The remaining variables of job satisfaction, morale, stress and burnout, job proficiency, and supervisory attitudes are more difficult to conceptualize. True, each of these persons may tell us how they feel about their work, whether they feel stressed or burned out, whether they have high or low morale, whether they are proficient at their work, and whether they approve of how they are supervised. What if they all say they like their jobs and have high morale? What if they all deny that they are stressed or burned out? What if they all say they are proficient in the performance of their work tasks? What if they all like their supervisor and approve of how they are supervised? Are we to assume that all of these persons surveyed are equal on each of these variables? While all of these persons may be equivalent to one another on each of these properties, social scientists generally assume that for any group, *there will be differences among individual members pertaining to their behavioral and attitudinal characteristics*. These differences may be either great or small, depending on the variables or characteristics examined.

Thus depending on how we choose to conceptualize job satisfaction, some of these persons will have higher levels of it compared with other persons. Variation in the level of morale will also be observed among these individuals. They will differ in their job performance, with some persons performing better or worse than others. We may even find that although all appear to like their supervisors and how they are supervised, some of these persons may not like these supervisors as strongly as the other persons. Typically, we will create measuring instruments for these different variables. These measures will likely consist of questions or statements, and these persons will differ in their agreements or disagreements with these statements. We will make inferences from their responses about whether they possess these characteristics or properties to high or low degrees. This is a basic task of measurement that will permit us to classify people differently and make distinctions between them on various dimensions.

OPERATIONALIZING VARIABLES

Nominal and Operational Definitions

The process whereby variables are brought into the empirical world where they can be manipulated or controlled is *operationalization*. The operational definition is the function of operationalization. Operational definitions of variables may be understood by comparing them with *nominal definitions*.

The explication of theories is heavily dependent on the extensive use of nominal definitions. Nominal definitions of terms are those definitions we might find in an ordinary desk dictionary. All attitudinal terms are defined by other terms that are considered synonymous with them. This establishes a circularity or merry-go-round of terms that is disturbing to many criminologists, since these terms are seldom defined in a uniform fashion. No consistent meaning is assigned to many of these terms, so that one, and only one, meaning can be measured by independent investigators. An attitudinal example is *anxiety*. Using the latest version of *Webster's New World Dictionary*, anxiety is defined as "the state of being uneasy, apprehensive, or worried about what may happen; misgiving; a thought or thing that causes this; an eager and often slightly worried desire." If we look up the word *misgiving*, we find that it means "a disturbed feeling of fear, doubt, apprehension." When we look up the word *apprehension*, we find that it means "foreboding, fear, dread." When we look up the word *fear*, we find that it means "to be uneasy, anxious, or doubtful, to expect with misgiving." And when we look up the word *uneasy*, we find that it means "disturbed by anxiety or apprehension." In other words, according to this dictionary, *anxiety is defined as anxiety*. Such circularities in nominal definitions of things are commonplace.

Nominal definitions of variables suffice at the outset for linking ideas with one another logically. For instance, "Bureaucratic settings are characterized by adherence to rules and impersonality. The greater the bureaucratic operations, the greater the impersonalization. Probationers often require personalized treatment in order to complete their probation sentences satisfactorily. Personalized treatment is less likely to occur in a highly bureaucratized probation office. The greater the bureaucracy of a probation office, the less individualized and personalized the treatment received by probationers from their probation officers. The less personalized the treatment received by probationers, the more likely they will re-offend or recidivate." All of this "theorizing" is done using nominal definitions of terms. Seemingly, we "know" what impersonal relations implies and what individualized treatment is. We can understand how probation office policies may inadvertently contribute to greater rates of probationer recidivism. But all of this theorizing is articulated through the use of nominal definitions of terms.

Theories are constructed largely of nominal definitions and logical abstract linkages between different concepts. Logical interrelationships between variables are outlined, largely through the use of nominal terms and how they are intrinsically associated with other nominal terms. However, to test our theories, we must bring our terms into the empirical realm. The term *empirical* means "amenable to our senses" in some respect. If we can see something, or smell it, or taste it, or hear it, it is said to be in the empirical realm. Bringing terms into the empirical realm generally involves the measurement process, or the assignment of numbers to varying degrees of personal and/or social properties. Transforming nominal definitions into an empirical form or rendering them as measurable quantities is to operationalize them. Thus *operational definitions are quantifications of nominal definitions*. Kerlinger (1965:34) defines an operational definition as "one that assigns meaning to a . . . variable by specifying the activities or "operations" necessary to measure the . . . variable."

If we wanted to devise an operational definition of anxiety, for example, we would come up with something like "anxiety is what an anxiety test measures." The anxiety test we might devise consists of agreement or disagreement with several statements that appear logically related to our nominal definition of anxiety. Certain responses are designated as "anxiety" responses, whereas other responses would be "nonanxiety" responses. For instance, Janet Taylor (1953) investigated anxiety and formulated an operational definition of it. Prior to creating this definition, however, she examined numerous psychoneurotic patients at a large state mental hospital. She reasoned that one of the best places to find anxious people would be a mental hospital. The patients she investigated had previously been diagnosed by psychiatrists as either psychotic or neurotic and suffering from considerable anxiety. Taylor observed these patients, their behaviors, and ailments. On the basis of her observations of large numbers of anxious persons and their behaviors, she created a manifest anxiety scale consisting of 50 statements with "true–false" responses. A few of the 50 items Taylor used to measure anxiety are shown below. "True" or "anxious" responses are indicated in parentheses following each item:

1. I am often sick to my stomach. (True)
2. I am about as nervous as other people. (False)
3. I blush as often as others. (False)
4. I have diarrhea once a month or more. (True)
5. When embarrassed, I often break out in a sweat, which is very annoying. (True)
6. Often my bowels don't move for several days at a time. (True)
7. At times I lose sleep over worry. (True)
8. I often dream about things I don't like to tell other people. (True)
9. My feelings are hurt easier than most other people. (True)

The idea behind this scale and others like it is that *the greater the number of anxious responses, the greater the degree of anxiety*. Taylor's anxiety scale ranged from "0" (no anxiety) to "50" (high anxiety). This score range was achieved by assigning 1 point to each "anxious" response, and assigning no points to a non-anxious response. When administered to samples of persons in different social contexts, most of their anxiety scores generally range from 14 or 15 to 35 or 40. Few persons ever have scores below 10 or above 40. Notice that the nine items above reflect different attitudes and behaviors. Psychological, social, and biological dimensions of anxiety are tapped by this measure. Irregular bowel or bladder functioning, loss of sleep, excessive worry, and greater sensitivity about one's thoughts and dreams seem to be closely correlated with anxiety. These characteristics are called *concomitants* of anxiety, primarily because they have been found to be closely correlated with it.

It should be noted that Taylor used psychoneurotic patients at a mental hospital exclusively for the purpose of identifying characteristics of anxiety and to devise her scale items. Later, she administered the scale to persons *outside* the hospital setting, in work environments and elsewhere. She found that anxiety could be used as an indicator of personal and social reactions to changes in one's work environment or family stability. The same principles that pertained to the development of Taylor's anxiety scale are also generalizable or applicable to constructing scales of burnout, stress, the nature of the probation officer–probationer relation, or any other attitudinal variable of interest to criminologists and criminal justice scholars.

The nominal definition–operational definition distinction is also understood by the distinction made between *concepts* and *constructs*.

Concepts

Concepts are terms in our language that have direct empirical referents. When we say the terms "book," "desk," or "blackboard," we can point to objects that these terms represent. Thus any book may be a direct empirical referent of the term *book*. We would say that the term *book* is a concept, since it has some distinctive object as its direct empirical referent.

Constructs

Constructs are terms in our language that do not have direct empirical referents. All attitudes are constructs, since we must rely on indirect evidence of their existence. When we say the word *anxiety*, we cannot point to some specific referent of it. However, we can point to an *anxiety scale* as the referent. The scale itself contains specific behaviors that are concomitants of the term. Occasionally, the term *epistemic correlate* has been used to characterize the components of operational definitions. Thus it is likely that underlying many attitudinal phenomena are numerous epistemic correlates. As an example, Taylor's manifest anxiety scale described above consisted of 50 epistemic correlates of anxiety.

The work of criminologists and criminal justice scholars involves the widespread investigation of constructs. Some variables, such as recidivism rate, age, gender, fractured family, or race/ethnicity, are more directly defined and amenable to measurement than other variables, such as anxiety, psychotic–aggressive personality, stress and burnout, political conservatism, offender dangerousness, reactive depression, extroversion, and acceptance of responsibility. These are just a few of the many constructs that have been gleaned from recent issues of *Criminal Justice Abstracts*, and they reflect the diversity of subject matter studied by social scientists.

Whereas most of the instruments that are devised to conceptualize these and other variables are of the paper–pencil variety and often administered in a questionnaire format, some attitudinal variables may be measured through other creative means. For example, Thompson, Dabbs, and Frady (1990) studied 17 adult male first-offenders who were exposed to a 90-day shock incarceration program. The program was modeled after a military boot camp, and offenders were examined over time regarding their stress levels and self-concepts pertaining to social status. These researchers found, for instance, that these offenders' stress levels were lowest and their perceptions of social status were highest at the time of their admission to the boot camp. However, stress for most program participants heightened during the first four weeks, and their social status perceptions decreased during the same period. Eventually, their stress levels dropped and social status perceptions increased.

These researchers were able to chart these changes by testing saliva samples and varying levels of testosterone concentrations. Levels of testosterone appeared to decrease in response to increased stress and loss of social status, coincidentally during the first four weeks of boot camp. Eventually, testosterone levels for most participants increased, varying positively with decreased stress and higher perceptions of social status. Although this particular means of tracking stress is not unique, it is imaginative and suggests alternative ways of evaluating attitudinal dimensions. Furthermore, precise levels of testosterone can be measured or gauged.

Summarizing briefly, we construct our theoretical schemes and use nominal definitions liberally as a way of logically relating attitudes and behaviors. When hypotheses are derived for empirical test, we must devise operational definitions for the terms used in our hypotheses. Operational definitions of terms are created by using epistemic correlates or observable characteristics that can be empirically determined. Although some of our terms used may be concepts, inasmuch as they have direct empirical referents, other terms we use must be conceptualized as constructs. Constructs involve the use of indirect indicators of phenomena of interest to us. Operationalization is the process of developing operational definitions from nominal ones. Operationalization is also described as establishing constructs for some of the less empirical terms used in our theories.

Some variables are more a part of our empirical world (concepts) than are other variables (constructs). Concepts and more elusive variables (constructs) are brought into the empirical world through quantification, where numbers are ultimately assigned. The fact that some of these variables are less tangible than others (e.g., attitudes, the psyche, stress), the numbers assigned to such intangible phenomena will vary in their meaning. Four different meanings have been assigned to numbers that represent social and psychological phenomena. These meanings are described as *levels of measurement* and are crucial to our data presentation, analysis, and interpretation.

LEVELS OF MEASUREMENT

Four levels of measurement have been distinguished: the *nominal, ordinal, interval,* and *ratio* levels. Some investigators have used other labels to describe these levels of measurement, including *classifiables* or *countables, rankables,* and *measurables* (Peatman, 1963). In one sense, numbers pretty much mean the same thing from one application to the next. Higher-level mathematics, for instance, utilizes numbers that have a consistent meaning, regardless of their application. In another sense, numbers mean different things, depending on what they are used to represent. When numbers are assigned to social and psychological variables, they take on different meanings depending on how the variable has been measured. If we assign a "1" to a male and a "2" to a female, for example, the "1's" and "2's" will have a different meaning compared with the "1's" and "2's" we use in our description of ages. We will not be able to average the "1's" and "2's" assigned to gender categories, for example, since these numbers are simply used to distinguish males and females in our sample from one another. However, numbers assigned various ages can be summed and averaged. Thus numbers are interpreted differently according to what they stand for in criminological research.

In this section, several popular levels of measurement are presented. This arrangement of levels moves from low to high, beginning with the nominal level, and ending with the ratio level. The importance of distinguishing between different levels of measurement is that researchers have a greater range of data analysis and statistical test options where higher measurement levels can be assumed to underlie the data they have obtained. The fewest analytical options are associated with the nominal level of measurement, whereas the greatest number of options would be associated with the ratio level of measurement. Each of these levels of measurement is described below.

Nominal Level of Measurement

The lowest level of measurement is the *nominal level*. This level involves the classification or categorization of variables into nominal *subclasses*. *Gender*, for instance, has two nominal subclasses: male and female. *Political affiliation* has several nominal subclasses, including Democrat, Republican, Independent, and Communist. Delinquency may be treated as a nominal-level variable, where different types of delinquent conduct can be distinguished. *Felony* and *misdemeanor* are two nominal subclasses on the *type of crime* variable. Different types of deviant behavior also may be placed into nominal subclasses. When numbers are assigned to these nominal subclasses, the numbers mean nothing more than to differentiate one subclass from another. Thus nominal-level measurement is highly qualitative and serves to distinguish between people according to discrete attributes.

Ordinal Level of Measurement

A higher level of measurement compared with the nominal level, the *ordinal level* of measurement not only allows researchers to distinguish between persons according to certain attributes, but the numbers assigned certain attributes are considered either higher or lower compared with one another. Socioeconomic status is generally considered measured according to the ordinal level of measurement. Supreme Court justices may be ranked higher than university professors or district attorneys or correctional officers. The numbers assigned these various professions or occupations permit researchers to say that a "1" is higher or lower than a "2," which may be higher or lower than a "3," and so on. Other variables that might be measured according to an ordinal scale might be police professionalism, correctional officer work satisfaction, prisonization, ego strength, and a force continuum. Most attitudinal variables are considered measurable according to ordinal scales.

It is important to recognize that the assignment of numbers to data measured according to an ordinal scale permits researchers to make "greater than" or "less than" distinctions between scores or values. We cannot determine actual distances between scores on a scale. Consider the following intensity continuum of police professionalism:

Low professionalism   High professionalism

```
———————/——/———————————————/——/————————————————————/———
     15   25                        26   30                              31
```

Points or units to the far left are toward the "low professionaliam" end of the continuum, whereas points or units toward the far right are toward the "high professionalism" end of the continuum. Therefore, some police officers are more professional than others. Some officers are less professional than others. However, we cannot say *how much more* professional or less professional these officers are from each other. Note that these points are not equidistant from one another. The scores of 15 and 25 are close together, while the scores of 25 and 26 are far apart. This is the nature of ordinal scales. Ordinarily, we can say that one score is higher or lower in relation to other scores, but we are not permitted to say "how much higher" or "how much lower" these scores are from other scores. In other words, the magnitude of differences between scores on an ordinal scale has little meaning other than to locate scores relative to others along a continuum. There is no standard distance between units along the horizontal axis of the ordinal continuum above.

This particular feature of ordinal scales limits the options available to researchers for data analysis and statistical applications. Some statistical procedures require that we can specify the magnitude of score differences for certain arithmetic operations, such as averaging, square root functions, summing, multiplying, and dividing. Thus averaging numbers derived from ordinal scales is not a legitimate arithmetic function. However, as we will see in later chapters, there are conventional applications of certain statistical measures that require a higher level of data than that obtained by ordinal scales. There are several reasons for these conventional misapplications of statistical procedures, and they will be discussed subsequently.

Interval Level of Measurement

Data measured according to the *interval level* of measurement are also assigned numbers. These numbers permit nominal differentiations between values. Further, these numbers permit determinations of "greater than" or "less than." Additionally, these numbers have equal spacing along an intensity continuum, and researchers may say that there are specified distances between units. In the study by Thompson, Dabbs, and Frady (1990), for example, levels of testosterone in saliva specimens provided by several boot-camp "shock probationers" would be measurable according to an interval scale. Thus if we had several boot camp participants' testosterone levels indicated by scores on a testosterone scale, we might see something like this:

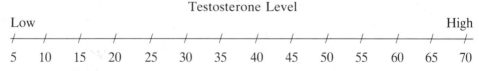

Testosterone Level

Low													High
5	10	15	20	25	30	35	40	45	50	55	60	65	70

The hypothetical testosterone level continuum above is gradated according to 5-point intervals. These intervals are considered equal distances from each other. The distance between 5 and 10, for example, would be identical to the distance between 50 and 55. The distance between 10 and 30 would be equal to the distance between 50 and 70. This equal spacing of interval scales is desirable, because it permits us to use statistical procedures and other data analysis techniques that involve arithmetic operations such as averaging and square rooting. Comparing our hypothetical police professionalism scale with this hypothetical testosterone-level scale, we would not be able to determine meaningful average police professionalism scores, whereas we would be able to compute meaningful average testosterone level values.

Statistical measures and techniques are often organized according to different levels of measurement. Therefore, we must consider how variables are measured before we decide which statistical procedures to apply. If a statistical procedure happened to require that our data be measured according to an interval scale, we would not be in a good position to apply this measure if the underlying levels of measurement achieved were either ordinal or nominal at best. Consider the following summary of permissible actions that we may take in Table 9.1, depending on the level of measurement we may assume with the data collected.

Table 9.1 says that analytical tools and statistical procedures may be used according to whether certain levels of measurement have been achieved. The characteristics of all lower levels of measurement are embodied within higher levels of measurement. Therefore, the interval level of measurement may also be treated as an ordinal scale, and it may be divided nominally. However, if we elect to divide interval scales according to some lower-level-of-measurement standard, we lose a certain amount of information. In the case of reducing an interval scale to a nominal one, we lose the equal spacing between units as well as the "greater than" or "less than" qualities it possesses. This is throwing away valuable data. Researchers may be faulted for "underutilizing" analytical techniques if they have the data to warrant applications of procedures suitable for higher measurement levels. A case of underutilization would be to take various age scores for some sample of elements and divide them into two categories, "old" and "young." By dichotomizing such values, we destroy the interval features of the scores. The statistical measures we might apply to such dichotomies may not be as sophisticated as measures that require the interval level of measurement for their application.

Alternatively, some researchers attempt to do too much with the data they have collected. If they apply a statistical technique or analytical procedures to data measured according to an ordinal scale, where those procedures require at least an interval scale, they are violating one assumption underlying those tech-

TABLE 9.1 LEVELS OF MEASUREMENT AND STATISTICAL APPLICATIONS

If the measurement level required by our statistical tests is:	we may apply:
1. Nominal	1. Nominal-level procedures
2. Ordinal	2. Either nominal- or ordinal-level procedures
3. Interval	3. Either nominal- or ordinal- or interval-level procedures
4. Ratio	4. Either nominal- or ordinal- or interval- or ratio-level procedures

niques or procedures. In the social sciences, this is a common occurrence and has come to be regarded as conventional. The frequent application of averages or means to data measured according to ordinal scales, such as attitudinal scores, is typical of such a violation. If we observe police professionalism scores of 10, 20, 25, 30, and 15, for example, their sum is 100. The average score would be 100 divided by the number of scores. Since there are five scores, the average score would be computed as follows: 100/5 = 20. The average professionalism score is 20. What does 20 mean? Not much. Again, the reason is that for averages to be computed, scale scores must be equal distances from one another along a continuum. We can see above that the hypothetical police professionalism continuum does not have equal spacing along the intensity continuum. Nevertheless, attitudinal scores are frequently averaged by researchers.

Therefore, two major pitfalls to be avoided by researchers are:

1. Underutilizing information collected by using lower-level-of-measurement tests and procedures with higher-level-of-measurement data
2. Overanalyzing data by applying tests requiring higher levels of measurement to data measured according to lower levels of measurement.

Ratio Level of Measurement

The *ratio level* of measurement is identical to the interval level of measurement, with one exception. The ratio level of measurement assumes an absolute zero on some ratio continuum. Income is a ratio-level variable, since income may be measured according to a scale having an absolute zero. Persons can have no money. Where an absolute zero is assumed, values may be proportionately related to other values. Therefore, $50 is to $100 as $10,000 is to $20,000. Interval scales lack an absolute zero, and therefore ratio statements are not permissible with such scales.

However, *no* procedure discussed in this book and in most other texts on statistics and methodology requires levels of measurement beyond the interval level. For instance, while income is actually measurable according to a ratio scale, it is treated as though it were interval. Since income has ratio-level properties, it also embraces properties of all other lower levels of measurement, including the interval, ordinal, and nominal levels. Table 9.1 illustrates this point.

TYPES OF SCALING PROCEDURES FOR MEASURING VARIABLES

The measurement of social and psychological variables may be accomplished by applying several popular methods devised by researchers. These include (1) Likert scaling, or the method of summated ratings; and (2) Thurstone scaling, or the method of equal-appearing intervals.

Likert Scales

Rensis Likert (pronounced "Lick-ert") (1932) was instrumental in devising the *method of summated ratings* as a means of distinguishing between persons according to differing degrees of ordinal-level characteristics. Subsequently labeled a *Likert scale*, this procedure is probably the most popular attitudinal scaling method used in criminology and other social sciences today.

Likert scales are easy to identify in the research literature. We may identify them according to the response patterns that accompany attitudinal items in questionnaires geared to measure ordinal-level attitudinal phenomena. Respondents are provided with a list of statements with which they agree or disagree to varying degrees of intensity. For example, the following items are typical Likert-style items,

where:

SA   = strongly agree
A   = agree
U,A = undecided, probably agree
U,D = undecided, probably disagree
D   = disagree
SD   = strongly disagree

Check (or select) the response that fits you best.

1. Firearms ownership in the United States should be limited to law enforcement officers and military personnel.
   (SA) (A) (U,A) (U,D) (D) (SD)
2. The right to bear arms is fundamental for all U.S. citizens.
   (SA) (A) (U,A) (U,D) (D) (SD)
3. When guns are outlawed, only outlaws will have guns.
   (SA) (A) (U,A) (U,D) (D) (SD)
4. There is a high relation between access to firearms and violent crime.
   (SA) (A) (U,A) (U,D) (D) (SD)
5. Firearms don't kill people; other people kill people.
   (SA) (A) (U,A) (U,D) (D) (SD)
6. Children should receive firearms instruction when they are very young.
   (SA) (A) (U,A) (U,D) (D) (SD)

These items obviously have something to do with firearms ownership and use in the United States. The categories of "strongly agree," "agree," "undecided, probably agree," "undecided, probably disagree," "disagree," and "strongly disagree" comprise a gradated pattern. Respondents choose the response that best fits them. These responses are *weighted* numerically. Depending on the choices one makes, the weights of selected responses are *summed* to yield a *raw score:* hence the term *summated ratings*.

An assumption made by researchers is that those persons who favor or disfavor gun control to varying degrees will select more-or-less intense responses for each question. Those strongly in favor of gun control and limiting firearms possession only to law enforcement officers and military personnel would tend to agree with items 1 and 4, and they would tend to disagree with the other items. Those favoring gun ownership and private use of firearms would tend to agree with items 2, 3, 5, and 6, and they would probably disagree with items 1 and 4. This scheme is not foolproof, however, since those favoring private ownership of firearms may not want small children to be exposed to them. Also, persons who agree that constitutional guarantees mandate private ownership and use of firearms may not agree that when guns are outlawed, only outlaws will have guns or that there is a strong relation between accessibility of firearms and violent crime.

A prevailing belief of researchers is that there is a fairly constant correspondence between the attitudes manifested by people and their behaviors. Therefore, it is often assumed that

$$\text{attitude } X \rightarrow \text{behavior } X'$$

where X is a particular attitude expressed and X' is the behavior that corresponds with that attitude. Thus, if some persons indicate strong prejudicial attitudes toward members of a minority group, it is assumed that they will probably discriminate or act differently toward those minorities. The attitude–action relationship is not consistent, however. Currently, considerable controversy exists about how accurately attitudinal measures actually forecast behaviors corresponding with those attitudes. This problem is examined at length later in this chapter as a measurement issue.

To illustrate the application of Likert scaling, we must begin with a nominal definition of some phenomenon. Suppose that we wish to measure police officer professionalism. We might define police officer professionalism nominally as the adoption of a set of attitudes and values by police officers, where those attitudes and values are consistent with a professional ideology (Crank, Regoli, Culbertson, and Poole, 1987:1). Professionalization has been conceptualized as the process of legitimation that an occupation goes through as it endeavors to improve its social status. Crank, Regoli, Culbertson, and Poole indicate that efforts toward conceptualizing police professionalism have focused on recruitment and training practices as well as management policies of police departments (1987:1).

It is significant to note that a clear, concise nominal definition of police professionalism does not exist in the paragraph above. This is not intended to be critical of Crank, Regoli, Culbertson, and Poole, since their extensive research efforts have been designed to devise such a concept and measure it. The fact is that many nominal definitions, including the one for police professionalism, are elusive, vague, and nonspecific. We might suspect as much, considering our earlier attempt to define *anxiety* using the *Webster's New World Dictionary* as our source. Further, this author researched ten separate articles where police professionalism was studied and was used in all article titles. No article contained a definition of police professionalism, not even a vague, elusive, or nonspecific one. It was as if everyone knew what it meant and thus that it did not need to be defined. Nevertheless, these articles discussed police professionalism at length, including factors associated with it, how it develops, and how it influences officer performance in the field.

However, from the statements about police professionalism provided by Crank, Regoli, Culbertson, and Poole, we can glean that police professionalism has something to do with rigorous selection and training procedures for police officers. Perhaps acquiring more education, or achieving high scores on various fitness and situational tests, is regarded by many as evidence of police professionalism.

In any case, once we have given a term a nominal definition, the next step is to give the term some "body" through the creation of an operational definition of it. Regoli, Crank, Culbertson, and Poole (1987) attempted this particular task, although they were interested primarily in exploring the relation between police professionalism and cynicism. They devised various statements believed to be indicative of police professionalism. Some of the statements they devised are shown below.

Police Professionalism Scale

1. I systematically read the professional journals (e.g., *Police Chief*).
2. I regularly attend professional meetings at the local level.
3. Although I would like to, I really don't read the police journals (e.g., *Police Chief*) too often.
4. Some other occupations are actually more important to society than mine is.
5. Other professions are actually more vital to society than mine.
6. The importance of being a police officer is sometimes overstressed.
7. There is really no way to judge fellow police officers' competence.
8. There is not much opportunity to judge how another police officer does his/her work.
9. My fellow police officers have a pretty good idea about each other's competence.

Thus a strict operational definition of police professionalism would be: "Police professionalism is what the police professionalism scale measures."

Accompanying each item might be the following responses and numerical weights:

Strongly agree	Agree	Undecided, probably agree	Undecided, probably disagree	Disagree	Strongly disagree
6	5	4	3	2	1

or

Strongly agree	Agree	Undecided, probably agree	Undecided, probably disagree	Disagree	Strongly disagree
1	2	3	4	5	6

These two response patterns are designed to accompany positively worded and negatively worded statements, such as "I like my job" or "I hate my job." Regarding the police professionalism scale above, items 1, 2, and 9 appear favorably worded, while the other items are somewhat negatively worded. If a police officer strongly agrees with statement 1, "I systematically read the professional journals," we might interpret this response as a sign of the officer's professionalism or commitment to the profession of policing. Also, if the police officer's response is strong disagreement to item 7, "There is really no way to judge fellow officers' competence," this response suggests that "professional" criteria exist whereby officers may be evaluated objectively. We might interpret agreements with items 3, 4, 5, 6, 7, and 8 as indicative of low professionalism, since the importance of the police officer role compared with other professions and occupations is played down, or perhaps objective criteria do not exist to evaluate this role.

The "weights" associated with each response reflect different intensities of agreement or disagreement with these statements. This particular weight arrangement is a six-point response pattern. The reversed weights shown in the example above are useful whenever we wish to interrupt the monotony of the same response pattern. Also, those who answer these statements may do so with little interest or enthusiasm. Sometimes, respondents do not read the statements carefully, and they rush through the questionnaire checking the first answers to all questions. A careful inspection of item weights associated with the responses they select may tell the researchers whether their responses are valid or whether they should be questioned. For instance, if someone says "strongly agree" to the statement "I love my job," and later that same person says "strongly agree" to the statement "I hate my job," this suggests a problem. Specifically, it suggests a *response set* or *set response*, where respondents rush through their questionnaires and check the first responses they encounter. They do this simply to "get it over with quickly." For all practical purposes, their responses to the questionnaire are worthless because they took no interest in completing it and giving truthful responses. This issue is addressed later in the section dealing with measurement issues.

Returning to our example of police professionalism and the scale items that comprise it, we have hypothetically assigned a six-point response pattern to the nine items above. This means that the most points one may receive per item answered is 6, and the least number of points is 1. If nine items comprise the scale of police professionalism, we may quickly calculate the range of raw scores that officers may receive when they respond to these scale items. We may multiply the largest weight, 6, by the number of items on the scale. This is (6)(9 items) = 54. Multiplying the number of scale items by the smallest weight, 1, will give us (1)(9 items) = 9. If we designate 6 to be indicative of a high degree of professionalism and 1 to be indicative of a low degree of professionalism, the range of responses for this particular set of items will be from 9 (low professionalism) to 54 (high professionalism).

For example, if 10 officers respond to these nine items, they might receive the following raw scores: 14, 22, 25, 29, 32, 33, 33, 40, 44, and 49. These are ordinal-level scores, since they were derived from a Likert scale. These raw scores may be grouped into different categories (low professionalism, 9 to 25; medium or moderate professionalism, 26 to 35; and high professionalism, 36 to 54). This categorization is mostly arbitrary, depending on the number of officers who respond and the overall raw scores they receive for this measure.

So far, what have we done to measure police professionalism?

1. We devised a nominal definition of police professionalism.
2. We created several items or statements that appeared to correlate highly with the nominal meaning of the term.
3. We devised a six-point response pattern for all items.
4. We assigned item weights to the different responses.
5. We administered the set of items to 10 police officers.
6. We summed each officer's weights for the nine items and determined their total scores.
7. We devised three intensity categories to portray police professionalism, according to the distribution of their raw scores.

There is nothing magical about any of this. The items that have been created were literally the products of the researchers' thoughts. They formulated items that they believed would closely parallel what they meant by police professionalism. But this does not necessarily mean that they derived the *best* items or the *only* items.

Numbers of items. This nine-item scale is only one of many scales that we might construct to measure police professionalism or any other attitudinal variables. We might create 35 statements or 100 statements. We might even use one statement to measure this and other phenomena. We might furnish officers with the following statement: "I consider myself a true police professional." The response might be a simple "yes" or "no." Of course, not many police officers are going to say that they are not professional. We will expand the number of items used to measure any phenomenon in order to create a wider range of response over which these officers may be distributed. This will enable us to obtain some meaningful variation on this variable and correlate the raw scores with scores on other variables. There is no limit to the number of items researchers may use whenever they create Likert scales. Of course, larger numbers of items may wear out respondents. They may approach a 50-page questionnaire with apathy or resistance, whereas they might feel more comfortable with a 10-page or shorter questionnaire.

Forms of response. The particular form of response for Likert scaling is not restricted to the agree–disagree variety. *Any* response pattern that can be gradated (very strong/very weak, increasing/decreasing, very positive/very negative, more/less) may be adapted to fit the Likert pattern. The most common response pattern is the agree–disagree format shown above, however.

There is little uniformity pertaining to the number of response categories, and there is no uniformity regarding the number of statements researchers may use to measure things. Decisions about the number of items and the particular response patterns to be used are made by the researcher. Consideration is given to the size of the group where the measure will be administered. If the researcher's intention is to administer the measure to thousands of people, more statements will be required to render a desirable degree of precision regarding the raw scores obtained. Perhaps more responses per item will be required as well.

For example, if we expand the number of items from 9 to 25, our range of response becomes $(1)(25) = 25$ (low) to $(6)(25) = 150$ (high). If we expand the number of items to 50, we have a range of from 50 to 300, using a six-point response pattern. Or we can devise a 10-point response pattern with 10 items and have a low score of 10 and a high score of 100 (1×10 and 10×10).

Sometimes the Likert format may be used to characterize attitudes of persons toward particular issues or programs. Kaci and Tarrant (1988:192) studied the attitudes of prosecuting attorneys and probation departments toward diversion programs for persons charged with spousal abuse in domestic violence cases. They were able to solicit opinions from district attorneys' offices in two California counties concerning various attitudes toward diversion programs. They devised categories such as those shown below.

Very high rating of diversion, highly effective

Good opinion of diversion, somewhat effective

Guarded opinion of diversion, possibly effective

Totally negative opinion of diversion, ineffective program

No opinion of diversion

The proportion or percentage of responses of district attorneys were charted for each of these categories. In the study by Kaci and Tarrant, they found that a majority of district attorneys rated diversion programs as highly effective or somewhat effective on the basis of these percentage distributions. This is a type of Likert pattern that appears to have some utility in portraying respondent opinions.

Meaning of raw scores derived from Likert scales. Provided that the items on a Likert scale are true indicators of the phenomenon to be measured (this is a validity question and is explored at length in Chapter 10), what do the raw scores mean? Raw scores by themselves mean relatively little. Raw attitudinal scores are of the greatest value whenever they are compared with one another. Thus persons who receive raw scores of 50 or lower on some attitudinal scale may be predicted to behave differently in some social situation from those who receive raw scores of greater than 50.

A hypothetical example illustrates how we might use scores from a Likert scale. Suppose that we administer our nine-item police professionalism scale to a random sample of 100 police officers of the Los Angeles Police Department, and that they receive raw scores ranging from 9 to 54. Further suppose that we determine that approximately 50 of these officers have scores of 32 or lower, and the other half of our sample has scores above 32. If we decide to see whether professionalism is associated with the rate of citizen complaints filed against these police officers, we might devise a table such as that shown in Table 9.2

Table 9.2 is a hypothetical cross-tabulation of police professionalism with citizen complaint filings against officers. According to these hypothetical figures, we might determine that officers with high professionalism scores tend to have low numbers of citizen complaints filed against them, whereas officers with low professionalism scores tend to have high numbers of citizen complaints filed against them. These findings might serve to strengthen our belief that we have measured police professionalism with these items. In short, the more professional police officers happen to be, the less likely they will engage in unprofessional behaviors that elicit citizen complaints. This is one way that these Likert-type scores can be used and interpreted.

The "cutting points" we used to determine "high professionalism," "low professionalism," "high citizen complaint filings," and "low citizen complaint filings" were not determined magically either. Usually, researchers determine these cutting points where the samples can be conveniently divided in logical ways. If our 100 police officers are distributed widely from scores of 9 to 54, we can use the point that divides them into halves as our cutting point. Perhaps that dividing line is the raw score of 32, where half of our officers are below this point and the other half of them are above this point.

Also, suppose that we tally the number of complaints for all officers and determine that an average of three complaints are filed against officers during the year. We might note that some officers have 10 complaints filed against them, while some officers have no complaints filed against them. Thus we might arbitrarily say that those officers who have three or more complaints filed against them will be in the "high complaint" group, while those receiving two or fewer complaints will be in the "low complaint" group. This distinction will enable us to cross-tabulate these results as shown in Table 9.2. Thus the five officers with high professionalism scores also have high numbers of complaints filed against them: three or more. The 45 officers with high professionalism scores have low numbers of complaints filed against them: two or less.

"Don't know" or "undecided" responses. The response scenarios provided in the examples above did not contain "don't know" or "undecided" response

TABLE 9.2 HYPOTHETICAL DISTRIBUTION OF CITIZEN COMPLAINTS FILED AGAINST POLICE OFFICERS MANIFESTING HIGH AND LOW AMOUNTS OF PROFESSIONALISM[a]

		Police professionalism		
		High (33+)	Low (32 or less)	Total
Citizen complaint filings	High (3+)	5	35	40
	Low (2 or less)	45	15	60
	Total	50	50	100

[a] Measured by nine-point professionalism scale, where 32 or lower means low professionalism, and 33 or higher means high professionalism.

options. The major concession to the "undecided" category was two "middle-of-the-road" categories designated as "undecided, but probably agree" and "undecided, but probably disagree." This arrangement was deliberate. The reason is as follows.

Typically, many Likert scales contain "undecided' or "don't know" categories. Thus we might see a response pattern like this:

Strongly agree	Agree	Undecided	Disagree	Strongly disagree
5	4	3	2	1

Notice that the "undecided" category above has been "weighted" with a "3." The same would be true of a "don't know" response. Some of the social sciences have reported a general trend in America toward noncommittal responses or middle-of-the-road opinions about things. Thus if persons are provided with a "don't know" or "undecided" option, they will probably take it. It is a "safe" response. Unfortunately, it has no weight or value. Persons who honestly "don't know" or are "undecided" are neither in agreement with an issue nor in disagreement with it. When these categories are assigned weights, the resulting point totals or raw scores lose a certain amount of their meaning.

Suppose that someone responds to a scale with 10 items, where the five-point response pattern shown above is used. A possible score range of 10 to 50 exists. It is possible for someone to obtain a score of 30 strictly on the basis of checking the "undecided" response category for each of the 10 scale items. This score is contrasted with others near it, where persons have received individual item weights of 4, 5, or 2. These other weights are meaningful, reflecting one's intensity of attitude toward something. Rather than run the risk of winding up with meaningless "30" scores in a scale such as this, the "undecided, but probably agree" and "undecided, but probably disagree" options are created. This gives persons an opportunity to say they are undecided, but it also gives them a chance to lean one way or another in terms of their attitudinal intensity.

This means forcing them to make a choice one way or another. Although many respondents apparently have no serious objections to these forced choices, a few respondents have been known to write "don't know" or "undecided" in capital letters in the margins of their questionnaires, or perhaps a string of profanity in response to these forced-choice scenarios. The presumption made by researchers who study attitudes, however, is that people generally have attitudes, one way or another, about various issues. The "undecided, probably agree/disagree" choices simply make it easier for them to make a middle-of-the-road decision with some degree of commitment. Further, it permits researchers to give meaningful weights to these middle categories.

Several exotic techniques have been proposed to deal with "don't know" or "undecided" responses, such as assigning these items the "average" weight otherwise assigned to the other items where persons actually express "agree" or "disagree" choices. This is tantamount to putting words in the respondents' mouths and creating artificial scores for them. Thus this alternative is discouraged. It is preferable to provide "forced-choice" responses and risk offending a few respondents while obtaining meaningful responses rather than to use "don't know" categories and assign meaningless weights to these choices.

Missing items. What do you do when respondents leave certain items blank and fail to answer them? First, do not put words in their mouths by creating artificial responses for them based on their responses to the completed items. There are different kinds of "missing item" situations. Did the respondent skip one item in a 10-page questionnaire? Did the respondent skip one page of a 10-page questionnaire? Did the respondent skip four pages of a 10-page questionnaire? Any respondent who skips one or more pages when completing a questionnaire is rushing through it and probably not taking it seriously. One page skipped may be accidental. Two or more pages skipped is apathy and carelessness.

The recommended solution when one page is skipped is to survey the contents of the page. If a portion of a scale is on the page, that scale should be dropped from the questionnaire. If several key questions are on the page, such as age, years of education, gender, and socioeconomic status, it might be a good idea to throw out the questionnaire completely. It is better not to have the additional questionnaire as a part of your collected data where strong evidence exists that the respondent did not take the study seriously. Skipped pages or numerous skipped items should tell you something. Dropping such questionnaires from your study makes your study better and more reliable anyway.

The recommended solution when one or two items are skipped is to determine if those items are a part of a scale. If they are part of a scale, drop the scale from the questionnaire. This type of omission frequently accounts for odd sample analyses in articles and reports. A researcher may indicate that 600 persons were surveyed and responded. But a table included in the report may show income averages for 590 persons. This probably means that 10 persons did not disclose their incomes to the investigator. The same thing may happen with other variables in other tables. Do not be disturbed when reading reports and different sample sizes are reported for different tabular analyses. Omissions of questions by respondents are common occurrences.

Strengths and advantages of Likert scales. Some of the major advantages of summated rating scales are:

1. *Likert scales are easy to construct and interpret.* Because researchers combine their professional experience with logic to derive items from an abstract theoretical universe of some trait, it is not too difficult to construct a questionnaire as a measure. Researchers are at liberty to word statements derived in any manner they choose, provided that they adhere to a logical standard of continuity between the trait being measured and the items used to measure it. Scoring Likert scales is easy, also. Further, statements can be worded negatively or positively, and numerical weights can be assigned to any common Likert response format. It is a simple matter to sum the responses to individual statements and derive a total score or raw score that may be compared with other scores from the same scale. The larger (or smaller) the score, the more (or less) the subject possesses the attribute being measured, according to the logic underlying this scaling procedure.

2. *Likert scaling is the most common scaling format used in criminology and criminal justice.* Likert summated rating measures are most frequently applied in social research. The ease of application and simplicity of interpretation are factors that make this scaling procedure especially attractive. The popularity of this measurement form is evidenced by its widespread conventional use in criminology and criminal justice.

3. *Likert scaling is flexible.* The flexibility of these scales is unattained by any other attitudinal scaling procedure yet devised. Researchers are at liberty to include in their measures as many or as few items as they choose. Because each item is presumed to count equally in the measure of some phenomenon, increasing the number of statements or responses to statements will increase the instrument's ability to disclose differences in the trait measured as group size increases.

4. *Summated rating scales lend themselves to ordinal-level measurement.* Numerous ordinal-level statistical procedures exist for assessing variations and patterns in social and psychological phenomena. Some researchers erroneously apply interval-level statistical measures to these data based on summated ratings. Certain mathematical operations are simply not permissible unless a particular measurement level has been attained. Averaging scores, for example, is most meaningful when data have been measured according to an interval scale. Since Likert scaling is ordinal-level measurement at best, averaging of derived scale scores is not recommended.

5. *Likert scales are similar to other forms of attitude measurement, such as Thurstone scaling or Guttman scaling.* Inspections of scores derived by other scaling procedures show that Likert scaling yields raw scores that are roughly equivalent with those obtained by alternative means.

Weaknesses of Likert scales. Weaknesses of Likert scales include the following:

1. *No consistent meaning can be attached to the raw scores derived by such measurement.* There is little that can be said about raw scores by themselves. Raw scores vary according to the number of statements devised and the extensiveness of response patterns used. This adds to the inconsistency of things as well. Summated rating measures are useful primarily when they permit comparisons to be made between individuals.

2. *It is assumed that each item in the measure has identical weight in relation to every other item. This is not necessarily a valid assumption.* Certain statements compared with other statements may have greater meaning or relevance to the trait being measured. Different persons may possess a given attitude to the same degree, although they may respond differently to common items on the measure. It is difficult, if not impossible, to ensure that each item counts the same as every other item.

3. *Persons receiving the same score on a measure do not necessarily possess the trait or attitude to the same degree.* This means that our measures are never as precise as they could be. Raw scores are crude estimates of people's location on intensity continuums.

4. *The validity of summated ratings is questionable.* Because the process of deducing items from an abstract universe of traits is a logical one, the possibility always exists that some items may be wrongly included in the measuring instrument at any given time. How do we know that we are measuring what we say we are measuring? The validity of our measures (discussed at length in Chapter 10) is generally determined by comparing score results with manifest behaviors of respondents in prediction situations. This is not an infallible process.

Thurstone Scales

A second type of measuring technique is *Thurstone scaling*. Another term for it is *equal-appearing interval scaling* (Thurstone and Chave, 1929). This technique probably rates second in overall social science usage to Likert scaling, although probably fewer than 10 percent of all researchers might be inclined to use it. Thurstone scaling differs from the Likert summated rating format by supplying each attitudinal statement with a specific scale value that stands for the intensity of the statement itself. Thus, instead of deriving a total score from accumulated item weights in the case of Likert scales, Thurstone scales would use intensity values associated with two or three items selected by respondents from a larger list of items. Consider the following five statements:

(10.5) **1.** Life imprisonment might be an acceptable punishment for child sexual abusers.

(2.1) **2.** Convicted child sexual abusers should be treated like any other convicted felons.

(3.4) **3.** Most child sexual abusers suffer from psychological problems and should be hospitalized rather than imprisoned.

(1.8) **4.** I would allow former convicted child sexual abusers to work as custodians in large apartment complexes with large numbers of children.

(8.3) **5.** Child sexual abuse is itself an aggravating factor in any prosecution for child sexual abuse.

The five statements above are hypothetical items that might be used to measure district attorneys' attitudes toward prosecuting child sexual abusers. Supposedly, these items are designed to reflect different intensities or degrees to which persons hold one view or another toward some idea, issue, person, or group. The values in parentheses are item weights or intensities assigned through a simple but rather elaborate judging procedure. In this hypothetical example, the larger the value, the more intense one's position toward the prosecution of child sexual abusers. Persons who would select item 1, for example, would probably press the prosecution of alleged child sexual abusers more vigorously than would those who might select item 4.

Consider several statements designed to measure one's degree of racial prejudice:

1. I would consider living next door to members of race X'.
2. I would consider marrying a member of race X.
3. I would bar members of race X from my church.

It is apparent that each of these items reflects a different degree of acceptance or hostility toward members of race X. We might consider the most accepting item to be number 2, where one might agree to marry persons from race X. The least accepting item might be 3, where respondents would not permit members of race X to belong to their churches.

Therefore, instead of furnishing respondents with a questionnaire consisting of various Likert-type items with which they must agree or disagree, researchers using Thurstone scales would provide them with a list of items from which they would choose two or three that they agree with the most. These items would already have weights assigned that reflect each item's intensity.

How do researchers devise these Thurstone scales? Thurstone recommended that investigators begin by creating a large number of statements that they believe correlate closely with the trait to be measured. Thurstone recommended that about 100 statements should be constructed. Next, at least 25 judges should inspect these items and sort them into various intensity categories. Thurstone recommended 25 judges, although he later indicated that fewer judges could accomplish the task adequately. The intensity categories into which these items might be sorted would consist of seven, nine, or 11 categories.

Who are the judges, and how are the categories conceived? Originally, Thurstone envisioned using university professors who taught psychology courses as judges. He believed they would be able to sort items of different intensities into appropriate categories, largely because of their training and expertise in attitudinal measurement. Since it was quite difficult to get these individuals to perform such sorting chores, this qualification was later relaxed. Currently, anyone may be a judge and sort these items, including introductory students in criminology courses. Sorting was simplified by providing "judges" with boxes containing various numbers of slots. Judges would be handed items individually typed on strips of paper. They would be asked to read each item and place it in one of seven, nine, or 11 categories, ranging from "low intensity" to "high intensity." These slots or categories would be numbered, and it would be easy to calculate the average weight for each item according to the categories it was assigned by the judges.

Consider the following simplified example. Suppose that we were to ask 25 judges to sort 10 statements into seven categories. We might designate each statement by letters: items A, B, C, D, E, F, G, H, I, and J. We would hand each judge slips of paper containing each statement. Each judge would sort the statements into the various categories or slots according to each item's intensity (in the judge's opinion or "judgment"). Following are the data for statement A and the number of judges who sorted it into various categories.

Category	Number of Judges Placing Item A in Category	Category Multiplied by Number of Judges
1	5	5
2	2	4
3	6	18
4	8	32
5	3	15
6	0	0
7	1	7
	25	81

Hypothetical statement A, whatever it might be, has been rated by 25 judges and placed into one of seven categories. The categories into which it has been placed by these judges are used to "weight" statement A. Thus category numbers are multiplied by the number of judges placing statement A into those categories. These are the products shown in the far-right column. To determine an item's "average weight," we compute a simple average, or $81/25 = 3.2$. Statement A's weight is 3.2.

After all items have been sorted and assigned numerical weights, it is possible to select approximately 20 or 30 of these statements for use in our final question-naire. Some statements will have weights in the range 6 to 7, while others will have weights in the range 1 to 2. The objective in our statement selections is to include statements having weights that span the spectrum from 1 to 7. For instance, suppose that we select the statements shown in Table 9.3 from an original list of 100 statements.

TABLE 9.3 TWENTY HYPOTHETICAL STATEMENTS TAKEN FROM AN ORIGINAL LIST OF 100 STATEMENTS, WITH ITEM WEIGHTS

Statement	Weight	Statement	Weight
1	6.8	11	3.9
2	6.2	12	3.4
3	5.9	13	3.2
4	5.6	14	2.8
5	5.2	15	2.7
6	5.0	16	2.2
7	4.8	17	1.9
8	4.6	18	1.8
9	4.2	19	1.6
10	4.1	20	1.2

The different weights accompanying the 20 items in Table 9.3 are derived from judges' ratings measured by us earlier. Note that there is a broad diversity of weights, ranging from a low of 1.2 to a high of 6.8.

The next step is to ask a sample of respondents to select two or three statements from this list that best reflect their position or attitudes or sentiments. Thurstone recommended that respondents select at least three statements. Theoretically, if these statements are accurate reflections of one's sentiments, persons will select statements having similar weights. For instance, persons who select item 1 as closest to their opinion about something might also be expected to select items having weights close to that item's weight, or 6.8. These items are nearest to the person's attitude. It is unlikely that persons will select item 1, with a weight of 6.8, and item 20, having a weight of 1.2, since these weights are at such different points on the intensity spectrum. According to these different weights, they indicate basically different points of view.

Suppose that a female respondent selects items 1, 5, and 6 as the three statements that suit her best. We would take the weights associated with these statements and average them. Respectively, the weights would be 6.8, 5.2, and 5.0. Averaging these values, we would have (6.8 + 5.2 + 5.0)/3 or 17/3 = 5.7. Thus 5.7 would be the final raw score we would use for this person.

Individual raw scores may be compared with one another and are theoretically reflective of differences in the degree or intensity of the attitude expressed. Thurstone believed that the weight assigned each scale item is a better way (than Likert scaling, for instance) of assessing attitudinal variations among people and plotting their differences along some attitudinal continuum. One assumption he made was that the resulting weights would enable researchers to approximate the interval level of measurement with the collected data. He used the term *equal-appearing intervals* to describe positions of these points along a continuum. To Thurstone, his scale of attitudinal intensity would look something like this:

Low 1————2————3————4————5————6————7 High

Subsequently, Thurstone changed his mind about the equal-appearing nature of spacing between items on these scales. He said that the interval level of measurement would be "approached" rather than actually achieved by such a scaling method. A subsequent comparison of Likert and Thurstone scales and their relative accuracy for measuring the same variables was made by Edwards and Kenney (1946). They reported no significant differences in the accuracy of the two scaling methods. Therefore, the greater time and effort required to formulate Thurstone scaling does not necessarily result in greater accuracy of attitudinal measurement, as Thurstone anticipated. Likert scaling is much easier and has equivalent accuracy.

Three points should be made about applying Thurstone scaling in criminological research. First, it is not acceptable to place item weights on questionnaires so that respondents can see them. Many researchers who use Thurstone scaling to measure attitudes often include such weights, since this makes the scoring process much easier for them. But to include these weights conspicuously causes respondents to focus more on the weights than on the items. Some bias may be incurred as a result.

A second problem pertains to the items subsequently selected by respondents as most typical of them. Some disturbing patterns may result. For instance, suppose that persons A and B chose items 1, 6, and 20 from Table 9.3 as most typical. These items have weights of 6.8, 5.0, and 1.2, respectively. The weights sum to 13.0, and the average for persons A and B would be 13/3 = 4.3. Next, suppose that persons C and D picked items 8, 9, and 10, with respective weights of 4.6, 4.2, and 4.1. These weights, summed, equal 12.9. The average of these three weights would be 12.9/3 = 4.3. The two average weights for persons A and B and for persons C and D would be 4.3. However, if we compare the spread of weights for both pairs of subjects, it is apparent that there is more homogeneity in response weights for C and D than for A and B. The greater the differences among item weights selected by various persons, the greater the *unreliability* of the Thurstone scale. It is presumed that no such wide variations among weights will occur. However, they do occur occasionally.

Finally, when Thurstone scaling is used, some researchers are inclined to believe that they have actually achieved the interval level of measurement with their scales. This is not so. The scale scores are at best ordinal. Nevertheless, there are misleading calculations and operations in the construction of Thurstone scales that lead researchers to erroneous conclusions. The averaging of judges' sortings of items and the averaging of item weights selected by respondents suggest that it is also appropriate to average the final raw scores. Again, as was the case with raw scores derived from Likert scaling, averaging is not recommended for derived scores from Thurstone scales.

Advantages and strengths of Thurstone scaling. Thurstone scales have the following advantages and strengths:

1. *Thurstone-derived scales enable researchers to differentiate between large numbers of people regarding their attitudinal positions.* When item weights are averaged, a greater variety of attitudinal positions is revealed than with Likert-type scale values. This would seemingly have the advantage of making it possible to render finer distinctions between people according to the attitudes they possess.

2. *Another argument in favor of using Thurstone-derived scales is that judges— usually professional persons—have achieved a high degree of agreement on the items used, and hence they perform a screening function by eliminating the "bad" or "poor" items that produce little or no agreement.* Researchers might apply such scales with increased confidence that the items used have a greater claim to reliability than would be the case in Likert scale construction.

Weaknesses of Thurstone scaling. Thurstone scaling procedures have the following weaknesses and limitations:

1. *Thurstone scales are time-consuming to construct.* Investigators must solicit judges who must take the time to sort numerous items. Then scale values must be determined. Then respondents' item selections must be averaged to place them on an attitudinal intensity continuum. And we have not mentioned the time and effort of researchers, who must think up 100 items to begin with and then select the final items for inclusion on the questionnaires. The fact that no advantage in accuracy accrues to researchers from using Thurstone scaling suggests that Likert scaling would be preferable, because it is simpler to apply and manage.

2. *It is possible to derive identical scores based on widely divergent attitudinal views.* This is the problem noted above, where two different persons might receive identical scale scores but where the scores are made up of widely dispersed scale items with different intensity weights. Do these persons with the same scores actually hold the same attitudes to the same degree? We do not know. The fact that greater variation in score values results from one subject compared with another subject would seem to place the validity of this scale in question.

3. *There is no way to control the influence of a judge's bias in item sorting.* The personal biases of judges might interfere with their objectivity in making item categorizations. However, repeatedly, Thurstone scaling has yielded a high degree of consistency among judges when attitudinal items have been sorted.

4. *In reality, Thurstone scale values are no better at predicting behavior than Likert-based measures.* Because Likert measures are so much easier to construct and score, the logical preference would be to use Likert scaling over Thurstone-derived methods.

Other Types of Scaling Procedures

Several other types of attitudinal scaling procedures exist. It is beyond the scope of this book to cover all other types of procedures, but two alternative procedures will be mentioned here because of their utility in criminology and criminal justice: (1) Guttman scaling or the Cornell technique and (2) the semantic differential.

Guttman scaling. A third major scaling method is called *Guttman scaling* or *cumulative scaling*. Other popular terms that refer to it are the *Cornell technique* and *scalogram analysis*. Guttman (1944) devised a method of scaling that permits researchers to determine whether the items they use in their scales are actually unidimensional. *Unidimensional* items measure the same dimension of the same phenomenon. Thus a unidimensional scale would consist of several items that would assess one, and only one, dimension of an attitude.

By comparison, Likert and Thurstone scales are *multidimensional*, since several different dimensions are measured by various items included on these scales. The police professionalism scale, for instance, contained items that tapped whether officers read police journals, whether assessments of officer competence can be made, and whether officers attend professional meetings. These are obviously different dimensions of professionalism, and it is possible for someone to agree with one item but not the others. With Guttman scaling, however, it is assumed that all items reflect a single dimension of the trait measured. Applied to our police professionalism example, items on a Guttman scale of police professionalism might focus on professional meeting attendance, how often such meetings are attended, whether papers are presented at those meetings, whether police officers hold various positions at those meetings, and so on. All items would focus on one specific dimension of professionalism.

Edwards (1957:172) defines a unidimensional scale as follows: "In the case of attitude statements, we might say that this means that a person with a more favorable attitude score than another person must also be just as favorable or more favorable in his response to every statement in the set than the other person. When responses to a set of attitude statements meet this requirement, the set of statements is said to constitute a *unidimensional scale*" (emphasis in original).

Suppose that we were to ask respondents to either agree or disagree with the following five statements:

1. I would marry a member of race *X*.
2. I would allow a member of race *X* to attend my church.
3. I would allow a member of race *X* to live in my neighborhood.
4. I would allow a member of race *X* to live in my community.
5. I would allow a member of race *X* to live in my country.

All of these statements are indicative of the amount of social distance we will permit or accept between ourselves and members of race *X*. Guttman would argue that if we agree with item 1, it makes sense that we would also agree with items 2, 3, 4, and 5. Guttman said that if we assign a "1" to all agreements, a person's score on this scale of five items would be 5. Knowing the score of 5 would enable us to predict the person's response to all items. Knowing that the score on the scale is 4 would allow us to predict their responses as well. We would probably say that the person with a score of 4 picked items 2 through 5 and disagreed with 1. Knowing that a person's score is 1 would mean agreement with item 5 only.

Using these five statements, Guttman scaling or scalogram analysis may be illustrated. Table 9.4 shows these five statements of different attitudinal intensity for 15 persons. We have provided hypothetical responses for all 15 persons according to whether they agree or disagree with each item. The far left-hand column in Table 9.4 shows each individual, from 1 to 15. The next five columns show x's for either agreement or disagreement for each of the five items listed across the top of the table. In the far right-hand column of the table are total scale scores, ranging from a "high" of 5 to a "low" of 0. Horizontal lines have been drawn underneath the pattern of agreements for each item. When agreements end, lines are drawn. These are cutting points based on how these 15 persons responded to the five items. The statements have been arranged in the table from left to right on the basis of "most intense" to "least intense." Thus persons who agree with item 1 will probably agree with the other four items. This is the case for persons 1 and 2. However, persons 3 and 4 do not agree with item 1, although they do agree with item 2. They also agree with the remaining items of lesser intensity. When items on a scale vary in a gradated fashion such as those five items in Table 9.4, Guttman calls the scale a perfectly reproducible one. *Reproducible scales* are those where one's individual item responses can be reproduced fairly accurately with a knowledge of one's overall scale score. A perfect error-free response pattern is illustrated in Table 9.5.

Few perfectly reproducible scales actually exist in reality, however. Thus Guttman devised a *coefficient of reproducibility*, which would enable him to cal-

TABLE 9.4 ILLUSTRATION OF THE GUTTMAN CORNELL TECHNIQUE[a]

	Statement										
	1		2		3		4		5		
Individual	A	D	A	D	A	D	A	D	A	D	Score
1	×		×		×		×		×		5
2	×		×		×		×		×		5
3		×	×		×		×		×		4
4		×	×		×		×		×		4
5		×		×	×		×		×		3
6		×		×	×		×		×		3
7		×		×		×	×		×		2
8		×		×		×	×		×		2
9		×		×		×		×	×		1
10		×		×		×		×	×		1
11		×		×		×		×	×		1
12		×		×		×		×	×		1
13		×		×		×		×		×	0
14		×		×		×		×		×	0
15		×		×		×		×		×	0

[a] The horizontal lines (dashes) in the body of the table are defined as "cutting points" for each statement.

TABLE 9.5 ERROR-FREE SCALOGRAMATIC PRESENTATION

	Statement					
	(Most Intense)			(Least Intense)		
Individual	1	2	3	4	5	Score
1	+	+	+	+	+	5
2	−	+	+	+	+	4
3	−	−	+	+	+	3
4	−	−	−	+	+	2
5	−	−	−	−	+	1

culate the amount of error involved in reproducing any individual's response pattern to a set of items. This would ultimately tell Guttman whether he was measuring a single dimension of the variable or whether multiple dimensions were being measured. What does a scalogram with errors look like? Table 9.6 shows a pattern of responses with several errors for a sample of two persons.

In this small-scale example, two persons have identical scale scores of 4. However, notice that person 1 has agreed (indicated by a +) with items 1, 2, 4, and 5 but has disagreed with item 3. By the same token, person 2 has agreed with items 1, 3, 4, and 5 but has disagreed with item 2. These are errors, according to Guttman. We have circled them and will later refer to such errors in the computation of the coefficient of reproducibility. The coefficient of reproducibility is as follows:

TABLE 9.6 SCALOGRAMATIC PRESENTATION OF ERRORS

	Statement[a]					
	(Most Intense)			(Least Intense)		
Individual	1	2	3	4	5	Score
1	+	+	⊖	+	+	4
2	+	⊖	+	+	+	4

A plus indicates acceptance or agreement with statement; a minus, rejection or disagreement with statement. Circled responses indicate errors.

$$\text{coefficient of reproducibility} = 1 - \frac{\text{number of errors}}{\text{number of responses}},$$

where the number of responses equals the number of people times the number of statements. A larger-scale example illustrates this computation more clearly. Suppose that we observe a response pattern to five items for 10 people, as shown in Table 9.7. In Table 9.7, five errors have been circled. In order to detect errors, we usually arrange patterns by ranking their overall scale scores. Persons who have the same scores can be moved upward or downward among one another in order to minimize errors. Thus in Table 9.7, persons 2, 3, and 4 can be moved upward or downward in relation to each other to minimize errors. Note what would happen if we switched persons 2 and 3. *Two* errors in their response patterns would occur instead of one. Suffice it to say that the way they are presently arranged yields minimal errors in their response patterns. If we were to draw imaginary horizontal lines underneath each item cutting point, minuses ($-$) above those lines and pluses ($+$) below those lines would be errors. These are illustrated in Table 9.7. A total of five errors are shown in this table and have been circled. We may compute the coefficient of reproducibility as follows:

$$\text{coefficient of reproducibility} = 1 - \frac{5}{(10)(5)}$$

$$= 1 - \frac{5}{50}$$

$$= 1 - 0.10 = 0.90.$$

The coefficient of reproducibility would be 0.90 in this case. This would mean that we can reproduce these persons' individual scores with 90 percent accuracy. Guttman believed that 90 percent is an acceptable cutoff point and that coefficients below 90 percent are simply not reproducible or nonreproducible. Later, he changed his mind somewhat and allowed unidimensionality to be declared if scales could be reproduced with 80 percent accuracy. He called these *quasi-reproducible scales*. Apparently, not too many researchers were developing unidimensional scales with reproducibility coefficients of 0.90 or higher, so this rigorous standard was relaxed somewhat.

TABLE 9.7 ERROR ILLUSTRATION OF SCALOGRAM ANALYSIS

| | Statement[a] | | | | | |
| | (Most Intense) | | | (Least Intense) | | |
Individual	1	2	3	4	5	Score
1	+	+	+	+	+	5
2	+	⊖	+	+	+	4
3	−	+	+	+	+	4
4	−	+	+	+	+	4
5	−	−	+	+	+	3
6	−	−	+	+	+	3
7	−	⊕	−	−	+	2
8	−	−	−	⊕	+	2
9	−	−	−	⊕	−	1
10	−	−	−	−	⊕	1
Errors	0	2	0	2	1	

[a] A plus indicates acceptance or agreement; a minus, rejection or disagreement. Circled responses indicate errors.

Guttman believed that unidimensional scales are superior to multidimensional scales for several reasons. First, if we really develop a true measure of something, the scores yielded by the measure should reflect the attribute consistently. Also, if several dimensions are being tapped by the measure, it is entirely possible that items from some other attitudinal universe (the imaginary place from which items are derived or thought of by researchers in their construction of scale items) may be included in our multidimensional scales. Therefore, our multidimensional measures, including Likert and Thurstone scales, may suffer some inaccuracy. This is a debatable point and one beyond the scope of this book.

The reality of the situation suggests that most attitudes are multidimensional anyway. If someone is satisfied with their work, for instance, they usually are satisfied with it because of several desirable features, such as good working hours, long lunch breaks, good supervision, extensive fringe benefits, good work content, challenging tasks, good work associates, and reasonable commuting distances. Presently, it is unknown how extensively Guttman scaling is used in criminology and criminal justice. An inspection of a wide assortment of current criminal justice and criminology journals shows several articles where Guttman scaling procedures are used, however.

Strengths and Advantages of Guttman Scaling

Some of the advantages and strengths of Guttman scaling are:

1. *Guttman scaling demonstrates the unidimensionality of items in an attitudinal measure.* Guttman considers this feature of scalogram analysis desirable, although it remains to be seen whether Guttman scaling yields scores that are any more accurate than Likert or Thurstone scale scores.

2. *Assuming a scalable set of items used in an attitudinal measure, the researcher is in a good position to identify inconsistencies in responses of subjects and possible untruthful replies.* This desirable feature could enhance a researcher's confidence in the quality of information furnished by respondents.

3. *Guttman's procedure is relatively easy to use when applied to small numbers of items.* However, when the number of items exceeds 12, the technique becomes unwieldy.

4. *A person's response pattern may be reproduced with a knowledge of one's total raw score on the scale.* Likert and Thurstone scale scores are not reproducible, although this should not detract from their usefulness as attitudinal measures.

Weaknesses of Guttman Scaling

Some of the weaknesses of Guttman scaling are:

1. *The Guttman scaling technique fails to provide as extensive an attitudinal continuum as the Likert and/or Thurstone methods.* Thus if we were to attempt to apply Guttman scaling to a sample of 100 or more persons, there would be an excessive number of tied scores. The error rate for these tied scores would be quite difficult to determine, and the researcher would not know whether the scale items were truly reproducible.

2. *The Guttman procedure is most easily applicable to situations where the researcher has few items with dichotomous responses.* Although Guttman scales may be constructed where there are more than two responses, the complexity of scoring such instruments outweighs their usefulness as unidimensional measures.

The semantic differential. The *semantic differential* consists of a series of bipolar characteristics, such as hot–cold, popular–unpopular, witty–dull, cold–warm, sociable–unsociable. Osgood, Suci, and Tannenbaum (1957) say that the semantic differential is a useful measure of psychological, social, and physical objects to various respondents. According to these researchers, the semantic differential should represent three basic dimensions of a persons's attitude toward another person, group, or object. These dimensions are (1) *potency*, the strength or physical attraction of the object; (2) *evaluation*, the favorableness or unfavorableness of the object; and (3) *activity*, the degree of movement of the object. These researchers originally devised a list of 50 pairs of terms, called *scales*, and arranged them on a continuum, such as:

```
                        Neutral
       Witty ——————————————————————————— Dull
                1   2   3   4   5   6   7
    Friendly ——————————————————————————— Unfriendly
                1   2   3   4   5   6   7
```

and so on. Persons responding to the semantic differential would check the point on each of the continua that described their particular feelings toward the object or person or group. The marks can be scored easily.

Criminologists might apply the semantic differential and make up terms to suit their particular needs. Studies of juvenile delinquents may make use of the semantic differential to evaluate the desirability or repulsion of school or peer groups. Personality assessments can also be made. Subjects are asked to portray themselves as they believe that they are at present and how they would like to view themselves in the future. Treatment programs in community corrections agencies might benefit from such applications, since insight may be gained about various clients. The primary usefulness of the semantic differential is to assess the subject's perception of the attractiveness of social and personal objects according to several dimensions. This assessment, in turn, may lead to specifying reasons for certain behaviors manifested in relation to those objects or groups or persons, to the extent that attitudes and behaviors coincide with reality.

MEASURES OF CRIME AND CRIME RATES

An important dimension of the measurement of variables pertains to charting crime, delinquency, and other criminological phenomena over time and describing diverse components of the criminal justice system.

Crime Rate

What is the crime rate in the United States? The crime rate is reported by the FBI in the *Uniform Crime Reports* and other sources. It is given for different states, cities and towns, counties, and rural and urban areas. It is also provided for different types of crime and for crime generally. The crime rate is computed as follows:

$$\text{crime rate} = \frac{\text{number of crimes}}{\text{population}} \times 100,000.$$

For example, in 1988 there were 245,807,000 persons in the United States. During the year, there were 12,356,865 property crimes reported to the FBI, including burglary, larceny, and vehicular theft. Using these figures, we have

$$\frac{12,356,865}{245,807,000} \times 100,000 = 0.0502706 \times 100,000 = 5027.06.$$

This means that there were approximately 5027 crimes against property per 100,000 persons in 1988. There were 20,675 murders reported in 1988. Therefore, 20,675/245,807,000 × 100,000 = 0.00084 × 100,000 = 84 murders per 100,000 persons, and so on.

Caution should be exercised when interpreting official statistics such as crime rates. The limitations and strengths of such statistical compilations are documented extensively elsewhere. Most introductory criminal justice texts summarize the pitfalls of such measures. There are seasonal variations in different types of crime. Crime varies from city to city and from state to state. Reported crime does not reflect the amount of unreported crime, which from independent victimization reports is known to be extensive. Large numbers of arrests do not represent large numbers of convictions. Crime waves may be politically created. When law enforcement agencies report crime to the FBI annually, only the most serious crime is reported, even if more than one crime was committed during a particular incident. These are only a few of the sources of error that interfere with the accuracy of these crime figures.

Suppose that we wished to determine whether particular types of crime were increasing or decreasing, from one year to the next? In 1986 there were 11,722,700 property crimes reported in the United States. Also, there were 241,077,000 persons in the United States as provided by U.S. census estimates. What was the amount of increase in property crime between 1986 and 1988? We can calculate the percent change by using the following formulas:

$$\text{percent change} = \frac{(\text{quantity at time 2}) - (\text{quantity at time 1})}{\text{quantity at time 1}} \times 100$$

$$= \frac{12,356,865 - 11,722,700}{11,722,700} \times 100$$

$$= \frac{634,165}{11,722,700} \times 100$$

$$= 0.054 \times 100 = 5.4 \text{ percent.}$$

There was a 5.4 percent increase in reported property crimes from 1986 to 1988. Was this particular percent increase equivalent with the general population increase during the same period? The same formula may be used to answer this question. The U.S. population in 1986 was estimated to be 241,077,000. In 1988 it was estimated to be 245,807,000. Therefore,

$$\text{general population increase} = \frac{245,807,000 - 241,077,000}{241,077,000} \times 100$$

$$= \frac{4,730,000}{241,077,000} \times 100$$

$$= 0.0196 \times 100 = 1.96 \text{ percent.}$$

Thus between 1986 and 1988, the general population was estimated to increase slightly less than 2 percent, or 1.96 percent. Compared with the 5.4 percent increase in property crimes, it would appear that property crimes are increasing at a greater rate between 1986 and 1988 than the growth of the general U.S. population. At least the reporting of property crimes is increasing at a rate greater than U.S. population growth.

Ratios

Ratios are commonly used by criminologists and criminal justice scholars for various purposes. Suppose that we wished to determine the ratio of prison inmates to prison correctional officers. If the prison population consisted of 1500 prisoners and there were 500 correctional officers, the ratio of prisoners to correctional officers would be

$$1500 \text{ to } 500 \text{ to } 1 \quad \text{or} \quad \frac{1500}{500} \text{ to } 1 \quad \text{or} \quad 3 \text{ to } 1.$$

Thus there would be three prisoners per correctional officer. This might also be expressed as 3:1. Looking at it from the standpoint of the number of correctional officers to prisoners, we would have 500 to 1500 to 1, or 500/1500 to 1, or 0.33:1. A 1:1 ratio would mean one correctional officer per prisoner. We might find this sort of arrangement in a close-custody, maximum-security facility, although this would be a luxury for most penal institutions.

SOME ISSUES OF MEASUREMENT

Various measurement issues are discussed: (1) the attitude–action relation, (2) social desirability as a contaminating factor, (3) response sets and validity, and (4) the level of measurement–statistical choices relation.

Attitude–Action Relation

Social scientists presume that behind every action is an attitude related to it. The logic is that if these attitudes can be identified in advance and measured accurately, actions or behaviors can be predicted or anticipated. Sounds easy, doesn't it? It isn't. Unfortunately, the attitude–action relation is far from certain. For example, it is possible for persons to possess certain attitudes and not express behaviors consistent with those attitudes. Those who may be prejudiced toward certain racial or ethnic groups may not discriminate against those groups, since discrimination is prohibited by law. Also, persons may behave in certain ways which suggest that they possess certain attitudes when they do not possess them.

Criminologists do not terminate their investigations of factors that explain criminal behavior or delinquent conduct or spousal assault simply because there are questions about the attitude–action relation. The attitude–action controversy actually began many decades ago. An early article about the relation between attitudes that persons express and their accompanying actions was written by Richard LaPiere (1934). LaPiere was interested in determining whether people behave in ways consistent with the attitudes they express. He planned a research project where he traveled throughout various parts of the country. He questioned hotel and restaurant owners about whether they would serve certain minorities, such as blacks and Orientals. Overwhelmingly, the hotel and restaurant owners indicated to LaPiere and his assistants that they would not serve such persons. Several months later, LaPiere instructed black and Oriental couples to travel to these same hotels and restaurants and attempt to be served. LaPiere expected that in most instances, they would be refused accommodations or food services because of their minority status. Interestingly, over 90 percent of the minority couples said that they were served or accommodated without incident. This finding caused LaPiere and others to critically evaluate their earlier thoughts about attitudes and how behaviors might be affected or influenced by their presence or absence.

Despite the uncertainty of the attitude–action relation, a prevalent belief among criminologists and criminal justice scholars is that attitudes should be studied. A majority of empirical investigations in criminology and criminal justice reveal attitudinal factors that appear related to actions or behaviors observed. However, replication research or repeating studies under different conditions and in different time periods contributes to our knowledge stockpile. As we learn more about people and their behaviors, we refine our instrumentation and theoretical schemes to more sophisticated levels. Interestingly, several complex statistical tools have been useful in helping us to understand how numerous variables affect behavior. Multiple correlation, path analysis, and other correlational techniques have proved valuable in assisting us in building our theories of criminal behavior. These procedures are beyond the scope of this book but are found in more advanced texts.

If attitudes precede certain types of social conduct, it is imperative that we develop sound measures of these attitudes. Not only must we identify those attitudes most relevant in explaining certain behaviors, but we must measure these attitudes accurately and reliably. The validity of measures, or the extent to which our instruments actually measure what we say they are measuring, as well as the reliability of measures, or their consistency for applications over time, are the primary topics of Chapter 10. Several conventional procedures will be described that enable researchers to demonstrate whether their instruments are accurate and consistent attitudinal measures.

Because we deal largely with quantities that cannot be observed directly, many of our attitudinal measures are challenged by competing instruments. It is not unusual to see numerous ways of conceptualizing and measuring police officer professionalism, or burnout and stress among probation officers. Every researcher is potentially capable of devising new instruments to measure virtually any attitudinal phenomenon. However, some attitudinal instruments have acquired considerable popularity and are used frequently to measure certain attitudinal dimensions. In the area of personality assessment, for instance, criminologists and criminal justice scholars rely heavily on measures of personality such as the *Minnesota Multiphasic Personality Inventory* (MMPI) or *Cattell's 16 Personality Factor Inventory* (16 PF). Subparts of both of these personality assessment devices have been used by many researchers to assess one's ego strength, self-concept, self-assurance, and other personality dimensions for selected purposes. Treatment programs in community-based corrections agencies, mental hospitals, and prisons often rely on such measures for preliminary assessments of patients or inmates. Some of these devices are used for classification purposes, to segregate more potentially violent patients and prisoners from less violent ones.

Because there is no single device to measure any attitudinal phenomenon that has 100 percent acceptance in criminal justice and criminology, we must constantly be aware of the strengths and weaknesses of all measures as we use or develop them. Better instruments stand the test of time, through repeated applications. Few, if any, social scientists are prepared to declare a moratorium on questionnaire construction and instrumentation. The field is expanding rapidly and maturing. Experimentation is vital to its growth, and we must constantly subject to empirical test the theories we have devised and the measures we have created.

Social Desirability as a Contaminating Factor

When attitudinal measures are constructed, we rely on the honesty of respondents to provide us with truthful information about themselves. The more sensitive the questions, however, the more difficult it may be for others to disclose to us their personal thoughts and feelings. Earlier in this chapter, an example of measuring anxiety was provided. That example contained excerpted items from Janet Taylor's Manifest Anxiety Scale. Some of these items were personal statements about one's bowel and bladder habits. Some items required that persons disclose things about their dreams or worries or manners of sleep. All of these personal items are, to one extent or another, related to anxiety. However, respondents may be inhibited and hesitate to give honest responses about themselves. Who wants to say that their sleep is fitful and disturbed, that the palms of their hands perspire frequently, or that they have bowel or bladder trouble frequently? These traits are undesirable. Few persons want to be undesirable. Therefore, people may say things about themselves that are not true but desirable. Methodologists refer to this behavior as social desirability.

Social desirability is saying things or disclosing things about yourself in writing that you want others to hear or see or that are favorable or self-serving. Social desirability is perhaps the most important contaminating factor affecting any attitudinal measure. We have no way of preventing social desirability. No foolproof remedies exist to detect it. Some standardized personality assessment tools have built-in "lie" factors that seek to detect the influence of social desirability. Thus persons are suspected of giving socially desirable responses when they deny behaviors or thoughts that most persons experience at one time or another. Asking people whether they worry about things or think about trivial matters may prompt some respondents to deny that they worry about things or think about trivial matters. Almost everyone worries about things from time to time, and it is rare for anyone to avoid thinking about trivial things occasionally. The thinking behind the inclusion of such items on personality assessment devices is that if people lie about commonplace traits, they will probably lie about less commonplace traits, such as frequent bowel or bladder trouble or frequent fitful and disturbed sleep.

Therefore, any measure of attitudinal phenomena must be considered a candidate for contamination by social desirability the more it delves into deeply private and personal matters and opinions. Giving responses that you think the researcher wants to hear or that make you look good tend to detract from the accuracy and reliability of measures.

Response Sets and Validity

Another contaminating factor that was mentioned earlier in this chapter is the *response set* or *set response*. Set responses occur whenever respondents check all "agree" or "disagree" responses or use some other systematic response pattern in a self-administered questionnaire, regardless of statement or question content. Therefore, if respondents were presented with obvious contradictory statements, such as:

"My job completely lacks challenge and intrinsic interest,"
or
"My job is intellectually rewarding, challenging, and intrinsically interesting,"

a response set would be indicated if "strongly agree" were checked for both items. Usually, there is a systematic response pattern throughout one's entire questionnaire. A male respondent, for instance, may check "female," if "female" is the first space to be checked among the information items included in the questionnaire. The best thing to do with questionnaires where response sets are strongly suspected is to throw them out. The researcher's concerns should be about the *quality* of data collected, not the *quantity* of data collected. Detecting response sets whenever they occur is fairly easy if researchers have constructed their questionnaires creatively. This usually means that they have interrupted phrasings of items that purportedly measure the same thing, with reverse phraseology suggested by the two items above. The decision to reject questionnaires or data because of the strong likelihood of set responses rests with the individual researcher and is a judgment call that depends on each situation.

Level of Measurement – Statistical Choices Relation

Much has been made in this chapter of levels of measurement and a researcher's efforts to measure attitudinal phenomena at the highest measurement levels. This is because we normally convert our data collected into numerical quantities for subsequent analysis. We want our analyses of collected data to be legitimate analyses. The scientific community has generally agreed on the rules by which the scientific game should be played. If one or more of those rules are violated in the course of our research efforts, our research enterprise is weakened accordingly in terms of its scientific contribution and significance.

The most typical rule violation relating to attitudinal measurement is the use of certain statistical procedures that involve particular arithmetic operations, such as summing and averaging. The facts are simple. Regarding the data you have collected and how you measured the different variables, you have either achieved the required level of measurement to conduct these arithmetic operations or have not achieved the required level of measurement. The following hypothetical scenario illustrates a common occurrence in the social sciences whenever attitudinal variables are investigated.

Suppose that researchers study two samples and collect data about certain attitudes they possess. Suppose that Likert-type scales have been used to operationalize each of the attitudes investigated. At best, these researchers have achieved the ordinal level of measurement by using Likert scaling. They now have numerous raw scores over some range from low to high. How should these scores be analyzed?

Perhaps these data have been coded and stored in a computer. A subsequent statistical program package is run for these data, and much descriptive material about the two samples is generated. Since the computer package usually features programming that computes assorted statistical values for the data to be analyzed, the results of the analysis may be the equivalent of data overload. In other words, even if the researchers are interested in only one particular computation, the computer package churns out all sorts of additional information not otherwise requested or desired by these researchers. They did not ask for additional data analyses, but the computer gave it to them anyway.

Perhaps they scan the data analyzed by the computer and notice that the program computed sample means or averages for all variables, including the attitudinal ones. Of course, the computer also computed modes, medians, ranges, standard deviations, and other miscellaneous descriptors for the same data. It is sometimes difficult to resist the temptation to do something with the additional data not originally requested from the computer.

Suppose that attitude X was measured according to Likert scaling and became a part of the data the computer analyzed. Subsequently, attitude X for the two samples was examined, and the researchers determined the following about attitude X:

	Group 1	Group 2
Mean (average)	55.2	51.6
Mode	50.0	49.3
Median	54.7	52.1
Standard deviation	4.6	4.9
Range	29.0	31.0

The first three values reported above are called "measures of central tendency" because they describe points around which scores in the distribution tend to focus. (In Chapter 15 we describe these measures and illustrate their computation and meaning in detail.) The standard deviation and range are "measures of dispersion or variability" because they depict *how* the scores are distributed around those central points. The mean or average for each sample on attitude X is shown, together with the mode and median, respectively. These are other central tendency measures that reflect different things about the central tendency of distributions. For instance, the mode indicates which scores are most popular or occur most frequently. The median defines that point separating the distribution of scores into two equal parts. In the example above, the median for group 1 of 54.7 divides group 1 into two equal parts, so that 50 percent of sample 1 is below 54.7 and 50 percent is above 54.7.

Now, how does this relate to rule violations? Likert scaling procedures produce ordinal-level raw scores. These are rankables, where raw scores may be placed along an intensity continuum from low to high. Scores at one point on the continuum are either higher or lower than other scores, but we cannot say how much higher or lower. If we wanted to say how much higher or lower these scores were from others, we would need to achieve the next-highest level of measurement with these scores, or the interval level of measurement. If we had achieved the interval level of measurement for attitude X, it would be arithmetically permissible to say how much higher or lower these scores were from each other. Unfortunately, we have only achieved the ordinal level of measurement with these scores using our Likert-type instrument to measure attitude X. The central tendency measure of choice *should be* the median. The median fits ordinal-level data well. The mean does not fit because averaging ordinal-level scores is meaningless, something similar to averaging Social Security numbers.

As the researchers examine their data, they observe arithmetic similarities between the means and medians of scores for these two groups on attitude X. For group 1, for instance, the mean of 55.2 is not much different from the median of 54.7. Similarly, the average of 51.6 for group 2 is not all that different from the median of 52.1. Since there is an obvious similarity in the two values, and since other investigators are more likely to be familiar with the mean or average rather than median, it might be considered harmless to report the means for these groups instead of the medians.

If researchers regard this as harmless, they might also regard as harmless the idea of using a "difference between means" test to evaluate the significance of differences between these two groups, particularly now that they have two means to work with. There is such a test, and it, too, requires that researchers have interval-level data at their disposal. Thus bending the rules in one instance may lead to other instances of rule breaking.

How important is all of this for the measurement of attitudes? There are mixed opinions among social scientists about this matter. Some researchers do not consider these data treatments as significant. In a conventional sense, considerable rule breaking can be detected in many professional journals. Thus if we gauge the incidence of this type of rule breaking according to what others in the social sciences do, we may conclude that it is generally acceptable. Convention often compels us to follow procedures that have been used by others. Beyond this, some scholars contend that if we were to comply fully with all requirements for statistical applications, we would never be able to do research. This is because our investigations are imperfect in various respects. Seldom are all requirements of tests and procedures actually achieved. Therefore, some information (where some rules are violated) is better than no information (where no rules are violated). In sum, the importance of this section is that it cautions us to recognize the various limitations of our data collection and instrumentation and view our findings accordingly.

SUMMARY

Measuring variables in criminal justice and criminology is a complex task, especially regarding attributes that cannot be seen directly but are inferred from other traits or characteristics. Attitudinal phenomena are in this invisible class, although they appear to exert significant influence on our behaviors. Measurement is the assignment of numbers to social and psychological properties according to rules, and correlating these numbers with these properties symbolically. Another way of treating measurement is to define it as a process of differentiating between persons according to the properties they possess.

Measuring social and psychological phenomena involves transforming nominal definitions into operational ones. The process of operationalization is the numerical conversion of attitudinal phenomena. Depending on what they represent, numbers mean different things under different circumstances. Researchers have evolved four levels of measurement by which numbers can be categorized: nominal, ordinal, interval, and ratio. The lowest level of measurement; the nominal level, involves categorizations of data into discrete subclasses. Ordinal-level data permit ranking of numbers, while the interval and ratio levels permit more advanced arithmetic operations. Distinctions are also made between concepts, terms that have direct empirical referents, and constructs, which have indirect empirical referents.

Popular attitudinal scaling procedures include the method of summated ratings or Likert scaling, Thurstone scaling or the method of equal-appearing intervals, Guttman scaling or scalogram analysis, and the semantic differential. The most popular measure is Likert scaling, which is multidimensional. A unidimensional procedure is Guttman scaling. There is no special advantage gained by devising unidimensional scales, and the accuracy of these scales is approximately equivalent.

Several important issues relating to measurement include the supposed relation between attitudes and actions. Researchers believe that an association exists between attitudes and actions, although at times this association is not a consistent one. The accuracy of scaling procedures is inflenced by social desirability, where persons say what they think researchers want to hear or whatever is socially desirable, and set responses, where persons check "agree" or "disagree" responses for all items, regardless of their content. Misapplications of statistical procedures often occur when assumptions underlying these procedures are not met with the data measured. Attitudinal measures are for the most part measured according to ordinal scales, although certain statistical procedures require higher measurement levels for their meaningful application. Validity and reliability, examined at length in Chapter 10, are two important characteristics of all attitudinal measures and influence data quality as well.

QUESTIONS FOR REVIEW

1. What is measurement? Identify and discuss briefly several important functions of measurement.

2. What are Likert scales? Describe their construction briefly. What are some general strengths and limitations of Likert scales?

3. What are Thurstone scales? Compare their accuracy with Likert scales of the same attitudinal phenomena. Which scales seem more accurate to you? Why?

4. What are some general limitations and strengths of Thurstone scales?

5. Differentiate between concepts and constructs. How do these terms relate to operationalization?

6. Distinguish between an operational definition and a nominal definition. What are the purposes of each in social research? Explain.

7. What are three important issues relating to measurement? Discuss each issue briefly, noting why it is important and is considered an issue.

8. What are Guttman scales? What is the coefficient of reproducibility?

9. Contrast multidimensional and unidimensional scales. Which scales seem more realistic and easier to construct? Why?

10. What are the respective contributions of nominal and operational definitions in theory construction, verification, and hypothesis testing?

11. What are four levels of measurement? Which levels of measurement permit averaging and division?

12. Why are levels of measurement important in relation to statistical applications to collected data? How can misapplications of statistical procedures influence the meaningfulness of scientific findings? Give two hypothetical examples from your own reading in criminal justice.

13. What are two major contaminating factors in self-administered questionnaires? How does each factor function as a contaminating factor? Of the two factors, which is probably more important, and why?

14. What is the semantic differential? What are some possible applications of it in criminology? Give two examples.

15. How can social desirability be detected in a questionnaire? How can a set response be detected? Explain.

10

accuracy   consistency

Validity and Reliability of Measures

KEY TERMS

Concurrent validity
Construct validity
Content validity
Criterion validity
Face validity
Factor analysis
Factorial validity
Item analysis
Item discrimination analysis

Parallel forms of the same test
Pragmatic validity
Predictive validity
Reliability
Split-half method
Test–retest
Universe of items
Validity

INTRODUCTION

How do we know if our measures of criminological phenomena are accurate and consistent measures?   In this chapter we examine various methods for determining the accuracy of the instruments we construct to measure attitudinal phenomena. *The accuracy of any measure is known as its validity.   Also, several ways of assessing a measure's consistency are described. *The consistency of an attitudinal measure is known as its reliability. These particular properties of measuring instruments are vital to theory verification and to the entire research enterprise. If we use measures that either lack validity or reliability, we are unsure of what we are measuring. Our tests of hypotheses will lack credibility and it will be doubtful whether we can successfully test our theories where attitudinal dimensions are included.

First, four methods of assessing validity are examined. These methods use either logic or statistical procedures as means of determining whether instruments are reflecting accurately the variables purportedly assessed. Next, several procedures for determining a measure's reliability are presented. These procedures include both internal and external methods that seek to determine whether the raw scores we generate through out instrumentation may be interpreted consistently. It will become apparent that of the two test properties, validity is the more elusive, since a measure's validity can only be inferred indirectly and is not provable. In contrast, reliability assessments may be made directly, and the reliability of measures is provable.

VALIDITY DEFINED

✳ *Validity* is the property of a measuring instrument that allows researchers to say that the instrument is measuring what they say it is measuring (Selltiz et al., 1959). An instrument is said to be valid whenever it measures what we say it measures. If we say that an instrument measures trait X, an attitudinal variable or otherwise, our measuring instrument is valid to the extent that it truly measures trait X. If our instrument measures trait Y and not trait X, it is not a valid measure of trait X, even though we might think it is. Thus it is possible for instruments to be valid indicators of certain unknown variables when they are not particularly valid indicators of those variables we wish to define.

Measuring instruments are created by people. For example, our standards of weight and length are previously agreed upon standards. In early times, primitive cultures used the distance from the tip of one's thumb to the first thumb joint as a length standard. However, it was soon apparent that some people received more than others because their thumbs were longer. More objective measures were subsequently employed to measure length and weight. Currently, rulers are universally used to measure feet, inches, meters, and millimeters; assorted weights and scales are used to measure pounds, ounces, and grams.

The use of such objective measures leaves little room for dispute among most people. They have agreed that certain measuring instruments will be used to take into account various properties of objects, such as length and weight. We say that a ruler is a valid measure of feet to the extent that it is patterned after some commonly agreed upon standard that has been determined to measure feet. If the ruler is constructed of wood and if the wood gets wet, there is the possibility that due to shrinkage and warping of the instrument, the measure will not accurately reflect feet as it did previously. *All of our measuring instruments, without exception, are vulnerable to contamination from various sources outside (external), or inside* (*internal*) *to the instrument itself.* Various weights may become worn, and their precision as measures will be affected. The validity of any measure, therefore, is a variable property.

It is helpful to view validity relatively because there are serious doubts among some social scientists that there is anything such as absolute validity. Rather, we determine the *degree* of validity, and validity has little meaning apart from particular operations by which it is determined. Some measures of things have higher validity, some have moderate validity, and some have lower validity relative to other measures.

Assessing the validity of weights and measures is accomplished rather easily, since it is not difficult to compare certain instruments with those already in existence and accepted as standards. If certain rulers and weights correspond to the accepted standard measures, we conclude that our measuring instruments are valid. In criminology and other social sciences, however, it is somewhat more difficult to establish the validity of instruments that assess nonempirical phenomena such as attitudes, prestige, power, or peer group pressure. Because many types of attitudes are said to be important in predicting human behavior in various social contexts, it is necessary for social scientists to devise measures of these attitudes so that their usefulness as predictors can be assessed empirically.

Once a measure has been constructed for some attitude, there is usually no objective standard whereby it may be evaluated. We have no universally acceptable measure of burnout and stress or of police officer professionalism. If we devise scales for these variables, what good would it do to compare them with other scales of these phenomena already in existence? These other measures must also be assessed in their own right, in terms of the degree of validity they happen to manifest. How do criminologists know whether their measures possess validity?

Before we examine several ways of tapping this elusive instrument property, we need to consider the relation between the items included on a paper–pencil questionnaire measure and the *theoretical universe of traits and items* that may be used to measure that phenomenon. Figure 10.1 shows a theoretical universe of items that measure some variable, in this case, trait X. The universe of items does not exist in the real world. It is merely an *abstraction*. Thus it comprises an

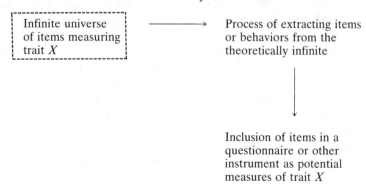

Figure 10.1 An illustration of the Process of Extracting Items from an Abstract and Infinite Universe of Traits Measuring Phenomenon X.

infinite universe of items and traits for any variable that has been nominally defined. Also theoretically, abstract universes of items and traits exist for all other variables that currently remain unknown or that we have not yet nominally defined.

Consider Figure 10.1. Researchers extract items from this abstract universe, almost wholly arbitrarily, although logic is an integral feature involved in their method of item or trait selection. Researchers have no way of proving that those items extracted are indeed from the universe of items that theoretically measures trait *X*. Thus investigators are in the difficult position of attempting to illustrate to others that the measures they have devised actually measure what they say they are measuring. The main arguments they cite supporting the validity of their instruments are founded almost entirely on logic and/or statistical support.

TYPES OF VALIDITY

There are four major methods for establishing a test's validity: (1) face or content validity, (2) predictive validity, (3) concurrent validity, and (4) construct validity. The labels applied to these types of validity are not uniformly used throughout the social sciences. Alternative terms are sometimes used, such as "criterion validity" and "pragmatic validity." Where appropriate, alternative terms will be noted where they might be substituted for some of the labels used to describe types of validity here.

Content Validity

Content or *face validity* is based on the logical inclusion of a sampling of items taken from the universe of items that measure the trait in question. The only way that content validity can be demonstrated is by examining the test or instrument items and comparing them with the universe of items that could theoretically be included, if known. On the basis of the items that comprise the instrument, researchers judge whether the test or instrument is valid according to its representative content. On the basis of the contents of the measure or on the "face" of it, do the items included seem logically related to the trait measured?

Content or face validity is exclusively a logical type of validity that any given measuring instrument may possess. For example, in the construction of verbal or quantitative tests such as the *Graduate Record Examination* (GRE), it is important that the test have content validity. It is essential that the items included on the test reflect the abilities and achievements of persons taking the test or their personal experience and professional background. If the examination were to emphasize a rather narrow treatment of mathematical skills rather than cover a broad spectrum of mathematical items (e.g., if the emphasis were on trigonometry rather than algebra, calculus, and/or simple arithmetic), the content validity of the measure as an index of general mathematical knowledge would be called into question. Specifically, we would challenge the test as a valid measure of general quantitative aptitude. Accordingly, if the verbal portion of the GRE emphasized only grammatical rules exclusive of reading comprehension and word understanding, we would seriously question whether it was a valid measure or indicator of one's verbal aptitude as it is generally understood or defined.

Therefore, for any given test or measuring instrument to have content validity, researchers must endeavor to ensure that the instrument contains a logical sampling of items from the so-called universe of items that presumably reflects the characteristic to be measured and correspond with it in some consistent fashion. In the classroom, for example, students might rationalize a poor performance on an examination by arguing that the instructor selected test items from book chapters that were not emphasized as important in class. If the test is supposed to cover the first five chapters of a book but only Chapter 1 has questions drawn from it, the test lacks content validity. It fails to have a representative sampling of items from the "universe of items" that could be utilized in the test's construction or any text material from the other four chapters.

Applied to attitudinal measures, face or content validity would be applied simply by inspecting a measure's content. On the face of the instrument, does the measure contain logical items that seem related to whatever the instrument purports to measure? If work satisfaction of probation officers is being assessed, the following items might appear on such an instrument administered to probation officers:

1. I would recommend this probation agency to my friends as a good place to work.
2. I would like to continue my present work arrangement for an indefinite period.
3. If I had the opportunity, I would leave this work to work in another organization doing entirely different things.
4. It would take a sizable change in pay to get me to move from my present position.
5. I don't get along well with my work associates.
6. I like my job more than most of my work associates like theirs.
7. My work assignments are boring and repetitious.
8. There are many things about my job that should be changed to make it more interesting to me.
9. There are many things about my job that I don't like.
10. My work is challenging and interesting.

It is apparent on the face of this instrument that these items are directed at one's work satisfaction and at different dimensions of one's work environment. These are just a few of the items that could be selected from the universe of items that purportedly measure job satisfaction. Our direct inspection of these items suggests that the instrument has at least content validity. This is a strictly logical analysis and conclusion.

Some problems with content validity. The fact that a measure appears to have content validity does not necessarily mean that we are indeed tapping the trait. In Chapter 9, problems occurred relative to social desirability and response sets as contaminating factors in attitudinal measurement. Certainly, these factors may be involved to varying degrees with the administration of any attitudinal scale, and we must expect a certain amount of social desirability to influence one's personal responses. If measures contain items that are so obvious about what they measure, it is relatively easy for respondents to fake their responses to these items or alter them in favorable ways. Therefore, some researchers resort to indirect means of assessing certain attitudinal variables. For instance, rather than asking persons if they are afraid of being confined in small places or of heights, they might ask persons whether they would like to be either a forest ranger or an accountant working in a small office. The indirect nature of this and other similar questions enables researchers to prevent respondents from knowing what the researchers are trying to measure. But the more indirect the questions or items, the greater the chance that some universe of items will be tapped other than the one associated with the variable to be measured. This problem is discussed later in connection with construct validity.

Another problem with content validity is that it is determined subjectively. Because content validity is dependent on the subjective professional judgment of the researcher to a large extent, what one person regards as high content validity might be regarded by another as low content validity. Consider the divergent views of teachers and students about the content validity of the same examination. The teacher may feel strongly that the test has high content validity, but the student may take issue with this belief for what are felt to be good reasons.

Content validity depends heavily on the quality of judgment of researchers. Whoever devises the measuring instrument must be careful to include as much as possible of a representative set of items that will measure the particular trait, whether it be verbal or quantitative aptitude, the degree of anxiety, or socioeconomic level.

Another problem concerns the reality of defining the universe of items from which the measuring instrument will be constructed. The universe of items may consist of all facts included in specific chapters of a textbook that students have been assigned. Or the universe of items may consist of all biological, social, and/or psychological features of anxiety. How does one go about identifying all of these features? For all practical purposes, anxiety has an infinite number of physiological, psychological, and social factors that may be extracted and included on an anxiety scale. Again, the judgment of researchers permits them to draw reasonably representative sets of items that measure the trait.

It is difficult to argue that a test does not have content validity, primarily because there is usually some resemblance of the items in the test to the trait presumably measuring it. Few measuring instruments, if any, are perfectly valid indicators of social and psychological traits. The general content validity of any test rests to a great extent on the skill and judgment of the constructor of the test. If poor judgment has been exercised (a factor that always exists as a possibility), the test or measure will probably have low content validity or no validity at all.

Pragmatic Validity

Perhaps the most useful and popular indicators of validity are *predictive* and *concurrent validity*. Both of these types of validity are forms of *pragmatic validity*. Pragmatism suggests that the validity of something can be assessed by whether or not it works. Does a particular attitudinal measure work in assessing a specific attitude? Two ways of demonstrating whether a measure works are to use the measure to forecast future behavior consistent with scores on the instrument, or correlating these instrument scores with some other concurrent activity at the same point in time. These two types of validation are predictive validity and concurrent validity.

Predictive validity. Predictive validity, also known as *criterion validity*, is based on the measured association between what an instrument predicts behavior will be and the subsequent behavior exhibited by an individual or group (Magnusson, 1967). For example, if we obtain from persons their attitudinal scores that purportedly reflect their degree of prejudice toward minority-group members (written expressions of what these persons might do if placed in a social situation requiring interaction with minority peoples), the relationship between their scores on the measuring instrument and their subsequent behaviors toward minority-group members will provide us with the necessary evidence of the predictive validity of the measure. If their scores indicate discriminatory behaviors, and if these subjects exhibit discriminatory behaviors toward one or more minority-group members, this is evidence that the test is measuring what we say it measures.

Suppose that we devise a measure of male chauvinism among personnel officers of several companies and find that some officers possess male chauvinistic attitudes to a high degree while others possess this characteristic to a low degree. A comparison of their subsequent hiring practices and their respective chauvinism scores might disclose much about the predictive utility of our measure. If those officers with high chauvinism scores have hiring records that show some gender discrimination (e.g., low numbers of female hires), and if those officers who have low chauvinism scores have hiring records showing more equitable hiring practices, our measure of male chauvinism would seem to have predictive validity.

Predictive validity is the simple correlation of predicted behavior with subsequent exhibited behavior. A high correlation or relationship between the predicted behavior and the behavior exhibited means that the measure possesses predictive validity.

Concurrent validity. Closely connected with predictive validity is concurrent validity. Concurrent validity differs from predictive validity in that the scores of predicted behavior are obtained simultaneously with the exhibited behavior. For instance, if we obtained manual dexterity and work efficiency scores from drill press operators in a factory, we might also obtain from their supervisors their productivity records. We can compare their productivity records directly with the manual dexterity and work efficiency scores to determine if there is concurrent validity. Again, as in the case of predictive validity, a high correlation or relation between the dexterity scores and high drill press productivity suggests that our measure has concurrent validity. Therefore, predictive validity forecasts expected behaviors in some future period, while concurrent validity is assessed by comparing test results with simultaneous behavior. Consider the hypothetical scores in Table 10.1.

In the example of hypothetical scores shown in Table 10.1, two measures have been obtained from a sample of delinquent boys. One measure we have presumably constructed is self-esteem; the other is perceived peer pressure. Wishing to validate our self-esteem scale, we might predict that those boys with lower amounts of self-esteem might be more receptive to peer pressures. Accordingly, we might suspect that as their scores on self-esteem increase, their perceived peer pressure scores might decrease. Also, as their self-esteem scores decrease, their perceived peer pressure scores might increase. Table 10.1 has been deliberately configured to demonstrate this. If these were actual scores of self-esteem and perceived peer pressure, we would consider this relation supportive of our theorizing. Also, our measure of self-esteem would appear to be validated by its correlation with perceived peer pressure.

Both predictive and concurrent validity are determined largely by statistical correlations, although we might conclude that our measures have these types of validity by visually inspecting the patterns of scores such as those displayed in Table 10.1. If there is a logical relation between these sets of scores, this is logical evidence of predictive and/or concurrent validity.

Some problems associated with predictive and concurrent validity. One of the major problems associated with predictive and concurrent validity is that simply observing a numerical association between a test score and actual individual or group behavior is no guarantee that the measuring instrument is a

TABLE 10.1   SELF-ESTEEM AND PEER PRESSURE SCORES FOR TEN DELINQUENT BOYS

Delinquent	Self-Esteem	Perceived Peer Pressure
1	42	28
2	45	27
3	47	25
4	49	24
5	52	23
6	55	21
7	56	20
8	58	20
9	59	19
10	61	16

valid indicator of the trait we have nomimally defined. It could be, for example, that our measure really is a valid indicator of something else closely related with the phenomenon we are investigating. Therefore, we might be led to suspect that our instrument is a valid measure of what we say it is, when in fact it may be a measure of something else. This problem always exists whenever attitudinal measures are constructed. There is no way we can ever be sure that we are measuring what we say we are measuring regarding attitudinal scales. However, we do consider as evidence of the potential validity of the instrument the relationship between the predicted and observed behavior in question. This should actually serve as a caution. Researchers must always be aware of the potential limitations of their measures. They should not be overconfident that they are measuring what they say they are measuring strictly on the basis of high correlations between predicted and observed behaviors.

In the case of gender and racial discrimination, another problem emerges. Since it is illegal to discriminate on the basis of gender and race, it is entirely possible to tap a gender or racial prejudice dimension with our devised instruments but not observe discriminatory behaviors. Thus people may have an amount of gender or racial prejudice, but they may not exhibit illegal behaviors of discriminating against persons because of their race or gender. Even if certain behaviors are not prohibited by law, social constraints exist to prevent certain discriminatory behaviors from being observed.

Another problem closely associated with pragmatic validation is the researcher's interpretation of exhibited behaviors by respondents as representing the predicted behavior. Some attitudinal measures are so abstract that several different kinds of interpretations of given behavior patterns could be made according to a variety of social researchers who define the situation. Again, the judgment of the researcher is a crucial element in determining the degree of pragmatic validity that exists.

Construct Validity

Construct validity is both a logical and a statistical validating method. Also known as *factorial validity*, construct validity is useful for measuring traits for which external criteria are not available, such as latent aggressiveness. This type of validity is determined through the application of *factor analysis*. Factor analysis is a statistical technique designed to determine the basic components of a measure (Blalock, 1970:97–102). For example, if we were to factor analyze a measure of police professionalism, we might find that the variable consists of three predominant factors: formal educational attainment, supervisory expectations, and promotional ambitions. Factor analysis is beyond the scope of this book, although we can discuss briefly what it does. If we devised a police officer professionalism scale that consisted of 50 items, the application of factor analysis might cause our scale to "factor" into three major parts, corresponding to educational attainment, supervisory expectations, and promotional ambitions. Thus we could see three distinct "clusters" of items that focus around these dimensions. An inspection of the individual items within each cluster should bear directly on those particular factors.

We could determine this relation in much the same way that we would use content or face validity to evaluate the contents of a scale.

A popular personality assessment device is Raymond Cattell's *16 Personality Factor Inventory*, developed at the Institute for Personality and Abilities Testing in Champaign, Illinois. Designated as the "16 PF," Cattell's inventory purportedly measures 16 separate personality dimensions. When factor analysis is applied to this measure, which consists of 187 questions, it factors into 16 separate parts, with 16 separate clusters of items. More advanced sources may be consulted for how factor analysis might be applied.

Some criticisms of construct validity. Construct validity can be used to demonstrate whether or not a measuring instrument is in fact measuring a particular phenomenon. If a measure is supposed to reflect only one dimension, and if factor analysis shows that more than one dimension of the variable is being measured, this raises serious questions about the instrument's validity.

Another problem is that construct validity requires a rather sophisticated statistical background on the part of the researcher in order to apply it manually. While statistical programs exist and have been adapted for computer use to facilitate one's computations, we must still possess interpretive skills to make sense out of what has been computed.

Further, because construct validity pertains almost exclusively to traits that are not directly observable, there is a greater risk that the instrument is actually measuring some other phenomenon closely related to the trait being investigated rather than the actual trait itself. Compared with predictive validity, for instance, there is no direct means to correlate actual behaviors with test scores as a way of demonstrating the construct validity of the instrument.

It was mentioned earlier that often, researchers will devise items that are indirect indicators of the traits they investigate. Thus rather than asking persons whether or not they like their work, researchers may ask them whether they would recommend the job to others as an indirect way of assessing their own job contentment or work satisfaction. For more deep-seated personality characteristics such as acrophobia (fear of heights) or claustrophobia (fear of small, enclosed places), indirect items are preferable. The use of indirect items is to discourage respondents from making socially desirable responses. We might ask someone if they are anxious or claustrophobic, for instance. It is likely that they will not be perfectly honest with us and say things that are socially desirable. However, if we ask indirect questions, they cannot easily determine what it is we are trying to assess. This is a case of the test-taker trying to outwit the tester. Indirect questions involve the tester attempting to outwit test-takers.

Consider the following item as an example.

121. I would rather:
(A) grow flowers; (B) add columns of numbers; (C) in between.

Presumably, if someone select (A) and prefers growing flowers over adding numbers, an inference might be made from this. Since "growing flowers" is a largely out-of-doors activity and "adding columns of numbers" is associated with in-door work, we might use this item to assess one's claustrophobic tendencies, if any. Bear in mind that we do not limit our inferences about one's behaviors to one item such as is indicated above. We might use multiple items, perhaps as many as 15 or 20, to ensure that our behavioral and attitudinal inferences are more valid ones. We are *not* going to conclude that because someone says she likes to grow flowers, she must be claustrophobic.

But the further away we get from the actual traits or characteristics we want to measure with the items we construct, the more likely it is that we might be tapping variables closely related to those we are investigating. Thus our indirect indicators of variables are helpful in the sense that they discourage test-takers from making socially desirable responses, but they are detrimental in the sense that we may be losing touch with the variables purportedly measured.

RELIABILITY DEFINED

Another important test property is reliability. The reliability of a measuring instrument is the ability of that instrument to measure consistently the phenomenon it is designed to measure (Selltiz et al., 1959). Reliability therefore refers to test consistency.

A practical example illustrating the usefulness of test reliability may be provided by a before–after study design. The before–after study design is geared to assess the impact of an experimental variable on a dependent variable between two time periods. Researchers select a social setting in which change is anticipated, and they observe group or individual behaviors both before and after the change occurs. Individuals' scores from both time periods are compared, and score differences are used as indicators of the impact of the change on the measured dependent variable.

Of course, in addition to the experimental variable, other factors may account for behavioral changes of individuals from one time period to the next. The problem of distinguishing between variables and the differential effects they have on factors is considered later in this chapter. For the present, we focus on behavior changes that occur principally as the result of experimental variables.

First, researchers theorize that when persons are exposed to particular stimuli, predictable changes will occur in certain of their attitudes and behaviors. A comparison of individual behaviors and attitudes both before and after the introduction of the stimulus or experimental variable should either confirm or refute our theorizing about the intended impact of change occurring as the result of the experimental variable. If a significant and predicted change in behavior is noted, the investigator usually interprets this as support for the theory. If no change in behavior occurs, the investigator considers this as evidence that the theory has been refuted, at least in this instance.

To measure specific behaviors of persons, potential measures of these behaviors are constructed and appear in various forms. The questionnaire is one major form of attitudinal measurement. Several statements are usually prepared that resemble the trait or traits under investigation. The respondents are asked to agree or disagree with specific statements or are obligated to say which statements are true of them. On the basis of respondents' overt reaction to these statements, researchers infer things about the extent to which these respondents possess some attitude or attitudes. The possession of particular attitudes is potentially indicative of behaviors corresponding to those attitudes, although as was noted in Chapter 9, there are contradictions in general attitude–action relationships.

WHY IS IT IMPORTANT TO HAVE RELIABLE MEASURES?

It is important to have reliable measures for at least two reasons: (1) reliability is a prerequisite for an instrument's validity; and (2) researchers want to be able to determine the effects of one variable on others. Reliable measuring instruments will enable researchers to draw tentative conclusions about the causal relationships between variables.

For the validity of a measuring instrument to be supported, it must be demonstrably reliable. Any measuring instrument that does not reflect some attribute consistently has little chance of being considered a valid measure of that attribute. For example, suppose that persons have conservative political views. A measure of conservatism would be regarded as unreliable if after repeated measures on the same persons, widely different conservatism scores were reported. This assumes, of course, that other variables did not intervene to cause changes in score results.

If it can be reasonably determined that individuals are relatively uninfluenced by extraneous variables that are a part of their environment from one instrument administration to the next, the chances for a measure to be considered unreliable are greatly increased if significant score differences are observed. The reliability of a measuring instrument is seldom, if ever, determined by examining responses from a single individual to that measure. Most often, evidence of reliability is gathered from large aggregates of persons.

Scores on a reliable measuring instrument will fluctuate only in response to some independent factor or condition causally associated with it directly or indirectly. Caution should be exercised in interpreting apparent relationships between two or more variables as causal relationships. If researchers observe a change in a person's score on some attitudinal dimension from one time period to the next, they want to be able to say that the score change is empirical evidence of the potential effect of one variable on the other.

Generally, if a factor X is introduced between two time periods, theoretically, certain changes in specific attitudinal dimensions that relate meaningfully to factor X should occur. For example, in many police departments in the United States, films and videotapes dealing with human relations skills are shown to units of officers as a part of their training and to enhance their interactions with the public. If officers manifest poor human relations skills in dealing with the public prior to seeing these films or videotapes, and if they are much improved in this respect after viewing the films and videotapes, this is considered to be tacit support for the assumption that the audiovisual aids helped to account for their behavioral change. Taken by itself, this does not prove that the audiovisual aids caused the changes in human relations skills, but it is nevertheless strong support for this contention. Figure 10.2 illustrates a conventional independent–dependent variable pattern, where one variable purportedly causes changes to occur in another variable.

Whereas Figure 10.2 shows only one score, most real-world applications use many scores in before–after research. In this hypothetical example, however, measures are taken in time 1 (t_1) and time 2 (t_2). Score differences are noted in a column to the far right. In this case, one score of 50 is observed for the dependent variable Y in time 1 and the score of 25 is recorded on the same measure of Y administered in time 2. The score difference of -25 is recorded. Between the two time periods, an experimental variable X is introduced. The score difference, -25, is presumed attributable to the introduction of variable X *if our measure of Y is reliable*. Again, some caution must be exercised when drawing causal inferences among variables. Several other factors may have accounted for this score difference. We examine phenomena that influence a measure's reliability and validity in a later section of this chapter.

TYPES OF RELIABILITY

Four methods of determining an instrument's reliability are presented here. These are divided into internal and external reliability checks or methods. Internal checks are those that establish reliability by inspecting the internal consistency of items; external checks use the entire measure against itself over time or through development of two or more equivalent measures of the same phenomena. Internal reliability checks include (1) the split-half method and (2) item discrimination analysis. External reliability checks include (1) test–retest and (2) parallel forms of the same test.

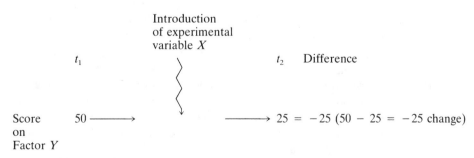

Figure 10.2   The Effect of An Experimental Variable X on Factor Y.

Internal Reliability Checks

One way of attacking the reliability problem of instruments is to examine the internal consistency of items used to construct them. Items that measure the same phenomenon should logically "cling together" in some consistent pattern. Persons who like their jobs are unlikely to give responses that would typify persons who do not like their jobs. The argument is that *persons with particular traits will respond predictably to items affected by those traits*.

Suppose that we were to construct a measure of some attitude and include 20 items in our instrument. These 20 items are statements with Likert-type agree– disagree responses. Ten of the items are positively worded, whereas the other 10 statements are negatively worded. Persons who have the attitude to either a high degree or a low degree should respond to all 20 items consistently, *provided that each of these items has been extracted from the same attitudinal universe*. Examining the internal consistency of the instrument enables researchers to determine which items are not consistent with the rest in measuring the phenomenon under investigation. The object is to remove those inconsistent items from the measure to improve its internal consistency. However, one preliminary caution is in order. Since most of our attitudinal measures are multidimensional, it may be possible for respondents to give positive responses to some items and negative responses to others. They might like their pay but not their work associates. Thus internal consistency may be more or less difficult to create, depending on the potential for these complex variations in item responses. Two categories of internal checks for reliability include the split-half method and item discrimination analysis.

Split-half method. The split-half technique is designed to correlate one-half of the test items with the other one-half. For instance, if we devised a 30-item scale, a suitable procedure for establishing the internal consistency of the test would be to divide the items into two equal parts and correlate them. Some researchers recommend numbering the items from 1 to N and correlating the odd-numbered items with the even-numbered ones.

There are no conventional standards that prescribe how to interpret the results of these correlations. One rule of thumb that might be applicable is to regard correlations of 0.90 or higher as indicative of high test reliability. The Kuder–Richardson 20 procedure may be applied here. Step-by-step directions for applying this advanced statistical procedure are presented in Magnusson (1967).

Applied to Likert-type scaling that we have examined in Chapter 9, recall that item weights are assigned on five- or six-point response patterns from "strongly agree" to "strongly disagree." If we took one-half of all test items and correlated them with the other one-half, we would be correlating item weights with one another. Theoretically, if a person receives a lot of "6's" and "5's" on one-half of the test, because of the responses given, there should be lots of "6's" and "5's" on the other half of the test if it is internally consistent. The Kuder–Richardson 20 procedure produces a correlation coefficient of the magnitude of relation between these two test halves.

Item discrimination analysis.   The second internal method of determining a test's reliability is called *item discrimination analysis*, sometimes simply *item analysis*. It is relatively simple to illustrate and understand, and complex statistical manipulations of data are not required.

For instance, let's assume that researchers have administered an attitudinal instrument to 100 persons. Further assume that the instrument contains 10 items, each having a six-point Likert-type response pattern of attitudinal intensity (i.e., strongly agree, agree, undecided, probably agree, undecided, probably disagree, disagree, and strongly disagree). If we weight each response per item according to a 1, 2, 3, 4, 5, and 6 intensity pattern (or, 6, 5, 4, 3, 2, and 1 in the case of negatively worded items), it would be possible for a person to obtain a maximum high score of $10 \times 6 = 60$ and a minimum score of $10 \times 1 = 10$. This would be the number of items times the largest weight for a single item. The scoring range would be between 10 and 60.

Logically, persons with larger overall scores on the instrument (e.g., 60, 59, 58, 56, etc.) would tend to respond to each item in such a way that the weight assigned each item response would probably be either a 4, 5, or 6. Persons with smaller overall scores of 10, 12, 15 and so on, would probably have small weights of 1, 2, or 3 associated with particular item responses. Sometimes, persons with overall larger scores will respond to an item and receive a 1, 2, or 3 instead of a 4, 5, or 6. By the same token, those with overall smaller scores might receive an item weight of 4, 5, or 6 instead of 1, 2, or 3. These response deviations are *inconsistencies*. If there are too many inconsistencies in any given response pattern for particular items, those items become suspect. An inconsistent item may not be from the same universe as the other items. Possibly the inconsistent item may be excluded from the rest to improve the internal consistency of the measure and thereby improve its reliability. To illustrate item inconsistencies, consider the hypothetical response patterns of 12 research participants to 10 items in a questionnaire designed to measure attitude A. These are shown in Table 10.2.

The body of Table 10.2 consists of weights assigned to each of the 10 items. Each column consists of the response pattern of different individuals to the 10 items. Note the consistency of subject 1 to all items except item 5. Note also the consistency of subject 2 (with opposite response patterns and indicating low attitudinal intensity) to all items except 5. Subject 3 is equally consistent in responses with the exception of item 5. When certain items stand out from the rest as being inconsistent, this may be considered evidence to challenge not only the reliability of the particular item, but also its validity. If items are to be discarded and total attitudinal scores are refigured on the basis of the new item composition and arrangement, the resulting score would be considered a more reliable estimate of the person's attitude A.

It is important to note that items having *consistently inconsistent* response patterns such as item 5 in Table 10.2 may not be unreliable items. If they are consistently inconsistent, we must examine the weight pattern we have assigned them. It may be that we mistakenly applied the 6, 5, 4, 3, 2, and 1 pattern to this item weight pattern when it should have received a 1, 2, 3, 4, 5, and 6 pattern. The wording of the item should be considered in relation to the weights we have

TABLE 10.2   EXAMPLE OF ITEM DISCRIMINATION ANALYSIS

Item	Subject											
	1	2	3	4	5	6	7	8	9	10	11	12
1	6	1	3	2	5	1	6	4	1	4	1	6
2	5	1	2	1	5	1	6	4	1	4	1	6
3	6	2	2	1	5	2	6	4	1	5	2	5
4	6	1	3	1	4	2	6	4	1	4	2	6
5	2	5	6	4	2	4	2	2	5	2	4	3
6	6	2	1	1	5	2	6	4	1	3	2	5
7	6	1	2	2	6	2	5	4	2	5	1	6
8	5	1	3	3	5	2	5	4	3	5	2	4
9	5	1	3	1	5	2	6	4	1	6	2	5
10	6	1	2	1	5	1	6	4	3	6	2	4

assigned. In short, we may have a reliable item. It may be that we simply assigned the wrong weights.

Another way of spotting inconsistent items is to deal with the discriminatory power of each item and reject those items that fail to discriminate between individuals possessing the attitudinal trait to a high or low degree, respectively. This method is as follows. We would first obtain responses from N individuals and rank them according to their total raw scores on the measuring instrument from high to low, or from the largest to smallest scores. Next, we would divide the total scores into upper and lower quartiles. The upper quartile would contain the upper 25 percent of all raw scores, while the lower quartile would contain the lower 25 percent of all raw scores. Those individuals in the center of the distribution or the central 50 percent would be excluded from further consideration according to this particular internal consistency procedure. The argument favoring their exclusion is that if the item discriminates, it is most observable in the case of extreme attitudinal intensity scores.

We now have two groups of respondents, representing both extremes of attitudinal intensity. As one example, suppose that we evaluated the hypothetical data presented in Table 10.2. Taking one item at a time on the measure, we could construct a table identifying the response weights of all individuals in the upper and lower quartiles. In Table 10.3, all responses to item 1 have been recorded for two groups of subjects in the upper and lower quartiles, considering their overall scores. This table has been constructed, based on an overall sample of 40 persons. Thus the upper and lower quartiles would consist of 10 persons each, since 10/40 = 25 percent. In this particular instance, note that the weights of persons in the upper quartile are considerably larger collectively than the weights shown for the subjects in the lower quartile. This is what we would expect logically for an item that discriminates between individuals possessing varying degrees of some attitudinal characteristic.

On the basis of the total scores persons receive for a set of attitudinal items, we may infer that their response for each item should be consistent with their overall responses. Therefore, persons identified as belonging to the upper quartile

TABLE 10.3 ILLUSTRATION OF ITEM DISCRIMINATION ANALYSIS FOR A SINGLE ITEM: RESPONSES OF UPPER AND LOWER QUARTILES TO ITEM 1

$N_1 = 10$ Upper Quartile	$N_2 = 10$ Lower Quartile
6	1
5	3
4	2
5	3
4	4
5	3
6	4
6	1
5	2
5	1
Sum of item scores = 51	Sum of item scores = 24
$\overline{X}_1 = 5.1$	$\overline{X}_2 = 2.4$

should have consistently larger weights assigned their responses for each item in the questionnaire, and those who belong to the lower quartile on the basis of their total score should have consistently smaller weights assigned each item. In the case illustrated in Table 10.3, item 1 (any item taken from the set of items in our measure of some attitude) appears to discriminate. We must verify this statement further, however.

The next step is to determine the *average weight* for item 1 among the subjects of the upper and lower quartiles. Averaging the weights of both groups, we have a mean of $\overline{X}_1$ (the average score for the upper quartile on item 1) = 5.1. The average or $\overline{X}_2$ for the lower quartile on the same item is 2.4. A visual inspection of the difference between the means of both groups would reveal that the item appears to discriminate between those who possess the trait to a high degree and those who possess it to a low degree.

We may continue our item analysis by selecting item 2, recording the response weights for all individuals in the upper and lower quartiles, determining the average response for both groups, and so on. Finally, we would generate a table containing the means and mean differences of the upper and lower quartiles of subjects for all 10 items, as shown in Table 10.4.

In Table 10.4, the column to the far right contains mean differences between the average weights of the upper and lower quartiles of respondents based on total scores to a measure of attitude X. (Although means are computed here for item discrimination purposes, the use of the mean for other functions is not recommended, since the interval-level-of-measurement assumption is violated). Notice that items 1, 4, 5, 7, 8 and 9 appear to discriminate between the two groups to varying degrees. These averages are consistent with what we would expect them to be. Note also that items 2, 3, and 6 do not appear to discriminate at all. In fact, item 6 contradicts slightly the way the average weights should logically be arranged in relation to one another. Predictably, averages for each item among

TABLE 10.4 COMPARISON OF THE UPPER AND LOWER QUARTILES

Item	Upper Quartile $\overline{X}_1$	Lower Quartile $\overline{X}_2$	Mean Difference $\overline{X}_1 - \overline{X}_2$
1	5.1	2.4	+2.7
2	4.6	4.5	+0.1
3	3.3	3.3	0.0
4	5.5	3.1	+2.4
5	4.8	1.8	+3.0
6	3.9	4.1	-0.2
7	5.0	4.0	+1.0
8	4.8	2.5	+2.3
9	4.9	2.8	+2.1
10	1.3	5.4	-4.1

the upper quartile of respondents should be larger compared with the averages of item weights for members of the lower quartile. Finally, observe that item 10 discriminates, but it does so *in reverse*!

There are several reasons why the item fails to discriminate as predicted. First, it could be a poor item and should not be included with the other items. It does not measure the phenomenon under investigation. Second, it may be that the researchers assigned the wrong weights to that particular statement. They must double-check the statement and response pattern assigned to it before throwing the item out altogether. It can be observed that if response weights have been assigned appropriately to that item, a correction will reinstate the item as a discriminating one. The function of item discrimination analysis is to improve the reliability of a test by eliminating those items that are inconsistent with the other items.

If researchers were to use item discrimination analysis, it would be advisable to begin by including a large number of items, at least in excess of 20. When item analysis is completed, several of the statements will be eliminated from the list because of their inability to discriminate between those individuals possessing variable amounts of the attitudinal trait under investigation. As a result of eliminating items, the range of response that is possible to achieve is narrowed. Considering the foregoing response pattern of 6, 5, 4, 3, 2, and 1, a 20-item questionnaire would yield a total response range of from 20 to 120. Decreasing the number of items from 20 to 10 will narrow the range of response from 10 to 60. Decisions to eliminate items are based in part on the following considerations:

1. The degree to which the item discriminates
2. The number of individuals to whom the instrument is administered
3. The degree to which precision is desired by researchers in their attempt to measure the attitudinal phenomenon

If researchers reject too many items, this increases the likelihood of larger numbers of tied scores among respondents. This narrows the latitude of flexibility in the data analysis stage and will affect tabular construction and significantly eliminate statistical test options. On the other hand, if too many items are retained, the chances increase of including items that discriminate poorly.

Choices as to which items should be retained and which ones should be excluded are almost always made arbitrarily by the researcher. Again, no specific conventional guidelines exist for making these kinds of decisions. Some researchers have advocated conducting statistical tests of significance of difference between two means as a way of introducing probability theory into their decision making to accept or reject specific attitudinal statements, but this is not recommended. Nevertheless, in Table 10.4, for example, items 1, 4, 5, 8, and 9 would probably be included in the final form of the measure of attitude A. The other items would either be excluded entirely or modified and reexamined within another subject situation. The decision to include specific items from Table 10.4 was based on an arbitrary mean difference of $+2.00$ or greater in the expected direction. This was purely arbitrary.

When the final items are chosen, it is possible to rescore the entire sample according to the remaining items. The results for all persons involved should be more reliable than before item analysis was applied. At least the internal consistency of the instrument has been improved significantly. And to that extent, the overall reliability of the instrument was strengthened.

A question may arise about why the middle 50 percent of persons was excluded from the original item analysis. The reason these persons are not included is that the upper and lower quartiles represent the extreme attitudinal intensities in either direction. Those persons in the middle of the distribution in terms of their overall scores are more likely to have response weights of 3 or 4 associated with each item. Thus the discriminatory ability of each item would be obscured by using these middle-of-the-road persons and their scores.

STRENGTHS AND WEAKNESSES OF ITEM DISCRIMINATION ANALYSIS

Some advantages of item discrimination analysis are that it assists researchers in eliminating unreliable items that are inconsistent with the rest. Also, internal consistency of any measure is strengthened. On the negative side, item discrimination analysis may result in the exclusion of items that truly measure the trait investigated. Some of those excluded items may be among the best indicators of the trait measured.

External Reliability Checks

External consistency procedures utilize cumulative test results against themselves as a means of verifying the reliability of the measure. Test results for a group of people are compared in two different time periods, or two sets of results from equivalent but different tests are compared. Two major methods of determining the reliability of a test by external consistency are test–retest and parallel forms of the same test.

Test–retest. The method of test–retest as a reliability measure is perhaps the most popular of all procedures discussed in this section. To determine the reliability of a measuring instrument using test–retest, an attitudinal measuring instrument is administered to a sample of persons at a given point in time. After a given time interval lapses (perhaps two to four weeks), the instrument is administered again to the same persons. The two sets of test results are correlated, and the resulting correlation coefficient is a measure of the reliability of the attitudinal measure. The higher the correlation between the two sets of scores, the more reliable the instrument. All of this assumes that nothing intervenes to influence test scores of these subjects between the two time periods. The logic is that if the measure is reliable, the score results should be equivalent or nearly equivalent in both time periods.

A reliable measure will reflect the characteristic to the same degree over two different time periods where no intervening variables can interfere significantly with test scores. A high correlation or similarity between the two sets of scores for the same individuals is considered as evidence of the instrument's reliability. Then, if researchers wish to use the instrument in an experimental situation, where some experimental variable is anticipated to elicit changes among respondents, the use of the reliable measure may yield score differences between the two time intervals that will probably be attributable to the experimental variable rather than to the unreliability of the instrument.

The test–retest reliability method is useful primarily in stable social situations where it is unlikely that the environment will change significantly from one test administration to the next (particularly over relatively short periods such as a few months). Ideally, for a measuring instrument to be demonstrably reliable, the researcher expects a situation similar to that shown in Table 10.5.

In the table, scores are shown in upper half for 10 individuals in a test–retest situation with no intervening variable occurring between the two test administrations. There are no differences between scores comparing the two time periods. In the lower half of the table, score changes over two periods are illustrated. Researchers want the measure to be reliable so that any score differences observed following the introduction of the experimental variable can tentatively be attributable to it. Score differences from one time period to the next should reflect actual differences in the trait being measured rather than the result of a chance fluctuation of an unreliable instrument.

Strengths and Weaknesses of the Test–Retest Reliability Method

Some of the major strengths of the test–retest method for determining reliability are that test–retest permits instruments to be compared directly against themselves. An instrument that performs unreliably in a test–retest situation may require some kind of item-by-item analysis, such as item discrimination analysis, to determine which items discriminate between those who possess the trait to varying degrees. Test–retest also most directly reveals the continuity of the measure over time. It it easiest to use in an external reliability check compared with other methods designed to perform the same function. Test–retest is quick and easy to apply,

TABLE 10.5. SCORES FOR TEN INDIVIDUALS ON MEASURE OF ATTITUDE A

Individual	t_1	t_2	Difference in Scores $t_1 - t_2$
	Experimental variable absent		
1	45	45	0
2	35	35	0
3	27	27	0
4	50	50	0
5	46	46	0
6	31	31	0
7	29	29	0
8	30	30	0
9	41	41	0
10	45	45	0
	Experimental variable present		
1	45	20	−25
2	35	18	−17
3	27	22	−5
4	50	31	−19
5	46	40	−6
6	31	22	−9
7	29	26	−3
8	30	29	−1
9	41	40	−1
10	45	38	−7

and it offers researchers the greatest degree of control over extraneous factors that might otherwise interfere with the instrument's reliability.

On the negative side, test–retest means that respondents will be able to see the same items again and perhaps recall how they responded originally. There is often a "strain for consistency" among respondents, and therefore even if they really feel differently in another time period, they will attempt to recreate their original responses from the first instrument administration. There is little researchers can do to prevent respondents from recalling their original responses to questions. One way of dealing with this problem is to lengthen the time interval between test administrations to several months. However, changes might occur among these persons over time as the result of natural causes and maturation. Conventionally, two to four weeks is considered an appropriate time interval between test administrations when applying the test–retest reliability check. There is no prescribed time interval that is universally accepted by all criminologists.

Another weakness of test–retest is that it is not foolproof. It is difficult for researchers to assess the impact of extraneous factors that might otherwise affect one's scores in two periods. A high correlation between two sets of scores is not absolute proof of the test's reliability, since consistencies may be the result of chance fluctuations. Also, when researchers enter social settings to administer

Types of Reliability

their instruments, their entry into these settings acts as an intervening variable that must be considered. Sometimes, after persons have had an opportunity to observe one's questionnaires and scales, they may not be receptive to reentry at a later date to complete the second phase of the test–retest sequence.

✳**Parallel forms of the same test.** A second major reliability check is the use of parallel forms of the same test. When researchers use parallel forms of the same test, they actually devise two separate measures of the same phenomenon. Previously mentioned was the 16 PF, a personality inventory developed by Raymond Cattell. This instrument has two versions, A and B. Both versions consist of 187 questions each that purportedly both measure 16 different personality dimensions. The two versions of the 16 PF are considered equivalent. Whenever factor analyses of these instruments are conducted, they "factor" or divide into 16 different parts. Interestingly, the items on form A that purportedly measure certain personality dimensions factor into the same areas as the items on form B that supposedly measure the same dimensions. Thus the two versions of the measure help to validate each other as well as to verify the reliability of each.

STRENGTHS AND WEAKNESSES OF THE PARALLEL FORMS METHOD

The primary advantage of devising two separate tests of the same attitudinal variable is that the instruments may be administered to the same audiences over different time periods without having to worry about recalling previous responses. The two versions of these measures are made up of entirely different items. It is impossible to recall how you responded to items you have not seen. Further, it is unnecessary to have "waiting periods" between test administrations to evaluate the measure's reliability. Basically, two forms of the measure are administered and their results are correlated.

On the negative side, it is quite difficult and time consuming to create two separate measures of the same attitudinal phenomenon. Some researchers have difficulty creating one measure. By doubling the number of items, the problems of establishing test validity and reliability are compounded, since more items are involved. Finally, it is difficult to establish the equivalency of two instruments that purportedly measure the same phenomena. What if the two measures correlate highly with one another? Does this mean that the measures are reliable? What if they measure different attitudes, although those different attitudes may be related to a degree? One test may measure factor X, while the other measures factor Y. A high correlation between the two measures does not automatically mean that the two instruments are measuring identical phenomena.

SOME FUNCTIONAL RELATIONSHIPS BETWEEN VALIDITY AND RELIABILITY

Of the two properties of measuring instruments, validity and reliability, the more important is reliability. There are several reasons for this. Before we examine these reasons, four general statements about the relation between validity and reliability may be made.

1. Valid instruments are always reliable instruments.
2. Instruments that are not valid may or may not be reliable.
3. Reliable instruments may or may not be valid.
4. Instruments that are not reliable are never valid.

These relationships between validity and reliability are important. Here is what each statement means. Statement 1 says that if you are really measuring whatever you think you are measuring, you are measuring it consistently or reliably. Statement 2 says that if you are not really measuring what you think you are measuring, you may or may not be measuring something else. If you *are* measuring something else, it is a valid measure of "something else," whatever that might be. If this is the case, the measure is reliable (this is the truthfulness of statement 1). In short, if we say we are measuring variable X but, in fact, we are measuring variable Y (which is closely related to X), we do not have a valid measure of X but we do have a valid measure of Y. We do not know that we have a valid measure of Y. We might think that our instrument measures X, but unknown to us is the fact that our instrument is really a valid measure of Y. If it is really a valid measure of Y (even though we do not know it), it is also a reliable instrument.

Statement 3 says that if we have a reliable measure, it may or may not be valid. What this means is that if we are measuring something consistently such as variable X (again, we might think that we are measuring variable X), the measure is valid. It may or may not be valid for whatever it is we think we are measuring. But at least we are measuring something consistently. We may not know what we are measuring, but at least it is significant; we can rely on it. The same thing is true about reliability. If our instrument exhibits reliability, we are measuring something. We may or may not be measuring what we think we are measuring, but we are definitely measuring something consistently.

Statement 4 says that if we do not have a reliable measure, we do not have validity. Thus reliability is a necessary prerequisite for an instrument's validity. Reliability is more important, therefore, since validity depends on the reliability of the measure. Any measure that lacks reliability also lacks validity. But any measure that lacks validity may or may not lack reliability. Again, "We don't know what we're measuring, but it is significant."

FACTORS THAT AFFECT VALIDITY AND RELIABILITY

Thus far we have examined validity and reliability in considerable detail and have considered several ways that these instrument properties may be assessed or determined. In this section we focus on several factors and conditions that affect significantly the validity and reliability of measures. These factors may be grouped into four broad headings: (1) the instrument and its contents, (2) environmental factors, (3) personal factors, and (4) researcher interpretations.

The Instrument and Its Contents

Whenever the validity and reliability of attitudinal measures are assessed, the first aspect to be scrutinized critically is the list of items included in the instrument. Are the items valid? Have they been drawn from the universe of traits and characteristics that measure the phenomenon under investigation? If the researcher has been careless and included items from a universe other than the one consistent with the trait designated in the theoretical scheme, the validity of the test will be seriously undermined. Apart from the logical and theoretical connection between the items included in the measure and the trait to be measured, other aspects of the test emerge as crucial as well. Some of these factors are:

1. *The length of the test.* A long instrument will sometimes cause respondents to give answers based on convenience rather than the way they really feel about things. Longer tests may become boring, and respondents begin to check the first responses they come to, as is the case with set responses.

2. *The cultural date of the test.* A test that uses words or phrases not used conventionally becomes increasingly unreliable and hence not a valid indicator of the trait in question. Using terms such as "ice box" to refer to "refrigerators" may create a misunderstanding between the meaning intended by the statement (defined by the researcher) and the way it is understood by respondents. The American Correctional Association and the American Jail Association have done much in recent years to improve the professional image of correctional officers who work in jails and prisons. In recent years, the term "guard," earlier used to refer to those who perform jail duties and monitor inmates, has been rejected as archaic and derogatory. In its place, the term "jail officer" is more respectful and dignified. The use of "guard" on a questionnaire to be administered to jail officers may be considered offensive by them. Thus unwittingly, researchers may evoke hostility from respondents because of the terms they use to characterize them and their work.

3. *Open-ended versus fixed-response questions.* Measures that utilize open-ended questions (questions that have respondents furnish written answers rather than check specific fixed alternatives) place a strong emphasis on the ability of respondents to express themselves in writing. One's educational sophistication becomes an important consideration. Because the type of response provided to open-ended questions determines the degree of intensity of some attitude possessed by respondents, it is clear that the ability to express themselves may seem to reflect differences in attitudes by persons of varying educational backgrounds when actually there are no differences.

4. *Mechanical factors.* Mechanical factors refer to instrument problems, including misspelled words, illegible words, missing pages, and poorly phrased items. All of these mechanical factors may cause some misunderstanding of instrument content, and this misunderstanding will detract from the instrument's validity and reliability. The same is true of face-to-face interviews. If researchers leave certain statements off their list of questions or if they use alternative words at random, the information solicited becomes less reliable, since respondents may make different interpretations of the questions asked. Ideally, the same administration conditions should prevail for each respondent. This uniformity would tend to minimize the possibility of errors due to differences in the way various subjects are approached by the investigator. Usually, pretests of instruments in smaller-scale pilot studies help to eliminate most of the mechanical deficiencies of measures.

Environmental Factors

Environmental conditions describe the conditions under which instruments are administered. These include (1) face-to-face interviews versus self-administered questionnaires and (2) the clarity of instructions for completing the instrument.

1. *Face-to-face interviews versus self-administered questionnaires.* Varying the degree of anonymity or confidentiality under which the instrument is administered may generate score differences for the same person under various test administration conditions. Persons sometimes report to an interviewer face-to-face feelings about things that are quite different from the feelings they would disclose in a more confidential, self-administered questionnaire situation where considerable anonymity exists.

2. *The clarity of instructions for completing the instrument.* If investigators fail to clarify the procedures to be followed in the completion of the instrument, there is a good chance that subjects will provide misleading information unintentionally.

Personal Factors

Some of the more relevant personal characteristics that impinge on the validity and reliability of measures are (1) the socioeconomic status of respondents; (2) age, gender, and maturity level; (3) ethnic and racial background; (4) memory or recall ability; and (5) social desirability.

1. *Socioeconomic status of respondents.* Occupation, educational level, income, and race/ethnicity are primary components of socioeconomic status. These factors may influence one's performance on any attitudinal instrument. Researchers should attempt to gear their instrumentation to closely approximate the socioeconomic level of the audiences they investigate. The cultural aspects of any measuring instrument will limit the generalizability and utility of it to particular social aggregates.

2. *Age, sex, and maturity level.* Like socioeconomic status, age and gender are important considerations in any instrument administration. Closely associated with age and gender are differences in maturity levels among respondents. The maturity level of intended respondents may influence the manner in which researchers are accepted and the degree of cooperation and interest demonstrated by participating subjects.

3. *Ethnic and racial background.* Although ethnicity and race are conventionally regarded as a part of socioeconomic status, it is worthwhile to note that ethnic background may account for certain misunderstandings pertaining to word choices in questionnaires. Different words may have different meanings and convey different ideas to people from different ethnic backgrounds as well as to persons of different socioeconomic statuses. In testing and measurement, researchers are increasingly moving toward the development of culture-free measures. They are learning more and more to appreciate the fact that tests often have built-in cultural biases that significantly affect our interpretations of results for different ethnic audiences.

4. *Memory or recall.* The ability of subjects to recall earlier responses on a before–after test administration may elicit responses consistent with earlier ones, regardless of whether or not the respondent's beliefs are the same in both periods. Parallel forms of the same test are used frequently to overcome the effects of memory or recall in test–retest situations, particularly if the span of time between test administration is short.

5. *Social desirability.* Many questionnaires have social desirability measures incorporated into them to ascertain the effect of this important variable on a subject's overall response pattern. Social desirability, responding in accordance with what subjects believe to be a desirable set of traits rather than what might be true of them, is a frequent test contaminator. In fact, some researchers have gone so far as to say that any given attitude is, in reality, an indication of what persons regard as socially desirable rather than what is actually true of them. Again, there is no way to determine the precise contribution made by social desirability in influencing a test's reliability and validity.

Researcher Interpretations

Finally, an important consideration in assessing an instrument's validity and reliability is the kind of interpretation made of results by researchers. Under this heading are included (1) the coding procedure and (2) interpretations of raw scores.

1. *Coding procedures.* Researchers are at liberty to code their information any way they wish. The validity and reliability of instruments often hinge, in part, on the coding pattern followed by investigators. Although this opportunity varies considerably from study to study, it is possible for researchers to code information in such ways so as to increase the chances of supporting one particular theoretical perspective or another. Objectivity in coding is encouraged, and it is recommended that researchers compare their own coding procedures with those used by other researchers who investigate similar phenomena. This will not guarantee that their coding procedures will be foolproof, but at least researchers can minimize the possibility that their own values and biases will enter the picture significantly when data are interpreted.

2. *Interpretation of raw scores.* Raw scores on any attitudinal measure are seldom meaningful apart from their comparison with other scores on the same scale. When researchers extract raw scores from a list of them, they run the risk of assigning meanings to scores that are quite different from the practical meanings those scores have in a comparative sense. Single-score interpretations should be made conservatively and tentatively. Sometimes, previous norms exist for specific instrument applications to certain types of audiences. These norms may be used for evaluations of scores on subsequent administrations, although researchers should not rely too much on such previous norms. It is likely that each test administration is somewhat different from previous test administrations and that the norms applicable in one setting may not be applicable to another setting.

SUMMARY

Two important instrument properties are validity and reliability. Validity is the property that enables researchers to specify what it is they are measuring with particular instruments. Reliability is the consistency property of measures, where scores mean pretty much the same thing from one test administration to the next unless affected by experimental variables or environmental changes affecting respondents.

Validity can never be proved. It can only be inferred on the basis of logical and/or statistical criteria. Four types of validation include content or face validity, predictive validity, concurrent validity, and construct validity. Reliability is a prerequisite for the validity of any measure. Thus it is weighed as the more important of the two properties of instruments. Reliability is determined by item discrimination analysis, the split-half method, test–retest, and parallel forms of the same test. These internal and external reliability checks exist as proof of a measure's reliability. Reliability can be proved and improved by these various checks.

General linkages between validity and reliability exist. Valid tests are always reliable tests. Tests that are not valid measures of one phenomenon may, in fact, be valid measures of other unknown phenomena. Therefore, we may say that tests that are not valid may or may not be reliable. Tests that are reliable are always valid measures of something, but we are not always sure what we are measuring. Thus reliable tests may or may not be valid, for designated attributes or variables. Finally, tests that are not reliable are never valid. For tests to have validity, reliability must exist.

Several different kinds of factors influence the validity and reliability of tests. The instrument itself, environmental factors, personal factors, and researcher interpretations all impact on a measure's validity and reliability in various ways. Test length, the cultural dating of tests, and mechanical factors, such as word choices, misspelled words, and missing pages, are test qualities that detract from validity and reliability. The socioeconomic status of respondents, their gender, ethnicity, and race, the nature of administration conditions, and social desirability are several other factors that influence instrument responses in certain ways and cause us to question the validity and reliability of the scales we devise.

QUESTIONS FOR REVIEW

1. What is reliability? How is it measured or determined? Describe two internal reliability methods.

2. What are four general relationships between validity and reliability? Discuss each briefly.

3. What is validity? How is it measured or determined? Identify four different methods for determining test validity. Is validity provable? Why or why not? Explain.

4. What are two external methods for determining a test's reliability? Discuss each.

5. Write a short essay on the importance of social desirability and how it might influence test results. How are reliability and validity influenced by social desirability?

6. What is meant by "environmental factors that impinge on a test's validity and reliability"? Discuss two of these factors.

7. What are five personal factors that influence the validity and reliability of tests?

8. Is it possible to have a valid test that is not reliable? Why or why not?

9. What is meant by a "mechanical factor" as it pertains to questionnaire construction?

10. How would the cultural dating of a test or measure influence its validity or reliability? Give an example.

11. Compare and contrast test–retest and parallel forms of the same test as reliability checks. What are the respective weaknesses and strengths of each?

—— 11 ——

Data Presentation and Descriptive Techniques

KEY TERMS

Bar graphs
Centiles
Collapsing tables
Control of variables
Crime clocks
Crosstabulations of variables
Cumulative frequency distributions
Deciles
Diagonal distributions of frequencies
Frequency distributions
Frequency polygons
Graphic presentation

Histograms
Interval midpoints
Ogive curves
Pie charts
Quartiles
Rows and columns
Spuriousness
2×2 tables
Upper and lower limits of intervals
Variables
Variable subclasses

INTRODUCTION

Any introduction to criminology or criminal justice course will expose students to diverse forms of graphic presentation. Graphic presentation includes charts, tabular materials, drawings of lines or bars, pie charts, and other visual material that assists us in describing what we have found. The idea that "a picture is worth a thousand words" is appropriate here. The *Uniform Crime Reports*, compiled by the FBI and published by the Department of Justice, is filled with graphic material about crime and crime trends. One glance at a well-illustrated graph or table can tell you much about whether certain crimes have increased or decreased over different time intervals. Popular periodicals such as *U.S. News and World Report*, *Time*, *Newsweek*, and the *Reader's Digest* feature numerous illustrations that inform us about such things as drug flow from South American countries, illegal immigration, violence among juveniles, prison and jail overcrowding, and public opinion or sentiment. These tables, graphs, charts, figures, and diagrams enhance our understanding of written material. Further, our efforts to build theories and test hypotheses are furthered by the strategic use of these materials.

In this chapter we describe several popular graphic techniques and methods that are used to illustrate published material in criminal justice and criminology. We should learn about this material for at least two reasons. First, we will be exposed to a great deal of written material where illustrations are used to highlight important points. We should be knowledgeable about how illustrative materials should be interpreted and how they enhance our understanding of subject matter. Second, we will be preparing reports, articles, and other writings ourselves. We want to maximize the reader's understanding of our own work, and graphic materials can assist us in achieving this objective.

In the first part of this chapter we describe various types of graphs, including line drawings and figures known as pie charts, bar graphs, histograms, and frequency polygons. In the second part of the chapter we examine tabular construction. We often create tables consisting of differing numbers of rows and columns. When our data are distributed throughout the tables we have created, they are amenable to certain statistical test applications, where we can evaluate the significance of what we have found. Throughout this chapter, conventional rules guide much of our graphic and tabular construction. Further, each of these illustrative techniques and methods has accompanying strengths and weaknesses.

GRAPHIC PRESENTATION

Graphic presentation consists of all tables, charts, illustrations, figures, and line drawings that depict how collected data are distributed or arranged. Usually, graphics are limited to the most important features of studies that deserve to be highlighted. Charts and graphs can show trends over time regarding the incidence of different types of crime and other variables. The "spread" or distribution of frequencies throughout tables can show the influence of certain variables on other variables, and whether associations exist. Informative summaries of statistical information, such as the proportionate distribution of race, gender, age, and type of offense associated with jail or prison inmate populations, enable researchers to design their own studies more effectively by isolating the most crucial factors for investigation. Below is a summary of some of the more important functions of graphic presentation.

FUNCTIONS OF GRAPHIC PRESENTATION

The major functions of graphic presentation include (1) enhancing articles, reports, and data summaries; (2) testing hypotheses derived from theories; (3) providing evidence of relationships between variables; (4) depicting trends and proportionate distributions; (5) influencing statistical test selections and applications; and (6) influencing policy decision making.

Enhancing Articles, Reports, and Data Summaries

It is helpful to provide line drawings and other illustrations to highlight the written words in technical reports. Those who read articles often analyze charts and graphs before digesting the written material. Much can be gained by paying attention to how variables are distributed. Readers may quickly grasp whether certain variables are important as explanatory factors and deserve to be studied further.

Testing Hypotheses Derived from Theories

Often, data are presented by researchers in tabular form for the purpose of testing hypotheses derived from theories. Depending on how such graphs and tables are constructed and arranged, investigators may be able to influence the significance of whatever they find. As we will see, it is fairly easy to "lie with statistics," and the manipulation of the same data in graphs and tables by two different researchers may yield opposite and contradictory results when analyzed. Several objective rules or conventional procedures have been established to minimize the bias that may be introduced by the different vested interests of researchers. However, not everyone adheres strongly to convention when presenting their data to others. At appropriate points in this chapter, conventional guidelines will be presented that are calculated to enhance the objectivity of data presentation.

Providing Evidence of Relationships between Variables

Tabular materials may illustrate relationships or associations between two or more variables. Thus we may be able to point at the distribution of tabular frequencies to show that one or more variables are related to each other in meaningful ways. Statistical tests may be applied to furnish independent numerical objectivity to our visual interpretations of tabular material.

Depicting Trends and Proportionate Distributions

Certain line drawings and graphs help to show whether variables change in certain directions over time. Is crime increasing in the United States? What is the proportion of mentally ill inmates among the entire U.S. jail population? How does the incidence of property crimes compare with violent crimes over time in specific cities or geographical regions? Which states have the highest execution rates? Graphic presentation illustrates this material easily.

Influencing Statistical Test Selections and Applications

For certain statistical tests to be applicable for our data analyses, various "distributional" assumptions may be required. Some statistical procedures presented in Chapter 17 require that the sample data be distributed in the form of a *bell-shaped curve* of *normal distribution* (see Chapter 16). If our line drawings of raw scores show curves or distributions other than "normal" ones, we have failed to meet at least one statistical test assumption. Our choices of *central tendency* and *dispersion* or *variability* measures often depend on how our data are distributed or arranged as well (see Chapter 15). If some raw scores among our collected data are quite different from the others or are "deviant scores" (e.g., most of 100 scores in some hypothetical distribution fluctuate between 10 and 30, but three of these scores are 80, 85, and 90 and are considered "deviant scores"), we would want to apply the central tendency measure that works best with these deviant scores. Otherwise, applications of the other central tendency measures to our data with deviant scores would be distorted or misleading. "Seeing" the distribution in graphic form influences our statistical test selections.

Influencing Policy Decision Making

Intervention programs that are intended to change behavior may be adopted on a large scale by communities if positive results can be illustrated by investigators. For example, researchers may believe that a particular elementary school juvenile counseling and therapy method for youths considered "at risk" is useful for reducing their inclination to become delinquent. Graphic presentations of samples of "high-risk" youths exposed to the intervention program or therapy may eventually illustrate low numbers of delinquent youths over time. Thus the community may adopt the intervention in schools as a general policy. Low recidivism rates among parolees and probationers may be attributable to lower probation and parole officer caseloads and more intensive supervision. Therefore, attempts may be made to keep officer caseloads low in an effort to decrease recidivism among clients.

TYPES OF GRAPHIC PRESENTATION

The following types of graphic presentation are illustrated: (1) pie charts, (2) bar graphs, (3) frequency distributions, (4) histograms, and (5) frequency polygons.

Pie Charts

Pie charts are circular graphs that portray either portions of 100 percent of some aggregate or the frequency of incidents. Figure 11.1 shows a *crime clock* of the incidence of robbery in the United States, while Figure 11.2 illustrates the proportion of minimum-, medium-, and maximum-security U.S. state prisons.

In recent years, the FBI has considered dropping crime clocks from its publication, the *Uniform Crime Reports*, because it is possible to misinterpret them

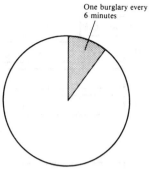

One burglary every
6 minutes

Figure 11.1 Crime Clock. [*From the FBI Uniform Crime Report Bulletin* (Washington, D.C. U.S. Government Printing Office.)

easily.   When certain crimes are represented as occurring every few minutes, this refers to the total number of those crimes during the year divided into the total number of minutes in that same time interval.   It does not mean that if there is a rape every 20 minutes in the United States, rapes occur in Denver, Colorado or Sioux Falls, South Dakota every 20 minutes.   Rather, national figures are portrayed.   There are seasonal fluctuations in these crime rates as well.   More frequent use of pie charts is made to portray proportions of selected populations with particular characteristics.

Few restrictions exist pertaining to pie charts, their construction, and their application.   The major shortcoming of them is the number of segments into which they may be divided conveniently.   Too many segments create a "cluttered" pie chart.   A rule of thumb governing the maximum number of divisions for portraying data would be six.   Beyond six divisions, it is difficult for researchers to label each sector in the chart adequately.   Their use may be extended to virtually any variable and its subdivisions.

Bar Graphs

Bar graphs are either vertical or horizontal "bars" that portray the frequency of values on some variable.   Figure 11.3 shows three separate bar graphs that portray national geographical distributions of (1) jails, (2) jail inmates, and (3) jail officers

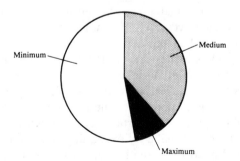

Figure 11.2 Pie Chart Showing U.S. State Prison Classifications.

Types of Graphic Presentation

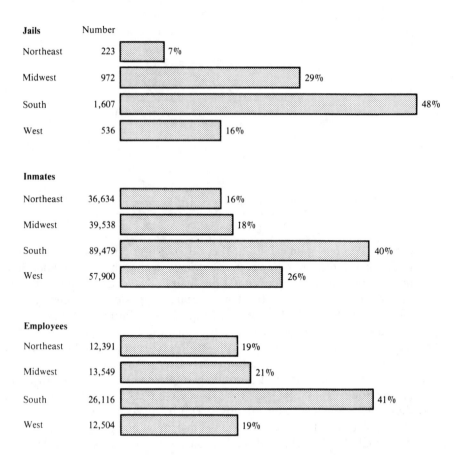

Figure 11.3 Regional Distributions of Jails, Inmates, and Jail Employees, 1988.
(Source: U.S. Dept. of Justice, *Census of Local Jails, 1983, Vol. I, The Northeast
Data for Individual Jails.* [Washington, D.C.: Bureau of Justice Statistics, 1988].
(cover)).

(U.S. Department of Justice, 1988:cover). We can determine at a glance that the
South accounts for nearly one-half (48 percent) of all U.S. jails, followed by the
Midwest, West, and Northeast. However, only 40 percent of all jail inmates are
in southern jails. Interestingly, the west has only 16 percent of all jails but 26
percent of all jail inmates. Although more information would be needed to interpret these data accurately, we might conclude initially that perhaps the South
has more and smaller jails compared with other regions. The population density
of jails is perhaps highest in the northeast, where only 7 percent of all U.S. jails
house 16 percent of all jail inmates. Further, the South seems understaffed, with
about 41 percent of all jail officers to service 48 percent of the jails. By contrast,
the Northeast has 19 percent of the nation's jail officers to service only 7 percent
of the nation's jails. These statements are nothing more than preliminary interpretations we might make by examining such graphic material. The entire document would need to be read carefully for us to appreciate fully the significance
of the distributions of these figures.

Bar graphs can be used to illustrate trends, such as increases or decreases in crime rates over time. An imaginative use of bar graphs is the portrayal of various forms of delinquent conduct for both males and females. Figure 11.4 shows proportionate distributions of male and female juveniles for overall delinquency and for specific types of offenses within uniformly drawn horizontal bars. Much like pie charts, the area within each bar represents 100 percent of each type of offense. Shaded areas are used to represent proportions of either males or females within each offense category.

Bar graphs do not need to consist of uniformly drawn bars. For example, we might construct a bar graph such as the one shown in Figure 11.5 to depict the incidence of crime across various social classes. In this instance, we have simply constructed vertical and horizontal axes, with high and low crime rates illustrated on the vertical axis, and social class, arranged from low to high, across the horizontal axis. The widths of the vertical bars in this case reflect either smaller or larger proportions of persons in different social classes. The wide flexibility of bar graphs and their lack of restrictions for any particular measurement level (e.g., nominal, ordinal, interval, or ratio) make them attractive illustrative devices in research reports and articles.

Frequency Distributions

One of the more important illustrative tools available to researchers is the frequency distribution. Frequency distributions are arrangements of raw scores from high to low, according to intervals of a designated size.

Construction of frequency distributions.
The construction of frequency distributions is one of the first things on a researcher's agenda after data have been collected. Investigators organize their data in some meaningful way in order to make sense out of it. Suppose that an investigator conducted interviews with 15

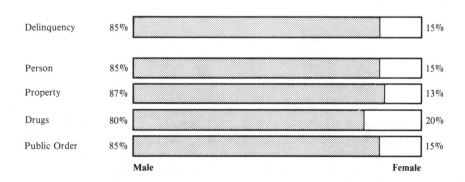

Figure 11.4 Offense Characteristics of Delinquency Cases by Sex, 1985. (*Source:* U.S. Department of Justice, *Juvenile Court Statistics, 1985* [Washington, D.C., 1989], p. 21.)

Types of Graphic Presentation

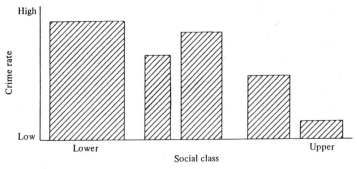

Crime rate

Low

Lower

Social class

Upper

Figure 11.5 Bar Graph Reflecting Social Class and Crime.

probation officers. The investigator determined from interviews that the ages of the probation officers were as follows: 35, 49, 62, 55, 41, 40, 35, 31, 30, 26, 29, 39, 39, 36, and 48. Taken as an aggregate, these ages are diverse and do not tell us much about these officers. Some organization of these ages is necessary.

Perhaps the investigator decides to arrange these ages as shown below. The data have been arranged into a frequency distribution of various age categories, and the *frequency* of each age has been placed in the appropriate category created. We can gain a better impression of the age distribution of these officers and see that the most popular age category is 35 to 39. Few officers are over age 50.

Age Category	Number of Officers (Frequency), f
25–29	2
30–34	2
35–39	5
40–44	2
45–49	2
50–54	0
55–59	1
60–64	1
Total (N) = Σf (sum of frequencies) = 15	

Depending on the size of one's sample, we will treat the data as either *ungrouped* or *grouped*. Ungrouped data analyses involve dealing directly with raw scores, without any attempt to order or arrange them from low to high or high to low. Grouped data analyses are arrangements of data into intervals of various sizes for better data management. A rule of thumb applied to making the ungrouped/grouped data decision is to "group" the data whenever one's sample size is 25 or larger ($N > 25$—read "N is greater than 25"). For sample sizes less than

25, treating data in ungrouped or grouped form is optional for the researcher, although it is probably best to deal with smaller samples in ungrouped fashion. The logic underlying "grouping" larger sample sizes is that the data are made more manageable for purposes of description, analysis, and statistical test applications. After arranging many scores into a frequency distribution of them, researchers can "see" the spread of scores or their distributional properties. Particular statistical tests and descriptive measures are suggested by different types of distributional arrangements.

In the example above where probation officers' ages were arranged into several age categories, only 15 ages were involved. While it was helpful to organize these data into several age categories and enabled us to "see" the spread of raw age scores, we could have left these scores as they were and computed various descriptive measures such as the "average" or *mean* (see Chapter 15). This would be following the rule of thumb noted above to deal with samples smaller than 25 in ungrouped form. As we will see in later chapters, statistical procedures are often designed for application to samples of specified sizes. Usually, statistical procedures have operating ranges of certain sample sizes where their meaningfulness and application are maximized. Thus there are statistical tests for small-sample situations and for large-sample applications. Further, various descriptive techniques have alternative formulas for their application to data in either ungrouped or grouped form. Because of the diversity of studies that are conducted in criminal justice and criminology, it is important for researchers to be familiar with both types of data management whenever large or small samples are encountered. A larger-sample example will illustrate the greater ease of data management whenever raw scores are grouped.

In Table 11.1 are 82 hypothetical scores on an achievement test administered to prison inmates who are enrolled in a GED program. The larger the score, the higher the performance on the achievement test. Table 11.1 does not make a lot of sense as shown. The raw scores are in *disarray*. We might profit by arranging the individual scores from high to low, but because of the large sample size, $N = 82$, this would be time consuming. Our decision is to arrange these data into a certain number of intervals of some size so that we can manage the data more easily. We will follow the steps below to create a frequency distribution for these data.

TABLE 11.1 UNGROUPED LISTING OF 82 HYPOTHETICAL ACHIEVEMENT TEST SCORES FOR PRISON INMATES

326	322	349	358	343	390	345	322	333	335	338	338	339
349	350	351	365	371	356	344	355	345	344	340	359	351
356	381	375	371	370	360	365	378	390	349	341	346	362
324	381	327	348	367	368	369	371	382	369	387	345	330
327	346	344	332	330	330	344	348	354	358	366	366	367
389	388	324	322	339	368	373	378	377	382	383	345	365
345	369	340	358									

Types of Graphic Presentation

1. *Identify the largest and smallest raw scores in the distribution.* In this case, an inspection of Table 11.1 shows that the largest score is 390, while the smallest score is 322.

2. *Divide the difference between the largest and the smallest scores by 15.* The difference in the scores, 390 and 322, is $390 - 322 = 68$. Dividing 68 by 15, we would have $68/15 = 4.5$. We divided the score difference by 15 because of a conventional rule. The conventional rule is that we should construct frequency distributions that contain from 10 to 20 intervals of some size. Frequency distributions with fewer than 10 intervals "compact" our data into too few categories, and we cannot evaluate clearly how the scores are distributed. Frequency distributions with more than 20 intervals are spread out too thinly, and again, we cannot evaluate clearly how the scores are distributed. The figure, 15, is selected as a happy medium, an arbitrary number between 10 and 20 intervals. When we divide the distance between the largest and smallest scores in the distribution by 15, this gives us a value, 4.5, that is near a "desirable interval size."

We may evoke another conventional rule about our interval size choice. Conventional interval sizes are 1, 2, 3, 4, 5, 10, 20, 30, 40, 50, 100, 200, 300, 400, 500, and so on. If we are dealing with decimals, rates, or proportions, our interval sizes may be 0.1, 0.2, 0.3, 0.4, 0.5, 0.01, 0.02, 0.03, 0.04, 0.05, and so on. In the example above, the value 4.5 is midway between an interval size of 4 and an interval size of 5. If we choose the interval size 5, we will have fewer intervals of size 5. If we choose 4, we will have more intervals of size 4. It is unusual and unconventional to have intervals of size 4.5, 7, 9, 13, or some number other than those noted here. This does not mean that unusual interval sizes *cannot* be chosen, but our computational work and general data management will be somewhat more complicated. In this case, let's use the interval size, 5, to create a frequency distribution for the data (raw scores) in Table 11.1.

3. *The next step is to decided where to begin our intervals and which numbers to use.* It is conventional to construct our first interval so that (1) the first number in it is a multiple of the interval size and (2) the largest or smallest score is included in the interval. Since our interval is 5, examples of multiples of size 5 would be 5, 10, 15, 20, 320, 330, 345, and 365. We examine our data and determine that the smallest score is 322. The largest score is 390. Therefore, we may begin our interval construction with either 320–324 or 390–394. Both of these intervals begin with a multiple of size 5, and each contains either the smallest or largest values among the scores in Table 11.1. The interval 320–324 contains the smallest scores in the distribution and is considered the "bottom" of it. The interval 390–394 is the "top" of the distribution, since it contains the largest scores. Suppose that we decided to begin with the interval 320–324.

4. *Our next step is to establish all intervals beginning with 320–324 and to continue constructing intervals until we have reached and included 390–394.* This is illustrated in Table 11.2.

5. *The fifth step is to enter the numbers of raw scores from Table 11.1 into their appropriate intervals in Table 11.2.* A raw score of 369 belongs in the interval 365–369, whereas the raw score 370 belongs in the interval 370–374. These frequencies have been entered into their appropriate intervals as shown. Finally,

TABLE 11.2 FREQUENCY DISTRIBUTION OF 82 ACHIEVEMENT SCORES FOR PRISON INMATES, CONSTRUCTED FROM RAW SCORES IN TABLE 11.1

Interval	Frequency, f	
320–324	5	("bottom" of distribution)
325–329	3	
330–334	5	
335–339	5	
340–344	8	
345–349	12	
350–354	4	
355–359	7	
360–364	2	
365–369	12	
370–374	5	
375–379	4	
380–384	5	
385–389	3	
390–394	2	("top" of distribution)

$$\sum f = 82 = N$$

we sum the frequencies as a check on our work to see that we have tabulated them correctly.

The rationale for beginning our intervals with a multiple of the interval size is simple. We may easily check the accuracy of our interval construction by scanning the first numbers in all intervals. Each is a multiple of the interval size of 5. Had we made one interval 365–370, our next interval would have been 371–374. Both of these intervals are improper because they are both the wrong size. The interval 365–370 might look as though it is of size 5, but it is of size 6. The scores 365, 366, 367, 368, 369, and 370 may be included in it. The other interval, 371–374, contains only four scores: 371, 372, 373, and 374. We can easily detect our error, since 371 is not a multiple of our interval size, 5. Another reason for verifying the consistency among the intervals we have constructed is that the interval size, i, is often a key term in descriptive and inferential statistical formulae. Therefore, if we are careless about how our intervals are constructed, we will eventually obtain erroneous statistical results. The importance of accuracy in the construction of frequency distributions cannot be overestimated. If in doubt about the size of any interval, some advice from a late statistics professor is relevant here: Use your fingers and count how many scores are contained in it.

Now we may examine Table 11.2 and determine several things. First, we have 15 intervals. Had we used the interval size 4 in constructing our intervals, there would have been slightly more intervals than 15. Also, the first interval constructed would have been 320–323. The value 320 is a multiple of the interval size, 4, and the interval 320–323 is of size 4 and contains the smallest score of 322. Our next interval would have been 324–327. Another feature of Table 11.2 is

Types of Graphic Presentation

that two intervals, 345–349 and 365–369, contain the most frequencies. Later, when we construct a line drawing of the scores shown in Table 11.2, two high peaks will be observed, reflecting the two intervals that contain the most frequencies. As mentioned earlier, this feature of the distribution will influence our choice of descriptive measures and statistical tests.

It is important to note that you have two options for arranging your data. You can arrange them as shown in Table 11.2, where the interval containing the smallest scores (the "bottom" of the distribution) is physically at the top of the page, or you can reverse your arrangement so that the "bottom" of the distribution is at the bottom of the page. Table 11.3 shows a reversal of information shown in Table 11.2.

This particular point is worth mentioning, since many students "lock" into either one way of constructing these intervals or the other. This is like "trained incapacity," where someone becomes proficient at solving problems only one way and cannot cope with other easy strategies for problem solving. Later, when they encounter distributions of scores that are arranged differently from what they have learned, they may make procedural mistakes associated with the computational requirements of certain inferential and descriptive statistical procedures. Either way of presenting your data is acceptable here. Some persons are more comfortable working with data as distributed in Table 11.3, whereas other researchers prefer the arrangement in Table 11.2. Take your pick. But whichever arrangement you choose, be mindful of this in your computational work, especially work involving calculations of descriptive statistics presented in Chapter 15. Be able to recognize which "end" of the distribution of scores is the "top" and which is the "bottom."

TABLE 11.3 INTERVAL REARRANGEMENT FROM THE DATA IN TABLE 11.2

Interval	f	
390–394	2	("top" of distribution)
385–389	3	
380–384	5	
375–379	4	
370–374	5	
365–369	12	
360–364	2	
355–359	7	
350–354	4	
345–349	12	
340–344	8	
335–339	5	
330–334	5	
325–329	3	
320–324	5	("bottom" of distribution)
	$\sum f = 82$	

Some characteristics of frequency distributions. To solve various problems, including determining various central tendency or dispersion values such as means or standard deviations, it is imperative that one acquire a familiarity with different aspects of frequency distributions. It is necessary to understand how to determine interval upper and lower limits as well as their midpoints. This assumes that the data are treated as though they are measured according to an interval scale, although frequency distributions may be created for data measured according to lower levels of measurement (e.g., nominal and ordinal).

Technically, intervals in frequency distributions extend from their lower limits to their upper limits. For example, technically, the interval 335–339 extends from 334.5 (its lower limit) to 339.5 (its upper limit). Thus if we subtract the lower limit from the upper limit of any interval, our result will be the interval size, or 339.5 − 334.5 = 5. Midpoints of intervals are those points within intervals that divide the intervals into two equal parts. If the interval is of size 5, a point within the interval is the midpoint where 2.5 values are on one side and 2.5 values are on the other. We determine interval midpoints easily by taking one-half of the interval size and either (1) adding it to the lower limit of the interval or (2) subtracting it from the upper limit of the interval. Thus if our interval is 335–339, we take one-half of the interval size of 5, 5/2 = 2.5, and add this amount to 334.5 (the lower limit), or 334.5 + 2.5 = 337. The alternative is to subtract one-half the interval size from the interval upper limit, or 339.5 − 2.5 = 337. Thus 337 is the interval midpoint. Table 11.4 shows some examples of intervals of different sizes, upper and lower limits of these intervals, interval midpoints, and the actual interval sizes for each interval shown.

Upper and lower limits of intervals are particularly meaningful when we deal with data that are continuously distributed. All too often we deal with scores in whole-number form, such as 10, 200, 85, or 350, although data are sometimes presented in decimal form, such as 10.3, 200.889, 85.0035, and so on. If we had an array of values expressed in decimal form, we would need to have some system whereby these scores could be assigned to one interval in our frequency distribution or another. For instance, if we observed the value 324.7, would this value belong in the interval 320–324 or in the interval 325–329? We may examine the upper and lower limits of these two intervals, which would be 319.5–324.5 and 324.5–329.5. Notice that the upper limit of the interval 320–324 is identical with the lower limit of the interval 325–329 (324.5). In the case of our score of 324.7, it

TABLE 11.4 INTERVAL SIZES, UPPER AND LOWER LIMITS, AND MIDPOINTS

Interval	Lower Limit	Upper Limit	Midpoint	Interval Size
15–19	14.5	19.5	17	5
500–509	499.5	509.5	504.5	10
0.21–0.23	0.205	0.235	0.22	0.03
1460–1479	1459.5	1479.5	1469.5	20
0.0058–0.0061	0.00575	0.00615	0.00595	0.0004

would belong in the interval 325–329, since the interval technically extends from 324.5 to 329.5.

If we encounter values that occur directly on the line between one interval or another, such as the value 324.5, does it belong in the interval 320–324 or in the interval 325–329? At this point we will invoke a *rounding rule*, which means that if our value is located exactly between two other values or is an equal distance from each, we will round the value either upward or downward, in favor of one of the values. *The rounding procedure followed in this book is to round our values in the direction of the nearest even number.* Thus 324.5 would be rounded to 324 rather than 325, since 324 is the nearest *even* number. There is nothing sacred about this rounding rule. It is simply a matter of author preference in this case. It is important that we agree at the outset about our rounding rule, since answers to numerical questions at chapter ends have been rounded in the direction of the nearest even number. Student answers will more likely match those in the textbook if this rounding rule is followed. The answer itself is not "more right" or "more wrong" if rounded in the other direction, however.

Some examples of rounding according to the nearest even number are presented below.

Value	Rounded to:
324.5	324 (nearest even number)
329.5	330 (nearest even number)
324.4	324 (324.4 is closer to 324 than to 325)
329.4	329 (329.4 is closer to 329 than to 330)
329.6	330 (329.6 is closer to 330 than to 329)

We would engage in such rounding merely to determine which interval to locate our raw scores that may be in decimal form. Most researchers express raw scores in whole numbers, although from time to time, decimal values occur and we must have a rule for dealing with them.

Regarding interval midpoints, these values are important because they express the "average" value found in each interval. For example, the intervals 320–324 and 330–334 have interval midpoints equal to 322 and 332. These are the representative values of any frequency found in those intervals. For instance, in Table 11.2 these two intervals contained five scores each. When grouped data are presented, it is assumed that the interval midpoints typify the scores found in the intervals. Therefore, all five scores in each of the intervals are regarded as 322 and 332, respectively.

This feature highlights an important drawback of grouping data into intervals such as those in Table 11.2. Whenever data are grouped into intervals, a certain amount of *precision* is lost in our resulting calculations. What if the interval 320–324 had five scores in it equal to 320? And what if the interval 330–334 had five scores equal to 334? In the first instance, we would be *overestimating* the average values of interval frequencies with 322. In the second instance, we would be *underestimating* the average values of interval frequencies with 332. This imprecision is a common feature of grouped data. Statisticians believe that for any given frequency distribution, most of the imprecision is "canceled out" by overestimating and underestimating, such as that shown here. Obviously, the *most precise* calculations would be to deal directly with raw scores and not group them into intervals. But our data management would become unwieldy. Imagine dealing with 82 raw scores directly, or 300 scores, or 500 scores! It is considered a fair trade-off, whereby we *lose* a certain amount of precision in our numerical calculations of such values as means and standard deviations, but we *gain* by rendering our data in a more manageable form for making such calculations. We also gain by being able to "see" the distribution of scores and making informed statistical test choices.

Cumulative frequency distributions. Before we leave the subject of frequency distributions, several additional operations must be described. For instance, we may create *cumulative frequency distributions* from any frequency distribution we have constructed. Table 11.5 is a cumulative frequency distribution constructed for the data in Table 11.2.

As can be seen from Table 11.5, cumulative frequency distributions are simply distributions of frequencies, where the frequencies from successive intervals are added to those totaled from previous intervals. This operation has been illustrated. Cumulative frequency distributions assist researchers in determining the accuracy of their computations. They provide an independent means for showing that all frequencies have been counted. A knowledge of the total frequencies can be used to locate easily the point most central to the distribution. In Table 11.5, for instance, there are 82 frequencies. Half of these frequencies would be 82/2 = 41

TABLE 11.5 CUMULATIVE FREQUENCY (cf) DISTRIBUTION FOR THE DATA IN TABLE 11.2

Interval	f	cf
320–324	5	5
325–329	3	8 (3 frequencies added to previous 5)
330–334	5	13 (5 frequencies added to previous 8)
335–339	5	18 (5 frequencies added to previous 13)
340–344	8	26 (8 frequencies added to previous 18)
345–349	12	38 (12 frequencies added to previous 26)
350–354	4	42 (4 frequencies added to previous 38)
355–359	7	49 (7 frequencies added to previous 42)
360–364	2	51 (2 frequencies added to previous 49)
365–369	12	63 (12 frequencies added to previous 51)
370–374	5	68 (5 frequencies added to previous 63)
375–379	4	72 (4 frequencies added to previous 68)
380–384	5	77 (5 frequencies added to previous 72)
385–389	3	80 (3 frequencies added to previous 77)
390–394	2	82 (2 frequencies added to previous 80)
	$\sum f = 82$	$cf = 82$

Types of Graphic Presentation

frequencies. This sum of 41 frequencies is closest to 42 frequencies, located in the interval 350–354. Thus the central point in the distribution is probably near the midpoint of that interval, 352. This would be the approximate point where the entire distribution of 82 scores is separated into two roughly equal parts. A measure of central tendency that depicts such a point is known as the *median*, described in Chapter 15.

Centiles, deciles, and quartiles. Additional features of frequency distributions are points that separate those distributions into different proportions. Proportions are determined by dividing a part of the sum of frequencies by the sum of frequencies. For example, if we wanted to know what proportion 20 scores were of 50, we would divide 20 by 50, or 20/50 = 0.40. In this case, 0.40 is the proportion of scores that 20 is of 50. If we multiply this proportion, 0.40, by 100, we can easily convert the proportion to a *percentage*. Therefore, (100) (0.40) = 40 percent. Twenty scores is 40 percent of 50 scores. We can also accomplish this by moving the decimal point two spaces to the right and adding the word *percent*. Thus 0.40 becomes 40.0 percent. Conventionally, in article and report writing, "percent" is usually spelled out rather than using the "%" sign.

If we wanted to determine those points below or above which a certain *proportion* of scores would be found, we would compute *centiles*, *deciles*, or *quartiles*. In any frequency distribution, there are points below and above which a certain proportion (or percentage) of scores will be found. A specific point in a distribution below which a given proportion of scores will be found is called a *centile* and designated symbolically by the letter "C." Centiles divide distributions of scores into increments of 1 percent. Particular subscripts are added to C to indicate the specific centile. For example, C_{18} is the 18th centile, and 18 percent of all scores in the distribution would be located below it. C_{35} is the 35th centile, and 35 percent of all scores in the frequency distribution would be found below it. Another way of dividing the distribution of scores into different parts is to use *deciles*, designated symbolically by the letter "D." Deciles divide distributions of scores into increments of 10 percent. D_2 is the 2nd decile, and 20 percent of the scores in the distribution would be located below this point. D_8 would be the 8th decile, and 80 percent of the scores would be located below it. Conversely, 20 percent of all scores would be located *above* it.

The third way of dividing frequency distributions is according to *quartiles*, designated symbolically by the letter "Q." Quartiles divide distributions into increments of 25 percent. Q_3 is the third quartile, and 75 percent of all scores in the distribution lie below it. Conversely, 25 percent of the scores lie above this point. Table 11.6 illustrates centiles, deciles, and quartiles, their relation with one another, and the percentages of scores below various points.

Centiles, deciles, and quartiles are computed easily and will be useful for understanding various central tendency and dispersion measures presented in Chapter 15. They are also useful for other methodological operations as well. Their computation will be illustrated by using the cumulative frequency distribution shown in Table 11.5.

Suppose that we wish to compute the fifth decile, D_5. An examination of Table 11.6 will show that this point is also equivalent with the 50th centile, C_{50}, and the second quartile, Q_2. We begin our computations by determining the proportion of 82 scores in Table 11.5 occurring below the fifth decile. This figure is determined by multiplying 82 by 0.50, or $(82)(0.50) = 41$ scores. Therefore, there are 41 scores below D_5. We will examine Table 11.5 and determine the sum of scores below and closest to 41. There are 38 scores in the interval 345–349. The next interval, 350–354, contains the scores we need to acquire our 41 scores. However, the interval contains four frequencies. We only need three of them. We may apply the following formula to complete our computations:

$$LL' + \frac{fn}{ff}(i),$$

where LL' = lower limit of the interval we are entering to obtain the frequencies we need to get our desired number of frequencies

fn = frequencies we need

ff = frequencies found in the interval

i = interval size

Determining D_5, we have

$$D_5 = 349.5 + \frac{3}{4}(5)$$

$$= 349.5 + 3.8$$

$$= 354.3$$

The fifth decile is 354.3. This is also the fiftieth centile, C_{50}, and the second quartile, Q_2. Fifty percent of all scores in the distribution are located below 354.3.

TABLE 11.6 CENTILES, DECILES, AND QUARTILES IN A HYPOTHETICAL DISTRIBUTION OF SCORES, EQUIVALENCIES, AND PROPORTIONS OF SCORES BELOW PARTICULAR POINTS

Interval	Quartiles	Deciles		Centiles
Highest scores	Q_4 =	D_{10}	=	C_{100} (point leaving 100% of scores below it)
.		D_9	=	C_{90} (point leaving 90% of scores below it)
.		D_8	=	C_{80} (point leaving 80% of scores below it)
.	Q_3		=	C_{75} (point leaving 75% of scores below it)
.		D_7	=	C_{70} (point leaving 70% of scores below it)
.		D_6	=	C_{60} (point leaving 60% of scores below it)
.	Q_2 =	D_5	=	C_{50} (point leaving 50% of scores below it)
.		D_4	=	C_{40} (point leaving 40% of scores below it)
.		D_3	=	C_{30} (point leaving 30% of scores below it)
.	Q_1		=	C_{25} (point leaving 25% of scores below it)
.		D_2	=	C_{20} (point leaving 20% of scores below it)
.		D_1	=	C_{10} (point leaving 10% of scores below it)
Lowest scores				

Suppose that we wanted to compute C_{80}, or that point below which 80 percent of all scores is found. We would first determine how many scores are below the 80th centile, or $(82)(0.80) = 65.6$. We need to find that point leaving 65.6 scores below it. We determine from the cumulative frequency distribution in Table 11.5 that 63 scores are found in the interval 365–369, the cumulative frequencies that are below and closest to 65.6 desired frequencies. The next interval, 370–374, contains five frequencies. We need 2.6 of these five frequencies to obtain our desired 65.6 frequencies. We may calculate C_{80} as follows:

$$C_{80} = 369.5 + \frac{2.6}{5}(5)$$

$$= 369.5 + 2.6$$

$$= 372.1$$

The 80th centile, C_{80}, is equal to 372.1. There are 80 percent of all scores in the distribution located below 372.1. This point is also the equivalent of the eighth decile, D_8. At the end of this chapter are various problems that can be worked for practice and to enhance your understanding of the concepts presented here. Answers to all numerical questions are given at the end of the book.

In each of the examples above, the frequencies we sought for the eightieth centile were rounded to the nearest *tenth* (65.6) rather than to the nearest *whole number* (66). Most numerical problems at chapter ends have been rounded to the nearest tenth, unless other instructions have been given. To maximize the meaningfulness of centile, decile, and quartile computations, it is preferable that researchers have interval-level data at their disposal. However, these values are frequently computed for data measured according to ordinal scales, such as attitudinal phenomena.

Histograms and Frequency Polygons

Histograms and frequency polygons are graphic portrayals of data that have been presented in frequency distributions. Figure 11.6 is a histogram of the frequencies shown in Table 11.2. The horizontal axis in the histogram marks off various intervals beginning with 320–324 in the far left corner and ending with 390–394 to the far right. Graph paper is useful for such drawings and interval designations. The vertical axis to the left represents the number of frequencies found in each interval in Table 11.2. Vertical bars similar to those found in bar graphs have been drawn for each interval, and the height of each vertical bar is determined by the number of frequencies found. Notice in Figure 11.6 that the vertical bars have been drawn such that the *centers* of the bars are interval midpoints. The height of the first vertical bar to the far left is "5," since there are five frequencies found in the interval 320–324. The height of the bar in the interval 345–349 is "12," since there are 12 frequencies found in that interval.

Figure 11.7 shows a frequency polygon drawn from the histogram in Figure 11.5 and from the data originally presented in Table 11.2. In the case of the frequency polygon in Figure 11.7, points at the centers and tops of the vertical

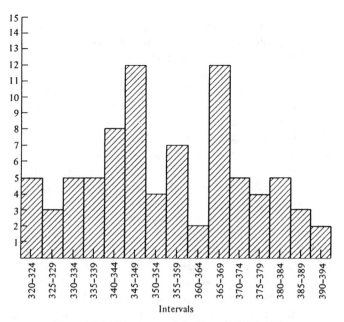

Figure 11.6 Histogram of the Data in Table 11.2.

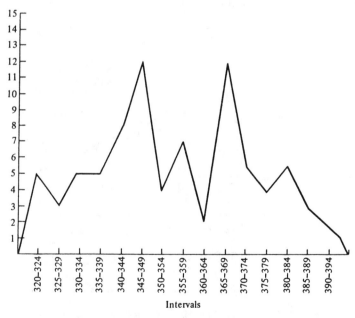

Figure 11.7 Frequency Polygon for the Data in Figure 11.6.

Types of Graphic Presentation

bars of the histogram shown in Figure 11.6 have been connected by straight lines. Note also that the "ends" of the frequency polygon to the far left and far right have been "tied down" to the horizontal axis at fictitious interval midpoints in the extremes of the distribution. Although there are no intervals 315–319 or 395–399, the frequency polygon is nevertheless "tied down" to the horizontal axis at the midpoints of these next intervals progressing to the left and to the right for the purpose of completion.

It will be recalled that the distribution of scores in Table 11.2 contained two intervals with frequencies of 12 each. It was suggested then that a subsequent histogram or frequency polygon would show at least two high peaks reflecting these large numbers of frequencies. Both the histogram in Figure 11.6 and the frequency polygon in Figure 11.7 show these prominent points.

Both histograms and frequency polygons provide readers with rapid visual inspections of how data are distributed in frequency distributions. Thus the distribution of scores shown in Table 11.2 is not approximately bell-shaped or "normal." Our inspection of the drawings of this distribution of scores shown in Figure 11.7 would rule out the application of certain statistical tests, since bell-shaped distributions of scores are required for some of these applications. Also, certain measures of central tendency and dispersion would be preferred over others, given the "spread" of these scores that we can see graphically portrayed. Compared with histograms, frequency polygons have the added advantage of being superimposed on one another where different distributions of scores are involved. Therefore, if we had scores from two or more distributions, several frequency polygons could be superimposed on one another for comparative purposes. The FBI uses these overlays to illustrate comparative crime trends over time. For instance, Figure 11.8 shows trends in victimization rates from 1973 to 1986.

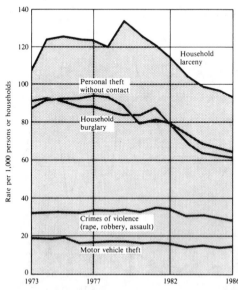

Figure 11.8 Trends in Victimization Rates, 1973–1986. U.S. Department of Justice, *BJS Data Report, 1987*. Washington, D.C.: Bureau of Justice Statistics, 1988:8.

If we were to construct a frequency polygon for cumulative frequency distributions, we would create what is known as an *ogive curve*. An example of an ogive curve is shown for some fictitious data in Figure 11.9. The construction of an ogive curve for the cumulative frequency distribution shown in Table 11.5 is left as an exercise. The shape of this distribution should resemble that shown in Figure 11.9.

Ogive curves are useful for illustrating how rapidly scores increase from low to high over a designated range. Sometimes, offenders are charted over time according to how many months or years lapse between their probation or parole and their commission of new crimes (recidivism). Ogive curves may also be superimposed on one another, and we might learn, for instance, whether parolees recidivate more or less rapidly compared with probationers. The horizontal axes in such curves would consist of months lapsing since probation or parole, while the vertical axis would portray the frequency of probationers or parolees who are charged with new crimes. Of course, these figures may be presented in some other tabular form. But ogive curves provide an immediate visual impression and comparison.

Other Types of Graphic Presentation

Stick figures, drawings of persons of different sizes, and dollar signs are also used by social scientists to illustrate population increase, gross national products, expenditures for justice purposes, or prison–jail inmate population comparisons. Creative graphics may be used in various combinations to illustrate trends, such as the escalation of the number of inmates on death rows throughout the United States as well as those states where the death penalty is used as the maximum punishment. Figure 11.10 shows two alternative graphic illustrations used in tandem for this purpose.

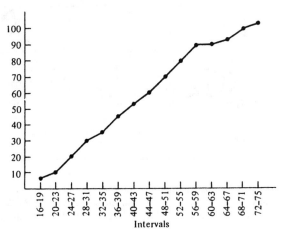

Figure 11.9 Ogive Curve for Cumulative Frequency Distribution Shown in Table 11.5.

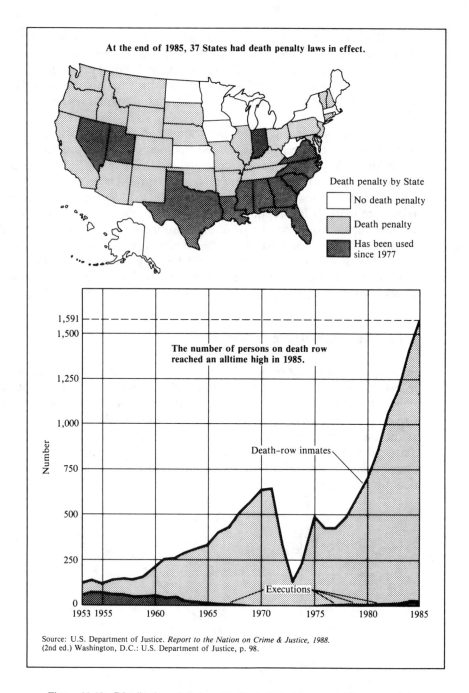

Figure 11.10 Distribution of States with Capital Punishment and Increase of Inmates on Death Row. U.S. Department of Justice. *1988 Report to the Nation on Crime and Justice* (2nd ed.) Washington, D.C. U.S. Department of Justice, p. 98.

Cross-Tabulation and Complex Variable Interrelationships

Cross-tabulations of variables represent arrangements of two or more variables in tables of size 2 × 2 or larger, and where one of the variables has been designated as independent. Table 11.9 shows some fictitious data arranged in a 2 × 2 table.

TABULAR PRESENTATION

By far the most popular method of presenting data in research articles and reports is through tabular presentation, where tables of various sizes are used for descriptive and other informative purposes. Tables may be small or large, simple or complex, depending on the research purposes of investigators and the elaborateness of the data they are presenting. Tables consist of various *rows* and *columns*, designated as size $r \times c$. These rows and/or columns depict *variables*, and the particular divisions on rows and/or columns depict *subclasses* of variables, or variable subclasses.

The smallest tables used in research contain either one row or one column, divided into two subclasses. Thus these smallest tables are either of size 2 × 1 or 1 × 2. For illustrative purposes, some fictitious data have been presented that portray the distribution of conviction offenses for a sample of state prison inmates. Tables 11.7 and 11.8 show examples of these smallest table sizes.

Notice for each of these tables, percentages have been calculated for the property and violent inmate categories. An inspection of articles and reports in a wide array of professional journals will disclose several stylistic differences in how data are arranged in tabular form. Although each journal has specific requirements about how to construct tabular material, there is a convention often followed regarding the percentaging of one's data. This convention is that *we should percentage in the direction of the independent variable.* In Tables 11.7 and 11.8, only one variable has been portrayed—conviction offense. In one-variable tables, it makes little difference whether we percentage in one direction or the other. However, for larger tables where *cross-tabulations* are involved, it does make a difference, at least *conventionally*.

TABLE 11.7 DISTRIBUTION OF A HYPOTHETICAL SAMPLE OF STATE PRISON INMATES, BY CONVICTION OFFENSE, ILLUSTRATED WITH A 2 × 1 TABLE

Conviction Offense	N	Percent
Property	250	68.4
Violent	115	31.6
Total	365	100.0

TABLE 11.8 DISTRIBUTION OF A HYPOTHETICAL SAMPLE OF STATE PRISON INMATES, BY CONVICTION OFFENSE, ILLUSTRATED WITH A 1 × 2 TABLE

	Conviction Offense		
	Property	Violent	
N's =	250 (68.4%)	115 (31.6%)	Total N = 365 (100%)

In Table 11.9, *gender* has been cross-tabulated with *type of delinquent offense* and has been designated as the independent variable. Notice also that the table has been percentaged in the direction of the independent variable, *gender*. Had the table been constructed where *type of delinquent offense* had been placed across the top of the table and *gender* down its left-hand side, *type of delinquent offense* would be treated as influencing one's gender. As Table 11.9 is currently presented, however, *gender* is the variable used to account for variation on the *type of delinquent offense* variable. This particular presentation of the data is conventional and makes more sense, although not all researchers follow such a convention. If several professional journals were scanned, they would disclose a variety of tabular styles, although a majority of tabular styles would probably be consistent with the conventional independent–dependent variable layout as shown in Table 11.9. Thus following this particular convention permits readers to make easier and more systematic interpretations of tabular material. Again, not all researchers follow this tabular style.

Table 11.9 also shows that four table cells have been identified with the letters *a*, *b*, *c*, and *d*. This is because several statistical tests and measures of association are constructed, especially for data presented in 2 × 2 tabular form, and these letters have symbolic significance in various statistical formulae. In Chapter 16 and 17 we present some of these tests and measures.

When reading Table 11.9, we can see that of our 340 juveniles, they are almost evenly distributed according to gender (180 males and 160 females). Property offenders account for 44 percent of our sample, while violent offenders account for 56 percent of it. However, we have percentaged in the direction of the independent variable, *gender*, and therefore, we can say that 83 percent of our male juveniles are violent offenders, whereas 75 percent of our female juveniles are property offenders. Our initial impression is that our sample of female juveniles commits more property offenses than violent offenses. Just the opposite impression is drawn about our sample of male juveniles, where most appear to have

TABLE 11.9 EXAMPLE OF A 2 × 2 TABLE

Dependent variable		Independent variable (Gender)		
		Males	Females	Total
(Type of	Property	30a (17%)	120b (75%)	150 (44%)
delinquent	Violent	150c (83%)	40d (25%)	190 (56%)
offense)	Total	180 (100%)	160 (100%)	340 (100%)

committed violent offenses. Tentatively, gender appears to explain whether or not one will tend to be a violent or a property offender.

Although caution has been recommended in earlier chapters regarding drawing hasty conclusions about cause–effect relationships between variables, we may at least *infer* that some causality exists between *gender* and *type of delinquent offense* in Table 11.9. Causing us to make this inference about a possible relation between these two variables is the particular arrangement of frequencies throughout the cells in this table. Notice that the preponderance of frequencies "bunch up" in cells *b* and *c*. Relatively fewer frequencies are found in cells *a* and *d*. This *diagonal distribution of frequencies* is important as well as desirable, since it permits us to make direct inferences about how the variables might be related to each other. The other desirable diagonal arrangement that would permit such relational inferences would be for the majority of the table frequencies to "bunch up" in cells *a* and *d*. Using the 2 × 2 tabular case to illustrate desirable and undesirable distributions of frequencies, we have the following two desirable distributions:

(a)				(b)	
45	15			10	72
a	*b*			*a*	*b*
10	65			85	14
c	*d*			*c*	*d*

These distributions are considered desirable not only because tentative causal inferences between variables may be drawn, but because *directionality of the relationship* between variables may be determined. In the case of the data distributed in table (a), cells *a* and *d* contain the most frequencies. If these frequencies were placed in Table 11.9, we would conclude tentatively that male juveniles and property offenses appear related, while female juveniles and violent offenses appear related. Note that the distribution of frequencies in table (b) is more similar to the actual distribution shown in Table 11.9, where the frequencies "bunch up" in cells *b* and *c*.

The following four tabular arrangements of frequencies are less desirable:

(c)		(d)		(e)		(f)	
75	68	10	15	66	10	3	85
a	*b*	*a*	*b*	*a*	*b*	*a*	*b*
13	15	43	55	75	12	4	71
c	*d*	*c*	*d*	*c*	*d*	*c*	*d*

The primary reasons that these four tabular arrangements are undesirable are because the frequencies in each table "bunch up" on either one or the other subclasses of either the independent or dependent variables and the directionality of relationship between variables cannot easily be determined. In short, there is little variation on either the independent or dependent variables. For instance, in the first table (c), the frequencies tend to "bunch up" on the first subclass of the dependent variable, cells a and b. In the table (d), the frequencies "bunch up" on the second subclass of the dependent variable in cells c and d. In the latter two tables, (e) and (f), the frequencies bunch up on the first and second subclasses of the independent variables (cells a and c and cells b and d, respectively).

This lack of variation in either the dependent or independent variable fails to provide us with an adequate opportunity to evaluate the impact of either variable on the other. This would be the same as beginning a study by declaring that we want to observe the impact of an intensive supervised probation program on recidivism among probationers compared with a program involving standard probation. We might obtain a large sample of probationers, but in creating our tables for these probationers and identifying their degree of recidivism, we may find that only a small proportion of probationers are involved in intensive supervised probation programs. Alternatively, we might find that the particular sample we have collected exhibits a low rate of recidivism across the board. Thus, it is imperative for researchers to ensure that ample representations of elements will be available to have more desirable tabular distributions. Statisticians recommend that proportionate breakdowns on the independent variable should be approximately 50–50, or close to it. Equal divisions on the dependent variable are also desirable, although dependent variables are often more difficult to control than are independent variables.

Whenever less desirable tabular distributions of frequencies are encountered, and the preponderance of frequencies is found on one or the other subclasses of independent or dependent variables such as those illustrated above, researchers may make proportionate analyses of their data and determine whether greater proportions of persons with specific characteristics share other designated attributes. For example, suppose that we investigated two samples of 100 first-degree murderers each in selected states that use the death penalty as the maximum punishment. One sample consists of convicted offenders who killed police officers during the commission of their crimes, whereas the other sample consists of convicted offenders who killed store clerks, innocent bystanders, or relatives during the commission of their crimes. We observe the results of jury deliberations in all cases and cross-tabulate both samples of convicted murders with the nature of punishment imposed. Keeping our problem simplified, suppose that only two punishment options exist. These options are "life without parole" and the "death penalty." Perhaps our belief is that those convicted of murdering police officers will be more likely to receive the death penalty compared with those convicted of killing nonpolice officers. Our data might appear as follows:

| | | Victim of convicted murderer | | |
		Police officer	Non/police officer	Total
Punishment imposed by jury	Life without parole	14	26	40
	Death penalty	86	74	160
	Total	100	100	$N = 200$

Perhaps we are disappointed at first because there is no diagonal relation between the punishment imposed and whether the murder victim was a police officer. For *both* samples, the death penalty was more frequently imposed, and our cell frequencies "bunched up" on the second subclass of the dependent variable, the *death penalty* as punishment. However, we can examine the proportionate distribution of the imposition of the death penalty and see whether or not those convicted of murdering police officers received it more frequently than the other sample of convicted murderers. In the table above, we can see that 86 percent of those convicted of murdering police officers received the death penalty, whereas only 74 percent of those convicted of murdering nonpolice officers received it. This is an obvious proportional difference and is generally consistent with what we originally anticipated, despite the fact that both samples of murderers tended to receive the death penalty anyway. Statistical tests may be applied to this table to determine whether 86 percent is significantly different from 74 percent. After all, this difference may be due to chance, not to whether police officers were the murderer's victims. In this case, a statistical test, the Z test for differences between two proportions, discussed elsewhere (Champion, 1981:227–230; Siegel, 1956), could be used as a numerical measure of the significance of difference between these two proportions in a statistical sense. Thus if diagonal relations between variables are nonexistent, we can usually adopt "plan B" methods to evaluate proportionate differences. Alternative problem solutions are useful whenever tables such as (c), (d), (e), and (f) above are encountered.

It is relatively easy to illustrate directionality and association between variables by using the 2×2 tabular case for our example. However, when tables are constructed larger than 2×2, it becomes increasingly difficult to "see" relations between variables or to infer the directionality of an association. An example of this more difficult chore might be illustrated by a 5×5 table. Consider the following hypothetical table, where data have been distributed across five rows and five columns:

| | Independent variable | | | | | |
	(Low) Col. 1	Col. 2	Col. 3	Col. 4	(High) Col. 5	Total
Dependent variable (Low)						
Row 1	18	28	36	15	19	116
Row 2	31	22	19	45	28	145
Row 3	16	18	18	14	21	87
Row 4	31	29	20	15	12	107
Row 5	16	19	30	40	60	165
(High) Total	112	116	123	129	140	620

It is quite difficult to determine whether any directional relation exists between the independent and dependent variables in this table. The frequencies appear scattered and do not seem to occur in any patterned relation.

Not all larger tables exhibit this much disarray, however. Following is a 5×5 table where directionality is more visually apparent:

Independent variable

Dependent variable	(Low) Col. 1	Col. 2	Col. 3	Col. 4	(High) Col. 5	Total
(Low) Row 1	6	15	19	30	50	120
Row 2	8	16	20	28	31	103
Row 3	10	6	20	16	15	67
Row 4	30	16	12	10	8	76
Row 5 (High)	70	40	20	16	3	149
Total	124	93	91	100	107	515

In this particular 5×5 tabular scenario, we can see that as we move across the five columns on the independent variable from left to right, there are few frequencies in the first few columns, but these frequencies increase in successive columns as we move to the right (e.g., 6, 15, 19, 30, and 50 as frequencies across row 1, and 8, 16, 20, 28, and 31 as frequencies across row 2). However, in row 3, there is an inconsistent pattern in the distribution of frequencies across the five columns (10, 6, 20, 16, and 15, moving from left to right). In rows 4, and 5, however, there are initially larger numbers of frequencies to the far left, although these frequencies decrease systematically as we move to the right across other columns (30, 16, 12, 10, and 8 in row 4, and 70, 40, 20, 16, and 3 in row 5, moving from left to right).

We would be able to say that for this particular table, higher scores on the independent variable are associated with lower scores on the dependent variable, while lower scores on the independent variable are associated with higher scores on the dependent variable. A rough line has been drawn around the preponderance of frequencies in the table, showing an approximately diagonal relation. Unfortunately, relationships between variables in many of these larger tables are not seen as clearly whenever real data are presented and discussed in articles, reports, or research summarizations.

When we *increase* the number of variables to be cross-tabulated, we make it possible to *control* for the influence of these additional variables on the remaining variables. We may observe a tentative association between some hypothetical variables in the following 2×2 table:

		Status of mother		
		Works	Does not work	Total
Status of children	Delinquent	100	50	150
	Nondelinquent	50	100	150
	Total	150	150	300

At first glance at the information above, it appears to make a difference whether mothers work or do not work and whether their children are or are not delinquent. Although it is entirely possible that the working/nonworking status of mothers is highly influential on whether their children become delinquent, we may wish to explore other factors to evaluate their potential impact on our initial observation. Perhaps we decide to examine the influence of "continuous adult supervision" on the incidence of delinquency among the children involved in this research. Maybe research suggests that continuous adult supervision of children is a more important determinant of a youth's delinquency or nondelinquency rather than the working/nonworking status of mothers. We can reconstruct the data above in the following table.

| | | Continuous Adult supervision of children | | | | |
| | | Yes | | No | | |
		Mother works	Mother does not work	Mother works	Mother does not work	Total
Status of	Delinquent	0	0	100	50	150
children	Nondelinquent	50	100	0	0	150
	Total	50	100	100	50	300

Now, we have an entirely different picture of the role of working mothers in relation to the delinquency/nondelinquency of their children. After we have added the third variable, "continuous adult supervision," it would seem that the more important factor here is whether or not the children are continuously supervised by adults, regardless of whether or not their mothers work. This also illustrates *spuriousness*, or *the presence of a supposed association between two variables that is actually the result of a third, perhaps unknown, variable*. Notice that all of the delinquent children are found under the category where children are not continuously supervised by adults, and that all of the children who are not delinquent are under the "continuous adult supervision" category. Although this finding does not prove a relation between the continuity of adult supervision and delinquency/nondelinquency, it seems to rule out the status of working mothers as an explanatory factor.

In the event that our tables are too large and unwieldy, such as the first 5 × 5 table above containing 620 frequencies in disarray, it is possible to "collapse" these tables to create smaller and more meaningful ones. *Collapsing tables means to reduce either the number of rows or the number of columns or both and combine the total frequencies into smaller numbers of cells.* Suppose that the column designations for the first 5 × 5 table were "strongly agree," "agree," "undecided, probably agree," "disagree," and "strongly disagree." Further suppose that the row designations were "very favorable," "favorable," "undecided, probably favorable," "unfavorable," and "very unfavorable." We could collapse the data into a 3 × 3 table to see whether our results are more meaningful. We might decide to collapse the columns as follows: place the "old" columns 1 and 2 into "new" column 1, the "old" column 3 into a "new" column 2, and the "old" columns 4 and 5 into a "new" column 3. Further, we might decide to collapse our rows as follows: We will combine our "old" rows 1, 2, and 3 into a "new" row 1, "old" row 4 into a "new" row 2, and the "old" row 5 into a "new" row 3. These collapsed data would be illustrated below (the old row and column totals are shown in parentheses in each of the nine cells of the new, collapsed 3 × 3 table):

(Collapsed table)
or
Independent variable

Dependent variable	(Agree) Col. 1	Col. 2	(Disagree) Col. 3	Total
(Favorable) Row 1	(18 + 28 + 31 + 22 + 16 + 18) = 133	(36 + 19 + 18) = 73	(15 + 19 + 45 + 28 + 14 + 21) = 142	348
Row 2	(31 + 29) = 60	= 20	(15 + 12) = 27	107
Row 3 (Unfavorable)	(16 + 19) = 35	= 30	(40 + 60) = 100	165
Total	228	123	269	= 620

or
Independent variable

Dependent variable	Agree		Disagree	Total
(Favorable)	133	73	142	348
	60	20	27	107
Unfavorable	35	30	100	165
Total	228	123	269	= 620

The pattern above has simplified the task of "seeing" relationships between these variables, if any. However, an inspection of the distribution of frequencies shows no meaningful pattern. There are 133 frequencies (persons) who tend to "agree" on the independent variable, while they are "favorable" on the dependent variable. However, 142 persons who "disagree" on the independent variable are also "favorable" on the dependent variable. It is possible that we might collapse these data differently and generate more meaningful patterns of frequencies. But collapsing of categories on either the independent or dependent variables should be done in a logical fashion. It would be illogical, for instance, to combine "un-favorables" with "favorables" on the dependent variable or to combine "agrees" with "disagrees" on the independent variable here.

Other Forms of Tabular Presentation

Many other forms of tabular presentation exist. Often, these tables illustrate trends or present informative figures. *The Sourcebook of Criminal Justice Statistics— 1989* (Flanagan and Maguire, 1990) contains hundreds of tables about all aspects of the criminal justice system, including crime trends and case information. For example, Table 11.10 shows the number of days between arrest and conviction for various crimes disposed of by state courts during 1986.

An inspection of Table 11.10 breaks these data down into total cases by type of offense and method of conviction (i.e., whether a jury or bench trial was conducted, and whether a guilty plea was entered through plea bargaining). Both average (mean) and median figures are presented, expressed in numbers of days from arrest to conviction. Explanatory notes in the table indicate the meaning of the median for purposes of reading the table as well as the meaning of other tabular notations. Murder cases seem to take the longest to resolve, with an overall

TABLE 11.10 NUMBER OF DAYS BETWEEN ARREST AND CONVICTION FOR FELONY CASES DISPOSED OF BY STATE COURTS, BY OFFENSE AND METHOD OF CONVICTION, UNITED STATES (ESTIMATED IN DAYS), 1986

| Most Serious Conviction Offense | Total | Estimated Number of Days between Arrest and Conviction for Cases Disposed by: | | | Guilty plea |
| | | Trial | | | |
		Total	Jury	Bench	
Average number of days	166	184	195	159	164
Murder[a]	274	279	280	272	257
Rape	210	239	242	220	192
Robbery	173	186	185	189	172
Aggravated assault	178	197	185	228	174
Burglary	142	131	144	107	143
Larceny[b]	151	138	165	111	154
Drug trafficking	172	217	209	235	168
Other felonies	171	181	197	149	169
Median number of days	123	141	162	105	120
Murder[a]	220	212	219	206	212
Rape	184	216	216	162	159
Robbery	122	110	110	107	125
Aggravated assault	140	175	176	158	132
Burglary	101	102	131	60	102
Larceny[b]	105	113	140	63	107
Drug trafficking	127	177	177	162	123
Other felonies	125	130	144	108	124

Source: U.S. Department of Justice. *1990 Sourcebook of Criminal Justice Statistics*. Washington, D.C.: U.S. Department of Justice, p. 518.

Note: The median number of days marks the point below which and above which 50 percent of all cases fall. Data are based on 57 percent of the estimated total 582,764 convicted felons.

[a]Includes nonnegligent manslaughter.
[b]Includes motor vehicle theft.

average of 274 days from arrest to conviction. Burglary convictions account for the cases most rapidly resolved, taking an average of 142 days from arrest to conviction. In almost every type of criminal case, the mean number of days to dispose of each case was higher than the median number of days. This suggests that jury trials for a portion of these cases may have prolonged the length of time needed to conclude them. Averages are influenced greatly by deviant scores or, in this case, a few extraordinarily long, drawn-out trials. In Chapter 15 we discuss means or averages at length and compare their strengths and weaknesses as central tendency measures with medians.

Tables may present trend information, such as the rates associated with the use of plea bargaining over time, or the proportion of civil and criminal cases in federal courts across several decades. The *Uniform Crime Reports* publishes tabular information about index crimes in most U.S. cities and counties on an annual basis. Certain statistical procedures are best illustrated through the use of diagrams, such as is the case with path analysis. *Path analysis* is a statistical technique that shows the sequential influence of multiple variables on some type of behavior or attitude. Figure 11.11 shows a path diagram indicating a relation between police officer training and intervention and the type of response of police officers to spousal abuse.

Breci (1989) was interested in the effectiveness of police department training programs in responding to reports of spousal violence. In recent years, various jurisdictions have enacted laws that provide for officers to make mandatory arrests of spouses who physically abuse their mates. Previously, an officer's discretionary authority was exercised at alleged spousal abuse crime scenes, where officers might attempt to encourage spouses to work out their differences. Under these previous interventions, arrests of one or both spouses were discretionary, influenced greatly by an officer's perception of the situation and its seriousness. Mandatory arrest policies have been promoted for such incidents as a deterrent to the incidence of spousal abuse. The Attorney General's Task Force on Family Violence (1984) recommended to police departments that arrest should be the preferred response in cases of family violence.

Breci believed that an officer's training or lack of training would significantly affect how spousal violence reports would eventually be handled. He postulated that untrained officers would be more likely to follow mandatory arrest guidelines, whereas trained officers would be more likely to exercise their discretion and possibly resist arresting either spouse when spousal violence was reported. The path diagram used by Breci was helpful in showing the relation of various factors to an officer's actual response. Factors in the diagram include an officer's skill and training, intervention techniques and skills, value of training, and role in family fights. As Breci anticipated, trained officers were more likely to circumvent administrative policies relating to arrests of spouses when responding to reports of family violence, and they were more inclined to exercise their own discretion rather than follow mandatory procedures as untrained officers appeared inclined to do.

Countless other types of tables will be encountered as students examine the research literature in criminology and criminal justice. It is imperative that all material presented in tables be examined carefully, particularly the table headnotes

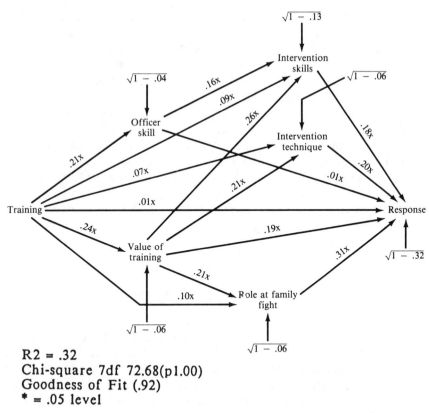

$\sqrt{1-.13}$

Intervention skills

$\sqrt{1-.04}$

.16x

.09x

Officer skill

.26x

$\sqrt{1-.06}$

Intervention technique

.18x

.21x

.07x

.21x

.01x

.20x

.01x

Training

Response

.24x

.19x

.31x

$\sqrt{1-.32}$

Value of training

.21x

.10x

Role at family fight

$\sqrt{1-.06}$

$\sqrt{1-.06}$

R2 = .32
Chi-square 7df 72.68(p1.00)
Goodness of Fit (.92)
* = .05 level

Figure 11.11 Path Coefficients Illustrating the Impact of Training on Values and Response (Source: Michael G. Breci "The Effects of Training on Police Attitudes Toward Family Violence: Where Does Mandatory Arrest Fit In?" *Journal of Crime and Justice*, 12:35-49 (p. 46) 1989.)

and footnotes. This material clarifies these tables and often explains tabular inconsistencies compared with the original research plans. However, tabular materials should also be regarded as instructive aids in understanding what has been presented. Some professionals might pay little attention to the bulk of any written report, however. They may scan the abstract, statement of the problem, and conclusions to gain a rapid impression of what was done and found. Where the research of others is used as a basis for one's own research plans, however, these other materials should be given more than cursory inspection.

DECIDING HOW BEST TO PRESENT YOUR INFORMATION GATHERED

There are no rules of thumb governing how much graphic materials are ideal for any research report or article. One guideline is that such materials should not appear to be "thrown in" or frivolous. Editors of professional journals generally favor shorter publications rather than longer ones. Excess graphic presentation and use of tabular materials may be distracting. Many articles are written without graphic material. Qualitative research projects (see Chapter 8) rely heavily on interpretations of social actions and descriptions of attitudes. In short, it is not a requirement of social scientific writing that such materials must always be supplemented with tables or graphs.

Decisions about the inclusion of graphs or tabular materials depend, in large part, on the nature of one's research. If samples of elements are studied and described, summary tables are helpful in portraying various features of the sample, including average age, prior record, educational training, gender, and a host of other factors. This material is also presented in written form, as authors describe the essential aspects of their graphic and tabular presentations. Studies that investigate trends, such as whether there is a rise in juvenile violence or female criminality over time, might profit from including summary tables of crime rates across several years.

SUMMARY

Graphic presentation consists of all tables, charts, illustrations, and line drawings that depict how collected data are distributed or arranged. The functions of graphic presentation include enhancing articles and reports, testing hypotheses derived from theories, providing evidence of relationships between variables, depicting trends and proportionate distributions, influencing statistical test selections, and influencing policy decision making.

Several types of graphic presentation include pie charts, bar graphs, frequency distributions, histograms, and frequency polygons. Pie charts are circular graphs that portray either proportions of 100 percent or the frequency of incidents such as burglary or robbery. Bar graphs may be either vertical or horizontal bars that portray the frequency of values on some variable. Frequency distributions are orderly arrangements of raw scores from high to low or low to high, according to invervals of specified sizes. These intervals have upper and lower limits and midpoints. These values are used to calculate centiles, deciles, and quartiles. Centiles divide distributions into 1 percent increments, while deciles and quartiles divide distributions of scores into increments of 10 and 25 percent, respectively. Conventional rules specify recommended interval sizes, with a range of intervals from 10 to 20.

Histograms are similar to bar graphs, although histograms are always vertically drawn. The horizontal axis in histograms represents intervals or values, while the vertical axis represents frequencies and determines the height of vertical bars. Frequency polygons are drawn from histograms. These consist of line drawings that link the centers of the tops of histogram bars with one another and are tied down at the extreme left and right of a score distribution. Other graphics include maps of geographical territories and line charts superimposed on one another to connote crime trends or other data that vary over time.

The most popular form of data presentation is the use of tables and cross-tabulations of variables. The smallest table sizes, represented by the expression, $r \times c$, are 1×2 or 2×1, where r designates the number of rows in the table and c designates the number of columns. The smallest cross-tabulated table is 2×2, a table having two rows and two columns. Larger tables with more rows and columns may be constructed. Sometimes, larger tables are unwieldy and may be collapsed. Collapsing means to reduce the number of cells in tables and combine the frequencies from the collapsed cells into fewer cells. Collapsing is done in accordance with a logical plan, where blended categories are meaningfully related with one another. Collapsing helps researchers to gain a clearer perspective about how frequencies in tables are distributed.

The most fruitful distributions of frequencies in tables are diagonal. Diagonal distributions of frequencies enable researchers to identify possible relationships between variables and establish causality. Sometimes, additional variables are introduced in tables as controls, in an effort to see which variables have the most explanatory value. Desirable diagonal relations between variables may not always exist in tables. Researchers often shift to different types of analyses of data, whenever frequencies on one or more variables "bunch up" on one or another variable subclass. These analyses become proportional analyses, where differences between proportions are examined. Some research is conducted without relying on graphic presentation. Reasonable use should be made of tables and graphs, and only to highlight the most important aspects of one's research.

QUESTIONS FOR REVIEW AND PROBLEMS TO SOLVE

All answers to numerical problems are given at the end of the book.

1. Under what conditions might a researcher benefit from treating a set of scores in grouped fashion in a frequency distribution?

2. What guidelines exist for constructing frequency distributions and determining the sizes of intervals?

3. Construct a frequency polygon for the following frequency distribution

Interval	f
10–14	6
15–19	7
20–24	13
25–29	8
30–34	6
35–39	10
40–44	19
45–49	15
50–54	7
55–59	3
60–64	9
65–69	12
70–74	13
75–79	5
$\Sigma f =$	133

4. Determine upper and lower limits for the following intervals.
   (a) 90-109
   (b) 1500–1599
   (c) 0.20–0.29
   (d) 0.0055–0.0059
   (e) 136–139
   (f) 200–249

5. Given the following array of scores, construct a frequency distribution beginning with the interval 30–39.

33	44	57	39	92	111	103	152	188	159	57	45	50	60
70	42	79	68	62	165	158	35	49	82	95	99	102	
91	94	39	40	110	115	56	84	137	126	145	176	164	
138	156	148	186	67	58	92	30	49	90	54	87	96	76
94	100	103	100	105	110	110	182	167	173	128	119		
177	115	115	83	49	68	58	190	187	154	139	150	112	

6. For the data you have arranged into a frequency distribution in Problem 5, determine the following centiles, deciles, and quartiles.
   (a) C_{27}
   (b) Q_3
   (c) D_8
   (d) C_4
   (e) D_5
   (f) Q_1
   (g) C_{90}
   (h) D_3

7. Given the following information, construct a pie chart.

Larceny	35 percent
Burglary	42 percent
Rape	20 percent
Homicide	3 percent

What are some major restrictions governing the use of pie charts? What are some of their intended applications?

8. Convert the following proportions to percentages.
   (a) .0036
   (b) .1560
   (c) .9700
   (d) .1158
   (e) .5550
   (f) .0004

9. Identify interval midpoints for the frequency distribution you constructed in Problem 5.

10. What is an ogive curve? Construct an ogive curve for the data presented in the frequency distribution in Problem 5.

11. What are desirable distributions of frequencies in 2 × 2 tables? Give two examples different from those in this book, using hypothetical variables.

12. What are some conventional rules governing the construction of $r \times c$ tables?

13. What is spuriousness? How can it be detected?

14. Collapse the following information into a 2 × 2 table, using a logical collapsing procedure.

	Variable X			
	Very strong	Strong	Weak	Very weak
Very high	30	20	15	10
High	20	15	10	5
Low	10	20	30	40
Very low	5	15	20	60

Variable Y

Illustrate your new table. Briefly explain the rationale for collapsing your table into a 2 × 2 form. Is there any kind of directionality apparent as the result of the collapsed 2 × 2 table? What interpretation can you make of the relation between variables X and Y?

12

Computers in Criminal Justice and Criminology

New Unit

KEY TERMS

Cursor

Directory

Disk drive

Floppy disk

Hard drive

Icon

Kilobytes (K)

Matrix of intercorrelations

Megabytes (Mb)

Modem

Mouse

Personal computer (PC)

Prompts

Shotgunning

INTRODUCTION

Dramatic improvements are being made, probably daily, in the technological sophistication of every academic field. Criminology and criminal justice are no exceptions. The advent of personal computers (PCs), their reduced cost, and widespread availability, together with an endless variety of statistics and graphics packages and programs, have enabled scientists to make data analyses and presentations that would have been undreamed of 10 years ago. Convincing evidence from the criminological literature suggests that both the theoretical and methodological sophistication of criminology and criminal justice have improved significantly in recent years (Holmes and Taggart, 1990).

In this short chapter we describe available computer technology and some of the tasks that PCs can perform for researchers. Several examples are provided to illustrate the types of analyses that investigators may make of their data, as well as how such data can be tabulated and presented. Because such a wide array of programs exists for most PCs, and because these programs and "packages" feature "finished products" on their covers, consumers are sometimes lulled into thinking that this computer gadgetry can do virtually everything for them. This is not so. Computers are tools. Like any tool, a computer's use is enhanced by a skilled craftsman who knows what to do with it. One objective of this chapter is to highlight certain strengths and weaknesses of computers for researchers. Thus far, computers have been unable to do all of our thinking for us. Human intervention is still required for interpreting findings, making sense of numerical results, and defining proper types of analyses that fit the data we have collected.

The chapter organization is as follows. First, we look at existing computer technology and several popular computer programs for use by researchers. Next, we examine some of the output from computers and what might be done with it. Although computers do much for investigators, they do have their limitations. Some of the major limitations and strengths of computer applications are described. Finally, we consider the future of computers in criminological research.

TYPES OF COMPUTERS

One of the first inexpensive computers for personal use was made available by Apple Computer, Inc. in the late 1970s. IBM developed its own version of a PC for home use. In an almost geometric progression, a variety of PCs from many different companies has been created in recent years. Major organizations, such as AT&T, Toshiba, Mitsubishi, Sony, Emerson, Hewlett-Packard, and Boeing, have developed versions of PCs that are generally compatible. Dozens of lesser known companies have recently manufactured "clones" or generic versions of computers from some of these larger organizations, such as IBM. Suffice it to say that for the "uninitiated" in the computer world, the world seems like a "Tower of Babel."

It is beyond the scope of this book to discuss computer languages or programming. Further, no attempt will be made to "sell" readers on any particular program discussed here. However, the fact is that many computer programs are currently available that feature picture-book illustrations as simple guides for their use. The Macintosh computer, for example, uses icons or graphic symbols to instruct users how to proceed. Most other computers, such as IBM, offer similar, simplistic programming instructions through their own icon language, including word processing programs, systems, and utilities such as *Microsoft Works*, *Microsoft Windows*, *Wordstar*, *WordPerfect*, and *Aldus PageMaker*. Database and spreadsheet programs are also available in a variety of formats, including *Lotus 1-2-3*, *dBase III*, *III+ or IV*, *Alpha Three*, *Personal Decision*, *Javelin Plus*, *Excel* (Microsoft), *Silk*, *VP-Planner*, *PC File Plus*, *Reflex*, *Clipper*, and *Omnis Quartz*. Figures 12.1 and 12.2 illustrate icon formats from two different computer systems.

Figure 12.1 illustrates an icon arrangement from a Macintosh computer. PC users "point" at individual icons with "mouses" or hand-operated devices that move an arrow around the monitor/screen, and particular programs or functions are activated. A drawing of an IBM PC with a mouse attachment is shown in Figure 12.3. Figure 12.2 is an example of a WordPerfect icon arrangement for particular word-processing functions. Again, mouses may be used to access these functions or utilities. PC users may also activate these functions with their PC keyboards.

One of the simplest utilities programs available for the IBM or IBM-compatible PC is *Microsoft Works*. Microsoft Works is a four-part software program that features word processing for letter writing and report preparation, a database for names and addresses or categories of things, a spreadsheet for income tax work, budgeting, and expense tabulation, and communications, which enables PC users to connect their computers with computers elsewhere, perhaps in other cities or countries, through the use of *modems*. A modem is a telephonic device that transmits information from one computer to another. Thus some criminologists may use modem access data sets from archives such as the National Archive of Criminal Justice Data at Ann Arbor, Michigan. Organizations with available data sets will usually charge nominal fees for providing this information to researchers. Further, beyond the initial cost of purchasing modems, many of which are under $200, using modems is about as expensive as using your telephone for long-distance calls.

The *System Menu* for Microsoft Works is shown in Figure 12.4. When this menu is displayed, researchers may use the mouse to operate their own software or some of the programs available within Microsoft Works itself.

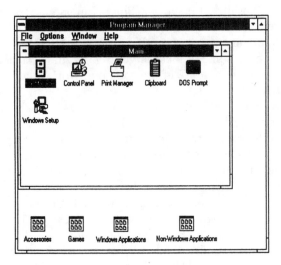

Figure 12.1 AT&T icon illustration.

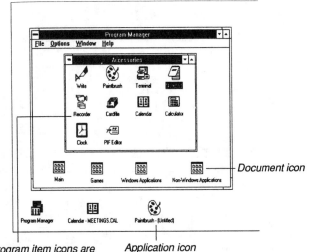

Application icon

Document icon

Figure 12.2 Microsoft Works icon illustration.

PC users may learn about their PCs by selecting *tutorials*, which are almost
always provided with any computer and computer program. These tutorials are
simple, step-by-step, instructional programs that provide users with hypothetical
examples about how to use their machines and programs. A system tutorial for
the Microsoft Works is shown in Figure 12.5. Notice that the tutorial uses icons
as visual indicators of different instructional functions.

Figure 12.6 shows a sample screen display when the PC user selects "Your
Software" from the original four choices shown in Figure 12.4. The mouse is used

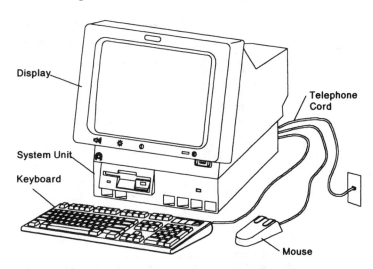

The IBM Personal System/1™ computer

Figure 12.3 PC with mouse.

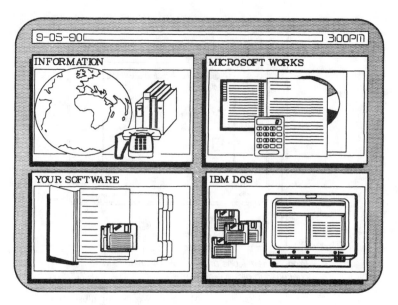

Figure 12.4   Microsoft Works system menu.

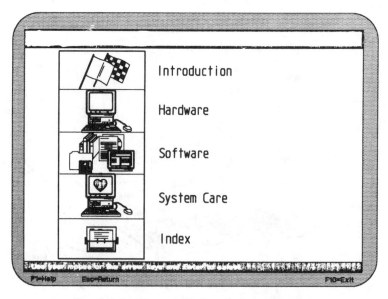

Figure 12.5   Microsoft Works system tutorial with icons.

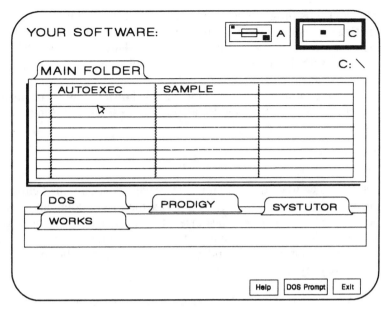

Figure 12.6 Screen display for "Your Software."

to point to programs desired. In this case, "SYSTUTOR" is the file users would select if they wanted to learn more about how their PC works. Other programs are shown, such as "DOS" (for "Disk Operating System") and "WORKS" (for "Microsoft Works") that may be chosen, depending on the interests of the user.

For IBM and IBM-compatible systems, more sophisticated "computer language" is often used to obtain file information or issue commands for report preparation and data analyses. Notice in Figure 12.6 that two "boxes" are shown in the upper right-hand corner, designated "A" and "C." These are different "drives" or disk drives that may be chosen. These drives use either $5\frac{1}{4}$- or $3\frac{1}{2}$-inch "floppy disks" which are inserted into slots. An example of a slot is shown for drive A in Figure 12.6. Thus investigators can insert their own floppy disks into a drive connected to their PCs and either run programs or record or retrieve information on these disks. Drive C is known as a *hard drive*, which is a self-contained unit that is capable of storing large amounts of information.

The total amount of information that can be stored on such drives is determined by the *size* of the drive. *Size* is measured in terms of megabytes (Mb). Common sizes of hard drives are 20, 30, 40, and 80 Mb. For comparative purposes, a complete textbook of 500 pages uses about 2 Mb. Conceivably, you could store seven or eight textbooks on a 20-Mb hard drive.

However, these hard drives also contain programs that enable researchers to perform various data analysis and word-processing functions. Some of these programs consume considerable space on these hard drives. For example, if researchers purchased the basic software and several tabular, graphics, and statistical packages from SPSS, Inc. in Chicago, Illinois (a popular program is known as the Statistical Package for the Social Sciences, and it will be illustrated later in this chapter), this program consumes about 13 Mb of space. Therefore, users anticipating extensive statistical and methodological applications will probably need PCs with an available space of at least 30 Mb. This way, they will have room on their hard disks for the computer package and a place to store their tabulated information once it has been generated.

Some sample computer language is shown below. For instance, if PC users select drive C with their mouse arrow, they will see a "prompt" on the screen such as

```
C:\>
```

which is a C disk drive prompt. They will see a blinking "cursor" in front of the arrow pointing to the right. They can then issue commands by using particular letter combinations. For instance, they are currently in the C directory or hard drive. If they want to change to drive A, they can type in "CD" and other appropriate information, and they will immediately be in drive A. Therefore, they would type the following:

```
C:\> CD A:   or   C:\> A:
```

(which means "Change directories. Go to directory A")
The next "prompt" would therefore be

```
A:\>
```

(which means that they are now in directory A).

IBM and most other computer manufacturers attempt to keep their computer language simple. IBM uses abbreviations of simple expressions, such as

```
C:\> MD
```

for "Make directory," if you want to create a new directory, or

```
C:\> CHKDSK
```

for "Check disk," if you want to see if the disk is defective or examine its contents.

Suppose that PC users have files, perhaps a book chapter, research article, or some other report stored in directory A? They can retrieve this file by typing in the appropriate letter combination as a "command." All files in any directory in the computer have letter combinations assigned to facilitate their retrieval by the PC. If an article on child sexual abuse is stored in directory A, which may be on a floppy disk, this file can be retrieved. If users are unsure of what is in the directory in drive A, they can see the disk contents by typing the following:

```
A:\> DIR
```

(which means essentially "Let me see the directory!")

The computer will display all files included on the disk inserted into drive A. Perhaps three files will be displayed as follows:

```
CORREC.DBF      44K    12/21/89
PROBAT.WKS      13K    01/21/91
EXAMSS.WPS      25K    09/02/91
```

These symbols are "computerese" for the different files the user has created. CORREC.DBF is probably a file having to do with corrections. It might be a list of references stored in a database format. The PROBAT.WKS might be an article on probation stored in Microsoft Works, while the EXAMSS.WPS might be a statistical examination stored in the word processor file. The "K" reference shows the "size" of the file in terms of kilobytes. Kilobytes are subdivisions of megabytes, where 1000 kilobytes = 1 Mb. Again, for purposes of comparison, a journal-length article of approximately 15 pages would probably take up about 25K to 35K, while a 40-page textbook chapter might be 90K or 100K. In this particular book, for instance, Chapter 1 was 49K, while Chapter 5, a much longer chapter, was 129K.

In the example above, if users want to access their file labeled "CORREC.DBF," they would type

```
C:\> CORRECT.DBF
```

and the file would eventually appear on the screen. The PC user could then type in new information, make new file or database entries, or any other changes, and store the new information back on the disk. Many PC users store their information, articles, reports, and other data on floppy disks in either the 5$\frac{1}{4}$- or 3$\frac{1}{2}$-inch formats. This saves valuable space on their PC hard drives, which they might wish to use for various kinds of programs.

Returning to the "Tower of Babel" referred to above, this relates to the fact that several different computer programs exist that utilize different computer language. Therefore, if PC users have an Apple computer and prepare documents on disks in a program format known as *Appleworks*, this Appleworks-developed disk format would be unreadable by an IBM PC. Inserting the Appleworks-based disk into an IBM disk drive would yield a message such as "Getting Errors Trying to Read Disk at Slot A; Retry? Abort? Fail?". By the same token inserting an IBM-formatted disk into an Apple computer disk drive would yield a similar message. The "Tower of Babel" example simply means that different computers cannot "talk" with one another directly.

Until recently, this was a major problem for most PC users. If they chose IBM products to use, those products could not be used with Apple products. Or if they chose Macintosh products, they could not use IBM products or Apple products, and so on. However, several inexpensive "bridge programs" have been created, so that for the most part, these communication problems no longer exist. Today, almost any computer can receive and read information generated on disks by other computers. For a modest fee, software programs may be purchased that enable PC users to translate data from one computer into readable language for another, previously incompatible, computer. An example from my own writing experiences helps to illustrate both the original problem and the solution.

For many years, I used an Apple II(e) computer for manuscript preparation. The software program was Appleworks. Publishers would receive my written materials on hard copy: that is, printed pages from my computer printer. Eventually, the publishers began requesting that I submit my work on computer disks, if possible. In this way, the editorial staff could work with the disks directly and implement manuscript changes more rapidly without having me make the changes and resubmit the manuscript. But my computer disks were in Appleworks format, and these publishers did not have the capability to translate the disks into a usable IBM format.

In the late 1980s, Applied Engineering, a computer components corporation in Texas, marketed a *Transporter*, a hardware device that translates IBM-formatted disks into an Appleworks-readable format, and vice versa. The Transporter is like a disk drive, requiring users to insert their floppy disks to be either read or copied from one type of computer language into another. However, in the early 1990s, a program known as *CrossWorks* was developed and marketed by Softspoken, Inc. of Raleigh, North Carolina. This program enables users to connect their Apple or Apple-compatible computers directly, by a special cable device, to an IBM or IBM-compatible computer. Crossworks permits each computer to send information to the other, regardless of the basic "language" difference. Thus Apple-to-IBM or IBM-to-Apple transformations were made possible. Of course, the Crossworks program requires two adjacent computers, one Apple and one IBM, although accessory 50-foot extension cables exist if there are minor "distance" problems. Despite this limited inconvenience, both types of computers can receive information precisely in the language in which it was originally formatted. Therefore, all underlining, boldfacing, paragraph breaks, and other editorial features are exchanged fully from one machine to the other and read by each as such.

This illustration applied only to the Apple–IBM translation problem. Additional software presently exists to link almost every type of computer with all others. For example, Macintosh has developed *MacLink*, which permits Macintosh computers to translate their disks into readable IBM language, and vice versa. And not all of these programs involve linking cables such as was the case with the Apple and IBM systems.

The discussion above serves to illustrate that today, PCs of almost every type and brand may be used by researchers for wordprocessing and statistical/methodological purposes. "Language problems" between different computer systems no longer hinder one's work. In short, you no longer have to be a computer programmer or necessarily computer-wise to use available software for data analysis purposes.

For our purposes, we are interested in both report preparation and analyzing data we have collected. For our data to be analyzed, we must first transmit it into some statistical *package* that can perform various desired calculations. The word *package* is often used to describe statistical programs, since they contain many features, such as cross-tabulation functions, descriptive statistical functions, correlation functions, and significance test computations. All of these features combine into a software "package" available to researchers. The best known and most widely used statistical package is the Statistical Package for the Social Sciences (SPSS), marketed by SPSS, Inc. in Chicago, Illinois.

The SPSS programs available through SPSS, Inc. include (1) statistics, (2) advanced statistics, (3) trends, (4) data entry, (5) categories, (6) graphics, (7) mapping, and (8) Harvard graphics. In order to use these programs, users must purchase the SPSS base program. These programs are not cheap. To obtain all programs available through SPSS, Inc., individual PC users might have to spend nearly $3000, although separate programs can be purchased for a few hundred dollars each. Obviously, purchasing the SPSS package is something only professional researchers might want to do, and even then, their purchases may be limited only to those packages that would involve heavy use. For criminologists, these packages might include the statistics/advanced statistics, trends, and tables packages. Demographers might purchase the map package and perhaps the graphics package. SPSS, Inc. provides a wide array of software to accommodate most needs of social researchers. In addition, some of their software is used extensively by corporations and large-scale organizations for quality control functions, inventory, resource planning, urban planning and public policy decision making, and periodic reporting.

Every statistical procedure to be described in subsequent chapters is included in the SPSS statistical/advanced statistical packages. Often, universities will have copies of these programs, so that faculty and students may use them for their research projects.

It is important to note, however, that this SPSS package is available exclusively for small-scale PC users, for home or office use. SPSS, Inc. features other versions of their programs for *mainframe computer systems* in computer centers at major colleges and universities.

When researchers collect data, they code and tabulate the data. Usually, they prepare sheets with numerical entries. Suppose that investigators obtained a sample of 50 probation officers and had descriptive information about them from questionnaires. They might enter such information into whatever statistical program they are using, whether it is SPSS, or Statpro, or dozens of other statistical packages presently available for home use.

Entering data into statistics packages involves a similar sequence of steps, regardless of the package used. First, researchers must create variables, or variable labels, for their statistics programs that match those used in their questionnaires or interviews. As they create these variables, such as age, gender, socioeconomic status, or political affiliation, they also create subclasses, or value labels, for each of these variables. From previous chapters we have seen how subclasses and value labels are created, such as "male" and "female" as relevant subclasses for the "gender" variable.

After all relevant variables in one's study have been identified, the researchers enter the numerical information from the questionnaire responses into each variable for each person. Let's use a small-scale example to illustrate what is usually done.

Below are five variables: *age* (old/middle-aged/young), *gender* (male/female), *community background* (urban/rural), *type of crime* (felony/misdemeanor), and *race* (black/white/Hispanic/other). On the left are questionnaire items for these variables. On the right are "columns" in the particular statistical program for each person where these values (codes) are entered. Each variable is expressed in a different column. For example, these five variables are expressed in columns 1, 2, 3, 4, and 5 as shown. The accompanying codes are numerical indicators of the appropriate variable subclass. In parentheses to the right of each variable are suggested variable labels that researchers might use to represent each. Subsequent data analyses will express these variables in this "variable label" language. Thus a cross-tabulation of TYPCRIM and COMBAC would be a cross-tabulation of "type of crime" with "community background."

Variable and code	Statistical package coded entry and column number	
	Code	*Column #*
Gender (GEN)		
Male (1) ——————————>1		1
Female (2)		
Age (AGE)		
Old (1)		
Middle-aged (2) ——————————>2		2
Young (3)		
Community background (COMBAC)		
Urban (1) ——————————>1		3
Rural (2)		
Type of crime (TYPCRIM)		
Felony (1)		
Misdemeanor (2) ——————————>2		4
Race (RACE)		
Black (1)		
White (2)		
Hispanic (3) ——————————>3		5
Other (4)		

We can see from the codes entered into our statistical package above that our first element (person) is a middle-aged, urban, Hispanic male who has committed a misdemeanor. Our next entry might be a young, white, rural female who has committed a felony. Under real circumstances, we will ordinarily use *many* variables, perhaps 30 or more, in our study. We may have to enter information for about 200 to 300 persons or more into the statistical program.

Once these numerical data have been entered into the statistical program, we may enter commands that instruct our statistical program to perform various functions. For instance, the program will tabulate all responses and show us how many males and females there are in the sample. These will be expressed as both frequencies and percentages. Similar tabulations will be compiled for all other variables. We may then cross-tabulate our information, seeing how many persons with rural backgrounds have committed felonies or misdemeanors, or whether our age categories seem to tabulate closely with other variables. We may see, for example, whether persons in different age categories seem to be differentiated according to crime seriousness (i.e., felony or misdemeanor).

It is beyond the scope of this book to provide an in-depth coverage of specific computer languages for any given statistical package, since so many different packages are presently available. The intent here is simply to show the flexibility inherent in these existing programs and statistical packages. Later in this chapter, several illustrations of computer output will be provided so that you can see cross-tabulations of variables and displays of statistical tests and correlation coefficients.

CAN COMPUTERS DO EVERYTHING FOR YOU?

No, they cannot. As tools, computers can help us do many things with the data we have collected. Printed materials from computers, *printouts*, contain considerable useful information. This information is sometimes interpreted by the computer in the sense that probabilities are provided or statements about statistical significance are made. However, it is up to individual researchers to make decisions about the usefulness of the available information and how best to interpret it.

Some people believe that "if computers print it out, it must be significant." But the decision-making capabilities of computers are limited. Computers lack imagination. In short, computers do precisely what they are instructed to do and whatever they are capable of doing. This means that they will literally do whatever they are programmed to do, depending on the software used and the functions to be performed. Frequently, computers will perform certain functions *literally* that make absolutely no sense to us. An example of such literal functioning is provided below.

Suppose that we were to enter data into a computer program such as the SPSS. We might enter information that would identify each of our elements. For instance, if we had 200 persons in our sample, we would number each 001, 002, 003, up to 200. These three-digit identification numbers would be entered to identify particular persons. Other than serving to differentiate these persons from one another, these ID numbers have no other value. Further suppose that we enter information about one's race/ethnicity, gender, educational level, prior criminal record, six or eight personality characteristics, occupational/professional affiliation, years on the job, job satisfaction, self-concept, religion, socioeconomic status, political affiliation, and 10 or so other variables. As we have seen from the discussion above, we would create variable labels and values for each variable subclass. Thus our data entry would consist of entering numbers into our SPSS program that refer to a wide variety of things, from a person's ID to a person's years of education.

Next, we instruct the computer to run certain statistical analysis programs. For example, we might command that the computer determine means or averages for all variables. This means that means will be computed for *all* variables literally, including gender and race/ethnicity. If we assign a "1" to males and a "2" to females, what does an *average gender* of 1.3 mean? By the same token, if we assign "1" to black, "2" to white, "3" to Hispanic, and "4" to "other," what would be the significance of a mean race/ethnicity of 2.4? Is this someone who is somewhere in between a white and Hispanic?

The computer does not discriminate. To computers, numbers are numbers are numbers are numbers. Researchers designate different variables (variable labels) and *subclasses* of those variables. They assign numerical quantities to these subclasses. Computers manipulate *only* these numbers. Computers do not "understand" that "1's" and "2's" in some cases refer to males and females and should not be averaged. Computers "understand" only that they should average *all* numbers on each variable category, regardless of what the numbers represent. Researchers must examine these numbers and interpret them appropriately. As you might suspect, researchers wind up with much more information than they really want from computers. Although it is possible to instruct computers to analyze specific variables, it is sometimes easier to use the "shotgun" approach and have the computer perform the same functions for all variables. The time taken to reprogram computers for special analysis functions may not be worth it.

In my own graduate student years at Purdue University, I went to the computer center and asked computer programmers to enter my dissertation data into their mainframe computer for various statistical analyses. Later, they gave me a box of printout materials that was perhaps a foot high. I was able to salvage about 10 meaningful pages out of the entire box and had to discard the rest as waste. The computer had averaged *everything*, including numbers standing for city names, street names, gender classifications, racial categories, religious categories, and even respondent identification numbers.

In their own ways, computers are designed to be helpful to researchers. For instance, investigators who wish to have computers print out cross-tabulated tables for them will run the appropriate programs. Some computer programs not only print out the tables requested, but they will also "collapse" these tables and give you different, condensed versions of them. This is one way that computers compensate for performing certain types of statistical tests that require minimal cell frequencies. A hypothetical example is provided below.

Jane Smith, a criminologist, has some data pertaining to job satisfaction and years of education for a sample of correctional officers. These data are shown in Table 12.1. Both variable subclasses have been numbered to show what the computer "sees." This is the table that Smith wanted. But she notices that the computer has printed out a second table, the one shown in Table 12.2.

Jane notices that the new table generated independently by the computer program represents a "collapsing" of the first three *education* subclasses into one category, while the fourth subclass is in a category by itself. For the *job satisfaction* variable, the first five subclasses have been combined into one general category, while the sixth subclass is in a category by itself. Jane scratches her head in bewilderment. The computer has just combined apples and oranges. Notice that the new categorization on the *job satisfaction* variable has combined "satisfied" with "dissatisfied" subclasses. This is meaningless.

TABLE 12.1 JOB SATISFACTION AND YEARS OF EDUCATION FOR 100 CORRECTIONAL OFFICERS

Job Satisfaction	Years of Education			
	12 or less (1)	13–14 (2)	15–16 (3)	17+ (4)
Very satisfied (1)	3	0	5	2
Satisfied (2)	2	0	0	4
Undecided, probably satisfied (3)	0	2	0	8
Undecided, probably dissatisfied (4)	4	11	0	7
Dissatisfied (5)	0	0	8	5
Very dissatisfied (6)	11	10	8	9

The point is that computers will do much for you, but they cannot yet think independently and interpret your findings for you. Researchers must still perform this task. Hopefully, this book will assist investigators in this respect.

COMPUTER OUTPUT AND WHAT TO DO WITH IT

As has been seen, computers often conduct analyses of data beyond those specific analyses desired by investigators. Simply, many software packages have built-in analysis procedures beyond those of interest to the researcher. Further, most investigators have a curiosity to explore whatever has been generated as computer output. Therefore, while a specific table has been printed, other tabular distributions and data arrangements have perhaps been plotted and printed as well. To guard against delving into this superfluous information (which is all it is), it is recommended that investigators refer directly to whichever hypotheses they are testing. A specific table or set of tables will be useful for determining support or lack of support for one's developed hypotheses. These are "natural" constraints that are pretty much self-imposed. In effect, the researcher says, "I want to test this hypothesis. Therefore, I will inspect the table that relates directly to it." Later, after one's hypotheses have been tested, other inspections of the computer

TABLE 12.2 COLLAPSED VERSION OF TABLE 12.1

Job Satisfaction	Years of Education	
	16 or Less (1–3)	17 or More (4)
(1) through (5)	35	26
(6)	30	9

printout information might be in order. We should not discount entirely the superfluous information that the computer has provided us. Recalling the serendipitous nature of criminological research, certain findings may be observed that are important in their own right. We may decide to cite and discuss these additional findings.

At least one temptation relating to computer printouts should be avoided, however. This is known as *shotgunning*. The term is derived from the fact that whenever a shotgun is fired, the buckshot leaves a fairly wide pattern around whatever it hits. Applied to criminological research, an example of shotgunning would be to run a statistical program on the computer, where a matrix of intercorrelations is generated. A *matrix of intercorrelations* is a table of correlation coefficients, where all variables have been correlated with each other. Thus, a fairly high correlation between one's height and weight might be anticipated. Further, we might expect that the greater presence of police officers in certain neighborhoods might act as a deterrent to criminal activity. Therefore, a correlation might be observed between greater law enforcement activity and lower amounts of crime.

Some researchers use the shotgun approach by inspecting these matrices of intercorrelation. They might circle all large coefficients, where a high degree of association might be indicated. Then, they trace these coefficients back to a specific pair of variables. Next, they might attempt to build a theory or develop an explanation for the particular associations they have observed. Compared with how criminological research ought to be done and the manner in which it should proceed, this is the equivalent of working backwards with the data. Therefore, researchers first look at their findings and then attempt to explain them. This is like watching a basketball game, waiting until the game is over, and then predicting the final score.

A matrix of intercorrelations can be of value to researchers, but it must be used appropriately. Simply circling all coefficients of association that appear "large" or significant, "shotgunning," may yield many coefficients that are nonsensical. Some of the circled coefficients may represent relationships between city names and gender, or between one's numerical ID and race, or between city size and religion. Therefore, researchers should be selective in their examinations of such matrices, which illustrates several things of importance. First, if we were interested in determining the association between drug use and prior record for a sample of probationers, inmates, or felons in general, the material in Figure 12.7 would help us to determine (1) whether an association exists, (2) the strength of the association, and (3) the significance of the association statistically.

Figure 12.7 is a cross-tabulation where the variables "drug use" and "prior record" have been abbreviated into computerese, "PRCORD" and DRGUSE." In the upper left-hand corner of the table are abbreviations for *row percentages* (ROW PCT), *column percentages* (COL PCT), and *total percentages* (TOT PCT), which indicates the percentage of frequencies in each cell compared with the total of 128 felons. The columns are the "yes" and "no" categories on the "prior record" variable, while the rows are the "no" and "yes" categories on the "drug use" variable. In each cell, actual frequencies are shown. Clockwise, these are

DRGUSE [DRUG USE]   BY   PRCORD [PRIOR RECORD]

```
                              PRCORD
          COUNT     I
          EXP VAL   I
          ROW PCT   I
          COL PCT   I    YES            NO          ROW
          TOT PCT   I           1               2   TOTAL
                  ---------+--------------+----------------
DRGUSE         1   I     29      I      34      I    63
              NO   I     35.4    I      27.6    I    49.2 %
                   I     46.0 %  I      54.0 %  I
                   I     40.3 %  I      60.7 %  I
                   I     22.6 %  I      26.6 %  I
                   +--------------+----------------
               2   I     43      I      22      I    65
             YES   I     36.6    I      28.4    I    50.8 %
                   I     66.2 %  I      33.8 %  I
                   I     59.7 %  I      39.3 %  I
                   I     33.6 %  I      17.2 %  I
                   +--------------+----------------
          COLUMN
          TOTAL          72             56           128
                         56.2 %         43.8 %       100.0 %
```

CHI-SQUARE	D.F.	SIGNIFICANCE
5.202	1	.02202

STATISTIC	SYMMETRIC	WITH DRGUSE IND	WITH PRCORD IND
LAMBDA	0.34831	0.41355	0.28226
UNCERTAINTY COEFFICIENT	0.00263	0.00356	0.22611
SOMERS' D	0.21745	0.21732	0.11138

STATISTIC	VALUE	SIGNIFICANCE
PHI	0.24567	0.03314
CONTINGENCY COEFFICIENT	0.19761	0.02241
KENDALL'S TAU B	0.31464	0.03345
KENDALL'S TAU C	0.29465	0.02116
PEARSON'S R	0.45829	0.00012
GAMMA	0.15495	0.06455

Figure 12.7 Hypothetical example of a computer printout crosstabulating prior record with drug use for 128 felons.

29, 34, 43, and 22, respectively. Immediately beneath these frequencies are "expected" frequencies based on the marginal totals. (Don't worry about these values; since we examine the chi-square statistic in detail in Chapter 17.) These expected frequencies are what would ordinarily be in those cells according to "chance": 35.4, 27.6, 36.6, and 28.4.

Computer Output and What to Do With It   **319**

The third value in each cell is the row percentage of the cell frequencies. For example, the first cell contains 29 frequencies in a row containing a total of 63 frequencies. Thus 29/63 = 46.0 percent. The fourth value in each cell is the column percentage of the particular frequencies found in the cell. Again, in the first cell, there are 29 frequencies, and there are a total of 72 frequencies in the first column as shown. Therefore, 29/72 = 40.3 percent. The final value is the percentage of any given cell frequencies in relation to the total of 128 frequencies. The first cell contains 29 frequencies, and 29/128 = 22.6 percent. As you can see, percentages have also been computed for the row totals and the column totals.

Beneath the table are printed various statistical values and correlation coefficients. In fact, there is considerably more information given than we actually need. However, this will be a good illustration of the usefulness of some of this printout information.

Note that a chi-square statistical value of 5.202 is shown. This is a measure of the statistical significance of the distribution of these frequencies throughout the table. These values are explained or cited in Chapter 17, and it is not necessary at this point to have a full understanding of what each means. The importance of this illustration is that some of this information is useful while the rest is not.

Immediately adjacent to right of the chi-square value is a column, D.F., "degrees of freedom." *Degrees of freedom* are determined by the number of rows minus 1 multiplied by the number of columns minus 1, or $(r - 1)(c - 1) = (2 - 1)(2 - 1) = 1$. Since there are two rows and two columns, there is only 1 degree of freedom. The next column shows the significance or probability associated with our chi-square value of 5.202. In this case, it is 0.02202. Normally, probabilities are rounded to the nearest hundredth, 0.02 in this case. Again, the computer has carried out the computational work to more "places" than were necessary.

Beneath these values are various statistics. In this case, all of these statistics are actually different measures of association which have been computed for the same data in the table. Note that each measure yields a different amount of association as indicated by the different coefficient values. Immediately to the left of certain of these measures (e.g., lambda, the uncertainty coefficient, and Somers' *d*) are "symmetric" values as well as "asymmetric" values, such as "with drug use as the independent variable" (WITH DRUSE IND) and "with prior record as the independent variable" (WITH PRCORD IND). These particular measures of association yield different values depending on which variable is used in the table as independent or dependent. In the printout in Figure 12.7, "prior record" was used as the independent variable and "drug use" was used as the dependent variable. The three measures of association for which this information has been provided have such interpretations. The remaining six measures of association listed at the bottom of the printout (e.g., phi, the contingency coefficient, Kendall's tau *b* and tau *c*, Pearson's *r*, and gamma) do not have asymmetric interpretations. All are symmetric measures of association. Thus only their magnitudes and significance are listed.

The interesting thing about all seven measures of association that have been printed out here for us is that only three of them can be computed legitimately for the data in their present form. These measures include lambda, phi, and the coefficient of contingency. The *best* measure of association of these three is lambda. It has *both* a symmetric and asymmetric interpretation.

What about the remaining measures of association? Recalling our discussion of levels of measurement in Chapter 9, the variables in Figure 12.7 have been dichotomized into "yes" and "no", both for "prior record" and "drug use." Therefore, at best we are analyzing two variables measured according to a nominal scale. Both of the Kendall measures, tau *b* and tau *c*, are applicable for two-variable situations where each variable has been measured according to an ordinal scale. This is also true of gamma and Somers' *d*. Pearson's *r* may be computed only when both variables are measured according to an interval scale. Four other stringent assumptions also underlie the appropriate application of this *r* value. In short, the values and probabilities printed out for the Kendall measures, gamma, Somers' *d*, and the Pearson *r* are meaningless.

Novice researchers without statistical training might be inclined to believe that because these additional coefficients were computer-generated, they must also be acceptable measures that describe the data in the table. Obviously, this is not the case, since there are several totally inappropriate measures included in the printout. What should the researcher do with this additional information? Ignore it. Throw it out.

In the following chapters, statistical material is presented that will enable readers to make decisions about whatever they observe. Decision-making criteria are made explicit for each statistical procedure and measure of association presented. Certain conventions are highlighted that pertain to how data should be presented as well as analyzed. Suggested applications of different statistical procedures in criminology and criminal justice are also described. Therefore, the remainder of the book will prepare students for interpreting their findings and making sense out of computer printout information such as the sample illustration shown in Figure 12.7.

COMPUTERS AND THE FUTURE OF CRIMINAL JUSTICE RESEARCH

No crystal ball is needed to anticipate the future of computer use in criminal justice research. Existing software programs available from different sources can do almost every type of data analysis imaginable. Minimal familiarity with computers is required to use such software meaningfully. However, elementary and middle school children are currently being exposed to computers in classrooms as learning tools. Successive generations of students will be increasingly computer-wise.

Criminology and criminal justice benefit greatly from such technological change. More sophisticated data analyses among these scholars generally permit the development of more sophisticated explanatory schemes or theories. More variables are subject to statistical control in prediction situations, and researchers will be able to greatly expand their present knowledge of social events. It is likely that as more investigators utilize modems or telephonic links with national data archives and other sources, data retrieval and researcher access to such information will be made easier.

SUMMARY

Dramatic changes are occurring within criminology and criminal justice as computers and computer software are made increasingly accessible to larger numbers of researchers. Computer programs are available today for virtually every type of data analysis that an investigator might wish to conduct. The most commonly available computers, personal computers, currently offer a wide-ranging list of statistical packages and programs designed to tabulate and analyze data. Graphics packages are also available, so that researchers may depict trends and other illustrative materials in their writing to make their reports more informative.

Modems provide linkages with major research archives throughout the United States. The National Archive of Criminal Justice Data in Ann Arbor, Michigan is one of several sources of data sets available to researchers for analysis. Costs associated with the use of such material are nominal. One of the most popular statistical packages is the SPSS, the Statistical Package for the Social Sciences, marketed by SPSS, Inc. in Chicago, Illinois. Many other types of statistical packages are available through local software distributors.

Computers perform diverse functions for researchers relating to analyses of their data. In fact, computer programs written for analyzing data often provide us with superfluous information that we probably do not need. Investigators need to be familiar with various statistical procedures and measures of association, including the conditions and restrictions governing their application in criminology. Computers cannot do everything for investigators. Although some decision making is done by computers, much interpretive action is required by investigators to make the most sense out of computer printouts. The future of computers in criminal justice research is positive. It is a certainty that our current level of data analysis and scientific inquiry will be elevated to new levels of sophistication as we explore the many uses of computers in social research.

QUESTIONS FOR REVIEW

1. What are icons, and what are their functions for personal computers?
2. In what sense can computers "talk" with one another? What evidence exists to indicate greater convergence of computer languages among the many different types of computers that presently exist?
3. What are disk drives? What are some common sizes of disks used in various types of disk drives?
4. What are hard drives? Why are they important for research purposes?
5. In what respects do computers provide more information than you really need? Give an illustration.
6. In what sense is a computer too accommodating with the information it produces? In what ways can researchers be misled by computer results?
7. What are some problems associated with computer "collapsing" of cells in cross-tabulations of data?

8. What is the relevance of levels of measurement for the types of statistical tests that are provided in statistics packages in computer programs?

9. What is a matrix of intercorrelations? What is shotgunning?

10. In what respect is researcher coding of variables misused or misinterpreted by statistical programs available for computers? Give two examples.

13

Hypothesis Testing
and Theory Verification

KEY TERMS

Hypotheses of association

Hypotheses of difference

Hypothesis sets

Null hypotheses

Point estimate hypotheses

Research hypotheses

Statistical hypotheses

Working hypotheses

INTRODUCTION

In this chapter we examine hypotheses, various testable statements that are derived from our theories. [Hypotheses are the means whereby our theories are tested. Hypotheses vary in their complexity and wording, and thus several different kinds of hypotheses are described. Conventional use of hypotheses in research suggests that these statements should be implicitly or explicitly presented in pairs or hypothesis sets. Hypothesis sets, including the conventional pairing of research and null hypotheses, are examined and several examples from the research literature are provided.

Hypotheses perform several important functions. Their use in criminological research signifies more elaborate or sophisticated research plans, where investigators are interested in description and experimentation. Hypotheses may contain one or several variables.   As we add variables to hypothesis statements, these statements become increasingly complex and more difficult to test.   Both one- and k-variable hypothesis statements are illustrated.

Although it is possible to verify or refute theories without deriving hypotheses from them to test, it is a widely accepted practice to use hypotheses for theory verification purposes.   Also, whenever hypotheses are subject to empirical test, researchers use probability theory as a means of minimizing guesswork and subjectivity when interpreting scientific results.   Hypothesis-test outcomes are evaluated in terms of the adequacy of the theory from which they were derived, the quality of instrumentation and sample selected, and other factors.   Several considerations relevant for interpreting the results of hypothesis tests are presented and examined.

HYPOTHESES AND THEORY

Hypotheses are tentative statements about something the validity of which is generally unknown. For example, to declare that "upper-class people have fewer delinquent children than lower-class people" might be construed as an hypothesis concerning the effect of social class on delinquent behavior. Whether or not this is a statement of fact or a hypothesis depends on how much we know about the social class–delinquency relation and whether the declarer actually knows if the statement is true.   If the statement reflects the investigator's "hunch" about the social class–delinquency relation, the statement is largely hypothetical.   However, if census data exist to show clearly that large proportions of delinquents are found in lower-class families and small proportions of them are found in upper-class families, these data provide empirical support for the authenticity of the statement.

Many facts that we recite today were hypotheses in earlier times.   For example, we know a great deal more about marijuana today than we did in the 1930s. Some persons believed that marijuana caused irreversible mental illness and insanity.   Others believed that it led to sexual promiscuity.   Today, although it is unlawful to use marijuana in any U.S. jurisdiction, we understand that it impairs our judgment and depth perception, although it does not appear to cause irreversible mental illness, insanity, or sexual promiscuity.

Another example pertains to the relation between broken homes and delinquency.   Children from broken homes (either by desertion or divorce) were believed to be likely candidates for delinquency.   Religious leaders promoted the importance of family stability and unity as a way of preventing children in those families from acquiring delinquent behaviors and characteristics.   Single-parent adoptions of children were unheard of in most jurisdictions, because the conventional two-parent family was believed most therapeutic for children.   Today, however, several states permit single-parent adoptions of children, since the evidence that single-parent families are unhealthy for child-rearing has been inconclusive and contradictory.

Many of our present beliefs have been shaped by previous verifications of theories about things.   Much uncertainty remains about different types of behaviors and social events, however. [Below are examples of hypotheses that might be tested in criminological and criminal justice research today:]

1. *Female correctional officers have the same stress levels compared with male correctional officers.*
2. *Crime rates in neighborhoods decrease as police visibility increases.*
3. *Criminal court judges in the South are more lenient than criminal court judges in the North in sentencing elderly offenders.*
4. *The greater the numbers of correctional officers supervising prisoners, the fewer the numbers of inmate disturbances.*
5. *Jurors are more sympathetic to female defendants than they are to male defendants.*
6. *Increasing the punitive fines for committing crimes will decrease the crime rate.*
7. *Felons who participate in community-based correctional programs will have lower rates of recidivism than will incarcerated felons who are paroled.*
8. *Crime rates vary inversely with the amount of money spent on crime prevention.*
9. *Females charged with felonies have a better chance of obtaining pretrial release than do males charged with the same crimes and having similar criminal histories.*
10. *Offenders on probation with electronic monitoring will have fewer program violations than will offenders on standard probation.*

[Hypotheses may pertain to anything. There are no restrictions about what can be hypothesized. Hypotheses do not necessarily have to be true, however. In fact, the truth of many hypotheses formulated by researchers is often unknown. *Hypotheses, therefore, are tentative statements about things that researchers wish to support or refute.*]

The 10 hypotheses listed above have been studied and subject to verification by various researchers in recent years. Some of these statements have been investigated more often than others. Thus our degree of certainty about any given statement is based, in part, on the amount of confirming evidence that we can compile about it. Also, each of these statements is derived from a larger theoretical scheme. If we are examining the effectiveness of various probation programs, for instance, we might theorize about the amount of control exerted over probationers by using home confinement and/or electronic monitoring as means of verifying their whereabouts and otherwise keeping track of their movements. One statement we might test would be whether those on standard probation might be more likely than those subject to more intensive monitoring, especially electronic monitoring, to commit new crimes.

It might also be believed that fining offenders might function to reduce their recidivism. Currently, the Internal Revenue Service and Drug Enforcement Administration, together with the U.S. Department of Justice, seize assets of drug dealers and those who traffic in illegal drugs. These assets might include automobiles, boats, airplanes, homes, and other types of property, in addition to large sums of money used for illicit drug transactions. In 1991, for instance, the Department of Justice claimed that several billion dollars had been used to improve law enforcement effectiveness, and that much of this money was from illegal drug transactions and property seizures. It might be hypothesized, therefore, that hitting drug dealers in their pocketbooks might have a deterrent effect on their propensity to violate the law.

Each hypothesis is closely connected with a theoretical scheme that provides an explanatory and predictive framework for it. An hypothesis is like an advance forecast, since a certain outcome is anticipated or expected. The theoretical rationale is such that it explains how it came to be so that the hypothesis might be true. It may be helpful to review briefly Chapters 2 and 3, particularly the functions of theory and derivations of hypotheses from theory.

TYPES OF HYPOTHESES, HYPOTHESIS CONSTRUCTION, AND HYPOTHESIS SETS

Several different kinds of hypotheses are used in criminological research. The primary types of hypotheses examined here are (1) research hypotheses and (2) null hypotheses. A third type of hypothesis is the statistical hypothesis, which is a numerical expression of both research and null hypotheses.

Research Hypotheses

Hypotheses that are derived from the researcher's theory are called either *research hypotheses* or *working hypotheses*. Social scientists believe that their research hypotheses are true since they are derived logically from theoretical schemes constructed by these researchers. These hypotheses are believed true to the extent that the theories from which they were derived are true.

Because theories are, in a sense, suppositions about the true nature of things and thus considered tentative statements about reality until they have been verified to the scientist's satisfaction, the hypotheses derived from theory must also be regarded as tentative suppositions about things until they have been tested. *Testing hypotheses* means to subject them to some type of empirical confirmation or disconfirmation. For example, testing the hypothesis "The average income expectation of boys in a poverty area is $1000 per month as adults" might be done by entering a poverty area, obtaining a sample of male youths, and asking them questions about their monthly income expectation as adults. If most of the boys tell us that their income expectation is around $1000 per month, our hypothesis about their income expectation is confirmed, at least in this instance. If their reports are substantially more or less than $1000, our hypothesis is disconfirmed, refuted, or not supported, again in this instance. *It is important to understand that hypothesis tests under any condition or in any situation, regardless of the magnitude of a study, are not conclusive proof of the truthfulness of the hypothesis.* Replication research is advised, where one's research is repeated again and again under different circumstances and in different geographical areas. If sufficient numbers of samples of boys continue to report income expectations of $1000 as adults, our hypothesis gradually becomes a factual statement. In time, there will be no further need to test it.

Null Hypotheses

In a sense, null hypotheses are the reverse of research hypotheses, although this is not entirely accurate. Null hypotheses are also statements about the reality of things, except that they serve to refute or deny whatever is explicitly stated in a given research hypothesis. To continue with our example above, if investigators state in their research hypothesis that "the average income expectation of boys in a poverty area is not $1000 as adults," the appropriate null hypothesis to accompany this research hypothesis is "the average income expectation of boys in a poverty area *is* $1000 as adults." If investigators subsequently find out that boys in a poverty area have income expectations considerably more (or less) than $1000 as adults, the null hypothesis can be rejected and the research hypothesis will be supported.

Another way of looking at research and null hypotheses is that both statements are directly contradictory of one another and cannot coexist as true. Therefore, if one of the statements is true, the other statement must be false. If one of the statements is false, the other statement must be true. If we show that the statement "the average income expectation of boys in a poverty area is not $1000 as adults" is false, this statement can be rejected. Then we conclude that *it must be true* that "the average income expectation of boys in a poverty area is $1000 as adults" is true and should be supported. Confirming one statement denies the other. Denying one statement confirms the other.

Null hypotheses are usually paired with specific research hypotheses, such as the 10 statements used as examples above. These statements have been re-created below, and null hypotheses have been devised for each in the sets below. Notice the wording of both hypotheses in these hypothesis sets.

HYPOTHESIS SET 1

1. *Research hypothesis: Female correctional officers have the same stress levels as male correctional officers.*

1'. *Null hypothesis: Female correctional officers have different stress levels compared with male correctional officers.*

HYPOTHESIS SET 2

2. *Research hypothesis: Crime rates in neighborhoods decrease as police visibility increases.*

2'. *Null hypothesis: Crime rates in neighborhoods either increase or remain the same as police visibility increases.*

HYPOTHESIS SET 3

3. *Research hypothesis: Criminal court judges in the South are more lenient than criminal court judges in the North in sentencing elderly offenders.*

3′. *Null hypothesis: Criminal court judges in the South are equally or less lenient than criminal court judges in the North in sentencing elderly offenders.*

HYPOTHESIS SET 4

4. *Research hypothesis: The greater the numbers of correctional officers supervising prisoners, the fewer the numbers of inmate disturbances.*

4′. *Null hypothesis: The greater the numbers of correctional officers supervising prisoners, the numbers of inmate disturbances will either remain the same or be greater.*

HYPOTHESIS SET 5

5. *Research hypothesis: Jurors are more sympathetic to female defendants than they are to male defendants.*

5′. *Null hypothesis: Judges are equally or less sympathetic to female defendants than they are to male defendants.*

HYPOTHESIS SET 6

6. *Research hypothesis: Increasing the punitive fines for committing crimes will decrease the crime rate.*

6′. *Null hypothesis: Increasing the punitive fines for committing crimes will either increase the crime rate or exert no effect on it.*

HYPOTHESIS SET 7

7. *Research hypothesis: Felons who participate in community-based correctional programs will have lower rates of recidivism than those of incarcerated felons who are paroled.*

7′. *Null hypothesis: Felons who participate in community-based correctional programs will have the same rates of recidivism or higher rates of recidivism than incarcerated felons who are paroled.*

HYPOTHESIS SET 8

8. *Research hypothesis: Crime rates vary inversely with the amount of money spent on crime prevention.*

8′. *Null hypothesis: Crime rates either vary directly or do not vary at all with the amount of money spent on crime prevention.*

Types of Hypotheses, Hypothesis Construction, and Hypothesis Sets

9. *Research hypothesis: Females charged with felonies have a better chance of obtaining pretrial release than do males charged with the same crimes and having similar criminal histories.*

9'. *Null hypothesis: Females charged with felonies have either the same chance or a poorer chance of obtaining pretrial release than do males charged with the same crimes and having similar criminal histories.*

HYPOTHESIS SET 10

10. *Research hypothesis: Offenders on probation with electronic monitoring will have fewer program violations than will offenders on standard probation.*

10'. *Null hypothesis: Offenders on probation with electronic monitoring will either have the same or greater program violations than will offenders on standard probation.*

In each of the hypothesis sets above, the null hypothesis was constructed directly from the wording of the research hypothesis. Notice that if we refute any of the null hypotheses, the accompanying research hypothesis will have to be true, at least under those specific test circumstances. Why should we do all of this in the first place? After all, we have a perfectly good theory that we have constructed. We have extracted various hypothesis statements from it to test. Why not test them and let it go at that?

Before these questions are answered, we must also accept the fact that *null hypotheses are strictly hypothetical models used to test research hypotheses indirectly.* Thus in reality, they were never intended to exist on their own. We make up null hypotheses directly from research hypotheses. Then, we test null hypotheses. As the result of our tests of null hypotheses, we make decisions about research hypotheses. Rejecting a specific null hypothesis, or throwing it out, or refuting it, or disconfirming it means that we support the specific research hypothesis that was used originally to construct that null hypothesis. If we *fail to reject* a null hypothesis, we *fail to support* the specific research hypothesis from which that null hypothesis was created. We *never* "accept" or "support" or "confirm" null hypotheses—they do not exist in reality, except as indirect tests of the real research hypotheses that we have formulated. The following relation is helpful in understanding what is meant by rejecting and failing to reject null hypotheses, and these two alternative consequences for specific research hypotheses:

Our decision about the null hypothesis is:	Our decision about the research hypothesis is:
Reject it ⟶	Support it
Fail to reject it ⟶	Fail to support it

By now, you are probably thoroughly bewildered by these last few paragraphs, and it is expected that you will eventually ask the question, "Why do criminologists want to bother with so-called null hypotheses anyway?" "Why don't they test their research hypotheses directly and be content with that?" These questions have been asked time and time again by every student confronting null hypotheses for the first time. There are four reasons why null hypothesis models are used, most of which may not answer these questions to your satisfaction.

1. *Because criminologists and other social scientists define their roles as being more detached and objective about phenomena compared with laypeople, it would appear as though they were not behaving objectively if they sought to prove true those statements they believed to be true initially.* Therefore, trying to show the truthfulness of research hypotheses would imply to some people, at least, a definite bias toward trying to confirm one's suppositions and possibly ignoring those things that would tend to refute one's beliefs. Null hypotheses assist researchers, therefore, because such hypotheses are denials of what is believed to be true. If investigators are able to reject or refute null hypotheses, their case for supporting their research hypotheses is strengthened as a result.

2. *It "seems" easier to prove something false than to prove it true.* There are those who contend that it is easier to find fault with something (i.e., an idea, belief, or hypothesis) than to look for those things that would support it. Whatever the relative merits of this argument, the null hypothesis is believed to be the tool that should act as the true indicator of things until proven otherwise.

3. *It is conventional to use null hypotheses in criminological and criminal justice research.* The key word here is *convention*. It is conventional in social research of any kind to use null hypotheses in conjunction with research hypotheses. Most social scientists use null hypotheses in their own research and in their articles published in professional journals. The fourth reason below illustrates why null hypotheses have become conventional for criminologists.

4. *Null hypotheses fit the probability model underlying hypothesis testing.* Under a probability theoretical model, hypotheses have a likelihood of being either true or false. The null hypothesis is an expression of one possible alternative outcome of our social observations. The probability model specifies that the null hypothesis may be either true or false. Another alternative hypothesis about our social observations is the research hypothesis. Research hypotheses are "grounded" in and derived from theory. Research hypotheses also have a probability of either being true or false. Thus the null hypothesis logically specifies a hypothetical social condition that may or may not be true, and that may be subject to empirical verification or refutation. Neither the research hypothesis nor the null hypothesis is absolutely true or false under any given test conducted. Both probabilities (being either true or false) always coexist for each type of hypothesis.

Statistical Hypotheses

For our purposes, we will distinguish a third type of hypothesis, known as a *statistical hypothesis*. *Statistical hypotheses are statements about statistical populations that on the basis of information obtained from observed data, one seeks to support or refute* (Winer, 1962). Statistical populations refer either to people or things. It is generally the case when testing hypotheses that our observations about people or things are reduced in some way to numerical quantities and symbolic expressions. For instance, suppose that we are concerned about age differences between two groups of persons. We hypothesize that one group is older than the other. To test our research hypothesis, which might be "group 1 is older than group 2," we create a null hypothesis, which becomes "group 1 is the same age as or younger than group 2."

To subject these hypotheses to an empirical test, we would obtain age values for groups 1 and 2, average the ages, and assess the average age difference by applying a statistical test of significance. (See Chapter 17 for discussions of statistical tests of significance.) In effect, we are transforming both our research and null hypotheses into statistical hypotheses so that they can be tested by numerical means. (It should be noted that it is not always possible to quantify certain research and null hypotheses about things. Statistical hypotheses are restricted in their application, therefore. These applications and restrictions are discussed in Chapter 17.)

A statistical hypothesis concerning the difference in average ages between groups 1 and 2 can be represented symbolically. Below are both verbal and symbolic expressions of the hypotheses above:

VERBAL EXPRESSION OF NULL AND RESEARCH HYPOTHESES

Null hypothesis, H_0: Group 1 is the same age as or younger than group 2.

Research hypothesis, H_1: Group 1 is older than group 2.

STATISTICAL AND SYMBOLIC EXPRESSION OF NULL AND RESEARCH HYPOTHESES

Statistical null hypothesis, H_0: $\overline{X}_1 \leq \overline{X}_2$

Statistical research hypothesis, H_1: $\overline{X}_1 > \overline{X}_2$

where H_0 denotes the symbol for the null hypothesis

H_1 denotes the symbol for the research hypothesis

$\overline{X}_1$ is read "X bar sub one" and is the average age or mean for group 1

$\overline{X}_2$ is read "X bar sub two" and is the average age or mean for group 2

The symbols $>$ and $\leq$ mean "greater than" and "equal to or less than."

In the examples above, H_0 denotes the null hypothesis, which says that the mean or average age of group 1 is equal to or less than the mean or average age of group 2. The research hypothesis, H_1, says that the average age of group 1 is greater than the average or mean age for group 2. Sometimes, the designations H_1 and H_2 are used to signify the null and research hypotheses. The *notation systems* or symbolic portrayals of such statistics such as the average or mean, and even research and null hypothesis designations, differ from one textbook to the next. Most books use the H_0 and H_1 designation, however, and thus this format is considered conventional.

Notice in the example above that the null hypothesis does *not* say simply that group 1 is younger than group 2. Rather, it says that group 1 is either younger or the same age as group 2. Think about which hypothesis would be supported if an investigator rejected a null hypothesis that said: "group 1 is younger than group 2." If this statement were not true, it would be true that either "group 1 is older than group 2" or that "group 1 is the same age as group 2." To guard against this imprecision, the null hypothesis is carefully worded "group 1 is *the same age as or younger than* group 2." This is an "equal to or less than" type of arrangement between the two samples, and thus the symbol $\leq$ (equal to or less than) is used. If this statement is rejected, the only remaining option is that group 1 is older than group 2, and the symbol $>$ (greater than) would be applicable.

Two conventional symbol combinations used by criminologists and criminal justice scholars are intended to illustrate directionality and nondirectionality. *Directionality* is intended to signify that one value is greater or less than another, whatever the values happen to be. Anytime the "greater than" ($>$) or "less than" ($<$) signs are used in a hypothesis set, it can safely be assumed that a directional test of some hypothesis is being made. That is, the researcher is interested in saying whether or not two or more values differ in specified directions. If the hypothesis set contains "equal to" ($=$) or "not equal to" ($\neq$) signs, this means the hypothesis test is nondirectional. In this case, investigators are only interested in whether differences exist among observed values, not in whether they differ in any particular direction. Thus in the hypothesis set above relating to the average ages of two groups, the hypothesis set was directional, since "greater than" and "less than" signs were used. A nondirectional hypothesis set is the following:

H_0: "Group 1 is equal to group 2."
H_1: "Group 1 is different from group 2."

Symbolically expressed, these hypotheses become

H_0: $\overline{X}_1 = \overline{X}_2$
H_1: $\overline{X}_1 \neq \overline{X}_2$

As we will see in Chapter 16 and 17, nondirectional hypothesis tests are also known as "two-tailed" tests, while directional hypothesis tests are designated as "one-tailed" tests. The "tails" refer to areas of sampling distributions of statistics and are reserved for more specialized discussion in Chapter 16, where their meaning is clarified.

Statistical hypotheses are usually established to indicate (1) differences between two or more groups regarding some trait or characteristic that they possess; (2) associations between two or more variables within one group or between several groups; and (3) point estimates of certain population characteristics, such as average values.

Summarizing briefly, three classifications of hypotheses exist that are important to criminologists and other social scientists. These are research hypotheses, null hypotheses, and statistical hypotheses. As a result of one's theorizing, research hypotheses are derived. Null hypotheses are established conventionally in accordance with how various research hypotheses are stated. Null hypotheses are hypothetical models established so that research hypotheses may be tested indirectly. Numerical and symbolic expressions of research and null hypotheses are called statistical hypotheses. Statistical hypotheses are those ultimately subjected to some sort of empirical test. On the basis of one's observations and the test of statistical hypotheses, tentative conclusions are reached about null hypotheses, and ultimately, about research hypotheses. If certain null hypotheses are not refuted by evidence found by researchers, certain accompanying research hypotheses are not supported. However, if certain null hypotheses are rejected by evidence found by investigators, certain accompanying research hypotheses are supported. Supporting any research hypothesis derived from some theory is considered partial support for that theory.

Hypotheses are comprised of variables. Hypotheses may contain a single variable, two variables, or k or more than two variables. Hypotheses containing more than two variables are considered complex hypotheses and are more difficult to test. This is because the interrelatedness of more than two variables acting simultaneously is more difficult to assess quantitatively and theoretically. Table 13.1 shows the general relation between research, null, and statistical hypotheses.

Where Do Hypotheses Come From?

Scanning various professional journals will expose any student to a wide variety of studies, each with its array of hypotheses and theory. People often ask, "Where do those hypotheses come from?" Quite simply, hypotheses come from our thoughts about things. Hypotheses are generated in graduate student "bull sessions," conversations and discussions between students and faculty, from random observations and reflections about life as people go to and from work, and of course, they are deduced from theory. Because of the diverse circumstances under which hypotheses are formulated, it stands to reason that there will be a wide variation in the quality of hypotheses.

TABLE 13.1 RELATION BETWEEN RESEARCH, NULL, AND STATISTICAL HYPOTHESES

H_1	H_0	H_1 and H_0
Research hypothesis	Null hypothesis	Statistical hypothesis (symbolically expressed)
Two groups differ according to age.	Two groups do not differ regarding age.	$H_0: \overline{X}_1 = \overline{X}_2$ $H_1: \overline{X}_1 \neq \overline{X}_2$
↓	↓	↓
(Derived from theory)	(Created from research hypothesis)	If conclusion is to reject null hypothesis, research hypothesis is supported.

Also, there is variety associated with the standards that criminologists employ to determine whether hypotheses are good or bad, useful or not useful. It is possible, for example, for two different researchers working independently to derive similar hypotheses from a common theory, although they might word their hypotheses differently and/or they might select different circumstances under which to conduct their empirical tests. The evaluation of hypotheses is quite often a relative matter. What one social scientist might regard as a good hypothesis might be judged as bad by another social scientist. We do not want to convey the impression that social science advances purely on the whims and personal preferences of criminologists and criminal justice scholars. What is important to understand here is that there are flexibility and latitude that enable social investigators to design studies in unique ways and to give hypothesis wording their personal style. Further, investigators may design their studies any way they wish and specify the empirical tests to be conducted in accordance with their personal and professional standards. Although personal standards of researchers vary, there are conventional guidelines followed by most investigators. So despite the diversity in methodological inquiry, there is a high degree of uniformity regarding the application of certain methodological guidelines.

Hypothesis Formulation: Good, Better, and Best

The "goodness" or "badness" of any particular hypothesis is dependent on the relative circumstances of the theory from which it was derived. One way of evaluating hypotheses generally is in terms of the amount of information they provide about phenomena. Consider the example below of three statements, each stating a simple relationship between two variables, X and Y.

A: X and Y are associated.
B: X is related to Y.
C: As X increases, Y decreases.

Notice that for hypothesis A, a simple statement of relationship is provided. Nothing is indicated *about* the relationship other than the fact that X and Y are associated. From the way this statement is worded, we know little or nothing about which variable has more of an impact on the other in a causal sense. We are cautious anyway about making statements of a causal nature, since causality is so difficult to establish in any type of social research. Clues about which variables tend to influence others may, of course, be found in the theoretical scheme. This explanatory framework shows linkages among variables and specifies how each relates with the others. However, examining statement A above gives us no clue as to which variable might be independent or dependent.

Statement B is more informative, "X is related to Y," since it mildly implies that Y influences values of X. If we wished to mildly imply that X influences Y, we might rephrase this hypothesis as "Y is related to X." Statement B is considered an improvement over statement A. However, statement C is the most informative of the three statements. This statement indicates that increasing values of X seem to elicit changes on the Y variable; namely, Y values decrease as X values increase.

Which of these hypotheses is best? Ordinarily, we might choose the most informative hypothesis if specific directionality of the relationship between the two variables is indicated. The objectives of one's research come into play here as well. If the research is primarily exploratory or descriptive, statement A or B might be suitable, given our immediate lack of awareness of how X and Y are related with one another. However, if extensive investigations have been conducted of variables X and Y, statement C would be best since it is the most informative. Investigators would tend to select hypothesis statements such as statement C, since their research designs would be more experimental in nature.

FUNCTIONS OF HYPOTHESES

Theories are relatively elaborate tools we use to explain and predict events. Social scientists develop theories to account for social and psychological phenomena, and then they devise a means whereby these theories can be tested and subjected to verification or refutation. Seldom do researchers actually test their entire theories directly. Most of the time, they conduct tests of specific hypotheses derived from theory. These hypotheses pertain to different parts of the theory, and if they "test out" and are supported by the evidence researchers find, their theories are supported in part.

Usually, it takes many tests of different hypotheses derived from the theory to test it adequately and determine its predictive value and adequacy as a tool of explanation for events. One major function of hypotheses, therefore, is to make it possible to test theories. In this regard, an alternative definition of a *hypothesis* is a statement of theory in testable form. All statements of theory in testable form are called hypotheses.

Sometimes, certain hypotheses are not associated with any particular theory. It could be that as a result of some hypothesis, a theory eventually will be devised or constructed. Consequently, another function of hypotheses is to suggest theories that may account for some event. Although it is more commonplace that research proceeds from theories to hypotheses, occasionally the reverse is true. Social investigators may have some idea about why a given phenomenon occurs, and they hypothesize several things that relate to it. They judge that some hypotheses have greater potential explanatory value than others, and as a result, they may construct a logical system of propositions, assumptions, and definitions linking their explanation of the event to the event itself. In other words, they create a theory. Working from hypotheses back to some theory is not necessarily poor methodology. Eventually, investigators are going to have to subject their resulting theory to empirical test anyway, to determine its accuracy. The predictive value of the theory may be evaluated at that time.

Hypotheses also perform a descriptive function. Each time hypotheses are tested empirically, they tell us something about the phenomena they are associated with. If the hypothesis is supported, our information about the phenomenon increases. Even if the hypothesis is refuted, the test tells us something about the phenomenon that we did not know before. Even the inventor who discovers 600 ways of doing something wrong learns something as a result of these frustrating experiences. The accumulation of information as a result of hypothesis-testing reduces the amount of ignorance that we may have about why certain social events occur in given ways.

For criminologists, therefore, the major functions of hypotheses are that they:

1. Test theories
2. Suggest theories
3. Describe social phenomena

Several secondary functions of hypotheses may be mentioned. As one result of testing certain hypotheses, social policies may be formulated in communities, penal institutions may be redesigned or revamped, teaching methods may be altered or improved, solutions to various kinds of social problems may be suggested and implemented, delinquents and criminal offenders may be treated differently, and supervisory practices may be changed in organizations. Testing hypotheses refutes certain "commonsense" notions about human behavior, raises questions about the explanations we presently use to account for things, and most generally alters our orientation toward our environment in various ways. All hypotheses relate to our knowledge of things, and as this knowledge changes, we change also.

SINGLE-VARIABLE, TWO-VARIABLE, AND K-VARIABLE HYPOTHESES

Hypotheses are distinguished according to whether they contain single variables, two variables, and k variables.

Single-Variable Hypotheses

Single-variable hypotheses are often known as *point estimate hypotheses*. Researchers are interested in forecasting certain values associated with populations of elements. They might predict various population values, such as the average age of some population. Subsequently, they might obtain a sample of persons from that population and make a comparison of their sample mean with the hypothesized population mean. These are single-variable hypotheses, since the only variable is the predicted mean value for the population. An example of a single-variable hypothesis might be

"The average age of the inmate population of prisons is 30."

Two-Variable Hypotheses

If we add a second variable and construct new statements, we will have two-variable hypotheses. All 10 hypotheses presented earlier in this chapter are examples of two-variable hypotheses. If we wanted to make a two-variable hypothesis out of the one-variable hypothesis above, we might differentiate inmates according to whether they are in prisons or jails. Our new two-variable hypothesis might be:

"Jail inmates tend to be younger than prison inmates."
or
"The average age of jail inmates is less than the average age of prison inmates."

k-Variable Hypotheses

When we construct hypotheses with three or more variables, we have complex hypotheses that are quite difficult to test. For example, we might have the following:

"Correctional officer job effectiveness varies according to one's job satisfaction, which varies inversely with the closeness of supervision officers receive from their correctional officer supervisors."

This hypothesis is difficult to test for several reasons. First, we may find that, indeed, job effectiveness and job satisfaction may be related as we have predicted. However, it may be that the type of supervision may have nothing to do with job satisfaction or with job effectiveness. To solve the problem of testing this hypothesis, it is recommended that this hypothesis be broken down into two separate hypotheses, which each can be tested independently. These two hypotheses would be:

"Correctional officer job effectiveness and job satisfaction are related."

"Correctional officer job satisfaction varies inversely with the closeness of supervision received by correctional officer supervisors."

If a third hypothesis is desirable linking job effectiveness with closeness of supervision, we can state:

"Correctional officer job effectiveness varies inversely with the closeness of supervision received by correctional officer supervisors."

HYPOTHESIS TESTING

When we "test hypotheses" *we subject them to some kind of empirical scrutiny to determine if they are supported or refuted by collected evidence.* If we are testing hypotheses about delinquents, we usually will need to go out and study a sample of delinquents to collect evidence relative to our hypotheses about them. If we are studying correctional officers or probationers, we need to obtain samples of correctional officers from a prison or prisons or probationers from one or more probation programs. Actually, testing hypotheses involves several tasks. These are listed below.

1. *A real social situation is needed that will provide a reasonable testing ground for the hypotheses.* Testing grounds are actual social settings where data exist pertaining to the hypotheses to be tested. These "grounds" may be probation agencies, jails, community corrections agencies, city or county courts, or any other location containing people with information we need to test our hypotheses.

2. *Investigators must make sure that their hypotheses are testable.* This means that only *empirical phenomena* should be selected for study. It makes no sense to ask questions that cannot be answered with our present instrumentation. Hypotheses containing variables that cannot be measured are also not amenable to empirical test. For example, if we hypothesize that "evil spirits cause delinquency," this statement is incapable of being refuted. It cannot be supported either, but it cannot be refuted. This and similar statements are outside the realm of scientific inquiry, because one or more variables are simply not amenable to empirical measurement.

For instance, in 1947, Hans Von Hentig wrote about western outlaws and observed that some of them had red hair. Von Hentig presented some spectacular observations about red hair and lawbreaking behavior to a convention of psychologists, and he claimed to identify an internal motivator that, he said, precipitated abnormal and even criminal behavior. This phenomenon, he said, was "accelerated motor innervation," some mystical central nervous system phenomenon that seemed closely associated with red body hair. However, Von Hentig never outlined clearly how accelerated motor innervation could be measured or taken into account by other scientists. Thus there was no way to refute Von Hentig's claims.

Many social scientists regarded Von Hentig's research as far-fetched, and some even suggested that his work might even aggravate the unfavorable stereotype of the "hot-tempered redhead." Von Hentig's work clearly rested outside the realm of scientific inquiry. This does not mean that sometime in the future, we might discover ways of measuring accelerated motor innervation empirically. For the time being, however, we must reject his explanation, since it lies outside the realm of empiricism. The lesson to be learned here is to confine theorizing to those phenomena that can be taken into account empirically.

3. *Investigators should devise and use measures of the phenomena of interest so that these phenomena may be quantified easily.* Each variable must be operationalized in order that objective, numerical assessments may be made of the worth of the hypothesis. An assortment of statistical tests exists for hypothesis-testing purposes.

INTERPRETING THE RESULTS OF HYPOTHESIS TESTS

Whenever hypotheses in one's research are tested, it is usually the case that *several* hypotheses are either confirmed or refuted rather than single-hypothesis tests.

There is no fixed number of hypotheses that researchers must test, since different theories vary in their detail and sophistication. Some theories are more elaborate and yield more testable hypotheses than other, less elaborate theories. An extreme might include tests of 100 or more hypotheses in a single study. More common, however, are hypothesis-test situations involving 10 or fewer hypotheses. Again, there are no conventional rules about how many hypotheses we should test.

To illustrate how we might judge the results of hypothesis tests in the general case, let's assume that we are testing 10 hypotheses from a given theory in our research project. We have constructed a theory to explain relationships between certain variables, we have collected relevant data, and on the basis of our analysis of that data, we have *tentatively* concluded certain things about our findings. Since hypotheses are predictions of what we believe will be found, based on the validity of our previous theorizing about phenomena, either some or all of our hypotheses may "test out" and be supported, or some or all may not "test out" and be refuted. Three possible outcomes or scenarios might be anticipated:

1. All of our hypotheses tested are supported by whatever we find.
2. None of the hypotheses we are testing are supported by whatever we find.
3. Some of the hypotheses we are testing are supported by our findings, while the remaining hypotheses are not supported.

Neophyte researchers will probably make the following interpretations of these outcomes:

Outcome 1: If all hypotheses being tested are supported, it might be assumed that the theory from which the hypotheses were derived is true.

Outcome 2: If none of the hypotheses tested are supported, it might be assumed that the theory from which these hypotheses were derived is not true.

Outcome 3: The most perplexing outcome, partial support of the theory through supporting some hypotheses and refuting others, might be interpreted as "faulty theorizing." Perhaps our theory is faulty in certain respects, particularly those respects relevant to those research hypotheses that were refuted rather than supported.

We must be careful not to attach too much significance to our hypothesis-test outcomes. After all, we are testing our hypotheses using various samples of elements that may or may not be representative of the general population about which we seek information. Some researchers blindly claim that their theories are valid if all of their hypotheses are supported. Other researchers "throw in the towel" and proclaim their theories "untrue" if their hypotheses are all refuted. Neither of these conclusions is warranted. This is because there are so many factors that influence hypothesis-test outcomes. The adequacy of one's theory is only one factor. We may have a perfectly good theory but poor methodology. We may have perfectly good theory, perfectly good methodology, but a poor, unrepresentative sample. We may have perfectly good theory, perfectly good methodology, a perfectly good sample, but poor instrumentation and measures of our phenomena studied. We may choose the wrong statistical tests to apply when analyzing our data. We may apply interpretive standards that are too rigorous. Suffice it to say that we may unintentionally commit any number of errors or experience any number of problems in the course of implementing our research plans.

If you turn to various professional journals and inspect the contents of different articles, you will often find that the authors of those articles have incorporated various safeguards into their studies. These warnings are similar to product liability statements, where manufacturers want consumers to know, in advance, whether their products contain substances that have been known to produce adverse side effects, whether some assembly is required, or whether there are sharp edges that might be harmful to children. Product liability-type statements in criminological research warn "consumers" or readers about a study's flaws. Some common phrases are, "These findings should be cautiously viewed," "Further study is recommended," or "Some suggestions for future research include. . . ." Specific drawbacks of the research or study limitations are cited, such as: "The sample analyzed in the present study consisted of only 35 percent of the original 500 persons selected randomly. Thus there is a question about how reliable the sample is in relation to its parent population." Or, "Evidence emerged to indicate that our measures lacked reliability. Further research is needed where more precise indicators of these phenomena can be constructed and applied." These writers are calling our attention to one or more "faults" of their studies. This is acceptable, since no study is perfect per se.

The point is that *we should not attach too much importance to any study*. It is best to interpret research findings from any particular study in a more general context. Thus how do these study results *compare* with the findings of similar studies? Considering *several* studies of the same subject matter, how does any new study support, refute, or modify what is generally believed about the phenomena under investigation? Regardless of the outcome of any given test of hypotheses (i.e., outcomes 1, 2, and 3 above), therefore, researchers should always raise questions about each of the following problem areas: theory, sampling, measurement, data collection, statistics, and participant involvement. Raising such questions will enable researchers to:

1. Improve the quality and meaning of the interpretation of any hypothesis test
2. Evaluate the relative importance of a given hypothesis test for theory building
3. Determine the degree to which the study supports the work of others
4. Determine the reliability of the explanation of events that are either explicitly or implicitly stated by the hypotheses

Theoretical Considerations

Judging the results of one's hypothesis tests involves evaluating the adequacy of the theory from which the hypotheses were derived. Was the theory coherent, logical, and meaningful, and did it include measurable phenomena? Was it too broad or too narrow? Was the theory comprehensive enough to take into account certain intervening variables but narrow enough to be fruitful as a predictive tool? Was the theorizing consistent with what has been found in the research literature on the subject? Were the hypotheses formulated correctly, and did they contain variables that were included in the theory?

Sampling Considerations

How representative was the sample of the population from which it was drawn? If questionnaires were mailed to respondents, was there any nonresponse? How much? What importance would nonresponse have on the hypothesis-test outcomes, if any? Was the sample adequately selected? Did sample elements possess the necessary information relative to the hypothesis tests and theoretical questions?

Measurement Considerations

Were the measures used valid and reliable? What tests were conducted by the investigators to demonstrate the reliability and validity of the measures and other instrumentation? How closely connected were the operational definitions of terms to the nominal definitions derived in the theory?

Data Collection Procedures as a Consideration

Were the data collection procedures necessarily the best ones to use given the problem investigated? Would other data collection methods have yielded more fruitful results? If secondary sources were used, how reliable were those secondary sources? Was triangulation employed by investigators to improve their data accuracy and validity?

Statistical Considerations

Were appropriate statistical tests selected for data description and analysis given the quality and randomness of the sample obtained? Was the level of significance appropriate given the sample size and generalizability desired? Were all statistical assumptions satisfied so that the meaning of the measures applied was maximized?

Participant Involvement as a Consideration

Were respondents coerced into participating in the study or was their involvement voluntary? What degree of anonymity was provided by researchers to enhance response objectivity? Was there anything unusual about how respondents were questioned, observed, or otherwise studied that might interfere with our appraisal of the findings?

SUMMARY

Hypotheses are testable statements that are derived from theories. Varying in their complexity and tentativeness, hypotheses describe relationships between variables and are predictive of various social and psychological outcomes. Hypotheses are capable of refuting theories, making inferences about population values, specifying differences between two or more samples, and depicting variable interrelationships. Different types of hypotheses include research hypotheses, which are derived from theory; null hypotheses, which are constructed from research hypotheses; and statistical hypotheses. Null hypotheses are artificially created and are used conventionally and in conjunction with probability theory. Research and null hypotheses are often presented in pairs and tested in sets of hypotheses.

Hypotheses vary in the degree of information they provide about relations between variables. Less descriptive hypotheses are associated with exploratory and descriptive research, while more descriptive hypotheses are associated with experimental research. Hypotheses test theories, suggest theories, and describe social phenomena. They may contain single variables and act as hypotheses of point estimation, or they may contain two or more variables. Those hypotheses containing three or more variables are considered complex and difficult to test. Testing hypotheses involves a real social situation and investigating empirical phenomena that can be measured or quantified.

Outcomes of hypothesis tests depend on many factors, including theory adequacy, representativeness of the sample, type of respondent involvement, the validity and reliability of measuring instruments, and statistical sophistication. Data collection procedures also influence the quality of data obtained as well as hypothesis-test results. Subsequent investigations of the same or similar phenomena are ordinarily recommended, since single studies rarely are conclusive about variable interrelationships.

QUESTIONS FOR REVIEW

1. What is a hypothesis? How are hypotheses used in social research?
2. What are some major functions of hypotheses?
3. Identify and describe three different types of hypotheses. What is a hypothesis set? Give three examples different from the book and selected from your inspection of the research literature.
4. What is the relationship between hypotheses and theory? Discuss.
5. Where do hypotheses come from?
6. What is the basic rationale for using null hypotheses instead of testing research hypotheses directly?
7. Does any particular study stand as the definitive work in any given subject area? Why or why not? Explain.

8. Describe how research hypotheses should be interpreted if:
    (a) Particular null hypotheses are rejected.
    (b) Particular null hypotheses are not rejected.
    Why don't we "accept" null hypotheses? Explain.

9. What are three types of statistical hypotheses? Give some examples.

10. Using X and Y as two variables, describe three different types of relationships between X and Y that reflect three different degrees of knowledge about their relation.

11. Below are several research hypotheses. Write null hypotheses for each.
    (a) The mean for group 1 equals or exceeds 20.
    (b) Two groups differ in their average age.
    (c) Probation officers have higher job satisfaction than that of parole officers.
    (d) Suicide rates are the same between jail inmates and prison inmates.
    (e) Suicide rates vary inversely with social cohesion.
    (f) As variable X increases, variable Y decreases.
    (g) There is a positive relation between variables X and Y.

12. Construct three complex hypotheses relating any three variables of your choice. Indicate in a subsequent discussion why such hypotheses are more difficult to test than either one- or two-variable hypotheses.

13. Why was Hans Von Hentig's research on western outlaws generally rejected by the scientific community? What is the significance of Von Hentig's study for hypothesis testing and empiricism? Discuss.

14. What are some major considerations that must be made regarding outcomes of hypothesis tests? Discuss each briefly.

PART 4

Statistics: Descriptive Procedures

In Part IV we introduce the subject of statistics as they are applied in criminological research. In the four chapters in this part we examine different descriptive functions performed by statistics. In Chapter 14 we distinguish between population parameters and sample statistics. Different meanings of statistics are presented, and several key functions of statistics are discussed, including description and inference. Statistical applications sometimes assist us in establishing causal relationships between two or more variables. However, utilizing statistical procedures requires that certain assumptions be satisfied to comply with particular arithmetic requirements. Several assumptions are discussed, including randomness, sample size, and levels of measurement. Finally, we overview how statistics are used in criminal justice and criminology.

In Chapter 15 we illustrate several popular statistical measures of central tendency and dispersion or variability. Central tendency depicts those points in distributions of scores around which other scores tend to focus, while variability shows how scores are distributed about these points. Measures of central tendency include the mode, median, and mean, while the range and standard deviation are described as measures of variability. For each of these measures, a discussion of their weaknesses, strengths, and assumptions is presented.

In Chapter 16 we present the unit normal distribution and discuss its utility in criminological research. This is a key concept and considerable attention is devoted to it. Standard scores and their derivation are described and illustrated with examples drawn from the criminal justice literature. Various applications of the unit normal distribution in criminological research are presented. Underlying our statistical decision making are decision rules that we must establish in advance of our hypothesis tests. Several of these decision rules are identified and discussed, including sampling distributions of statistics, levels of significance, and regions of rejection or critical regions.

In Chapter 17 we discuss the basics of statistical inference and how criminologists and others can generalize from their samples to larger populations of elements. Two types of statistical inference are presented: point estimation and interval estimation. While point estimation is less popular, it is useful for illustrating the type of statistical decision making that will be relevant for statistical test applications. The more useful type of inference, interval estimation, is illustrated. Also, two major classes of statistical procedures are described. These include parametric and nonparametric procedures. These classes of procedures are described in detail, together with a discussion of their strengths and limitations in social research.   Several criteria are presented concerning which tests investigators might use for particular types of data analysis.   Also examined are several common assumption violations accompanying parametric and nonparametric test applications.   The chapter concludes with several examples of both parametric and nonparametric statistical procedures.

14

Statistics in Criminal Justice and Criminology

KEY TERMS

Description

Element

Estimation

Inference

Level of measurement

Nonparametric procedures

Parameter

Parametric procedures

Population

Purist

Randomness

Robustness

Sample

Sample size

Sampling fraction

Statistic

INTRODUCTION

Between 1976 and 1985, robberies in the United States decreased by about 22 percent (Flanagan and Jamieson, 1988:13). Also in 1985, property crimes outnumbered violent crimes by 9:1. Further, between 1976 and 1985, rapes in the United States increased by about 38 percent (Flanagan and Jamieson, 1988:14). Studies also show that approximately 10 to 20 percent of those defendants on pretrial release are arrested again for other crimes while awaiting trial (Flanagan and Jamieson, 1988:45). In 1983 there was one adult probationer for every 109 adults in the United States. By 1985, this figure had risen to 1 adult on probation for every 94 persons in the nation (Flanagan and Jamieson, 1988:104). Between 1974 and 1985, the one-day count of all juveniles in custody rose by 9 percent in relation to the average national daily population increase of 6 percent during the same period (Flanagan and Jamieson, 1988:105). In 1987, females comprised only 7 percent of all incarcerated state prison inmates. Also, 65 percent of the state prisons in the United States in 1987 were designed to house fewer than 500 inmates (Flanagan and Jamieson, 1988:107).

You have just been deluged by *statistics*. All of the statements in the paragraph above reflect statistical information about prisoners, juveniles, incarcerated female offenders, probationers, and crime rates. The *Uniform Crime Reports* and *National Crime Survey*, together with the *Report to the Nation on Crime and Justice* source from which the information above was taken, are compendiums of statistical information about criminals, crime rates, and victims of crime. In this chapter we introduce you to the field of statistics, although you will soon discover that the word *statistics* has several different meanings and more extensive applications in criminological and criminal justice research beyond the descriptive statements presented above. First, statistics is explored according to the different functions it performs in the research process. Beyond merely describing things, statistics extends to a wide variety of tests and measures that help us to make decisions about whatever we observe. Accordingly, there are assumptions we must address that underlie statistical applications.

Criminal justice experts and criminologists ordinarily study samples of persons in their investigations. These samples are often described through the use of statistical information such as that above. In addition, researchers seek information about entire populations (e.g., all probation officers, all police officers, all state prison inmates, all female juvenile offenders), and they frequently use samples of persons drawn from these populations to make inferences about populations from which they were drawn. Thus statistics performs both descriptive and inferential roles. Additionally, correlations are investigated between different combinations of variables. There exists many correlational techniques of use to criminologists and others for drawing causal inferences between different variables selected for investigation. Therefore, this chapter is an overview of the various meanings of statistics, how statistics function to benefit us in our research endeavors, and how they might be applied to solve various problems in criminal justice and criminology.

WHAT ARE STATISTICS?

In the general case, *statistics* is the body of methods and procedures used to assemble, describe, infer something from, or make decisions about the distribution of numerical data. Numerical data refer to any information we might collect about people and their characteristics (e.g., age, gender, religion, race, ethnicity, socioeconomic status, criminality, probationary status, and crime patterns). An examination of these data by persons skilled in data analysis and interpretation will yield statistical information or results that can be presented to others for their consideration and/or action.

All of us are consumers of statistical information in one form or another, and some of us are also generators of statistical information, as we do research and conduct scientific investigations of criminological phenomena. We learn about statistics in our early years, as we compile batting averages of our favorite baseball players, yardage gained by our favorite football players, as well as our own performance characteristics in various sports. We learn to evaluate things on the basis of statistical information. We might choose not to purchase certain automobiles because of poor statistics demonstrated by performance tests conducted by independent consumer agencies. We may or may not be admitted to colleges or universities, depending on our grade-point averages and entrance examination scores compared with national norms. Most likely we are quite familiar with what statistics can do for us by describing things. Fewer of us are familiar with what statistics can do for us in making decisions about the social or psychological events we observe. Some preliminary distinctions are in order.

STATISTICS AS CHARACTERISTICS

One way of viewing statistics is to compare samples in relation to populations. *Populations* represent a broad class of persons about which we seek information. Sometimes, we use the term *element* to refer to all persons in the population. Actually, "element" may refer to either people or things. Thus 90 elements may mean that we have 90 light bulbs. For our present purposes, however, elements will always refer to persons. Populations of relevance to those conducting criminal justice or criminological research might include all correctional officers in the United States, all county jail officers, all police officers in municipalities, all federal judges, all district attorneys and their assistants, all defense attorneys, all probation or parole officers, all robbers, all rapists, or all murderers.

Seldom do we investigate all elements in the population, however. It would be unwieldy for even the most financially endowed organizations or corporations to study all probation officers in the United States at any given point in time. Even the U.S. Bureau of the Census fails to study every family in the United States from one decade to the next. Rather, we find it more convenient (and less expensive) to study samples of elements. *Samples* consist of proportions of any given population. Thus rather than study all probation officers in the United States, we might elect to study a sample of probation officers taken from the states of Georgia, Florida, Alabama, Pennsylvania, and New Jersey. Our investigation objectives, personal or agency resources, and other practical criteria will dictate how large our samples of elements will be. Our intent is to obtain samples that are *representative* of the populations from which they were drawn, according to certain relevant characteristics. Unfortunately, there are no means whereby we can *guarantee* the representativeness of any sample we choose to study. Thus we are left with statements such as, "Our sample seems to have these characteristics; therefore, it is possible or likely that the population has these same or similar characteristics as well." Of course, much depends on *how* a sample is drawn from its population initially. (Different sampling procedures were discussed in detail in Chapter 5.)

Population Parameters

Population parameters are characteristics of populations. In criminal justice and criminology, for instance, population parameters might be the average annual caseload of *all* probation officers in the United States, the average age of *all* state inmates, the offense profile of *all* juvenile delinquents adjudicated delinquent within a given time period, or the average salaries of *all* municipal police officers nationally. The list of population parameters and accompanying population characteristics is limited only by our imaginations.

Sample Statistics

Sample statistics are characteristics of samples. Therefore, the average annual caseload of a sample of California probation officers, the average age of a sample of Louisiana prison inmates, the offense profile of a sample of Detroit juvenile delinquents, or the average salaries of a sample of Decatur, Georgia police officers are statistics or sample characteristics.

We determine the *scale* of our investigations. We may wish to limit our analyses to all persons of a certain type in a single community or part of the community. Or we may wish to study the national population of persons possessing certain characteristics. The important thing is that *we* decide or determine how broad our population base will be. In turn, the scope or limits of our target population will help us determine how large our sample size ought to be. (Again, it may be helpful to review the fundamentals of sampling presented in Chapter 5.)

FUNCTIONS OF STATISTICS

Statistics that we have mentioned thus far have been largely descriptive. But there are other meanings of statistics beyond simple description. One useful way of viewing statistics is to regard them as a set of tools to be used for various purposes. (In Chapter 15 we discuss descriptive statistics in detail.) While some of these purposes may include description, other purposes may be to enable us to make *inferences* about population parameters by using sample statistics as *estimates* of them. (In Chapter 17 we discuss statistical inference in detail.) Also, there are statistical procedures that disclose how closely related two or more variables happen to be. These are *correlational* measures, and within limits, they permit us to infer causal connections between things. However, we must be cautious regarding statements of causality. Correlations between two or more phenomena imply causality but do not prove its existence. (In Chapter 17 we discuss measures of association or correlation.) Finally, another purpose of statistics is decision making about differences that we observe between two or more groups of elements.

Description

The descriptive function of statistics is well known. We can learn much about samples of elements based on descriptive information obtained about them. For example, if we know about some of the more relevant characteristics of certain types of prison inmates, we might be able to determine with greater accuracy the type of intermediate punishment program they should eventually be assigned. We might make strategic changes in police patrol styles in given cities as the result of learning which patrol styles seem to influence crime prevention the most. Such information would pertain to fluctuations in crime rates in relation to different police patrol styles. Thus description not only informs; it also influences policy decisions by various criminal justice agencies. Studying the use of electronic monitoring and home confinement on a sample of Nebraska delinquent youths, for instance, and their relative avoidance of delinquent activity might prompt us to make the use of electronic monitoring of delinquent youths more widespread.

Inference

Another important function of statistics is inference. We may infer things about populations by studying samples taken from them. Of necessity, our inferences are not absolutely perfect, since we do not ordinarily have access to the entire population of elements we study. However, if we use certain types of sampling plans, such as probability sampling, we can make statements, couched in a probabilistic context, about certain populations based on our sample statistics. Thus we say "There is a 95 percent likelihood that the population of police officers in Newark, New Jersey is similar in certain characteristics shared by a sample of Newark, New Jersey police officers." We never make any inferential statement about a population with absolute certainty. There is always a persistent element of uncertainty associated with our inferential remarks or implications. In Chapter 17 we will see that there are different types of statistical inference, and that each has limitations and strengths. For the present, however, it is important only to recognize inference as one important function of statistics.

Establishing Causality through Correlation

Certain statistical procedures are correlational, in that they demonstrate apparent relationships or associations between two or more variables. Suppose that we are interested in devising a risk assessment instrument to be used by parole boards in determining an inmate's early release potential. We may assemble statistical data about a large sample of parolees and determine that those who return to prison because of one or more parole program violations also share certain characteristics. We might find, for instance, that a majority of these parolee-recidivists are younger, male, black, unemployed or underemployed, alcohol and/or drug abusers, of lower socioeconomic status, and have earlier histories as juvenile offenders. Should we conclude from these findings that these variables "cause" recidivism? And should we deny parole in the future to those inmates who possess these characteristics? No. Further analysis may show that many "successful" parolees also have these same characteristics. There are any number of variables that may be used to explain recidivism behavior of designated parolees. We are only scratching the surface by referring to a limited number of social and personal traits as possibly causally related to recidivism. Obviously, if two variables are unrelated statistically, no causal relation exists between them. However, it is important to establish an initial connection between variables as a basis for establishing an eventual causal relation.

The general discussion of measures of association or correlation in Chapter 17 indicates that depending on how certain variables are measured and the level of measurement which is assumed to underlie them, some measures are more useful or appropriate than others. Several criteria exist for assessing the utility of particular measures of association for our research problems. Assorted assumptions, weaknesses and strengths, and/or advantages and disadvantages of these procedures obligate us to make choices for particular correctional applications.

Tests of Significance and Statistical Decision Making

One of the most useful functions of statistics relates to decisions about what we have found. *Statistical tests are procedures we use to assist us in making objective appraisals of the significance of the data we have collected.* Perhaps we might examine labor turnover among paraprofessionals in several community corrections agencies. In certain agencies with higher labor turnover, we may discover that the agency administrators obligate staff to complete extensive paperwork and comply rigidly with program requirements. In other agencies with lower turnover, we may find less demanding administrators who expect less compliance with agency rules from their subordinates. Do significant differences exist in labor turnover among paraprofessionals in the different agencies, controlling for type of administrative style? Although we may observe different rates of paraprofessional turnover, certain statistical procedures may be applied to provide us with a numerical appraisal to accompany our subjective opinions about these differences.

How do we know whether intensifying face-to-face contacts between probation officers and their clients will have any appreciable effect on probationer recidivism? We might view recidivism rates of two or more different probation programs and note differences among them. Is the difference we observe "significant"? We may "think" or "believe" or have a "gut feeling" that the differences we observe are significant, but a statistical procedure applied to these data will provide independent numerical evidence to confirm or refute our feelings or views. These statistical decision-making procedures are not substitutes for good thinking. Rather, they perform "supporting roles" in the research enterprise.

All statistical decision making involves probability theory. A common example illustrating probability theory is flipping a coin. When a coin is flipped, the result will be "heads" or "tails." There is a 50–50 chance that a "head" will occur or that a "tail" will occur. If the coin is flipped 100 times, it is expected *by chance* that there will probably be 50 heads and 50 tails. However, if the 100 flips yielded 51 heads and 49 tails, this would not be a substantial departure from our "expected" 50–50 split. We might expect or anticipate this outcome or would not be particularly disturbed by it. What if we observed 99 heads and 1 tail, for example? Would this result be expected? Probably not. This is a departure not expected according to chance. At some point we need to decide where these departures are "significantly different" from our chance expectations of 50–50. Is a 60–40 split significant? Is a 75–25 split significant? Where should this line be drawn? The statistical procedures we apply to assess the differences we observe between groups on certain measured characteristics simply tell us whether the differences are "chance differences" or probably attributable to something else. The "something else" might be administrative differences as in the paraprofessional labor turnover example above or different amounts of intensive supervised probation accounting for variations in recidivism rates among samples of probationers.

But statistical significance is not everything. Frankly, statistical significance is often overrated by researchers, since certain findings may be statistically significant, but at the same time, they may not mean much to us in any practical sense. Increasing our sample sizes does much to influence the significance of whatever we observe. If our sample sizes are large enough, any differences we observe will be statistically significant. For instance, if we were to study 10,000 probationers, 5000 involved in probation program A and 5000 involved in probation program B, it may be that A has a 29.9 percent recidivism rate, while B has a 30.1 percent recidivism rate. This minor variation, 0.2 percent, may be judged statistically significant according to specific tests we apply. But most, if not all researchers would conclude that for all practical purposes, the two programs are the same regarding their recidivism rates. Thus there is a substantive or "practical" significance that we must consider in addition to the significance associated with statistical tests. In short, we do not want to be in the position of saying, "It is statistically significant, but it doesn't mean anything." More will be mentioned in Chapter 16 about the influence of sample-size fluctuations on statistical significance.

MEETING THE ASSUMPTIONS

All statistical procedures, even descriptive ones, have various assumptions that must be met before they may be applied appropriately. It is much the same as playing a game with rules decided in advance. If one or more players chose to ignore certain rules of the game, the outcome would be questionable, possibly meaningless. All statistics are data sensitive, in a sense. That is, for them to be maximally efficient in serving their intended purposes, they depend on how the data are measured and distributed, among other things. However, there are diverse points of view about the importance of meeting all assumptions associated with particular tests before they are applied.

For example, suppose that I wished to describe the proportionate distribution of male and female inmates of county jails. I could simply determine the proportion of males and the proportion of females, convert this information to percentages, and present this as a part of a larger report on jail conditions. However, someone might wish to describe this same information differently. Or a computer program might print out unwanted information such as the "average gender" in county jails. After all, computers are not in the position of "knowing" what numbers stand for that are used to express subclasses on different variables. Computers are "number crunchers," and they process any information they are fed. It makes no difference to computers if a "1" stands for a male, a "2" for a female, and so on. If the operating computer program is designed to produce averages or means for each variable, it might kick out a 1.2 as the "average gender" of county jail inmates. What does this mean? Nothing, obviously. This example is closely linked with "levels of measurement," a topic discussed at length in Chapter 9.

The two extreme points of view relating to meeting the assumptions are as follows. First, there are those who contend that no statistical test or descriptive procedure should be applied if one or more assumptions associated with the procedure are not met fully and completely. Thus if we wanted to apply a test to some data, but the test required data measured according to an interval scale, we may only have attitudinal data or data measured according to an ordinal scale at our disposal. Because of this single assumption violation, researchers in this first "camp" would reject the test for use in this instance. They would look further for a test applicable for data measured according to an ordinal scale. In other words, they would look for a test that not only would answer their research questions, but also one that would fully satisfy the requirements or assumptions underlying the test selected. In some circles, these researchers are termed *purists*.

At the other extreme are those investigators who ignore the assumptions associated with particular tests, throw caution to the wind, and apply any test they wish to any data they may have, regardless of whether the assumptions associated with the test have been satisfied. In psychology and other related fields, the term *robustness* has been coined for statistical test applications where certain assumption violations are evident. Robustness is the ability of any given statistical test or procedure to yield results under adverse circumstances (i.e., where one or more assumptions are not satisfied) comparable to the results that might have been obtained if those same assumptions had been satisfied. For example, if I wished to apply statistical test A to some data I have collected, I see that test A requires satisfaction of three assumptions in order to be applied appropriately. For my own application, I know that I have failed to meet two of these three assumptions. But I may proceed anyway and apply the test, arguing that the test is "robust" regarding those particular assumption violations. That is, I believe that my results will not be affected seriously by applying this test, despite the fact that two important assumptions of it remain unsatisfied.

These are extreme points of view, and each side has supporting evidence that is more or less convincing. In reality, it is unlikely in a philosophical sense that certain assumptions can ever be met fully. As was seen in Chapter 5, for instance, randomness is desirable for enhancing the representativeness of a sample in relation to the population from which it was drawn. However, most researchers disclose that they experience varying amounts of nonresponse, where certain persons selected originally did not respond to their questionnaires or interviews. What do you call a sample of a random sample? I do not know, but you certainly cannot call it random. Yet most researchers present their information in academic journals and other periodicals or give papers at professional meetings, where they refer repeatedly to their "random samples." Over the years, it has become conventional in various professions to use the term *random sampling* rather loosely. Everyone recognizes the adverse implications of nonresponse for the representativeness of the sample ultimately obtained, although this fact is glossed over rather hurriedly in many presentations and publications.

Perhaps the most practical advice to provide here, considering such opposing views, is to do the most you can with your data under the circumstances, acknowledging the limitations of your study as you become aware of them. My own leanings are toward the purist side, although I can appreciate the relative merits of the robustness argument. The research process is an ongoing enterprise, and hundreds of thousands of studies on different subjects will be conducted over time. It is through the accumulation of literature on a given topic that we move toward certainty about the topics we investigate. Regardless of particular methodological pitfalls in any specific study, time has a habit of revealing trends that indicate the most feasible solutions to criminological problems or questions. The format followed below is to highlight "ideal" considerations and assumptions that precede a test's appropriate application. Appropriateness of application is obviously relative, however, depending on the point of view that one adopts relative to the extreme positions above. One general assumption apart from those discussed below is that there will almost always be ideal–real departures or gaps in the research enterprise. We learn ideal ways to proceed, but we are prepared to accept and interpret real occurrences or events that frustrate our attainment of ideal procedures and applications of them. Three assumptions associated with most statistical tests and procedures include (1) sample size, (2) randomness, and (3) level of measurement. For certain tests, other assumptions may be applicable. These are discussed in Chapter 17.

Sample Size

Most statistical procedures were originally designed for samples of varying sizes. Some procedures are designed for small group research and are intended to be applied when the combined sizes of two groups do not exceed 12 persons. For many researchers, these small-sample tests are not particularly useful, since applications of them to much larger sample sizes are unwarranted and unwieldy. Other procedures have been designed for large-sample applications, where the sample size is 200 or larger. There is no precise "cutting point" differentiating large samples from small ones. Largeness or smallness lies in the eyes of the beholder and is relative. Thus the sample-size recommendations in this book are crude indicators of a test's applicability for certain types of data analysis. These recommendations are "rules of thumb" from which departures may occur. However, substantial departures from these recommendations may cause distortions to occur in one's statistical results. If the numerical results are seriously distorted, misinterpretations or erroneous interpretations of statistical significance may be made.

If we were to determine that 75 percent of the police officers we interviewed prefer Smith and Wesson handcuffs to other brands, the fact that our sample consists of *four* police officers would deflate the credibility of our original statement. It makes sense, for instance, to establish lower limits when percentaging data or determining proportions. Often, these lower limits have been set at 50 persons. If we percentage significantly fewer persons than 50 of them, our percentages will be increasingly misleading or unreliable. At the upper end of the sample-size continuum it can be demonstrated that if our sample sizes are large enough, virtually *any* statistical observation we might make will be significant statistically. The rationale for this statement is provided in Chapters 16 and 17. Thus many of the statistical procedures discussed in this book have what I term "reasonable operating ranges." What this means is that each test is maximally meaningful when applied under certain sample-size conditions. Radical departures from these "reasonable operating ranges" may result in meaningless results.

One rule of thumb about sample size is that the *sampling fraction* should be approximately $\frac{1}{10}$. This means that ideally, if our population size is 1000, we should draw $\frac{1}{10}$ of 1000, or 100, for our desired sample size. This $\frac{1}{10}$ sampling fraction rule of thumb breaks down when our population size is enormous. If the population size is 15 million, for instance, we would never be expected to obtain a sample size of 1.5 million, or $\frac{1}{10}$ of it. We can usually accomplish our research objectives with samples much smaller than $\frac{1}{10}$ of the population, especially if our population is large. The $\frac{1}{10}$ rule of thumb is probably applicable up to a population size of 2500. This would mean that we would attempt to obtain 250 persons in our resulting sample. Considering the nonresponse expected, we would probably end up with far fewer elements than 250. Beyond a population size of 2500, however, researchers should use their own judgment. In this book, at least, large sample sizes are 100 or more, although this figure is purely arbitrary.

Randomness

Randomness was discussed at length in Chapter 5. Randomness was the primary means of control for obtaining probability samples. All statistical procedures relating to statistical inference require (ideally) the assumption of randomness associated with the sample selected. However, this is a key assumption that is frequently violated. Depending on the degree of the violation, it is up to the researcher to provide an appropriate, preferably conservative, interpretation of test results. Nonresponse affects the representativeness of the sample in relation to the population from which it was drawn. The greater the nonresponse, the greater the unrepresentativeness.

Experience has shown that much research is published in leading criminal justice and criminology journals where nonresponse (to mailed questionnaires, for instance) has been as high as 70 percent or more. This means that only 30 percent of one's original sample responds. In a mailed questionnaire situation (a common, inexpensive data collection method discussed in Chapter 6), for example, this would mean a 30 percent return rate. If 100 questionnaires had been mailed to a random sample of respondents, only 30 questionnaires would be returned. Again, what would you label the sample of 30? Would it still be random? Would it necessarily be representative of the population from which it was drawn? How representative were the originally drawn 100 names to whom the questionnaires were sent? The answer is that we do not know how representative our original sample was, and we do not know the precise influence of nonresponse on the representativeness of the remaining 30 elements in our sample. In any case, it should not be called a random one.

Level of Measurement

Levels of measurement were discussed in Chapter 9. Commonly identified levels of measurement include the nominal, ordinal, interval, and ratio levels. Each statistical test, both descriptive and inferential, as well as all correlational procedures are designed where particular levels of measurement are assumed. For all practical purposes, we may ignore the ratio level of measurement, since no statistical procedure in this book requires it. For each statistical procedure or correlational technique, therefore, it is important that we know in advance the recommended level of measurement associated with the ideal test application. We may get by with "underapplying" statistical tests (i.e., applying a test that only requires data measured according to an ordinal or nominal scale to data measured according to an interval scale), but we are treading on dangerous ground whenever we "over-apply" a test (i.e., applying a test that requires data measured according to an interval scale to data measured according to nominal or ordinal scales).

More than any other assumption, this one is the most troublesome in crim-inological research. Reasons for this statement are based on information presented in later chapters. It is necessary first to have an elementary statistical foundation in order to appreciate the importance of the level of measurement assumption for specific test applications. One reason may be advanced initially, however. In beginning statistics courses, we are exposed to "standard" tests and procedures that have broad applications, not only in criminal justice and criminology, but in physics, agriculture, chemistry, bacteriology, and other sciences. Many of these "standard" tests are useful, provided that we satisfy the assumptions associated with them. But the kind of data we study often make it difficult for us to satisfy some or all of these assumptions. We deal with people, not chemicals in a test tube or measured amounts of fertilizer distributed over several similar land plots. Naturally enough, we are inclined to use those procedures we have learned. Often, however, we must bend certain rules in order for the tests to be applied, especially to attitudinal data, socioeconomic information, or nominal characteristics such as race, religion, ethnicity, political affiliation, or type of criminal offense.

Other Assumptions

Besides sample-size requirements or limitations, the level of measurement assumption, and the randomness factor, some tests and procedures require that additional assumptions must be satisfied before the test may be ideally applied. In Chapter 15 we present several measures of central tendency and dispersion. These are measures that describe distributions of scores according to certain values around which the scores tend to be distributed (central tendency), and *how* or in what ways the scores tend to be distributed around these central points (dispersion, variability). One of the measures of dispersion or variability is called the variance, and its magnitude reflects score dissimilarity. That is, if we had a sample with widely divergent scores on some measured characteristic, the "variance" would be fairly large. On the other hand, if we had a sample where the scores on some measured characteristic were fairly uniform or homogeneous, the "variance" would probably be small. It is a requirement of some procedures that if two or more samples are being compared on some measured characteristic, their variances should be similar. This is referred to as "homogeneity of variances." There are statistical tests or procedures that determine whether homogeneity of variances exists among several samples under investigation. If we wished to apply a statistical test requiring homogeneity of variances as one of its ideal assumptions, and if we lacked homogeneity of variance with the data we possessed, our application of that test to the data might yield unreliable results. Keep in mind, however, that one extreme view mentioned above would argue that certain tests are "robust" with respect to violations of the homogeneity of variance assumption. Thus you will frequently see tests applied to data under less than ideal circumstances. These test applications are conventional, in part, and reflective of the robustness position, in part.

Another assumption accompanying several statistical tests is that the measured characteristic under investigation should be distributed in a particular way so as to yield a "bell-shaped" or normal curve. In Chapter 16 we discuss normal distributions, how they are derived, and their importance to investigators in both descriptive and inferential work. For the present, bell-shaped distributions have many scores near the central point and gradually, fewer scores, tapering off toward the low and high ends of the score distribution. An example of what a normal curve looks like is shown in Figure 16.1. Often, tests that can only be used with a normal distribution of scores are termed *parametric*, while those tests that do not require normally distributed scores are *nonparametric*. Several of these procedures will be illustrated in Chapter 17.

For certain correlational procedures, other assumptions may be required in addition to several of those mentioned above. It is appropriate that these assumptions be noted when the particular correlational procedures are presented. Their presentation here would be premature and might be confusing to those encountering statistical procedures for the first time.

OVERVIEW OF STATISTICS AND THEIR APPLICATION IN CRIMINAL JUSTICE AND CRIMINOLOGY

The fields of criminal justice and criminology utilize statistical procedures extensively. Applications of statistical procedures in these disciplines include descriptions of samples from populations of elements, inferential work, decision making about differences among samples investigated, and correlational computations. The *Uniform Crime Reports*, *National Crime Survey*, and *Report to the Nation on Crime and Justice* are only a few of the many publications distributed by government agencies annually about crime and criminals in the United States. The U.S. Department of Justice and Bureau of Justice Statistics distribute large amounts of material monthly, about different dimensions of crime, criminals, juveniles, and victims. Many of these reports are summaries of research conducted by persons working under the auspices of government research grants.

Among the many topics these publications address are prisoners and prisoner characteristics, probationers and parolees in the United States, criminal victimization figures, criminal defense for the poor or indigent, felony laws among the states, drug law violators, drug use and crime, drunk driving, elderly victims, households touched by crime, jail inmates and their characteristics, juvenile records and record-keeping systems, population density in state prisons, recidivism of young parolees, seasonality of crime victimization, setting prison terms, sentencing outcomes in felony courts, federal civil justice systems, time served in prison and on parole, tracking white-collar offenders, sentencing and time served, sentencing practices in various states, the prosecution of felony arrests, pretrial release, detention, bail reform, public access to criminal history record information, historical statistics on prisoners in state and federal institutions, and international crime rates. The Rand Corporation, Vera Institute, and other private organizations distribute vast amounts of informative material concerning crime, criminals, victims, and crime patterns.

Those who conduct research in criminal justice and criminology are often affiliated with universities or colleges in professorial capacities. These scholars are often expected to do research in addition to teaching courses. However, many investigators are employed as researchers for governmental or private corporations and agencies. These individuals identify problems for investigation, design research plans, collect data, analyze collected information, and publish their findings in articles, books, or technical reports. Often, these researchers extend statistical applications to tests of hypotheses and theories. Samples of elements are selected or designated, and certain of their characteristics are described and/or measured. Depending on the interests of the researcher, any topic may become a target for criminological inquiry or an object of interest to criminal justice scholars. Chapter 3 provided a vast list of topic areas that are commonly investigated by these researchers.

Those interested in juvenile delinquency, for instance, may wish to explore plausible explanations of delinquency through analyses of samples of delinquents and nondelinquents in a given jurisdiction. Their theories may suggest that delinquents possess certain characteristics not ordinarily possessed by nondelinquents. Or these designated characteristics may be more prevalent among delinquents than among nondelinquents. Statistical tests of significance can answer questions about differences among samples according to these and other measured characteristics.

Certainly those interested in devising inmate classification schemes and risk prediction instruments want to know which factors or characteristics are highly correlated with one's future dangerousness. Correlational procedures or measures of association may be used to provide numerical evidence of such relationships.

We have already alluded to the use of statistical procedures in evaluation research, where the effectiveness of various programs, including home confinement or house arrest, electronic monitoring, furloughs, work release, halfway houses, intensive supervised probation programs, and a host of other community-based correctional services may be measured by particular statistical applications. Recidivism is often used to determine whether one program is more successful than another. Other criteria are used as well. For example, how effective is a community-based correctional agency for assisting parolees and others in finding employment? Effectiveness in placing clients in various types of jobs might be one way of measuring whether certain types of programs are working. Again, statistical tests may be used to answer these questions and to furnish confirming numerical evidence to support our personal beliefs. But as we have seen in past chapters, the research we conduct and statistical tests we subsequently apply in data analyses may refute our personal beliefs. Thus we retain a high degree of objectivity in our investigations and interpret whatever we find according to objective criteria. Statistical tests help us to maintain our objectivity.

The statistical procedures to be described in the following chapters are not comprehensive. Some procedures used by those in criminal justice and criminology are complex and require statistical sophistication well beyond that required to understand the material to be presented here. Other sources must be consulted for these more elaborate technical procedures. Over the years, various fields in social science have become heavily quantitative, moving toward statistical applications that permit complex variable manipulations, so that more complex theories may be subjected to empirical test. In this book we emphasize the basic statistical procedures as well as several specialized tests and measures. All of these procedures are included in most standard statistical packages for computer systems. Thus a familiarity with these procedures will enable students to acquire a better understanding of computer printouts and make more informed interpretations of their data during different phases of their research work.

SUMMARY

Statistics has several meanings. In one sense, statistics defines characteristics of samples of persons, commonly referred to in research as elements. When entire populations of persons or elements are investigated, their characteristics are designated as parameters. Another meaning of statistics is a broad assemblage of tests and procedures that describe samples of elements and permit inferences to be made from these samples to larger populations from which they were drawn. Statistics also includes those procedures that permit researchers to make decisions about their observations or collected data. Some statistical procedures may be used for correlational purposes, where certain variables are related to others. Numerical expressions of the degree of association between variables are statistical expressions.

Functions of statistical procedures include description, inference, decision making, and correlation. The descriptive function of statistics enables investigators to illustrate the data they have collected graphically and/or numerically. On the basis of sample statistics, estimates of population parameters are made and evaluated within certain probability limits. Hypothesis testing is accomplished by applying certain statistical procedures to data. Numerical results of such applications provide both an independent and an objective appraisal of what one has found. Further, statistical procedures permit numerical computations of the degree of association existing between two or more variables. These numerical expressions and final products may be interpreted according to conventional guidelines or other criteria.

Applications of statistical tests, particularly ideal applications, involve several assumptions. Each statistical procedure, test, or correctional technique requires that certain assumptions be satisfied. Randomness is a requirement of most statistical procedures. Further, each procedure or test assumes a particular level of measurement relating to the measured variable under investigation. Also, these statistical tests often are recommended for samples of certain sizes. Thus there are recommended "reasonable operating ranges" for ideal statistical applications. Meeting or satisfying a test's assumptions is considered a prerequisite for proper application of that statistical test. There are contrasting views, however, in that some investigators, known as purists, believe that no test should be applied to criminological data if *any* assumption is violated. Contrarily, there are those who favor applying tests to data despite occasional assumption violations. They argue that a test's robustness or ability to withstand certain assumption violations and render reliable results is preferred to applying no statistical tests or lesser known tests. Both positions have merit.

There are many applications of statistical procedures in criminology and criminal justice. Government publications are distributed regularly that describe crime, crime patterns, criminals and their characteristics, victimization figures, and a host of other material. Much of this material describes samples or populations of designated elements, such as inmates of prisons or jails, probationers or parolees, or households affected by crime. Also, researchers use statistical procedures to describe whatever they have found and to make decisions about differences among samples they study. Correlational techniques are used as well to provide a foundation for establishing causality between variables. Thus statistics and methods are closely intertwined in several important respects.

QUESTIONS FOR REVIEW

1. What is meant by the term *statistics*? Briefly describe at least two uses of the term for those interested in criminal justice and criminology.

2. Distinguish between *statistic* and *parameter*. Write a short paragraph about the relation between statistics and parameters in research work. Relate this discussion to inference.

3. What is robustness? What does robustness have to do with applying statistical tests to collected data? Is everyone in agreement about robustness and subsequent statistical test applications? What other positions might be cited here that differ in viewpoint about the robustness argument?

4. How is sample size related to statistical test assumptions?

5. Why is it important that researchers obtain random samples of elements in their research work? Explain briefly.

6. What is nonresponse? How does it influence the representativeness of one's sample in relation to some population from which it was drawn?

7. What is meant by a "reasonable operating range" associated with particular statistical tests?

8. What are four general functions of statistical procedures? Describe each briefly.

9. Each statistical procedure has an accompanying recommended level of measurement. Why should the level of measurement be relevant here? How might a statistical test be overapplied? How might a statistical test be underapplied? Relate each of your answers to the level of measurement assumption.

10. What is a sampling fraction? Is there a conventional sampling fraction used in social science? Under what circumstances might a researcher consider departing from the recommended or conventional sampling fraction? Explain.

15

Descriptive Statistics: Central Tendency and Dispersion

KEY TERMS

Arbitrary reference point
Average deviation
Deviation score
Dispersion or variability
Grand mean
Interquartile range
Mean
Mean of means
Median

Mode
Quartile deviation
Range
Semi-interquartile range
Standard deviation
10–90 range
Variance
Weighting

INTRODUCTION

This chapter is about descriptive statistical measures. Two types of descriptive measures are illustrated here. One is central tendency. Measures of central tendency describe the points in a distribution of scores around which other scores tend to focus. Sometimes these values are "popular," meaning that they occur with great frequency but may not be exactly in the center of a distribution of scores.

Sometimes scores that depart markedly from other scores might "pull" upward or downward the rest of the scores when they are averaged. Three measures of central tendency discussed here include the mode, the median, and the mean. Additionally, the mean of means is described. This is a measure used when researchers have means from several different samples and wish to average them.

The second block of descriptive statistical measures consists of measures of dispersion or variability. These measures describe the manner or way in which scores are focused around some central tendency measure we have used. Some of these measures describe distances over which an array of scores is spread. The variability measures presented here include the range, the average deviation, the variance, and the standard deviation. Together with various graphic procedures illustrated in Chapter 11, these measures of central tendency and dispersion provide investigators with much valuable information about the persons they study.

DESCRIPTIVE STATISTICS

Descriptive statistics include any statistical measure that characterizes persons, their behaviors, or things that happen to them, according to particular variables. Some of the many variables investigated by criminologists and criminal justice scholars include age, gender, race/ethnicity, socioeconomic status, prior record, type of crime, juvenile adjudicatory dispositions, peer-group influence, cultural deprivation, achievement motivation, family stability, recidivism rates, religious affiliation, religiosity, degree of alcohol and/or drug abuse, political affiliation, employment status, burnout and stress, professionalism, type of sentencing scheme, police officer discretion, force used in effecting arrests, probation or parole officer caseloads, crime trends, jury size, type of criminal trial, risk assessment scores, inmate adjustment, style and intensity of police patrol, sentencing disparities, length of prison terms, and state speedy-trial provisions.

Descriptive statistics may be used to describe samples of elements at a single point in time. They may also be used to chart various trends over many time periods, as in the case of changing crime rates annually reported in the *Uniform Crime Reports* (UCR). As we have seen, the UCR utilizes many forms of graphic presentation to illustrate crime and crime trends, including pie charts, crime clocks, bar graphs, and histograms. Numerical information, crime rates, and the actual incidence of crime are also included in this report. Researchers make various uses out of this information. Some investigators analyze this information further as a means of testing certain theories they have devised about crime control or prevention. In Chapter 8 we described several ways of utilizing secondary source material for research purposes. Below are two types of descriptive measures: measures of central tendency and measures of dispersion or variability.

MEASURES OF CENTRAL TENDENCY

Measures of central tendency are ill-named, in a sense, since it would be expected that they disclose central points in a distribution of scores or the measured values on some characteristics that we are investigating. Only one of three presented in this section have this property: the median. It is a value representing the midpoint or halfway mark in an array of scores from low to high. The other measures, the mode and mean, may or may not reflect the centrality of score distributions. These distinctions will become more apparent in the discussion to follow. Generally, measures of central tendency reflect points around which other scores tend to focus. But as has been mentioned above, these points may not be located at central points in distributions of measured values.

Modes, Medians, and Means

Modes, medians, and means are the most common measures of central tendency, and each has a different significance for us. In the following section we proceed as follows. First, each of these measures is illustrated for both ungrouped and grouped data applications. Then, a summarization is provided, highlighting each measure's underlying assumptions, weaknesses, strengths, and possible applications. To conclude the section, we examine briefly the grand mean or mean of means, applicable whenever we wish to average two or more means.

Mode. It will be recalled that a numerical distinction between data in ungrouped and grouped forms is that data are treated as ungrouped if the number of scores is 25 or fewer. If more than 25 scores are examined, researchers tend to group them into intervals of various sizes in order to simplify data analysis and computational work. For data in *ungrouped* form, the *mode* is defined as the value or values occurring most frequently in a distribution. In the following distribution of raw scores:

10 10 11 12 14 14 14 15 15 15 15 16 16 16 17 18 19 20

the value 15 would be designated as the mode, since it occurs more than any other value or four times. While the values 14 and 16 occur three times each, they do not occur as frequently as 15. However, suppose that we were to observe a variation of the distribution above such as the following:

10 10 11 14 14 14 14 15 15 15 15 16 16 16 16 17 18 19.

We would designate the values 14, 15, and 16 as modes, since each occurs most frequently in the distribution of scores. *Conventionally*, there is a limit placed on the numbers of values that are designated as modes. We may define up to three values as modes, but if more than three values occur in a distribution (e.g., if there were four 10's, four 11's, four 12's, four 13's, and four 14's), we would simply say, "There is no mode." This is a conventional rule of thumb that is followed by many researchers.

If we should have data in *grouped* form, where our scores are arranged into a frequency distribution, the *mode* would be defined as the midpoint of the interval containing the most frequencies. Again, we would apply the conventional rule of thumb used for ungrouped data, meaning that we would identify up to three interval midpoints as being modes, but if there were more than three intervals containing the most frequencies, we would declare that there is no mode for these data. Again, it is conventional to do so. A distribution of scores grouped into intervals of size 5 is shown in Table 15.1. Note that the interval 75–79 contains 12 frequencies. Thus the interval midpoint, 77, would be the mode for these data. This also illustrates what was mentioned earlier, that central tendency measures are not necessarily "centrally located" within the distribution. In this instance, the interval 75–79 is at the far end of this distribution rather than in the center of it. The mode defines the most popular value, therefore, not necessarily the most central one. If we observed a variation of the distribution above such as the one shown in Table 15.2, several modes would be defined. In this instance, there are three intervals that contain the most frequencies, and thus their interval midpoints, 47, 62, and 77, respectively, would be reported as the modes for this distribution. Also, if more than three intervals contained the most frequencies, we would simply say, "There is no mode for these data."

Median. The median is the midway point in a distribution. It is defined as the value that divides a distribution of scores into two equal parts. For ungrouped data such as the following 17 scores:

15   16   17   18   19   20   21   22   23   24   25   26   27   28   29   30   31

the median would be the central score or 23. If several values near the center of the distribution were identical such as the following array:

15   16   17   18   19   20   21   22   22   22   25   26   27   28   29   30   31

we would simply designate "22" as the median for these data. Some textbooks apply a grouped-data procedure for determining medians for ungrouped data, where several scores near the center of the distribution are identical, such as those above. This is not recommended here, however. Simply conclude that the median is 22, since so many "22's" hover around the center of the distribution. Incidentally, if we were to change the score of 31 to 100, we would have

15   16   17   18   19   20   21   22   22   22   25   26   27   28   29   30   100.

The median would still be 22, since the central arrangement of scores is unaffected by the *deviant* or quite different score of 100 compared with the rest of the scores.

TABLE 15.1 FREQUENCY DISTRIBUTION WITH ONE MODE

Interval	f
45–49	7
50–54	3
55–59	5
60–64	3
65–69	7
70–74	2
75–79	12

TABLE 15.2 FREQUENCY DISTRIBUTION SHOWING THREE MODES

Interval	f
45–49	12
50–54	5
55–59	7
60–64	12
65–69	3
70–74	6
75–79	12

It will be seen that deviant scores such as the example above illustrates have no impact on medians. However, deviant scores in a distribution tend to pull means upward or downward, depending on whether the deviant scores are extremely large or extremely small. This effect of deviant scores on means but not on medians is discussed in greater detail in this section's summary.

For grouped data, the median is again defined as that point dividing a distribution into two equal parts. However, the median is somewhat more complicated to compute where grouped data are involved. An illustration of the median for grouped data is shown in Table 15.3. To compute the median for the grouped table in Table 15.3, we may find it useful to construct a *cumulative frequency distribution*. This is merely a distribution where the frequencies in previous intervals are added to successive intervals. The third column shows the cumulative frequency distribution based on the distribution of frequences in the second column (f). The cumulative frequency distribution will assist us in determining which interval contains the median or central point in this distribution of scores. We must divide our total number of frequencies by 2, or 151/2 = 75.5. This means that our median value will be that which divides our distribution of scores such that 75.5 scores are above that value and 75.5 scores are below that value. Examining Table 15.3, we see that 75.5 is slightly above the cumulative frequencies shown in the interval 560–569. We may seek our median in the next interval, 570–579. We proceed as follows.

First, we enter that interval from the lower limit of it, 569.5. We will add to that value the frequencies we need, 0.5 (one-half of one frequency), divided by the number of frequencies found in that interval, 15, and multiply the result by the interval size, 10. The formula is

$$\text{median} = LL' + \frac{fn}{ff}\,(i),$$

where LL' = lower limit of the interval we need to enter to obtain the frequencies
we need to acquire half of them
fn = frequencies we need in the interval
ff = frequencies found in the interval
i = interval size

Thus, using the values from Table 15.3, the median computation is as follows:

$$\text{median} = 569.5 + \frac{.5}{1.5}\,(10)$$

$$= 569.5 + \frac{5}{15}$$

$$= 569.5 + .3$$

$$= 569.8.$$

The median for these data is 569.8. This is the point that divides the distribution into two equal parts. Note that had we wished to compute a mode for the same

TABLE 15.3 MEDIAN FOR GROUPED DATA

Interval	f	cf
500–509	8	8
510–519	17	25
520–529	14	39
530–539	3	42
540–549	10	52
550–559	11	63
560–569	12	75
570–579	15	90
580–589	12	102
590–599	9	111
600–609	15	124
610–619	15	139
620–629	12	151
	$\Sigma f = \overline{151}$	

data in Table 15.3, it would have been the midpoint of the interval containing the most frequencies, in this case 510–519, which contains 17 frequencies. The midpoint of this interval is 514.5. Observe that the mode is quite different in magnitude compared with the median, and that it is well away from the center of the distribution, not particularly representative of the central tendency of it.

Mean. The best known and popular measure of central tendency is the mean. The mean or average is the arithmetic average of all scores in a distribution. It is the sum of the scores divided by the number of scores. Thus if we observed the following array of 11 scores in ungrouped form:

$$15 \quad 16 \quad 17 \quad 18 \quad 19 \quad 20 \quad 21 \quad 22 \quad 23 \quad 24 \quad 25$$

the mean would be the sum of these scores, 220, divided by the number of scores, 11, or 220/11 = 20. In this particular situation, the median would also be 20, since it is the point dividing the 11 scores into two equal parts, located precisely in the center of the distribution. There is at least one important difference between the median and the mean, however. Suppose that we were to change the score of 25 to 250. Although this would continue to have no effect on the median (either extremely large or small scores), the mean would be "pulled" upward, toward the deviant score of 250. The new sum of scores would be 445. Dividing this new sum by the number of scores would be 445/11 = 40.4. This would be the *true* average or mean, although the mean of 40.4 would be atypical of any score in that distribution. The presence of deviant scores tends to distort the mean more-or-less considerably, depending on their magnitude. Therefore, whenever deviant scores are present in a distribution, the median would be preferred, since it is nearly immune to distortions resulting from such deviant scores.

The mean for grouped data is slightly more complicated to compute. The computation of the mean for grouped data is illustrated below. Table 15.4 shows

TABLE 15.4 ARBITRARY-REFERENCE-POINT METHOD OF MEAN COMPUTATION WITH AN ARRAY OF 116 SCORES

Interval	f	x'	fx'
325–329	6	6	36
320–324	10	5	50
315–319	11	4	44
310–314	3	3	9
305–309	12	2	24
300–304	2	1	2
295–299	6	0	0
290–294	10	−1	−10
285–289	9	−2	−18
280–284	4	−3	−12
275–279	8	−4	−32
270–274	15	−5	−75
265–269	11	−6	−66
260–264	9	−7	−63
	$\Sigma f = 116$		$\Sigma fx' = -111$

a frequency distribution containing 116 scores and the arbitrary-reference-point method for mean computation. The arbitrary-reference-point method involves selecting an interval, normally one near the "center" of the distribution, as the one designated as containing the arbitrary reference point. In this instance, the interval 295–299 is selected. There is nothing sacred about this selection. It is simply an interval near what appears to be the center of the distribution. Virtually *any* interval could have been selected, since the arbitrary-reference-point procedure is self-correcting and yields the same mean value each time. However, an interval near the center of the distribution is selected primarily to minimize our mathematical computations. We may designate the midpoint of this interval, 297, as the MP' or arbitrary reference point.

Notice in Table 15.4 that two additional columns have been constructed. These columns are labeled x' and fx', respectively. The x' column designates a "0" (zero) placed adjacent to the interval we selected originally as that containing the arbitrary reference point. We may number away from "0" in both directions (toward the "top" and "bottom" of the distribution) as follows: $-1, -2, -3, -4$, and so on, until the "bottom" of the distribution is reached (i.e., that interval containing the smallest scores). Also, we number 1, 2, 3, 4, and so on, until the "top" of the distribution is reached (i.e., that interval containing the largest scores). It is important to take into account *how* the intervals have been arranged so that we do not erroneously number the x' column $-1, -2, -3$, and so on, toward the "top" of the distribution, and 1, 2, 3, and so on, toward the "bottom" of the distribution.

Once these x' values have been placed adjacent to each interval, the interval frequencies, f, are multiplied by the x' values as shown in a column labeled fx'. The negative sum of products is offset by the positive sum of products to yield a sum of fx'. In this instance, the sum is -111, since the negative sum of products is greater than the positive sum. Using the information from Table 15.4, we may apply the following formula.

$$\overline{X} = MP' + \frac{\Sigma fx'}{N} \ (i),$$

where MP' = midpoint of the interval we selected as the arbitrary reference point
$\Sigma fx'$ = sum of the products of frequencies and their adjacent x' values
N = sample size
i = interval size

With this information, we have

$$\overline{X} = 297 + \frac{-111}{116} \ (5)$$

$$= 297 + \frac{-555}{116}$$

$$= 297 - 4.8$$

$$= 292.2.$$

The mean for these data in Table 15.4 is 292.2. Again, it makes no difference which interval we select as the one containing the arbitrary reference point, since the computational formula is self-correcting. Changing the location of the arbitrary reference point either upward or downward will modify the resulting fx' value as well as the MP', and the self-correcting nature of the formula will be readily apparent.

Grand mean. Occasionally, researchers may wish to average several means for various purposes and determine a *grand mean*. They may be interested in whether several different groups of employees in a police agency vary in their work output from overall employee performance. If certain groups are below agency standards or norms, officials may wish to improve the group's performance by implementing new incentive systems or different types of supervision or leadership. Averaging two or more means is also a step involved in the computation of certain statistical tests of significance, such as the *F* test for analysis of variance. Thus for at least these two reasons it is important to understand grand mean computations.

The "mean of means" or grand mean is illustrated below. Suppose that we observed the following means for three groups of 10 employees each:

Group	Mean
1	15
2	12
3	9
	$\Sigma = \overline{36}$

In this example, the sum of the individual means = 36. We may simply divide the sum of means by 3, or 36/3 = 12. The grand mean = 12. However, if the groups contain unequal numbers of elements or are of different sizes, we must take into account each group's size before completing our computational work. For instance, if group 3 above consisted of 25 employees but group 1 consisted of only five employees, our original grand mean would be erroneous, since we would be giving equal weight to the means of groups consisting of 25 and 5, respectively. We would seriously underrepresent group 3 and overrepresent group 1 in our calculations. The correct procedure would be to *multiply* each mean by the number of elements in the sample. Once these products were determined, we would sum the products and divide by the sum of all sample elements. For instance, given the same information above but changing the sample N's, we would have the following.

The grand mean would be 420/40 = 10.5. This smaller grand mean or mean of means is correct, since it takes into account the proportionate weight of each sample size. Thus because there are considerably more persons in group 3, the smallest mean of 9 receives greater weight. Accordingly, the least weight is given the first group mean of 15, since there are only five persons in group 1. Researchers refer to this process as "weighting." We have weighted each mean by its respective sample size. Grand means are symbolically expressed as $\overline{X}_T$, where the subscript "T" indicates the overall mean of means.

Group	Size (N)	Mean ($\overline{X}_i$)	$(N)(\overline{X}_i)$
1	5	15	75
2	10	12	120
3	25	9	225
	$\Sigma N = 40$		$\Sigma (N)(\overline{X}_i) = 420$

Assumptions, Advantages, and Disadvantages of Measures of Central Tendency

Applying the mode, median, and mean correctly is governed by several factors. First, the level-of-measurement assumption should be met for each measure. Accordingly, the nominal, ordinal, and interval levels of measurement, respectively, are required for computing the mode, median, and mean. Thus the mean is subject to the most rigorous test of an interval scale underlying the attribute or characteristic measured. The mode is least rigorous, applicable to data measured according to nominal scales. Since virtually all attitudinal scales devised thus far are measurable according to an ordinal measurement scale at best, the median is perhaps most appropriate for situations where attitudes are investigated. Age, years of educational attainment, income, and sentence lengths in months or years are examples of variables that may be assessed readily by an interval scale.

However, great license has been taken regarding applications of the mean to ordinal, and sometimes nominal, scales. A common reason researchers have given for doing this over the years is that we are most familiar with the mean or average and least familiar with modes and medians. Another reason is that the mean will permit applications of more complex, and informative, statistical tests of significance compared with the array of tests available for nominal and ordinal data applications. Thus it is routine in social research to find an endless number of instances where means have been used and where the attainment of an interval scale for some measured variable is questionable.

Since this practice is so widespread and cuts across virtually all social science fields, including criminology and criminal justice, it is fruitless to condemn it. Rather, it is important to recognize the limitations and problems that arise or are associated with misapplications of the mean. Relying on the assumption that some information, however erroneous or misleading, is better than no information, we may *interpret* our findings as well as the findings reported by others accordingly. Where it is suspected that means have been computed for data measured according to nominal or ordinal scales, cautious and conservative interpretations of these data are recommended. This reflects the purist philosophy. Obviously, there are wide-ranging opinions about measures and tests and their legitimate applications under certain conditions.

As measures of central tendency, the mode, median, and mean have different advantages. Some of these have already been illustrated by examples. The mode is indicative of the most popular value, although we know that this popular value may not be located near the center of the distribution. The median is the central value, identifying a point dividing the distribution of scores into two equal parts. The mean is the average value, although it is easily influenced upward or downward by the presence of deviant large or small scores. If deviant scores existed in a distribution, the median would be preferred over the mean. Therefore, in this sense, the median is more stable than the mean.

However, another meaning of stability raises the mean to greater standing compared with the mode or median. Suppose that researchers were in possession of data from several samples of elements. They might have data from 10 groups. Thus there would possibly be 10 sample modes as well as 10 sample medians and means. If we were to examine the variation among the sample modes, medians, and means, the *least amount of variation* would probably occur among the sample means. This means that there would be greater similarity among means (i.e., mean values would be more homogeneous, nearly identical) than among sample modes or medians. For statistical inference purposes (see Chapter 17), the mean would be more desirable than the mode or median because of this advantage. In later chapters we will see that the mean is used, together with a measure of dispersion or variability, for statistical inference purposes.

Because of the mean's utility in relation to statistical inference, this provides an additional reason for why researchers are inclined to use means in their work under questionable circumstances. Simply, more can be done with data where means are computed. Statistical inference work, making statements about population values based on sample statistics, is facilitated when the mean is used. Many investigators consider this advantage, together with the sheer popularity of the mean, as offsetting strengths compared with the questionable practice of using means for data analyses where lower levels of measurement have been achieved.

MEASURES OF DISPERSION

Measures of dispersion or variability describe how scores are distributed around certain central tendency values. Consider the following example, where two sets of scores are presented. The means are the same for both distributions, but the scores are distributed differently, more or less scattered around the same point.

Distribution 1: 55 56 57 58 59 60 61 62 63 64 65
Distribution 2: 10 20 30 40 50 60 70 80 90 100 110

In both distributions, the means = 60. However, the scores in distribution 1 are closely distributed about the mean of 60, while they are more sparsely distributed around 60 in the second distribution. Graphically portrayed in the form of frequency polygons (see Chapter 11 for review), these two distributions will be narrowly and widely dispersed, respectively. (In Chapter 16 we introduce various shapes of curves that indicate different formations of frequency polygons based on several alternative score distributions.)

To maximize our descriptive information about any array of scores, we must know *both* the central tendency and variability (dispersion) of it. Useful measures of dispersion include the range and standard deviation. Other measures exist and some will be discussed briefly in this section. One of these other measures is the average deviation discussed below. Although the average deviation is seldom used today in criminological research, it illustrates the concept of deviation scores. This concept is important for understanding the standard deviation. The standard deviation is the preferred measure of variability in much the same sense as the mean is the preferred measure of central tendency.

Range

The range for ungrouped distributions of scores is the distance between the lower limit of the smallest score and the upper limit of the largest score. If we observed the following distribution of scores:

11 12 13 14 15 16 17 18 19 20

the range would be $20.5 - 10.5 = 10$. Sometimes, investigators compute the range as the largest score minus the smallest score plus "1", or $20 - 11 + 1 = 9 + 1 = 10$. This method also takes upper and lower limits of scores into account by combining each into the "1". The range defines the distance over which all scores (100 percent) in the distribution are spread. The use of upper and lower limits of scores is meaningful only when the researcher has data measured according to an interval scale. (A brief review of upper and lower limits of scores in Chapter 11 might be helpful.)

For grouped data, the range is either (1) the distance between the midpoints of extreme intervals or (2) the distance between the upper limit of the interval containing the largest scores and the lower limit of the interval containing the smallest scores. Both computations of the range for grouped data are presented in various statistics texts. Computational procedure 2 above seems more popular than procedure 1. Table 15.5 shows an hypothetical distribution and the range computation using both methods 1 and 2.

Both methods for the range computation are illustrated in Table 15.5. Note that for method 1, midpoints of the extreme intervals (those containing the largest and smallest scores) are identified, the difference computed, and "1" added, yielding a range = 19. The second method is the difference between the upper and lower limits of the extreme intervals, or $47.5 - 26.5 = 21$. Either 19 or 21 is reported as the range. Sometimes investigators compute both as a check on their work. The difference between them will always be the equivalent of the interval size, in this case "3." Observe that the upper limit of 21 minus the lower limit of 19, $21.5 - 18.5 = 3$.

Other Ranges

Besides the range, which describes the distance over which 100 percent of the scores is distributed, other ranges include the 10–90 or interdecile range, the interquartile range, and the semi-interquartile range or quartile deviation. The 10–90 range or interdecile range is the distance between the 10th and 90th centiles, and it describes the distance over which the middle 80 percent of all scores is spread. The interquartile range is the difference between the first (Q_1) and third (Q_3) quartiles and is the distance over which the middle 50 percent of the scores is spread. Finally, the semi-interquartile range is one-half of the distance of the interquartile range, or $Q_3 - Q_1/2$.

The major reason for using these alternative ranges rather than the range itself is that sometimes, deviant scores in a distribution may distort the range value. This distortion may mislead researchers into thinking that most scores are distributed over a large distance. In reality, however, most scores might be closely grouped with one another, with only a few scores being extremely large or small

TABLE 15.5 DISTRIBUTION OF SCORES AND TWO RANGE COMPUTATIONS

Interval	f	
45–47	5	Range (method 1) = 46 − 28 + 1
42–44	7	= 18 + 1 = 19
39–41	8	
36–38	4	
33–35	3	Range (method 2) = 47.5 − 26.5 = 21
30–32	5	
27–29	6	
	$\Sigma' f = \overline{38}$	

compared with the rest. For example, if investigators examined 100 scores, where 98 scores were between 15 and 35, scores of 95 and 96 would mean a reported range of 81 or 82. Close inspection of the distribution of scores would show that most were within a range of 21, not 81 or 82. Therefore, a compensation is made for these deviant scores. Thus when deviant scores are encountered, researchers may decide to report the distance over which the middle 80 or 50 percent of scores is spread. These alternatives are more reliable or stable indicators than the range itself.

One comment is in order about the semi-interquartile range or quartile deviation. In past years, some investigators have erroneously assumed that the semi-interquartile range is somehow analogous to the standard deviation presented below. This is untrue. There is no mathematical connection between these different measures. For all practical purposes, the semi-interquartile range or quartile deviation is meaningless, despite its attempted dignification by using the appellation "quartile deviation." This best illustrates the power of *convention* in statistics, where certain procedures are sometimes adopted for use for no logical reason other than that other people use those procedures.

Average deviation and deviation scores. The average deviation is slightly more meaningful compared with the quartile deviation. It is the average variation of scores about the mean of the distribution. This is illustrated below by a simple example.

$$15 \quad 16 \quad 17 \quad 18 \quad 19 \quad 20 \quad 21 \quad 22 \quad 23 \quad 24 \quad 25$$

The 11 scores above have a mean = 20. Each score "deviates" from the mean of 20, either positively or negatively, a certain distance. This distance is measured by a deviation score, x'. For these 11 scores, x' values have been computed as follows:

Score	x'
15	-5
16	-4
17	-3
18	-2
19	-1
20	0
21	$+1$
22	$+2$
23	$+3$
24	$+4$
25	$+5$
	$\Sigma x' = \overline{0}$

Note that the x' for the score of 15 = -5, since 15 is 5 points below the mean of 20. The score of 24 has an x' value = $+4$, since 24 is 4 points above 20, and so on. The score of 20, which occurs at the same point where the mean is found,

Measures of Dispersion

has an $x' = 0$ since there is no deviation from the mean. As a check on one's work, the sum of the x' values always equals "0," provided that we begin our computations with a correct mean value.

To compute the average deviation for these data, we must ignore the signs (either $+$ or $-$) associated with each deviation score and compute the sum of the absolute $|\cdot|$ departures from the mean. These absolute deviations from the mean are:

Score	$|x'|$
15	5
16	4
17	3
18	2
19	1
20	0
21	1
22	2
23	3
24	4
25	5
	$\Sigma\,|x'| = \overline{30}$

The absolute departures of all scores from the mean, summed, would be $5 + 4 + 3 + 2 + 1 + 0 + 1 + 2 + 3 + 4 + 5 = 30$. We must divide this sum by the total number of scores, N, in order to obtain the average deviation. With an $N = 11$, this becomes $30/11 = 2.7$. The scores fluctuate about the mean of 20 an average of 2.7 points. This is what is meant by the average deviation.

Again, for various reasons, the average deviation was believed for many years to be an approximation of the standard deviation. It seems that researchers wanted an approximation of the standard deviation without having to compute it formally. Instead, values with little meaning, including the average and quartile deviations, were often reported erroneously as approximations of the standard deviation. Suffice it to say that these alternatives failed the test of consistency that characterizes the true standard deviation. That is, when investigators knew average or quartile deviation values for several different distributions of scores, these values lacked comparative utility. They could not be compared meaningfully with one another. Over time, the standard deviation emerged as the most consistent variability measure. In Chapter 16 we illustrate this desirable property in depth. For our purposes in the present chapter, we focus on the computation of the standard deviation for both ungrouped and grouped data as well as a preliminary interpretation of it.

Variance and standard deviation. Based on our knowledge of the average deviation and the meaning of deviation scores, the standard deviation may be determined by following a series of related steps. As we work from our original data used in the average deviation problem above, our series of steps will take us first through a solution of the variance. Once the variance has been determined, we may square root this value. The result is the standard deviation. Using the information from the average deviation example above and extending our computational work to square each deviation score and sum these squared scores, we have

Scores	$|x'|$	$(|x'|^2)$
15	5	25
16	4	16
17	3	9
18	2	4
19	1	1
20	0	0
21	1	1
22	2	4
23	3	9
24	4	16
25	5	25
220	30	$\Sigma x^2 =$ 110

With a knowledge of the number of scores, 11, and the sum of the squared deviation scores, we may determine the variance by dividing the squared deviation score sum by N. We may use the following expression:

$$s^2 = \frac{\Sigma x^2}{N},$$

where Σx^2 is the sum of the squared deviation scores and N is the number of sample elements. Carrying out this computation yields $110/11 = 10$. The variance is 10. The square root of the variance is the standard deviation, s. Thus $\sqrt{10} = 3.2$.

A shortcut for computing the standard deviation for ungrouped data is as follows. This method eliminates the necessity of first determining the sample mean and then determining deviation scores. We may work directly with the raw scores and the squares of the raw scores. For the data above, we would have the following:

Scores, X_i	Squares of Scores, X_i^2
15	225
16	256
17	289
18	324
19	361
20	400
21	441
22	484
23	529
24	576
25	625
$\Sigma X_i = $ 220	$\Sigma X_i^2 = $ 4510
$N = 11$	

For these data, we may apply the following formula to compute our sum of squared deviation scores, Σx^2.

$$\Sigma x^2 = \Sigma X_i^2 - \frac{(\Sigma X_i)^2}{N},$$

where ΣX_i^2 = sum of the squared raw scores
ΣX_i = sum of the raw scores
N = number of scores

Substituting these values for formula symbols, we have

$$\Sigma x^2 = 4510 - \frac{(220)^2}{11}$$

$$= 4510 - \frac{48,400}{11}$$

$$= 4510 - 4400$$

$$= 110.$$

Again, the sum of squared deviation scores = 110. The same result was obtained when the mean and deviation scores were used. The main advantages of the latter method are that we do not need to compute a mean first, we avoid possible rounding error in the event our mean is not a whole number, and our computational work is greatly simplified. Using the sums of scores and the sums of the squared scores is recommended. The table of squares and square roots, Table A1 in Appendix A, may be used to expedite the computation of standard deviations for ungrouped data.

For data in grouped form, the standard deviation procedure appears considerably more complex than it really is. Actually, we perform all functions used for computing the mean for grouped data presented earlier in this chapter. In addition, we add another column, as illustrated in Table 15.6.

The final column in Table 15.6 eliminates the minuses from our computational work. Actually, we multiply each value in the x' by the adjacent values in the fx' column. These computations have been illustrated. Next, we sum these products. We use the following formula to derive the sum of squared scores:

$$\Sigma x^2 = (i)^2 \left[\Sigma fx'^2 - \frac{(\Sigma fx')^2}{N} \right],$$

where i = interval size
$\Sigma fx'^2$ = sum of products of the fx' and x' columns
$\Sigma fx'$ = sum of products of the f and x' columns
N = sample size

TABLE 15.6 DATA FROM TABLE 15.4 RECAST TO ILLUSTRATE THE ARBITRARY-REFERENCE-POINT METHOD OF THE STANDARD DEVIATION COMPUTATION WITH AN ARRAY OF 116 SCORES

Interval	f	x'	fx'	$(x')(fx')$ or fx'^2
325–329	6	6	36	216
320–324	10	5	50	250
315–319	11	4	44	176
310–314	3	3	9	27
305–309	12	2	24	48
300–304	2	1	2	2
295–299	6	0	0	0
290–294	10	−1	−10	10
285–289	9	−2	−18	36
280–284	4	−3	−12	36
275–279	8	−4	−32	128
270–274	15	−5	−75	375
265–269	11	−6	−66	396
260–264	9	−7	−63	441
	$\Sigma f = \overline{116}$		$\Sigma fx' = \overline{-111}$	$\Sigma fx'^2 = \overline{2141}$

From the information in Table 15.6, we have

$$\Sigma x^2 = (5)^2 \left[2141 - \frac{(-111)^2}{1161} \right]$$

$$= 25 \left(2141 - \frac{14{,}462}{116} \right)$$

$$= 25(2141 - 124.7)$$

$$= 25(2016.3)$$

$$= 50{,}407.5.$$

In order to compute s, we apply an earlier formula,

$$s = \sqrt{\frac{\Sigma x^2}{N}} = \sqrt{\frac{50{,}407.5}{116}}$$

$$= \sqrt{434.5} \quad \text{(also the variance, } s^2\text{)}$$

$$= 20.8.$$

The standard deviation for these data is 20.8.

The principal reason why the standard deviation is the best measure of variability, especially in inferential work, is that under most circumstances, it has a consistent meaning from one distribution to the next. One standard deviation value of 5.1 for one distribution of scores means the same thing as 15.3 means for another distribution of scores. A standard deviation of 200 in a third distribution of scores would have an equivalent meaning as well. This property of *consistency of interpretation* makes the standard deviation distinctive among other variability measures.

When applied to any distribution of raw scores, the standard deviation usually refers to a given distance on either side of the mean, which will include a specific proportion of scores. Thus if we knew that the mean for a distribution of scores were 100 and the standard deviation were 10, a specific proportion of scores would be included between the mean of 100 and one standard deviation above or below the mean, or from 90 to 100 and from 100 to 110. It will be seen in Chapter 16 that generally, a knowledge of the mean and standard deviation for *most* distribution of scores will permit us to determine the likely or expected proportion of scores between any pair of points in that distribution. For instance, we could determine the proportion of scores between 85 and 120, between 60 and 62, or between 140 and 175. For the present, it is important only to recognize the importance of this property of consistency.

Assumptions, Advantages, and Disadvantages of Measures of Dispersion

All measures of dispersion or variability discussed in this section assume the interval level of measurement associated with the variable under investigation. The range is a useful computation for establishing the size of intervals in the construction of frequency distributions for grouped data. However, it fluctuates according to the presence of deviant or especially large or small scores in any distribution. Thus in this sense it is considered an unstable measure of variability. Researchers have attempted to compensate for the presence of deviant scores by moving "into" distributions from their upper and lower extremes and calculating distances over which a certain proportion of the central scores are spread. These adjustments or compensations are the 10–90 range and the interquartile range. Respectively, they reflect distances over which the central 80 percent and 50 percent of scores are spread.

Measures such as the semi-interquartile range (quartile deviation) and the average deviation have been created primarily as less cumbersome methods for approximating standard deviation values. However, there is no mathematical relation between the standard deviation and either the semi-interquartile range or the average deviation. These alternative measures illustrate primarily the power of convention and the previously popular application of less meaningful measures. The average deviation serves an important function, however, in that it illustrates the meaning of deviation scores. Utilizing deviation scores helps us to understand more fully such computations as the variance and standard deviation.

Ordinarily, the usefulness of the variance is largely related to other tests of statistical significance, such as the F test for analysis of variance. The square root of the variance is the standard deviation. This measure of variability is important because it has a consistent interpretation and is maximally useful when combined with the mean in statistical inference problems. To obtain a more complete understanding of the standard deviation and what it can do for researchers in such problems, we must first consider particular distributions of scores and how these distributions occur around central tendency points. This topic is explored in detail in Chapter 16.

SUMMARY

Central tendency and variability or dispersion are two important properties of distributions of scores. Researchers seek to describe those points around which other scores seem to focus. Three measures are available for this objective. These include the mode, median, and mean. The mode is the most popular value, not necessarily the most central one. It is most frequently used when researchers have nominal data to analyze. The median is that point dividing a distribution of scores into two equal parts. It is associated with data measured according to an ordinal scale. It is considered the most stable measure of central tendency, since its magnitude is unaffected whenever deviant scores are present in the distribution. Deviant scores are extremely large or small values apart from the majority of other scores.

The mean or arithmetic average is the most popular and well-known measure of central tendency. However, it is sensitive and is influenced greatly by the presence of deviant scores. In this sense it is less stable than the median. But in another sense, it is the most stable measure. Whenever several samples of elements are examined and modes, medians, and means are determined for them, there is less variation among sample means than among the other two central tendency measures. Thus it is considered most stable when used as an estimate of its counterpart in the population, the population mean. Frequently, researchers may wish to compute the grand mean or "mean of means." The grand mean is the average of two or more sample means. If the sample sizes vary, each mean is weighted by its respective sample size in order for an accurate grand mean to be computed. The grand mean is a useful computation for other procedures and tests of significance discussed in later chapters, such as the F test for analysis of variance.

Measures of dispersion or variability reflect the way in which scores are distributed around various central tendency measures. These include the range, 10–90 range, interquartile range, semi-interquartile range or quartile deviation, average deviation, variance, and standard deviation. The range defines the distance over which 100 percent of the scores is distributed. It is primarily useful for determining interval size for grouped data. It is the most sensitive and unstable measure of variability, however. This is because deviant scores influence the range's magnitude easily. As a means of compensating for deviant scores in a distribution, researchers have created the 10–90 range and interquartile range, respectively. These yield distances over which the central 80 percent and 50 percent of the scores are spread. Therefore, any deviant scores in a distribution are virtually ignored by these computations.

The power of convention is illustrated by the use of the semi-interquartile range or quartile deviation and the average deviation. Believed to be approximations of standard deviations in past years, these measures have little practical meaning. Also, they have imprecise and inconsistent interpretations. Thus their usefulness in statistics is nil. The primary utility of the average deviation is that it introduces the concept of a deviation score. Deviation scores are the distances of various scores from the mean of their distributions.

By far the most useful and informative measure of variability is the standard deviation or square root of the variance. Standard deviations disclose various proportions of scores in a distribution occurring between different pairs of points. Thus if we know the standard deviation for a distribution, we will probably know the proportion of scores lying between the mean of the distribution and one or more standard deviations above or below it. Used in tandem with the mean, the standard deviation is essential to statistical inference and several tests of significance. The usefulness of the standard deviation in statistical inference and hypothesis testing is illustrated more fully in Chapters 16 and 17.

QUESTIONS FOR REVIEW AND PROBLEMS TO SOLVE

1. Given the information below compute the values requested.

Interval	f
640–643	8
644–647	10
648–651	3
652–655	2
656–659	9
660–663	14
664–667	12
668–671	11
672–675	9
676–679	15
680–683	14
684–687	12
688–691	5
	$\Sigma f = \overline{124}$

(a) The variance and standard deviation.
(b) The 10–90 range.
(c) The semi-interquartile range.

2. Given the following information, determine the values requested.

Interval	f
550–554	2
545–549	3
540–544	6
535–539	8
530–534	4
525–529	6
520–524	19
515–519	0
510–514	0
505–509	4
500–504	5
	$\Sigma f = \overline{57}$

    (a) The mode.
    (b) The median.
    (c) The mean.

3. For the following ungrouped data, determine the mode, median, and mean.

$$8 \quad 9 \quad 10 \quad 11 \quad 12 \quad 13 \quad 14 \quad 14 \quad 15 \quad 20$$

4. Given the following information, determine the mode, median, and mean.

$$15 \quad 17 \quad 17 \quad 18 \quad 22 \quad 68 \quad 120 \quad 15 \quad 60 \quad 45 \quad 13 \quad 19$$

$$26 \quad 31 \quad 28 \quad 15 \quad 22 \quad 29 \quad 41 \quad 95$$

5. In what sense is the median more stable as a measure of central tendency than either the mode or mean? In what sense is the mean more stable than the median?

6. Given the following information, determine the grand mean.

Sample	N	Mean
1	52	47.8
2	65	28.3
3	29	52.5
4	70	40.1
5	10	65.3
6	23	55.4

7. Given the following information, determine the mean and median.

$$55 \quad 75 \quad 82 \quad 41 \quad 28 \quad 41 \quad 55 \quad 67 \quad 69 \quad 75 \quad 78 \quad 75$$

$$55 \quad 24 \quad 38 \quad 42 \quad 46 \quad 49 \quad 57 \quad 76$$

8. Given the following information, determine the mode, median, and mean.

Interval	f
115–119	5
120–124	10
125–129	11
130–134	15
135–139	10
140–144	9
145–149	10
150–154	7
155–159	8
160–164	13
165–169	3
170–174	6
175–179	4
	$\Sigma f = \overline{111}$

9. Compute the range, standard deviation, and average deviation for the following distribution of scores.

2 5 7 8 8 8 9 12 13 13 13 14 15 15 16

10. Compute the standard deviation and range for the following distribution.

3 8 12 14 9 16 12 29 58 22 4 14 14

11. Determine the 10–90 range, the standard deviation, and interquartile range for the distribution below.

Interval	f
900–909	3
910–919	7
920–929	13
930–939	14
940–949	15
950–959	4
960–969	10
970–979	15
980–989	10
990–999	11
1000–1009	5
1010–1019	10
	$\Sigma f = \overline{117}$

12. Given the following information, determine the range and standard deviation.

21 21 35 36 38 39 40 41 42 42 43

55 66 66 67 67 67 71 75 78

16

The Normal Curve and Sampling Distributions

KEY TERMS

Asymptotic property
Bell curve
Critical region
Decision rules
Expected value of a statistic
Kurtosis
Leptokurtosis
Mesokurtosis
Normal curve
Normality
Platykurtosis

Region of rejection
Sampling distribution of a statistic
Skewness
Standard error
Standard error of the mean
Standard normal distribution
Standard score or value
Unbiased estimate
Unit normal distribution or normal distribution
Z score, Z value

INTRODUCTION

Criminologists and criminal justice scholars are interested in generalizing their studies of samples of elements to larger populations of them. In Chapter 5 our attention was focused on different types of sampling plans that social scientists use in their research work. Some of these plans, probability sampling plans, are especially useful because they permit us to generalize about the characteristics of populations of elements based on the distribution of sample characteristics. These sampling plans include simple random sampling, proportionate and disproportionate stratified random sampling, and cluster, area, or multistage sampling. These sampling plans enhance our likelihood of drawing samples that are representative or typical of their respective populations. Although no sampling plan ever guarantees that any sample will be truly representative of the population from which it is drawn, at least the use of probability sampling plans increases this likelihood.

Whenever probability sampling plans are used for research purposes, investigators wishing to make inferences about population values may be able to utilize the unit normal distribution for some of their generalizations. Over the years, social scientists have found that many distributions of characteristics based on probability samples tend to resemble the unit normal distribution in form. In fact, they have been able to use several features of unit normal distributions in their research work for making inferential statements about population parameters within a probabilistic context. For instance, it has been found that if the unit normal distribution is approximated by several different distributions of raw scores, those scores may be standardized and compared with one another by using the unit normal distribution as the comparative standard.

In this chapter we examine the unit normal distribution and describe this important comparative function. Further, the unit normal distribution yields a "normal" or bell-shaped curve representing the total area covered by any set of scores. It has been found that different areas of the unit normal distribution include constant proportions of curve area, and that these constant proportions of curve area may have extended application to particular distributions of our raw scores. Standardized values associated with the unit normal distribution have been derived and tabled so that social scientists can easily understand and apply them.

In Chapter 14, various assumptions underlying the legitimate application of statistical tests were presented. One of these assumptions pertained to the distributions of raw scores that we might analyze. Specifically, some of our statistical tests require that our raw scores should be distributed in a fashion similar to the unit normal distribution or bell-shaped curve. If our distributions of scores do not resemble this bell-shaped curve, we cannot use the standardized properties of unit normal distributions profitably in our own data analyses. But employing a probability sampling plan, where elements have an equal and independent chance of being included, enhances the likelihood that our samples of element characteristics will approximate the unit normal distribution or normality. The more our distributions of scores approximate the unit normal distribution in form, the more we can use this distribution for generalization or inferential purposes.

The unit normal distribution is also resembled by certain sampling distributions of statistics. It we use particular statistical procedures that have sampling distributions approximating normality, our inferential work is improved and our generalizations about population parameters are rendered more meaningful. The notion of a sampling distribution is illustrated and discussed as well as its importance for researchers. Finally, the use of unit normal distributions extends into the area of hypothesis testing. Certain types of hypotheses about population parameters have *decision rules* that influence our judgments and inferences. We examine decision rules and see how they relate closely to sampling distributions of statistics. Because normality is an important assumption underlying several statistical procedures, understanding this chapter is especially crucial for understanding various applications of statistical tests in Chapter 17.

THE NORMAL CURVE

The unit normal distribution does not exist in the real world. Rather, it is a *theoretical distribution*, existing only in theory. Statisticians and mathematicians have created the unit normal distribution theoretically by using the following formula:

$$Y = \left(\frac{1}{\sigma\sqrt{2\pi}}\right) e^{-\frac{1}{2}\left(\frac{\bar{X}-\mu}{\sigma}\right)^2}$$

where $\pi = 3.1416$
$e = 2.7183$
σ = parameter equal to the standard deviation of the distribution
μ = parameter equal to the mean of the distribution
X = abscissa—measurement or score marked on the horizontal axis
Y = ordinate–height of the curve at a point corresponding to an assigned value of X

Figure 16.1 illustrates the unit normal distribution derived by the formula above. Because the "curve" drawn for this distribution appears bell-shaped, it is sometimes known as the *bell curve*. Other names for the unit normal distribution are the *normal distribution*, the *standard normal distribution*, or simply, the *normal curve*. In this chapter, the term *unit normal distribution* will apply specifically to this mathematically derived curve.

Since other distributions of raw scores may resemble the unit normal distribution by their "bell-curve" shape, these other distributions of scores are often said to be "normal in form." In fact, researchers often refer to their distributions of raw scores as *normal* or having the characteristics of a *normal distribution*. Whenever they make these statements, their intention is to indicate that their distributions of raw scores approximate the unit normal distribution in their shape

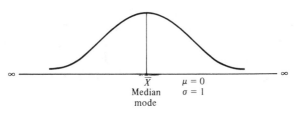

$\bar{X}$ $\mu = 0$
Median $\sigma = 1$
mode

Figure 16.1 Unit normal distribution.

or form. Thus it may be said that there is only one unit normal distribution, the one that is theoretically derived. But an infinite number of normal distributions of raw scores exists in the real world that appear to approximate the unit normal distribution.

Characteristics of the Unit Normal Distribution

Several features of the unit normal distribution are important for us to learn. These features are:

1. *The curve of the unit normal distribution, known as the normal curve, is bell-shaped and perfectly symmetrical.* The highest point of the curve is at the center of it, and the ends of the curve or "tails" taper off in opposite directions in an identical manner.

2. *The tails of the curve, extending to the left and right, continuously approach the horizontal axis, but they never touch it. Thus these tails extend toward infinity.* A close examination of Figure 16.1 reveals this feature of the curve. This is known as the *asymptotic property* of the unit normal distribution and discloses one departure of this theoretical distribution from actual distributions of raw scores. In the real world, actual distributions of raw scores have low and high points or limits. There are lowest and highest scores in a distribution, and thus the horizontal axis is reached at both ends by the tapering tails of curves drawn for distributions of raw scores.

3. *The mean, median, and mode all occur at the same point on the unit normal distribution, which is at the precise center of it or highest point. Thus these central tendency measures calculated for the unit normal distribution are exactly equal to one another.*

4. *Because the median is located at the center of the unit normal distribution, and because the unit normal distribution is perfectly symmetrical, the distribution is divided into two equal parts, with the area to the left of the median equaling the area to the right of it.* These two areas are each equal to one-half of the total area under the normal curve, or 50 percent of it.

5. *The total area under the curve is equal to unity or 1.0000 or 100 percent. Various proportions of curve area located either to the left or right of the mean are equal to various portions of 1.0000, such as .4000, .3425, or .2618.* Four-place decimal values representing various proportions of curve area are used because Table A.3 of Appendix A, areas under the normal curve, is expressed proportionately to four places.

6. *The two parameters or characteristics of the unit normal distribution are the mean,* μ (read "mu"), which is equal to "0" and the standard deviation, σ (read "sigma"), which is equal to "1." Because the curve is perfectly symmetrical and the mean is located where the median occurs that divides the distribution into two equal parts, identical standard deviation values to the left or right of the mean cut off identical portions of curve area in opposite directions.

STANDARD SCORES AND THEIR INTERPRETATION

Because the unit normal distribution is central to discussions of many statistical tests and statistical inference generally, considerable attention will be given to working with the table of areas under the normal curve, Table A.3. In fact, much of the busy work pertaining to determining normal curve areas presented here is for the purpose of increasing your facility in using Table A.3 profitably, not only for purposes of statistical inferences, but also for purposes of statistical decision making.

While the unit normal distribution exists only in theory, criminologists and other have found over the years that the distributions of a wide variety of variables often approximate the unit normal distribution in their central tendency and dispersion. For instance, police professionalism might be approximately normally distributed in given samples of law enforcement officers, with most officers exhibiting a moderate amount of professionalism and a few officers exhibiting very high and very low degrees of it. Various attitudes that have been converted into numerical quantities appear to be normally distributed in various samples. Distribution of scores that approximate several of the characteristics of the unit normal distribution are said to be normally distributed. And statements that can be made about the unit normal distribution can also be applied to distributions of scores that approximate it. In short, if we have a distribution of attitudinal scores that is approximately normal in form (e.g., resembling the form of the curve illustrated in Figure 16.1), we can say things about the distribution of attitudinal scores that can also apply to the unit normal distribution. The functional utility of the unit normal distribution is illustrated below.

Standard Scores

Various points along the horizontal axis of the unit normal distribution cut off various portions of curve area. These points are referred to as *standard values* or *standard scores*. They are most often designated by Z; hence they are also known as Z scores. Standard scores or Z values depict both the *direction* and *distance* of a given point along the horizontal axis of the unit normal distribution in relation to its mean, μ, 0. This distance is measured in terms of standard deviation units of 1 because one of the parameters of this distribution is $\sigma = 1$. Figure 16.2 shows the unit normal distribution with various Z values depicted.

Each of the Z values in Figure 16.2 cuts off a *constant* proportion of curve area. Each of these values is a given distance from the $\mu = 0$ expressed in sigmas of 1. Each of these Z values may be translated as shown in Table 16.1.

Further, we can identify the curve area proportions cut off by given Z values by turning to Table A.3. The left-hand column contains Z values expressed to the nearest tenth. Values across the top of the table provide additional precision to the nearest hundredth. Therefore, if we are looking up a Z value of 1.68 in this table, we must first find 1.6 down the left-hand column and then 0.08 across

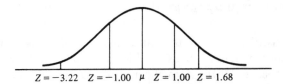

Figure 16.2 Unit normal distribution with Z values depicted.

$Z = -3.22$ $Z = -1.00$ μ $Z = 1.00$ $Z = 1.68$

the top of the table. Where these values intersect in the body of the table identifies the proportion of curve area lying between $\mu = 0$ and a Z value of 1.68, or .4535. This proportion also may be expressed as percentage. In other words, approximately 45 percent of the curve area lies between the mean of 0 and a Z of 1.68 (which is 1.68σ's above the mean). The proportion, .4535, represents the amount of curve area between these two points, as illustrated in Figure 16.3.

In Figure 16.3, an additional Z value of -1.68 has been provided to illustrate that because of the *symmetry* of the unit normal distribution, *identical Z values lying in opposite directions away from the $\mu = 0$ cut off identical proportions of curve area*. Thus the $Z = -1.68$ cuts off .4535 of the curve area to the left of μ just as a $Z = 1.68$ cuts off .4535 of the curve area to the right of μ. Generally, *all* negative Z values occur below or to the left of the mean, μ, while *all* positive Z values occur to the right of or above μ. A Z value that occurs directly on the mean would be a $Z = 0.00$. Z values are ordinarily expressed to the nearest hundredth, as the Z values in Table A.3 are presented. In fact, *it a useful rule of thumb that in any subsequent statistical application, statistical results are ordinarily expressed to the nearest place commensurate with values shown in various statistical tables in Appendix A*. Therefore, if we want to identify the proportion of curve area cut off by *any Z* value, regardless of whether it is above (positive) or below (negative) the mean, we simply examine the *absolute Z* value shown in Table A.3. A Z value of 1.00 cuts off .3413 of the curve area, while a Z value of -1.00 cuts off the same amount of curve area, .3413, in the opposite direction. Additional examples of Z values of different magnitudes and in different directions from μ are shown in Table 16.2.

The proportions of curve area shown in Table 16.2 are *constant proportions* that have been derived from the proportions tabled in Table A.3. They are constant proportions included between $\mu = 0$ and some designated number of sigmas (σ's) above or below the mean. Another way of looking at these is to

TABLE 16.1 DIRECTION AND DISTANCE OF Z VALUES FROM MEAN OF UNIT NORMAL DISTRIBUTION

Z value	Direction and distance from $\mu = 0$ in sigmas equal to 1
1.00	1.00 σ's or 1.00 σ above the mean
-1.00	-1.00 σ's or 1.00 σ below the mean
1.68	1.68 σ's or 1.68 σ's above the mean
-3.22	-3.22 σ's or 3.22 σ's below the mean

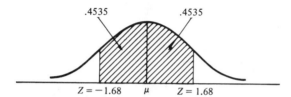

.4535 .4535

$Z = -1.68$ μ $Z = 1.68$

Figure 16.3 Z values of the unit normal distribution.

regard them as *standard proportions*. These standard proportions always exist for each sigma (σ) departure from the mean of the unit normal distribution. If we encounter distributions of scores in our research that are approximately normally distributed, we can make fairly reliable estimates about the proportion of scores included within a given distance of the mean, whatever it might be, in terms of standard deviation units or values.

Suppose that we were to draw a random sample of elements from a population and construct a frequency distribution of ages for the sample. Table 16.3 shows a frequency distribution of ages for a sample of 199 elements. These age values have also been arranged into a "curve" of ages shown in Figure 16.4.

Figure 16.4 is nothing more than a frequency polygon for these data, and we have merely "smoothed out" the lines connecting the various frequencies in each interval. It will be observed that the curve for these data is bell-shaped and appears normal in form. Statements that can be made about the unit normal distribution may also apply to this distribution of 199 ages *to the extent that this distribution is also approximately normal in form.* How do we know whether our distributions of raw scores are normal? Some preliminary computations for the data in Table 16.3 will show that the mean, mode, and median are identical, or 52. The standard deviation for these data, s, is 20.8. Knowing the mean and standard deviation of any distribution that is approximately normally distributed will enable us to determine several important things about the distribution. For instance, we can determine the approximate proportion of ages that occurs between the mean, 52, and one standard deviation of 20.8 above or below 52. Given an $\overline{X} = 52$ and $s = 20.8$, we will know that .3413 or approximately 34 percent of all 199 ages should

TABLE 16.2 PROPORTIONS OF CURVE AREA CUT OFF BY GIVEN Z VALUES

Z value	Proportion of curve area from mean to Z value
2.26	.4881
-2.26	.4881
-3.14	.4992
.03	.0120
1.45	.4265
1.96	.4750
2.33	.4901
-2.33	.4901

Standard Scores and Their Interpretation

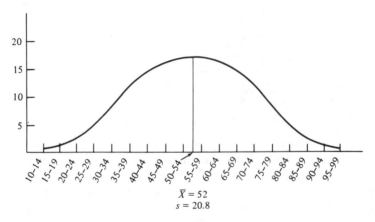

Figure 16.4 Frequency polygon, smoothed out, for data in Table 16.3.

probably occur between 52 and 20.8 points above or below 52. We know this because (1) our distribution of ages is approximately normally distributed, and (2) 0.3413, the curve area for the unit normal distribution, lies between a $\mu = 0$ and 1σ to either the left or right of μ.

A Z value of $+1.00$ or -1.00 cuts off .3413 of the curve area or approximately 34 percent of it. Therefore, a point in our distribution of ages that is 1 standard deviation (s) above or below the mean (X) will cut off and include an identical proportion of .3413, or 34 percent. The point of -1.00 on the unit normal distribution is analogous to the point 31.2 on the distribution of ages, which is one standard deviation (s) of 20.8 below the mean of 52 (i.e., $52 - 20.8 = 31.2$). The Z value of -1.00 is 1σ below the mean of 0, whereas the value, 31.2, is one standard deviation of 20.8 ($-1.00s$) below the mean of 52. Thus 31.2 is at the same point along the horizontal axis of its distribution as -1.00σ is along the horizontal axis of the unit normal distribution. If we were to superimpose the two distributions on one another, these points, $-1.00s$ and -1.00σ, would be identical. This statement holds to the extent that our distribution of scores is normal in form or approximates the unit normal distribution with its characteristics.

Referring to the information in Table 16.3, if we know that a given person's age is 75, for instance, we can determine the proportion of persons in the sample who are between the ages of 52 and 75. First, we must convert our age "score" of 75 to a standard score or Z value. Once we have made this conversion, we can determine easily the amount of curve area lying between the mean, 52, and the observed age, 75. This is accomplished with the following Z score formula:

$$Z \text{ score} = \frac{X_i - \overline{X}}{s},$$

where X_i = any raw score in a frequency distribution
$\overline{X}$ = mean of the distribution
s = standard deviation of the distribution

TABLE 16.3 FREQUENCY DISTRIBUTION OF AGES FOR 199 ELEMENTS

Interval	f
10–14	3
15–19	7
20–24	9
25–29	12
30–34	13
35–39	14
40–44	15
45–49	16
50–54	17
55–59	16
60–64	15
65–69	14
70–74	13
75–79	12
80–84	9
85–89	7
90–94	3
95–99	2
	$\Sigma f = 199$

Given a $\overline{X} = 52$ and $s = 20.8$, we compute the Z score for our age of 75 as follows:

$$Z = \frac{75 - 52}{20.8}$$

$$= \frac{23}{20.8}$$

$$= 1.11.$$

The Z value associated with our raw score (age) of 75 is 1.11. Turning to Table A.3, we determine that .3665 of the unit normal curve area lies between 0 (the mean) and a $Z = 1.11$. In the general case, raw scores for any distribution may be converted to Z scores by using the Z-score formula above. Once we have converted raw scores to Z scores, we can use Table A.3, the table of areas of the normal curve, as a way of knowing about where our raw scores might be located in any distribution.

Comparison of Standard Scores by Using the Unit Normal Distribution

One of the major uses of Z scores is to make comparisons of persons of different abilities and skills. Criminologists might wish to compare elementary and secondary school students who either have or have not committed prior delinquent acts. Self-report information can disclose profiles of offending juveniles even if they have never had direct contacts with police. Different aptitude tests that measure totally different attributes, such as mathematical or verbal skills, can be compared, and educational contrasts between different categories of children may be made. Analyses of scores that reflect different aptitudes and skill levels may enable interventionists to make a difference in children's lives. Perhaps special programs might be devised to assist children to improve in areas where they appear deficient.

For example, suppose that we subjected a single student to a battery of four different aptitude tests. It is assumed that these four aptitude tests have also been administered to large classes of students in the school, although we are now focusing our interest on the performance of a single student. Suppose that the student's scores on these four tests, labeled tests A, B, C, and D are those shown in Table 16.4.

It is apparent from a preliminary examination of these scores that the largest score for the student, 3000, was achieved on test B, while the smallest score was received on test D (15). But our preliminary appraisal would be in error. We cannot make such direct comparisons of test scores from different tests, since each test may be quite different from the others in terms of difficulty, conditions of administration, ability level of other students taking the test, the score range, and several other factors. To obtain a crude appraisal of our student's test performances, we must convert all four test scores into standard scores or Z scores. But to make this conversion, we must first know the means and standard deviations of all four tests. Table 16.5 shows the student's raw scores on tests A, B, C, and D, together with the class means and standard deviations on all four tests. Additional information in Table 16.5 are Z scores that have been calculated for each raw score.

To determine the person's standard scores for the four tests, the Z-score formula presented earlier is used. Using the formula

$$Z = \frac{X_i - \overline{X}}{s}$$

we can determine the Z values shown in Table 16.5 as follows:

Test A: $(25 - 20)/5 = 5/5 = 1.00 = Z_1$
Test B: $(3000 - 3300)/300 = -300/300 = -1.00 = Z_2$
Test C: $(150 - 165)/7.5 = -15/7.5 = -2.00 = Z_3$
Test D: $(15 - 12)/1 = 3/1 = 3.00 = Z_4$

TABLE 16.4 FOUR TEST SCORES

Test	Raw score
A	25
B	3000
C	150
D	15

TABLE 16.5 TESTS, RAW SCORES, Z SCORES, STANDARD DEVIATIONS, AND MEANS

Test	Raw score	Mean	Standard deviation	Z score
A	25	20	5	1.00
B	3000	3300	300	-1.00
C	150	165	7.5	-2.00
D	15	12	1	3.00

Next, we can place each of these Z scores on the unit normal distribution as shown in Figure 16.5. A visual inspection of Figure 16.5 discloses that the student did best on test D, having a standard score (Z score) of 3.00. The student did worst on test C, where a standard score (Z score) of -2.00 was received. Thus the student did best, relative to other class members, on test D, although this test had the smallest raw score of 15. The student's "worst" performance, compared with other students who took the test, occurred on test C, coincidentally the test evidencing the student's largest raw score. Specifically, the Z score of 3.00 tells us that the raw score of 15 was 3 standard deviations of "1" above the mean of 12. We can now see, with the other means and standard deviations for comparison, that the score of 3000 was actually below the mean of its distribution for test B, 3300, by one standard deviation of 300. This raw score of 3000 received a standard score or Z score of -1.00. Since test C showed that the student's score, 150, was actually 2 standard deviations of 7.5 below the class mean of 165, we might persuade the student to remedy this deficiency by means of a special curriculum or counseling. Of course, these test scores are not the only criteria we would use in advising students or diagnosing their weaknesses and strengths. Such diagnoses are more complicated than that. But at least these scores are of some assistance in helping us to highlight one's skill levels and deficiencies.

This is the comparative function served by the unit normal distribution. We may convert any raw scores from any distribution into Z scores for comparative purposes. The unit normal distribution is the "common denominator" for all distributions of scores that tend to approximate it in form. Additionally, once we have determined Z scores for any set of raw scores, it is possible to determine other interesting information as well. For instance, we will be able to determine (1) the amount of curve area above or below (to the left or right of) given Z values, and (2) the amount of curve area lying between two Z values.

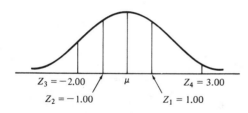

$Z_3 = -2.00$ μ $Z_4 = 3.00$
$Z_2 = -1.00$ $Z_1 = 1.00$

Figure 16.5   Unit normal distribution showing four Z scores.

Standard Scores and Their Interpretation

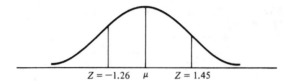

Figure 16.6 Unit normal distribution showing two Z values.

Determining Curve Area to the Left or Right of a Z Value

Two Z values of 1.45 and -1.26 are shown in Figure 16.6. Suppose that we want to know how much curve area lies below (or to the left of) each of these Z values. For the Z value of 1.45, we first determine the amount of curve area (from Table A.3) between the mean, 0, and a $Z = 1.45$. The amount of curve area between the mean, 0, and the $Z = 1.45$ is equal to .4265. Since we are concerned about all of the curve area lying to the left of a $Z = 1.45$, we must not ignore the entire left half of the curve, which contains .5000 of curve area. Remember that the unit normal distribution is divided into two perfectly equal parts of .5000 each. Thus we should add .5000 to .4265, giving us .9265, the total amount of curve area lying to the left of the $Z = 1.45$. This is the shaded portion of curve area shown in Figure 16.7.

For the $Z = -1.26$, this Z value lies to the left of the mean, 0. We want to know how much curve area lies to the left of this Z value. Again, we must first determine how much of the curve area lies between the Z score of -1.26 and the mean, 0. From Table A.3 we determine that the proportion is .3962. We are now ready to solve this problem. Since .3962 is the *known* portion of curve area lying to the left of the mean, 0, *and* since we know that the total amount of curve area lying to the left of the mean, 0, is .5000 or half of the distribution, we simply solve for the unknown. This involves *subtracting* .3962 from .5000, or .5000 $- .3962 = .1038$. This is the shaded portion of curve area shown in Figure 16.8.

As additional examples, suppose that we are interested in determining the amount of curve area to the *right* of the same Z scores above, $Z = 1.45$ and $Z = -1.26$. These presently unknown areas of the unit normal distribution are shown as shaded portions in Figures 16.9 and 16.10.

Using our knowledge of the unit normal distribution, we must determine the amount of curve area lying between each of the Z values and the mean, 0. This is simple, since these are the same proportions of curve area that we determined earlier, or .4265 between the mean, 0, and a $Z = 1.45$, and .3962 between the mean, 0, and a $Z = -1.26$. To find how much curve area lies to the right of a $Z = 1.45$, we *subtract* the area .4265 from .5000, or .5000 $- .4265 = .0735$. This is the amount of curve area lying to the right of a $Z = 1.45$. Again, we are taking

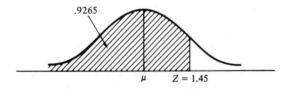

Figure 16.7 Unit normal distribution showing the curve area to the left of Z = 1.45.

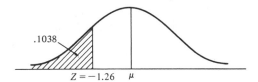

Figure 16.8 Unit normal distribution showing the curve area to the left of $Z = -1.26$.

what we know and solving for the unknown. For the second task of finding the curve area to the right of a $Z = -1.26$, we *add* .3962 to .5000, the total amount of curve area lying to the right of the mean, 0. This becomes .5000 + .3962 = .8962. Thus about 7 percent of the curve area is found to the right of a $Z = 1.45$, while about 90 percent of the curve area lies to the right of a $Z = -1.26$.

Determining Proportions of Curve Area between Two *Z* Values

If we wanted to determine the amount of curve area *between* two Z values, we would first determine the amount of curve area between each and the mean, 0. Suppose that we had the Z values of -1.55 and 1.86, respectively. The amount of curve area included between the mean, 0, and -1.55 is equal to .4394 (from Table A.3). The amount of curve area between the mean, 0, and 1.86 is .4686. Summing these two proportions will give us the total amount of curve area between the two Z scores. This is the shaded portion shown in Figure 16.11, or .9080.

If the two Z scores happen to both occur to the right or left of the mean, 0, we would again determine for each the amount of curve area between them and the mean, 0. Thus if we had Z scores of -1.23 and -2.66, we would again determine the proportionate amount of curve area between each and the common mean of 0. The Z value, -1.23, cuts off .3907 of the curve area, while the Z value, -2.66, cuts off .4961 of curve area. In this case, to find the proportion of scores between the two Z values, simply determine the difference between these proportions. Here we have .4961 − .3907 = .1054. Almost 11 percent of the curve area occurs between Z scores of -1.23 and -2.66. This is the shaded portion of the unit normal distribution shown in Figure 16.12.

What if we are reading a research report and discover that the author has presented only Z scores for samples of elements rather than raw score information? What if we want to know what the sample raw scores happen to be in order to compare them with our own samples of elements? This operation would involve converting Z scores or standard scores back into raw score form. This procedure is illustrated below.

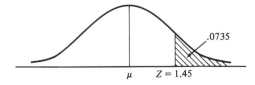

Figure 16.9 Unit normal distribution showing the curve area to the right of $Z = 1.45$.

Standard Scores and Their Interpretation

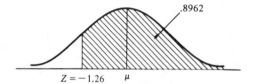

Converting Z Scores into Raw Scores

The conversion of Z scores into raw scores is relatively easy. We might wish to make this conversion if those who read our material are not familiar with standard scores. To transform Z scores into raw scores, we must know the original mean, $\overline{X}$, and the original standard deviation, s. With these two pieces of information, any Z score from that distribution may be converted back into its original raw score form. The formula we would use is illustrated here:

$$X_i \ (raw \ score) = \overline{X} + (Z)(s),$$

where $\overline{X}$ = original mean
 s = original standard deviation
 Z = standard score to be transformed

For instance, suppose that one of our sample elements had a Z score of 1.50. If the mean and standard deviation of the distribution where that Z score was obtained were 65 and 4, respectively, we could determine that person's original raw score as follows:

$$X_i = 65 + (1.50)(4)$$
$$= 65 + 6$$
$$= 71.$$

The person's original raw score would be 71. If someone else had a Z score of -2.75, we would determine their original raw score the same way. The computation would be

$$X_i = 65 + (-2.75)(4)$$
$$= 65 + (-11)$$
$$= 65 - 11$$
$$= 54.$$

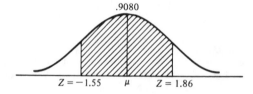

Figure 16.11 Unit normal distribution showing the curve area between the Z values -1.55 and 1.86.

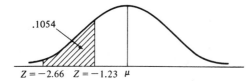

Figure 16.12 Unit normal distribution showing the curve area between $Z = -1.23$ and -2.66.

The person's original raw score is 54. In the second raw score computation, note that we had to subtract the product from the mean of the distribution, since we had a negative Z value associated with the original raw score above. This negative Z value meant that the person's raw score occurred below the mean. What if another person's Z score were 0.00? No computation would be necessary, since a Z score of 0.00 lies directly on the mean of the distribution. In this case, if the mean of the original distribution were 65, the raw score would also be 65. This could be done by inspection.

Standard Scores and Nonnormal Distributions

When investigators can assume normality in comparative analyses of different distributions of raw scores, the mean and standard deviation are always used to provide systematic and consistent interpretations of raw scores from one distribution to the next. Unfortunately, researchers cannot always assume normality about the data they have collected. Some types of score arrangements are encountered from time to time that are not normal in form. Two kinds of conditions may exist that render distributions of scores nonnormal. These conditions are known as skewness and kurtosis. *Skewness* refers to situations where scores in the distribution "bunch up" to the far left or right of the distribution rather than are spread out in a bell-shaped fashion. *Kurtosis* refers to curve peakedness, where the scores may be "bunched up" near the center of the distribution, where the scores may be spread out too thinly, and where the scores are distributed irregularly so that they yield a "bulgy" appearance when curved. Normal distributions are relatively free of both skewness and kurtosis. Skewness and kurtosis are illustrated below.

Figures 16.13 and 16.14 show two types of skewed distributions. Figure 16.13 shows positive skewness, and Figure 16.14 shows negative skewness. Note that in Figure 16.13, the scores appear to bunch up toward the left end of the distribution, and the tail of the curve tapers off toward the right. In Figure 16.14, the scores

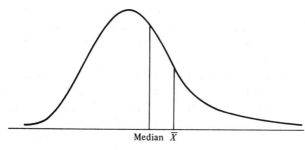

Median $\bar{X}$

Figure 16.13 Distribution that is positively skewed.

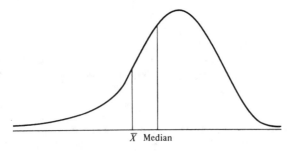

Figure 16.14 Distribution that is negatively skewed.

$\overline{X}$ Median

appear to be "bunched up" toward the right end of the distribution, and the curve tail tapers off toward the left. In Figure 16.13, the mean is larger than the median, while in Figure 16.14, the mean is smaller than the median.

How do we know if any distribution of scores is skewed? Can skewness be measured? Skewness for any distribution may be computed as follows:

$$\text{skewness} = \frac{3(\overline{X} - \text{Mdn})}{s},$$

where $\overline{X}$ = mean
  Mdn = median
  s = standard deviation
  3 = a constant

If the mean for a distribution were 30, the median were 27, and the standard deviation were 2, skewness for the distribution would be computed as follows:

$$\text{skewness} = \frac{(3)(30 - 27)}{2} = \frac{(3)(3)}{2} = \frac{9}{2} = +4.50$$

Skewness for this distribution is +4.50. The distribution is positively skewed, and we know that it probably looks much like the distribution shown in Figure 16.13. We know that some amount of skewness exists, since the mean and median are different. But how much skewness is too much skewness? Since perfectly normal distributions have no skewness (the mean and median are identical in the unit normal distribution, since they occur at the same point on the horizontal axis of it), an arbitrary rule of thumb exists that if skewness for any distribution exceeds +1.00 or -1.00, too much skewness exists for the distribution to be considered normal. If too much skewness exists, our statements about Z scores and the proportions of curve area they represent are inaccurate. Skewed distributions do not permit accurate use of Table A.3. For example, if we defined two identical distances of 2 standard deviations from the mean of a skewed distribution in opposite directions, the area cut off from the mean to a $Z = -2.00$ would not be identical to the curve area cut off from the mean to a $Z = +2.00$.

Kurtosis refers to curve peakedness and consists of three types: (1) leptokurtosis, (2) platykurtosis, and (3) mesokurtosis. *Leptokurtic distributions* are "tall" distributions, *platykurtic distributions* are "flat" distributions, and *mesokurtic distributions*, although the most normal-appearing of the three, have irregular

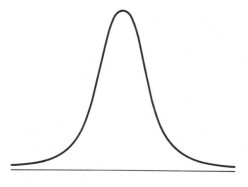

Figure 16.15 Leptokurtic distribution.

distributions of frequencies and appear bulgy. These three types of distributions are illustrated in Figures 16.15, 16.16, and 16.17.

As in the case of skewness, any attempt to apply the table of areas of the normal curve, Table A.3, would be unsuccessful and misleading, since these distributions are not normally distributed. Thus if a researcher calculated the curve area lying 1σ to the left or right of the mean of the unit normal distribution, the result would be .3413, as shown in Table A.3. This is the area cut off by a Z score of ± 1.00. However, a skewed distribution or one exhibiting substantial kurtosis would not contain .3413 of curve area from the mean to a Z value of ± 1.00. The curve areas in these nonnormal distributions would be unequal to .3413.

Under certain conditions, distributions may appear to have one type of kurtosis or another, but in fact, they may be normal in form. Thus we must be careful to distinguish between leptokurtic-appearing, mesokurtic-appearing, and platykurtic-appearing normal distributions and those distributions that are truly leptokurtic, mesokurtic, or platykurtic. The latter distributions are not normal ones, whereas the former distributions might be normal. If researchers suspect that substantial kurtosis exists for any given distribution of scores so that normality may not be assumed, direct tests may be made. Direct counts of raw scores lying between two points in the distribution of scores can determine whether the actual area of the curve matches the tabled area for the unit normal distribution as shown in Table A.3. Thus the researcher can count the number of scores within one standard deviation on either side of the mean. The total area within a $Z = -1.00$ and a $Z = 1.00$ is .3413 + .3413 = .6826 or about 68 percent of the total curve area on the unit normal distribution. The researcher's distribution of raw scores should have about 68 percent of all scores within one standard deviation on either side of the actual mean. If the mean is 50 and the standard deviation is 10, about 68 percent of all scores *should* occur between 40 and 60, points exactly one standard deviation below and above the mean of 50. You can count the number of scores

Figure 16.16 Platykurtic distribution.

Standard Scores and Their Interpretation

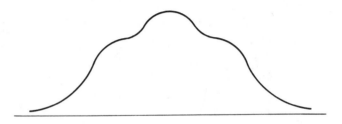

Figure 16.17 Mesokurtic distribution.

and see if they represent 68 percent of the scores. Minor departures from 60 percent will not necessarily disqualify the distribution from being designated as normal. However, if there is an appreciable discrepancy, kurtosis and/or skewness probably exists.

APPLYING THE NORMAL CURVE IN CRIMINAL JUSTICE RESEARCH

In research projects in criminal justice and criminology, the unit normal distribution is used for comparing scores taken from different distributions. These scores may be aptitude scores, attitudinal scores, test results involving the effectiveness of rehabilitative or treatment programs, recidivism statistics, or any other measured variable.

Another application of the unit normal distribution pertains to statistical inference and decision making about hypotheses. In addition to being useful for comparative purposes in educational testing and diagnostic activities, the unit normal distribution serves a probability function. Proportions of curve area can be translated into probabilities. Scores that occur within one standard deviation on either side of the mean have a 68 percent chance of occurring within this general area. In short, the proportions of curve area encompassed by any standard score or Z value can be translated into probabilities. Scores found in the extremes of the distribution (i.e., in the tails to the left or to the right) are less plentiful compared with scores near the center of the distribution, and therefore there is a much lower probability associated with their occurrence.

For some of the statistical procedures presented later, a Z value will be the result of a statistical test application. We will evaluate each Z value according to where it is located on the unit normal distribution. A probability will be assigned that will tell us how significant the Z value is within a chance or probability context.

DECISION RULES

Whenever statistical tests are made of any hypothesis set, the results of those tests are interpreted by researchers. The results may lead the investigator to believe that the null hypothesis is not true and ought to be rejected. Or the result may indicate that the null hypothesis cannot be rejected. Guiding the investigator's decision making about the outcomes of these statistical tests and how such outcomes should be interpreted are *decision rules*.

Decision rules consist of a set of conditions specified in advance of statistical tests that define how test outcomes should be properly interpreted. If investigators were to proceed with hypothesis testing without using a set of decision rules, the results would be subject to any interpretation the investigator would care to make. One researcher's interpretation of a test outcome would be just as valid as any other researcher's interpretation of it. This is because no standards would exist to function as objective or impartial arbiters about what is found and how it should be interpreted. Decision rules are therefore employed to minimize the subjectivity and guesswork that might otherwise exist. Following the canons of scientific inquiry, researchers are obligated to abide by certain decision rules when judging hypothesis test results or outcomes. Decision rules include the following: (1) the sampling distribution of statistics, (2) the level of significance, and (3) the critical region or region of rejection.

Sampling Distributions of Statistics

All known statistics have sampling distributions. Therefore, all statistics presented in Chapter 15, including the mode, median, mean, standard deviation, interquartile range, and range, have sampling distributions. *Sampling* distributions of statistics are distributions of all possible values a given statistic may assume when computed for samples of specified sizes drawn from populations of specified sizes. This concept is a very important one and this discussion must be followed carefully.

If an investigator had a population of 300 elements and drew a random sample of 20 elements from that population, this would be only one sample of many samples that could be drawn from that population. We can calculate how many possible samples of a given size could be drawn from a population of a given size by the following formula:

$$N^n$$

where N is the population size and n the sample size. Using this formula, given a population size $= 300$ and a sample size $= 20$, we would have 300^{20} samples. We can appreciate this better by using a smaller-scale example. Suppose that the researcher had a population of 10 and a sample size of 3. Under this condition, how many possible samples of size 3 could be drawn from a population of 10? This is worked out as follows:

$$10^3 = (10)(10)(10) = 1000 \text{ samples}$$

Thus 1000 samples of size 3 could be drawn from a population of 10. Of course, throughout this book we have been discussing sample sizes of several hundred persons taken from populations numbering in the thousands or millions. Imagine how many samples of size 500 could be drawn from a population of 100,000. This would be $100,000^{500}$, or $(100,000)(100,000)(100,000). . .$, until 500 products had been obtained. It staggers the imagination to contemplate just how many different samples of 500 could conceivably be drawn from that original population of 100,000!

But returning to our smaller-scale example of drawing all possible samples of size 3 from a population of 10 persons, we know that we would be able to draw 1000 samples of size 3. Let us assume that for each sample of size 3 drawn from this population of 10, we compute a mean, median, a standard deviation, and a range. Therefore, after we obtain all 1000 of our samples, we would have 1000 means, 1000 medians, 1000 standard deviations, and 1000 ranges. Now, if we were to arrange all of these values into frequency distributions, we would have a frequency distribution of 1000 means, 1000 medians, 1000 standard deviations, and 1000 ranges. Each of these four frequency distributions would be called sampling distributions of these statistics. In other words, the frequency distribution of all 1000 means we computed would be the sampling distribution of the mean. The frequency distribution of all 1000 standard deviations we computed would be the sampling distribution of the standard deviation, and so on.

In each of the cases described above, researchers have arranged all observed statistical values into a frequency distribution. The sampling distribution of means is the distribution of all possible values that the mean can be for samples of a specified size (in this case, 3) drawn from a specified population (in this case, 10). The sampling distribution of standard deviations is the distribution of all possible values that the standard deviation can be for samples of a specified size (again, 3) drawn from a specified population (again, 10).

These sampling distributions can be illustrated, on a small scale by the following example. Suppose that we had a population of six probation officers from an intensive supervised probation program and caseloads for each officer. We might designate these officers by a different letter, such as *A, B, C, D, E,* and *F*. To the right of each probation officer, caseloads are indicated. Caseloads refer to the number of probationers each probation officer supervises. Table 16.6 shows these probation officers and their respective caseloads. Officer *A* has a caseload of 10, officer *B* has a caseload of 11, and so on. Also indicated is the population mean $\mu = 12.5$.

TABLE 16.6 CASELOADS FOR A
POPULATION OF SIX PROBATION
OFFICERS

Officer	Caseload
A	10
B	11
C	12
D	13
E	14
F	15
	$\mu = 12.5$

Now, although in the present case we know all of the population values as well as the actual population mean, most of the time in actual research projects these facts are *unknown*. The main reason we sample from larger populations is to learn about these population characteristics and estimate them without having to study entire populations. In this case, however, our intent is to illustrate how a sampling distribution is constructed and how it appears.

Suppose that we wish to draw a sample of size 2 from this population of six officers. Using the earlier formula, the possible numbers of samples of $n = 2$ that could be drawn from a population of $N = 6$ would be N^n or $(6)^2 = 36$ possible samples. Using the different letter combinations from Table 16.6, the following sample combinations may be generated:

AA	*BA*	*CA*	*DA*	*EA*	*FA*
AB	*BB*	*CB*	*DB*	*EB*	*FB*
AC	*BC*	*CC*	*DC*	*EC*	*FC*
AD	*BD*	*CD*	*DD*	*ED*	*FD*
AE	*BE*	*CE*	*DE*	*EE*	*FE*
AF	*BF*	*CF*	*DF*	*EF*	*FF*

After these 36 samples of size 2 have been drawn, the researcher computes all the sample means. These means would be portrayed symbolically as $\overline{X}_1, \overline{X}_2$, and so on, until $\overline{X}_{36}$ is reached. These are illustrated below. Notice that there are letter combinations of *AA, BB, CC, DD, EE,* and *FF.* This is possible because of *sampling with replacement* where elements once selected for inclusion in a sample are replaced in the population and may be drawn again. Sampling with replacement permits such samples and includes them in the possible number of different samples of a given size that can be drawn from a population of a given size. Sampling with replacement is a necessary assumption underlying random sampling, since it enables researchers to assume that their population elements have had an equal and an independent chance of being selected. (It may be helpful to review the randomness discussion presented in Chapter 5.) To the far right of these mean symbols are the actual mean values computed for all samples. The smallest mean is $\overline{X}_1 = 10.0$, while the largest mean is $\overline{X}_{36} = 15.0$.

$\overline{X}_1$	$\overline{X}_2$	$\overline{X}_3$	$\overline{X}_4$	$\overline{X}_5$	$\overline{X}_6$	10.0	10.5	11.0	11.5	12.0	12.5
$\overline{X}_7$	$\overline{X}_8$	$\overline{X}_9$	$\overline{X}_{10}$	$\overline{X}_{11}$	$\overline{X}_{12}$	10.5	11.0	11.5	12.0	12.5	13.0
$\overline{X}_{13}$	$\overline{X}_{14}$	$\overline{X}_{15}$	$\overline{X}_{16}$	$\overline{X}_{17}$	$\overline{X}_{18}$	11.0	11.5	12.0	12.5	13.0	13.5
$\overline{X}_{19}$	$\overline{X}_{20}$	$\overline{X}_{21}$	$\overline{X}_{22}$	$\overline{X}_{23}$	$\overline{X}_{24}$	11.5	12.0	12.5	13.0	13.5	14.0
$\overline{X}_{25}$	$\overline{X}_{26}$	$\overline{X}_{27}$	$\overline{X}_{28}$	$\overline{X}_{29}$	$\overline{X}_{30}$	12.0	12.5	13.0	13.5	14.0	14.5
$\overline{X}_{31}$	$\overline{X}_{32}$	$\overline{X}_{33}$	$\overline{X}_{34}$	$\overline{X}_{35}$	$\overline{X}_{36}$	12.5	13.0	13.5	14.0	14.5	15.0

TABLE 16.7 SAMPLING DISTRIBUTION OF $\overline{X}$'s FOR SAMPLES OF SIZE 2 FROM A POPULATION OF SIZE 6

Observed $\overline{X}$'s	f	Proportion	Probability
10.0	×	$\frac{1}{36}$	0.03
10.5	× ×	$\frac{2}{36}$	0.06
11.0	× × ×	$\frac{3}{36}$	0.08
11.5	× × × ×	$\frac{4}{36}$	0.11
12.0	× × × × ×	$\frac{5}{36}$	0.14
12.5	× × × × × ×	$\frac{6}{36}$	0.16
13.0	× × × × ×	$\frac{5}{36}$	0.14
13.5	× × × ×	$\frac{4}{36}$	0.11
14.0	× × ×	$\frac{3}{36}$	0.08
14.5	× ×	$\frac{2}{36}$	0.06
15.0	×	$\frac{1}{36}$	0.03
	$\Sigma f = 36$	$\frac{36}{36}$ or 1.00	1.00

Next, the researcher constructs a simple frequency distribution of these sample means, as shown in Table 16.7. The resulting frequency distribution of sample means is called the sampling distribution of the mean for samples of size 2 drawn from a population of size 6. It is possible for the researcher to determine any other statistic desired for these samples of size 2 and arrange those statistical values obtained into a similar frequency distribution of them. In these cases, the researcher would have sampling distributions of whatever statistic has been computed, such as the sampling distribution of the standard deviation, the sampling distribution of the median, or the sampling distibution of the mode.

The sampling distribution of the mean shown in Table 16.7 has several desirable properties. For one thing, this distribution is approximately normal in form, in that it resembles the unit normal distribution. In the example shown in Table 16.7, these frequencies have been plotted into the curve shown in Figure 16.18. Although in this small-scale example the smoothed curve is more triangular than normal, this curve actually becomes smoother, more bell-shaped,

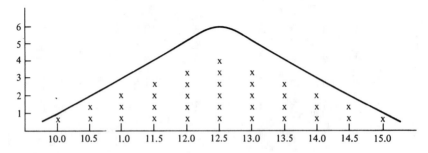

Figure 16.18 Curve drawn for the data presented in Table 16.7.

and approaches normality as larger sample sizes are drawn from larger population bases.

Generally, whenever one's sample size is greater than 30, the normality approximation is quite close. In fact, the mean is the *only* statistic presented in Chapter 15 that has a sampling distribution that is normal in form or approximates the unit normal distribution. This means that the sampling distributions of the standard deviation, mode, median, variance, or average deviation are not normal in form.

Another characteristic of the sampling distribution of means is that its mean or average (in this case, the average of all 36 sample means) is equal to the original population mean, μ. Notice in Table 16.6 that the probation officer population mean caseload = 12.5. Computing a mean for the means shown in Table 16.7 also yields a mean = 12.5. Thus it can generally be said that *the mean of the sampling distribution of the means is equal to the population mean*. This is a very important statement. No other statistic we have presented can make this claim. For example, the mean of the sampling distribution of standard deviations is *not equal to* the population standard deviation. The mean of the sampling distribution of sample modes is *not equal to* the population mode.

Whenever a statistic has a sampling distribution whose mean (expected value) is equal to the parameter it is designed to estimate, we say that the statistic is an *unbiased estimate* of its population parameter. The statistic, the mean, is an unbiased estimate of the population parameter, μ, because the mean has a sampling distribution whose mean is equal to the population mean. However, the standard deviation is not an unbiased estimate, since it has a sampling distribution whose expected value (mean) is not equal to the population standard deviation. In fact, most sample standard deviations are *smaller* than the expected value of the sampling distribution of standard deviations. This is because the sampling distribution of the standard deviations is positively skewed.

Focusing on the sampling distribution of the sample means, it has two parameters. It has a mean and a standard deviation. But because we are discussing *sampling* distributions of *statistics* and not simply *sample* distributions of *raw scores*, we give special names to these parameters: expected value and standard error, respectively. Expected values are means of sampling distributions of statistics. Standard errors are standard deviations of sampling distributions of statistics. Therefore, whenever you see terms such as *expected value* or *standard errors*, you know that sampling distributions of statistics are being discussed.

Looking at these terms another way, the expected value of the mean is the mean of the sampling distribution of sample means; the expected value of the standard deviation is the mean of the sampling distribution of sample standard deviations; and so on. The expected value of the sampling distribution of means is simply equal to μ, the same notation we use to denote the population mean.

Standard error terms are somewhat more complicated to define. As we have seen, standard errors are standard deviations of sampling distributions of statistics. The standard error of the mean is the standard deviation of the sampling distribution of sample means. To compute the standard error of the mean, we may use the following formula:*

$$s_{\bar{x}} = \frac{s}{\sqrt{N - 1}},$$

where s is the sample standard deviation and N is the sample size. In the illustration of six probation officers above, if we had the sample of two elements, A and F, for example, with caseloads of 10 and 15, respectively, the resulting $s_{\bar{x}}$ would be equal to 2.5, as an example. (You can prove this as an exercise.)

The sampling distribution of sample means is therefore normal in form and has the parameters, μ and $s_{\bar{x}}$. In the general case, it may be illustrated by Figure 16.19. Note the two parameters, μ and $s_{\bar{x}}$. Almost always, the sampling distribution of means is bell-shaped, symmetrical, and approximates the unit normal distribution. It is also a probability distribution. Referring to Table 16.7, for example, the observed mean of 10.0 occurs once in 36 times. The observed mean of 12 occurs five times out of 36 times. These occurrences of various means have been illustrated as proportions to the center right, and ultimately, as probabilities to the far right. These probability values are the likelihoods that samples of size 2 will be drawn, having those means associated with them. Thus the probability of drawing a random sample of size 2 (from that original population of size 6) with a mean = 10.0 is .03, or 3 times in 100. The probability of drawing a random sample of size 2 (from that original population of size 6) with a mean = 12.5 is .16, or 16 times in 100.

Continuing to refer to Table 16.7, what would be the probability of drawing a sample of size 2 from that original population of 6, where the mean would be *either* 10.0, 10.5, or 11.0? To answer this question, we would simply *sum* the individual probabilities associated with the occurrence of each value. In this case, .03 + .06 + .08 = .17. The probability of getting a sample of size 2 from that population of 6, where the mean would be either 10, 10.5, or 11, would be 17 times in 100, or 17 percent. Another way of saying this would be that the odds of getting a 10, 10.5, or an 11 as a mean for a sample of size 2 drawn from that population of size 6 would be 17 times in 100.

Notice that the means occurring most frequently in the distribution shown in Table 16.7 are those at or near the population mean of 12.5. This is called the *area of high probability*. If you were a betting person, you would expect that in any random draw of 2 elements from the original population of 6, you would probably get a mean whose value was somewhere close to the population mean of 12.5, rather than draw one of those extreme samples with a mean of either 10 or 15. Those means in the "tails" of the distribution occur in *low probability areas*.

---

*Sometimes, the standard error of the mean is described in statistic books as $\sigma_{\bar{x}}$. This particular expression assumes that we somehow have a knowledge of the actual population standard deviation. Thus we might be able to compute $\sigma_{\bar{x}}$ by using the formula, $\sigma/\sqrt{N}$, where σ is the known population standard deviation and N is the sample size. However, since we are attempting to estimate these values by using sample statistics, it is unlikely that we will *ever* know the population standard deviation and *not* know the population mean we are attempting to estimate. Thus for the sake of reality, we will use only the symbol $s_{\bar{x}}$.

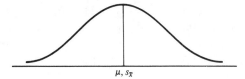

Figure 16.19 Sampling distribution of means.

$\mu, s_{\bar{x}}$

Up to now, we have been dealing with a small-scale example, a situation where we know all about the population characteristics as well as the values of all possible statistics for samples of a given size that could be drawn from it. Fine. But what about the real world? When are we ever going to know all about the population and all possible samples that could be drawn from it? We will *never* know, unless of course we study the entire population of elements. The fact is, we will only draw *one* sample in most of our research investigations, not 36 or 10,000 or them, and we will have absolutely no idea of whether our sample mean is close to or far away from the population mean or the expected value of the sampling distribution of means.

But at this point, we may take advantage of what we have learned about the unit normal distribution and apply it to our sampling distribution of sample means. What have we learned? First, the unit normal distribution has tabled standard Z scores that cut off certain proportions of curve area. For instance, we know that within one standard deviation, σ, on either side of the mean, μ, is located .3413 of the curve area on the unit normal distribution. Since our sampling distribution of means is also normal in form, let's superimpose it over the unit normal distribution and see what happens. Figure 16.20 shows our sampling distribution of sample means superimposed over a unit normal distribution. However, we have substituted the standard error of the mean, $s_{\bar{x}}$, for the standard deviation term, σ, on the unit normal distribution.

The standard error of the mean functions in precisely the same way on the sampling distribution of the mean as the standard deviation does on the unit normal distribution. Whereas the standard deviation on the unit normal distribution cuts off a portion of curve area that might contain a portion of raw scores, the standard error of the mean cuts off curve area on the sampling distribution of means that contains a portion of all sample means. In this case, if we move one standard error of the mean to the left and to the right of the population mean, μ, we will cut off .3413 + .3413 = .6826, or about 68 percent of all sample means. The terms $-1.00s_{\bar{x}}$ and $+1.00s_{\bar{x}}$ on the sampling distribution of the means are analogous to -1.00σ and $+1.00\sigma$ on the unit normal distribution. This fact underscores the similarity between the unit normal distribution and the sampling distribution of means. It is also indicative of why researchers often prefer to compute means in

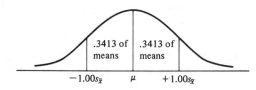

.3413 of means | .3413 of means

$-1.00s_{\bar{x}}$ μ $+1.00s_{\bar{x}}$

Figure 16.20 Sampling distribution of means superimposed over unit normal distribution.

Decision Rules

their statistical inference and estimation work compared with other statistics they could use. The fact that the unit normal distribution principles can apply to sampling distributions of means supplies researchers with an important advantage that they would not have if other sampling distributions of statistics were used.

Levels of Significance

As a second decision rule, the *level of significance* is the probability that a researcher assigns to the decision made about any hypotheses tested. The researcher is interested in rejecting null hypotheses and supporting research hypotheses. Research hypotheses have usually been derived from theoretical schemes that are believed to be reasonably sound explanations of phenomena. If research hypotheses are supported or confirmed by observed data, there is a good chance that theories from which those hypotheses were derived are also confirmed or supported by the researcher's findings. But as we have seen in an earlier discussion, it is conventional to test null hypotheses directly and to infer support or lack of support for some alternative research hypothesis as the result of rejecting or failing to reject some null hypothesis counterpart.

In advance of any statistical test, the researcher specifies a probability (P), known as the level of significance at which the null hypothesis is tested. Usually, this probability is set at 5 percent or 1 percent as a matter of convention, although other probability levels may be set. The probability, P, refers to the amount of error the researcher is willing to accept in a subsequent decision about null hypothesis tests. Specifically, if the researcher decides on the basis of empirical evidence or data collected that the null hypothesis is not true and should be rejected, a probability of error, P, would accompany this decision. If the level of significance were set at .05 or 5 percent, there would be a 5 percent chance of the researcher being wrong if the decision is to reject the null hypothesis and support the research hypothesis. If this level of significance is lowered to .01 or a 1 percent chance, there is a 1 percent chance that the researcher is wrong if the decision is to reject the null hypothesis and support some alternative research hypothesis. Levels of significance *always* accompany such hypothesis tests. Also, the probability of being wrong, P, can only be increased or decreased. It can never be eliminated completely.

Type I and Type II Errors and Hypothesis Tests

Table 16.8 provides a more complete picture of statistical decision making and the probable implications of these decisions for hypothesis tests. We always make the assumption that the null hypotheses being tested are potentially both true or false. We must make this assumption, since we never know absolutely that our collected data or samples are perfectly representative of their populations or the phenomena we are investigating. The investigations we usually conduct are simply single instances of tests of theories. We lack the certainty of knowing that our particular research represents a true picture of reality. Therefore, a probability must always

TABLE 16.8 TYPE I AND TYPE II ERRORS IN STATISTICAL DECISION-MAKING SITUATIONS

	H_0 is:	
	True	False
Decision is to: Reject H_0	Type I error, α	$1 - \beta$
Fail to reject H_0	$1 - \alpha$	Type II error, β

exist that any hypotheses we test may or may not be true, regardless of the outcomes of such hypothesis tests and the decisions we make about those outcomes.

If we decide on the basis of collected data that the null hypothesis we are testing should be rejected, there is always some likelihood that we are wrong in our decision. This is one source of error, known as *type I error* or *alpha (α) error*, shown in Table 16.8. Type I error is the probability of rejecting a null hypothesis when it is true and should not be rejected. This is also the level of significance at which our hypotheses are tested, or the *P* (probability) that we have designated.

A second type of error exists as well. This is known as *type II error*, or *beta (β) error*. What if we test the null hypothesis and fail to reject it? What if it is false and ought to be rejected? In this case, we have committed the error of failing to reject a false hypothesis. Type II or β error is the probability of failing to reject the null hypothesis when it is false and ought to be rejected. The computation of type II error is complicated and beyond the scope of this book. Nevertheless, we can consider its relevance for hypothesis testing.

Our objective is to minimize *both* type I and type II errors whenever we test hypotheses. We can minimize type I error simply by reducing the level of significance to a smaller value, from .05 to .01. But when we do this, we influence the amount of type II error we will incur. Usually, whenever type I error is lowered, type II error is raised. There is not a perfect one-to-one relationship between these types of error, however. Type II error is influenced only indirectly by type I error. But the general nature of this influence is to increase type II error whenever type I error is lowered.

The conventional significance levels of .05 and .01 have been selected by many researchers because they offer reasonable amounts of error (type I error) and keep type II error to a minimum. (Additional reasons for selecting these particular significance levels are discussed later.) However, we can influence type II error another way besides changing the amount of type I error. *We can increase our sample size.* Generally, as our sample sizes are increased, the amount of type II error decreases, regardless of what our levels of significance happen to be. Sample sizes of 500 have less type II error associated with them than do samples of size 50. This occurs because of the amount of sampling error involved in our research projects. Usually, larger *N*'s have smaller sampling error, and smaller sampling error usually means less type II error.

An examination of Table 16.8 also shows $1 - \alpha$ values and $1 - \beta$ values. These are probabilities that we wish to maximize in our research work. The probability $1 - \alpha$ is the probability of failing to reject the null hypothesis when it is true and should not be rejected. The probability $1 - \beta$ is the probability of rejecting the null hypothesis whenever it is false and ought to be rejected. $1 - \beta$ is also known as the measure of the power of any statistical test. The *power of a statistical test* is the ability of the test to reject false null hypotheses. It makes sense that if we can reduce type II or β error by increasing our sample size, we can also increase accordingly the power of any statistical test by using precisely the same strategy. This follows as the result of the β *error/1 - β error* relation. Decreases in one probability will result in increases in the other probability. The power of statistical tests is often used as a basis for selecting certain tests over others. When data are analyzed, several statistical tests might be applicable. However, each test differs regarding its power to reject false null hypotheses. Thus, among other things, researchers usually attempt to use the most powerful statistical procedures when testing hypotheses. However, given the many circumstances that accompany hypothesis testing, other considerations may be more important than test power (e.g., level of measurement assumed, type of sample, sample size, and arrangement of data or how they are presented).

Regions of Rejection in Hypothesis Tests

A third decision rule is the specification of a *critical region* or *region of rejection*, which is an area on the sampling distribution of sample means. The sampling distribution of means is used here because our hypothesis test deals with observed sample means; other sampling distributions of statistics would be used if the other sample statistics were used in hypothesis tests. The area designated as the critical region on our sampling distribution of means is determined directly by our choice of the level of significance for hypothesis tests. If we have selected the .05 level of significance (also known as $\alpha = .05$ or the amount of type I error), 5 percent of the sampling distribution of means will comprise the critical region. If the .01 level of significance has been chosen, 1 percent of the sampling distribution of means will make up the critical region or region of rejection.

These critical regions or regions of rejection are located in the "tails" or extremes of sampling distributions. Consider the following hypothesis set as an illustration of how we would identify critical regions on the sampling distribution of means:

$$H_0: \mu = 75$$
$$H_1: \mu \neq 75$$
$$P \leq .05 \quad (\text{also}, \alpha = .05)$$

H_0, the null hypothesis, says that the population mean is equal to 75. The research hypothesis, H_1, says that the population mean is not equal to 75. The level of significance is set at .05. Here, the mean of 75 is actually a guess, or more accurately, our *estimate* of the population mean, μ. Since the mean of the sampling distribution of means (the expected value) is also equal to μ, H_0 is also specifying that the expected value of the mean is equal to 75. Figure 16.21 shows a sampling distribution of sample means with our guessed or estimated $\mu = 75$ at its center, as illustrated. Interestingly, we do not need to know the value of all sample means to construct our sampling distribution of means. We know that in most cases, it will be normal in form.

An area of the sampling distribution of means will be designated as the critical region. We know that 5 percent of the area of this distribution will be set aside as the critical region. This is because we set the significance level at .05. We also know that the area will be located in either one or both tails of the distribution. Notice that the null hypothesis says that the population mean is *equal to* 75, and that our research hypothesis is that the population mean is *not equal to* 75. Thus we conceivably could reject the null hypothesis by finding a sample mean that is substantially higher or lower than 75. Since we are not concerned about the *direction* of the departure of our sample mean from the hypothesized population mean, we will establish critical regions in *both* tails of the distribution to the far left and far right. This is easily accomplished by halving our level of significance, .05, and placing each half, .025, in both of the extreme tails. This has been done in Figure 16.21. These shaded areas that contain .025 each of the total amount of curve area are our critical regions or regions of rejection. If we find that our sample mean is in either of these shaded areas, we will reject the null hypothesis and conclude, with some amount of error (type I error), that the population mean is not equal to 75. This is why these regions are called "regions of rejection," because they result in rejecting null hypotheses. Any sample mean occurring in either of these regions is considered significantly different from the hypothesized μ value.

But how do we know whether our observed sample mean is significantly different from the hypothesized μ value? When do we know whether our observed sample means lie in the critical regions of sampling distributions we have specified? Again, we will use our knowledge of the unit normal distribution to answer these questions. We will proceed systematically with a hypothetical research problem to illustrate the solution to our apparent dilemma.

Suppose that researchers are conducting a study of stress among correctional officers and are specifically interested in the influence of intervention methods whereby stress can be reduced. In this hypothetical situation, researchers have identified a population of correctional officers in a large Midwestern state where a popular stress index has been administered to officers annually. During the preceding year, correctional officers in the state were exposed to an educational program designed to equip them with coping strategies to combat stress. The

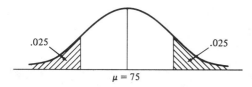

Figure 16.21 Sampling distribution of means showing critical regions.

educational program, a three-week course, is highly experimental, and no previous information is available about it and whether it has been found effective in other settings. Because the researchers have access to previously published reports about all state correctional officers and their stress levels for previous years, they know that the stress level, as measured by the popular stress index, has averaged about 100 for the population. Believing that the educational experience will change stress levels among officers for the current year, the researchers decide to draw a random sample of current officers who have had the educational course and see whether there are significant differences in their stress levels compared with previous years.

The researchers decide to test the following hypothesis set:

H_0: $\mu = 100$

H_1: $\mu \neq 100$

$P \leq .05$

The research hypothesis says that the mean stress level for correctional officers will not be equal to 100. The null hypothesis, therefore, is that the average stress level for officers will be equal to 100. The level of significance used for this hypothesis test is .05. Suppose that the researcher obtains a random sample of 50 correctional officers from the state roster and calculates the average stress score for the sample. In this case, suppose that the sample mean, $\overline{X}$, is 108. The question to be answered is whether 108 is significantly different from the hypothesized μ of 100. We know that 108 is different from 100. But is 108 significantly different from 100 so that it lies in the region of rejection on the sampling distribution of the sample means?

A sampling distribution of means is constructed by the researcher. The hypothesized μ under H_0 is supplied and critical regions for the distribution indicated. These regions are shown in Figure 16.22. To determine whether our *observed* mean of 108 lies in either of the rejection regions of this distribution, we must assign 108 a Z score. Also, we must assign Z values to those points along the horizontal axis of the sampling distribution of means that identify the critical regions of it.

First, each of the critical regions of our sampling distribution of means contain .025 of curve area, or one-half of .05, the level of significance chosen. Since the unit normal distribution is also approximated by this sampling distribution, we may apply what we have learned abut it to solve this particular part of our problem. The question becomes, what Z value cuts off a proportion of curve area from the

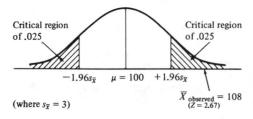

Critical region of .025

Critical region of .025

$-1.96 s_{\overline{x}}$ $\mu = 100$ $+1.96 s_{\overline{x}}$

(where $s_{\overline{x}} = 3$)

$\overline{X}_{observed} = 108$
$(Z = 2.67)$

Figure 16.22 Sampling distribution of means showing critical values.

mean to some point to the left or right of the mean that leaves 2.5 percent of the curve area in the tails of the distribution? We know that 50 percent or .5000 of the curve area of the unit normal distribution is found on either side of the mean of it. Therefore, if we know that 2.5 percent or .0250 of curve area lies in either tail, .4750 (.5000 − .0250 = .4750) is the amount of curve area between the mean, 0, and those particular points to the left and right of μ. We can examine Table A.3 and find a proportion in the body of the table that corresponds most closely to .4750. In this case, we find .4750 exactly. We note the Z value that intersects this proportion and determine it is 1.96. Therefore, our Z values corresponding to the critical values along the horizontal axis of our unit normal distribution are + and −1.96. In other words, on the unit normal distribution, we would move 1.96σ's of 1 to reach a point to the left and right of μ = 0 that would cut off .4750 of the curve area, leaving .0250 in each tail. On the sampling distribution of sample means, we would move along the horizontal axis of the distribution in terms of *standard error of the mean* units. Thus + or −1.96$s_{\bar{x}}$'s would define points to the left and right of our μ = 100 that mark off the two critical regions. These points are illustrated in Figure 16.22, and the shaded areas are the two critical regions. Also, these points are referred to as *critical values of Z*, since they identify critical regions of sampling distributions.

Assigning our observed mean of 108 a Z value requires that we have a knowledge of the value of the standard error of the mean. Assume that we have already determined the sample standard deviation, s, and that s = 21. With s = 21 and N = 50, the standard error of the mean, $s_{\bar{x}}$, is equal to

$$s_{\bar{x}} = \frac{s}{\sqrt{N-1}}$$

$$= \frac{21}{\sqrt{50-1}}$$

$$= \frac{21}{\sqrt{49}}$$

$$= \frac{21}{7}$$

$$= 3.$$

The standard error of the mean = 3. Using this standard error term, we can convert our observed mean of 108 in a Z value by using a formula similar to the one used to convert raw scores into Z scores. In this case, we can give our observed sample mean a Z score as follows:

$$Z = \frac{\overline{X}_{obs} - \mu}{s_{\bar{x}}},$$

where $\overline{X}_{obs}$ = observed sample mean
μ = hypothesized population mean
$s_{\bar{x}}$ = standard error of the mean

Using the information we have, the Z value for our observed mean of 108 becomes

$$Z = \frac{108 - 100}{3}$$

$$= \frac{8}{3}$$

$$= +2.67.$$

The Z value associated with our observed mean of 108 is 2.67. This is also known as our *observed value of Z*. Since this Z value of 2.67 equals or exceeds the absolute critical value of Z, + or −1.96, we may reject the null hypothesis and support the research hypothesis that the population mean is different from 100. Of course, there is a 5 percent chance that we are wrong in making this conclusion, because .05 was our chosen level of significance (type I error).

Generally, the values of Z that identify critical regions on sampling distributions are called critical values of Z. Any time an observed Z value (associated with an observed $\overline{X}$ value) equals or exceeds the critical value of Z (as established by the level of significance, or α), the null hypothesis being tested can be rejected at the level of significance indicated. The amount of error we incur in this decision is equal to or smaller than the level of significance we originally selected.

The foregoing problem was solved by translating our observed mean into a Z value and comparing that Z value with a critical value of Z established to identify the critical regions on the sampling distribution of means. We can also solve this problem by translating critical values of Z into a form that can be compared directly with our observed mean of 108. For instance, the critical values of Z for the .05 level of significance in the earlier problem were −1.96 and +1.96, respectively. These Z values are a given distance from the hypothesized μ value of 100. Specifically, these points are 1.96 standard errors of the mean above and below the hypothesized mean of 100. If our standard error of the mean = 3, these points are (1.96)(3) above and below 100. Thus if $s_{\overline{x}}$ = 3, then $100 \pm (1.96)(3) = 100 \pm 5.88$, or 94.12 and 105.88. The value 94.12 is 1.96 standard errors of the mean (of 3) below 100, while 105.88 is 1.96 standard errors of the mean (of 3) above 100. Does our observed mean of 108 fall below 94.12 or above 105.88? Yes. In the general case, the following formula may be used to identify these critical points:

$$\mu \pm (s_{\overline{x}})(Z),$$

where μ = hypothesized population mean under H_0
$\quad s_{\overline{x}}$ = standard error of the mean
$\quad Z$ = critical value of Z identifying the critical region(s)

The example above involved a prediction of stress levels of correctional officers, where the researchers were not concerned about the direction of difference between the observed sample mean and the hypothesized population mean. This situation is called a *two-tailed hypothesis test*, since two tails of the sampling distribution of the mean are involved as critical regions. The two-tailed nature of the statistical test was made, in large part, because the educational program these researchers studied was a highly experimental one. No one could anticipate whether it would have negative or positive results. Thus simple differences were predicted. What if these researchers believed that the educational program would *reduce* stress? Perhaps the program had been used previously by other states as a part of their program of correctional officer training. Under this circumstance, and anticipating that the educational program might actually reduce officer stress levels, these researchers might make a one-tailed or directional prediction instead of a two-tailed, nondirectional one. An example of a one-tailed test application is illustrated below.

Suppose that all information from the original problem above is the same in this case, except that these researchers observe a sample mean of 90 for these 50 officers instead of 108. Prior to drawing the sample of officers, however, these researchers construct the following hypothesis set:

H_0: $\mu \geq 100$

H_1: $\mu < 100$

$P \leq 0.05$

Notice in this hypothesis set that the notation is different regarding the prediction made about μ. In this case, the null hypothesis says that "the population mean is equal to or larger than 100," while the research hypothesis says that "the population mean is less than 100." Because this hypothesis set indicates the direction of difference expected, it is a *one-tailed test* rather than a two-tailed one. We still have the .05 level of significance as our P, except that this time, instead of halving this value, we will place *all* of it in one tail of the curve or the other. Which tail of the sampling distribution will contain the critical region in a one-tailed test situation? Our H_1 will answer this question. Always look at the research hypothesis to ascertain which tail of the curve will be used for the critical region whenever a one-tailed test of a hypothesis is being made. In this case, the research hypothesis says that the population mean will be "less than 100," so we will place all 5 percent of the level of significance in the left tail of the sampling distribution. This is illustrated in Figure 16.23.

Again, we place our hypothesized μ of 100 on the sampling distribution of means as shown in Figure 16.23. However, this time we are dealing with only one tail of the curve—the left tail. Notice in Figure 16.23 that .05 of the curve area occurs in the shaded area or critical region. We can again apply some of our knowledge about the unit normal distribution to solve our problem. We know that 50 percent, or .5000, of curve area on the unit normal distribution lies to the left of the mean of 0, and that .0500 remains in the left tail (the shaded portion

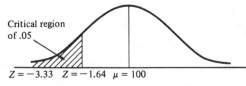

Critical region of .05

$Z = -3.33$ $Z = -1.64$ $\mu = 100$

$\overline{X}_{observed} = 90$

Figure 16.23 Sampling distribution for one-tailed test.

from Figure 16.23). Thus from the mean of the unit normal distribution to this point cuts off .5000 − .0500 = .4500 of curve area. Looking at Table A.3, we are interested in the Z value that cuts off .4500 of curve area, leaving .0500 in the left tail of the curve. We attempt to find the closest proportion to .4500. This presents us with an instructive problem here. Notice in the body of Table A.3 that there is no .4500. However, two proportions are found that are identical distances from .4500. We find .4495 and .4505. These are associated with Z values of 1.64 and 1.65, respectively. Which one should we choose? When we are the same distance from the desired proportion we are seeking in Table A.3, always select the Z value that ends in an even digit. Again, this is an arbitrary selection, but it will make your answers correspond with various normal curve exercises at chapter ends. In this case, will pick the Z value associated with .4495, since it is 1.64, an even Z value.

In Figure 16.23, the critical value of Z, −1.64, has been located to the left of the mean of 100. The Z value carries a minus (−) sign since the Z value is to the left of or below μ. Next, we must assign a Z value to our observed mean = 90. In this case, we will use the same Z score formula used in our earlier two-tailed problem:

$$Z = \frac{90 - 100}{3}$$

$$= \frac{-10}{3}$$

$$= -3.33.$$

Our observed Z value is −3.33. If the critical value of Z, −1.64, is equaled or exceeded by our observed Z value, we may reject the null hypothesis and support the research hypothesis, that the population mean is less than 100. Clearly, −3.33 is to the left of −1.64, and we may say that 90 is significantly different from 100. We run a 5 percent risk of being wrong in making this statement, according to the significance level we have used.

Again, we may convert our critical Z value into a form that will enable us to compare it directly with the observed mean of 90. Our critical Z value is −1.64, which means that it is 1.64 standard errors of the mean below the hypothesized μ of 100. If our "standard error of the mean" term is 3, the critical region is 1.64 of these 3's below 100. Accordingly (1.64)(3) = 4.92. Then, 100 − 4.92 = 95.08. The critical value (expressed in terms similar to mean values) is 95.08. Is our observed mean of 90 equal to or smaller than 95.08? Obviously. Therefore, there are two ways of resolving this problem and testing our hypotheses.

All hypothesis tests that utilize the signs "less than" (<) and "greater than" (>) are directional or one-tailed tests. All hypothesis tests that use the signs "equal to" (=) and "not equal to" (≠) are two-tailed or nondirectional tests. In all two-tailed tests, the critical region is dispersed evenly in both tails of the sampling distribution. In one-tailed tests, the critical region is determined by the direction predicted under the research hypothesis. If the research hypothesis uses "greater than," the right tail of the sampling distribution will contain the critical region. If the research hypothesis uses "less than," the left tail of the curve contains the critical region.

Sample-Size Considerations

Increasing one's sample size through any probability sampling procedure generally decreases the amount of sampling error incurred. In turn, the amount of statistical test power increases, and β error or type II error is reduced. In Chapter 17, statistical tests of significance are presented and discussed. The significance of any observed numerical value associated with any statistical test is, in part, a function of the sample size. Generally, the larger the sample size, the more significant one's findings will be statistically. Thus it will be important for researchers to distinguish between *statistical significance* and *substantive significance* or "practical" significance.

It is entirely possible that if one's sample sizes are large enough, *all* reported statistical values will be significant, at least in a probabilistic sense. Therefore, we should not be overly impressed with large sample sizes and lengthy discussions of their statistical significance. The sheer magnitude of samples will cause significance to occur, although it will not be that meaningful. The statement "What we have observed is statistically significant, but it doesn't mean anything" applies here. We must evaluate both the statistical significance of whatever we find and the practical significance that our findings have for social applications.

Sample-size considerations are relevant for the present discussion of sampling distributions of statistics, since larger sample sizes *decrease* the size of standard errors of means. Since standard errors of means are the units of measurement along the horizontal axes of sampling distributions of means, the significance of observed means is evaluated according to how many standard errors of the mean they are apart from hypothesized means. The larger the sample, the smaller the standard error of the mean, and the more "significant" the difference between the observed and hypothesized means.

In our previous examples, where population means of 100 were hypothesized regarding stress levels of correctional officers, observed means of 90 and 108 were used. In each of these cases, reported Z values associated with these means were considered significantly different from the hypothesized population means. If our sample sizes were inflated from 50 to 50 million, as an exaggerated illustration, observed means of 100.1 or 99.9 would be significantly different from the hypothesized mean of 100 as well. However, we would not pay much attention to these negligible differences. Again, we might observe statistical significance associated with our results, but it may not mean anything of any practical significance.

SUMMARY

The unit normal distribution is a mathematically derived, theoretical distribution that serves both a comparative and a probability function. In research work, criminologists often approximate the unit normal distribution with their distributions of raw scores that have been collected. To the extent that similarities occur between these distributions and the unit normal distribution, many statements about the unit normal distribution can also apply to those distributions of raw scores that approximate it. Some of the characteristics of the unit normal distribution are that it is bell-shaped, symmetrical, and has as its primary parameters a mean of 0 and a standard deviation of 1.

For comparative purposes, researchers may translate their raw scores into standard scores. Not all distributions of scores are normal in form, however. Distributions may be skewed, where scores tend to "bunch up" toward the left or right ends of the distribution, or kurtosis or curve peakedness may exist. Three types of kurtosis are leptokurtosis, mesokurtosis, and platykurtosis. Any distribution of scores that has substantial kurtosis or skewness is not normal in form.

Decision rules are always specified in advance of statistical tests. One decision rule is specifying a sampling distribution of a statistic, such as the mean. Sampling distributions of statistics are distributions of all possible values that those statistics may assume when based on samples of a specified size and drawn from a specified population. Some sampling distributions approximate the unit normal distribution. The sampling distribution of the mean is a normal distribution with a mean and a standard deviation. Means of sampling distributions of statistics are called expected values; their standard deviations are called standard errors. With a knowledge of the sampling distribution of means, hypotheses about population means may be tested.

All statistical tests have two types of error: type I or α error and type II or β error. Type I error occurs whenever null hypotheses are rejected but should not be rejected. Type II errors occur whenever null hypotheses are not rejected and should be rejected. Both types of errors always exist in any hypothesis test. Researchers may influence, either directly or indirectly, the amounts of these errors. Type I error is also known as the level of significance, a second decision rule. Levels of significance are probabilities set for purposes of hypothesis testing. These levels of significance also identify a third decision rule, known as a critical region or region of rejection on sampling distributions. Whenever researchers observe sample means that fall in rejection regions of sampling distributions, they may reject null hypotheses and support their research hypotheses. In the following chapter, we examine different types of statistical inference that utilize the principles learned here.

QUESTIONS FOR REVIEW AND PROBLEMS TO SOLVE

1. Determine the proportion of curve area lying to the right of the following Z values.
   (a) 1.45
   (b) −2.33
   (c) .00
   (d) .40
   (e) 1.99
   (f) 1.00

2. Determine the proportion of curve area lying between the following pairs of Z values.
   (a) -1.95 and -1.26
   (b) -1.66 and 1.66
   (c) 2.11 and $.04$
   (d) 2.33 and 2.44

3. Convert the following raw scores to Z scores, where the observed mean $= 115$ and the standard deviation $= 10$.
   (a) 156
   (b) 115
   (c) 100
   (d) 85

4. Convert the following Z scores to raw scores, where $\overline{X} = 220$ and $s = 15$.
   (a) -5.55
   (b) 1.44
   (c) 3.11
   (d) $.00$

5. Determine the proportion of curve area lying to the left of the following Z values.
   (a) $.32$
   (b) -2.18
   (c) $.99$
   (d) $-.03$
   (e) 1.11
   (f) 2.23
   (g) $-.81$
   (h) 1.00

6. Determine the raw score associated with each of the following Z values, given an $\overline{X} = 40$ and an $s = 4.2$ (round your raw scores to the nearest whole number).
   (a) -1.09
   (b) $.11$
   (c) $.99$
   (d) -6.00
   (e) $.00$
   (f) -2.26

7. Determine the amount of curve area lying between the following Z values.
   (a) $.26$ and 1.21
   (b) 1.09 and -2.18
   (c) $.00$ and 1.00
   (d) 1.45 and -1.02
   (e) 2.32 and 2.33
   (f) 2.88 and -1.18
   (g) 1.86 and -1.23
   (h) $-.09$ and -1.10

8. Transform the following raw scores into standard scores, given $\overline{X} = 400$ and $s = 32$.
   (a) 442
   (b) 496
   (c) 448
   (d) 411
   (e) 465
   (f) 480

9. With $\overline{X} = 60$, and $s = 4$, what percentage of scores theoretically lies above the following values?
   (a) 64
   (b) 49
   (c) 46
   (d) 55

10. If the standard error of the mean $= 3$ and the hypothesized population mean $= 68$, what would be the Z value associated with the following observed sample means?
    (a) 68
    (b) 90
    (c) 55
    (d) 65
    (e) 40

11. Differentiate between type I and type II errors. Who determines each type of error? How can these types of errors be minimized? Explain.

12. How does the level of significance we select relate to critical regions on sampling distributions?

13. For the following six population scores, construct a sampling distribution of means, based on samples of size 2.

Person	Score
A	20
B	22
C	24
D	26
E	28
F	30

Construct a frequency distribution of your sample means.

14. Under what circumstances are both tails of sampling distributions of statistics used in hypothesis testing? Explain.

15. Why is the critical region also known as the "region of rejection"? Explain.

17

Statistical Inference: Point Estimation, Confidence Intervals, and Tests of Significance

KEY TERMS

Chi-square test
Confidence interval
Curvilinearity
Degrees of freedom
Estimation
Goodness of fit
Inference
Interval estimation
Linearity
Measure of association
Nonlinearity

Nonparametric statistical tests
One-tailed test
Parametric statistical tests
Point estimation
Proportional-reduction-in-error (PRE)
Standard error of a statistic
Statistical inference
t test
Two-tailed test
Z test

INTRODUCTION

Criminologists and others investigating the characteristics of samples usually want to generalize their results beyond the samples studied. Studies of prison inmates, juvenile delinquents, correctional officers, judges, district attorneys, public defenders, halfway house volunteers, or those working in private, community-based facilities are conducted generally for purposes beyond mere description. Although describing the characteristics of samples is an important task of researchers, a general objective of social scientists is to relate their knowledge so that statements may be made about the population generally. Whatever investigators find relating to a sample of public defenders in Columbus, Ohio, for example, might be applicable to studies of public defenders throughout the remainder of the state. As we have seen, researchers cannot guarantee the representativeness of typicality of any sample they study in relation to the population from which the sample was drawn, but they *can* enhance the likelihood that it is generalizable to the population through the use of probability sampling plans and randomness in element selection.

This chapter is about two types of statistical inference: point and interval estimation. First, these different types of statistical inference are described, together with a rationale for their use, by criminal justice professionals and others. Examples from the criminological literature will be used to enhance the meaningfulness of these procedures.

Additionally, in this chapter we include a brief discussion of tests of significance. These tests are applied to one or more samples of elements, and they vary in their application according to the type of data collected by researchers as well as the nature of the samples studied. Two broad divisions of statistical tests are parametric and nonparametric. Examples of each of these types of tests are defined and described. Each division has certain strengths and weaknesses. Sample applications of these procedures are illustrated from the research literature in criminology and criminal justice. Finally, a brief discussion of measures of association is presented. Measures of association are intended to reflect how closely two or more variables vary or are "in step" with one another.

STATISTICAL INFERENCE

Statistical inference is the process of estimating population parameters by examining sample statistics. Ideally, populations are identified in advance and samples of elements are drawn from populations. Researchers may then hypothesize about the parameters of the population and test these hypotheses by investigating various sample characteristics and comparing these with their hypothesized estimates.

PURPOSES OF STATISTICAL INFERENCE

The purposes of statistical inference are to (1) test unlimited numbers of hypotheses about population values, (2) determine likely limits within which population parameters occur, and (3) advance our knowledge about population characteristics.

Types of Statistical Inference

Two alternative forms of estimation exist: point estimation and interval estimation. Both types of estimation involve sample statistics or information generated from samples. However, *point estimation* involves a forecast or prediction about some hypothesized population parameter, whereas *interval estimation* uses an observed sample statistic to generalize about related population parameters. For several reasons discussed below, point estimation is relatively unpopular compared with interval estimation. This is why it receives less coverage in most texts where both types of estimation are discussed. Nevertheless, it provides a convenient illustration of hypothesis testing.

Point estimation. We have already had a taste of point estimation in the discussion of critical regions in Chapter 16. Point estimation is the process of forecasting or predicting the value of a population parameter and then comparing the particular sample statistic counterpart with it. For instance, we might predict that the population $\mu = 100$, as we did in the example used in Chapter 16. Then we draw a sample of elements and compare our sample mean with the population mean. The degree of discrepancy between our observed $\overline{X}$ and the hypothesized μ will indicate the accuracy of the inference or estimation. In short, we estimate a "point" at which we believe the population mean, μ, occurs. We then compare this *point estimate* with an actual observed sample mean value, $\overline{X}$, to determine the accuracy of the estimate. Accordingly, estimates may be made about population standard deviations, modes, medians, or 10–90 ranges. Sample standard deviations, modes, medians, and 10–90 ranges are used as our observed sample statistics to compare with predictions of population parameters.

The primary problems with point estimation are that (1) we must guess what the population parameters are in advance, and (2) unless we know a great deal about the population we are studying, we will have little basis for justifying the guesses we make. In the problem of point estimation discussed in Chapter 16, a "guess" was made about the stress levels of a population of correctional officers in a particular state, and a statistic from a sample of correctional officers was used to compare with this estimate. The basis for this "guess" was previous information about known stress levels of correctional officers from former years. If we had *no* previous information about the population or if our general knowledge about it were limited, we would have no logical basis for our predictions. Actually, using information about correctional officer stress levels from previous years does not truly legitimize our estimates for later years, either. Each year is a new one, and whatever "levels of stress" existed in earlier years are no longer applicable for later years. Therefore, point estimates are like stabs in the dark. Nevertheless, in the absence of any other information, information about a population for previous years is better than no knowledge at all.

The purpose of statistical inference is to learn about population parameters by studying samples drawn from them. Initially, we assume *no* knowledge of the population or its characteristics. This is why point estimation is troublesome for so many researchers, because a question always exists as to where our point estimates come from. More often than not, the population parameters about which we seek information are unknown. We draw samples of elements from populations to learn more about certain population parameters. It is no coincidence that we use the sample mean as an estimate of the population mean, since the mean has a sampling distribution that is normal in form. The principles of the unit normal distribution apply to it, and we can benefit from this knowledge.

Briefly reviewing what we learned in a portion of Chapter 16, we know that the sampling distribution of means is generally normal in form. It is perfectly symmetrical. Most statements that can be made about the unit normal distribution can also apply to any normal distribution of scores, including certain distributions of sample statistics, such as the sampling distribution of the mean. While the horizontal axis of the unit normal distribution is measured according to standard deviation (σ) units of 1 as they depart from the μ of 0, the sampling distribution of means is measured according to standard errors of the mean, $s_{\bar{x}}$, in relation to the population mean, μ. We know that means of sampling distributions of statistics are called *expected values*, and standard deviations on these distributions are called *standard errors*.

Finally, we know that whenever the expected value of any statistic equals the population parameter that that statistic is intended to estimate, the statistic becomes an *unbiased estimate* of that population parameter. All sample statistics have corresponding population parameters. We know that the mean of the sampling distribution of means, μ, is always equal to the actual population mean, μ. Therefore, the sample mean, $\overline{X}$, is an unbiased estimate of the population μ. All other statistics discussed in Chapter 15 are *not* unbiased estimates of their respective population parameters, because despite the fact that they all have sampling distributions, they *do not have* sampling distributions with means equal to those corresponding parameters.

Point estimation is illustrated by the following problem. Suppose that investigators wish to study the influence of new sentencing guidelines on reductions in sentencing disparities that have previously been attributed to gender, race, ethnicity, and socioeconomic factors. Sentencing disparities exist whenever several convicted offenders in the same jurisdiction are sentenced to widely different prison terms by the same judge, despite the similarity of their conviction offenses and prior records. A blatant example is sentencing two convicted male robbers, one black and one white, to terms of 10 and 5 years, respectively. Both offenders have similar criminal records, are about the same age, and the circumstances of their instant offense are nearly identical. Yet the black offender receives a sentence twice as harsh as that of the white offender.

Suppose that a jurisdiction is selected where indeterminate sentencing has been used previously to sentence offenders. Indeterminate sentencing is a sentencing scheme that permits wide judicial discretion in imposing sentence lengths. In the most recent year, suppose this jurisdiction has implemented a new guidelines scheme for sentencing convicted offenders. This scheme of guidelines provides a range of months within which judges should sentence offenders, depending on the seriousness of their acts and prior records. The prevailing belief among officials in that jurisdiction is that the new guidelines will minimize previous sentencing disparities that were considered discriminatory.

Previous information available from this fictitious jurisdiction shows that sentencing disparities according to race averaged about 12 months, or 1 year. In other words, sentences for black offenders who were convicted of the same crimes as white offenders received an average of 12 additional months as punishment over the incarcerative terms imposed on convicted whites. Using this "previous information" as the basis for our current estimates, we obtain a sample of black and white convicted offenders in that jurisdiction and determine their conviction offenses and sentences imposed under the new guidelines. Under point estimation, we predict as our projected amount of sentencing disparity the following, as illustrated by our hypothesis set:

H_0: $\mu \geq 12$ months
H_1: $\mu < 12$ months
$P \leq .05$ (one-tailed test)

The research hypothesis says that the average sentencing disparity between black and white offenders in this jurisdiction will be less than 12 months. Based on this research hypothesis, we derive a null hypothesis that says that the average sentencing disparity will either equal or exceed 12 months. A one-tailed hypothesis test is being made here, since we reasonably expect disparities in sentences between black and white convicted offenders to be minimized under the new sentencing guidelines.

Further information available, based on the samples of offenders we have selected, is given, that the observed $\overline{X} = 6.5$, which represents the current amount of sentencing disparity under the new guidelines, and a standard error of the mean, $s_{\overline{x}} = 2.00$, based on the magnitude of the standard deviation and sample size obtained.

First, the hypothesis set is tested using the .05 level of significance, and a one-tailed or directional prediction is being made. Therefore, we would follow the steps outlined below to test our hypothesis.

1. Construct a sampling distribution of means.
2. Place the population mean of 12 months at the center of this sampling distribution.
3. Identify the critical region in left tail of this distribution as containing the 5 percent of error consistent with the .05 level of significance used. The left tail is chosen because under the research hypothesis, the direction of difference hypothesized is below or to the left of 12 months.
4. Identify a Z value from Table A.3 that corresponds with the .05 level of significance or leaves 5 percent of the curve area in the left tail of the sampling distribution. In this case, the Z value leaving 5 percent of the curve area in the left tail of the curve also cuts off .4500 of curve area from the mean of 12 to that point, or $Z = -1.64$. This becomes our *critical value of Z* for the 0.05 level of significance, making a one-tailed test.
5. Assign our observed mean of 6.5 a Z value, using the standard error of the mean term, 2.00. This Z value will represent the distance 6.5 is from the forecast mean of 12. The computational work is simple, consisting of

$$\text{Observed } Z = \frac{\overline{X} - \mu}{s_{\overline{x}}},$$

where $\overline{X}$ = observed sample mean

μ = hypothesized population mean

$s_{\overline{x}}$ = standard error of the mean

or $(6.5 - 12)/2.00 = -5.5/2 = -2.75$. The observed $Z = -2.75$.

6. Compare the observed mean with the hypothesized mean and evaluate its significance. Since our observed Z value, -2.75, is in the predicted direction under H_1 and equals or exceeds the critical value of $Z = -1.64$, we may reject H_0 and support the research hypothesis. In this case, although disparities in sentencing continue to exist, they appear to have minimized significantly, at least according to these test results. Also, there is a 5 percent chance that we are wrong (the α level or level of significance chosen) in making this conclusion based on these findings. This concludes our point estimate test.

Interval estimation and confidence intervals. Interval estimation can be used to answer the same question raised in the point estimation example. However, for various reasons described below, interval estimation is superior to point estimation. The logic of interval estimation is as follows.

If we obtain a sample of elements (by using a probability sampling plan) and compute various statistics for it, there is a strong likelihood that our sample statistics are close to their parametric counterparts in the population. For example, a sample $\overline{X}$ is probably near the true population μ value on the sampling distribution of sample means. A sample median is probably near the true population median value. In fact, for any random sample of elements we select, any mean we compute is more likely to be closer to the population mean than far away from it.

Recalling the nature of the sampling distribution of means, we may say with considerable assurance (and confidence) that there are far more sample means occurring in and around the center of the distribution than occur in its extremes. We might designate the general area near the center of the sampling distribution of means as an area of high probability. Similarly, we may designate the tails of the sampling distribution of means as areas of low probability. The area of high probability near the center of the distribution is where a majority of sample means are located. Relatively few means are found in the extremes of the distribution. Utilizing what we know about the sampling distribution of means and the unit normal distribution it approximates, about 68 percent of the sample means lie within $+$ or $-1.00s_{\overline{x}}$ on either side of the population μ. This is because approximately 68 percent of the normal curve area lies between -1.00σ and $+1.00\sigma$ on either side of μ on the unit normal distribution.

To make this statement, we do not have to know the value of μ for the sampling distribution of means. We merely need to know that the sampling distribution of means is normal in form. A given distance to the left or to the right of the unknown μ value will cut off a certain amount of curve area, which is also equivalent to a portion of mean values occurring there. Therefore, whenever we draw a random sample of elements from a designated population, the probability is in our favor of obtaining a sample with a $\overline{X}$ that is nearer μ than far away from it. It is logical to assume that if we place our observed $\overline{X}$ value on the horizontal axis of the sampling distribution of sample means, it will probably be near μ, the true population mean. Furthermore, if we advance a short distance to the left *and* to the right of our observed $\overline{X}$, it is probable that the true μ value will be overlapped. In short, an *interval* can be created around our observed $\overline{X}$ value which will probably include or overlap the population μ at some point. The interval created around an observed $\overline{X}$ value is referred to as a *confidence interval* and is the subject of interval estimation.

Confidence intervals are designated distances above and below an observed sample $\overline{X}$ value that have a specified likelihood of overlapping the true μ value at some point. Confidence intervals are labeled as 95 percent confidence intervals, 90 percent confidence intervals, 99 percent confidence intervals, and so on. These percentage values refer to the likelihood that any given confidence interval we determine will overlap the true population mean, μ.

Since the true population mean is almost always unknown, we are never absolutely sure that any confidence interval we construct will truly overlap μ. As a way of illustrating the logic of confidence interval construction, imagine that researchers were to draw all possible samples of size 50 from a population of 2000. As we have discussed earlier, there would be N^n or 2000^{50} samples that could be drawn. Furthermore, suppose that researchers were to compute a mean for each of the samples drawn. Obviously, this would require much work, but eventually, researchers would have 2000^{50} $\overline{X}$'s.

Next, imagine that a 95 percent confidence interval were to be constructed around each and every one of the 2000^{50} sample means. There would be 2000^{50} confidence intervals constructed. Since all of these would be 95 percent confidence intervals, we could say with certainty that 95 percent of these confidence intervals would overlap the true population μ at some point. We could also say with certainty that 5 percent of these confidence intervals would not overlap μ.

Had we created 99 percent confidence intervals for all observed mean values, we would have 2000^{50} 99 percent confidence intervals. We could say that 99 percent of them would overlap μ at some point, and that 1 percent of them would not overlap it. Had we created 80 percent confidence intervals for all of our observed $\overline{X}$ values, 80 percent of those confidence intervals would overlap the population mean and 20 percent of them would fail to overlap it. The confidence interval that we designate defines the percentage of confidence intervals that would overlap the true population mean value if we were to construct such intervals for all possible $\overline{X}$ values that could be computed.

What does the researcher do in reality? Usually, one sample is drawn randomly rather than 10 samples or 1000 samples. The researcher observes a single

$\overline{X}$ rather than 2000[50] of them. A single confidence interval of some magnitude is created around that single observed $\overline{X}$. The researcher then specifies the likelihood associated with that confidence interval (e.g., 99 percent, 90 percent, 95 percent) of overlapping the true (and unknown) population μ value. The researcher is never in the position of knowing which sample has been drawn from all possible samples that could be drawn. Therefore, the researcher cannot possibly know which mean has been obtained from all possible means that could have been computed. Again, probability works in the researcher's favor here. We do know that the random draw of a single sample will stand a better chance of being near the population mean rather than far away from it on the sampling distribution of sample means. Therefore, the probability that the sample mean lies near the population mean is in our favor. Therefore, a confidence interval we construct around that mean will be more likely to overlap μ at some point than not to overlap it.

Suppose that the researcher has drawn a random sample of 226 elements and has observed a sample $\overline{X} = 25$ and a sample $s = 5$. Further suppose that the researcher wants to construct a 90 percent confidence interval about the observed $\overline{X}$ of 25. The 90 percent confidence interval is constructed as follows:

$$90 \text{ percent confidence interval} = \overline{X}_{obs} \pm (s_{\overline{x}})(Z),$$

where $\overline{X}_{obs}$ = observed sample mean

$s_{\overline{x}}$ = standard error of the mean

Z = standard score associated with cutting off one-half of the confidence interval percent (in this case, 90 percent/2 = 45 percent or .4500)

Using the information provided by the hypothetical example above, we have

$$90 \text{ percent confidence interval} = 25 \pm \left(\frac{5}{\sqrt{226 - 1}}\right)(1.64)$$

$$= 25 \pm \left(\frac{5}{15}\right)(1.64)$$

$$= 25 \pm (.33)(1.64)$$

$$= 25 \pm .54$$

$$= 24.46 \text{ to } 25.54$$

The 90 percent confidence interval around the observed mean of 25 extends from 24.46 to 25.54 and has a 90 percent chance of overlapping the population μ at some point. We used the sample size and standard deviation to derive our standard error of the mean value.

In the general case, if we wish to construct any confidence interval around any observed $\overline{X}$, the following formula could be used:

$$? \text{ percent confidence interval} = \overline{X}_{obs} \pm (s_{\overline{x}})(Z),$$

where $\overline{X}_{obs}$ = observed mean

$s_{\overline{x}}$ = standard error of the mean

Z = standard score associated with cutting off normal curve area equal to one-half of whatever percent the confidence interval happens to be

To determine which Z value should be used in this formula, we must first divide the percent of the confidence interval desired by 2. If we are computing the 90 percent confidence interval, we would divide 90 percent by 2 or 90 percent/2 = 45 percent (.4500); if we are computing the 80 percent confidence interval, we would divide 80 percent by 2 or 80 percent/2 = 40 percent (.4000); and so on. Once we have determined this result, we may look up the equivalent Z value in Table A.3. This is the Z value cutting off one-half of the confidence interval percentage we have designated. The Z value cutting off .4500 (from the mean of 0 to that point) is 1.64, while the Z value cutting off .4000 (from the mean of 0 to that point) is 1.28.

Given an observed $\overline{X}$ = 25 and $s_{\overline{x}}$ = .33, we could determine the following confidence intervals as shown:

$$95 \text{ percent confidence interval} = 25 \pm (.33) (1.96)$$

$$= 24.35 \text{ to } 25.65$$

$$99 \text{ percent confidence interval} = 25 \pm (.33) (2.58)$$

$$= 24.15 \text{ to } 25.85$$

$$80 \text{ percent confidence interval} = 25 \pm (.33) (1.28)$$

$$= 24.58 \text{ to } 25.42$$

In each of these cases, we have added to and subtracted from the observed mean the product of the $s_{\overline{x}}$ and the Z value associated with cutting off one-half of whatever the confidence interval percent happens to be. The 95 percent confidence interval above means that there is a 95 percent chance that the true and unknown population μ lies somewhere between 24.35 and 25.65. The 99 percent confidence interval means that there is a 99 percent chance that the true and unknown population μ lies somewhere between 24.15 and 25.85. Finally, the 80 percent confidence interval means that there is an 80 percent chance or likelihood that the true and unknown population mean μ lies somewhere between 24.58 and 25.42.

It will be observed that the confidence interval gets larger as the percentage increases. Also, the confidence interval decreases in magnitude as the percentage decreases. This reflects either an increase or decrease in our "confidence" that the population mean will be found within any given confidence interval. Thus we are provided with another reason for the use of the term "confidence interval."

Confidence intervals have the distinct advantage over point estimation of providing a *range* wherein the population μ might occur. We begin our estimation with an observed $\overline{X}$ value and create an interval around it that probably overlaps μ. This is superior to the method of guessing a population mean value in advance, with little or no information, and then comparing a sample mean with our point estimate.

It is helpful to compare point estimation with interval estimation on a problem we have already solved involving forecasts of population values. Regarding the hypothetical problem of sentencing disparities discussed earlier under point estimation, we forecast a population mean of 12 months, indicating the disparity in sentence lengths between convicted black and white offenders. Under a new sentencing guidelines scheme, it was anticipated that sentence lengths would be more equivalent as disparities probably due to racial factors diminished. One one-tailed test was made which predicted that under new guidelines, disparities in sentence lengths between black and white offenders would be less than 12 months.

In the following scenario, let's assume the same information as given in the original problem, where our predicted $\mu = 12$ months, observed $\overline{X} = 6.5$ months, and $s_{\overline{x}} = 2.00$. However, we will generate the following two-tailed hypothesis set, where direction is not forecast:

H_0: $\mu = 12$ months

H_1: $\mu \neq 12$ months

$P \leq .05$ (two-tailed test)

The research hypothesis says that the average length of sentencing disparity (measured in months) will be different from 12 months, while the null hypothesis says the average disparity will be equal to 12 months. This forecast is based on previous information about sentencing in the jurisdiction studied. The same level of significance, .05, is used in this case. But because the direction of difference is not predicted, a two-tailed or nondirectional test is conducted. This means that we will have to split our significance level of .05 into two equal parts and place each part in the two tails of our sampling distribution of means. This will require that we locate a Z value that cuts off .4750 of curve area in both directions from the mean, leaving .0250 in each tail of the curve as the rejection regions or critical regions. This Z value is ± 1.96 and is designated as our critical value of Z for the .05 level of significance, using a two-tailed test.

Since we already know that our observed $\overline{X} = 6.5$ months and has an observed Z value associated with it of -2.75, we need only ask whether -2.75 equals or exceeds the critical values of ± 1.96. Yes, the $Z = -2.75$ is in the rejection region to the far left of -1.96. Thus we may reject the null hypothesis and conclude (with 5 percent error) that the sentencing disparity in that jurisdiction is not equal to 12 months.

Interval estimation may be used to answer the same question of whether the new guidelines have had any impact on sentencing disparities between convicted black and white offenders. In this case, we will not hypothesize anything. Rather, we will obtain our sample, compute our mean of 6.5 and standard error of the mean $= 2.00$, and construct a confidence interval around our observed $\overline{X} = 6.5$.

To make a test commensurate with the .05 level of significance used in the point estimate problem, we select a percent confidence interval that corresponds with the probability of .05. In this case, the probability is 95 percent. Therefore, we are seeking the 95 percent confidence interval around the observed $\overline{X} = 6.5$. Taking our given information, we have

$$95 \text{ percent confidence interval} = 6.5 \pm (2.00)(1.96)$$

$$= 6.5 \pm 3.92$$

$$= 2.58 \text{ to } 10.42.$$

Our 95 percent confidence interval extends from 2.58 to 10.42. We may say, with 95 percent confidence, that the population mean is overlapped by this interval 95 percent of the time. Notice that our original population mean of 12 months is *outside* this confidence interval. *Any* population mean that occurs outside confidence interval ranges is considered significantly different from the sample mean. We are answering essentially the same question about differences in sentence lengths, except that we are solving this problem by using alternative strategies.

Further note that the Z value chosen for our 95 percent confidence interval problem was the same value that was selected for a two-tailed hypothesis test at the .05 level of significance. This is the general relation between point estimation and interval estimation. Two-tailed point estimation is the functional equivalent of interval estimation, where the same levels of significance are involved. Levels of significance and confidence interval percentages are linked as follows:

90% confidence interval = .10 level of significance, two-tailed test

95% confidence interval = .05 level of significance, two-tailed test

80% confidence interval = .20 level of significance, two-tailed test

99% confidence interval = .01 level of significance, two-tailed test

and so on.

Summary Comparison of Point and Interval Estimation

Summarizing the basic differences between point and interval estimation, point estimation involves making a prediction about an unknown population parameter, drawing a random sample, determining the appropriate corresponding statistic, and making a comparison of this statistic with what was hypothesized as the population mean. Interval estimation involves no advance prediction of population values. Rather, interval estimation involves drawing a random sample of elements, computing sample statistics, and establishing probable ranges within which the population parameters will occur. Interval estimation deals with what is *known:* namely, the values of sample statistics. Point estimation involves dealing with what is *unknown:* population parameters. The main function of point estimation in recent years is to illustrate hypothesis testing and the meaningfulness of statistical significance and critical regions on sampling distributions.

PARAMETRIC AND NONPARAMETRIC STATISTICAL TESTS AND DECISION MAKING IN CRIMINAL JUSTICE

Tests of significance, sometimes known as "tests of significance of difference," may apply in cases involving single samples of elements. Two or more samples of elements may be involved for two-sample and k-sample statistical tests. Further, in the two- and k-sample cases, specialized tests of significance have been designed to work with independent samples as well as related samples.

What does "difference" refer to in tests of significance of difference? The term *difference* refers to the discrepancy between what researchers observe and what might be expected according to chance. In single-sample situations, researchers want to know whether their observed sample values or statistics differ from some hypothesized population parameter. Point estimation is closely linked with various significance tests. When we were concerned in the hypothetical situation above about whether sentencing disparities were reduced under a sentencing guidelines scheme, we wanted to know whether 6.5 months was significantly different from 12 months as hypothesized. This difference of 5.5 months appeared significant. Whether or not we realized it, we applied a statistical test of significance or difference (a Z test in this case) to our point estimation problem. We evaluated the significance of the difference between our sample observation, $\overline{X} = 6.5$ and the hypothesized population mean, 12 months, and determined that it was significant statistically, with a 5 percent chance of being in error.

What if we observed several different samples of elements? What if we observed public defenders from several different cities and were concerned with whether they varied significantly in their general competence when representing indigent clients? A statistical test of significance of difference could be applied here. Provided that we had a reasonable measure of attorney competence, we could determine if several samples of public defenders differed significantly on the competency variable. Numerical values resulting from our statistical test application could be assessed, and we could conclude, with some error, whether the different samples of attorneys actually differed significantly in their degree of competency.

The questions of whether one sample differs from what we hypothesize or whether two or more samples of elements differ according to selected measured variables are *not* the questions we attempt to answer when we apply statistical tests of significance of difference. We can see whether or not samples differ from one another. We can see whether 6.5 months differs from 12 months, or whether our competency measures for several different samples of public defenders yield different values. These observed differences are obvious or apparent. The questions we want answered pertain to the *statistical significance* of the differences in the scores we observe. Therefore, we may observe differences in competency ratings between two or more groups of public defenders, but these differences may not be *significant statistically*. We may see differences in months reflecting sentencing disparity from one type of sentencing scheme to another, but these differences may not be *significant statistically*. The decision rules we formulate also function as guidelines whereby we can evaluate the significance of whatever we find. *We normally and conventionally establish decision rules in advance of any hypothesis test we make, and on the basis of our decision rules, we decide to reject or fail to reject null hypotheses and support or fail to support corresponding research hypotheses.*

Two major categories of statistical tests of significance of difference exist: parametric and nonparametric. *Parametric statistical tests* are those that either require or have (1) randomness or a probability sampling plan, (2) a normal distribution underlying the characteristic or variable measured, (3) the interval level of measurement associated with the measured variable, and (4), sample sizes of 30 or larger. They are further characterized as having high test power relative to rejecting false null hypotheses.

Because of the fact that many variables studied by criminologists, criminal justice professionals, and social scientists in general do not achieve the interval level of measurement for selected variables or have normally distributed samples of elements to study, parametric statistical test choices may often be inappropriate ones. For instance, attitudes are popular investigative topics. Do probation officers with high client caseloads have higher or lower burnout scores than those of probation officers with lower client caseloads? Does police chief cynicism vary according to years in grade as chief? Do attitudes of delinquents change over time as the result of various intervention programs? All of these studies and thousands of others are concerned, at least in part, with attitudes of sample elements. Judging from reviews of recent criminological literature, since the most popular measures of attitudes today are Likert or summated rating scales (e.g., strongly agree, strongly disagree), Thurstone scales ("equal-appearing," interval scales), Guttman scales (i.e., the Cornell technique, unidimensional scaling), and the semantic differential, all of these scaling methods yield scores measured at best according to the ordinal level of measurement.

Also, many of the samples investigated by criminal justice professionals exhibit distributions of scores that depart markedly from normality and do not approximate the characteristics of the unit normal distribution. Examples of parametric statistical tests include the t test and Z test for significance of difference between means, the F test for analysis of variance, and the Newman–Keuls procedure.

A second major category of statistical procedures consists of *nonparametric statistical tests*. Nonparametric statistical tests assume or require randomness or a probability sampling plan. They are characterized as being applicable to situations where sample sizes may be quite small, where the level of measurement is usually, though not always, normal or ordinal, and where normality is not assumed to exist regarding distributions of raw scores. Compared with parametric tests, they are designed to answer similar questions, although they are less powerful regarding rejections of false null hypotheses.

Sometimes, nonparametric tests are called "distribution-free" statistics. This should not be interpreted to mean that there are no distributional assumptions underlying these tests. As we have seen, all statistics have sampling distributions. What "distribution-free" means in this case is a relaxation of the normal distribution assumption. In short, nonparametric tests do not require that researchers have sample scores that are normally distributed. Another designation of many of these tests is that they are "goodness-of-fit" procedures. The "goodness-of-fit" label means the "fit" between some chance occurrence or what would be expected according to chance and whatever scores happen to be observed. Flipping a coin 100 times, for instance, might be expected to yield 50 tails and 50 heads. However, a real distribution of 100 coin flips may yield 55 tails and 45 heads. Is the 55–45 difference different from what would be expected according to chance, namely, 50–50? Goodness-of-fit tests assess the significance of such differences. Examples of goodness-of-fit procedures include the chi-square test, Mann–Whitney U test, Kruskal–Wallis H test, and McNemar test for two related samples.

Advantages and Disadvantages of Parametric and Nonparametric Tests

Parametric tests of significance or statistical procedures are well-known tests. In fact, they are *so* well-known that they have often obscured the importance of utilizing more appropriate nonparametric tests under certain study conditions. Parametric tests are more sensitive regarding one's statistical observations. Therefore, if researchers were to simultaneously apply parametric and nonparametric procedures to the same sets of scores for two or more samples of elements, they would be more likely to reject false null hypotheses with their parametric test results rather than with their nonparametric test results. This reflects the general difference that parametric tests are more powerful than nonparametric tests. However, the significance of this difference in test power between parametric and nonparametric procedures is often exaggerated.

Several nonparametric statistical procedures have power levels that are almost equivalent to those associated with parametric tests. Since a test's power may be increased by increasing one's sample size, it is possible to make certain nonparametric test applications about as powerful as their parametric counterparts. Nonparametric tests have fewer restrictive assumptions associated with their application. Most are rapid to compute and easy to apply to a wide variety of social and psychological investigations. The use of nonparametric statistics in the social sciences generally has been increasing steadily over the years. Our increased familiarity with such procedures and a greater recognition of the tasks they can potentially accomplish accounts for such increased use of them in criminal justice and criminology.

If anything, nonparametric statistical tests are more conservative procedures compared with their equivalent parametric counterparts. Thus if there are serious questions raised about whether one or more assumptions have been violated in conjunction with the use of certain parametric tests, a safe course to follow would be to use a corresponding nonparametric procedure for a more conservative answer to one's research questions.

SOME EXAMPLES OF PARAMETRIC STATISTICAL TESTS

Two tests are presented in this section. The first, the Z test, relates closely to point estimation. Another well-known procedure for single-sample tests of significance is the t-test. Both of these procedures are designed to test hypotheses about population means and whether observed sample means are different from them. They differ primarily according to how the significance of the respective Z and t values may be interpreted.

Z and t Tests

The t test is perhaps the best single-sample test of significance of difference where data are measured according to an interval scale. The Z test and t test share the *same* formula:

$$Z \text{ or } t = \frac{\overline{X}_{\text{obs}} - \mu}{s_{\overline{x}}},$$

where $\overline{X}_{\text{obs}}$ = observed sample mean
μ = hypothesized population mean
$s_{\overline{x}}$ = standard error of the mean, $(s/\sqrt{N - 1})$

One frequently ignored technical distinction between the Z and t tests is that the Z test requires knowledge of the *population standard deviation*, whereas the t test requires only a knowledge of the *sample standard deviation*. Since it is unlikely that estimates about population means will ever be made when the population standard deviation is known, either the Z or t test is applied conventionally using the *sample standard deviation* for both applications. One additional difference between the two procedures is that for Z-test applications, the unit normal distribution is used for interpretive purposes. For t-test applications, the t distribution is used to interpret observed t values. Whenever the sample size investigated exceeds 120, both of these distributions are identical, meaning that the Z and t critical values for different levels of significance and for both one-and two-tailed tests are the same. But for situations involving analyses of smaller sample sizes, critical values yielded by the t test are generally *larger* than those disclosed by applications of the Z test. A special t table has been provided in Table A.5 for easy interpretation. The meanings of both t and Z values are illustrated by the following example.

MacKenzie and Shaw (1990) studied inmate adjustment and change resulting from a Louisiana shock incarceration program known as the *Intensive Motivational Program of Alternative Correctional Treatment* (IMPACT). The program consists of two phases, where offenders are placed in shock incarceration from 90 to 180 days in a "rigorous boot-camp atmosphere" in the first phase (p. 127), and an intensive supervised parole program in the second phase. Among other things, the shock incarceration experience conducted by "drill instructors" was designed to modify inmate behaviors and provide them with positive reinforcement and prosocial attitudes.

Suppose that MacKenzie and Shaw wanted to determine if the prosocial attitudes and social adjustment of a sample of inmate IMPACT participants tended to be *higher* than for the general prison population not exposed to IMPACT. Such a finding might prove valuable in showing the effectiveness of IMPACT for subsequent adjustment to life on the "outside" through supervised parole. Suppose that a measure of prosocial attitudes and social adjustment exists, the Prosocial Attitude and Social Adjustment Scale (PASSAC), and that it has been applied to populations of Louisiana prison inmates in previous years. Further assume that in previous years, the population mean on PASSAC has been 64, a relatively low degree of prosocial attitudes and social adjustment. The following hypothesis set is constructed:

H_0: $\mu \le 64$
H_1: $\mu > 64$

$P \le .05$ (one-tailed test)

The hypothesis set says the following. The null hypothesis, H_0, says that the population mean, μ, on PASSAC will be equal to or smaller than 64, while the researcher hypothesis says that μ will be greater than 64. A directional prediction is made under H_1 that for an observed sample of IMPACT participants, their prosocial attitudes and social adjustment will be higher than the predicted population mean of 64. It will be assumed that a significant difference of scores in the predicted direction under the research hypothesis will be indicative of the effectiveness of the IMPACT program. Suppose that the following information has been obtained, based on a sample of 41 IMPACT inmates: $\overline{X}_{obs} = 68.5, s = 12.2, N = 41$. A t test is conducted, yielding the following t observed:

$$t = \frac{68.5 - 64}{12.2\sqrt{41 - 1}}$$

$$= \frac{4.5}{1.94}$$

$$= 2.320.$$

The observed value of t is $2.320 = t_{obs}$.

To determine the statistical significance of our observed t value, we must turn to Table A.5. This table contains critical values of the t statistic that must be equaled or exceeded by our observed t values in order for our observed t values to be significant at the levels of probability indicated across the top of the table. Note in Table A.5 that both one- and two-tailed probabilities are provided. Since our hypothesis set is being tested at the .05 level of significance for a one-tailed or directional test, we locate the .05 one-tailed probability across the top of the table. Next, we must determine *degrees of freedom.*[*]

Degrees of freedom, df, are located down the left-hand side of Table A.5. We determine the appropriate df for one-sample tests by the formula $N - 1$, where N = the sample size. (The uppercase N is used here to refer to sample sizes, since most formulae use this uppercase designation. It is understood that most, if not all, of our work deals with samples of elements rather than populations of them.) In this case, degrees of freedom are $N - 1$ or $41 - 1 = 40$ df. Where df = 40 and the .05 level of significance for a one-tailed test *intersect* in the body of the table defines the *critical value of t* that we must equal or exceed with our *observed t value*. The critical value found where these values intersect is 1.684.

Does our observed $t = 2.320$ equal or exceed the critical value of 1.684? Yes. Therefore, we may reject H_0 and conclude tentatively that the sample mean, 68.5, is larger than and significantly different from the hypothesized population mean of 64. It appears that the IMPACT program may be influential in increasing inmate prosocial attitudes and social adjustment or PASSAC scores. Of course, there is a 5 percent chance that we might be wrong in rejecting H_0, however. (A two-tailed or nondirectional test of the same hypothesis set would have required equaling or exceeding a critical value of $t = 2.021$. See if you can find this critical value in Table A.5.)

Had we applied the Z test to the problem above, we would have used the unit normal distribution or values of Z from Table A.3. How would we know which Z value to use as our critical Z value? Again, our observed t value, 2.320, would be treated precisely as a Z value and interpreted accordingly. Since the .05 level of significance is being used in this hypothesis test, and a one-tailed or directional test is involved, we would identify a Z value that would cut off 45 percent of the curve area in one direction or the other, leaving 5 percent of the curve area in one tail. Under the research hypothesis specified in the problem above, the right tail of the unit normal distribution would contain the critical region. The critical value of Z would be 1.64, the Z value cutting off 45 percent of the curve area between the mean of 0 and a $Z = 1.64$. If our observed Z is equal to or larger than the critical Z value of 1.64, we may reject the null hypothesis and conclude H_1. In this case, an observed $Z = 2.320$ does equal or exceed the critical value of $Z = 1.64$. Conventional levels of measurement chosen by researchers are .05 and .01.

Notice two important points about what we have done in our applications of t and Z tests. The first point is that we have carried out the observed t value *three places*, to *2.320*. This was done because the critical t values in Table A.5 are also expressed to three places. Thus our comparisons are conveniently made, without having to worry about rounding. In this hypothesis-test situation, rounding would not have made a significant difference. In other tests of hypotheses, however, borderline decisions often have to be made. It is best to express your observed

---

[*]Degrees of freedom are frequently used for the purpose of entering statistical tables and determining critical values. They are almost always designated as "df" and refer to the number of values in a set of them which are free to vary. Different ways of determining degrees of freedom are calculated whenever tabular distribution of frequencies are analyzed.

Some Examples of Parametric Statistical Tests

statistical values to the *same number of places* as those same critical values of statistics are expressed in the appendix interpretative tables.

The second point is to notice the similarity between the t and Z critical values. The critical value of t was 1.684; the critical Z value was 1.64. Remember that t critical values will tend to be larger than Z critical values whenever samples are smaller than 120. In this case, our hypothetical sample size of IMPACT inmates was 41. Had the sample size been 121, $N - 1 = 120$ would have been our df for the problem above, using the t table. The critical t value would have been 1.658, somewhat closer to Z than was found when df equaled 40. Notice also that the infinity (∞) line in Table A.5 does virtually equal Z values for equivalent significance levels. In the infinity case, the t value becomes 1.645, about what our critical Z value would be if the unit normal distribution were used instead of the t distribution.

Another fact worth noting is that in the df column in Table A.5, precise degrees of freedom between points 30 and 40, 40 and 60, and 60 and 120 are not provided. Thus, if researchers do not have the exact df as shown in the table, *always* choose the smaller df point in the table rather than the larger one. This is a conservative move and yields slightly larger critical t values to equal or exceed with our observed t values. You are actually making it slightly more difficult to reject null hypotheses, but in close-call situations, it is better to err on the conservative side rather than to be accused of deliberately choosing a critical value that will result in the support of your research hypotheses. Although a headnote explains what to do when this situation occurs in Table A.5, an example is provided below.

A brief example illustrating our choices is if we happen to observe a $t = 1.690$, with 35 degrees of freedom, for the .05 level of significance and a one-tailed hypothesis test. As you can tell by inspecting df values in Table A.5, there is no df = 35. You must decide between df = 30 and df = 40. If you choose df = 40, the critical value of t that you must equal or exceed is 1.684. With df = 30, the critical value of t is 1.697. You will reject H_0 under the first condition but not under the second. What should you do? Several exotic suggestions have been proposed over the years, including interpolating. But in view of the characteristics of the t distribution, interpolation is totally inappropriate. The safest course is to choose df = 30 and decide *not* to reject H_0. If your observed and critical values of statistics are that close together, you probably have observed a chance difference anyway.

Table A.5 provides only one "side" of the t distribution. Since it is perfectly symmetrical, as is the unit normal distribution and also has $\mu = 0$, the other "side" of it is identical to the side shown in this table. We may assign negative $(-)$ t values to those values below the mean of 0 or to the left of it, and positive t values occurring above 0 or to the right of it. This fact is especially important whenever one-tailed hypothesis tests are made.

"Coming or Not Coming from the Same Populations"

Sometimes, interpretations of statistical test results are couched in seemingly unusual language. This "unusual" language might go something like this: "We reject the null hypothesis and conclude that our sample comes from a different population." Another way of saying this is that "The two means (i.e., $\overline{X}$ and μ) come from different populations." Both of these phrases are confusing to beginning students. Remember that statistical inference is the process of saying something about a population of elements based on samples drawn from it. The sample mean is considered the "best estimate" of the hypothesized population mean. When we conduct t or Z tests and find that the two means differ from one another, saying that one mean is not from the same population as the other is the same as saying that they are different.

This phraseology is better understood with a two-sample example. If we drew samples from two classes of criminal justice students, one class from the University of California–Irvine (UCI) and the other from the University of Kentucky (UK), the two samples of students would obviously be independent of one another. Measuring these students on a variable such as their *level of criminal justice aptitude* or their *knowledge of the history of criminology* would probably yield different average scores for the two samples. If we designate the UCI class as N_1 and the UK class as N_2 and their respective means as $\overline{X}_1$ and $\overline{X}_2$, it is assumed that these respective $\overline{X}$'s are estimates of the two populations of UCI and UK scores on these measured variables. Thus $\overline{X}_1$ is an estimate of μ_1, and $\overline{X}_2$ is an estimate of μ_2.

Since we are dealing with sample means, however, we are using them as estimates of their respective $\overline{X}$'s to find whether the μ's difer. If the sample $\overline{X}$'s differ, it will be assumed that the populations from which the samples were derived also differ. Thus we will say that the two samples *come from different populations* on their average "knowledge of criminology history" scores or their "criminal justice aptitude" score averages. If our test of significance shows that the two $\overline{X}_k$'s (where k = the different samples) do not differ from one another significantly, we say that the two samples *come from the same population* regarding the distributions of those variables: their "criminal justice aptitude" or their "knowledge of criminology history." Obviously, the UCI and UK students come from different *school* populations, but their history or aptitude score distributions are sufficiently similar (or different) to conclude that their population distributions of those scores are similar (or different).

Assumptions, Advantages, and Disadvantages of *Z* and *t* Tests

The assumptions of the Z and t tests include (1) randomness, (2) the interval level of measurement underlying the characteristic measured, and (3) a normal distribution associated with the observed scores.

The primary advantages of the t and Z tests are: (1) they are easy to use; (2) tables of critical t and Z values exist for quick and convenient interpretations of observed t and Z values; (3) there are no sample-size restrictions; (4) these tests are well-known and conventionally applied in social scientific work; and (5) these tests have high power at rejecting false null hypotheses. However, there are some strong disadvantages associated with t and Z test applications. Purists might be inclined to disfavor using these procedures, particularly when attitudinal scores are analyzed. The rigorousness of these tests works to their detriment, since they both require that the data analyzed be measured according to interval scales. Popular attitudinal scales such as Likert, Thurstone, and Guttman scaling yield, at best, scores measured according to ordinal scales. Thus applications of t and Z tests to attitudinal information should be treated cautiously and conservatively.

An additional disadvantage of these tests is the assumption requiring normality of distributions of scores. Although we have found that comparatively few researchers actually verify how the scores they analyze are distributed, it is unlikely that normality is achieved in a significant number of these projects. Of course, randomness is seldom achieved in a "perfect" sense, so we must consider multiple assumption violations whenever these tests are applied. Nevertheless, these tests continue to be popular and exhibit widespread application in the social sciences, including criminology and criminal justice, and it is difficult to counter such conventional usages effectively.

Another weakness is that applications of t or Z whenever there are deviant scores present in one's distributions of raw scores analyzed are unreliable. This is because of the distorting impact or effect of deviant scores on the mean. There are no sample-size restrictions regarding the application of t or Z. Use the t table, Table A.5, whenever your sample sizes are 120 or less. Use either Table A.5 or Table A.3 whenever your sample sizes exceed 120 appreciably. However, for extremely large samples of elements, perhaps N's of 500 or larger, standard error terms are greatly decreased. This means that whatever we observe using the t or Z tests will probably be statistically significant, but the substantive meaning of such results may be minimal. Thus we must apply good judgment in determining whether the findings have substantive merit.

GOODNESS-OF-FIT AND NONPARAMETRIC STATISTICAL TESTS

Many nonparametric statistical procedures are known as "goodness-of-fit" tests. "Goodness-of-fit" refers to the "fit" between what is observed and what might be expected according to chance. Another way of viewing goodness-of-fit is as the "fit" between an *observed set of frequencies* and an *expected set of frequencies*. An extreme hypothetical situation serves to illustrate what is meant by goodness of fit. Suppose that we possessed information about a sample of 100 convicted rapists in North Dakota. Further suppose that we knew absolutely nothing about the characteristics of rapists, including their probable gender. (Sometimes the examples we use may seem far-fetched, but in order to understand certain statistical concepts and remember them, these examples are useful.)

Expected distributions or sets of frequencies are often defined by the number of categories into which they are arranged. For instance, if we distributed 300 persons across three categories, we might "expect" 100 persons to be in each of the categories. Our "expected frequencies" would be defined by taking the number of persons, N, and dividing this by the number of categories into which they are dispersed, k, or N/k. If $N = 300$ and $k = 3$, then $300/3 = 100$ frequencies. Thus we would "expect" 100 persons to be in each of the three categories. Applying N/k to the present hypothetical example of North Dakota rapists, we may wish to disperse them into two categories, male and female. To determine how many male and female rapists would be expected to occur "according to chance," we would apply N/k or $100/2 = 50$ to yield the following:

Expected Number of Male and Female Rapists, N		
Male	Female	
50	50	$N = 100$

Thus it would appear from these expected "cell" frequencies that there would be 50 male and 50 female rapists *according to chance*. Again, chance is defined in this instance according to the number of categories into which our data have been divided and our sample size, or N/k. When we tabulate the actual numbers of North Dakota rapists who are male and female, we might observe the following distribution:

Observed Number of Male and Female Rapists, N		
Male	Female	
90	10	$N = 100$

These frequencies are known as our "observed" frequencies, since they are what we actually observe when we tabulate our collected information. The "goodness-of-fit" then becomes the discrepancy between what is observed and what is expected according to chance. Therefore, we would compare the expected 50–50 split with our observed 90–10 split to see the degree of goodness-of-fit. Obviously, there is poor goodness-of-fit between these observed and expected call frequencies. *The greater the discrepancy between what we expect and what we observe, the more significant our observations statistically.* This is important. In the instance above, we would probably conclude that proportionately more of our North Dakota rapists are males rather than females. And if we had applied a goodness-of-fit statistical test to evaluate the discrepancy we observed between the expected and observed cell frequencies, our test results would probably have been significant statistically.

One nonparametric test of significance is presented here: the chi-square test for a single sample. This test is designed for applications where researchers have one or more samples of elements under investigation.

Chi Square for a Single Sample

The chi-square statistic, χ^2, is the most popular goodness-of-fit statistic used in social science literature today. An example from criminal justice literature illustrates the test application.

Adams and Vogel (1986) investigated prostitution, sentencing patterns of those arrested and convicted for the crime, and citizen awareness of its incidence in a North Carolina jurisdiction. Among other objectives, the researchers sought to determine whether there were significant differences between first-offenders (arrested prostitutes) and the frequency with which warnings/releases, fines, or probation were used as optional punishments. First offenders are often treated leniently by judges, although the types of leniency/punishment might vary. Using this idea for our example and a hypothetical sample of 192 convicted prostitutes in a particular North Carolina jurisdiction, we might generate the following hypothesis set:

H_0: There is no difference in the type of punishment imposed on first-offender prostitutes.

H_1: There is a difference in the type of punishment imposed on first-offender prostitutes.

$P \leq .001$ (two-tailed test)

This is a two-tailed or nondirectional test, since no attempt is made to predict the direction of difference associated with the three punishment categories. Table 17.1 shows a hypothetical sample of 192 arrested prostitutes according to whether they have been given warnings by judges and released, whether they have been convicted and ordered to pay fines, or whether they have been convicted and granted probation. This table has been constructed so as to show both the observed and expected frequencies distributed throughout the three punishment categories.

In Table 17.1, both the observed and expected frequencies are presented. The expected frequencies for the three categories have been determined by using N/k, where N is the sample size of numbers of prostitutes ($N = 192$) and k is the number of punishment categories (i.e., whether these prostitutes received warnings and were released, were fined, or received probation). In this case, the expected frequencies were determined as $192/3 = 64$ frequencies per category as illustrated. The formula for the chi-square test for a single sample is as follows:

$$\chi^2 = \frac{(O_k - E_k)^2}{E_k},$$

TABLE 17.1. OBSERVED AND EXPECTED FREQUENCIES FOR A HYPOTHETICAL SAMPLE OF 192 NORTH CAROLINA PROSTITUTES ACCORDING TO PUNISHMENT SEVERITY

First-Offenders	Warning/ Release	Fine	Probation	Total
Observed frequency	121 (63%)	40 (21%)	31 (16%)	192 100%
Expected frequency	64	64	64	192

O_k is the observed frequencies in the kth cell and E_k is the expected frequencies in the kth cell. For the data in Table 17.1, we may carry out our computations as follows:

$$\chi^2 = \frac{(121 - 64)^2}{64} + \frac{(40 - 64)^2}{64} + \frac{(31 - 64)^2}{64}$$

$$= \frac{(57)^2}{64} + \frac{(24)^2}{64} + \frac{(33)^2}{64}$$

$$= \frac{3249}{64} + \frac{576}{64} + \frac{1089}{64}$$

$$= 50.766 + 9.000 + 17.016$$

$$= 76.782$$

The observed chi-square (χ^2) value = 76.782.

To determine the significance of this observed χ^2, we turn to Table A.4. Across the top of the table are two-tailed probabilities. Down the left-hand side of the table are degrees of freedom, df. For the single-sample application of χ^2, df $= k - 1$, where k is the number of categories into which the sample has been divided. In this case, $k = 3$, so df $= k - 1$ or $3 - 1$, or 2 df. Entering Table A.4 with 2 df at the .001 level of significance with a two-tailed test of the hypothesis, we determine where these values intersect in the body of the table. This defines the critical value of χ^2, or 13.815. If our observed χ^2 value equals or exceeds 13.815, we can reject H_0 and support H_1. Since our observed χ^2 value of 76.782 equals or exceeds the critical value in Table A.4, we support H_1: that there is a difference among first-offender prostitutes and the type of punishment they receive.

Headnote instructions in Table A.4 are useful for using the table for one-tailed hypothesis tests. Whenever one-tailed χ^2 applications are desired for single-sample tests, it is necessary to inspect the observed distribution of frequencies to see whether the distribution is in the direction predicted under H_1. Had we predicted that first-offender prostitutes would tend to receive warnings rather than fines or probation, for instance, our data would have been in the "correct" or predicted direction under H_1. One-tailed tests always require careful inspection of the distribution of observed cell frequencies to make sure they are in the predicted direction as specified in our H_1's.

Assumptions, Advantages, and Disadvantages of the Chi-Square Test

Three assumptions underlie proper application of the chi-square test: (1) randomness, (2) the nominal level of measurement, and (3) a sample size equal to 25 or larger. The chi-square test is easy to apply and interpret. It has both one- and two-tailed applications and may be applied to any data in categorical form. An interpretive table (Table A.4) exists for a rapid determination of critical values of this statistic. A major weakness of the chi-square test is the sensitivity of the test to very small and very large samples. The reasonable operating range for this test is sample-size variation from 25 to 250.

An example of the influence of sample-size changes on the magnitude of the observed chi-square value may be provided by doubling the observed frequencies in Table 17.1. Thus, instead of having observed frequencies of 121, 40, and 31, respectively, we would have 242, 80, and 62. We would still have $k = 3$, but we would now be dealing with a sample size double that of 192 or (2) (192) = 384. This would mean that our calculated expected cell frequencies would be 384/3 = 128. If we were to carry out our chi-square computations on this enlarged sample size, the original observed χ^2 of 76.782 would double to 153.564. (The truthfulness of this statement is left for you as a mathematical exercise.)

If you entered Table A.4 with this new value, you might be mistakenly impressed by it, since the largest critical value in the entire table is 59.703 (lower right-hand corner). Remember, however, that the *same* proportionate distribution of frequencies would exist as before, and that *nothing* had actually changed except the fact of *doubling* our cell frequencies. But seemingly, our result would appear to be "more significant" statistically than was originally observed. What is actually occurring here, however, is the dramatic distortion of the original chi square value resulting from its application to a much larger sample size.

Two additional recommendations must be made. First, percentages have been computed for the observed frequencies in Table 17.1. This has been done to illustrate a point. Many researchers erroneously conclude that the chi-square test may be applied to *percentages* meaningfully. This is not true. Such applications would be as though these researchers had a sample size of 100 (100 percent). Every time chi square is computed for percentage values, the sample size for each variable subclass changes to 100, consistent with 100 percent. *Do not compute chi square percentages.* The second admonition pertains to expected cell frequencies. *The chi-square statistic should not be applied to any tabular situation where one or more of the expected cell frequencies is smaller than* 5. The reason for this is simply that you would obtain a distorted chi-square value that might be misinterpreted as a "significant" difference when no significant difference exists.

A wide array of both parametric and nonparametric statistical tests may be found in several introductory statistics texts. Often, these tests are accompanied by discussions of their underlying assumptions and suggested applications. It is beyond the scope of this book to provide an extensive coverage of such tests, but a basis for understanding and applying these other tests has been provided in the discussion above. Beyond tests of significance that may be used for hypothesis-testing purposes, researchers may also wish to determine how variables are correlated or associated. To answer questions about the degree to which variables are "in step" or correlated, various *measures of association* are available. In the final section, a general discussion of association will be provided, including the meaning, nature, direction, significance, and strength of association.

MEANING OF CORRELATIONS, ASSOCIATIONS, AND RELATIONSHIPS

Numerical expressions of the degree to which two variables are "in step" or fluctuate predictably with each other are known as *coefficients of association*. Procedures that yield these coefficients are called *measures of association*. Tests of theory or theoretical schemes often involve measures of association. To what extent do two variables vary with one another? To what extent does a relationship exist between one variable and another? For instance, it might be believed that an association exists between poverty and crime. It may appear that those in lower socioeconomic statuses have higher arrest rates than those in higher socioeconomic statuses. An association would be said to exist between poverty and crime.

In another instance, it might be believed that increasing the number of street lights in a given section of a city will decrease the amount of crime in that section. Subsequently, if researchers observe that well-lighted sections of the city have proportionately fewer crimes committed than do poorly lit city sections, one conclusion drawn might be that an association exists between the incidence of crime and the amount of city lighting.

Measures of association, also known as *relationships* and *correlations*, furnish the platform for making causal statements about variables. Although these terms (relationship, correlation, association) are used interchangeably in criminological research, there are some subtle differences between them. "Association" is preferred because it implies causality the least. "Relationship" and "correlation" imply causality more strongly. Because cause–effect relations between variables are quite difficult to establish empirically, the simple appearance of an association between variables may be misleading. This apparent association is insufficient to assume that a causal relation exists between the variables. Ultimately, we are interested in establishing causal relations between variables. This is what our work is about. But causal models take time to build. Our knowledge of which factors influence others in predictable ways is incomplete at present. Therefore, we approach the task of observing associations between variables with a certain degree of caution and conservatism.

Associations between variables may be described according to (1) the strength of association, (2) the direction of association, (3) the statistical significance of an association, and (4) the predictive utility of the association.

Strength of Association

There are several ways of describing associations between variables. One way is to discuss variable associations in terms of the *strength of the association*. A strong association between variables is gauged according to how closely we approach either +1.00 (a perfect positive association) or −1.00 (a perfect negative association). No association is indicated by 0. Association coefficients are either positive or negative and are typically expressed to the nearest hundredth. From a conventional standpoint, coefficients of association of ± .30 or larger are considered to be "good" in criminological literature. The following crude guide may be used to assess the general strength of association coefficients.

±.00 to .25: no association or low association (weak association)

±.26 to .50: moderately low association (moderately weak association)

±.51 to .75: moderately high association (moderately strong association)

±.76 to 1.00: high association (strong association) up to perfect positive or negative association

Figures 17.1 and 17.2 illustrate (1) a perfect positive association between variables X and Y, and (2) a perfect negative association between variables X and Y. In Figure 17.1, a unit increase in variable X is followed by a unit increase in variable Y. Plotting the intersection points as shown enables us to draw a straight line representing the perfect association between these hypothetical variables. Since this line is fairly straight, it is also considered to be *linear*. *Linearity is a "straight-line" relation between variables.* For example, if a new crime occurs in a given neighborhood for each street light we remove, there will be a linear relation between the number of street lights and the amount of crime. If we observe a 1-inch growth in a plant for each quart of water we give it, a linear relation exists between the amount of water fed to a plant and the amount of growth. Figure 17.2 shows that for each unit increase in variable Y, a unit decrease occurs in a variable X. Plotting the intersecting points in this figure also shows a straight line, but in the opposite direction to that shown in Figure 17.1. This is also a linear association, but in this case it is a perfect negative or *inverse* association.

Nonlinear associations between variables are represented by lines drawn from intersection points that are not aligned in a straight-line fashion. Figure 17.3 represents a *curvilinear* association between variables X and Y. It is probably true that few, if any, variable interrelationships in criminology and criminal justice are truly linear. But for certain measures of association, such as the well-known Pearson r, it is assumed that linearity exists between variables. Thus if linearity

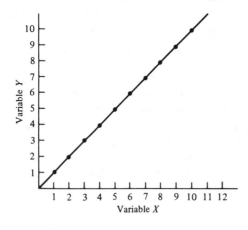

Figure 17.1 Perfect positive association between variables X and Y.

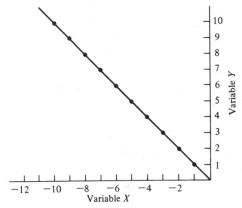

Figure 17.2 Perfect negative (inverse) association between variables X and Y.

does not exist, at least one underlying assumption of this measure of association is not met, and the application of the measure is questionable.

Direction of Association

We can also discuss association in terms of *direction*. If we were to discuss both the strength and direction of .32, for example, this would be a "moderately low (moderately weak) positive association." An association coefficient of $-.55$ would be a "moderately strong (moderately high) negative or inverse association."

Statistical Significance of Association

Another way of discussing association is in terms of its *statistical significance*. Each measure of association can be evaluated in terms of how "significant" the departure of the observed coefficient is from 0. Therefore, practically all measures of association have tests of significance accompanying them. If researchers observe a coefficient of .83, for example, they might say that this coefficient is significant at the .05 level of significance. But as we will soon see, tests of significance applied to measures of association are frequently misleading and inappropriate. A measure's significance depends in large part on the sample size investigated. Larger

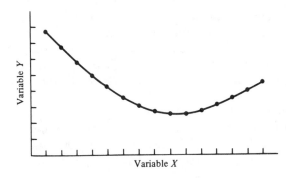

Figure 17.3 Curvilinear association between variables X and Y. Values on variable Y tend to decrease for a time as the values on variable X increase. While X continues to increase, the values on Y begin to increase after a time as well.

Meaning of Correlations, Associations, and Relationships **449** sample sizes will yield greater statistical significance in the same way that larger sample sizes operated to yield greater statistical significance in tests of significance of difference.

An example of how the statistical significance of a measure of association can be badly misinterpreted is the hypothetical case of observing a coefficient = .01, the amount of association between variables X and Y. This means that there is almost no association between the two variables. Using our crude interpretive table above, we might say there is a low positive association between the two variables. Suppose that our sample size is 2000. A sample size this large may reduce our sampling error to such a degree that when we assess how different .01 is from .00 or the .00 − .01 difference, we may conclude that our association coefficient of .01 is significant at the .05 level of significance. So what?

Proportional-Reduction-in-Error (PRE), Explanation, and Prediction

We are directly interested in the predictive power or explanatory utility associated with certain variables in relation to others. If we are concerned about juvenile delinquency, for example, what good will it do for us to know how socioeconomic status or peer-group pressure contribute to delinquency? What kind of association exists between delinquency and broken homes?

These prediction situations involve associations between variables. But our interest is in forecasting accurately anticipated behaviors of persons based on our previous knowledge of other crucial variables. We would like to be able to say, "If X, then Y." Certainly, a juvenile delinquency rehabilitation center would like to "cure" all delinquents who participate in the center's program. Of course, this example assumes perfect prediction. Unfortunately, our predictions of these and other behaviors are more or less imperfect. Whatever we fail to predict accurately is called *error*. Therefore, we devote much time to identifying, measuring, and utilizing variables that will minimize errors in our prediction schemes.

Using certain measures of association in our research will often serve the function of telling us how much error we have accounted for in predicting particular behavioral outcomes. Recalling an example used in a previous chapter, suppose that we are interested in the association between delinquency and whether children are or are not continuously supervised by adults. We may believe that children who are continuously supervised by adults will have little or no opportunity to commit delinquent acts. Those youths who do not have continuous adult supervision may be in a better position to commit delinquent acts if they choose to do so. Therefore, we predict initially that delinquency will depend on whether or not children are under continuous adult supervision. We expect to find the association between these two variables, *delinquency* and *degree of adult supervision*, as shown in Table 17.2.

In Table 17.2, we have samples of 50 delinquents and 50 nondelinquents. We cross-tabulate them according to whether or not they are continuously supervised by adults. Under an error-free model that we might construct, we would find all delinquent youths not subject to continuous adult supervision, whereas we

TABLE 17.2. ERROR-FREE RELATION BETWEEN DELINQUENCY AND CONTINUITY OF ADULT SUPERVISION OVER YOUTHS

| | Continuous adult supervision | |
	Yes	No
Delinquent	0	50
Nondelinquent	50	0

would find all nondelinquent youths under continuous adult supervision. There are no "errors." But what if we observe something "less than perfect," such as the cross-tabulation shown in Table 17.3?

Table 17.3 contains 15 "errors." There are five youths who are delinquent but who are also continuously supervised by adults. There are 10 nondelinquent youths who are not supervised continuously by adults. These 15 youths are "errors," in that they depart from our perfect forecast as shown in Table 17.2. Although our knowledge of whether or not the youths are continuously supervised by adults did not result in perfect prediction in this case, we *did* manage to account for a large amount of the "error" we would have without this knowledge. We accounted for 85 of the cases of delinquents and nondelinquents, but we failed to account for the remaining 15 cases.

If we had predicted that all youths in our sample of 100 were delinquent, we would have been wrong 50 times, since 50 of these youths turned out to be nondelinquent. Accordingly, had we predicted that all 100 youths would be nondelinquent, we would have made 50 errors, since 50 of the youths turned out to be delinquent. With a knowledge of continuous or noncontinuous supervision, however, we have minimized our prediction error as follows:

$$\frac{\text{original error} - \text{error with continuous adult supervision variable}}{\text{original error}} (100)$$

$$= \frac{50 - 15}{50} (100)$$

$$= \frac{35}{50} (100)$$

$$= 70 \text{ percent.}$$

By using the adult supervision variable, we have reduced our error in predicting delinquency for these 100 youths by 70 percent. Instead of committing 50 errors as we did originally, we commit only 15 errors using a predictor variable such as adult supervision. We have reduced the actual number of errors from 50 to 15, a 70 percent error reduction. This *proportional-reduction-in-error* is conventionally designated as PRE. Some measures of association have PRE interpretations; other measures do not have them. Generally, measures of association

TABLE 17.3. IMPERFECT RELATION
BETWEEN DELINQUENCY AND CONTINUITY
OF ADULT SUPERVISION

	Continuous adult supervision	
	Yes	No
Delinquent	5	40
Nondelinquent	45	10

having PRE interpretations are preferred over those not having such interpretations. Thus whether measures have PRE interpretations becomes one of the criteria we use to select our measures of association to apply in our analysis of data.

PRE is perhaps the most important criterion used for discussing coefficients of association. We may compare variables to see which are better predictors of phenomena than other variables. In most cases, those measures of association that have PRE interpretations usually have *symmetric* PRE interpretations. This means that whether we use variable X as a predictor of variable Y or variable Y as a predictor of variable X, both scenarios will yield identical coefficients of the same magnitude. In a few cases, some measures of association have *both symmetric* and *asymmetric* interpretations. When measures have asymmetric interpretations, this means that we can determine *which variable is the better predictor of the other*. For instance, if we used variable X as a predictor of Y and then use variable Y as a predictor of X, coefficients of *different magnitudes* will be yielded by our computations. This occurrence is from a measure of association with an *asymmetric* interpretation. One such measure is *lambda, the coefficient of predictability*. It has *both* asymmetric (directional) and symmetric (nondirectional) interpretations.

In popular statistical programs and "packages," such as the Statistical Package for the Social Sciences (SPSS), as many as 30 different measures of association may be calculated. Not all of these measures are suitable for a particular research problem, however. As is the case with different tests of significance, each measure of association has advantages, disadvantages, assumptions, and limited applications. Depending on the data we have collected, we may or may not be able to apply certain measures.

For instance, specialized measures of association exist to determine degrees of association between pairs of variables, where one is measured according to one level of measurement (e.g., nominal, ordinal, interval) and the other is measured according to a different measurement level. Two-variable level of measurement combinations, such as nominal–ordinal, nominal–interval, and ordinal–interval, have special correlational techniques associated with them, such as *theta* (the coefficient of differentiation), *eta* (the correlation ratio), and Jaspen's *M* (Champion, 1981). When we identify the level of measurement attained for any particular two-variable combination, therefore, certain measures of association are applicable, while other measures are not applicable. Therefore, it is *not* the case that all measures of association have blanket application to a common research problem or data set. It is beyond the scope of this book to provide an in-depth discussion of measures of association. These are normally included in basic statistics courses that often accompany the first methods course. More extensive discussion of different measures of association may be found in several introductory statistics books, some of which are listed in the Bibliography, Appendix D.

WHICH TESTS SHOULD YOU USE?

The artful nature of criminological research is such that blanket generalizations about statistical applications that cover all types of situations are unwarranted. Choices of statistical tests for particular applications should be made carefully, in part, by weighing both the strengths and weaknesses of different procedures under consideration. Compared with procedure A, for example, procedure B may be more powerful. But procedure B may require normality of distribution, whereas procedure A has no such prerequisite. Procedure A may be easier to apply directly to raw scores, whereas procedure B may require that data be transformed into ranks or different kinds of categories. Procedure B may yield distorted results if sample sizes are too small or too large, whereas procedure A may be applicable to samples of diverse sizes without incurring substantial distortion effects.

In many cases, statistical tests have been tailor-made for particular kinds of research problems. But you must pay attention to the assumptions underlying each test before deciding whether it can be applied. Researchers run certain risks by applying tests where the assumptions of those tests have not been fully satisfied.

Three Common Assumption Violations

Perhaps the three most frequent assumption violations committed by many researchers are (1) violating the level of measurement assumption, (2) violating the normality assumption, and (3) violating the randomness assumption.

The level of measurement assumption associated with statistical tests pertains to how raw scores have been obtained and measured. If the scales used to quantify these scores are ordinal scales, treating these scores as though they are interval-level scores is an assumption violation. How serious an assumption violation is this? Few researchers would attach much meaning to averaged Social Security numbers. Few researchers would attach much meaning to 3.2 as the "average religion" for some sample, or somewhere between a Catholic and a Protestant. These examples relate to averaging nominal-level variables. Perhaps averaging ordinal-level variables is less serious. In Chapter 9 we described levels of measurement and their importance for researchers. There is no doubt that certain arithmetic operations applied to certain kinds of data have questionably meaningful results. Yet, when the literature is surveyed, numerous instances are found where means or averages have been applied to attitudinal information. One might conclude that it is conventional to treat ordinal-level variables as though they were actually measured according to interval scales.

Choices of statistical tests are justified to a great degree by the nature of data collected and what researchers want to do with the data. Perhaps a parametric test might furnish certain results that cannot be provided by nonparametric procedures. However, every parametric procedure has a nonparametric counterpart that is designed specifically to be applied when certain assumptions, such as the interval level of measurement, are not satisfied. The parametric t test has an equivalent nonparametric counterpart, the Mann–Whitney U test. Similarly, the parametric F test for analysis of variance has a nonparametric counterpart, the Kruskal–Wallis H test (Champion, 1981). Thus with alternative nonparametric tests available that can answer the same kinds of questions as parametric tests, why would researchers knowingly choose tests that violate the level-of-measurement assumption when other tests exist that do not violate it? The most plausible answer is *convention*. Thus inappropriate statistical tests are often selected simply because many other researchers also choose them.

A second important assumption underlying parametric tests is *normality*. Raw scores should be distributed in a fashion similar to the unit normal distribution in order for a parametric test's meaning to be maximized. However, few researchers ever take the time to assess how their sample raw scores are distributed. The normality assumption is often ignored. One reason it is ignored is because researchers assume it has been met as the result of the randomness initially used to select their samples. But we have seen that randomness merely enhances the chances of getting a distribution of scores that may be normal in form. No guarantees exist that normality will occur for any raw score distribution, regardless of how the sample is drawn. If it is true that the normality assumption is seldom checked (no one knows how much or how little verification is actually conducted among criminologists concerning the normality of their distributions of raw scores studied), and if it is also true that the main reason for this lack of "quality control" is the presumption that randomness will likely yield normality, an even greater problem probably exists.

This "greater problem" pertains to the third type of assumption violation: failure to meet the randomness requirement in obtaining probability samples. Almost every research project exhibits some amount of nonresponse. The mailed questionnaire, perhaps one of the cheapest and most popular methods of data collection, has nonresponse ranging from 20 to 80 percent. Typical nonresponse rates are variously given as 30 percent, 40 percent, or 50 percent. Some researchers appear genuinely excited when they obtain response rates from mailed questionnaires that are in excess of 50 percent. Therefore, we may conclude that true random samples are usually not obtained, at least not complete ones. That is, those random samples originally sought by researchers and clearly delineated by them are often short a certain percentage of respondents or elements.

How should we label "samples of random samples"? Should we continue to call samples "random" even though only 50 or 60 percent of all selected elements respond? Again, the literature is replete with examples of this problem furnished by seasoned professionals. Usually, a short paragraph in one's research article is devoted to how the sample was obtained. Where nonresponse occurs, some note may be made of it. But a typical conclusion is that those who did not respond probably would not have affected the outcome of findings anyway. This is a curious statement. How does anyone know what the nonrespondents were like and whether their responses would have influenced the final results? Perhaps the nonresponse problem is a matter of degree, and perhaps, if a 10 percent nonresponse rate occurred, the addition of the remaining 10 percent of all randomly selected elements would not make a great deal of difference. But where should the line be drawn? What if the nonresponse is one-third of all originally selected elements? What if the nonresponse is one-half of all originally selected elements?

The problem of assumption violations and what to do about them is a difficult one and not easily resolved. Convention encourages that procedures be followed because many professionals follow them. Certain statistical procedures are well-known, and therefore, they should be applied. The attempt to use randomness in one's sample selection probably means that normality will be achieved in some distribution of scores, doesn't it? Certainly, a little nonresponse will not make much difference to our final results.

But let us recall that the research enterprise is like a chain of interconnected links. The strength of each link determines the strength of the chain. Statistical tests are only one link in this research chain. No research project will succeed or fail simply because of statistical misapplications. But our research chain may be strengthened or weakened by our choices if it is decided that statistical tests should be applied. There are both qualitative and quantitative research choices, and statistical applications may be inappropriate for certain types of projects.

The perspective adopted here is a conservative one. If serious assumption violations exist regarding the application of certain statistical procedures, serious thought should be given to selecting alternative statistical procedures where these assumptions are either not violated or not violated to the same degree. A clear preference exists for parametric tests to be applied, provided that all of their requisite assumptions are satisfied. They are the most powerful and most sensitive tests for our statistical purposes. But if any one or more assumptions associated with these tests are violated, serious consideration should be given to choosing equivalent nonparametric tests that are designed to accomplish the same function. This is the safe, conservative alternative. However, as we have seen, convention is a powerful force that often causes researchers to make statistical test selections on the basis of their popularity and usage rather than on the basis of technical assumptions. This issue remains controversial and otherwise unresolved.

SUMMARY

Statistical inference is the process of estimating population parameters by studying the characteristics of samples or sample statistics. Researchers engage in two types of estimation in the course of their inferential work. Point estimation involves stating in advance a hypothetical population value and comparing it with a sample statistic as its counterpart in a subsequent sample randomly drawn. Interval estimation is the preferred alternative, inasmuch as the researcher obtains an estimate of the range around an observed sample mean that has a strong likelihood of overlapping or including the population mean.

Population values are the targets of estimation work. Sample statistics function as estimates of population parameters. Normally, probabilities are assigned to the intervals estimated by the researcher, which specify a likelihood of including population parameter values.

Statistical tests of significance of difference are grouped according to whether they are parametric or nonparametric procedures. Parametric tests ordinarily are more powerful, assume normality about distributions of raw scores to which they are applied, and often require the interval level of measurement underlying the scores examined. They are considered popular and quite sensitive in hypothesis testing. Two parametric tests are the Z test and the t test. Nonparametric tests, such as the chi-square test, are considered less rigorous than parametric tests. Generally, they have fewer restrictive assumptions underlying them. For instance, they do not require normality of score distributions when they are applied. They are comparatively less powerful and designed largely for data measured according to nominal or ordinal scales. Most parametric tests have nonparametric counterparts. Nonparametric tests are preferred whenever several assumptions associated with parametric tests are violated. Besides tests of statistical significance, researchers apply measures of association to determine how two or more variables are correlated or are "in step" with one another. Different measures of association exist, depending on the levels of measurement achieved by the different variables to be correlated.

QUESTIONS FOR REVIEW AND PROBLEMS TO SOLVE

1. Differentiate between parametric and nonparametric statistical tests. What are some identifying characteristics of each?
2. What is a confidence interval? Give an example.
3. What is the difference between point estimation and interval estimation? Which method of estimation is preferred, and why?
4. Given $s_{\bar{x}} = 2.55$, $N = 108$, and $\overline{X}_{obs} = 100$, determine the following.
   (a) 90 percent confidence interval.
   (b) 80 percent confidence interval.
   (c) 99 percent confidence interval.
5. With $\overline{X}_{obs} = 100$, $N = 65$, and $x = 24$, determine the following.
   (a) 95 percent confidence interval.
   (b) 80 percent confidence interval.
   (c) 85 percent confidence interval.
6. Determine the confidence intervals for each of the following, where $\overline{X}_{obs} = 330$, $s = 25$, and $N = 145$.
   (a) 88 percent confidence interval.
   (b) 95 percent confidence interval.
   (c) 70 percent confidence interval.

7. On the basis of the magnitudes of the confidence intervals you established in Problem 6, what can be said generally about increasing and decreasing the percentages of confidence intervals you have determined and the likelihood that the population mean is overlapped? Explain.

8. Identify the Z values you chose for solving Problems 5 and 6.

9. With $s = 15$, $N = 220$, and $\overline{X}_{obs} = 122$, determine the following.
   (a) 85 percent confidence interval.
   (b) 95 percent confidence interval.
   (c) 65 percent confidence interval.

10. You have the following information: $\overline{X}_{obs} = 25$, $s_{\bar{x}} = 3$. You have previously hypothesized the population mean to be 30. Using the .01 level of significance, conduct a two-tailed test Z test to see whether 25 is significantly different from 30 at the .01 level. Next, construct a confidence interval around the observed mean $= 25$. What Z value did you use for this confidence interval? What is the relation between two-tailed hypothesis tests of point estimation and confidence interval problems relating to the same sample means and identical significance levels?

Appendix A

Statistical Tables

TABLE A.1 Table of Squares and Square Roots From 1–1000.

N	N²	√N	N	N²	√N
1	1	1.0000	29	841	5.3852
2	4	1.4142	30	900	5.4772
3	9	1.7321	31	961	5.5678
4	16	2.0000	32	1024	5.6569
5	25	2.2361	33	1089	7.7446
6	36	2.4495	34	1156	5.8310
7	49	2.6458	35	1225	5.9161
8	64	2.8284	36	1296	6.0000
9	81	3.0000	37	1369	6.0828
10	100	3.1623	38	1444	6.1644
11	121	3.3166	39	1521	6.2450
12	144	3.4641	40	1600	6.3246
13	169	3.6056	41	1681	6.4031
14	196	3.7417	42	1764	6.4807
15	225	3.8730	43	1849	6.5574
16	324	4.0000	44	1936	6.6332
17	289	4.1231	45	2025	6.7082
18	324	4.2426	46	2116	6.7823
19	361	4.3589	47	2209	6.8557
20	400	4.4721	48	2304	6.9282
21	441	4.5826	49	2401	7.0000
22	484	4.6904	50	2500	7.0711
23	529	4.7958	51	2601	7.1414
24	576	4.8990	52	2704	7.2111
25	625	5.0000	53	2809	7.2801
26	676	5.0990	54	2916	7.3485
27	729	5.1962	55	3025	7.4162
28	784	5.2915	56	3136	7.4833

N	N²	√N	N	N²	√N
57	3249	7.5498	85	7225	9.2195
58	3364	7.6158	86	7396	9.2736
59	3481	7.6811	87	7569	9.3274
60	3600	7.7460	88	7744	9.3808
61	3721	7.8102	89	7921	9.4340
62	3844	7.8740	90	8100	9.4868
63	3969	7.9373	91	8281	9.5394
64	4096	8.0000	92	8464	9.5917
65	4225	8.0623	93	8649	9.6437
66	4356	8.1240	94	8836	9.6954
67	4489	8.1854	95	9025	9.7468
68	4624	8.2462	96	9216	9.7980
69	4761	8.3066	97	9409	9.8489
70	4900	8.3666	98	9604	9.8995
71	5041	8.4261	99	9801	9.9499
72	5184	8.4853	100	10000	10.0000
73	5329	8.5440	101	10201	10.0499
74	5476	8.6023	102	10404	10.0995
75	5625	8.6603	103	10609	10.1489
76	5776	8.7178	104	10816	10.1980
77	5929	8.7750	105	11025	10.2470
78	6084	8.8318	106	11236	10.2956
79	6241	8.8882	107	11449	10.3441
80	6400	8.9443	108	11664	10.3923
81	6561	9.0000	109	11881	10.4403
82	6724	9.0554	110	12100	10.4881
83	6889	9.1104	111	12321	10.5357
84	7056	9.1652	112	12544	10.5830

N	N^2	$\sqrt{N}$	N	N^2	$\sqrt{N}$
113	12769	10.6301	141	19881	11.8743
114	12996	10.6771	142	20164	11.9164
115	13225	10.7238	143	20449	11.9583
116	13456	10.7703	144	20736	12.0000
117	13689	10.8167	145	21025	12.0416
118	13924	10.8628	146	21316	12.0830
119	14161	10.9087	147	21609	12.1244
120	14400	10.9545	148	21904	12.1655
121	14641	11.0000	149	22201	12.2000
122	14884	11.0454	150	22500	12.2474
123	15129	11.0905	151	22801	12.2882
124	15376	11.1355	152	23104	12.3288
125	15625	11.1803	153	23409	12.3693
126	15876	11.2250	154	23716	12.4097
127	16129	11.2694	155	24025	12.4499
128	16384	11.3137	156	24336	12.4900
129	16641	11.3578	157	24649	12.5300
130	16900	11.4018	158	24964	12.5698
131	17161	11.4455	159	25281	12.6095
132	17424	11.4891	160	25600	12.6491
133	17689	11.5326	161	25921	12.6886
134	17956	11.5758	162	26244	12.7279
135	18225	11.6190	163	26569	12.7671
136	18496	11.6619	164	26896	12.8062
137	18769	11.7047	165	27225	12.8452
138	19044	11.7473	166	27556	12.8841
139	19321	11.7808	167	27889	12.9228
140	19600	11.8322	168	28224	12.9615

N	N²	√N	N	N²	√N
169	28561	13.0000	197	38809	14.0357
170	28900	13.0384	198	39204	14.0712
171	29241	13.0767	199	39601	14.1067
172	29584	13.1149	200	40000	14.1421
173	29929	13.1529	201	40401	14.1774
174	30276	13.1909	202	40804	14.2127
175	30625	13.2288	203	41209	14.2478
176	30976	13.2665	204	41616	14.2829
177	31329	13.3041	205	42025	14.3178
178	31684	13.3417	206	42436	14.3527
179	32041	13.3791	207	42849	14.3875
180	32400	13.4164	208	43264	14.4222
181	32761	13.4536	209	43681	14.4568
182	33124	13.4907	210	44100	14.4914
183	33489	13.5277	211	44521	14.5258
184	33856	13.5647	212	44944	14.5602
185	34225	13.6015	213	45369	14.5945
186	34596	13.6382	214	45796	14.6287
187	34969	13.6748	215	46225	14.6629
188	35344	13.7113	216	46656	14.6969
189	35721	13.7477	217	47089	14.7309
190	36100	13.7840	218	47524	14.7648
191	36481	13.8023	219	47961	14.7986
192	36864	13.8564	220	48400	14.8324
193	37249	13.8924	221	48841	14.8661
194	37636	13.9284	222	49284	14.8997
195	38025	13.9642	223	49729	14.9332
196	38416	14.0000	224	50176	14.9666

N	N^2	$\sqrt{N}$	N	N^2	$\sqrt{N}$
225	50625	15.0000	253	64009	15.9060
226	51076	15.0333	254	64516	15.9374
227	51529	15.0665	255	65025	15.9687
228	51984	15.0997	256	65536	16.0000
229	52441	15.1327	257	66049	16.0312
230	52900	15.1658	258	66564	16.0624
231	53361	15.1987	259	67081	16.0935
232	53824	15.2315	260	67600	16.1245
233	54289	15.2643	261	68121	16.1555
234	54756	15.2971	262	68644	16.1864
235	55225	15.3297	263	69169	16.2173
236	55696	15.3623	264	69696	16.2481
237	56169	15.3948	265	70225	16.2788
238	56644	15.4272	266	70756	16.3095
239	57121	15.4596	267	71289	16.3401
240	57600	15.4919	268	71824	16.3707
241	58081	15.5242	269	72361	16.4012
242	58564	15.5563	270	72900	16.4317
243	59049	15.5885	271	73441	16.4621
244	59536	15.6205	272	73984	16.4924
245	60025	15.6525	273	74529	16.5227
246	60516	15.6844	274	75076	16.5529
247	61009	15.7162	275	75625	16.5831
248	61504	15.7480	276	76176	16.6132
249	62001	15.7797	277	76729	16.6433
250	62500	15.8114	278	77284	16.6733
251	63001	15.8430	279	77841	16.7033
252	63504	15.8745	280	78400	16.7332

(*continued*)

N	N²	√N	N	N²	√N
281	78961	16.7631	309	95481	17.5784
282	79524	16.7929	310	96100	17.6068
283	80089	16.8226	311	96721	17.6352
284	80656	16.8523	312	97344	17.6635
285	81225	16.8819	313	97969	17.6918
286	81796	16.9115	314	98596	17.7200
287	82369	16.9411	315	99225	17.7482
288	82944	16.9706	316	99856	17.7764
289	83521	17.0000	317	100489	17.8045
290	84100	17.0294	318	101124	17.8326
291	84681	17.0587	319	101761	17.8606
292	85264	17.0880	320	102400	17.8885
293	85849	17.1172	321	103041	17.9165
294	86436	17.1464	322	103684	17.9444
295	87025	17.1756	323	104329	17.9722
296	87616	17.2047	324	104976	18.0000
297	88209	17.2337	325	105625	18.0278
298	88804	17.2627	326	106276	18.0555
299	89401	17.2916	327	106929	18.0831
300	90000	17.3205	328	107584	18.1108
301	90601	17.3494	329	108241	18.1384
302	91204	17.3781	330	108900	18.1659
303	91809	17.4069	331	109561	18.1934
304	92416	17.4356	332	110224	18.2209
305	93025	17.4642	333	110889	18.2483
306	93636	17.4929	334	111556	18.2757
307	94249	17.5214	335	112225	18.3030
308	94864	17.5499	336	112896	18.3303

N	N^2	$\sqrt{N}$	N	N^2	$\sqrt{N}$
337	113569	18.3576	365	133225	19.1050
338	114244	18.3848	366	133956	19.1311
339	114921	18.4120	367	134689	19.1572
340	115600	18.4391	368	135424	19.1833
341	116281	18.4662	369	136161	19.2094
342	116964	18.4932	370	136900	19.2354
343	117649	18.5203	371	137641	19.2614
344	118336	18.5472	372	138384	19.2873
345	119025	18.5742	373	139129	19.3132
346	119716	18.6011	374	139876	19.3391
347	120409	18.6279	375	140625	19.3649
348	121104	18.6548	376	141376	19.3907
349	121801	18.6815	377	142129	19.4165
350	122500	18.7083	378	142884	19.4422
351	123201	18.7350	379	143641	19.4679
352	123904	18.7617	380	144400	19.4936
353	124609	18.7883	381	145161	19.5192
354	125316	18.8149	382	145924	19.5448
355	126025	18.8414	383	146689	19.5704
356	126736	18.8680	384	147456	19.5959
357	127449	18.8944	385	148225	19.6214
358	128164	18.9209	386	148996	19.6469
359	128881	18.9473	387	149769	19.6723
360	129600	18.9737	388	150544	19.6977
361	130321	19.0000	389	151321	19.7231
362	131044	19.0263	390	152100	19.7484
363	131769	19.0526	391	152881	19.7737
364	132486	19.0788	392	153664	19.7990

N	N²	√N	N	N²	√N
393	153664	19.8242	421	177241	20.5183
394	155236	19.8494	422	178084	20.5426
395	156025	19.8746	423	178929	20.5670
396	156816	19.8997	424	179776	20.5913
397	157609	19.9249	425	180625	20.6155
398	158404	19.9499	426	181476	20.6398
399	159210	19.9750	427	182329	20.6640
400	160000	20.0000	428	183184	20.6882
401	160801	20.0250	429	184041	20.7123
402	161604	20.0499	430	184900	20.7364
403	162409	20.0749	431	185761	20.7605
404	163216	20.0998	432	186624	20.7846
405	164025	20.1246	433	187489	20.8087
406	164836	20.1494	434	188356	20.8327
407	165649	20.1742	435	189225	20.8567
408	166464	20.1990	436	190096	20.8806
409	167281	20.2237	437	190969	20.9045
410	168100	20.2485	438	191844	20.9284
411	168921	20.2731	439	192721	20.9523
412	169744	20.2978	440	193600	20.9762
413	170569	20.3224	441	194481	21.0000
414	171396	20.3470	442	195364	21.0238
415	172225	20.3715	443	196249	21.0476
416	173056	20.3961	444	197136	21.0713
417	173889	20.4206	445	198025	21.0950
418	174724	20.4450	446	198916	21.0950
419	175561	20.4695	447	199809	21.1187
420	176400	20.4939	448	200704	21.1424

N	N²	√N	N	N²	√N
449	201601	21.1896	477	227529	21.8403
450	202500	21.2132	478	228484	21.8632
451	203401	21.2368	479	229441	21.8861
452	204304	21.2603	480	230400	21.9089
453	205200	21.2838	481	231361	21.9317
454	206116	21.3073	482	232324	21.9545
455	207025	21.3307	483	233289	21.9773
456	207936	21.3542	484	234256	22.0000
457	208849	21.3776	485	235225	22.0227
458	209764	21.4009	486	236196	22.0454
459	210681	21.4243	487	237169	22.0681
460	211600	21.4476	488	238144	22.0907
461	212521	21.4709	489	239121	22.1133
462	213444	21.4942	490	240100	22.1359
463	214369	21.5174	491	241081	22.1585
464	215296	21.5407	492	242064	22.1811
465	216225	21.5639	493	243049	22.2036
466	217156	21.5870	494	244036	22.2261
467	218089	21.6102	495	245025	22.2486
468	219024	21.6333	496	246016	22.2711
469	219961	21.6564	497	247009	22.2935
470	220900	21.6795	498	248004	22.3159
471	221841	21.7025	499	249001	22.3383
472	222784	21.7256	500	250000	22.3607
473	223729	21.7486	501	251001	22.3830
474	224676	21.7715	502	252004	22.4054
475	225625	21.7945	503	253009	22.4277
476	226576	21.8174	504	254016	22.4499

10,000 Samp. 1,000

TABLE A.2
Random Numbers.

10097 32533	76520 13586	34673 54876	80959 09117	39292 74945
37542 04805	64894 74296	24805 24037	20636 10402	00822 91665
08422 68953	19645 09303	23209 02560	15953 34764	35080 33606
99019 02529	09376 70715	38311 31165	88676 74397	04436 27659
12807 99970	80157 36147	64032 36653	98951 16877	12171 76833
66065 74717	34072 76850	36697 36170	65813 39885	11199 29170
31060 10805	45571 82406	35303 42614	86799 07439	23403 09732
85269 77602	02051 65692	68665 74818	73053 85247	18623 88579
63573 32135	05325 47048	90553 57548	28468 28709	83491 25624
73796 45753	03529 64778	35808 34282	60935 20344	35273 88435
98520 17767	14905 68607	22109 40558	60970 93433	50500 73998
11805 05431	39808 27732	50725 68248	29405 24201	52775 67851
83452 99634	06288 98083	13746 70078	18475 40610	68711 77817
88685 40200	86507 58401	36766 67951	90364 76493	29609 11062
99594 67348	87517 64969	91826 08928	93785 61368	23478 34113
65481 17674	17468 50950	58047 76974	73039 57186	40218 16544
80124 35635	17727 08015	45318 22374	21115 78253	14385 53763
74350 99817	77402 77214	43236 00210	45521 64237	96286 02655
69916 26803	66252 29148	36936 87203	76621 13990	94400 56418
09893 20505	14225 68514	46427 56788	96297 78822	54382 14598
91499 14523	68479 27686	46162 83554	94750 89923	37089 20048
80336 94598	26940 36858	70297 34135	53140 33340	42050 82341
44104 81949	85157 47954	32979 26575	57600 40881	22222 06413
12550 73742	11100 02040	12860 74697	96644 89439	28707 25815
63606 49329	16505 34484	40219 52563	43651 77082	07207 31790
61196 90446	26457 47774	51924 33729	65394 59593	42582 60527
15474 45266	95270 79953	59367 83848	82396 10118	33211 59466
94557 28573	67897 54387	54622 44431	91190 42592	92927 45973
42481 16213	97344 08721	16868 48767	03071 12059	25701 46670
23523 78317	73208 89837	68935 91416	26252 29663	05522 82562
04493 52494	75246 33824	45862 51025	61962 79335	65337 12472
00549 97654	64051 88159	96119 63896	54692 82391	23287 29529
35963 15307	26898 09354	33351 35462	77974 50024	90103 39333
59808 08391	45427 26842	83609 49700	13021 24892	78565 20106
46058 85236	01390 92286	77281 44077	93910 83647	70617 42941
32179 00597	87379 25241	05567 07007	86743 17157	85394 11838
69234 61406	20117 45204	15956 60000	18743 92423	97118 96338
19565 41430	01758 75379	40419 21585	66674 36806	84962 85207
45155 14938	19476 07246	43667 94543	59047 90033	20826 69541
94864 31994	36168 10851	34888 81553	01540 35456	05014 51176
98086 24826	45240 28404	44999 08896	39094 73407	35441 31880
33185 16232	41941 50949	89435 48581	88695 41994	37548 73043
80951 00406	96382 70774	20151 23387	25016 25298	94624 61171
79752 49140	71961 28296	69861 02591	74852 20539	00387 59579
18633 32537	98145 06571	31010 24674	05455 61427	77938 91936
74029 43902	77557 32270	97790 17119	52527 58021	80814 51748
54178 45611	80993 37143	05335 12969	56127 19255	36040 90324
11664 49883	52079 84827	59381 71539	09973 33440	88461 23356
48324 77928	31249 64710	02295 36870	32307 57546	15020 09994
69074 94138	87637 91976	35584 04401	10518 21615	01848 76938

Source: The Rand Corporation, *A Million Random Digits* (New York: The Free Press, 1955). By permission of the publishers.

Statistical Tables   App. A

(continued)

09188	20097	32825	39527	04220	86304	83389	87374	64278	58044
90045	85497	51981	50654	94938	81997	91870	76150	68476	64659
73189	50207	47677	26269	62290	64464	27124	67018	41361	82760
75768	76490	20971	87749	90429	12272	95375	05871	93823	43178
54016	44056	66281	31003	00682	27398	20714	53295	07706	17813
08358	69910	78542	42785	13661	58873	04618	97553	31223	08420
28306	03264	81333	10591	40510	07893	32604	60475	94119	01840
53840	86233	81594	13628	51215	90290	28466	68795	77762	20791
91757	53741	61613	62269	50263	90212	55781	76514	83483	47055
89415	92694	00397	58391	12607	17646	48949	72306	94541	37408
77513	03820	86864	29901	68414	82774	51908	13980	72893	55507
19502	37174	69979	20288	55210	29773	74287	75251	65344	67415
21818	59313	93278	81757	05686	73156	07082	85046	31853	38452
51474	66499	68107	23621	94049	91345	42836	09191	08007	45449
99559	68331	62535	24170	69777	12830	74819	78142	43860	72834
33713	48007	93584	72869	51926	64721	58303	29822	93174	93972
85274	86893	11303	22970	28834	34137	73515	90400	71148	43643
84133	89640	44035	52166	73852	70091	61222	60561	62327	18423
56732	16234	17395	96131	10123	91622	85496	57560	81604	18880
65138	56806	87648	85261	34313	65861	45875	21069	85644	47277
38001	02176	81719	11711	71602	92937	74219	64049	65584	49698
37402	96397	01304	77586	56271	10086	47324	62605	40030	37438
97125	40348	87083	31417	21815	39250	75237	62047	15501	29578
21826	41134	47143	34072	64638	85902	49139	06441	03856	54552
73135	42742	95719	09035	85794	74296	08789	88156	64691	19202
07638	77929	03061	18072	96207	44156	23821	99538	04713	66994
60528	83441	07954	19814	59175	20695	05533	52139	61212	06455
83596	35655	06958	92983	05128	09719	77433	53783	92301	50498
10850	62746	99599	10507	13499	06319	53075	71839	06410	19362
39820	98952	43622	63147	64421	80814	43800	09351	31024	73167
59580	06478	75569	78800	88835	54486	23768	06156	04111	08408
38508	07341	23793	48763	90822	97022	17719	04207	95954	49953
30692	70668	94688	16127	56196	80091	82067	63400	05462	69200
65443	95659	18288	27437	49632	24041	08337	65676	96299	90836
27267	50264	13192	72294	07477	44606	17985	48911	97341	30358
91307	06991	19072	24210	36699	53728	28825	35793	28976	66252
68434	94688	84473	13622	62126	98408	12843	82590	09815	93146
48908	15877	54745	24591	35700	04754	83824	52692	54130	55160
06913	45197	42672	78601	11883	09528	63011	98901	14974	40344
10455	16019	14210	33712	91342	37821	88325	80851	43667	70883
12883	97343	65027	61184	04285	01392	17974	15077	90712	26769
21778	30976	38807	36961	31649	42096	63281	02023	08816	47449
19523	59515	65122	59659	86283	68258	69572	13798	16435	91529
67245	52670	35583	16563	79246	86686	76463	34222	26655	90802
60584	47377	07500	37992	45134	26529	26760	83637	41326	44344
53853	41377	36066	94850	58838	73859	49364	73331	96240	43642
24637	38736	74384	89342	52623	07992	12369	18601	03742	83873
83080	12451	38992	22815	07759	51777	97377	27585	51972	37867
16444	24334	36151	99073	27493	70939	85130	32552	54846	54759
60790	18157	57178	65762	11161	78576	45819	52979	65130	04860

TABLE A.2

(continued)

03991	10461	93716	16894	66083	24653	84609	58232	88618	19161
38555	95554	32886	59780	08355	60860	29735	47762	71299	23853
17546	73704	92052	46215	55121	29281	59076	07936	27954	58909
32643	52861	95819	06831	00911	98936	76355	93779	80863	00514
69572	68777	39510	35905	14060	40619	29549	69616	33564	60780
24122	66591	27699	06494	14845	46672	61958	77100	90899	75754
61196	30231	92962	61773	41839	55382	17267	70943	78038	70267
30532	21704	10274	12202	39685	23309	10061	68829	55986	66485
03788	97599	75867	20717	74416	53166	35208	33374	87539	08823
48228	63379	85783	47619	53152	67433	35663	52972	16818	60311
60365	94653	35075	33949	42614	29297	01918	28316	98953	73231
83799	42402	56623	34442	34994	41374	70071	14736	09958	18065
32960	07405	36409	83232	99385	41600	11133	07586	15917	06253
19322	53845	57620	52606	66497	68646	78138	66559	19640	99413
11220	94747	07399	37408	48509	23929	27482	45476	85244	35159
31751	57260	68980	05339	15470	48355	88651	22596	03152	19121
88492	99382	14454	04504	20094	98977	74843	93413	22109	78508
30934	47744	07481	83828	73788	06533	28597	20405	94205	20380
22888	48893	27499	98748	60530	45128	74022	84617	82037	10268
78212	16993	35902	91386	44372	15486	65741	14014	87481	37220
41849	84547	46850	52326	34677	58300	74910	64345	19325	81549
46352	33049	69248	93460	45305	07521	61318	31855	14413	70951
11087	96294	14013	31792	59747	67277	76503	34513	39663	77544
52701	08337	56303	87315	16520	69676	11654	99893	02181	68161
57275	36898	81304	48585	68652	27376	92852	55866	88448	03584
20857	73156	70284	24326	79375	95220	01159	63267	10622	48391
15633	84924	90415	93614	33521	26665	55823	47641	86225	31704
92694	48297	39904	02115	59589	49067	66821	41575	49767	04037
77613	19019	88152	00080	20554	91409	96277	48257	50816	97616
38688	32486	45134	63545	59404	72059	43947	51680	43852	59693
25163	01889	70014	15021	41290	67312	71857	15957	68971	11403
65251	07629	37239	33295	05870	01119	92784	26340	18477	65622
36815	43625	18637	37509	82444	99005	04921	73701	14707	93997
64397	11692	05327	82162	20247	81759	45197	25332	83745	22567
04515	25624	95096	67946	48460	85558	15191	18782	16930	33361
83761	60873	43253	84145	60833	25983	01291	41349	20368	07126
14387	06345	80854	09279	43529	06318	38384	74761	41196	37480
51321	92246	80088	77074	88722	56736	66164	49431	66919	31678
72472	00008	80890	18002	94813	31900	54155	83436	35352	54131
05466	55306	93128	18464	74457	90561	72848	11834	79982	68416
39528	72484	82474	25593	48545	35247	18619	13674	18611	19241
81616	18711	53342	44276	75122	11724	74627	73707	58319	15997
07586	16120	82641	22820	92904	13141	32392	19763	61199	67940
90767	04235	13574	17200	69902	63742	78464	22501	18627	90872
40188	28193	29593	88627	94972	11598	62095	36787	00441	58997
34414	82157	86887	55087	19152	00023	12302	80783	32624	68691
63439	75363	44989	16822	36024	00867	76378	41605	65961	73488
67049	09070	93399	45547	94458	74284	05041	49807	20288	34060
79495	04146	52162	90286	54158	34243	46978	35482	59362	95938
91704	30552	04737	21031	75051	93029	47665	64382	99782	93478

TABLE A.3

Areas Under the Normal Curve: Fractions of Unit Area from 0 to Z.

The Z values are expressed to the nearest hundredth. The left-hand column contains the first two digits of the Z value. The values across the top of the table are third digits. To determine the proportion of curve area from the mean to a Z = 1.45, find 1.4 down the left-hand column. Next, find .05 across the top of the table. Where these values intersect in the body of the table defines the proportion of curve area. In the case of a Z = 1.45, the proportion of curve area is .4265.

Z	0.00	0.01	0.02	0.03	0.04	0.05	0.06	0.07	0.08	0.09
0.0	0.0000	0.0040	0.0080	0.0120	0.0160	0.0199	0.0239	0.0279	0.0319	0.0359
0.1	.0398	.0438	.0478	.0517	.0557	.0596	.0636	.0675	.0714	.0753
0.2	.0793	.0832	.0871	.0910	.0948	.0987	.1026	.1064	.1103	.1141
0.3	.1179	.1217	.1255	.1293	.1331	.1368	.1406	.1443	.1480	.1517
0.4	.1554	.1591	.1628	.1664	.1700	.1736	.1772	.1808	.1844	.1879
0.5	.1915	.1950	.1985	.2019	.2054	.2088	.2123	.2157	.2190	.2224
0.6	.2257	.2291	.2324	.2357	.2389	.2422	.2454	.2486	.2517	.2549
0.7	.2580	.2611	.2642	.2673	.2704	.2734	.2764	.2794	.2823	.2852
0.8	.2881	.2910	.2939	.2967	.2995	.3023	.3051	.3078	.3106	.3133
0.9	.3159	.3186	.3212	.3238	.3264	.3289	.3315	.3340	.3365	.3389
1.0	.3413	.3438	.3461	.3485	.3508	.3531	.3554	.3577	.3599	.3621
1.1	.3643	.3665	.3686	.3708	.3729	.3749	.3770	.3790	.3810	.3830
1.2	.3849	.3869	.3888	.3907	.3925	.3944	.3962	.3980	.3997	.4015
1.3	.4032	.4049	.4066	.4082	.4099	.4115	.4131	.4147	.4162	.4177
1.4	.4192	.4207	.4222	.4236	.4251	.4265	.4279	.4292	.4306	.4319
1.5	.4332	.4345	.4357	.4370	.4382	.4394	.4406	.4418	.4429	.4441
1.6	.4452	.4463	.4474	.4484	.4495	.4505	.4515	.4525	.4535	.4545
1.7	.4554	.4564	.4573	.4582	.4591	.4599	.4608	.4616	.4625	.4633
1.8	.4641	.4649	.4656	.4664	.4671	.4678	.4686	.4693	.4699	.4706
1.9	.4713	.4719	.4726	.4732	.4738	.4744	.4750	.4756	.4761	.4767
2.0	.4772	.4778	.4783	.4788	.4793	.4798	.4803	.4808	.4812	.4817
2.1	.4821	.4826	.4830	.4834	.4838	.4842	.4846	.4850	.4854	.4857
2.2	.4861	.4864	.4868	.4871	.4875	.4878	.4881	.4884	.4887	.4890
2.3	.4893	.4896	.4898	.4901	.4904	.4906	.4909	.4911	.4913	.4916
2.4	.4918	.4920	.4922	.4925	.4927	.4929	.4931	.4932	.4934	.4936
2.5	.4938	.4940	.4941	.4943	.4945	.4946	.4948	.4949	.4951	.4952
2.6	.4953	.4955	.4956	.4957	.4959	.4960	.4961	.4962	.4963	.4964
2.7	.4965	.4966	.4967	.4968	.4969	.4970	.4971	.4972	.4973	.4974
2.8	.4974	.4975	.4976	.4977	.4977	.4978	.4979	.4979	.4980	.4981
2.9	.4981	.4982	.4982	.4983	.4984	.4984	.4985	.4985	.4986	.4986
3.0	.4987	.4987	.4987	.4988	.4988	.4989	.4989	.4989	.4990	.4990
3.1	.4990	.4991	.4991	.4991	.4992	.4992	.4992	.4992	.4993	.4993
3.2	.4993	.4993	.4994	.4994	.4994	.4994	.4994	.4995	.4995	.4995
3.3	.4995	.4995	.4995	.4996	.4996	.4996	.4996	.4996	.4996	.4997
3.4	.4997	.4997	.4997	.4997	.4997	.4997	.4997	.4997	.4997	.4998
3.6	.4998	.4998	.4999	.4999	.4999	.4999	.4999	.4999	.4999	.4999
3.9	.5000									

Source: Harold O. Rugg, *Statistical Methods Applied to Education* (Boston: Houghton Mifflin Company, 1917), Table III, pp. 389–390. With the permission of the publishers. Reprinted by permission from *Statistical Methods*, 6th edition, by George W. Snedecor and William G. Cochran. © 1967 by the Iowa State University Press, Ames, Iowa.

TABLE A.4
Distribution of χ^2.

Degrees of freedom are defined as $k - 1$ for single samples, where $k =$ the number of categories into which the data are divided. For 2×2 tables or larger, df $=$ (rows $- 1$) (columns $- 1$). Probabilities for a two-tailed test are shown across the top of the table. For one-tailed test interpretations, simply halve the probability shown; i.e., .10 (two-tailed) becomes .10/2 $=$ .05 for a one-tailed probability.

df	.99	.98	.95	.90	.80	.70	.50	.30	.20	.10	.05	.02	.01	.001
1	.0³157	.0³628	.0³393	.0²158	.0642	.148	.455	1.074	1.642	2.706	3.841	5.412	6.635	10.827
2	.0201	.0404	.103	.211	.446	.713	1.386	2.408	3.219	4.605	5.991	7.824	9.210	13.815
3	.115	.185	.352	.584	1.005	1.424	2.366	3.665	4.642	6.251	7.815	9.837	11.345	16.268
4	.297	.429	.711	1.064	1.649	2.195	3.357	4.878	5.989	7.779	9.488	11.668	13.277	18.465
5	.554	.752	1.145	1.610	2.343	3.000	4.351	6.064	7.289	9.236	11.070	13.388	15.086	20.517
6	.872	1.134	1.635	2.204	3.070	3.828	5.348	7.231	8.558	10.645	12.592	15.033	16.812	22.457
7	1.239	1.564	2.167	2.833	3.822	4.671	6.346	8.383	9.803	12.017	14.067	16.622	18.475	24.322
8	1.646	2.032	2.733	3.490	4.594	5.527	7.344	9.524	11.030	13.362	15.507	18.168	20.090	26.125
9	2.088	2.532	3.325	4.168	5.380	6.393	8.343	10.656	12.242	14.684	16.919	19.679	21.666	27.877
10	2.558	3.059	3.940	4.865	6.179	7.267	9.342	11.781	13.442	15.987	18.307	21.161	23.209	29.588
11	3.053	3.609	4.575	5.578	6.989	8.148	10.341	12.899	14.631	17.275	19.675	22.618	24.725	31.264
12	3.571	4.178	5.226	6.304	7.807	9.034	11.340	14.011	15.812	18.549	21.026	24.054	26.217	32.909
13	4.107	4.765	5.892	7.042	8.634	9.926	12.340	15.119	16.985	19.812	22.362	25.472	27.688	34.528
14	4.660	5.368	6.571	7.790	9.467	10.821	13.339	16.222	18.151	21.064	23.685	26.873	29.141	36.123
15	5.229	5.985	7.261	8.547	10.307	11.721	14.339	17.322	19.311	22.307	24.996	28.259	30.578	37.697
16	5.812	6.614	7.962	9.312	11.152	12.624	15.338	18.418	20.465	23.542	26.296	29.633	32.000	39.252
17	6.408	7.255	8.672	10.085	12.002	13.531	16.338	19.511	21.615	24.769	27.587	30.995	33.409	40.790
18	7.015	7.906	9.390	10.865	12.857	14.440	17.338	20.601	22.760	25.989	28.869	32.346	34.805	42.312
19	7.633	8.567	10.117	11.651	13.716	15.352	18.338	21.689	23.900	27.204	30.144	33.687	36.191	43.820
20	8.260	9.237	10.851	12.443	14.578	16.266	19.337	22.775	25.038	28.412	31.410	35.020	37.566	45.315
21	8.897	9.915	11.591	13.240	15.445	17.182	20.337	23.858	26.171	29.615	32.671	36.343	38.932	46.797
22	9.542	10.600	12.338	14.041	16.314	18.101	21.337	24.939	27.301	30.813	33.924	37.659	40.289	48.268
23	10.196	11.293	13.091	14.848	17.187	19.021	22.337	26.018	28.429	32.007	35.172	38.968	41.638	49.728
24	10.856	11.992	13.848	15.659	18.062	19.943	23.337	27.096	29.553	33.196	36.415	40.270	42.980	51.179
25	11.524	12.697	14.611	16.473	18.940	20.867	24.337	28.172	30.675	34.382	37.652	41.566	44.314	52.620
26	12.198	13.409	15.379	17.292	19.820	21.792	25.336	29.246	31.795	35.563	38.885	42.856	45.642	54.052
27	12.879	14.125	16.151	18.114	20.703	22.719	26.336	30.319	32.912	36.741	40.113	44.140	46.963	55.476
28	13.565	14.847	16.928	18.939	21.588	23.647	27.336	31.391	34.027	37.916	41.337	45.419	48.278	56.893
29	14.256	15.574	17.708	19.768	22.475	24.577	28.336	32.461	35.139	39.087	42.557	46.693	49.588	58.302
30	14.953	16.306	18.493	20.599	23.364	25.508	29.336	33.530	36.250	40.256	43.773	47.962	50.892	59.703

Probability

Source: Ronald A. Fisher and Frank Yates, *Statistical Tables for Biological, Agricultural and Medical Research*, published by Longman Group Ltd., London (previously published by Oliver & Boyd, Edinburgh). By permission of the authors and publishers. Table V. Reprinted from *Basic Statistical Methods* (2nd ed.), N. M. Downie and R. W. Heath, Harper & Row, 1965.

Statistical Tables   App. A

TABLE A.5

Degrees of freedom (df) are defined as $N - 1$ for a single sample. For two-sample tests, df = $(N_1 - 1) + (N_2 - 1)$, where the N's are the respective sample sizes. When the exact df cannot be located down the left-hand side of the table, use the smaller df for locating significant t values. For example, if the researcher has df = 110, use 60 df for entering the table. This renders the decision somewhat more conservative. Any observed t value that equals or exceeds the value shown in the body of the table for any df is significant statistically at the probability level shown at the top of the table.

df	Level of significance for one-tailed test					
	.10	.05	.025	.01	.005	.0005
	Level of significance for two-tailed test					
	.20	.10	.05	.02	.01	.001
1	3.078	6.314	12.706	31.821	63.657	636.619
2	1.886	2.920	4.303	6.965	9.925	31.598
3	1.638	2.353	3.182	4.541	5.841	12.941
4	1.533	2.132	2.776	3.747	4.604	8.610
5	1.476	2.015	2.571	3.365	4.032	6.859
6	1.440	1.943	2.447	3.143	3.707	5.959
7	1.415	1.895	2.365	2.998	3.499	5.405
8	1.397	1.860	2.306	2.896	3.355	5.041
9	1.383	1.833	2.262	2.821	3.250	4.781
10	1.372	1.812	2.228	2.764	3.169	4.587
11	1.363	1.796	2.201	2.718	3.106	4.437
12	1.356	1.782	2.179	2.681	3.055	4.318
13	1.350	1.771	2.160	2.650	3.012	4.221
14	1.345	1.761	2.145	2.624	2.977	4.140
15	1.341	1.753	2.131	2.602	2.947	4.073
16	1.337	1.746	2.120	2.583	2.921	4.015
17	1.333	1.740	2.110	2.567	2.898	3.965
18	1.330	1.734	2.101	2.552	2.878	3.922
19	1.328	1.729	2.093	2.539	2.861	3.883
20	1.325	1.725	2.086	2.528	2.845	3.850
21	1.323	1.721	2.080	2.518	2.831	3.819
22	1.321	1.717	2.074	2.508	2.819	3.792
23	1.319	1.714	2.069	2.500	2.807	3.767
24	1.318	1.711	2.064	2.492	2.797	3.745
25	1.316	1.708	2.060	2.485	2.787	3.725
26	1.315	1.706	2.056	2.479	2.779	3.707
27	1.314	1.703	2.052	2.473	2.771	3.690
28	1.313	1.701	2.048	2.467	2.763	3.674
29	1.311	1.699	2.045	2.462	2.756	3.659
30	1.310	1.697	2.042	2.457	2.750	3.646
40	1.303	1.684	2.021	2.423	2.704	3.551
60	1.296	1.671	2.000	2.390	2.660	3.460
120	1.289	1.658	1.980	2.358	2.617	3.373
∞	1.282	1.645	1.960	2.326	2.576	3.291

Source: Abridged from Ronald A. Fisher and Frank Yates, *Statistical Tables for Biological, Agricultural and Medical Research*, published by Longman Group Ltd., London (previously published by Oliver & Boyd, Edinburgh). By permission of the authors and publishers. Table III. Reprinted from Sidney Siegel, *Nonparametric Statistics for the Behavioral Sciences* (McGraw-Hill Book Company, 1956) by permission of the publishers.

Appendix B

Answers to Numerical Problems

Chapter 11

4. (a) 89.5 and 109.5 (b) 1499.5 and 1599.5 (c) .195 and .295
 (d) .00545 and .00595 (e) 135.5 and 139.5 (f) 199.5 and 249.5
6. (a) 64.7 (b) 139.5 (c) 152.8 (d) 35.9 (e) 99.5 (f) 61.5 (g) 169.5
 (h) 69.5
8. (a) .36% (b) 15.6% (c) 97% (d) 11.58% (e) 55.5% (f) .04%
9. 34.5, 44.5, 54.5, 64.5, 74.5, 84.5, 94.5, 104.5, 114.5, 124.5, 134.5, 144.5, 154.5, 164.5, 174.5, 184.5, 194.5

Chapter 15

1. (a) $s = 13.9$ $s^2 = 193.21$ (b) 39.7 (c) 10.2
2. (a) 522 (b) 524.9 (c) 527
3. Mode = 14, median = 12.5, mean = 12.6
4. Mode = 15, median = 24, mean = 35.8
6. 42.5
7. Mean = 56.4, median = 55
8. Mode = 132, median = 142, mean = 143.8
9. Range = 13.7, $s = 3.9$, average deviation = 3.6
10. $s = 13.7$, range = 56
11. 10–90 range = 85.3, $s = 31.3$, interquartile range = 52.4
12. Range = 58, $s = 17.3$

Chapter 16

1. (a) .0735   (b) .9901   (c) .5000   (d) .6554   (e) .0233   (f) .1587
2. (a) .0782   (b) .9030   (c) .4666   (d) .0026
3. (a) 4.10   (b) 0   (c) -1.50 (d) -3.00
4. (a) 137   (b) 242   (c) 267   (d) 220
5. (a) .6255   (b) .0146   (c) .8389   (d) .4880   (e) .8665   (f) .9871
   (g) .2090   (h) .8413
6. (a) 35   (b) 40   (c) 55   (d) 15   (e) 40   (f) 31
7. (a) .2843   (b) .8475   (c) .3413   (d) .7726   (e) .0003   (f) .8790
   (g) .8593   (h) .3284
8. (a) 1.31   (b) 3.00   (c) 1.50   (d) .34   (e) 2.03   (f) 2.50
9. (a) .1587   (b) .9970   (c) .9998   (d) .8944
10. (a) 0   (b) 10.67   (c) -4.33 (d) -1.00 (e) -9.33

Chapter 17

4. (a) 95.82 to 104.18   (b) 96.74 to 103.26   (c) 93.43 to 106.57
5. (a) 94.12 to 105.88   (b) 96.16 to 103.84   (c) 95.68 to 104.32
6. (a) 326.76 to 333.24   (b) 325.92 to 334.08   (c) 327.84 to 332.16
8. (5a) 1.96   (5b) 1.28   (5c) 1.44   (6a) 1.56   (6b) 1.96   (6c) 1.04
9. (a) 120.55 to 123.45   (b) 120.02 to 123.98   (c) 121.06 to 122.94
10. + or -2.58 (critical value of Z for .01 level of significance, two-tailed test);
    Observed $Z = 1.67$; not significant
    Confidence interval = 99% CI = 17.26 to 32.74 (based upon a Z value of 2.58)

Appendix C

Bibliography

ADAMS, REED AND RONALD VOGEL. 1986. "Perceptional Foundations of Deterrence: The Case of Prostitution." *American Journal of Criminal Justice*, 10:131–139.

ANSON, RICHARD H. 1983. "Inmate Ethnicity and the Suicide Connection: A Note on Aggregate Trends." *The Prison Journal*, 12:191–200.

Attorney General's Task Force on Family Violence. 1984. *Final Report*. Washington, DC: U.S. Department of Justice.

BACKSTROM, CHARLES H. AND GERALD D. HURSH. 1963. *Survey Research*. Evanston, IL: Northwestern University Press.

BAHN, CHARLES AND JAMES R. DAVIS. 1991. "Social Psychological Effects of the Status of Probationer." *Federal Probation*, 55:17–25.

BAILEY, KENNETH D. 1987. *Methods of Social Research* (3rd ed.) New York: Macmillan.

BALL, RICHARD A. AND J. ROBERT LILLY. 1985. "Home Incarceration: An International Alternative to Institutional Incarceration." *International Journal of Comparative and Applied Research*, 9:85–97.

BECKER, GARY. 1968. "Crime and Punishment: An Economic Approach." *Journal of Political Economy*, 78:169–217.

BERNSTEIN, ILENE N., WILLIAM R. KELLY, AND PATRICIA A. DOYLE. 1977. "Societal Reaction to Deviants: The Case of Criminal Defendants. *American Sociological Review*, 42:743–755.

BERSANI, CARL, HUEY-TSYH CHEN, AND ROBERT DENTON. 1988. "Spouse Abusers and Court Mandated Treatment." *Journal of Crime and Justice*, 11:43–60.

BLACK, JAMES A. AND DEAN J. CHAMPION. 1976. *Methods and Issues of Social Research.* New York: Wiley.

BLALOCK, HUBERT M. JR. 1972. *Social Statistics* (2nd ed.). New York: McGraw-Hill.

BOHM, ROBERT M. 1987. "Myths about Criminology and Criminal Justice: A Review Essay." *Justice Quarterly*, 4:631–642.

BONJEAN, CHARLES M., RICHARD J. HILL, AND S. DALE MCLEMORE. 1967. *Sociological Measurement: An Inventory of Scales and Indices.* San Francisco: Chandler Publishing Company.

BOWDITCH, CHRISTINE AND RONALD S. EVERETT. 1987. "Private Prisons: Problems within the Solution." *Justice Quarterly*, 4:441–453.

BRECI, MICHAEL G. 1989. "The Effect of Training on Police Attitudes toward Family Violence: Where Does Mandatory Arrest Fit In?" *Journal of Crime and Justice*, 12:35–49.

BURGESS, ROBERT L. AND PATRICIA DRAPER. 1989. "The Explanation of Family Violence: The Role of Biological, Behavioral, and Cultural Selection." In *Family Violence*, ed. Lloyd Ohlin and Michael Tonry. Chicago: University of Chicago Press.

CHAMPION, DEAN J. 1981. *Basic Statistics for Social Research* (2d ed.). New York: Macmillan.

CHAMPION, DEAN J. 1988. "Private Counsels and Public Defenders: A Look at Weak Cases, Prior Records, and Leniency in Plea Bargaining." *Journal of Criminal Justice*, 17:253–263.

CHAMPION, DEAN J. AND ALAN M. SEAR. 1969. "Questionnaire Response Rate: A Methodological Analysis." *Social Forces*, 47:335–339.

CHARLES, MICHAEL T. 1989. "Research Note: Juveniles on Electronic Monitoring." *Journal of Contemporary Criminal Justice*, 5:165–172.

CLEMMER, DONALD C. 1940. *The Prison Community.* New York: Holt, Rinehart and Winston.

COHEN, MORRIS R. AND ERNEST NAGEL. 1934. *An Introduction to Logic and the Scientific Method.* New York: Harcourt, Brace.

COLEMAN, JAMES S. 1959. "Relational Analysis: The Study of Social Organizations with Survey Methods." *Human Organization*, 17:28–36.

COLEMAN, JAMES S., E. KATZ, AND H. M. MENZEL. 1957. "Diffusion of Innovation among Physicians." *Sociometry*, 20:253–270.

COLLEY, LORI, ROBERT G. CULBERTSON, AND EDWARD J. LATESSA. 1986. "Juvenile Probation Officers: A Job Analysis." *Juvenile and Family Court Journal*, 38:1–12.

CONLEY, J. A. (ed.) 1979. *Theory and Research in Criminal Justice: Current Perspectives.* Cincinnati, OH: Academy of Criminal Justice Sciences Series, Anderson Publishing Company.

CRANK, JOHN P., ROBERT M. REGOLI, ROBERT G. CULBERTSON, AND ERIC D. POOLE. 1987. "Linkages Between Professionalization and Professionalization among Police Chiefs." Unpublished paper presented at the Academy of Criminal Justice Sciences meetings, St. Louis, MO. (March).

CRANK, JOHN P. et al. 1986. "Cynicism among Police Chiefs." *Justice Quarterly*, 3:343–352.

CRESSEY, DONALD R. AND JOHN IRWIN. 1962. "Thieves, Convicts, and the Inmate Culture." *Social Problems*, 10:145–152.

CROUCH, BEN M. AND JAMES W. MARQUART. 1990. "Resolving the Paradox of Reform: Litigation, Prisoner Violence, and Perceptions of Risk." *Justice Quarterly*, 7 :104–123.

DEMARIS, ALFRED. 1989. "Attrition in Batterers' Counseling: The Role of Social and Demographic Factors." *Social Service Review*, 63:142–154.

DINGWALL, R. AND P. LEWIS (eds.) 1983. *The Sociology of the Professions*. New York: St. Martin's Press.

DIRENZO, GORDON J. (ed.) 1966. *Concepts, Theory, and Explanation in the Behavioral Sciences*. New York: Random House.

DURHAM, ALEXIS M. III. 1988. "Crime Seriousness and Punitive Severity: An Assessment of Social Attitudes." *Justice Quarterly*, 5:131–153.

EDWARDS, A. L. 1957. *The Social Desirability Variable in Personality Assessment Research*. New York: Dryden.

EHRLICH, I. 1975. "The Deterrent Effect of Capital Punishment: A Question of Life and Death." *American Economic Review*, 65:397–417.

EMPEY, LAMAR T. AND MAYNARD ERICKSON. 1972. *The Provo Experiment: Evaluation of Community Control of Delinquency*." Lexington, MA: Lexington.

FAGAN, JEFFREY, MARTIN FORST, AND T. SCOTT VIVONA. 1987. "Racial Determinants of the Judicial Transfer Decision: Prosecuting Violent Youth in Criminal Court." *Crime and Delinquency*, 33:259–286.

FISHMAN, JOSEPH F. 1934. *Sex in Prison*. New York: National Liberty Press.

FITZGERALD, JACK D. AND STEVEN M. COX. 1987. *Research Methods in Criminal Justice*. Chicago: Nelson-Hall.

FLANAGAN, TIMOTHY J. AND KATHERINE M. JAMIESON. 1988. *Sourcebook of Criminal Justice Statistics, 1987*. Albany, NY: The Hindelang Criminal Justice Research Center, The University of Albany.

FLANAGAN, TIMOTHY J. AND KATHLEEN MAGUIRE. 1990. *Sourcebook of Criminal Justice Statistics, 1990*. Albany, NY: Hindelang Criminal Justice Research Center.

FRAZIER, CHARLES E. AND DONNA M. BISHOP. 1990. "Obstacles to Reform in Juvenile Corrections: A Case Study." *Journal of Contemporary Criminal Justice*, 6:157–166.

FYFE, JAMES J. 1988. "Police Use of Deadly Force: Research and Reform." *Justice Quarterly*, 5:165–205.

GELLES, RICHARD J. AND HELEN MEDERER. 1985. "Comparison or Control: Intervention in the Cases of Wife Abuse." Paper presented at the Third Annual Conference for Family Violence Researchers. Durham, NH: University of New Hampshire. (July).

GOODE, WILLIAM J. AND PAUL K. HATT. 1952. *Methods in Social Research*. New York: McGraw-Hill.

GUNDERSON, D. F. 1987. "Credibility and the Police Uniform." *Journal of Police Science and Administration*, 15:192–195.

GURALNIK, DAVID B. 1972. *Webster's New World Dictionary of the American Language*. New York: World Publishing Company.

GUTTMAN, LOUIS. 1944. "A Basis for Scaling Qualitative Data." *American Sociological Review*, 9:139–150.

HAGAN, FRANK E. 1989. *Research Methods in Criminal Justice and Criminology*. New York: Macmillan.

HENDERSON, JOEL H. AND RONALD L. BOOSTROM. 1989. "Criminal Justice Theory: Anarchy Reigns." *Journal of Contemporary Criminal Justice*, 5:29–39.

HIRSCHI, TRAVIS AND HANAN C. SELVIN. 1967. *Delinquency Research: An Appraisal of Analytic Methods*. New York: Free Press.

HOLMES, MALCOLM D. AND WILLIAM A. TAGGART. 1990. "A Comparative Analysis of Research Methods in Criminology and Criminal Justice Journals." *Justice Quarterly*, 7:421–437.

HUMPHREYS, LAUD. 1970. *The Tearoom Trade*. Chicago: Aldine.

HYMAN, HERBERT. 1955. *Survey Design and Analysis*. Glencoe, IL: Free Press.

IRWIN, JOHN. 1970. *The Felon*. Berkeley, CA: University of California Press.

IRWIN, JOHN. 1980. *Prisons in Turmoil*. Boston: Little, Brown.

IRWIN, JOHN. 1985. *The Jail: Managing the Underclass in American Society*. Berkeley, CA: University of California Press.

JOHNSON, RICHARD E. 1986. "Family Structure and Delinquency: General Patterns and Gender Differences." *Criminology*, 24:65–84.

JOHNSTON, MILDRED E. 1988. "Correlates of Early Violence Experience among Men who are Abusive toward Female Mates." In *Family Abuse and its Consequences: New Directions in Research*, ed. Gerald T. Hotaling et al. Newbury Park, CA: Sage.

JUDD, CHARLES M., ELIOT R. SMITH, AND LOUISE H. KIDDER. 1991. *Research Methods in Social Relations*. New York: Holt, Rinehart and Winston.

KACI, JUDY HAILS AND SHIRA TARRANT. 1988. "Attitudes of Prosecutors and Probation Departments Toward Diversion in Domestic Violence Cases in California." *Journal of Contemporary Criminal Justice*, 4:187–200.

KEIL, THOMAS J. AND GENNARO F. VITO. 1989. "Race and the Death Penalty in Kentucky Murder Trials: An Analysis of Post-*Gregg* outcomes." *Justice Quarterly*, 7:189–207.

KELLING, GEORGE L. et al. 1974. *The Kansas City Preventive Patrol Experiment: A Summary Report and a Technical Report*. Washington, DC: The Police Foundation.

KENNEY, DENNIS JAY. 1986. "Crime on the Subways: Measuring the Effectiveness of the Guardian Angels." *Justice Quarterly*, 3:481–496.

KLOFAS, JOHN AND RALPH WEISHEIT. 1987. "Guilty But Mentally Ill: Reform of the Insanity Defense in Illinois." *Justice Quarterly*, 4:39–50.

KOHFELD, CAROL W. AND JOHN SPRAGUE. 1990. "Demography, Police Behavior, and Deterrence." *Criminology*, 28:111–136.

KOWALSKI, GREGORY S., ALAN J. SHIELDS, AND DEBORAH C. WILSON. 1985. "The Female Murderer: Alabama 1929–1971." *American Journal of Criminal Justice*, 10:75–104.

KRISBERG, BARRY et al. 1987. "The Incarceration of Minority Youth." *Crime and Delinquency*, 33:173–205.

LAPIERE, RICHARD, T. 1934. "Attitudes vs. Actions." *Social Forces*, 14:230–237.

LARZELERE, ROBERT E. AND GERALD R. PATTERSON. 1990. "Parental Management: Mediator of the Effect of Socioeconomic Status on Early Delinquency." *Criminology*, 28:301–324.

LEMERT, EDWIN M. 1951. *Social Pathology*. New York: McGraw-Hill.

LIKERT, RENSIS. 1932. "A Technique to Measure Attitudes." *Archives of Psychology*, 21, No. 140.

LONG, NIGEL, GEORGE SHOUKSMITH, KEVEN VOGES, AND SHANNON ROACHE. 1986. "Stress in Prison Staff: An Occupational Study." *Criminology*, 24:331–345.

LUCAS, WAYNE L. 1987. "Staff Perceptions of Volunteers in a Correctional Program." *Journal of Crime and Justice*, 10:63–78.

MACKENZIE, DORIS LAYTON AND JAMES E. SHAW. 1990. "Inmate Adjustment and Change During Shock Incarceration: The Impact of Correctional Boot Camp Programs." *Justice Quarterly*, 7:127–150.

MAGNUSSON, DAVID. 1967. *Test Theory*. Reading, MA: Addison-Wesley.

MARQUART, JAMES W. 1986. "Doing Research in Prison: The Strengths and Weaknesses of Full Participation as a Guard." *Justice Quarterly*, 3:15–32.

MARQUART, JAMES W. AND JULIAN B. ROEBUCK. 1986. "Prison Guards and Snitches." In *Dilemmas of Punishment: Readings in Contemporary Corrections.*" ed. K. C. Haas and G. P. Alpert. Prospect Heights, IL: Waveland Press.

MCSHANE, MARILYN D. 1987. "Immigration Processing and the Alien Inmate: Constructing A Conflict Perspective." *Journal of Crime and Justice*, 10:171–194.

MEADOWS, ROBERT J. AND LAWRENCE C. TROSTLE. 1988. "A Study of Police Misconduct and Litigation: Findings and Implications." *Journal of Contemporary Criminal Justice*, 4:77–92.

MEDNICK, S. A. AND J. VOLAVKA. 1980. "Biology and Crime." In *Crime and Justice: An Annual Review of Research*," eds. N. Morris and M. Tonry. Chicago: University of Chicago Press.

MERTON, ROBERT K. 1957. *Social Theory and Social Structure*. New York: Free Press.

MERTON, ROBERT K., M. FISKE, AND PATRICIA L. KENDALL. 1956. *The Focused Interview*. New York: Free Press.

MILL, JOHN STUART. 1930. A System of Logic. New York: Longmans.

MILLER, DELBERT C. 1977. *Handbook of Research Design and Social Measurement*. New York: David McKay Company.

MORN, F. T. 1980. *Academic Disciplines and Debates: An Essay on Criminal Justice and Criminology as Professions in Higher Education*. Washington, DC: Joint Commission on Criminology and Criminal Justice Education Standards.

National Archive of Criminal Justice Data. 1990. *Data Available from the National Archive of Criminal Justice Data*. Ann Arbor, MI: The Inter-University Consortium for Political and Social Research.

PEATMAN, JOHN G. 1963. *Introduction to Applied Statistics*. New York: Harper and Row.

RACHAL, J. VALLEY et al. 1975. *A National Study of Adolescent Drinking Behavior, Attitudes, and Correlates: Final Report*. Contract No. HSM-42-73-80, to the National Institute on Alcohol Abuse and Alcoholism. Research Triangle Park, NC: Research Triangle Institute.

REGOLI, ROBERT M., JOHN P. CRANK, ROBERT G. CULBERTSON, AND ERIC D. POOLE. 1987. "Police Professionalism and Cynicism Reconsidered: An Assessment of Measurement Issues." *Justice Quarterly*, a 4:257–286.

RILEY, MATILDA W. 1963. *Sociological Research*. New York: Harcourt, Brace.

ROSE, ARNOLD, M. 1965. *Sociology: The Study of Human Relations*. New York: Alfred A. Knopf.

SAMPSON, ROBERT J. 1986. "Crime in Cities: The Effects of Formal and Informal Social Control." In *Communities and Crime*, eds. Albert J. Reiss, Jr. and Michael Tonry. Chicago: University of Chicago Press.

SCHRAG, CLARENCE. 1961. "Some Foundations for a Theory of Corrections." In *The Prison: Studies in Institutional Organization*, ed. Donald R. Cressey. New York: Holt, Rinehart, and Winston.

SCHWARTZ, MARTIN D. 1988. "Ain't Got No Class: Universal Risk Theories of Battering." *Contemporary Crises*, 12:373–392.

SECHREST, D. K. 1989. "Prison 'Boot Camps' Do Not Measure Up." *Federal Probation*, 52:31–35.

SELLTIZ, CLAIRE, S. W. COOK, AND L. S. WRIGHTSMAN. 1976. *Research Methods in Social Relations*. New York: Holt, Rinehart, and Winston.

SELLTIZ, CLAIRE, et al. 1959. *Research Methods in Social Relations*. New York: Holt, Rinehart, and Winston.

SELTZER, JUDITH AND DEBRA KALMUSS. 1988. "Socialization and Stress Explanations for Spouse Abuse." *Social Forces*, 67:473–491.

SHAH, SALEEM A. AND LOREN ROTH. 1974. "Biological and Psychophysiological Factors in Criminality." In *Handbook of Criminology*, ed. Daniel Glaser. Chicago: Rand McNally.

SIEGEL, SIDNEY M. 1956. *Nonparametric Statistics for the Behavioral Sciences*. New York, NY: McGraw-Hill.

SMITH, R. L. AND R. W. TAYLOR. 1985. "A Return to Neighborhood Policing: The Tampa, Florida Experience." *Police Chief*, 52:39–44.

STEVENS, S. S. 1951. "Mathematics, Measurement, and Psychophysics." In *Handbook of Experimental Psychology*, ed. S. S. Stevens. New York, Wiley.

SYKES, GRESHAM. 1958. *The Society of Captives*. Princeton, NJ: Princeton University Press.

THOMPSON, KEVIN M. 1989. "Gender and Adolescent Drinking Problems: The Effects of Occupational Structure. *Social Problems*, 36:30–47.

THOMPSON, WENDY M., JAMES M. DABBS, AND ROBERT L. FRADY. 1990. "Changes in Saliva Testosterone Levels During a 90-Day Shock Incarceration Program." *Criminal Justice and Behavior*, 17:246–252.

THURSTONE, L. L. AND E. J. CHAVE. 1929. *The Measurement of Attitudes*. Chicago: University of Chicago Press.

Uniform Crime Reports. 1989. *Crime in the United States*. Washington, DC: U. S. Department of Justice.

U. S. Department of Justice. 1988. *Census of Local Jails, 1983, Vol. I, The Northeast Data for Individual Jails*. Washington, DC: U. S. Department of Justice, Bureau of Justice Statistics.

VANDERZANDEN, JAMES. W. 1984. *Social Psychology*. New York: Random House.

VON HENTIG, HANS. 1947. "Redhead and Outlaw." *Journal of Criminal Law and Criminology*, 38:6–10.

WALKER, ANNE GRAFFAM. 1986. "Content, Transcripts, and Appellate Readers." *Justice Quarterly*, 3:409–427.

WALTERS, GLENN D. AND THOMAS W. WHITE. 1989. "Heredity and Crime: Bad Genes or Bad Research?" *Criminology*, 27:455–485.

WALTERS, STEPHEN. 1988. "Correctional Officers' Perceptions of Powerlessness." *Journal of Crime and Justice*, 11:47–59.

WHITEHEAD, JOHN T. 1989. *Burnout in Probation and Corrections*. Cincinnati, OH: Anderson Publishing Company, 1989.

WILBANKS, WILLIAM. 1986. "Are Female Felons Treated More Leniently by the Criminal Justice System?" *Justice Quarterly*, 3:516–529.

WILLIS, C. L. 1983. "Criminal Justice Theory: A Case of Trained Incapacity?" *Journal of Criminal Justice*, 11:447–458.

WINER, BEN J. 1962. *Statistical Principles in Experimental Design*. New York: McGraw-Hill.

WISEMAN, JACQUELINE P. 1970. *Stations of the Lost: The Treatment of Skid Row Alcoholics*. Englewood Cliffs, NJ: Prentice Hall.

WOLFGANG, MARVIN E. 1983. "Delinquency in Two Birth Cohorts." In *Perspective Studies of Crime and Delinquency*, ed. Katherine Teilmann Van Dusen and Sarnoff A. Mednick.

WOLFGANG, MARVIN, ROBERT M. FIGLIO, AND THORSTEN SELLIN. 1972. *Delinquency in a Birth Cohort*. Chicago: University of Chicago Press.

WOLFGANG, MARVIN E. et al. 1986. *Violent Juvenile Crime: What Do We Know about It and What Can We Do about It?* Minneapolis, MN: Center for the Study of Youth Policy, Hubert H. Humphrey Institute of Public Affairs, University of Minnesota.

Cases Cited

Skinnar v. Oklahoma, 115 P. 2d 123 (1942)
Tennessee v. Garner, 105 S.Ct. 1694 (1985)

Subject Index

Murphy's Law 33, 117
  sampling 117
Murrow, Edward R. 147, 155
Mutual exclusivity 112 (*see also*
  Independent Samples)

*National Archive of Criminal
  Justice Data* 87, **306**
National Crime Survey 87, 147,
  160–168, 359
  example 161–168
  use of interviewing 147
National Institutes for Mental
  Health 160
National Institute of Justice 175
National Opinion Research
  Center 160
National Youth Survey 64, 147
  use of interviewing 147
Necessary conditions 34
Negative association (*see*
  Association)
New Jersey State Maximum
  Security Prison at Trenton
  58
New York 26–27
  probationers 26–27
New York Probation Department
  5, 26
New Zealand 60
  prison studies 60
Nominal definitions 199–200,
  209–210
Nominal level of measurement
  204 (*see also* Levels of
  Measurement)
Nonparametric procedures 358,
  434–436
  defined 435–436
Nonparticipant observation 179
  effects of observed on
    observers 182–183
  effects of observer on observed
    182–183
  studies of homosexuals 179
Nonprobability sampling plans
  102–110
  accidental sampling 103–104
  convenience sampling 103–104
  dense sampling 109–110
  distinguished from probability
    plans 103–104
  judgmental sampling 105–106
  purposive sampling 105–106
  quota sampling 107–108
  saturation sampling 109–110
  snowball sampling 108–109
  systematic sampling 104–105
Nonrespondents 142–143
  effects of 142–143
Nonresponse 6, 114–116, 142–
  143, 356
  adjustments for 114–116, 142–
    143
  defined 114
  randomness 356
Normal curve (*see* Normal
  Distribution)

Normal distribution 387–399
  asymptotic property of 388
  characteristics 388
  criminal justice applications
    402
  formula 387
  standard scores 389–402
"Not guilty by reason of
  insanity" pleas (NGRI)
  187–188
Null hypothesis 328–331 (*see also*
  Hypotheses)
  defined 328
  reasons for developing 331

Observation 175–189
  advantages and disadvantages
    180–183
  characteristics 175–176
  defined 175–176
  participant 177–179
  purposes 176
  types 177–179
Observed frequencies 442 (*see
  also* Goodness-of-Fit
  Tests)
Observed statistical values 416
Offenders 10–11
  electronic monitoring of 11
  sentencing 10
Ogive curves 287 (*see also*
  Cumulative Frequency
  Distributions)
Oklahoma 23
  prisoner sterilization 23
One-tailed tests (*see* Critical
  Regions)
Open-ended questionnaires 129–
  130, 262
  advantages and disadvantages
    132–133
  compared with fixed-response
    questionnaires 130
  defined 129–130
  effects on validity and
    reliability 262
Operational definitions 199–200
Operationalization 27, 199–203
  defined 199
Ordinal level of measurement
  204–205 (*see also* Levels
  of Measurement)
Oregon Youth Study 89–90
Overcrowing 194–195
Oversampling 115–116

Package (*see* **Statistical Package**)
Panels 64 (*see also* Survey
  Designs)
Parallel forms of the same test
  260 (*see also* Reliability)
Parameters 83–84, 350 (*see also*
  Population Parameters)
  compared with statistics 84
  defined 83, 350
Parametric procedures 358, 434–
  443
  defined 435

Parole boards 23
  behavioral prediction 23
Parolees 72–73
Parole officers 5–6, 15
  research examples involving
    5–6
  work roles 15
Paroulees 9
Participant observation 177–179,
  182, 183
  advantages and disadvantages
    180–182
  defined 177
  effects of observed on observer
    182–183
  effects of observer on observed
    183
  studies 177–178
Path analysis 35, 298–299
  illustrated 299
Personal Computers (PCs) (*see*
  Computers)
Peer-group influence 8, 20, 65
Pennsylvania 5
  probation officer research 5
Percentaging 289–290
  cross-tabulations of variables
    289–290
"Phantom effect" 75
Physicians 108
  studying with snowball
    sampling 108
Pie charts 270–271
  defined 270
  restrictions 271
Pilot studies 138
Platykurtosis 401
Plea bargaining 156–159
  interviewing 156–159
  studies of 156–159
Post estimation 425–428
  compared with interval
    estimation 433–434
  defined 425
Police officers 20, 29, 33, 43–44,
  74–75, 209–212, 247–248,
  293, 298
  crime deterrence 43–44
  cynicism 210–211
  murders of 293
  patrol units of 20, 74–75
  professionalism 29, 33, 209–
    212, 247–248
  resolving marital disputes 298
  studies of 20, 29, 33, 209–
    212
  training 298
  types of uniforms worn 29, 33
Policy decision making 270
  graphic presentation 270
Postage variations 115
  mailed questionnaire response
    115 (*see also* Mailed
    Questionnaires)
Population parameters 350
Populations of elements 67, 83–
  84, 349–350 (*see also*
  Elements)
  defined 83, 349

Positive association (*see* Association)
Potentates 117–118
  defined 117
  obtaining permission to sample 117–118
Potency 228 (*see also* Semantic Differential)
Potentates 117–118
Power of a test 412 (*see also* Type I and Type II Errors)
Pragmatic validity 245–247 (*see also* Concurrent Validity, Predictive Validity, Validity)
  concurrent 245–247
  predictive 245
Prediction 14, 22–23
  function of theory 22–23
  scientific inquiry 14–15, 22–23
  XYY theory 22
Predictive validity 245–247
  advantages and disadvantages 246–247
  defined 245
Pretests 138
Prison guards (*see* Correctional Officers)
Prisonization 58, 204
Prison overcrowding 20
Prisons 8, 12, 33, 57–58, 60, 87, 89–90, 94, 177–179, 194–195
  inmate suicides 33
  New Zealand 60
  overcrowding 194–195
  studies involving, 8, 12, 57–58, 87, 89–90, 177–179
  violence 94
Probability model 331
  null hypotheses 331
Probability sampling plans 89–102
  area sampling 98–102
  cluster sampling 98–102
  defined 89–91
  disproportionate stratified random 95–97
  distinguished from nonprobability plans 102–103
  multistage sampling 98–102
  proportionate stratified random 97–98
  randomness 91–94
  simple random 92–95
  stratified random 95
Probationers 111, 151–152, 195, 292
  recidivism rates 195, 292
Probation officers 5–6, 15, 20, 123–124, 195–197
  burnout 20
  caseloads 196–197
  client interaction 201
  male-female officer differences 5–6
  power 20

questionnaires used to study 123–124
research examples involving 5–6, 15
work roles 15
Probes 156–158 (*see also* Follow-Ups)
  interviewing 156–158
Problems (*see* Research Problems)
Professionalism 209–212, 214, 247–248
  construct validity 247–248
  crosstabulated with other variables 214–215
  scale to measure 210
Professional literature (*see* Journals)
Prompts 310–311 (*see also* Computers)
Proportional-reduction-in-error measures 450–453
  asymmetric interpretations 452
  computation 451
  defined 450
  error 450
  symmetric interpretations 452
  unexplained variation 451–452
  usefulness of 451–453
Proportionate stratified random sampling 97–98
  advantages and disadvantages 98
  defined 97
Propositions 19–22, 24
  defined 22
  examples 22
Prosocial Attitude and Social Adjustment Scale (PASSAC) 438
Public documents (*see* Secondary Source Analysis)
Public policy 8, 23
  impact of research, 8, 23
  sterilization of inmates 23
Pure research 7–8
  defined 7
Purposive sampling plans 105–106
  advantages and disadvantages 106
  defined 105

Qualitative research 9–10
Quantitative research 9–10
Quartiles 282–284
Quasi-reproducible scales 226 (*see also* Guttman Scales)
Questionnaire construction 135–140
Questionnaire content 141
Questionnaire length 136–137, 140–141, 262
  effects on reliability and validity 262
  response rates 140–141
Questionnaires 5–6, 51, 109–110, 114–115, 121–143, 216

administration 133–135
advantages and disadvantages 131–133
combined fixed-response and open-ended 129–130
combined with interviewing 122
combined with observation 122
construction 135–140
content 141
criminal justice research 122–124
cultural date of instruments 262
defined 121–122
face-to-face administration 134
fixed-response 125–128
follow-ups 109, 133
functions 124–125
length 136–137
mailed 5–6, 130
missing items 216
open-ended 129
response and nonresponse 114–116, 140–143
response sets 131
saturation sampling 109–110
self-administered 263
survey research 130
triangulation 122
uses 5–6, 122–124
Quota sampling plans 107–108
  advantages and disadvantages 107–108
  defined 107

Race 263
  effects on validity and reliability 263
Radical criminology (*see* Critical Criminology)
Rand Corporation 359
Random assignment 71–73
Randomness 91–94, 355–356
  defined 91
  equality of draw 91
  independence of draw 91
  nonresponse 356
  statistical test assumption 355–356
  ways of obtaining 92–94
Random numbers 92 (*see also* Tables of Random Numbers)
Range 373–374
  defined 373
Rankables 203 (*see also* Ordinal Level of Measurement)
Ratio level of measurement 207 (*see also* Levels of Measurement)
Ratios 230–231
Raw scores 208, 264, 407
  converting to standards scores 392–394
  meanings of 264
Recidivism 7, 9, 195–198, 292
  rates 198
  studies of 7, 9, 195–198

Name and Case Index